Studies in Manuscript Cultures

Edited by
Michael Friedrich
Harunaga Isaacson
Jörg B. Quenzer

Volume 10

Bidur Bhattarai
Dividing Texts

Bidur Bhattarai

Dividing Texts

Conventions of Visual Text-Organisation in Nepalese and North Indian Manuscripts

DE GRUYTER

ISBN 978-3-11-054307-0
e-ISBN (PDF) 978-3-11-054308-7
e-ISBN (EPUB) 978-3-11-054311-7
ISSN 2365-9696

Library of Congress Control Number: 2019915358

Bibliographic information published by the Deutsche Nationalbibliothek
The Deutsche Nationalbibliothek lists this publication in the Deutsche Nationalbibliografie; detailed bibliographic data are available on the Internet at http://dnb.dnb.de.

Printing and binding: CPI books GmbH, Leck

www.degruyter.com

Contents

1 **Introduction —— 1**
1.1 Conventions, labels and abbreviations —— **8**
1.2 Description of the manuscripts —— **16**
1.2.1 Nepalese manuscripts —— **16**
1.2.2 East Indian manuscripts —— **30**
1.2.3 West Indian manuscripts —— **37**

2 **Overall layout and possible reasons for its change in manuscript —— 42**
2.1 Writing support —— **42**
2.2 Scribal practice —— **43**
2.3 Text style —— **44**
2.4 Time and place of manuscript production —— **44**
2.4.1 Examples of layout in Nepalese manuscripts —— **45**
2.4.2 Examples of layout in East Indian manuscripts —— **58**
2.4.3 Examples of layout in West Indian manuscripts —— **68**
2.4.4 Layout – Overall conclusions —— **73**

3 **Use of symbols —— 75**
3.1 The term '*puṣpikā*' —— **75**
3.2 Use of symbols in manuscripts – Selected early examples —— **76**
3.3 Shape and size —— **80**
3.4 Types of symbols found in the same region or in more than one region —— **80**
3.5 Further types of symbols related to particular areas —— **107**
3.5.1 Symbols in Nepalese manuscripts —— **108**
3.5.2 Symbols in East Indian manuscripts —— **117**
3.5.3 Symbols in West Indian manuscripts —— **126**
3.6 Symbols and their functions in manuscripts —— **127**
3.6.1 Decorative-only symbols —— **128**
3.6.2 Structural and decorative symbols —— **135**
3.7 Symbols occurring together with foliation numbers —— **198**
3.7.1 Preliminary conclusions —— **206**
3.8 Symbols and other features as a means to connect separated parts of the manuscript —— **207**
3.8.1 An observation: Symbols and other features on folio in SP_1 and one of the folios in A 38/5 —— **207**
3.8.2 An observation: Symbols and other features in SP_3 and SP_4 —— **209**

3.9 Symbols and other features as a means to identify a change of scribe — 215
3.9.1 Symbols and other features in SP_1 — 215
3.9.2 Symbols and other features in SP_2 — 219
3.9.3 Symbols and other features in KT — 223
3.9.4 Symbols and other features in TSPV — 226
3.9.5 Symbols and other features in TUS — 229
3.9.6 Symbols and other features as means to identify a change of scribes – Preliminary conclusions — 231
3.10 Some preliminary conclusions on use of symbols — 232

4 Use of space — 233
4.1 Blank space — 233
4.1.1 Blank spaces in Nepalese manuscripts — 234
4.1.2 Blank spaces in East Indian manuscripts — 242
4.1.3 Blank spaces in West Indian manuscripts — 248
4.1.4 Blank space – Overall conclusions — 248
4.2 Gaps — 249
4.2.1 Gaps: type (a) — 250
4.2.2 Gaps: type (b) — 254
4.2.3 Gaps – Preliminary conclusion — 261

5 Use of colour — 262
5.1 Colours as text-related feature — 266
5.1.1 Overall conclusions on use of colours — 287
5.2 Scientific examination of manuscripts — 289
5.2.1 Preliminary conclusions on scientific examination of manuscripts — 300

6 Conclusions — 301

Appendices — 305
I. List of selected symbols and blank spaces in Nepalese manuscripts — 305
II. List of selected symbols and blank spaces in East Indian manuscripts — 345
III. List of selected symbols in West Indian manuscripts — 351

Preface

This book is a revised version of my PhD dissertation, which was defended at the Centre for the Study of Manuscript Cultures (CSMC) of the University of Hamburg in January 2016. It is also the outcome of the sub-project 'Dividing Texts: Conventions of Visual Text-Organization in North Indian and Nepalese Manuscripts up to ca. CE 1350' (B04) of the 'Sonderforschungsbereich 950 *Manuskriptkulturen in Asien, Afrika und Europa*' supported by the Deutsche Forschungsgemeinschaft (DFG) from 2011–2015.

The present volume focuses on the study of the visual organisation of manuscripts primarily from Nepal (particularly those originating in the Kathmandu Valley) and North-India (regions of Eastern, Western India), which were produced, largely on palm-leaves, between ca. 800–1300 CE. However, a few examples of birch-bark and paper manuscripts as well as inscriptions from the same regions or other regions, prior or later, to the aforementioned time-frame are also included. Most of those examples not belonging to the 'core' corpus of manuscripts analysed in this book have largely been recorded in the footnotes. Visual organisation is a significant aspect of any manuscript culture and its study helps obtain a broad knowledge of those artefacts, spanning from their production process to their usage. The study also takes into consideration the various techniques for dividing texts into sub-section and the practices used by scribes in the course of the manuscript's production, such as symbols, blank spaces, gaps, colours etc.

This book consists of six chapters. In the first chapter the introductory matters of the study are briefly mentioned providing notes on its methodology and the conventions that have been employed. The second chapter deals briefly with the overall layout of the manuscripts providing two examples for each manuscript from the 'core' corpus that has been analysed. The third chapter, the most significant of this volume, studies the use of symbols found in manuscripts. Chapter four examines, in detail, the use of space(s) in manuscripts as dividing devices. Chapter five focuses on the use of colours followed by preliminary results from scientific examination of manuscripts. The examination of selected manuscripts was carried out in cooperation with scientists affiliated to the Project Area Z of the CSMC at the National Archives, Kathmandu in 2013. The sixth chapter discusses possible conclusions. The latter, however, are to be taken as preliminary findings, for many questions remain unanswered and call for further research.

A caveat is in order here as the number of manuscripts focused on in this study represents a mere fraction of the enormous corpora of manuscripts that may be deemed pertaining to 'Indic' manuscript cultures. It is hoped this study will contribute some new insights into the studies of visual organisation and, possibly, inspire readers to undertake further research in the field. At the same time, remarks and suggestions may help improve the scope and content of this work.

https://doi.org/10.1515/9783110543087-202

Acknowledgements

This study could not have borne much fruit without various forms of support from numerous individuals, scholars, institutions, libraries, archives, etc. First and foremost, the work would have been impossible without the continuous support and invaluable supervision of Professor Dr Harunaga Isaacson (University of Hamburg). I wish to thank him very much not only for giving me the opportunity to work on the subject-matter of this book, but also for his constant support and encouragement during my work. His immense knowledge and guidance helped me at all stages of its research and throughout the book's preparation.

I would also like to express my sincere gratitude to Prof. Dr Jürgen Hanneder (University of Marburg), who as second supervisor kindly examined my PhD dissertation. He too, showed constant interest in my research, provided motivation and insightful comments right up to the book's completion. Furthermore, I would like to thank Prof. Dr Michael Zimmermann (University of Hamburg), one of the members of the examination committee of my PhD defence. His comments and suggestions were of great help in improving my work.

My sincere thanks also go to Prof. Dr Eva Wilden (University of Hamburg), who kindly granted me a three-month working contract in 2017 under the auspices of the NETamil project funded by the European Research Council (ERC). During which time, I was able to continue working on the book's completion. Likewise, my heartfelt thanks go to the CSMC, especially Prof. Dr Michael Friedrich for the various short-term working contracts between 2016–2017 which permitted me to carry out further work on the book.

Furthermore, I would like to take this opportunity to thank my friend and colleague Dr Giovanni Ciotti (University of Hamburg). Always interested in my work, he provided remarkable feedback during my PhD, and was someone with whom I was able, not only to discuss many specific details, but also widen the horizons of my approach to manuscript studies.

This book would not have arrived at this form without the support of the editors of the *Studies in Manuscripts Cultures* series of the University of Hamburg, namely the aforementioned Prof. Dr Michael Friedrich, Prof. Dr Harunaga Isaacson and Prof. Dr Jörg B. Quenzer. I thank them all for granting me the opportunity of publishing the work in this series and most notably for their learned comments and suggestions.

I am also thankful to Dr Sebastian Bosch (University of Hamburg), Prof. Dr Oliver Hahn (University of Hamburg), Emanuel Kindzorra, and Prof. Dr Ira Rabin (University of Hamburg) for their generous support regarding the section on the scientific examination of manuscripts. In 2013, Prof. Hahn, Emanuel Kindzorra, and Prof. Rabin conducted the material analysis of certain manuscripts in Kathmandu, assisting me in making new discoveries on the materials used in manuscripts. Dr Bosch shared his valuable expertise with me when I was engaged in finalising the section on scientific examination. Furthermore, I would also like to take the opportunity to thank Karsten Helmholz, Christina Kaminski and Dr Irina Wandrey (CSMC) for their generous administrative assistance for the preparation of the research trip to Nepal in 2013 and the late Dr Albrecht Hanisch (Nepal Research Centre/Nepalese-German Manuscript Cataloguing Project) for his organisational help before and during our trip to Kathamandu.

One other individual deserves special mention, namely Cosima Schwarke (CSMC), who took great care in the layout of this book and several vital administrative tasks. This book would not have achieved the form it has now without her insights. She also played an essential role in ensuring smooth communication between the editors of the series, de Gruyter, and myself during the volume's preparation. I am grateful to her for her great patience and support. Furthermore, my sincere thanks also go to de Gruyter Verlag and Florian Ruppenstein who took upon the book's publication tasks. I would also like to thank James Rumball who read through the English of this volume at its near-final stage and made many valuable suggestions.

The research undertaken for this book also received various kinds of support from several archives and libraries. My gratitude goes to the Kaiser Library (Kathmandu) and the members of its team for their helpfulness. In particular, I thank Mr Dashrath Mishra (Chief, Kaiser Library) for granting me the permission to publish folios or parts of folios of the manuscripts in the library's possession.

I would also like to express my gratitude to the National Archives (Kathmandu) and its team members, who always allowed me to conduct manuscript research, on the spot, and gave me permission to publish some of the folios from the archive's manuscripts. My thanks go to Prakash Darnal (Former Chief, National Archives), Jyoti Neupane, Manita Neupane, Saubhagya Pradhananga (Chief, National Archives), Niran Kumar Rajbamshi, Raju Rimal, Shivaram Sapkota, and Kumar Shrestha.

Thanks also go to the Bodleian Library (Oxford), especially Jen Burford, Gillian Grant and Samantha Sherbourne, and their team who were always supportive during the preparation of this volume and made digital images of a particular manuscript available to me and granted me the permission to use some of the folios or elements from them.

Similarly, my sincere gratitude goes to the British Library (London) and its team for their generous support, particularly Sandra Powlette and Chris Rawlings for making images of manuscripts available to me as well as granting me the permission to use a few folios or parts from them. Their help enabled me to conduct my research further.

I am also thankful to the Cambridge University Library, in particular, Domniki Papadimitriou, Johanna Ward and the whole team as well as the members of the 'Sanskrit Manuscripts Project' who were always supportive and provided me with the digital copies of manuscripts for my study and the permission to publish them in their entirety or in part for the present volume.

Furthermore, my sincere thanks also go to the Jinabhadrasūri Grantha Bhaṇḍāra (Jaisalmer), especially to Dhiraj Dharod and Muni Pundarikratnavijaya who helped me in many ways, making digital copies of manuscripts available to me during my research and giving permission to use folios of manuscripts or parts of them in this book.

Thanks also go to the General Library, University of Tokyo, the Hemacandrācārya Jaina Jñānamandira (Patan), the Nepalese-German Manuscript Cataloguing Project, the Schøyen Collection and its editor of texts of the Buddhist manuscripts, and the members of those institutions for producing digital copies of the manuscripts required for my study and granting me the permission to publish folios or extracts of them.

Many more friends and colleagues supported me during the preparation of this book. My thanks go to Dr Jung-Lan Bang, Dr Victor D'Avella (University of Hamburg), Dr Camillo Formigatti (University of Oxford), Shanshan Jia (University of Hamburg), Dr Andrey Klebanov (University of Kyoto), Jooyoung Lim (University of Hamburg), Dr Costantino Moretti (École française d'Extrême-Orient, Paris), Dimitri Pauls (University of Hamburg), Dr Ramhari Timilsina (University of Heidelberg) and Dr Judith Unterdörfler (University of Würzburg). I also thank all friends and members of the CSMC who supported me in numerous ways.

Last but not least, this work would have not been possible in the first place without the constant support of each member of my family, who assisted me in many more ways than can be stated here. I would like to thank all of them deeply.

1 Introduction

The number of literary cultures and literary languages of the Indian sub-continent is vast. Countless texts have been composed in dozens of languages, from Sanskrit, Middle-Indic, to the various New-Indic as well as Dravidian, Arabic, Persian and various other languages. Despite a major role played by orality up into the modern age, people of the sub-continent have written down texts for a long time; a practice that for many centuries largely involved the writing of manuscripts.

The number of manuscripts produced in the sub-continent is astounding[1] and is the result of a massive enterprise carried out over a large geographical area, the influence of which far exceeded the borders of the sub-continent, reaching out to large parts of Central Asia and South-East Asia[2] over a vast expanse of time. I will use the label 'Indic manuscript culture' to refer to a set of trans-regional practices of production and reception of written literature, of social institutions regulating such processes, and of materials used for writing.

The visual organisation of texts in manuscripts is at the centre of the present study.[3] This is an important aspect of any manuscript culture, just as the way in which texts are arranged, directly links scribes and readers. Through the study of visual organisation, we have also come to recognise that Indic manuscript culture is in fact a plethora of many manuscript cultures. They share much in terms of choice of material supports, writing techniques, and types of visual arrangements, but they are also characterised by as many unique features that can be perceived in practically each region and epoch.

As a consequence, in this study I focus primarily on a selection of manuscripts from a precise time span and geographical area. In particular, I have taken into account a selection of manuscripts mostly written on palm-leaves (*tālapatra*[4]

---

1 Sources about the estimate number of manuscript are in disagreement. On the one hand, Pollock 2006, 558 reports the estimate of the Indira Gandhi National Centre for the Arts according to which there are over thirty million manuscripts containing texts written in Sanskrit and vernacular languages, on the other, Goswamy 2006, 7 estimates there to be five million handwritten manuscripts. Neither Pollock nor Goswamy corroborate their statements with any further details. Furthermore, Pingree 2003, 46 estimates there to be about three million manuscripts related to the *jyotiḥ śāstra* ('astronomy') alone. However, to simply accept the lowest estimation, the number of existing manuscripts remains some millions; see also Wujastyk 2014, 160.

2 Ibid. 159.

3 In this study 'visual organisation' does not cover the iconography and illuminations in manuscripts. The present volume deals primarily with the visual text organisation and dividing devices in the manuscripts.

4 For instance, see Hoernle 1900, 1–2; Katre 1954, 6–7.

https://doi.org/10.1515/9783110543087-001

or *tādapatra*) produced between approximately 800–1300 CE in the Northern part of the sub-continent. This time frame has been chosen as after the 13th century, paper[5] production appears and slowly becomes the favoured writing material in most parts of South Asia (save in Sri-Lanka, South India etc.) gradually replacing earlier materials.[6]

For this study, I have selected and examined mainly 41 different manuscripts from Nepal[7] and North India but, in giving examples, refer to many more manuscripts and a few inscriptions. This corpus was chosen as the development of the various scripts used in these manuscripts shows similar characteristics. In these regions local varieties of scripts have developed from the northern variety of ancient Brāhmī script.[8]

From the core group of 41 manuscripts examined here, 22 are from Nepal and 19 from North India. Of the latter group, 12 manuscripts are from Eastern India (i.e. Bihar or Bengal etc.) and 7 manuscripts from Western India[9] (i.e. Gujarat or Rajasthan). This study investigates both single-text manuscripts (STMs) and multiple-text manuscripts (MTMs).[10] The latter includes manuscripts containing more than one text and were conceived as such (as opposed to composite manuscripts).

Further to temporal and spatial criteria, another criterion used for selecting the corpus scrutinised here is the literary genre to which the texts in the various manuscripts belong as well as their religious affiliation (e.g. Buddhist Sūtra, Buddhist Tantra, Jaina Sūtra, Kāvya, Mahābhārata, Āyurveda (medicine), Purāṇa, Śaiva Tantra etc.).

5 On the paper as writing support, see e.g. Katre 1954, 8–9.

6 See Janert 1995, 60; Formigatti, 2015, 29.

7 The label 'Nepal' in reference to medieval and pre-medieval manuscripts readers does not designate modern political Nepal, but specifically denotes the areas of Nepālamaṇḍala (for a detailed study and discussion of this, see Tamoṭa 2006) or regions of the pre-modern Kathmandu valley (see Regmi 1965 and 1966; Petech 1984) and its surrounding areas, before the three kingdoms were conquered by the Śāha dynasty in 1769. With the exception of a few, most of the manuscripts featured in the present study purport to date back to even earlier than the aforementioned time period. In this volume both labels 'Nepal' and 'Nepalese' have been used interchangeably. On the attribution of manuscripts, see also section 1.1 below.

8 On the Brāhmī script, see Bühler 1896, 45–59; Salomon 1998, 17–42; Wujastyk 2015, 163.

9 The labels 'East India' or 'Eastern India' here, roughly refer to the modern political areas of Bihar, Bengal (or West Bengal) etc. The labels 'West India' or 'Western India' in turn correspond to the modern political geographical area of Gujarat, Rajasthan etc. For the label 'Western India', see also Balbir et al. 2006, 61. On the attribution of manuscripts, see also section 1.1 below.

10 On the study of composite and multiple-text manuscripts comprising various areas such as Asia, Africa and Europe, see Friedrich/Schwarke 2016.

The claim here is not that all manuscripts belonging to one of these categories (time, place, etc.) will have the same visual organisation. However, it emerges that, if used as parameters for categorising manuscripts on a large scale, these criteria can offer a sound representation of the more widespread trends concerning the visual organisation of texts. Furthermore, certain features, in particular those closely connected to a specific religious affiliation may, at times, also have a ritual, performative significance.

The aim of this study is to understand how scribes organised the texts; how they demarcated the texts by means of different visual devices, such as symbols, blank spaces, colours and writing styles. However, visual organisation is not always just a mere device used for dividing the various levels of a text; it may be the effect or the manifestation of religious and literary textual traditions. It is for this reason that strategies of visual organisation in manuscripts should be examined in connection with the contents and contexts of each text.

In the last few decades, many systematic studies have been carried out in the field of manuscriptology. Indic manuscript culture is so vast and productive that there are still many questions to be asked and much research is yet to be carried out on a wide range of subjects. In the following, only the selected studies most closely related to the topics and areas of the study of the present book are to be mentioned. Other secondary literature briefly referring to elements that contain a limited relevance to the concerns of the present volume are of occasional mention, when pertinent to examples presented or issues under scrutiny.

In chapter 7 of G. Bühler's *Indische Palaeographie* ('Indian Palaeography') (1896, 83–87) Äussere Einrichtung der Inschriften und MSS. ('External organisation of inscriptions and MSS.'), the author refers to some elements relating to the area of this present study. Firstly, he introduces a few symbols and 'bildliche Darstellungen' ('pictorial depictions') under the sub-section Maṅgala und Verzierungen ('Maṅgala and ornaments') and provides interpretations. These, however, say not so much of the extensive further variety of the use of symbols to be evidenced in the present study. Secondly, he briefly mentions the use of free space 'größer Zwischenraum' ('big free space' categorised in this study as 'gaps', see section 4.2 below) between *pādas* ('quarter(s)') or half verses in some inscriptions, here too they are not investigated in depth. Furthermore, he also remarks on the use of 'yellow' pigment in the sub-section 'Correcturen, Auslassungen, Abkürzungen' ('Corrections, omissions, abbreviations') mainly emphasising corrections in inscriptions. His study and remarks on these items and detailed palaeographical evidence are occasionally referred to and his notes are discussed where relevant in this volume.

On more specific topics, H. Śākya (1973) only partly deals with symbols, focusing mainly on paleography. Nonetheless, his work provided a good starting point for further investigation in the field. In particular, he presents two tables[11] to provide an overview of some signs and symbols which he says have been adapted from manuscripts.[12] His study, however, does not discuss the symbols in any further detail. As evidenced and discussed in one of the sections in the present book (see section 3.6.2.1.6, Figs. 3.6.2.1.6-XXII–XXXIII), some of those symbols can be seen to be representations of specific religious emblems or elements about which he says nothing. As a result, some of those symbols are reproduced and presented to compare with symbols that appear in other Nepalese manuscripts.

G. Roth (1986), L. Sander (1986) and G. Bhattacharya (1995) examined mainly 'initial auspicious symbols' ('*mangala*', '*siddham*', '*bhale*' respectively) in manuscripts and/or inscriptions featuring key discussions on the terms in great detail.

In Roth's study on symbols, 'Mangala-Symbols' appear in Buddhist Sanskrit manuscripts and inscriptions are investigated. Here he deals largely with symbols appear primarily at the text's beginning. He used one of Śākya's tables (p. 85) as an appendix (plate no. I). This study, also briefly takes into account a few similar types of symbols, but includes many other symbols featured in MTMs or STMs.

Sander is particularly important for the present study for her examination of the 'initial' symbols appearing at the beginning of Buddhist manuscripts and inscriptions from Gilgit and Central Asia. Such symbols appear in the manuscripts of this study's corpus, not only at the beginning of the text but also at the end of chapters or texts. This study also presents and discusses some similar symbols, taking Sander's investigation and examples into consideration.

Bhattacharya has examined the *bhale* symbols often found largely at the beginning of Jaina (in Western Indian) manuscripts as well as in inscriptions. He worked specifically on manuscripts from Gujarat and Rajasthan dated between 15th to 19th century. He also includes examples from a few inscriptions.

Although Roth, Sander and Bhattacharya's work are of great significance for the studies of the symbols, their limited coverage of the usages of the symbols falls short in filling in the lacuna of visual representation in manuscripts.

H. Sarkar and B.M. Pande's (1999) study of inscriptions is of particular importance for this research. Primarily dealing with symbols and 'graphic representations' appearing in Indian inscriptions, they also included those used as dividing devices. They confirm to have collected data largely from the *Epigraphica Indica* (EI), but also from secondary sources. Although the present study does not

11 See Śākya 1973, 84–85.
12 In the manner of eye-copy forms.

deal with inscriptions directly, understanding the development of symbols in different writing materials is essential to it. The study of Sarkar and Pande and others as well as examples found in other inscriptions are refered to in the present study.

Furthermore, M. Pant (2000) is of notable significance. He records and describes some of the symbols and signs of the manuscript he used for his edition of *Jātarūpa's Commentary on the Amarakoṣa* precisely.[13] Until now such symbols have either been virtually neglected in editions or represented by modern symbols easily available in fonts. Therefore, Pant's approach to representing symbols is vital. Although Pant's attempt at recording and describing symbols has led scholars working in the field to think more carefully about the visual representation of manuscripts, his questioning of the visual organisation in manuscripts is of limited scope.

K. Weissenborn's (2012) work is also of note. Her work focuses on *Buchkunst aus Nālandā* ('Book Art from Nālandā'), largely examining manuscripts from one of the important eastern Indian Buddhist monasteries. Weissenborn's monograph provides two big symbols, she postulates can be found somewhere in a part of the text in one of her Buddhist manuscripts, and seven symbols appearing at the end of chapters in some manuscripts.[14] She labels the two large symbols 'Dharma-Räder' ('Wheels of Dharma') symbolizing them as such[15] and the seven symbols 'Rosette'.

J.P. Thaker's (2002) monograph (*Manuscriptology and Text Criticism*) contains topics of various kinds and provides some observations on some elements also related to this study. He briefly mentions symbols, for instance, but does not examine them in detail. Moreover, he writes about the use of colours providing different colouring agents, reasons etc. in his study (see section 5 below). On the possible highlighted elements he (p. 138) states that 'important notable words, phrases' etc. can be highlighted, however, aside from mentioning a few examples (such as foliations and symbols around string-holes) and the use of colour for corrections or deletions etc., he fails to indicate what important elements may appear highlighted in manuscripts and the reasons they are highlighted. Excluding a few examples, for most of his references, his focus was primarily on Jaina manuscripts or materials from West India, i.e. Gujarat or Rajasthan.

A recent and noteworthy publication is K. Einicke's (2009) monograph entitled *Korrektur, Differenzierung und Abkürzung in indischen Inschriften und Handschriften* ('Correction, Differentiation and Abbreviation in Indian Inscriptions and Manuscripts') which covers a large amount of materials of different areas and

13 See Pant 2000, part I, 78–79; part II, 9, 46, 48, 50, 56, 143, 325.

14 See Weissenborn 2012, 198, Abbildungen 69, 70.

15 Ibid. 84.

epochs. *Differenzierung* ('Differentiation'), in particular, the second part of Einicke's study, is related to the present study's interests. It should be noted that Einicke has used some data from the IndoSkript Project (2000–2005),[16] an electronic database of Indic palaeography. Data gathered and presented by the IndoSkript Project has benefited the present study too, to some extent with regard to symbols and examples from that project are referenced in the present study. Regarding symbols and other elements, Einicke (p. 5) writes she has excluded most of the symbols that appear at the end of chapters, texts etc. in her study for the following reasons.

> [...] in der Arbeit nicht aufgenommen wurden (unter anderem wegen der vorliegenden Menge von Beispielen) einfache *daṇḍas* oder Ornamentzeichen, die zwar auch der Textgliederung dienen, aber doch als solche leicht zu erkennen sind und hier nicht näher erläutert werden müssen.

> Simple *daṇḍas* or ornamental signs/symbols have not been recorded in my work (also due to the sheer quantity of examples). Although they also serve as demarcation devices, they are easy to recognise as such, and therefore, they do not have to be explained here in more detail.[17]

More recently, in her PhD thesis (*Selected Chapters from the* Tantrasadbhāva. *Based on the tradition of 11th century Śaiva Sanskrit Manuscript in Nepal*) carried out at the CSMC, J. Bang (2017) has presented a few *siddham* symbols and other symbols (e.g. 'Ornaments' in 30, Table I.4) from the manuscripts belonging to her text corpus and other Nepalese manuscripts dating from 9th to 12th century. Although her examples are mainly from manuscripts containing śaiva texts and she does not make detailed investigations into the symbols, her study and presentation of symbols are significant nonetheless, and are referred to here at times.

However, in the present study limited to small areas of the sub-continent and materials, the overall layout of the manuscripts of the 'core' corpus is presented and discussed which not all of the aforementioned studies included. Furthermore, taking examples and discussions of some of the aforementioned studies into account, this study focuses on a great number of symbols to be found in various parts of manuscripts and presents many of them for the first time in typological fashion to help obtain a better understanding of their development, use and visual organisation. In some cases possible meanings and reasons behind their drawing, their functions, and their relation to the contents or affiliations have also

16 For more details, see <http://userpage.fu-berlin.de/falk/index.htm> (last accessed on 04.11.2018).
17 The translation is mine.

been discussed and presented in detail in the present book. In addition some of the symbols have been presented and discussed for the first time that have not been included in other studies until now. Save for a few remarks here and there, symbols in most of the publications have often been considered just to be 'floral elements' or 'decorations' etc. with no recognition or identifying of the stylised forms of a particular object or other meaning behind their drawing. Therefore, the presentation, interpretation and discussion of some of symbols in this study proposes the reader to reconsider existing interpretations or understanding of symbols repeatedly treated merely as 'ornamental' features in publications.

It appears, aside from mere mentions on their appearance in some secondary studies without detailed information and a few presentations of examples of 'blank spaces' (e.g., those by Einicke from some manuscripts and inscriptions),[18] there are no other detailed studies in the field, of use of spaces ('blank spaces' and 'gaps') as a way of demarcating texts so far and to date, no further systematic research on this topic has been published. Similarly, it is to be noted that hardly any attention has been paid to the use of colour in manuscripts, save for mentioning its reasons for correction or deletion of the text (e.g. Bühler 1896, 86; Thaker 2002, 146; Einicke 2009, 35). In this respect, this study aims at providing a starting point for the investigation of the use of both spaces and colours as dividing devices for the texts in Indic manuscripts. Furthermore, during the project some composition of the writing materials was examined in cooperation with scientists affiliated to the CSMC who employed mobile and non-destructive equipment to analyse four manuscripts on site in Kathmandu. The main colouring substance in four manuscripts was examined, the drawing of a symbol in one manuscript, and the possible traces left from drawing tool use. The preliminary results of this scientific examination are included in this volume in the hope a further step can be taken in gaining a better understanding of the material composition and process of the production of manuscripts.

---

18 See Einicke 2009, 344 as "Zwei Doppeldaṇḍas ohne Zwischenelement" ('two double *daṇḍas* without the element in between'). Her examples can be found in 344–345 as SarIs(1002)_1, Ben2(1446)_41, Bir2(1834)_1, Bir3(1874)_22, Bir4.1(1884)_23, Bir4.2(1884)_21, Bir4.2(1884)_22, Bir5(1902)_19, Naj6(1582)_20, New16(1826)_3).

1.1 Conventions, labels and abbreviations

(1) Conventions

Various steps were undertaken during the analysis of the manuscripts and their elements in the present study. It should be noted that as all the manuscripts in the corpus bear no information of place of copying etc., it is difficult and challenging to attribute them to specific region or to associate them entirely to a specific area. Therefore, one must consider other features to be found in manuscripts or secondary references etc. for the potential of regional attribution or place of origin. Manuscripts that were produced or may have been produced in present-day Nepal, particularly in or around present-day Kathmandu valley, or produced even elsewhere that exhibit something of the customs, characteristics, flavour and so on of 'Nepalese writing' have been categorised in the present volume as 'Nepalese' manuscripts or manuscripts from 'Nepal'. Similar criterion have been applied in the attribution to regions of North India, such as 'East Indian' or 'West Indian', for all of these bear no precise information on place of production and so on.

Firstly, the manuscripts were grouped on the basis of their various features (e.g. palaeographical, layout-related evidence) and, generally, from other information available about them. They pertain to one of the following three geographical areas: (1) Nepal, (2) East India and (3) West India. In each group, the manuscripts are arranged in possible chronological order. Undated manuscripts, secondary references, palaeographical or other evidence are taken into consideration to provide an approximate date. The dates of such manuscripts are here refered as '9th', '9th c.' or 'ca. 9th c.'

If the beginning of a text has been preserved, part of the beginning of most manuscripts has been transcribed. Subsequently, symbols and blank spaces appearing in different parts of the manuscripts have been collected and listed in tables (some of the selected symbols and blank spaces are presented and discussed in sections, most of which are listed in the appendices below).[19] In addition, colophons and sub-colophons[20] were recorded and transliterated as they appear in the manuscripts (some of them are presented and discussed in sections below).[21] In a few cases, a part of the text of the succeeding chapter appearing immediately after the symbol or blank space has also been recorded.

19 See Appendices.

20 For the labels, see below and also section 3.1.

21 For example, see sections 3.6.2.4.1; 4.1.1–4.1.2 below.

The comparison between different kinds of symbols, blank spaces, sub-colophons, colophons and other textual parts has played a significant role in understanding the scribal practices in dividing texts at several levels.

In some manuscripts small gaps are used to divide smaller text units such as sentences, each *pāda* or the first and second half of the verse. Therefore, some parts of the text have been transcribed according to the layout using a separate sign in the transliteration to designate smaller gaps (for the sign, see on this page below). Recording the features of the manuscript in this way made it possible to group the occurrences according to their location or function.

To gain an understanding of the use of colour in manuscripts, some parts of the highlighted elements have been recorded. For the highlighted texts, red script has been used to denote them in the transcription. To understand the scribal practice and identify different hands, other features such as space-fillers and palaeographical evidence are crucial. Therefore, they too have been recorded from selected manuscripts. These are important elements when comparing the different scribal hands and their differing practice in manuscripts.

When reporting the (Sanskrit) texts found in manuscripts I only transliterate the text as it appears in the manuscript and do not attempt any corrections or emandations (except for the use of sic (!) sign in the transliteration) in the present book. The following symbols are to be noted in the transliteration.

<< >>	parts of an *akṣara* ('syllable'), an *akṣara* or words deleted by the scribe or by a later corrector; in all cases the << >> brackets have been used
?	uncertainty of folio number or sides of folio
...	part of the text that is not quoted or transliterated
+	*akṣara* lost due to physical damage or it is no longer readable, the number of the symbol represent the possible number of lost *akṣara*s
///	when big parts of the folios are broken off
- -	*akṣara*(s) left out by the scribe in the process of copying
(!)	sic
¦	line-filler sign or hyphen sign used before the string-holes or at the end of the line on the folio
␣	gap appearing between every *pāda*, or between the first and second halves of a verse, or between sentences
∽	space-filler

⊙	string-hole or text lines that are not conspicuously left clear around the string-holes on the folio
|⊙|	text lines are left clear from top to bottom around the string-holes on the folio
||⊙||	text lines are left clear from top to bottom on the string-hole spaces and one or more vertical ruling lines are used for each text-section on the folio
⊡	some lines have been left clear around the string-hole space and the uppermost or lowermost lines run across the whole folio, making the free space around the string-hole look like a square-shaped box
\ /	marginal or interlineal textual addition; it does not matter whether the addition was made by the first scribe himself or by a later individual
Text in red	(approximately) highlighted part of the text in the manuscript

In the present study, each manuscript included in my 'core' corpus is referred to by a specific siglum (see section 1.2 below). Many times I also refer to manuscripts or different elements of manuscripts that are not part of my 'core' corpus in order to emphasise or generalise a specific argument or topic. These manuscripts are indicated mainly by the title of the work they contain, their accession, catalogue (or reel number), and the name of the library, archive or institution (often in abbreviated form) that preserve them, but at times they are mentioned merely by the accession number of the manuscript, e.g. 'the manuscript of the *Saddharmapuṇḍarīka* (CUL Add.2197)' or simply with or without brackets '(CUL Add.2197)'. In this case, the manuscript is kept in the Cambridge University Library under the shelfmark Add.2197.

Symbols and other elements extracted from the manuscript and arranged in figures in the present work are indicated as follows: (1) siglum of the manuscript (this information is omitted if contextually clear); (2) folio number or image number (according to how the image file has been received from the library or archive if the foliation is not preserved); (3) line number in which (at first) symbols and other elements can be found; (4) the text part where they can be found; (5) the (possible) date of manuscript production (this information is also omitted if contextually clear). These data appear immediately after the symbol or other element in square brackets, for instance:

 [KT_87v2_BCC_924]

The symbol appears in the manuscript of the *Kiraṇatantra*, on folio 87 verso, in line number 2 before the chapter colophon. The date of the manuscript corresponds to 924 CE.

On the other hand, excerpts of symbols and blank spaces reported along with the text, chapter colophon or colophon[22] are indicated by the folio (or image number) and line number. These data are placed before symbols or blank spaces in square brackets. For instance:

[20r1]  *upāyakauśalyaparivartto dvitīyaḥ* 

In this case, the chapter colophon and symbols are found on folio 20 recto, in line number 1. The chapter colophon starts after the upper right double *daṇḍa* of the first symbol and ends before the upper left double *daṇḍa* of the second symbol.

Furthermore, symbols placed around the string-holes are indicated in two ways in the present work. If the folio of a particular manuscript contains only one string-hole, the symbol around it is indicated in a style similar to that described above in the case of KT (see p. 11 above), but without line number. For example:

 [TSa_10r_SH_1143]

The symbol appears in the manuscript of the *Tattvasaṃgraha*, around the string-hole on folio 10 recto. The date of the manuscript corresponds to 1143 CE.

22 On these, see 76–77 and section 3.1 below.

In the case of a folio with two string-holes, symbols around string-holes are indicated in a way similar to that used for TSa. However, two additional pieces of information are added to the entry before the date of the manuscript, e.g.:

[TSPV_36v_LSH_1143]

[TSPV_36v_RSH_1143]

Both symbols appear in the manuscript of the *Tattvasaṃgrahapañjikāvṛtti*, on folio 36 verso, around the left string-hole (LSH) and the right string-hole (RSH). The date of the manuscript corresponds to 1143 CE.

Furthermore, symbols appearing together with foliation numbers are indicated by giving the following data.

[TSa_10v_WF_1143]

The symbol appears together with the foliation (WF) number 10 on verso in the manuscript of the *Tattvasaṃgraha*.

In order to provide reliable statistics, *akṣara*s have been counted more than once from different lines on the same folio or different folios of the same manuscript. The sample number of *akṣara*s is given in the following way:

73 (2v1), 74 (26r5), 78 (32v1)

In this particular manuscript, 73 *akṣara*s appear on folio 2 verso in line 1, 74 *akṣara*s on folio 26 recto in line 5 and 78 *akṣara*s on folio 32 verso in line 1.

As far as foliation is concerned, if it is not preserved and there are doubts about the folio number, then only the number of the image is indicated, as this is found in the file provided by a particular institution or library. Often in an image with two sides (such as verso and recto or recto and verso) of two folios they are photographed together. This is denoted as follows:

101 (10b3)

In this case 101 *akṣaras* appear in line 3 on the lower folio (b) in the 10th image in which the sides of two folios are photographed together. Similarly 'a' stands for the side of the upper folio in the digitised image.

Selected symbols and blank spaces from each manuscript of my 'core' corpus used during my study have been organised in the appendix. The list of these items is merely to provide an overview of the occurrence of such elements in the manuscripts. They are arranged, when possible, in chronological order in each manuscript group (Nepalese, East Indian and West Indian). In the case of lost foliation or the folios of the particular manuscript that are very disordered and the correct order of the folios is uncertain, they have been recorded and organised according to the images received from the respective library or institution (as described 10–11 above). In the data, only the folio number or image number, the line in which they can be found, and the place where they appear in the text, are mentioned in square brackets.

In the present work I label the scripts[23] used in the manuscripts as follows: (1) 'Transitional Gupta': the script(s) found in the 9th c. Nepalese manuscripts; (2) 'Newari': the script(s) used after 10th c. onward in the Nepalese manuscripts; (3) 'Old Bengali': the script(s) used in all East Indian manuscripts (with one exception 'Rañjanā' in PR); and (4) 'Jaina Devanāgarī': the script(s) used in the West Indian manuscripts of my corpus.

(2) Labels

Some labels have been proposed for the structure and systematic approach being deemed suitable to the examination of various elements in the present volume.

Author line: A statement that may include, among other things, the name of the author of the work, e.g. *kṛtir iyam ācāryapādānām* ('this work [is] of venerable preceptor').

Benediction: A phrase that expresses the auspiciousness or prosperity etc. (for reader, scribe etc.) and is often found at the end of the text in manuscripts, e.g. *maṅgalaṃ bhavatu, śubham astu* ('may there be auspiciousness') etc.

---

23 One should note that in the present study I do not aim to define the scripts which can be universally applicable. As we know, for a particular script various names or 'local' names are suggested and sometimes used to denote (e.g. Transitional Gupta, Licchavi, Uttaralicchavi etc. for scripts that can be found mainly in 9th c. Nepalese manuscripts and Golamola etc. for scripts that are found largely in manuscripts of the Eastern Indian group, such as GV, HAP, LTṬ, STṬ, ḌVPṬ, HP).

Buddhist concluding formula: A statement that can be found in Buddhist texts, namely *idam avocad bhagavān* ... ('thus spoke the Bhagavān ...').
Buddhist opening phrase: An expression that can often be found in Buddhist texts, namely *evaṃ mayā śrutam* ... ('thus have I heard ...').
Buddhist verse (*pratītyasamutpāda***):** A verse that can often be found at the end of Buddhist texts, for example, *ye dharmā* ...[24]
Chapter colophon (or sub-colophon): A statement that indicates the end of a chapter or sub-chapter etc. It may begin with or without *iti* and contain the title of the work and/or title of the chapter and/or just chapter number, and end with or without the expression like *samāpta* ('completed' or 'concluded').
Colophon (or final colophon): A statement that states the completion of the work and can often be found at the end of the text in manuscripts. It may begin with or without *iti* and contain the title of work and end with or without expressions such as *samāpta, parisamāpta, saṃpūrṇa* ('concluded' or 'entirely completed') etc.
Invocation: A phrase that expresses respect to gods, goddesses, gurus, Buddhas etc. and found often at the beginning of the text or occasionally in other places in the text in manuscripts, for instance, *namaḥ sarvajñāya* ('homage to Sarvajña').
Opening formula: A phrase that starts, among others, with *atha khalu* ... ('now further/then ...') etc. in the text.
Post colophon: Lines that can be found (mainly) after the colophon containing various kinds of information such as copying place, date, purpose of the manuscript, king, donor, name of scribe etc.
Speaker indication: A formula that indicates the speaker in the text, e.g. *bhairava uvāca* ('Bhairava spoke').
Text-section: If the lines on folios have been left clear from text on the string-hole space from top to bottom and the text has been divided into two to three parts/sections according to the number of existing string-holes on the folio, I label this kind of text arrangement on folios as 'text-section' in the present book.
Topic change formula: Phrases that can be found in a particular place in the text and indicate the change of a topic or subject in the text, e.g. *ataḥ paraṃ pravakṣāmi* ... ('hereafter I will speak ...') etc.

---

24 For a detailed study of the verse, see Boucher 1991, 1–27. Generally the verse reads as follows, *ye dharmā hetuprabhavā hetuṃ teṣāṃ tathāgato hy avadat | teṣāṃ ca yo nirodha evaṃvādī mahāśramaṇaḥ* || 'Those *dharmas* which arise from a cause, the Tathāgata has declared their cause. And that which is the cessation of them, thus the great renunciant has taught' (translated in Boucher 1991, 11).

(3) Abbreviations

AAL	after author line
AB	after benediction
ABCF	after Buddhist concluding formula
ABOF	after Buddhist opening formula
AC	after colophon
ACC	after chapter colophon
ADL	after dating line
AI	after invocation
AOF	after opening formula
APS	after particular section
ASpI	after speaker indication
BAL	before author line
BB	before benediction
BBCF	before Buddhist concluding formula
BBOF	before Buddhist opening formula
BC	before colophon
BCC	before chapter colophon
BDL	before dating line
BI	before invocation
BMSC	Braarvig, Jens (Ed.) (2002–2016): "Buddhist Manuscripts in the Schøyen Collection", Vol. 1–4. In *Manuscripts in the Schøyen Collection*. Oslo: Hermes Publishing.
BOF	before opening formula
BPC	before post colophon
BPS	before particular section
BSpI	before speaker indication
CUL	Cambridge University Library
EI	*Epigraphia Indica*
Fig(s).	figure(s)
fol(s).	folio(s)
KL	Kaiser Library, Kathmandu
LS	Lakṣamaṇa Saṃvat
LSH	left string-hole
NAK	National Archives, Kathmandu
NGMCP	Nepalese-German Manuscript Cataloguing Project
NGMPP	Nepal-German Manuscript Preservation Project
NS	Nepāla Saṃvat
RSH	right string-hole
ŚS	Śaka Saṃvat
VS	Vikrama Saṃvat
WF	with foliation

1.2 Description of the manuscripts

In this section manuscripts from the 'core' corpus of the study alone have been listed with brief information provided about them. They have been arranged in three manuscript groups. In each group, the manuscripts have been recorded in a possible chronological order. As mentioned above, regarding undated manuscripts it is only a possible date that has been suggested. In the description (1) siglum for the manuscript, title of the text, place of storage and its accession number (followed by reel number etc. if available), (2) writing support, format, size and cover, and (3) condition, date, script and foliation have been mentioned.

1.2.1 Nepalese manuscripts

1.2.1.1 Manuscript SP_1

Title: *Skandapurāṇa*[25]
Place of storage: National Archives, Kathmandu
Accession no. 2/229
NGMPP reel no. B 11/4

Writing support, format, size and cover

Palm-leaf, *pothī*,[26] ca. 40 × 5 cm (some folios are smaller and taper at the edges). 268 folios (one folio of this manuscript can be found in A 38/5 and as it has been identified by scholars there are some folios of the recension of the *Pārameśvara(tantra)* in this manuscript) (see section 3.8.1).[27] There are two string-holes on each folio. The manuscript contains wooden covers which seem to be 'original'.

25 See Shastri 1905, Vol. 1, lii and 141–146; Bhaṭṭarāī 1988, 37 with siglum *kha*; Adriaensen et al. 1998, 32 with siglum SP_1. See also NGMCP entry at: <http://ngmcp.fdm.uni-hamburg.de/mediawiki/index.php/B_11-4_Skandapur%C4%81%E1%B9%87a> (last accessed on 10.09.2018). I am thankful to Prof. Harunaga Isaacson for sharing with me the digitised colour images of this manuscript.

26 For *pothī*, I refer to the study by Formigatti 2011, 29 where the term has been thoroughly discussed from an historical and material point of view.

27 See Adriaensen et al. 1998, 33. There may be around 6 fragmentary folios in the bundle of the manuscript that belong to this.

Condition, date, script and foliation

Incomplete; in most cases the margins are broken. Some folios are in a fragmentary condition. In many places parts of the folios are worm eaten. The manuscript is dated Mānadeva Saṃvat 234 (811 CE).[28] Transitional Gupta. Letter-numerical foliation is on the left-hand margin verso.[29] With but few exceptions all foliation has been lost. On some folios, figure-numerals have been added later above the left string-hole space (save for a few figure-numerals under the string-hole). Most are written in 'black ink' but some are in orange-like ink.

1.2.1.2 Manuscript PT

Title: *Pārameśvaratantra* (aka *Pauṣkarapārameśvara*)[30]
Place of storage: University Library, Cambridge
Accession no. MS Add.1049

Writing support, format, size and cover

Palm-leaf, *pothī*, ca. 38.5 × 3.8 cm. (some folios are smaller and taper at the edges). 62 folios (one fragmentary folio of the *Jñānārṇavamahātantra* is in the bundle of this manuscript). There are two string-holes on each folio. It is possible the manuscript did not include covers or they are lost or misplaced.

Condition, date, script and foliation

Incomplete; the margins are broken. Some folios are in a fragmentary condition. The manuscript is dated Mānadeva Saṃvat 252 (829 CE).[31] Transitional Gupta. Foliation is on the left-hand margin on the verso. The majority of the original foliation has not been preserved. Additional modern figure-numerals are written above the left string-hole and on the verso of many folios. Occasionally further additional modern

---

28 Different corresponding dates are suggested by scholars, e.g. Shastri 1905, lii as 659 CE; Adriaensen et al. 1998, 33 as 810 CE; Harimoto 2011, 90 as 811 CE. In the present study I follow the date verified by Harimoto 2011.

29 For the label 'letter-numerals' and examples, see Bendall 1883, liii; Kapadia 1973, 171–186; Balbir et al. 2006, 61–62.

30 See Bendall 1883, 27–28; Shastri 1905, lii; for the detailed information of this manuscript, see also Cambridge online entry at: <https://cudl.lib.cam.ac.uk/view/MS-ADD-01049-00001/1> (last accessed on 04.09.2018).

31 Different corresponding dates are suggested by scholars, e.g. Bendall 1992, 27 as 859 CE; Harimoto 2011, 90 as 829 CE. In the present study I follow the date verified by Harimoto 2011.

figure-numerals appear above or under the right string-hole on the recto of some folios, some of which have been crossed out.

1.2.1.3 Manuscript SS/N

Title: *Suśrutasaṃhitā*[32]/*Suśrutanighaṇṭu*[33]
Place of storage: Kaiser Library, Kathmandu
Accession no. 699
NGMPP reel no. C 80/7

Writing support, format, size and cover

Palm-leaf, *pothī*, ca. 53.5 × 4.4 cm (some folios are curved and taper at the edges). 127 folios extant. There are two string-holes on each folio. Manuscript includes wooden covers which seem to be original.

Condition, date, script and foliation

Incomplete; the margins of some folios are broken. Parts of the folios are worm eaten. Many folios are missing. The manuscript is dated Mānadeva Saṃvat 301 (878 CE).[34] Transitional Gupta. Original foliation is in letter-numerals on the left-hand margin verso. The manuscript also contains some extra 'supplementary' folios which bear letter-numerals following the duplication of some of the foliation numbers of the 'original' folios on the left-hand margin and letter-numerals again starting from 1–16 on the right-hand margin.[35]

---

32 See Klebanov 2010, 60 with sigla K, K_1, K_2; Harimoto 2011, 87–88; 2014, 1087–1093; 2016, 363–364; see also NGMCP entry at: <http://ngmcp.fdm.uni-hamburg.de/mediawiki/index.php/C_80-7_Su%C5%9Brutasa%E1%B9%83hit%C4%81> (last accessed on 05.09.2018). I am thankful to Dr Andrey Klebanov for sharing with me the digitised colour images of this manuscript. This manuscript (SS/N) has been registered in UNESCO's Memory of the World Register in 2013.
33 See Suvedī/Tivārī 2000, 7 with siglum *sau. ni. ha.* (*kha*).
34 Regarding the date of the manuscript, see Petech 1984, 29; Klebanov 2010, 66; Harimoto 2011, 88; 2014, 1087; 2016, 363–364.
35 Possibly the numbers 1–16 can be taken as an indication of the number of the folios inserted in the bundle later. The handwriting of the foliation of these parts is clearly different to those of other folios.

1.2.1.4 Manuscript SP_2

Title: *Skandapurāṇa*[36]
Place of storage: National Archives, Kathmandu
Accession no. 1/831
NGMPP reel no. B 12/3

Writing support, format, size and cover

Palm-leaf, *pothī*, ca. 53 × 4.4 cm (some folios are smaller and taper at the edges). 217 folios. There are two string-holes on each folio. The manuscript includes an original wooden front cover and one new wooden back cover. Red and yellow mixed colours are smeared on the outer part of the front cover. A small piece of paper has been stuck on the left side: this is a label containing information about the manuscript most likely put on the cover at the NAK for cataloguing purposes. On the back cover, however, there are no traces of pigment or similar items.

Condition, date, script and foliation

Incomplete; margins are broken. Parts of the folios are worm eaten. The manuscript is dated ca. 9th c.[37] Transitional Gupta. Letter-numerals on the left-hand margin on the verso. Most of the foliation has not been preserved. Figure-numerals have been added later in modern hand above the left string-hole and occasionally on the right margin on the verso.

1.2.1.5 Manuscript NTS

Title: *Niśvāsatattvasaṃhitā*[38]
Place of storage: National Archives, Kathmandu
Accession no. 1/277
NGMPP reel no. A 41/14

---

36 See Bhaṭṭarāī 1988, 36 with siglum *ka*; Adriaensen et al. 1998, 32 with siglum SP_2. See also NGMCP entry at: <http://ngmcp.fdm.uni-hamburg.de/mediawiki/index.php/B_12-3_Skandapur%C4%81%E1%B9%87a> (last assessed on 10.09.2018). I am grateful to Prof. Harunaga Isaacson for sharing with me the digitised colour images of this manuscript.

37 See Adriaensen et al. 1998, 32; Harimoto 2011, 92–93.

38 See Shastri 1905, lxxvii; Goodall et al. 2015, 104–108 with siglum N; Kafle 2015, 92 with siglum N. See also NGMCP entry at: http://ngmcp.fdm.uni-hamburg.de/mediawiki/index.php/A_41-14_Ni%C5%9Bv%C4%81satattvasa%E1%B9%83hit%C4%81 (last accessed on 05.09.2018). This manuscript has been registered in UNESCO's Memory of the World Register in 2013.

Writing support, format, size and cover

Palm-leaf, *pothī*, ca. 50 × 4 cm (some folios are smaller and taper at the edges). 114 folios. There are two string-holes on each folio. The manuscript includes wooden covers which seem to be orginal. The inner parts of both covers are illustrated.

Condition, date, script and foliation

Complete; margins are broken. Some folios are in fragmentary condition. In many places parts of the folios are worm eaten. The manuscript is thought to be ca. 9th c.[39] Transitional Gupta. The original foliation is written in letter-numerals on the left-hand margin and the majority of it has been lost. Modern figure-numerals added later can be found above and under the left string-hole in different hands. The upper one is written larger and in darker ink compared to the lower one. Several of both of the foliations added later have been crossed out.

1.2.1.6 Manuscript KT

Title: *Kiraṇatantra*[40]
Place of storage: National Archives, Kathmandu
Accession no. 5/893
NGMPP reel no. A 40/3

Writing support, format, size and cover

Palm-leaf, *pothī*, ca. 34.5 × 4.5 cm. 88 folios. There are two string-holes on each folio. The manuscript contains wooden covers and they seem to be original. A part of the upper right margin of the front cover and bottom right margin of the back cover is damaged.

Condition, date, script and foliation

Incomplete; some leaves are damaged. Parts of some of leaves are worm eaten. The manuscript is dated NS 44 (924 CE).[41] Newari. Letter-numerals on the left-hand margin on the verso.

---

39 Various dates are suggested by scholars, for instance, see Shastri 1905, lxxvii as ca. 8th c.; Goodall et al. 2015, 108 as 850–900 CE; Kafle 2015 as the date after the dated manuscript SS/N (i.e. 878 CE). For practical reasons, I refer to the date as ca. 9th c. in the present study.

40 See Shastri 1915, 99; Goodall 1998, lxxxiv–lxxxv with siglum N_1; see also NGMCP entry at: <http://ngmcp.fdm.uni-hamburg.de/mediawiki/index.php/A_40-3_Kira%E1%B9%87atantra> (last accessed on 05.09.2018).

1.2.1.7 Manuscript KV/UVDh

Title: *Kāraṇḍavyūha/Uṣṇīṣavijayadhāriṇī*[42]
Place of storage: National Archives, Kathmandu
Accession no. 3/359
NGMPP reel no. A 39/5 (1–2)

Writing support, format, size and cover

Palm-leaf, *pothī*, ca. 48 × 4.5 cm.[43] 57 folios (KV: 1v–52v3 and UVDh: 52v3–56r). There are two string-holes on each folio. Images of covers are not available.

Condition, date, script and foliation

Complete; in relatively good condition. A few leaves have been damaged at the margins. The writing is faded on folios 1v and 2r. The manuscript is dated NS 88 (968 CE). Newari. Original letter-numerals on the left-hand margin on verso and modern figure-numerals added later in modern hand above the left string-hole on verso.

1.2.1.8 Manuscript SP_3

Title: *Skandapurāṇa*[44]
Place of storage: Bodleian Library, Oxford
Accession no. MS Sansk a. 14 (R)

Writing support, format, size and cover

Palm-leaf, *pothī*, ? cm. 214 folios extant? There are two string-holes on each folio. Possibly new wooden covers.

41 See Goodall 1998, lxxxiv.

42 See NGMCP entry at: <http://ngmcp.fdm.uni-hamburg.de/mediawiki/index.php/A_39-5(1)_U%E1%B9%A3%E1%B9%87%C4%AB%E1%B9%A3avijayadh%C4%81ra%E1%B9%87%C4%AB> (last accessed on 05.09.2018).

43 NGMCP entry records the size of 31 x 4.5 cm, but we find in the catalogue card 48 × 4.5 cm. Given the size of the folios the latter measurement seems to be more convincing.

44 See Adriaensen et al. 1998, 33–34 with siglum SP_3.

Condition, date, script and foliation
Incomplete; some folios are broken on the left and right margins and a few folios are in fragmentary condition. The manuscript is thought to be ca. 10th c.[45] Newari. Letter-numerals on the left-hand margin on verso.

1.2.1.9 Manuscript SP₄

Title: *Skandapurāṇa*[46]
Place of storage: National Archives, Kathmandu
Accession no. 4/2260
NGMPP reel no. B 12/2[47]

Writing support, format, size and cover
Palm-leaf, *pothī*, ca. 41 × 4.5 cm.[48] 22 folios ('fragments'). There are two string-holes on each folio. The manuscript has new covers.

Condition, date, script and foliation
Incomplete; the manuscript is considerably damaged and it is already in fragmentary condition. The manuscript is thought to be 10th c.[49] Newari. Foliation is on the left-hand margin verso. The majority of the foliation has been lost.

1.2.1.10 Manuscript YY

Title: *Yogayājñavalkya*[50]
Place of storage: National Archives, Kathmandu
Accession no. 5/696
NGMPP reel no. A 51/12[51]

45 For a possible date, see Adriaensen et al. 1998, 33.
46 See Bhaṭṭarāī 1988, 37 with siglum *ga*; Adriaensen et al. 1998, 34 with siglum SP₄. See also NGMCP entry at: <http://ngmcp.fdm.uni-hamburg.de/mediawiki/index.php/B_12-2_Skandapur%C4%81%E1%B9%87a> (last accessed on 12.09.2018).
47 Note that this manuscript also contains another NGMPP reel number as A 1084/7.
48 This measurement is just based on the NGMCP card. None of the folios are in full size at present.
49 See Adriaensen et al. 1998, 34.
50 See NGMCP entry at: <http://ngmcp.fdm.uni-hamburg.de/mediawiki/index.php/A_51-12_Yogay%C4%81j%C3%B1avalkya> (last accessed on 13.09.2018).
51 Note that this manuscript also contains another NGMPP reel number as A 1161/3.

Writing support, format, size and cover

Palm-leaf, *pothī*, ca. 20.5 × 4 cm. 49 folios extant. The text of the YY ends on 43v. The other last six folios contain the texts of the *Gāyatrīnyāsa* and *Prāṇāgnihotra*. The very last folio is small and looks half-size compared to other folios. The folio is not numbered and usually contains two lines of writing on one side with the other side left blank aside from one invocation added later and the writing of the archival number in modern Devanāgarī added relatively later. The handwriting on the last folios seems clearly to be of a later period when compared to the handwriting of other folios in the YY. There are two string-holes on each folio (except for the very last small folio where there is only one string-hole). The manuscript has wooden covers which seem to be original.

Condition, date, script and foliation

Complete, in relatively good condition. On a few folios parts of the writing have faded (e.g. 1v, 6r, 5v, 8rv, 9r, 10r, 19r, 20v, 31rv, 32r, 40v, 41r, 42v). The manuscript is dated NS 144 (1024 CE). Newari. Letter-numerals on the left-hand margin verso.

1.2.1.11 Manuscript HV_1

Title: *Harivaṃśa*[52]

Place of storage: National Archives, Kathmandu

Accession no. 1/910

NGMPP reel no. A 29/4

Writing support, format, size and cover

Palm-leaf, *pothī*, ca. 55 × 4.5 cm. 333 folios. There are two string-holes on each folio. The manuscript has wooden covers which seem to be original.

Condition, date, script and foliation

Complete; in relatively good condition. A few leaves are broken. On a few folios parts of the writing have faded. The manuscript is dated NS 157 (1037 CE).[53] Newari. Letter-numerals on the left-hand margin.

---

52 See Shastri 1905, 1 and 25; see also NGMCP entry at: <http://ngmcp.fdm.uni-hamburg.de/mediawiki/index.php/A_29-4_Hariva%E1%B9%83%C5%9Ba> (last accessed on 13.09.2018).

53 Shastri 1905, 1 dates this manuscript NS 257 corresponding to 1137 CE. However, the manuscript is actually dated NS 157 (1037 CE), see 329r4 where the date is found.

1.2.1.12 Manuscript HY

Title: *Haṃsayāmala*[54]
Place of storage: National Archives, Kathmandu
Accession no. 1/1076
NGMPP reel no. B 28/33

Writing support, format, size and cover

Palm-leaf, *pothī*, ca. 29 × 4 cm (some folios are smaller and taper at the edges). 22 folios extant. There is one string-hole one third away from the left edge of the folio. The manuscript has new wooden covers.

Condition, date, script and foliation

Incomplete; margins are broken. Some parts of the folios are worm eaten. On a few folios the writing has faded (e.g. 9v, 10r 11v, 12r). The manuscript is dated NS 159 (1039 CE). Newari. Letter-numerical foliation on the left-hand margin verso. Most of the foliation has been lost due to the damage of leaves. A modern figure-numerical foliation added later appears under the string-hole.

1.2.1.13 Manuscript DDh

Title: *Dānadharma*[55]
Place of storage: National Archives, Kathmandu
Accession no. 1/1321
NGMPP reel no. A 27/2

Writing support, format, size and cover

Palm-leaf, *pothī*, ca. 43 × 4.5 cm. 69 folios. There are two string-holes on each folio. The manuscript contains wooden covers which seem to be original.

Condition, date, script and foliation

Incomplete; in good condition. The manuscript is dated NS 173 (1053 CE).[56] Newari. Letter-numerical foliation on the left-hand margin verso.

---

54 See NGMCP entry at: <http://ngmcp.fdm.uni-hamburg.de/mediawiki/index.php/B_28-33_Ha%E1%B9%83say%C4%81mala> (last accessed on 13.09.2018).

55 See Shastri 1905, 1 and 48; see also NGMCP entry at: <http://ngmcp.fdm.uni-hamburg.de/mediawiki/index.php/A_27-2_Mah%C4%81bh%C4%81rata> (last accessed on 08.09.2018).

1.2.1.14 Manuscript TS_1

Title: *Tantrasadbhāva*[57]
Place of storage: National Archives, Kathmandu
Accession no. 5/445
NGMPP reel no. A 44/2

Writing support, format, size and cover

Palm-leaf, *pothī*, ca. 56 × 5 cm. 186 folios. Small pieces of leaves can be found after the 'actual' folios 60, 99 and 125 on which one can see numbers written again '60', '99' and '125' on the left-hand margin. On these folios text is written only on one side with the other side blank. All contain a two-line text, and before and after the lines, 'x'-like insertion signs can are found. There are two string-holes on each folio. The manuscript has wooden covers and both seem to be original.

Condition, date, script and foliation

Incomplete; the manuscript is in relatively good condition and dated NS 217 (1097 CE).[58] Newari. Letter-numerical foliation on the left-hand margin verso.

1.2.1.15 Manuscript VDh

Title: *Viṣṇudharma*[59]
Place of storage: National Archives, Kathmandu
Accession no. 5/344
NGMPP reel no. A 10/6

---

56 Shastri 1905, I dates this manuscript NS 169 corresponding to 1049 CE. Actually this manuscript is dated NS 173 (1053 CE), see 69r5.

57 Part of the text of this manuscript and TS_2 (see below) was studied by my colleague Jung-Lan Bang (2017, 16 and 39–55) (TS_1 with siglum A and TS_2 with siglum B) in the course of her doctoral dissertation at the CSMC. I am grateful to her for sharing with me the digitised colour images of both manuscripts (TS_1 and TS_2). See also NGMCP entry at: <http://ngmcp.fdm.uni-hamburg.de/mediawiki/index.php/A_44-2_Tantrasadbh%C4%81va> (last accessed on 13.09.2018).

58 For the discussions of the manuscript date, see Petech 1984, 49–50 (as Friday, February 27th, 1097); Bang 2017 as 1097/8 CE. Here I refer to 1097 CE.

59 See Grünendahl 1983, 16–17 with siglum N8; see also NGMCP entry at: <http://ngmcp.fdm.uni-hamburg.de/mediawiki/index.php/A_10-6_Vi%E1%B9%A3%E1%B9%87udharma> (last accessed on 07.09.2018).

Writing support, format, size and cover

Palm-leaf, *pothī*, ca. 57.5 × 5 cm. 160 folios. There are two string-holes on each folio. The manuscript contains wooden covers which seem to be original. In addition, the inner parts of both covers are illustrated.

Condition, date, script and foliation

Complete; in relatively good condition. On some folios the writing has faded. The manuscript is possibly ca. 12th c.[60] Newari. Letter-numerical foliation on the left-hand margin verso and figure-numerical foliation on the right-hand margin verso.

1.2.1.16 Manuscript SSS

Title: *Siddhasārasaṃhitā*[61]
Place of storage: National Archives, Kathmandu
Accession no. 7/4
NGMPP reel no. A 45/4

Writing support, format, size and cover

Palm-leaf, *pothī*, ca. 55 × 5 cm. 54 folios. There are two string-holes on the folio. As I only had access to b/w images of this manuscript before preparing the current volume and the images include no pictures of the covers, it is difficult to make any statement on the condition of the covers at this moment.

Condition, date, script and foliation

Complete; leaves are broken. In many places parts of folios have been broken or are worm eaten on the margins. On one folio, the writing has faded (on 4r). The manuscript is dated NS 234 (1114 CE).[62] Newari. Letter-numerical foliation on the left-hand margin verso.

---

60 For possible manuscript dating, see Grünendahl 1983, 16–17.
61 See Emmerick 1980, 5 with siglum C; see also NGMCP entry at: <http://ngmcp.fdm.uni-hamburg.de/mediawiki/index.php/A_45-4_Siddhas%C4%81rasa%E1%B9%83hit%C4%81> (last accessed on 07.09.2018).
62 On the date of the manuscript, see Emmerick 1980, 5.

1.2.1.17 Manuscript AṣP$_1$

Title: *Aṣṭasāhasrikā Prajñāpāramitā*
Place of storage: National Archives, Kathmandu
Accession no. 5/195
NGMPP reel no. A 36/4

Writing support, format, size and cover

Palm-leaf, *pothī*, ca. 55.5 × 5 cm. 272 folios extant.[63] There are two string-holes on each folio. The manuscript has wooden covers and both seem to be original. The inner parts of both covers are illustrated and outer parts of covers contain traces of coloured paste that is largely of red and yellow hues.

Condition, date, script and foliation

Incomplete; some folios are broken. The manuscript is dated NS 271 (1151 CE). Newari. Letter-numerical foliation on the left-hand margin verso and figure-numerical foliation on the right-hand margin verso.

1.2.1.18 Manuscript HV$_2$

Title: *Harivaṃśa*[64]
Place of storage: National Archives, Kathmandu
Accession no. 1/455
NGMPP reel no. A 27/1

Writing support, format, size and cover

Palm-leaf, *pothī*, ca. 57.5 × 5 cm. 414 folios. There are two string-holes on each folio. The manuscript has wooden covers and they seem to be original. The inner parts of both covers are illustrated.

---

63 The actual existing folios are 272 not 255 as displayed on the NGMCP entry and catalogue card. 10 folios from 210–219 appear to be missing.

64 See Shastri 1905, 1 and 25; see also NGMCP entry at: <http://ngmcp.fdm.uni-hamburg.de/mediawiki/index.php/A_27-1_Hariva%E1%B9%83%C5%9Ba> (last accessed on 07.09.2018).

Condition, date, script and foliation
Almost complete; in relatively good condition. Some parts of the writing have faded on a few folios, e.g. 140v, 141r, 383r. The manuscript is dated NS 292 (1172 CE).[65] Newari. Letter-numerical foliation on the left-hand margin verso.

1.2.1.19 Manuscript SDhPS

Title: *Saddharmapuṇḍarīkasūtra*[66]
Place of storage: National Archives, Kathmandu
Accession no. 3/678
NGMPP reel no. A 37/2

Writing support, format, size and cover
Palm-leaf, *pothī*, ca. 54 × 5.5 cm. 134 folios (folios 1, 41, 112, 121, 124 are missing). There are two string-holes on each folio. The manuscript has wooden front and back covers. Both seem to be original. Inner parts of both covers contain illustrations.

Condition, date, script and foliation
Incomplete; some folios are broken. It is possible to date the manuscript ca. 12th c. Newari. Letter-numerical foliation on the left-hand margin and figure-numerical foliation on the right-hand margin verso.

1.2.1.20 Manuscript AṣP$_2$

Title: *Aṣṭasāhasrikā Prajñāpāramitā*
Place of storage: National Archives, Kathmandu
Accession no. 3/359
NGMPP reel no. A 35/9

Writing support, format, size and cover
Palm-leaf, *pothī*, ca. 59 × 6 cm. 38 folios extant. Many folios of the manuscript are missing or have most likely been misplaced in the bundle of other manuscripts. There are two string-holes on each folio. Covers.[67]

---

65 It seems that Shastri 1905, l did not notice the manuscript to be dated. The date is actually written in *bhūtasaṃkhyā* ('object or concrete numbers') on 416r4 and reads as follows *nayanagrahakara-varṣe* ('in the year 292').
66 See NGMCP entry at: <http://ngmcp.fdm.uni-hamburg.de/mediawiki/index.php/A_37-2_Saddharmapu%E1%B9%87%E1%B8%8Dar%C4%ABka> (last accessed on 08.09.2018).

Condition, date, script and foliation
Incomplete; margins are broken. It is possible to date the manuscript ca. 12th. Newari. Letter-numerical foliation on the left margin verso.

1.2.1.21 Manuscript SS

Title: *Sādhanasamuccaya*[68]
Place of storage: University Library, Cambridge
Accession no. MS Add.1648

Writing support, format, size and cover
Palm-leaf, *pothī*, ca. $12^{1/2} \times 2$ in (ca. 31.7 × 5 cm). 228 folios (folios are mostly regular). There are two string-holes on each folio. Wooden covers. They appear to be original.

Condition, date, script and foliation
Complete; in good condition. The manuscript is dated NS 336 (1216 CE).[69] Newari. Figure-numerical foliation on the left-hand margin verso.

1.2.1.22 Manuscript TS$_2$

Title: *Tantrasadbhāva*[70]
Place of storage: National Archives, Kathmandu
Accession no. 1/363
NGMPP reel no. A 44/1

Writing support, format, size and cover
Palm-leaf, *pothī*, ca. 34.5 × 5.5 cm. 140 folios. There are two string-holes on each folio. Wooden covers. The front cover seems to be new and the back cover original.

67 As has been reported in the NGMCP entry at: <http://ngmcp.fdm.uni-hamburg.de/mediawiki/index.php/A_35-9_A%E1%B9%A3%E1%B9%ADas%C4%81hasrik%C4%81_praj%C3%B1%C4%81p%C4%81ramit%C4%81>, the manuscript possibly has covers, but we did not find images of the covers in the digitised copies of the NGMPP reel A 35/9.
68 See Bendall 1883, xxviii and 154–155; see also at: <https://cudl.lib.cam.ac.uk/view/MS-ADD-01648/1> (last accessed on 08.09.2018).
69 On the discussion of the date of the manuscript, see Bendall 1883, xxviii and 154.
70 See NGMPP entry at: <http://ngmcp.fdm.uni-hamburg.de/mediawiki/index.php/A_44-1_Tantrasadbh%C4%81va> (last accessed on 08.09.2018). Part of the text was studied by my colleague Jung-Lan Bang (2017, 39–55 with siglum B) for her doctoral dissertation.

Condition, date, script and foliation

Incomplete; some parts of the margins of folios have been damaged. On some folios the writing is faded. It is possible to date the manuscript ca. 13th c. Newari. Letter-numerical foliation on the left-hand margin verso and figure-numerical foliation on the right-hand margin verso.

1.2.2 East Indian manuscripts

1.2.2.1 Manuscript PR

Title: *Pañcarakṣā*[71]

Place of storage: University Library, Cambridge

Accession no. MS Add.1688

Writing support, format, size and cover

Palm-leaf, *pothī*, ca. 56 × 5 cm. 69 folios (folio 27 is missing). There are two string-holes on each folio. Wooden covers, possibly original ones. Eight spots made of a reddish-like power/paste can be found on the outer part of the back cover.[72] However, there are no traces of pigment on the front cover.

Condition, date, script and foliation

Incomplete; in relatively good condition. Some parts of the leaves are worm eaten. Some of the writing on a number of folios is faded. The manuscript is

71 See Bendall 1883, 175; see also Cambridge entry for detailed information of this manuscript at: <https://cudl.lib.cam.ac.uk/view/MS-ADD-01688> (last accessed on 08.09.2018).

72 There are a few manuscripts containing the same text in which traces of pigment or other substance are found on the covers, e.g. on the outer part of the front cover of the manuscript of the *Pañcarakṣā* (NS 183 / 1063 CE) (NAK 3/688 / NGMPP B 30/45-B 31/1); on the outer part of the front cover of the manuscript of the *Pañcarakṣā* (CUL Add.1644) (NS 325 / 1205 CE), on the outer part of the front cover of the manuscript of the *Pañcarakṣā* (ca. 15th–16th c.) (NAK 5/7457 / NGMPP B 31/17) including a big bundle of threads bound on the right side; on the outer part of the back cover of the manuscript of the *Pañcarakṣā* (NS 655 / 1535 CE) (NAK 4/21 / NGMPP B 30/29); on the outer part of the front cover of the (birch-bark) manuscript of the *Pañcarakṣā* (ca. 16th c.) (KL 116 / NGMPP C 13/4) including bundles of threads bound on the left and right sides; on most of the outer part of the front cover of the (*nīlapatra*, i.e. 'black paper') manuscript of the *Pañcarakṣā* (ca. 16th–17th c.) (NAK 5/7633 / NGMPP A 139/2) including curds bound on the left side; on the outer part of the front cover of the (paper) manuscript of the *Pañcarakṣā* (NS 815 / 1695 CE) (CUL Or.2258); on the outer part of the front cover of the (paper) manuscript of the *Pañcarakṣā* (ca. 17th c.) (CUL Add.1164.1).

dated to 14th regnal year of Nayapāla of Bengal (1054 CE).[73] Rañjanā. Letter-numerical foliation on the left-hand margin verso and figure-numerical foliation on the right-hand margin verso. A figure-numerical foliation has been added above (on 1v, 2v, 3v, 4v, 8v, 11v, 12v) or below the right string-hole on the verso (on all remaining folios).

1.2.2.2 Manuscript AAĀ

Title: *Abhisamayālaṅkārālokā*[74]
Place of storage: National Archives, Kathmandu
Accession no. 3/738
NGMPP reel no. A 37/7

Writing support, format, size and cover

Palm-leaf, *pothī*, ca. 55 × 5 cm. 162 folios (folios 1, 137 and 138 are missing). There are two string-holes on each folio. Wooden covers. They seem to be original. The inner parts of both covers contain illustrations which are now partly faded.

Condition, date, script and foliation

Almost complete; in considerably good condition. Some of the leaves and the leave's margins are broken. The manuscript can probably be dated ca. 11th c.[75] Old Bengali. Figure-numerical foliation on the left hand-margin verso.

1.2.2.3 Manuscript GV

Title: *Guṇavatī* (aka *Mahāmāyāṭīkā*)[76]
Place of storage: Kaiser Library, Kathmandu
Accession no. 226
NGMPP reel no. C 25/7

---

73 Various dates have been suggested by scholars for the manuscript, e.g. Bendall 1883, 175 as ca. 1054 CE; Losty 1982, 31 1057 CE; Mevissen 1992, 415 1041 CE. More recently Dimitrov 2016 has provided a new chart on the Pāla chronology, see 747–756, Appendix 1 and Figure 9. For practical reasons in this volume I refer to the date suggested in 1883 by Bendall now verified.

74 See Tucci 1932, vi with siglum N.

75 For the discussion on dating this manuscript, see Delhey et al. 2015.

76 See Moriguchi 1989, 98 as catalogue no. 412. He appears to have taken the title directly ('*Mahāmāyatantraguṇavatiṭīkā*(!)') from the NGMPP card. However, the colophon giving the text title reads on 10r5–6 *guṇavatī nāma mahāmāyāṭīkā paṇḍitaratnākaraśā*[6]*ntipādānāṃ samāpteti*.

Writing support, format, size and cover
Palm-leaf, *pothī*, ca. 56.6 × 5.5 cm. 10 folios. There are two string-holes on each folio. The manuscript contains yellow painted new wooden covers.

Condition, date, script and foliation
Complete; in good condition. Parts of a few folios are worm eaten on the left. It is possible to date the manuscript ca. 12th c. Old Bengali. Figure-numerical foliations on the left and right-hand margins verso.

1.2.2.4 Manuscript HAP

Title: *Herukābhyudayapañjikā* (aka *Katipayākṣarā*)[77]
Place of storage: Kaiser Library, Kathmandu
Accession no. 229
NGMPP reel no. C 26/2

Writing support, format, size and cover
Palm-leaf, *pothī*, ca. 56.5 × 5.5 cm. 10 folios. There are two string-holes on each folio. The manuscript contains new, yellow-painted wooden covers.

Condition, date, script and foliation
Complete and in good condition. It is possible to date the manuscript ca. 12th c. Old Bengali. Figure-numerical foliations on the left and right-hand margins verso.

1.2.2.5 Manuscript LTṬ

Title: *Laghutantraṭīkā*[78]
Place of storage: Kaiser Library, Kathmandu
Accession no. 225
NGMPP reel no. C 25/6

77 See Moriguchi 1989, 144 as catalogue no. 609. A question mark is recorded after the text title '*Herukābhyudayamahāyoginītantrarāje katipayākṣarapañjikānāmaṭikā*'. The manuscript colophon on 10r2 reads *śrīherukābhyudayamahāyoginītantrarāje kumāracandrakṛtā katipayākṣarā pañjikā samāptā*. One may assume he was not certain of the actual title and took on a large part of the colophon without identifying the text title.

78 See Moriguchi 1989, 108 as catalogue no. 457. He records the title thusly *Lakṣābhidhānatantroddhṛtalaghvabhidhāna*. Here it appears he took most of the title from the colophon line without identifying the proper title. See Cicuzza 2001, 26 with siglum A.

Writing support, format, size and cover

Palm-leaf, *pothī*, ca. 56.3 × 5.5 cm. 30 folios (folio 22 is missing). There are two string-holes on each folio. The manuscript has yellow painted new wooden covers.

Condition, date, script and foliation

Nearly complete; in good condition. It is possible to date the manuscript ca. 12th c.[79] Old Bengali. Figure-numerical foliations on the left and right-hand margins verso.

1.2.2.6 Manuscript STṬ

Title: *Saṃpuṭatantraṭīkā* (aka *Prakaraṇārthanirṇaya*)[80]
Place of storage: Kaiser Library, Kathmandu
Accession no. 228
NGMPP reel no. C 26/1

Writing support, format, size and cover

Palm-leaf, *pothī*, ca. 56.5 × 5.3 cm. 11 folios. There are two string-holes on each folio. Manuscript contains yellow painted new wooden covers.

Condition, date, script and foliation

Complete and in good condition. It is possible to date the manuscript ca. 12th c. Old Bengali. Figure-numerical foliations on the left and right-hand margins verso.

---

79 Cicuzza 2001, 26 suggests the date for this manuscript as 13th–14th c. On palaeographical grounds, however, I consider this manuscript to be older, possibly one century older than the date Cicuzza suggests (Szántó 2012, 105 also suggests referring to Harunaga Isaacson to be the second half of the 12th c.). See also section 3.5.2 for observations on symbols and palaeography.

80 See Moriguchi 1989, 128 as catalogue no. 553. See also NGMCP entry at: <http://ngmcp.fdm.uni-hamburg.de/mediawiki/index.php/C_26-1_Sampu%E1%B9%ADatantra%E1%B9%AD%C4%ABk%C4%81> (last accessed on 08.09.2018).

1.2.2.7 Manuscript ḌVPṬ

Title *Ḍākinīvajrapañjaraṭippaṇī*:[81]
Place of storage: Kaiser Library, Kathmandu
Accession no. 230
NGMPP reel no. C 26/3

Writing support, format, size and cover

Palm-leaf, *pothī*, ca. 56 × 5 cm. 8 folios. There are two string-holes on each folio. The manuscript has modern, yellow-painted wooden covers.

Condition, date, script and foliation

Complete; in good condition. It is possible to date the manuscript ca. 12th c. Old Bengali. Figure-numerical foliations on the left and right-hand margins verso.

1.2.2.8 Manuscript AP

Title: *Abhayapaddhati* (aka *Buddhakapālamahātantraṭīkā*)[82]
Place of storage: National Archives, Kathmandu
Accession no. 5/21
NGMPP reel no. A 48/2

Writing support, format, size and cover

Palm-leaf, *pothī*, ca. 57 × 6 cm. 20 folios extant (folios 2, 6, 11, 16–17, 19 appear to be missing or misplaced). There are two string-holes on each folio. The manuscript has new wooden covers.

Condition, date, script and foliation

Complete; in good condition. The manuscript is purported to date from ca. 12th c.[83] Old Bengali. Figure-numerical foliations on the left and right-hand margins verso.

---

81 See Moriguchi 1989, 46 as catalogue no. 185. See also NGMCP entry at: <http://ngmcp.fdm.uni-hamburg.de/mediawiki/index.php/C_26-3_%E1%B8%8C%C4%81kin%C4%ABvajrapa%C3%B1jara%E1%B9%ADippa%E1%B9%87%C4%AB> (last accessed on 08.09.2018).

82 See Moriguchi 1989, 82 as catalogue no. 333; see also NGMCP entry at: <http://ngmcp.fdm.uni-hamburg.de/mediawiki/index.php/A_48-2_Abhayapaddhati> (last accessed on 08.09.2018).

83 Szántó 2012, 105 suggests referring to Prof. Harunaga Isaacson to be the second half of the 12th c.

1.2.2.9 Manuscript CPN

Title: *Catuṣpīṭhanibandha*[84]
Place of storage: Kaiser Library, Kathmandu
Accession no. 134
NGMPP reel no. C 14/11

Writing support, format, size and cover

Palm-leaf, *pothī*, ca. 55.5 × 5.5 cm. 53 folios (3 folios, namely 1, 39, 49 of this manuscript can be found in the bundle of the HP (KL 231 / NGMPP C 26/4)).[85] There are two string-holes on each folio. The manuscript has modern, yellow-painted wooden covers.

Condition, date, script and foliation

Incomplete; in good condition. ca. 12th c.[86] Old Bengali. Figure-numerical foliations on the left and right-hand margins on verso.

1.2.2.10 Manuscript HP

Title: *Hevajrapañjikā* (aka *Ratnāvalī*)[87]
Place of storage: Kaiser Library, Kathmandu
Accession no. 231
NGMPP reel no. C 26/4

Writing support, format, size and cover

Palm-leaf, *pothī*, ca. 55.5 × 5.2 cm. 25 folios extant (folios 1, 39, 49 of CPN (KL 134 / NGMPP C 14/11) are in this manuscript bundle). There are two string-holes on each folio. The manuscript has modern, yellow-painted wooden covers.

---

84 See Moriguchi 1989, 40 as catalogue no. 156 titled '*Catuṣpīṭhapañjikā*'; Szántó 2012, 100 with siglum 'K'.

85 Also one folio of the *Ḍākinīvajrapañjarapañjikā* (NAK 5/20 / NGMPP A 47/17) seems to be inserted in the manuscript bundle.

86 Szántó 2012, 105 suggests referring to Prof. Harunaga Isaacson to be the second half of the 12th c.

87 See Moriguchi 1989, 146 as catalogue no. 615; see also NGMCP entry at: <http://ngmcp.fdm.uni-hamburg.de/mediawiki/index.php/C_26-4(2)_Ratn%C4%81val%C4%AB_Hevajrapa%C3%B1jik%C4%81> (last accessed on 08.09.2018).

Condition, date, script and foliation
Complete; in good condition. It is possible to date the manuscript ca. 12th c. Old Bengali. Figure-numerical foliations on the left and right-hand margins verso.

1.2.2.11 Manuscript HTṬ

Title: *Hevajratantraṭīkā* (aka *Ṣaṭsāhasrikā*)[88]
Place of storage: Kaiser Library, Kathmandu
Accession no. 128
NGMPP reel no. C 14/6

Writing support, format, size and cover
Palm-leaf, *pothī*, ca. 29.5 × 5 cm. 33 folios (folios 2, 6, 8–18, 32–39, 42–46 are missing). There is one string-hole on each folio which appears to be a little more than one third part away from the left edge of the folio. The manuscript has modern, yellow-painted wooden covers.

Condition, date, script and foliation
Incomplete; some folios are damaged on the margins and parts of a few folios are broken. On a few folios some of the writing has faded (e.g. on 24v, 25r, 26v, 27r). The manuscript is thought to date from ca. 12th c.[89] Old Bengali. Figure-numerical foliations on the left and right-hand margins verso. A figure-numerical foliation on the upper-centre margin verso has been added later. There is another figure-numerical foliation on the upper-right margin verso on many folios and this appears, when the right side of the leaf is broken and the foliation on the right-hand has been lost.

---

88 See Moriguchi 1989, 146 as catalogue no. 614; Sferra 2009, 436 as siglum K^K.
89 On the date, Sferra 2009, 436.

1.2.2.12 Manuscript AT

Title: *Anāvilatantra*[90]
Place of storage: General Library, University of Tokyo, Tokyo
Accession no. MF14 63 014

Writing support, format, size and cover

Palm-leaf, *pothī*, ca. ? cm, 19 folios extant. There is one string-hole on the folio. At present we have no knowledge of the state of the covers.

Condition, date, script and foliation

Incomplete; in relatively good condition. Some of the folio margins have been broken. It is possible to date the manuscript ca. 12th c.[91] Old Bengali. Figure-numerical foliation on the left-hand margin verso. Most of the foliation has not been preserved.

1.2.3 West Indian manuscripts

1.2.3.1 Manuscript TSa

Title: *Tattvasaṃgraha*[92]
Place of storage: Jinabhadrasūri Grantha Bhaṇḍāra, Jaisalmer
Accession no. 377

Writing support, format, size and cover

Palm-leaf, *pothī*, ca. ? cm. 187 folios extant (folio 186 is missing). There is one string-hole on each folio. The manuscript seems to have included wooden covers.

---

90 Sanderson (2009, footnote 360) reports referring to the communication of Dr Péter-Dániel Szántó who identified the existence of the *Anāvilatantra* in the General Library of the University of Tokyo. I am thankful to Prof. Harunaga Isaacson for sharing with me the digitised colour images of this manuscript. B/w images of this manuscript are available at: <http://picservice.ioc.u-tokyo.ac.jp/03_150219~UT-library_sanskrit_ms/MF14_63_014~MF14_63_014/> (last accessed on 09.09.2018).

91 On palaeographical grounds this manuscript exhibits some similarities with the HTṬ. Therefore, it is also possible to date this manuscript ca. 12th c (for the palaeographical evidence, see section 3.5.2 below).

92 See Jambuvijay 2000, 40.

Condition, date, script and foliation

Incomplete; in good condition. The manuscript is dated VS 1200 (1143 CE). Jaina Devanāgarī. Letter-numerical foliation on the left-hand margin verso and figure-numerical foliation on the right-hand margin verso.

1.2.3.2 Manuscript TSPV

Title: *Tattvasaṃgrahapañjikāvṛtti*[93]
Place of storage: Jinabhadrasūri Grantha Bhaṇḍāra, Jaisalmer
Accession no. 378

Writing support, format, size and cover

Palm-leaf, *pothī*, ca. ? cm. 313 folios extant? (folios 61, 113, 302 and 311 appear to be missing). There are two string-holes on each folio. The manuscript seems to have included wooden covers.

Condition, date, script and foliation

Complete and in good condition. The manuscript is dated VS 1200 (1143 CE). Jaina Devanāgarī. Most of the manuscript has letter-numerical foliation on the left-hand margin verso and figure-numerical foliation on the right-hand margin verso. However, in some parts there are only figure-numerical foliations on both the left and right-hand margins. Further on, parts of the manuscript's left and right foliation numbers do not match with one another.

1.2.3.3 Manuscript HVM

Title: *Haravijayamahākāvya*[94]
Place of storage: Jinabhadrasūri Grantha Bhaṇḍāra, Jaisalmer
Accession no. 408

Writing support, format and size

Palm-leaf, *pothī*, ca. ? cm. 107 folios. There are two string-holes on each folio.

---

93 Jambuvijay 2000, 40.
94 Ibid., 43.

Condition, date, script and foliation

Complete and in good condition. The manuscript is dated VS 1228 (1171 CE). Jaina Devanāgarī. Letter-numerical foliation on the left-hand margin verso and figure-numerical foliation on the right-hand margin verso.

1.2.3.4 Manuscript PV

Title: *Praśnavyākaraṇa*[95]
Place of storage: National Archives, Kathmandu
Accession no. 4/149
NGMPP reel no. B 23/37

Writing support, format, size and cover

Palm-leaf, *pothī*, ca. 34 × 6 cm. 152 folios (folios 142, 143 are missing). There is one string-hole on each folio. At present we have no knowledge of the state of the covers.

Condition, date, script and foliation

Nearly complete; margins of some folios are damaged. The manuscript is purported to date from ca. 12th c.[96] Jaina Devanāgarī. Figure-numerical foliation on the left-hand margin verso.

1.2.3.5 Manuscript JKS/C

Title: *Jītakalpasūtra*/*Jītakalpacūrṇī*[97]
Place of storage: British Library Board, London
Accession no. Or. 1385

95 See Acharya 2007, 1–10; see also NGMCP entry at: <http://ngmcp.fdm.uni-hamburg.de/mediawiki/index.php/B_23-37_Pra%C5%9Bnavy%C4%81kara%E1%B9%87a> (last accessed on 03.01.2019)

96 For discussion of the manuscript's dating, see Acharya 2007, 4.

97 See Balbir et al. 2006, 31; see also JAINpedia for manuscript information and digital images at: <http://www.jainpedia.org/manuscripts/detail-view-meta/manuscript/jita-kalpa-sutra-or-1385/first-page.html> (last accessed on 09.09.2018).

Writing support, format, size and cover

Palm-leaf, *pothī*, ca. 30 × 5 cm. 77 folios. Some folios taper at the margins and at times in the middle part. Each folio has one string hole. At present we have no knowledge of the state of the covers. The manuscript most probably does not have covers.

Condition, date, script and foliation

Complete, but some leaves are broken and there is damage in many places. The manuscript has been dated VS 1258 (1201 CE). Jaina Devanāgarī. Letter-numerical foliation on the left-hand margin verso and figure-numerical foliation on the right-hand margin verso.

1.2.3.6 Manuscript TUS

Title: *Tattvopaplavasiṃha*[98]

Place of storage: Hemacandrācārya Jaina Jñānamandira, Patan

Accession no. 178 (2)

Writing support, format, size, cover

Palm-leaf, *pothī*, ca. 14 × 1.1/5 inches (ca. 35.5 × 3.8 cm). Some folios are smaller and taper at the edges. 176 folios. Each folio has one string hole. At present we have no knowledge of the state of the covers.

Condition, date, script and foliation

Incomplete and most of part of the first folio is damaged and the margins of other folios are also broken. The manuscript is dated VS 1349 (1292 CE).[99] Jaina Devanāgarī. Figure-numerical foliation on the right-hand margin verso and letter-numerical foliation on the left-hand margin verso.

1.2.3.7 Manuscript BCV

Title: *Bṛhaccūrṇivyākhyā*[100]

Place of storage: British Library Board, London

Accession no. Or. 1386

---

98 See Sanghavi/Rasiklal 1987, i.

99 Ibid., for the date of the manuscript.

100 See JAINpedia for further manuscript information, digital images and date at: <http://www.jainpedia.org/manuscripts/detail-view-meta/manuscript/brhaccurnivyakhya-or-1386/text-e8212be59a.html> (last accessed on 09.09.2018).

Writing support, format, size and cover

Palm-leaf, *pothī*, ca. 30 × 5 cm (some folios are smaller and taper on the edges). 78 folios. Each folio has one string-hole. At present we have no knowledge of the state of the covers.

Condition, date, script and foliation

Complete; in good condition. The manuscript purportedly dates from ca. 13th c. Jaina Devanāgarī. Letter-numerical foliation on the left-hand margin verso and figure-numerical foliation on the right-hand margin verso.

2 Overall layout and possible reasons for its change in manuscript

In most Indic manuscripts each folio contains several elements: one or more texts, blank margins, string-holes, symbols, 'gaps' and 'blank spaces'.[101] The elements distribution on the folio is in relation to one another and can be termed a layout, or *mise en page*. Here the script size, line numbering and justification are elements that are part of the layout. Several factors determined the layout of a manuscript, for instance the shape of the writing supports, scribal practice, and text style (i.e. whether or not the text is composed in verse or prose) etc.

This chapter's main objective is to investigate the various layout elements in the manuscripts selected for the study to highlight the similarities and differences characterising the layout of manuscripts according to the place of their production. At times it may offer the opportunity to gain more precise information on the period of production of the manuscripts within the time-frame of the 9th to 13th c. relevant to this study.

2.1 Writing support

The arrangement of texts, free spaces, etc. on a folio is closely related to the writing support on which the manuscript has been made. In this instance palm-leaf manuscripts have largely been used, all of which are in *pothī* format.[102] This means their length is longer than their breadth. The leaf shape has been adopted for writing, and the text often runs horizontally on each folio.[103]

According to its length, each folio can have one or two string-holes. A short leaf will usually have just one string-hole (see sections 2.4.1–2.4.3 for examples of layout below). Long leaves, usually have two string-holes (see sections 2.4.1–2.4.3 for examples below).[104]

---

101 In this work a small free space, used between smaller text units (such as sentences, *pāda*s or first and second halves of the *śloka*s) on the folio, has been categorised as a 'gap' (see section 4.2 for more details below). The free spaces left at the end of a (sub-)chapter, text demarcated by a set(s) of double *daṇḍa*s have been categorised as a 'blank space' (see section 4.1 for more detail below).

102 For *pothī*, see Formigatti 2011, 29.

103 On the discussion of the direction of writing, see Hoernle 1900, 131.

104 See Godakumbura 1980, IL in which the rule for fixing of the holes on the folio has been given (though some readings in the verse appear to contain errors; I have marked them with a

https://doi.org/10.1515/9783110543087-002

The text may run all along the length of the folio or may be divided into two or three text-sections.[105] In the latter, portions of the folio page are left clear intentionally, with no written text. These portions may occupy the entire space above and below the string-holes, or just a small area of the space around the string-holes (this smaller free space may take a kind of a 'square shape').

Furthermore, even in one manuscript, the shape of the leaves may vary considerably.[106] Some leaves may to an extent be regular and some appear slightly curved or taper on the left and right margins (e.g. see Figs. 2.4.1-II, 2.4.1-III, 2.4.1-V, 2.4.3-III, 2.4.3-VI, 2.4.3-VII below).[107] In such cases, scribes break the lines where they cannot write properly and insert space-fillers.[108] This results in widely different numbers of *akṣara*s per line, even on the same folio.

2.2 Scribal practice

Another important part of this study is the scribal practice, which may be directly related to the arrangement of the text and other features in manuscripts. If more than one scribe had been involved in the production of a manuscript, certain features may be perceived (e.g. script, overall layout etc.) as altered within the same manuscript. In such cases, one scribe may write the text carefully for his lines appear as straight, whereas another scribe may write in a less sophisticated way or not take the same pains to produce clear or regular writing, resulting in writing that appears to be of poor quality.

Regarding symbols, one scribe may draw them beautifully, but another may draw extremely simple ones, with little effort (even in the same manuscript). In other cases, the scribe may not draw symbols and leave blank spaces in their place (see section 4.1 below).

---

sic sign) as follows: *ayamena*(!) *caturbhāgaṃ tribhāgaṃ punar eva ca*[|]*ubhayoḥ sūtramadhyena tathā kuryāc chidralakṣaṇaṃ*(!)||; on the topic, see also Losty 1982, 7.

105 If the text lines are left clear from top to bottom on the string-hole space on the folio making the organisation of the text on the folio appear like a kind of column, it is categorised as a 'text-section' in the present study (see section 2.5 for more details below).

106 Regarding study of the writing support, especially palm-leaves and size, see Hoernle 1900.

107 See Thaker 2002, 143.

108 Space-fillers are normally found at the beginning or end of lines on the left or right side on the folio. Here scribes cannot write properly due to the format of leaf and thus place such symbols in order to indicate that a line or portion of text continues in another line of the same folio or in another folio. See Einicke 2009, 487 for the term 'Zeilenfüller'.

However, a scribe may write the text in three text-sections on a folio featuring two string-holes, while another may write the text in the same manuscript in only two text-sections in spite of the two string-holes (e.g. see section 3.9.3 below).

Also, a scribe may clearly divide smaller text units, such as *pāda*s or the first and second halves of *ślokas*,[109] leaving small but visible gaps between those parts of the text. In the same manuscript, however, another scribe may exhibit no interest in demarcating such kinds of text divisions (see sections 3.9.1 and 3.9.2 below).

2.3 Text style

The text style contained in a manuscript may be closely related to its layout. If the text is in verse, a scribe may write the text in to mirror the metrical scansion. Scribes may therefore leave small gaps either between the *pāda*s ('quarters') or only between the first and second half of the verse (see sections 4.2.1 and 4.2.2 below).

This phenomenon can be related to the level of each scribe's proficiency. We know that not all scribes were of the same level,[110] and that learned scribes were expected to have mastery in metrics.[111] Furthermore, it could well be that this way of dividing texts may be the result of the practice of writing under dictation.

2.4 Time and place of manuscript production

Certain layout features are clearly determined by the temporal and spatial setting of their production. The lines are written more regularly and the text is arranged carefully on the folio. In the corpus considered here, one sees that from the 10th c. onward the layout becomes gradually standardised.[112]

Furthermore, the site of manuscript production also bears a close relation to the text arrangement. A particular type of writing style, the overall page layout,

---

109 A *śloka* or *anuṣṭubh* (metre) contains total 32 syllables, each quarter consisting of eight syllables e.g. see Apte 1957, Appendix, 3. See also Steiner 1996 for a detailed study on *anuṣṭubh* metre.

110 For the qualifications and types of scribes, see Sarma 1992, 33–40. On scribes, see also Einicke 2009, 430–446; De Simini 2016, 96–102.

111 See Sarma 1992, 32–33: *chandolakṣaṇatattvajñaṃ satkaviṃ madhurasvaram* | *praṇaṣṭaṃ smarati granthaṃ śreṣṭhaṃ pustakalekhakam*(!) ||. We may at least deduce from this that a scribe was expected to know the metres and be a good poet.

112 I am not claiming here that this applies to all existing manuscripts for the regions. Exceptions and variations are always to be found.

or perhaps just a few features may have been developed and used solely in a specific area.

In the following, I will outline the overall layout of each manuscript from the three groups implemented in my analysis. I present the manuscripts in their possible chronological order, and specify the features that relate them to the regions of manuscript production.

2.4.1 Examples of layout in Nepalese manuscripts

The group of Nepalese manuscripts selected for this study consists largely of 22 manuscripts exhibiting a variety of layouts that were to become increasingly standardised within the period 9th to 13th c.

SP₁

SP₁ contains two string-holes per folio, each containing five to eight lines. The sample numbers of *akṣara*s per line are 96 (158v4, 159v2, 159v5, 186v4) (regarding the organisation of the *śloka*s by gaps in each text-section on the folio), 101 (10b3) and 99 (10b4) (without the division of *śloka*s by means of gaps). Not all folios are of the same size or shape: some taper at the edges and others are slightly curved. The text has been divided into three text-sections on each folio. On some folios, within each text-section, the first and second half of each *śloka* is further separated by a small gap (see sections 3.9.1 and 4.2.2 for more details below). If the *pāda*s are arranged within the frame of text-sections accordingly, each folio line contains three *śloka*s. With a few exceptions, at least two scribes appear to have worked on the production of the manuscript.[113] The overall layout of the manuscript can be seen as follows.

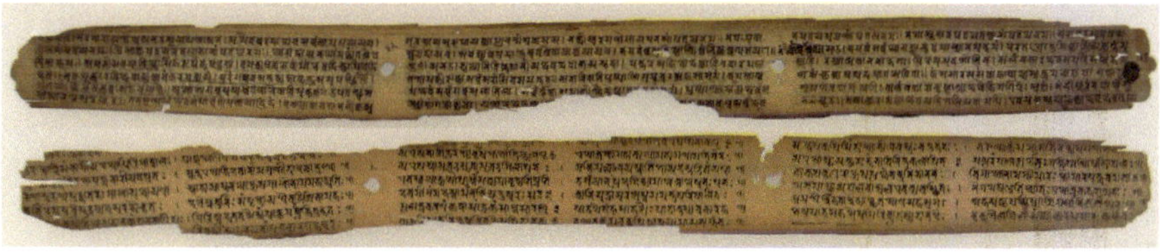

Fig. 2.4.1-I: Overall layout, fols.? (NAK image 71a, 74a) © NAK

113 This issue has been discussed thoroughly in section 3.9.1.

PT

PT has two string-holes per folio, each with three, five or seven lines. The sample numbers of *akṣara*s per line are 60 (14v4), 69 (17r3). The text has been divided into two or three text-sections (two text-sections on 22v, 35r, 37rv, 44rv, 46r, 47rv–51rv, 52r, 53r, 54rv–57rv etc. and three text-sections on 1v, 2r, 3rv, 4rv, 5v, 6rv, 7rv, 8rv, 9v, 10rv–14rv, 16rv–21rv, 22r, 23rv–34rv, 35v, 36rv, 39rv, 40rv–43rv, 52v, 53v, 62rv). The leaves are not of a uniform size (as can be seen in Fig. 2.4.1-II). Some of the folios taper at the edges and some folios are considerably curved. In many cases, this leads to irregularity of line-length, the number of lines per folio, and the number of *akṣara*s on the folio. A narrow, empty space has been left on the margins (concerning precise measurements of the script, text-sections, etc., see the Cambridge online catalogue entry). The overall layout of the manuscript can be seen in Fig. 2.4.1-II.

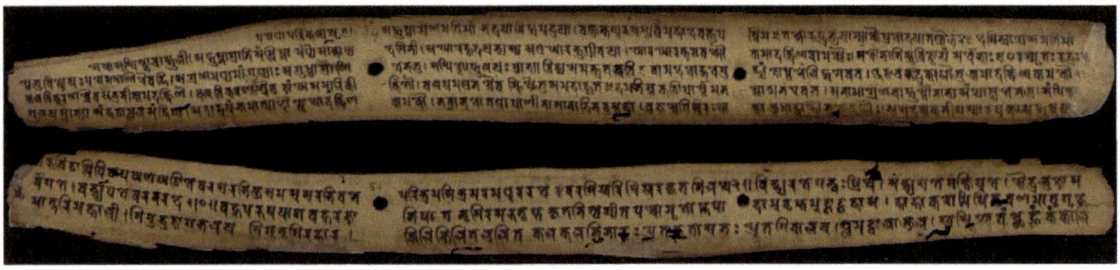

Fig. 2.4.1-II: Overall layout, fols. 34v, 51v © CUL

SS/N

SS/N has two string-holes per folio, each with seven to eight lines. The sample numbers of *akṣara*s per line are 88 (23v1), 110 (23v7), 98 (114v4). The text has been divided into three text-sections on each folio.[114] Folios are not of uniform size or shape. Some folios taper at the edges and a few others are slightly curved (e.g. Fig. 2.4.1-III). Small gaps have been used between the first and second halves of the *śloka*s or between 'sentences' on many folios (see section 4.2.1.2 below). Taking palaeography, symbol and space-filler, into account it may be assumed likely that four to five scribes could have worked on the manuscript's production. The overall layout in the manuscript may be seen as follows.

114 One should note that there are five folios on which the titles of the (sub-)chapters are written in the column structure. Two different hands are clearly evident on these folios. In comparison to the hands of the main text on other folios both hands on these folios look rather modern.

Fig. 2.4.1-III: Overall layout, fols. 119v, 130v © KL

SP₂

SP₂ presents two string-holes per folio, each containing four to seven lines per folio. The sample numbers of *akṣara*s per line are 96 (5a3), 95 (5a5), 94 (204a4). The text has been divided into three text-sections on each folio.[115] Some folios taper at the edges. On one folio *śloka*s have been divided precisely by small gaps within each text-section. At least two scribes may have worked on the manuscript production.[116] Two folios exemplifying the overall layout in the manuscript can be seen in Fig. 2.4.1-IV.

Fig. 2.4.1-IV: Overall layout, fols.? (NAK image 5a, 203a) © NAK

NTS

NTS has two string-holes per folio, each with five or six lines. The sample numbers of *akṣara*s per line are 97 (90v3), 99 (101v3), 106 (105r5) *akṣara*s. The text

115 On '1rv' the figure-numbers have been arranged in columns located between vertical lines. After most of these numbers there is no writing. However, a few of these numbers contain the titles of the chapters. It is likely the numbers without any writing were to have featured the titles. In comparison with hands of other folios, the hand on this folio looks rather modern. This might have been added comparatively later.

116 This has been discussed in detail in section 3.9.2 below.

has been divided into three text-sections on each folio. Some of the folios taper at the edges. Small gaps have been used between *pāda*s of the *śloka*s on some folios (see section 4.2.1.1 for more detail below). The overall layout in the manuscript can be seen as follows.

Fig. 2.4.1-V: Overall layout, fols. 99v, 100r © NAK

KT

KT presents two string-holes per folio, each containing five to seven lines per folio. The sample numbers of *akṣara*s per line are 47 (13v3), 61 (49v4), 58 (91v5). The text has been divided into two or three text-sections. At least three scribes may have worked on the production of the manuscript, evidenced by the layout and other features such as symbols and palaeography.[117] Examples of the overall layout in the manuscript can be seen as follows.

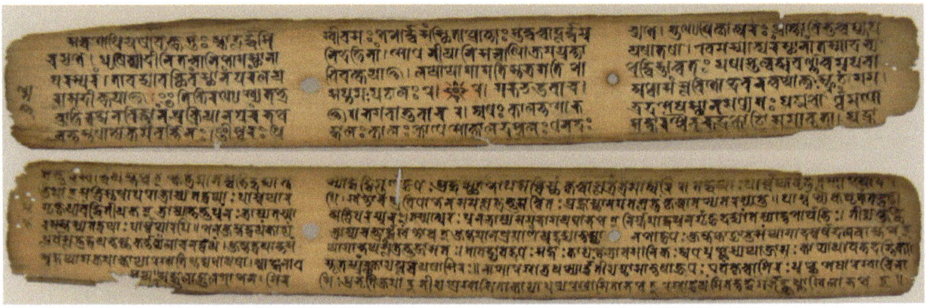

Fig. 2.4.1-VI: Overall layout, fols. 13v, 44v © NAK

117 This topic has been discussed in detail in section 3.9.3 below.

KV/UVDh

KV/UVDh contains two string-holes per folio, each with six lines. The sample numbers of *akṣara*s per line are 76 (4v1), 84 (54r1). Some folios taper at the edges. Symbols appear around the string-holes on the folio. The text has been divided into three text-sections on each folio, aside from 1v which is purported to have been added later (according to the palaeographical evidence) and on 55r where the text has been divided into only two text-sections. On 1v the uppermost and lowermost lines run across the whole folio. The writing here has faded considerably. On 55r, the two uppermost and two lowermost lines run across the right string-hole space and the left string-hole space is left clear of the text. A set of two parallel vertical ruling lines have been drawn after the left text-section, before and after the central text-section on 13r, in the outer part before the left text-section and after the right text-section on 17v. The overall layout in the manuscript can be seen as follows.

Fig. 2.4.1-VII: Overall layout, fols. 41v, 42v © NAK

SP_3

SP_3 has two string-holes per folio, each of five or six lines. The sample numbers of *akṣara*s per line are 108 (34r1), 98 (184v1), 100 (130v6). The text has been divided into three text-sections on each folio. Examples of the overall layout in the manuscript can be seen in Fig. 2.4.1-VIII. This and the following manuscript have been discussed in detail in section 3.8.2 below.

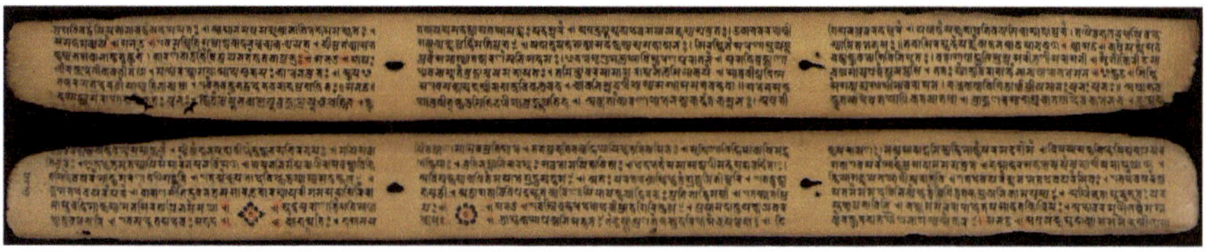

Fig. 2.4.1-VIII: Overall layout, fols. 46v, 48r © Bodleian Library, Oxford

SP₄

SP₄ presents two string-holes per folio, each containing five (on 250rv, 71rv, 254rv, 253rv, 248rv, 251rv, 249rv, 61rv, 256rv, 247rv) or six lines (on 63rv, 62rv, 10rv, 9rv, 5rv, 65rv, 68rv, 67rv, 66rv, 6rv, 230rv) lines per folio. The text has been divided into three text-sections. The overall layout in the manuscript can be seen as follows.

Fig. 2.4.1-IX: Overall layout fols. 61rv © NAK

YY

YY has two string-holes per folio (except for the very last small folio which only has one string-hole), each with six or seven lines. The sample numbers of *akṣara*s per line are 59 (5r1), 53 (4v1). The text has been divided into two text-sections on each folio. The space above and below the left string-hole has been left clear of text, however, the lines on the right string-hole space have not been left clear above and below the string-hole. The left text-section is considerably narrower than the right text-section. The overall layout in the manuscript can be seen as follows.

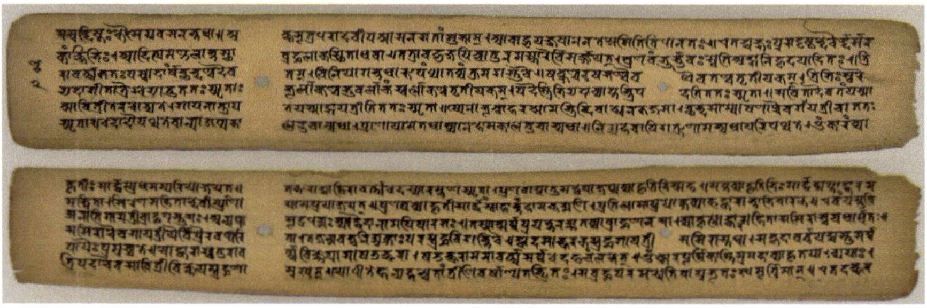

Fig. 2.4.1-X: Overall layout, fols. 12v, 13r © NAK

HV$_1$

HV$_1$ presents two string-holes per folio, each containing four or five lines per folio. The sample numbers of *akṣara*s per line are 96 (14v1–5), 93 (160r1), 88 (160r2), 104 (160r3), 95 (160r4), 96 (160r5). The text has been divided into three text-sections on each folio. The leaves are even and written in a regular way. Furthermore, the first and second halves of most of the *śloka*s on most of the folios have been divided by gaps in text-sections. Only on very few folios is the text not divided by any gaps. If the *pāda*s are organised within the frame of text-sections accordingly, mostly three *śloka*s appear per line (see section 4.2.2.3 for more detail below). Examples of the overall layout in the manuscript can be seen as follows.

Fig. 2.4.1-XI: Overall layout, fols. 169v, 170r © NAK

HY

HY has one string-hole per folio, each with three to six lines. The sample numbers of *akṣara*s per line are 57 (15v3), 59 (16r1). The folios do not have uniform size. Some of the folios taper at the edges and some folios are slightly curved (e.g. Fig. 2.4.1-XII).

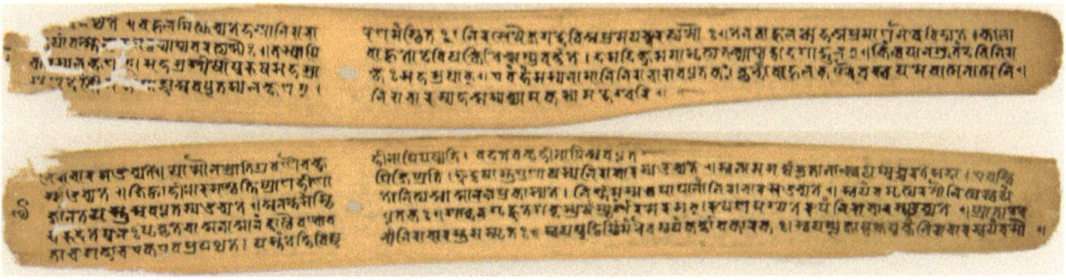

Fig. 2.4.1-XII: Overall layout, fols. 6v, 7v © NAK

The string-hole appears almost one third away from the left edge on the folio. The text has been divided into two text-sections on each folio. Lines are left clear from top to bottom on the string-hole space. The left text-section is considerably narrower than the right text-section. Examples of the overall layout in the manuscript can be seen in Fig. 2.4.1-XII.

DDh

DDh presents two string-holes per folio, each with four to five lines. The sample numbers of *akṣara*s per line are 73 (2v1), 78 (32v1), 74 (26r5). The text has been divided into three text-sections. The leaves are even and the lines are regular. Examples of the overall layout in the manuscript can be seen as follows.

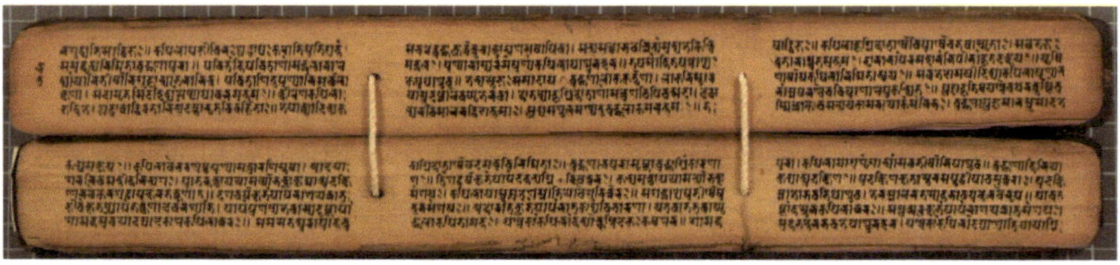

Fig. 2.4.1-XI: Overall layout, fols. 36v, 37r © NAK

TS₁

TS₁ has two string-holes per folio, each with six lines. The sample numbers of *akṣara*s per line are 110 (4r1), 107 (10v4), 105 (55v6). The text has been divided into three text-sections on each folio. Leaves are even and lines appear regular. The overall layout in the manuscript can be seen in Fig. 2.4.1-XIV.

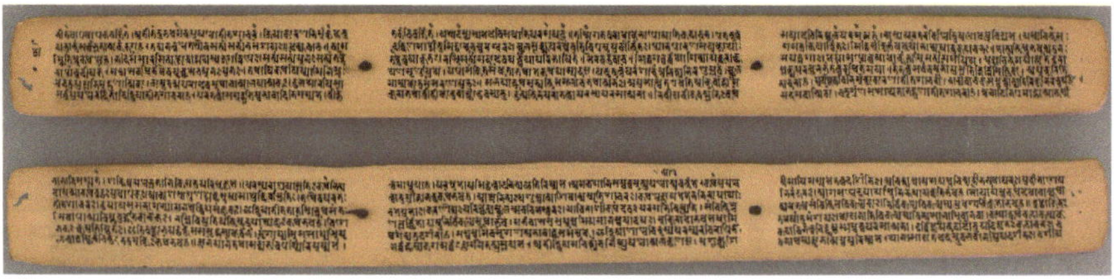

Fig. 2.4.1-XIV: Overall layout, fols. 10v, 11r © NAK

VDh

VDh contains two string-holes per folio, each mostly with five lines (except for four lines on 16r, 49v, 59rv, 89v, 160v). The sample numbers of *akṣara*s per line are 91 (28v1; with ruling-lines), 89 (60v2; with square-shaped string-hole space). Lines are left clear top to bottom on both string-hole spaces on some folios and the text appears divided into three text-sections on e.g. 2rv–24rv, 26rv–32rv, 33r, 34rv–38rv, 39r, 40rv–48rv, 49r, 50rv–52rv. Furthermore, there are no text-sections on e.g. 1v, 25rv, 33v, 39v, 49v, 53rv–160r, only a square-shaped free space has been left around both string-holes. Some of the folios (on e.g. 2r–24rv, 26rv–30rv) contain vertical ruling-lines and delimit text-sections. However, on most of the folios (1v, 25rv, 31r–160r) there are no ruling-lines. Examples of the overall layout in the manuscript can be seen as follows.

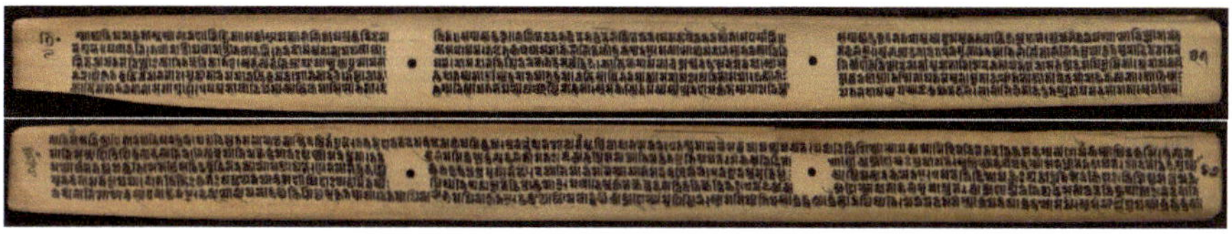

Fig. 2.4.1-XV: Overall layout, fols. 37v, 52v © NAK

SSS

SSS has two string-holes per folio, each with six lines (except five lines on 1v, 2rv, 3r, 4v). The sample numbers of *akṣara*s per line are 92 (2v1), 86 (34r6), 84 (53v1). The text has been divided into three text-sections on each folio (except on 54r on which lines run around the string-holes on the folio. On palaeographical grounds it seems that which is written from mid way of the second line text may be of a different hand).[118] The leaves are even and lines appear rather regular. Here is an example of the overall layout in the manuscript:

118 N.B. on fol. 1r a list of chapters written in modern hand and arranged in seven columns has been added later.

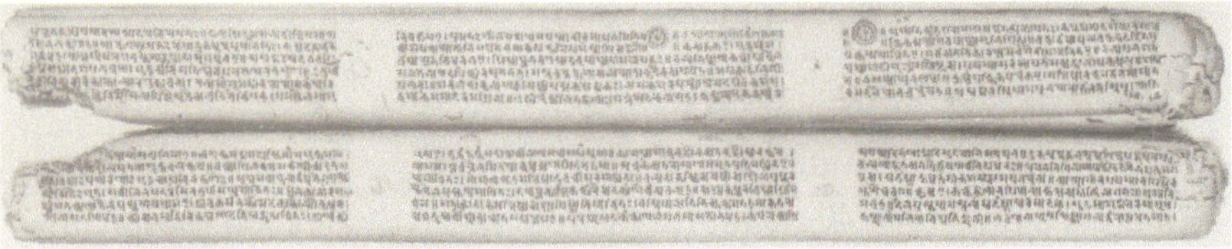

Fig. 2.4.1-XVI: Overall layout, fols. 33v, 34r © NAK

AṣP$_1$

AṣP$_1$ presents two string-holes per folio, each with mostly five (except for 6 lines on 197v, 204r, 206v, 226v, 237rv, 277v and 4 lines on the last folio 282v). Leaves are even and lines appear regular. The sample numbers of *akṣara*s per line are 94 (3v1), 107 (66v1), 104 (204v5). The text has been divided mainly into three text-sections (except on some folios where the first line runs across the right string-hole space on 46r, 136r, 204v, 237v, 238v, 268r, 281r, the last line across the string-hole space on 203v and both first and last lines across the right string-hole space on 66v, 233v, 201r, 204r). Examples of the overall layout in the manuscript can be seen in Fig. 2.4.1-XVII.

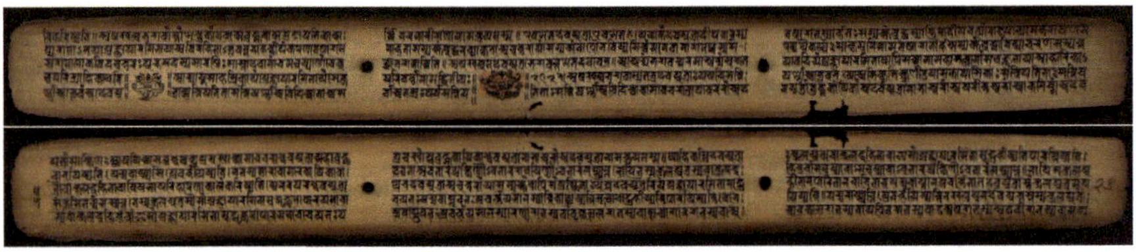

Fig. 2.4.1-XVII: Overall layout, fol. 26rv © NAK

HV$_2$

HV$_2$ contains two string-holes per folio, each with five lines (except six lines on 1v, 2rv). The sample numbers of *akṣara*s per line are 106 (3v1), 104 (90v1), 92 (100v5). The text has been divided into three text-sections on all folios (except on 416rv on which first line runs across the right string-hole space). The leaves are even and the lines are written in a regular form. The overall layout in the manuscript can be seen in Fig. 2.4.1-XVIII.

Fig. 2.4.1-XVIII: Overall layout, fols. 189v, 190r © NAK

SDhPS

SDhPS presents two string-holes per folio, each with six lines (except on 21r, 25v, 26r, 34r, 120v on which five lines can be found). The sample numbers of *akṣara*s per line are 122 (35v1), 106 (74v6), 94 (127v2). The text has been divided frequently into three text-sections (except on 9v, 133v on which text appears divided only into two text-sections). Leaves are to a great extent of uniform size and the lines are of regular form. On 138v, 139rv ruling-lines can be found and they delimit text-sections. Small gaps can be found between smaller text units such as the sentences on 125r–128r, 131r–132r. The overall layout in the manuscript can be seen in Fig. 2.4.1-XIX.

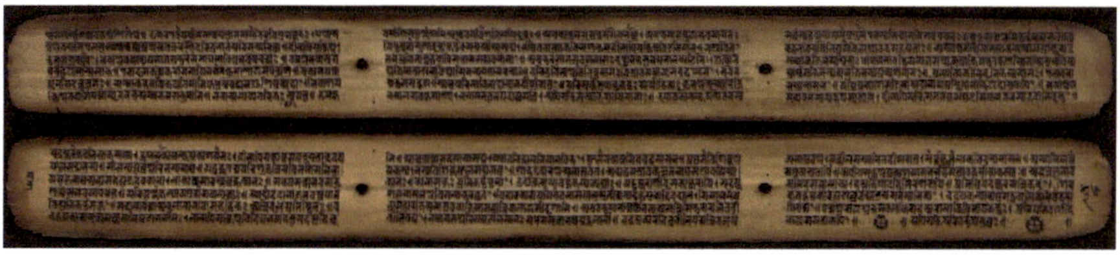

Fig. 2.4.1-XIX: Overall layout, fol. 36rv © NAK

AṣP$_2$

AṣP$_2$ has two string-holes per folio, each with mostly six lines (except seven lines on 69r, 177r and 179r). The sample numbers of *akṣara*s per line are 110 (60r1), 98 (60v3). The text has been divided largely into three text-sections (except on 60rv where the text has not been divided into text-sections; the uppermost and lowermost lines run across the whole folio, on 166r on which text appears divided only into two text-sections). The leaves are even and the lines appear regular. Below is the overall layout of the manuscript:

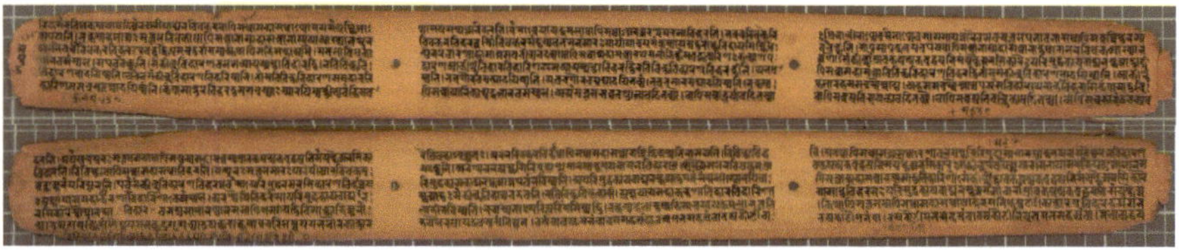

Fig. 2.4.1-XX: Overall layout, fols. 60v, 62r © NAK

SS

SS presents two string-holes per folio, each with six to seven lines. The sample numbers of *akṣara*s per line are 80 (1v1), 58 (37r5). The text has not been divided into text-sections on the folio. Square-shaped free space has been left around the left and right string-holes on each folio and on both sides the square-shaped free space is an area of five text-lines in height on the folio. The uppermost and lowermost lines run across the whole folio. On some folios the text is written in cursive style. The overall layout of the manuscript can be seen in Fig. 2.4.1-XXI.

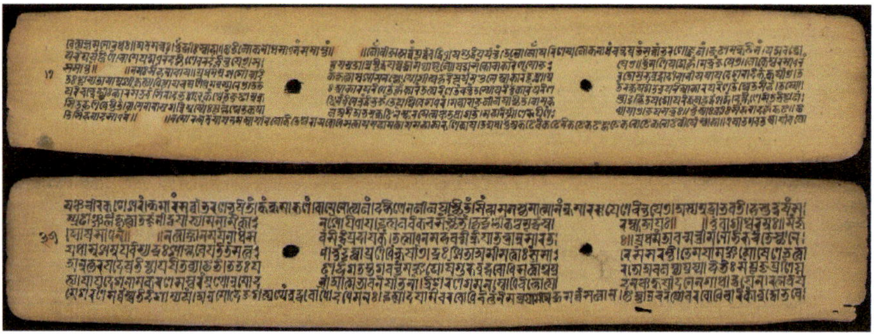

Fig. 2.4.1-XXI: Overall layout, fols. 17v, 35v © CUL

TS$_2$

TS$_2$ has two string-holes per folio, each with six lines. The sample numbers of *akṣara*s per line are 63 (9r1), 63 (22v1), 62 (50v1). The text has not been divided into text-sections on the folio. Only a square-shaped free space has been left around the left and right string-holes on each folio and on both sides, the square shaped area is four text-lines in height on the folio. The uppermost and lowermost lines run across the whole folio. Below is the overall layout of the manuscript:

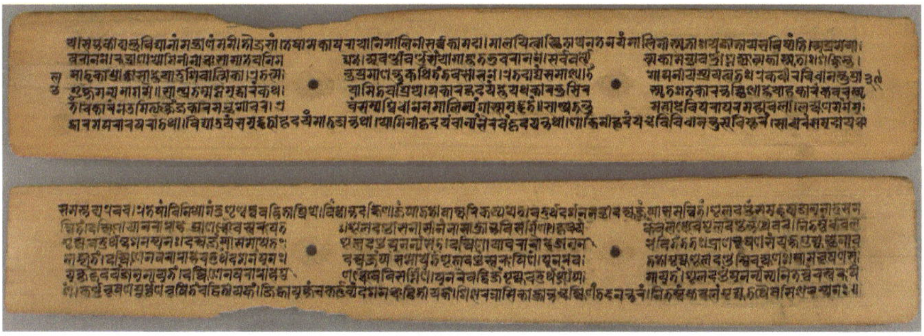

Fig. 2.4.1-XXII: Overall layout, fols. 39v, 40r © NAK

2.4.1.1 Layout in Nepalese manuscripts – Preliminary conclusions

All 9th c. Nepalese manuscripts (SP_1, SP_2, SS/N, NTS and PT) have two string-holes per folio and the text is largely divided into three text-sections.

The 10th c. manuscripts' (KT, YY, SP_3, SP_4, KV/UVDh) text are regularly divided into two or three text-sections. KT and YY have two string-holes per folio. Part of the text in KT is divided into two text-sections and a few other parts into three. In YY the text is divided into two text-sections only. It is also important to note that in those manuscripts with two string-holes and two text-sections, the space above and below the left string-hole is left clear of text.

Manuscripts from the 9th c. (SP_1, PT, SS/N, SP_2, NTS) do not feature regularly shaped leaves. Some leaves taper strongly at the edges and some leaves are extremely curved (folios of PT, SS/N). In these cases, the leaves' shape translates into an irregular number of lines per folio and *akṣara*s per line. However, the examples show that from the 10th c. onward the size of folios becomes more regular within each manuscript. The text is also written more uniformly to a degree. Lines appear straight. The number of lines per folio does not vary much.

Only in two Nepalese manuscripts of my corpus (SS, dated 1216 CE, and TS, ca. 13th c.) has the text not been divided into text-sections. Only a square-shaped free space has been left around both string-holes. Such a shape is obtained by leaving four to five lines of script clear (four lines in TS_2, and four to five lines in SS) around the string-holes, with only the first line and the last line of the page delimiting the upper and lower borders of the square.

Leaving gaps between sentences or *pāda*s of *śloka* was a frequent feature both in part or entirely in most of the 9th c. manuscripts (e.g. SP_1, SP_2, NTS, SS/N) (see section 4.2 below). At least two manuscripts contain puranic texts (i.e. SP_1, SP_2 from 9th c.) and one manuscript contains an epic text (i.e. HV_1 from 11th c.), *śloka*s have been divided using gaps in each text-sections. Vertical ruling lines have been used in manuscripts (e.g. VDh, SDhPS) on occasion.

2.4.2 Examples of layout in East Indian manuscripts

In the East Indian manuscripts group, of this study, I have largely analysed twelve manuscripts. Nine of them are purported to originate from present-day area of Bihar (possibly from Vikramaśīla),[119] the other three manuscripts from what today is the area of Bengal (PR from Bengal according to its colophon), or a nearby area. Firstly, the overall layout of each manuscript of this group has been presented in its possible chronological order, though none have been dated precisely (except PR) after which they are summed up by a few preliminary conclusions and notes on how some specific phenomena in the layout of this region's manuscripts indicating how the layout may be differentiated from the overall layout of the manuscripts from the other regions of my corpus (i.e. the layout of Nepalese and West Indian manuscripts).

PR

PR has two string-holes per folio, each with five lines (except six lines on 69v, 70r). The sample numbers of *akṣaras* per line are 106 (28v2), 110 (35v3), 110 (50v5). The text has been divided into three text-sections on each folio.[120] Each text-section has been demarcated by vertical ruling-lines on the folio. The lines are quite straight. No gaps can be found between sentences or verses on the folio (concerning precise measurements of the script and text-sections, etc., see the Cambridge online catalogue entry). The overall layout of the manuscript can be seen in Fig. 2.4.2-I.

---

119 Vikramaśīla was one of the important Buddhist monasteries in present-day Bihar which for various historical reasons is thought to have been destroyed around 12th c. On Vikramaśīla and its downfall, see Sanderson 2009, 89; Delhey et al. 2015, 121. Some of the manuscripts of this group have also been studied in Delhey 2015, 3–24 and in Delhey et al. 2015, 119–152 with regard to the composition of the material.

120 Miniatures of Buddhas, goddesses, *yoginīs* and a *stūpa* can be found in the centre part of text-sections on 1v, 2r, 19v, 20r, 45v, 46r, 64v, 65r, 66v, 67r, 69v, 70r.

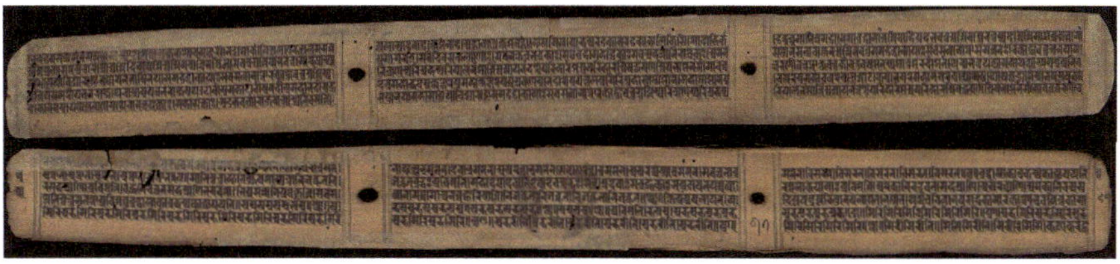

Fig. 2.4.2-I: Overall layout, fols. 26r, 67v © CUL

AAĀ

AAĀ presents two string-holes per folio, each with seven lines (except six lines on 34r, 59rv–60rv, 120rv–122rv, 134rv, 135r and eight lines on 143rv). The sample numbers of *akṣaras* per line are 125 (20v1), 116 (20v4), 127 (20v7). The folios are even and standardised. Ample free space has been left on the margins. The lines are quite regular and the text appears carefully justified. The text has not been divided into text-sections on the folio. Around both string-holes square-shaped free areas can be seen on each folio. Three lines have been left clear around both string-holes in height on each folio (except four lines on 34r and two lines on 59rv–60rv, 120rv–122rv, 134rv, 135r). The uppermost and lowermost two lines run across the whole folio. Figure-numerical foliation can be found on the left-hand margin on the verso. The use of space-fillers cannot be found in the manuscript. The overall layout in the manuscript can be seen as follows.

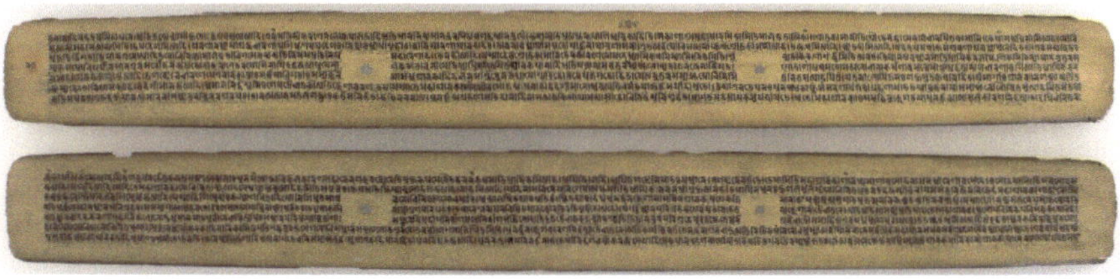

Fig. 2.4.2-II: Overall layout, fols. 35v, 36r © NAK

GV

GV contains two string-holes per folio, each with seven lines. The sample numbers of *akṣaras* per line are 123 (2v1), 107 (2v4), 114 (2v7). The shape of the folios is standardised and ample free space has been left on the margins. The text has not been divided into text-sections on the folio. Around both string-holes square-shaped free areas can be found on each folio. Three lines have been left clear of text around both string-holes on the folio. The uppermost and lowermost two lines run across the whole folio. Figure-numerical foliations can be found on the left and right-hand margins on the verso. No space-fillers can be found in the manuscript. The overall layout of the manuscript can be seen in Fig. 2.4.2-III.

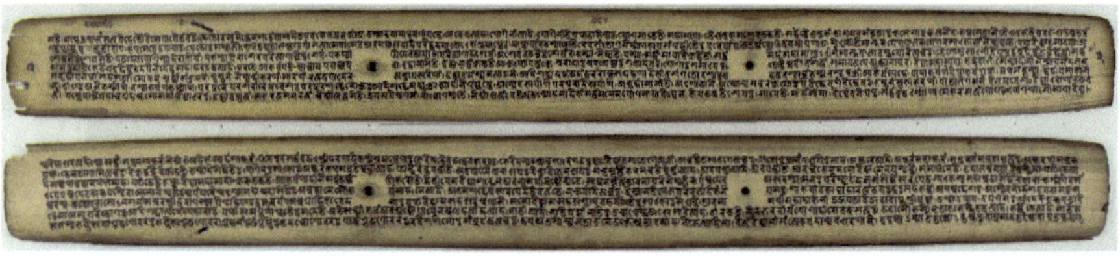

Fig. 2.4.2-III: Overall layout, fols. 3v, 4r © KL

HAP

HAP has two string-holes per folio, each with seven lines (except for the first folio (1r) and last one (10rv). On 1r there are three and a half lines and the text seems to have been written by the same hand later. There are two and over a half line on 10r and the text ends there. There is just one line on 10v.). The sample numbers of *akṣara*s per line are 143 (3v1), 126 (3v4), 133 (3v7). Folios are standardised and ample free space has been left on the margins. Lines are straight. The text has not been divided into text-sections on the folio. Around both string-holes square-shaped free areas have been left on each folio. Three lines are left clear around both string-holes on the folio. The uppermost and lowermost two lines run across the whole folio. Figure-numerical foliations can be found on the left and right-hand margins on the verso. There are no space-fillers in the manuscript. The overall layout in the manuscript can be seen in Fig. 2.4.2-IV.

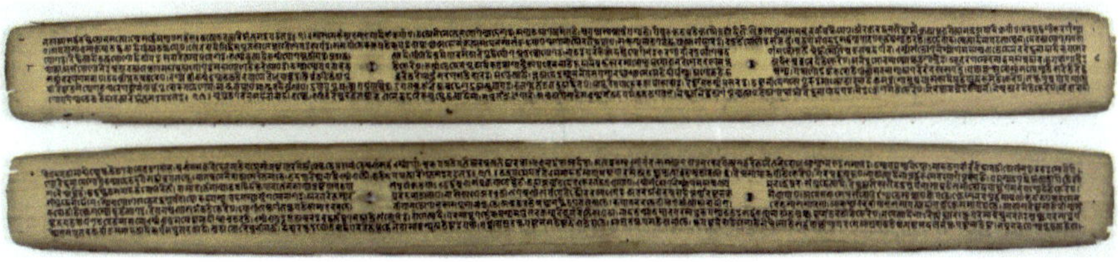

Fig. 2.4.2-IV: Overall layout, fols. 8v, 9r © KL

LTṬ

LTṬ has two string-holes per folio, each with seven lines. The sample numbers of *akṣara*s per line are 139 (5v1), 130 (5v4), 135 (5v7). The text has not been divided into text-sections on the folio. The folios are standardised and ample free space has been left on the margins. Around both string-holes square-shaped free spaces are left clear on each folio. Three lines have been left clear around both string-holes on the folio. The two uppermost and lowermost lines run across the whole folio. Figure-numerical foliations can be found on the left and right-hand margins on the verso. Space-fillers cannot be found in the manuscript. Below is the overall layout of the manuscript:

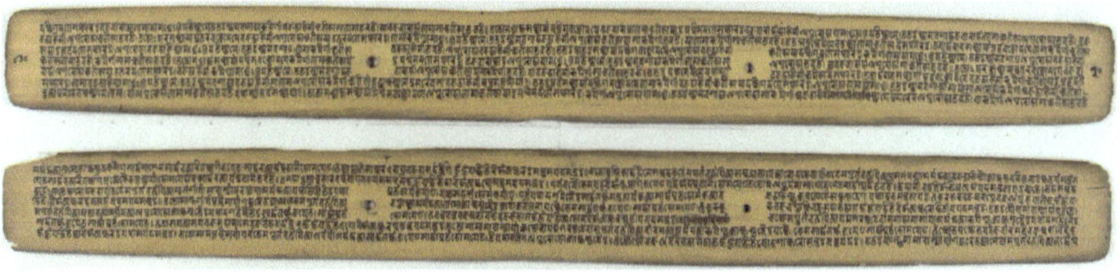

Fig. 2.4.2-V: Overall layout, fols. 20v, 21r © KL

STṬ

STṬ has two string-holes per folio, each with seven lines. The sample numbers of *akṣara*s per line are 136 (7v1), 118 (7v4), 124 (7v7). The text has not been divided into text-sections on the folio. Around both string-holes square-shaped free spaces have been left clear on each folio. Three lines are left clear around both string-holes on the folio (except 1v on which around the right string-hole just two lines are left clear in height). The two uppermost and lowermost lines run across the whole folio (except the right string-hole space on 1v). On 2r6, 2r7 a few *mantra*s can be found written in *kūṭākṣara*.[121] Figure-numerical foliations can be found on the left and right-hand margins on the verso. Space-fillers have not been used in the manuscript. Below is the overall layout of the manuscript:

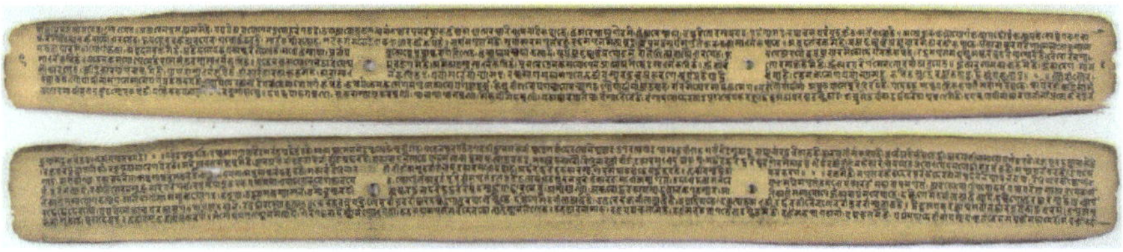

Fig. 2.4.2-VI: Overall layout, fols. 4v, 5r © KL

ḌVPṬ

ḌVPṬ contains two string-holes per folio, each with seven lines (except the last folio 8v on which only three lines can be found). The sample numbers of *akṣara*s per line are 121 (2v1), 111 (2v4), 118 (2v7). Ample free space has been left on the margins. The lines are regular and the text has been carefully justified. The text has not been divided into text-sections on the folio. Around both string-holes square-shaped free spaces can be seen on each folio. Three lines are left clear around both string-holes in height on each folio. The uppermost and lowermost two lines run across the whole folio. Figure-numerical foliations can be found on the left and right-hand margins on the verso. Space-fillers cannot be found in the manuscript. The overall layout in the manuscript can be seen in Fig. 2.4.2-VII.

121 Sometimes understood to be 'monogram' or '*mantra* monogram', which, literally means, 'heap syllable(s)' (see Hartmann 1998, 38). This label indicates special sets of visual configurations, in which syllables and syllable-like characters used in *mantra*s or *mantra*-like elements are written underneath one another, making them all look closely intertwined. See also Śākya 1973, 37–38; Rajbanshi 1974, 104–105.

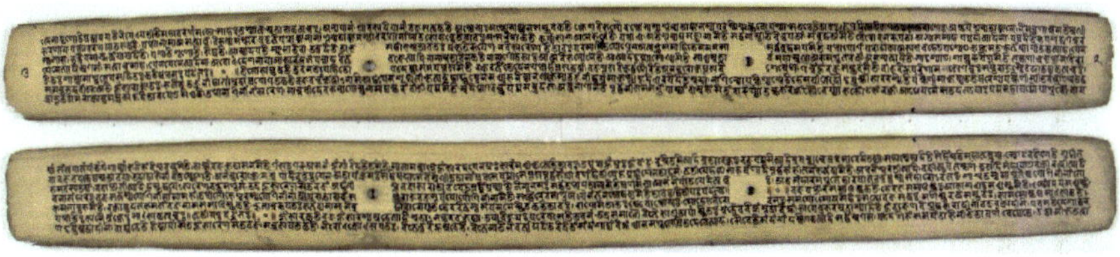

Fig. 2.4.2-VII: Overall layout, fols. 2v, 3r © KL

AP

AP has two string-holes per folio, each with seven lines (except for the last folio 28r). The sample numbers of *akṣara*s per line are 142 (9v1), 138 (9v4), 131 (9v7). Ample free space has been left on the margins. The lines are very regular and the text has been carefully justified. The text has not been divided into text-sections on the folio. Around both string-holes square-shaped free areas have been left clear on each folio. Three lines have been cleared around both string-holes in height on the folio. The uppermost and lowermost two lines run across the whole folio. Figure-numerical foliation can be found on the left-hand margin on the verso. Space-fillers cannot be found in the manuscript. The overall layout in the manuscript can be seen in Fig. 2.4.2-VIII.

Fig. 2.4.2-VIII: Overall layout, fols. 5v, 6r © NAK

CPN

CPN presents two string-holes per folio, each with seven lines (except last folio on which only six lines can be found). The sample numbers of *akṣara*s per line are 127 (4v1), 116 (4v4), 123 (4v7). Ample free space has been left on the margins. Lines are regular and the text has been carefully justified. The text has not been divided into text-sections on the folio. Around both string-holes square-shaped free areas can be seen on each folio. Three lines have been left clear around both string-holes in height of the folio. The two uppermost and lowermost lines run across the whole folio. A few *mantras* are written in *kūṭākṣara* on 8v3, 9r7, 10v5, 14v5, 14v6, 41v7, 52r4. Figure-numerical foliations can be found on the left and right-hand margins on the verso. Space-fillers cannot be found in the manuscript. The overall layout in the manuscript can be seen in Fig. 2.4.2-IX.

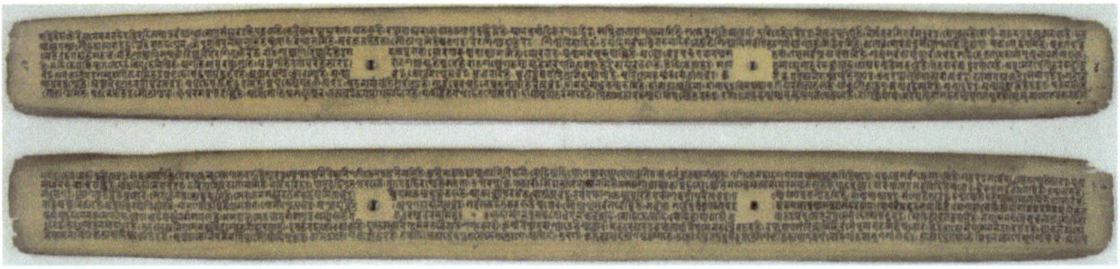

Fig. 2.4.2-IX: Overall layout, fols. 4v, 5r © KL

HP

HP has two string-holes per folio, each with seven lines (except last folio 23r on which only three lines can be found). The sample numbers of *akṣaras* per line are 153 (16v1), 133 (16v4), 142 (16v7). Ample free space has been left clear on the margins. The lines are very regular and the text has been carefully arranged. The text has not been divided into text-sections on the folio. Around both string-holes square-shaped free areas can be seen on each folio. Three lines have been left clear around both string-holes in height on the folio. The uppermost and lowermost two lines run across the whole folio. Figure-numerical foliations can be found on the left and right-hand margins on the verso. Space-fillers cannot be found in the manuscript. Below is the overall layout of the manuscript:

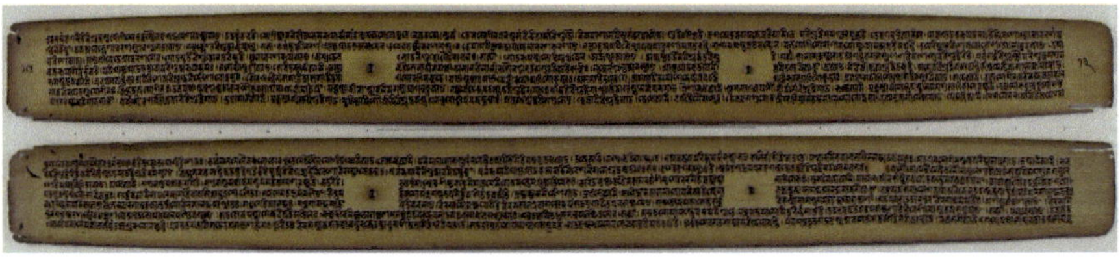

Fig. 2.4.2-X: Overall layout, fols. 13v, 14r © KL

HTṬ

HTṬ contains one string-hole per folio, each with six lines (except seven lines on 56v). The sample numbers of *akṣara*s per line are 54 (4v4), 59 (4v6). The text has not been divided into text-sections on the folio. Just two lines are cleared around the string-hole space. The uppermost and lowermost two lines run across the whole folio (except on folio 56v on which the lowermost three lines run across the whole folio). The text has been written mostly in cursive. No space-fillers can be found in the manuscript. The overall layout in the manuscript can be seen in Fig. 2.4.2-XI.

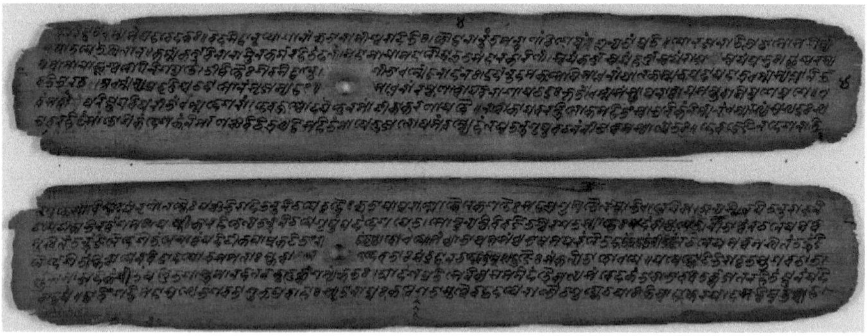

Fig. 2.4.2-XI: Overall layout, fols. 4v, 5r © KL

AT

AT has one string-hole per folio, each with five lines (except six lines on a few folios). The sample numbers of *akṣara*s per line are 52 (15?v1), 49 (15?v3) 47 (15?v6). The text has not been divided into text-sections on the folio. A part of the text is written in cursive. The overall layout can be seen in Fig. 2.4.2-XII.

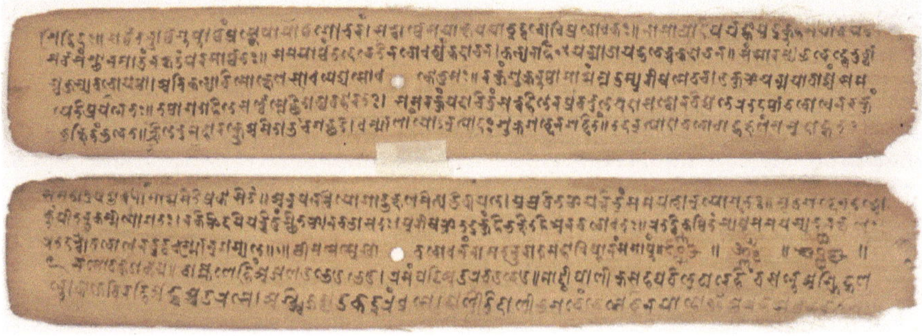

Fig. 2.4.2-XII: Overall layout, fols.? © General Library, University of Tokyo

The folios of the manuscripts which are supposed to have originated from Vikramaśīla (GV, HAP, LTṬ, STṬ, ḌVPṬ, AP, CPN, HP)[122] appear extremely uniform in shape. The folios are long and have almost identical size (e.g. length of manuscripts is 55–57 cm and height 5–6 cm[123]) and folios do not taper (so much) on the edges or they are not curved.[124]

2.4.2.1 Layout in East Indian manuscripts – Preliminary conclusions

All East Indian manuscripts contain square-shaped free space around both string-holes on the folio (except in HTṬ and AT, in which just one or two lines are left clear around the string-holes and the left area is not a square-shaped box, and PR in which lines are left clear above and below both string-holes of

122 In the manuscript of the *Pāramitāsamāsa* (NAK 5/145 / NGMPP A 39/9) which might also have originated from the same area (depending on the palaeography and occurrence of the symbols), there are seven lines per folio and three lines are cleared around both string-holes on the folio. The following manuscripts have an almost identical layout and palaeographical similarities, e.g. the manuscript of the *Ḍākinīvajrapañjarapañjikā* (NAK 5/20 / NGMPP A 47/17(1)) (preserved in Nepal), the manuscript of the *Kalyāṇakāmadhenuvivaraṇa* (NAK 5/20 / NGMPP A 47/17(2)) (folio 4 is kept in Nepal and all other folios are preserved in Tibet); the manuscript of the *Trisamayarājatantraṭikā* (NAK 5/20 / NGMPP A 47/17(3)) (folios 2, 3, 5–9, 11–15, 18, 19 are preserved in Nepal and folio 4 is found in Tibet) (on the identification of the corpus of many of these manuscripts by Harunaga Isaacson, see Delhey et al. 2015, footnote 13); the manuscript of the *Viṃśatividhi* (Tucci_MT 34 EE); the manuscript of the *Bhikṣuṇi-Vinaya*, see Roth 1970, plate 9A.1-6; the manuscript of the *Smṛtyupasthānasūtra*; the manuscript of the *Jñānaśrīmitranibandhāvalī* (18 A_Sāṅkṛtyāyana).

123 The size is based on the measurements of the catalogue cards of the NGMPP.

124 See also Delhey et al. 2015.

the folios). In most cases three lines have been left clear around both string-holes. The square shape is obtained with the first two lines and the last two lines of each page demarcating the upper and lower sides of the free space around the string holes. Although not directly related to the layout in the manuscripts a relatively important point is worthy of mention – many of the manuscripts of this group contain new covers, painted yellow (GV, HAP, LTṬ, STṬ, ḌVPṬ, CPN, HP, HTṬ). Except for the size of covers of HTṬ, the size and the shape of manuscript covers (GV, HAP, LTṬ, STṬ, ḌVPṬ, CPN, HP) are identical.

Ruling-lines are not found in the manuscripts of this region discussed in my corpus, except for PR in which they are used to demarcate text-sections. The number of lines should also be noted. In most manuscripts there are seven lines per folio, each of which is fairly straight. Both margins are carefully arranged so there are no space-fillers in any of the manuscripts, and a space of remarkably regular size is left blank on both left and right sides of the folio. Another conspicuous feature is also worthy of mention. Most of the manuscripts of this group contain figure-numerical foliations on both the left and right-hand margins (namely, GV, HAP, LTṬ, STṬ, ḌVPṬ, AP, CPN, HP).

Approximately the same number of *akṣaras* per line is found in many manuscripts of this group e.g. the average number of *akṣaras*: 116–127 in AAĀ, 114–123 in GV, 126–133 in HAP, 130–139 in LTṬ, 118–136 in STṬ, 111–121 in ḌVPṬ, 131–142 in AP, 116–127 in CPN, 133–152 in HP.

A symbol that looks like a '*siddham*' can be found at the end of the chapter or text in many manuscripts of this group (see section 3.4, type no. 45 and section 3.5.2 below). Their shape is near identical, and may perhaps be used to trace most of these manuscripts back to the same geographical area.

Finally, a feature concerning the genre of the texts found in the manuscripts of this group is worth noting: all texts have a Buddhist affiliation. Ten contain commentaries on Buddhist tantric texts (GV, HAP, LTṬ, STṬ, ḌVPṬ, AP, CPN, HP, HTṬ and AT).[125] PR contains a *dhāraṇī* and AAĀ contains a commentary to a Buddhist mahāyānic text.

125 It is also important to mention here that we find some characters which look Tibetan in at least three manuscripts of this group, namely, in GV, LTṬ and CPN. In all manuscripts they appear on 1r but aside from that the folios are fairly blank. In the case of GV we can see a short text part (in two lines) in the middle on the space between left and right string-holes on 1r. According to the appearance of characters it seems to be written in Tibetan script, though it appears that there was an attempt to deliberately erase parts of characters and a horizontal line in the script area is still visible in the first line of the text part that was perhaps used for the deletion. Furthermore, in LTṬ on 1r, which is also blank (except for a verse that appears in the middle on the space between left and right string-holes), we find under the verse a dark spot of

2.4.3 Examples of layout in West Indian manuscripts

I have examined seven manuscripts from West India. One manuscript contains a commentary of the *Haravijayamahākāvya* an epic poem. The other manuscripts largely contain texts (both *mūla* ('root') texts and commentaries) related to the Jaina tradition. The manuscripts can be dated 12th to 13th c. approximately. The manuscripts will be presented in (probable) chronological order, outlining their overall layout and providing examples for each manuscript.

TSa

TSa presents one string-hole per folio, each with four to six lines. The sample numbers of *akṣaras* per line are 61 (20v1), 62 (39v5), 64 (114v3). The text has been divided into two text-sections on each folio. The left text-section is narrower than the right text-section. Both text-sections are demarcated by vertical ruling-lines. A symbol can be found around the string-hole on each folio. The overall layout in the manuscript can be seen as follows.

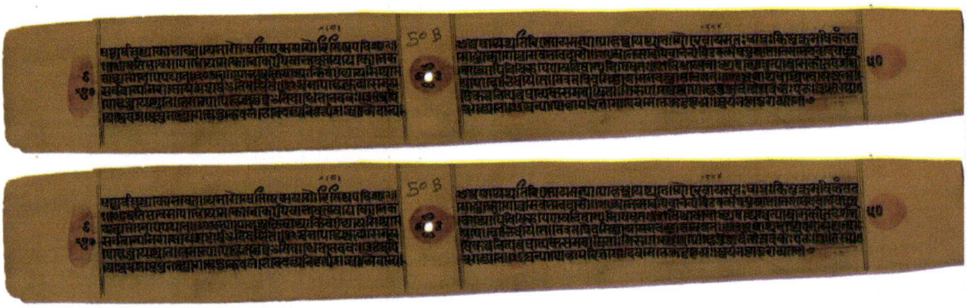

Fig. 2.4.3-I: Overall layout, fols. 50v, 84v © Jinabhadrasūri Jñāna Bhaṇḍāra, Jaisalmer

an ink-like element and parts of some curved lines at the bottom of the dark spot are still visible. It appears also that the line here was probably written in Tibetan script which someone intentionally tried to erase. As the spot appears to some extent in the same place on the folio like in GV and CPN (i.e. between left and right string-holes), we can assume that the writing was probably in Tibetan script as well. Similarly, in CPN on 1r, which is blank, we find a two-line short text portion in the middle on the space between left and right string-holes. It is also written in Tibetan script. The second line seems to have been erased intentionally. A horizontal line in the script area can be seen, which here too, was most probably used to mark the deletion. These examples of deletion may suggest how we are to think of the user of the manuscripts. It is likely at least to some extent that these manuscripts were in the hands of a reader of the Tibetan language or knower of Tibetan writing.

TSPV

TSPV has two string-holes per folio, each with three to nine lines. The sample numbers of *akṣara*s per line are 106 (18v2), 144 (37v5), 117 (144?v4), 118 (312v1). The text has been divided into three text-sections. All three text-sections are demarcated by vertical ruling-lines. Symbols can be found around both string-holes on each folio. At least four scribes may have worked on the manuscript production.[126] Above is the overall layout of the manuscript.

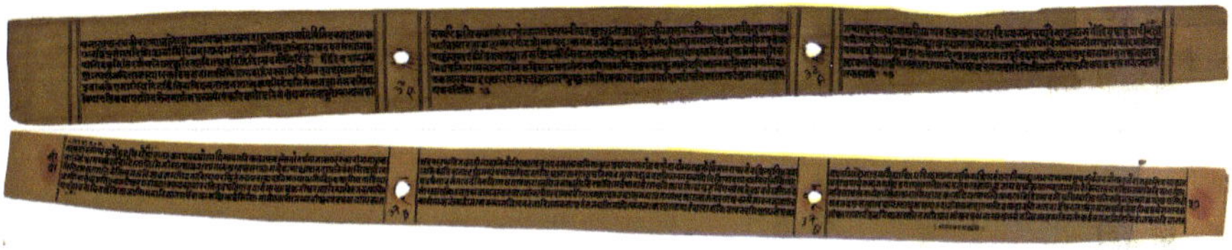

Fig. 2.4.3-II: Overall layout, fols. 32v, 37v © Jinabhadrasūri Jñāna Bhaṇḍāra, Jaisalmer

HVM

HVM contains two string-holes per folio, each with four to seven lines. The sample numbers of *akṣara*s per line are 179 (1v1), 189 (21v4), 96 (46v6). The text has been divided into three text-sections. All three text-sections are demarcated by vertical ruling-lines. Symbols can be found around both string-holes on each folio (see section 3.6.1 below). Both symbols around the string-holes seem to have been highlighted (see section 5.1). Furthermore, both foliations (letter-numeral on the left-hand and figura-numeral on the right-hand margin) have also been highlighted. The overall layout in the manuscript can be seen as follows.

Fig. 2.4.3-III: Overall layout, fols. 5v, 6v © Jinabhadrasūri Jñāna Bhaṇḍāra, Jaisalmer

126 This is discussed in detail in section 3.9.4 below.

PV

PV has one string-hole per folio, each with four to five lines. The sample numbers of *akṣaras* per line are 58 (18v1), 55 (74r1). The text has been divided into two text-sections on each folio. The left text-section is narrower than the right. Both text-sections are delimited by a set of double vertical ruling-lines. There is a symbol around the string-hole on each folio. A few tables and diagrams with *akṣaras* and figure-numerals are found in the manuscript (e.g. 87r, 89v, 90r and on a few last folios). The overall layout in the manuscript can be seen in Fig. 2.4.3-IV.

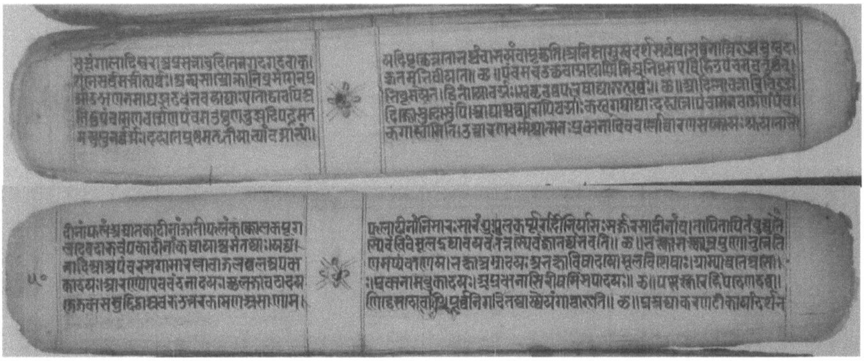

Fig. 2.4.3-IV: Overall layout, fols. 28r, 50v © NAK

JKS/C

JKS/C presents one string-hole per folio, each with two to eight lines. The sample numbers of *akṣaras* per line are 47 (20v1), 53 (22v1). The text has been divided into two text-sections on each folio. The left text-section is narrower than the right text-section. Both text-sections are demarcated by vertical ruling-lines. Furthermore, both foliations (letter and figure-numerals) have been highlighted. A symbol can be found around the string-hole on each folio and it appears highlighted. The overall layout in the manuscript can be seen in Fig. 2.4.3-V.

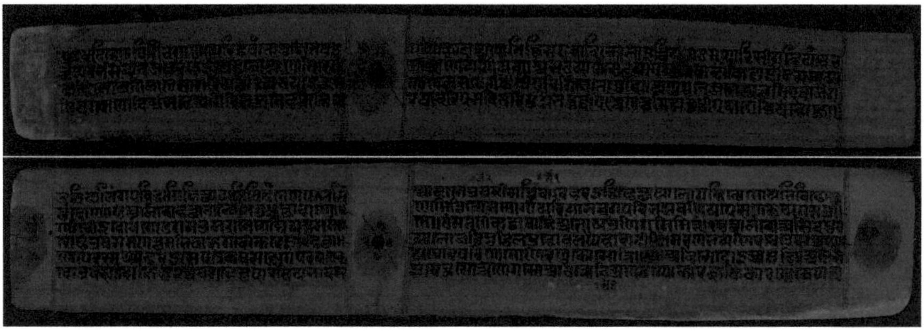

Fig. 2.4.3-V: Overall layout, fols. 23r, 60v © British Library Board, London

TUS

TUS contains one string-hole per folio, each with two to eight lines. The sample numbers of *akṣara*s per line are 50 (33v3), 57 (112v2). The text has been divided into two text-sections on the folio. The left text-section is narrower than the right text-section. Both text-sections are demarcated by vertical ruling-lines. A symbol can be found around string-hole on each folio and they appear highlighted. Both foliations (letter and figure-numerals) have also been highlighted. The overall layout in the manuscript can be seen in Fig. 2.4.3-VI.

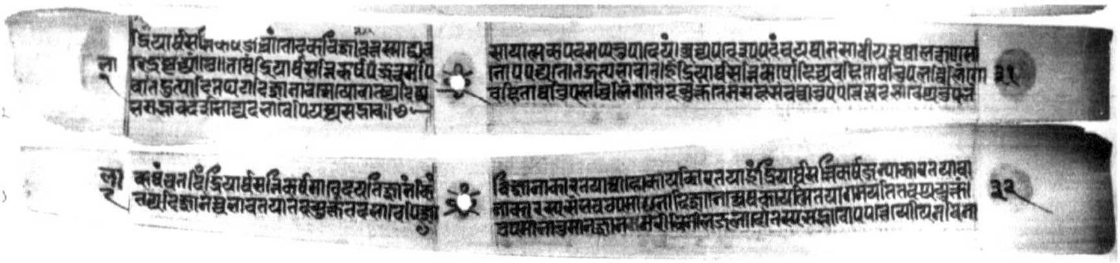

Fig. 2.4.3-VI: Overall layout, fols. 31v, 32v © Hemacandrācārya Jaina Jñānamandira, Patan

BCV

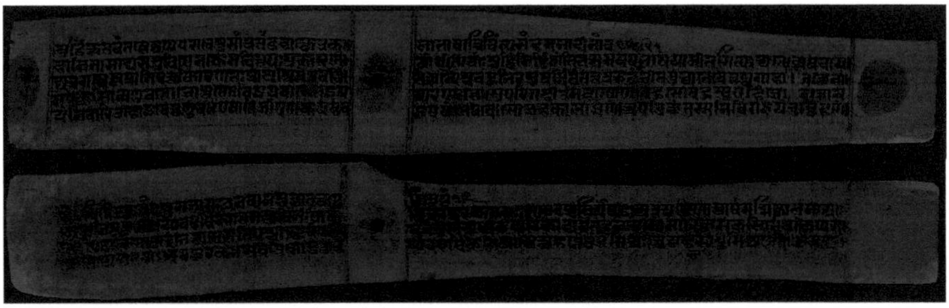

Fig. 2.4.3-VII: Overall layout, fols. 20v, 42r © British Library Board, London

BCV presents one string-hole per folio, each with three to seven lines. The sample numbers of *akṣara*s per line are 48 (11v1), 45 (70v1). The text has been divided into two text-sections on each folio. The left text-section is narrower than the right text-section. Both text-sections are delimited by vertical ruling-lines. A symbol can be found around the string-hole on each folio and they appear highlighted. Both foliations (letter and figure-numerals) have also been highlighted. The overall layout in the manuscript can be seen in Fig. 2.4.3-VII.

2.4.3.1 Layout in West Indian manuscripts – Preliminary conclusions

All manuscripts from this area contain vertical ruling-lines[127] on the folio and they demarcate each text-section. Although it is difficult to ascertain when and where the ruling-lines first appeared in Indic manuscripts, it is clear they have become a common scribal practice in manuscripts from West India.

Almost no gaps can be found either in prose passages or between verses. The number of lines per folio vary extremely, even within a single manuscript (e.g. HVM has four to seven lines, JKS/C two to eight lines, TSa four to six lines, TUS two to five lines, and BCV three to seven lines).[128] This latter feature is closely related to the shape of the leaf.

127 On the use of ruling-lines, see also Thaker 2002, 143.

128 See also further manuscripts from the same region, e.g., in the manuscript of the *Udbhaṭakāvyālaṅkāralaghuvṛtti* (VS 1160 / 1103 CE) (Jinabhadrasūri Grantha Bhaṇḍāra, Jaisalmer, no. 329) there are three to five lines per page; in the manuscript of the *Jayadevachandaḥ Śāstra* (VS 1190 / 1133 CE) (Jinabhadrasūri Grantha Bhaṇḍāra, Jaisalmer, no. 314/1) two to six lines per

According to the number of string-holes, one can find two or three text-sections on the folio (e.g. two text-sections can be found in TSa, PV, JKS/C, TUS and BCV and three text-sections in HVM and TSPV). Furthermore, all manuscripts contain simple symbols around the string-hole of each folio (see section 3.6.1 for more detail below). In all manuscripts the space surrounding the string-holes has been left clear from top to bottom. Regarding those with only one string-hole per folio, the hole appears at a distance of slightly more than a quarter of the whole folio starting from the left edge. As a result, the left text-section is always narrower than the right text-section (e.g. the text-sections in TSa, PV, JKS/C, TUS and BCV). A large free space often features on the left and right margins on the folio.

Foliation can be found on both margins in all the West Indian manuscripts of the corpus – letter-numerals on the left margin and figure-numerals on the right margin (except in PV where only figure-numerals can be found on the left margin) and both foliations are highlighted (see section 5.1 for more details below).

2.4.4 Layout – Overall conclusions

To provide easy reference for the readers, I will place the observations found above, on the general features of the manuscripts of the three areas, under consideration.

(a) Nepalese manuscripts exhibit a variety of layouts. They may have two or three text-sections per page or no text-sections at all. Ruling-lines and gaps (either between sentences or verse lines) occur occasionally. In addition, at times *śloka*s are arranged within text-sections by means of gaps. It is also important to note that two of the manuscripts with the *śloka* division by gaps within text-sections contain puranic texts (i.e. SP_1, SP_2) and the other one contains

page; in the manuscript of the *Sūtrakṛtāṅgasūtravṛtti* (VS 1200 / 1143 CE) (Jinabhadrasūri Grantha Bhaṇḍāra, Jaisalmer, no. 4) three to six lines per page; in the manuscript of the *Kalpalatāviveka* (*Kalpapallavaśeṣa*) (VS 1205 / 1148 CE) (Jinabhadrasūri Grantha Bhaṇḍāra, Jaisalmer, no. 317) two to seven lines per page; in the manuscript of the *Upadeśapadaprakaraṇalaghuṭīkā* (VS 1212 / 1155 CE) (Jinabhadrasūri Grantha Bhaṇḍāra, Jaisalmer, no. 214/1) three to six lines per page; in the manuscript of the *Ṣaḍāvaśyakasūtravṛtti* (VS 1298 / 1241 CE) (Jinabhadrasūri Grantha Bhaṇḍāra, Jaisalmer, no. 136/1) four to six lines per page; in the manuscript of the *Sthānāṅgasūtravṛtti* (VS 1300 / 1295 CE) (Jinabhadrasūri Grantha Bhaṇḍāra, Jaisalmer, no. 6) four to seven lines per page; in the manuscript of the *Praśnavyākaraṇadaśāṅgasūtravṛtti* (VS 1300 / 1295 CE) (Jinabhadrasūri Grantha Bhaṇḍāra, Jaisalmer, no. 23/3) two to four line per page.

an epic text (i.e. HV_1). One could argue that the texts written largely in one metre – as is the case with the Purāṇas and epic texts, which are composed almost exclusively in *śloka*s – fit the text-section layout suitably.

(b) The layout of manuscripts from East India, in particular those purported to be from Vikramaśīla, is very carefully organised. Most manuscripts contain seven lines per folio (except for PR, HTṬ and AT), and are usually written in a rather straight manner. No text-sections are found (with one exception in the corpus; the Bengali PR where the text is divided into three text-sections and each text-section demarcated by vertical ruling-lines). In most of the manuscripts square-shaped free space appears around both string-holes. For the free space around the string-holes, three lines have been left clear in height on the folio. There is ample free space on the margins of the folio. Clear visible gaps like those between sentences or *śloka*s in some Nepalese manuscripts are not found on the folio in East Indian manuscripts. In terms of the text genre, all manuscripts contain Buddhist (commentary) texts.

(c) In the West Indian manuscripts of my corpus, the text appears to be organised in two to three text-sections. While we find the use of vertical ruling-lines (occasionally) as well as in some Nepalese and East Indian manuscripts,[129] their use is consistent with all West Indian manuscripts of my corpus. Each text-section appears demarcated by vertical ruling-lines on the folio. Large margins can also be found in West Indian manuscripts. Foliations (both letter and figure-numerals) appear highlighted (see section 5.1 for more details). The symbols around the string-holes often appear highlighted. No use of blank spaces can be found at the end of the chapters or text in the manuscripts.

129 For example, in VDh, ruling-lines have been used partly. Furthermore, in the manuscript containing texts of the *Prajñāpāramitāstotra*, *Aṣṭasāhasrikā Prajñāpāramitā* and *Vajradhvajapariṇāmanā* (NS 135 / 1015 CE) (CUL Add.1643), one can also find the use of ruling-lines. Among the East Indian manuscripts, ruling-lines can be seen in the manuscript containing texts of the *Prajñāpāramitā* and *Aṣṭasāhasrikā Prajñāpāramitā* (1070 CE) (CUL Add.1464) (see also Bendall 1883, ii and 100).

3 Use of symbols

Symbols are found in manuscripts of – possibly – all cultures. Regarding Indic manuscripts, symbols are usually conspicuous features frequently found on the page and may be accurate representations or mere sketches of real objects taking on the appearance of abstract forms. Symbols may either serve as decorations and/or structuring devices, which sometimes signal the internal organisation of texts. At times, they may also have a particular religious or ritual significance, pertaining to specific faiths or schools of thought.

This chapter investigates the symbols found mainly in the manuscripts of my 'core' corpus referring to many more symbols from other manuscripts as well as some inscriptions. The aim is to discover whether certain symbols are characteristic of a particular region, epoch (largely within the time-frame 9th to 13th c.) etc. Thus, one cannot exclude the possibility that a specific workshop or group of scribes may have developed a specific way of drawing symbols, or that individual scribes may have developed their own style in the course of time.

3.1 The term '*puṣpikā*'

Without further ado, however, a note should be devoted to the Sanskrit term *puṣpikā*. This literally means (among other things) 'little flower'. However, it is also commonly used in the Indian sub-continent, at least from the 19th c. onward, to signify 'colophon', i.e. a short text providing information about the subject of a whole text or of one of its sections.[130]

In manuscripts containing a single text (STM) or more than one text, or multiple-text manuscripts (MTMs), the symbols are mainly embedded between double *daṇḍas*[131] placed either before or after a (sub-)chapter colophon or colophon; alternatively, they may appear both before and after these textual items. The

130 For the meaning of the term '*puṣpikā*', see Apte 1957, 1038 s.v. *puṣpikā*: "The last words of a chapter, which state the subject treated therein; e.g. *iti śrīmahābhārate śatasāhasryāṁ saṁhitāyāṁ vanaparvaṇi* &c. ... *amuko 'dhyāyaḥ*;" Tripāṭhī 1975, 41 states the following: "In many Indian languages the colophon is called puṣpikā. ... a colophon is often called 'iti śrī' because of its opening words. In Gujarati 'iti śrī' is also used in the general sense of 'en'"; Further, Das 2007, 37 understands the term '*puṣpikā*' as follows: "Most Orissan palm-leaf manuscripts have a *pushpika* (colophon) at the end, giving the name of the scribe and the date of copying ..."

131 It should be noted that there are also cases in which *daṇḍa*s are not used before and after the symbol see section 3.6.2.4.2 below where some of large symbols are delimited by a set of long vertical lines, but not sets of *daṇḍa*s.

https://doi.org/10.1515/9783110543087-003

variety of shapes of the symbols ranges from that of a dot, a simple circle, and more complex symmetrical figures, and representations of stylised flowers, realistic flowers etc. The term *puṣpikā* is generally used to label all these various shapes, however, in this work I introduce the following distinctions: the term 'symbol' to indicate all symbols or signs as a whole, the expression 'stylised *puṣpikā*' or 'florally stylised symbol' for symmetrical figures or symbols drawn in floral way, and 'realistic *puṣpikā*' for symbols more closely resembling real flowers containing stalks, leaves, sepals and buds etc. As certain symbols depict real or almost real flowers this is most likely why the term '*puṣpikā*' has been taken for their label.

The term *puṣpa*, literally 'flower', is used in modern times among other things to refer to a book that has been published in a *granthamālā* ('garland of books').[132] In this respect, one may draw a speculative parallel between the use of the terms *puṣpa* and *puṣpikā* and the size of the texts which they describe, i.e. a whole book, or a colophon or (sub-)chapter respectively.

3.2 Use of symbols in manuscripts – Selected early examples

If we try to find some of the oldest available evidence of the use of symbols by which texts or parts of texts have been divided/demarcated in Indic manuscripts, we may come across, the evidence offered by the Buddhist manuscripts from the Bāmiyān valley now part of the Schøyen Collection.[133] The manuscripts of the collection are thought to date approximately from ca. 2nd to 8th c.[134] the time period of which actually predates the one selected for this study.

Among the Schøyen manuscripts, a copy of an early commentary (MS 2373/1) written in 'Kuṣāṇa Brāhmī' script[135] presents a simple stylised *puṣpikā*.[136]

132 For example, in the book *Saṃskṛtaracanāprakāśaḥ* which was published in a series by the Mahendra Sanskrit University, we find: *śrīmahendrasaṃskṛtaviśvavidyālagranthamālāyāḥ pañcatriṃśaṃ puṣpam*. Literally meaning: 'The 35th flower of the garland of books of the Mahendra Sanskrit University.'

133 I am aware of the existence of the ancient Gandhāran Buddhist scrolls, some of which are thought to be older specimens than the manuscripts of this collection and contain some symbols at the end of the chapters etc. (see e.g. Baums 2014, 202 and Fig. 2). Most of these scrolls are written in the so called 'Kharoṣṭhī' script, in addition to the Brāhmī script. In the present study, I limit myself mainly to manuscripts written in the Brāhmī-related scripts or their northern, local derivatives.

134 See Braarvig et al. 2010, xvii.

135 See Sander 1968.

136 See IndoSkript, IS-Nr. 259.

This object is purportedly dates from ca. 2nd c.[137] In the last line one of the folio fragments (Plate XIII.1, 1 A) one small stylised simple *puṣpikā* can be found after double *daṇḍa*. This symbol consists of circles with a few lines or elements between them (see Fig. 3.2-I).

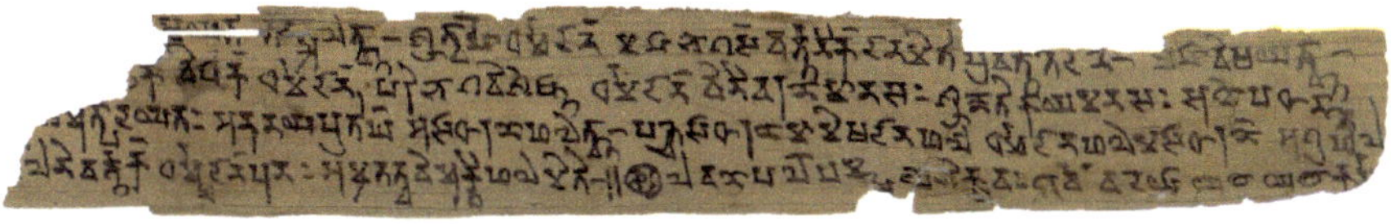

Fig. 3.2-I: An example of symbol in an earlier manuscript (reproduced by kind permission of editor from BMSC, 2002, Vol. II, Plate XIII.1, 1 A) © Jens Braarvig

The symbol appears after the word '*iti*' and is followed by '*lavaṇapalopamam* ...':

> /// lanivarttakaṃ dharmmadānaṃ punaḥ amṛtatvavimuktīphalam iti . 
> lavaṇapalopamam* yo bhikṣavaḥ evaṃ vadeyā yathā yathā ka[rma][138]

Another of the early examples of symbols used to divide texts in MTM is in the same collection in manuscript SC 2378. The manuscript is of Mahāyāna tradition and composed in 'Buddhist Hybrid Sanskrit' in the 'North Western Gupta' script[139] and thought to date from ca. 5th c. At the end of the Sūtra of the *Śrīmālādevīsiṃhanādanirdeśa*,[140] there are two symbols on 392r (in line nos. 3 and 4) that enclose one of the colophons. Some portions of the first symbol (in line 3) have been partially lost, in particular in the centre, due to the damages to the leaf, so the shape of the symbol is not fully detectable. However, the second symbol (in line 4) is visible. Slightly bigger than the first one it has a circle encircling the inner part of the symbol. Both symbols fit into one text line of the folio. Examples of these symbols can be seen on the folio shown in Fig. 3.2-II.

---

137 See BMSC, 2002, Vol. II, 249.
138 Aside from the double *daṇḍa* and symbol, I present the transliteration of the textual part following the convention of BMSC, 2002, Vol. II, 250.
139 See Sander 1968, Tafel 9–20.
140 See BMSC, 2000, Vol. I, 63–218.

Fig. 3.2-II: Symbols at the end of the text (reproduced by kind permission of editor from BMSC, 2000, Vol. I, Plate III, fol. 392r) © Jens Braarvig

 [141] [4] samāpta(ṃ) śrīmālādevīsiṃha[nāda]nirde[śa] O (sūtraṃ) [e](kayāna)ṃ

[ma](h)[opā](ya)vaitulye abhijñā[taṃ] śrī[mā]lā[sūtra]m etat*[142]  [143]

Enclosing colophons by means of symbols in MTMs, thus also demarcating the sections of a text, is a common feature of the manuscripts.

Another example of a beautifully drawn symbol is in one of the fragments written in the 'Gilgit/Bāmiyān Type I' script[144] of the *Vītaśokāvadāna* (MS 2380/6)[145] on the legend of king Aśoka. This manuscript is thought to date from ca. 6th c. The symbol appears after 'bhāṣaṭa:' and is placed between double daṇḍas (3 recto, MS 2380/6). It contains eight petals, encircled by another circle (see Fig. 3.2-III). A very similar symbol also containing eight petals can be found in some manuscripts of my corpus from Nepal (e.g. see Appendix I, SP_1 on 76b1, 96b1; SP_2 on 95v6 below).

Fig. 3.2-III: Symbol (reproduced by kind permission of editor from BMSC, 2000, Vol. I, Plate VIII,1, fol. 3r) © Jens Braarvig

141 See IndoSkript, Symbol: IS-Nr. 309.
142 Except for the symbols, here I present the transliteration of the textual part following the convention of BMSC, 2000, Vol. I, 67.
143 See IndoSkript, Symbol, IS-Nr: 309.
144 On the script, see Sander 1968.
145 See BMSC, 2000, Vol. I, 219–231.

/// +++ .. bhāṣata:  yadā rājñā aśok[en](a) ///[146]

An example of a symbol with 'double circles' can be found in the birch-bark manuscript MS 2385 on 26r1.[147] The editors of the text report there to be two texts within the manuscript, i.e. the *Bhaiṣajyagurusūtra* and the *Vajracchedikā Prajñāpāramitā Sūtra*.[148] The *Bhaiṣajyagurusūtra* ends with its 'sub-colophon' on folio 26r1 and, at the end of the sub-colophon, double circles are placed between double daṇḍas (see also section 3.4, type no. 6 below). After that the *Vajracchedikā Prajñāpāramitā Sūtra* begins with the invocation '*namo śākyamuna* ...'. This symbol can be seen in Fig. 3.2-IV.

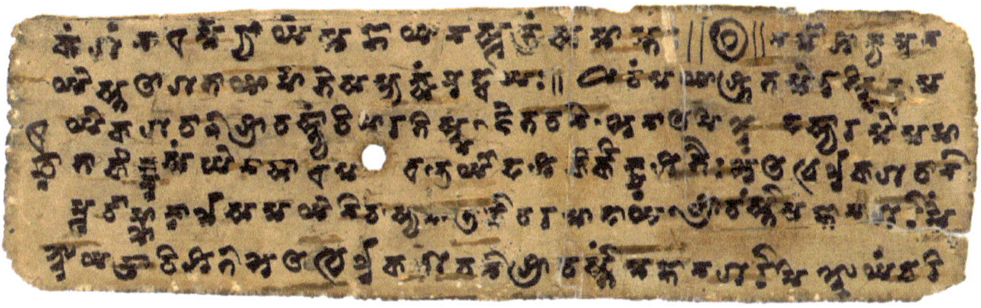

Fig. 3.2-IV: Symbol at the end of a particular text (reproduced by kind permission of editor from BMSC, 2016, Vol. III, Plate VII, fol. 26r) © Jens Braarvig

... nā<ma> dharma<pa>ryāyaṃ mahāyānasūtraṃ samāptaḥ [149] namo śākyamuna[150]

To conclude, evidence from the earlier manuscripts from Gilgit show that drawing different kinds of symbols at the end of chapters and texts with colophon or colophon-like statements predates the time-frame of 9th to 13th c. selected for my study.

146 Apart from using the symbol, I follow the transliteration of the textual part of BMSC, 2000, Vol. I, 222.
147 See BMSC, 2006, Vol. III, Plate VII. 1.
148 See BMSC, 2006, Vol. III, 89–132.
149 For examples of double circles, see below section 3.4, type no. 6.
150 Aside from the symbols and the omission of some parts of the text, I follow the transliteration of the textual part as BMSC, 2006, Vol. III, 95.

3.3 Shape and size

The symbols have different shapes even within the same manuscript. Some can have a simple shape, whereas others may have been drawn so skillfully they appear and could well be the work of a professional artist. Size can also vary greatly, even within the same manuscript. They may occupy the whole height of the folio (top to bottom) or just one line of the text on the folio. At times, they are drawn so small they are difficult to find on the folio.

Such variation in shape or size may also correspond to the differing degrees of emphasis given to the various levels of a text. Symbols appearing at the end of a chapter may be (slightly) bigger than those within a chapter, possibly hinting at a change in topic. Symbols placed almost at the end or actually at the end of a text accompanied by a colophon or other statements, are drawn more elegantly or larger than those at the end of a chapter or within the text (see section 3.6.2.4.1 below). A particular type of sequence or distribution of symbols may also be related to a specific tradition (see section 3.6.2.4.2 below).

Although changes in size and shape and the level of refinement of the symbols can be closely related to scribal habits (if the symbols are drawn by the scribes who copied the texts), such variations may at times provide specific information to the reader on the particular part of the text he/she is reading at that moment, should it be a chapter of the text or the end of the whole text (see sections 3.6.2.4.1 and 3.6.2.4.2 below).

In terms of the shape of the symbols and their production, it is fair to assume that in only in a few cases have the symbols been drawn with the help of tools, such as compasses, rulers, etc. At other times, particularly when a certain degree of accuracy is lacking, the symbols have been drawn freehand. To improve our understanding of the production of symbols, a specific example was examined during a field trip to Nepal (see section 5.2 for details below).

3.4 Types of symbols found in the same region or in more than one region

In this section I investigate the distribution of types of symbols. They can be found in various manuscripts originating from one particular area, or in several manuscripts across different areas or in manuscripts from different periods of time. Manuscripts belonging to the same religious tradition or containing texts of the same literary genre may also contain specific varieties of symbols.

In the following figures, I present some types of 'identical' or 'almost identical' symbols from manuscripts originating from the same area and from all the areas investigated in my study. As Indic manuscript culture is so rich in literature and production of artefacts, I am certainly not claiming to show all examples from all available manuscripts of particular areas or time periods here. In this section I present but a few selected symbols in the hope these examples will stimulate new ideas for future studies. I have selected mainly one symbol for each manuscript and arranged them in possible chronological order (see Figs. 3.4-I to 3.4-XLVII).

(1) These types of similar symbols can be seen in the following Figure. Here the symbol looks like a kind of 'dot'.[151] Please note that in manuscripts written in Śāradā script (from Kashmir) a dot or a dot-like element generally corresponds to '0'.[152] Examples of this type can be seen in Fig. 3.4-I.

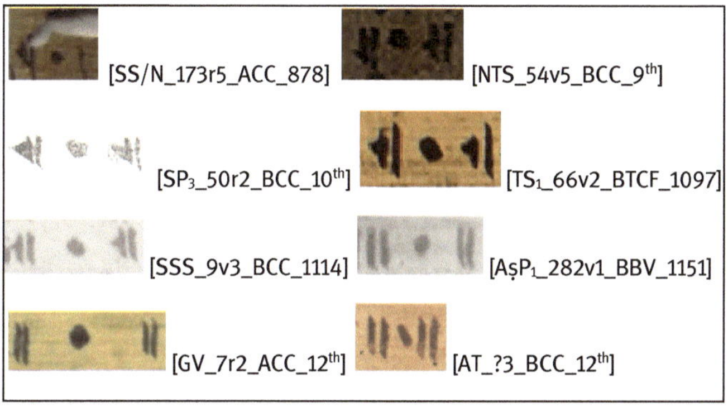

Fig. 3.4-I: Similar symbols

(2) One of the most popular types of the symbol is the simple circle,[153] often found in manuscripts before and/or after chapter colophons, colophons, in the parts of the

151 A similar dot can be found in the manuscript of the *Śivadharma* corpus (ca. 12th c.) (CUL Add.2102) on 278r3_ACC.

152 For example, see Grierson 1916, 698 the numerals for '10', '20', '30', '100', '1000'; Slaje 1993, 46 the numerals for '0' and '10'.

153 Simple circles can be found in the Vil̲avaṭṭi Grant of Pallava Siṃhavarman (446 CE), EI 24, IndoSkript, symbol, IS-Nr: 24; in the Badal pillar inscription of the time of Nārāyaṇapāla (860–917 CE), EI 2, No. 10, 160–167, Einicke 2009, 51, 284, 343 as NagIs3(860+)_1; in the manuscript of the *Saurasaṃhitā* (NS 69 / 949 CE) (NAK 1/1231 / NGMPP A 1161/6), Bang 2017, 30, Table I.4 (one circle as example); in the Kharepatan plates of Rattaraja (ŚS 930 / 1008 CE), EI 3, No. 40, 292–302, Mirashi 1977, CII 6, No. 41, 183–193, Einicke 2009, 55, 284, 343 as NagIs(1008)_2; in the manuscript of the *Kulālikāmnāyatantra* (NS 158 / 1037 CE) (NAK 5/877 / NGMPP A 41/3), Bang 2017, 30, Table I.4 (one circle as example); in the manuscript of the *Niśvāsamahātan-*

post colophonic statements etc.[154] In addition a circle or circle-like feature corresponds sometimes to the letter '*ṭha*'[155] or letter-numerals '0'.[156] Examples of the type of symbols can be seen in Fig. 3.4-II.

trāntargatapratiṣṭhātantra (NS 180 / 1060 CE) (NAK 1/279 / NGMPP A 41/15–A 42/1), Bang 2017, 30, Table I.4 (one circle as example); in the manuscript of the *Svacchandalalita* (NS 188 / 1068 CE) (NAK 1/224 / NGMPP B 28/18), Bang 2017, 30, Table I.4 (one circle as example); in the manuscript of the *Siddhāntasārapaddhati* (NS 197 / 1077 CE) (NAK 1/1363 / NGMPP B 28/29), Bang 2017, 30, Table I.4 (one circle as example); in the manuscript of the *Kubjikāmata* (NS 212 / 1092 CE) (NAK 1/1077 / NGMPP B 25/24), Bang 2017, 30, Table I.4 (one circle as example); in the manuscript of the *Siddhāntasārapaddhati* (NS 231 / 1111 CE) (NAK 5/743 / NGMPP B 28/19), Bang 2017, 30, Table I.4 (one circle as example); in the manuscript of the *Amarakoṣaṭīkā* (NS 239 / 1119 CE) (KL 560 / NGMPP C 121/1, Pant 2000, Einicke 2009, 150, 152, 154–155, 286, 344 as New10.1(1119)_11, New10.2(1119)_6, New10.3(1119)_1, New10.4(1119)_3; in the Copper Plate of the Vañapalli Grant of Sauryāditya (1020 CE), Sircar 1963–1964, IndoSkript, symbol, IS-Nr: 192; in the manuscript of the *Pañcarātramahājñāna* (NS 147 / 1027 CE) (NAK 1/1648 / NGMPP A 54/9), Einicke 2009, 143, 286, 344 as New4(1027)_1; in the Naḍagām Plates of Vajrahasta (ŚS 979 / 1058 CE), EI 4, IndoSkript, symbol, IS-Nr: 457; in the Copper-Plate of the time of Ānandadeva (NS 282 / 1161 CE), Pant/Sharma 1977, IndoSkript, symbol, IS-Nr: 752; in the manuscript of the *Śivadharmaśāstra* (NS 290 / 1170 CE) (NAK 1/1075 / NGMPP B 7/3), see Einicke 2009, 158, 286, 344 as New11(1170)_4. See also Śākya 1973, 85 the first symbol in the first row; Sarkar/Pande 1999, Fig. 15; 2–5.

154 See Bühler 1896, 85: "In späterer Zeit kommen gleichfalls bisweilen im Texte, nach grösseren Abschnitten und öfter am Ende von Documenten, Symbole vor, die meist sehr abgeschliffene Formen haben. Das gewöhnlichste besteht aus einem grossen Kreise mit einem kleineren, oder auch mit mehreren Puncten in der Mitte. Dieses kann entweder aus dem Dharmacakra entstanden sein, der sich noch vor CII, 3. Nr. 63, deutlich findet, oder aus dem Lotus, der auch vorkommt. Da der Kreis mit einem Puncte ⊙ dem alten *tha* entspricht, so werden andere, späteren *tha* ähnliche, oder gleiche Zeichen dafür gebraucht ..."; see Sarkar/Pande 1999, 55 with regard to the interpretation and meaning of circle, circle with dot or 'double circles' in inscription: "The majority of the highly abstract figures of the inscriptions share one common feature: a circle or a circle with a dot in the centre. As indicated, the circle possibly represents the thalamus on which other floral members stand and survive. It serves as a platform for the pollen-bearing stamen and the female-organ bearing carpel to unite. So, a circle with a dot or concentric circles represent union, procreation, proliferation and prosperity."

155 For the letter '*ṭha*', see Bühler 1896, Tafel II, row 19, Tafel III, row 17, Tafel IV, row 18 and Tafel V, row 21; Dani 1963, plate IIIa, Iva, Va, Via, VIIIa, IXa, Xia, XIIa, XIVa, XVIIa; Sander 1968, Tafel 1, 9, 21.

156 For the figure-numerals '0', see Bendall 1883, Table of Figure-numerals; Bühler 1896, Tafel IX.

[SP₁_224b3_ACC_811]   [PT_37r2_ACC_829]
[SS/N_159v1_BCC_878]   [NTS_15r5_BCC_9th][157]
[KT_87v2_ACC_924][158] [UVDh_56r3_AD_968]
[SP₃_123r6_ACC_10th]   [SP₄_274v5_ACC_10th]
[HV₁_313r2_ACC_1037]   [HY_22v5_AD_1039][159]
[DDh_4r4_BCC_1053]   [PR_67r2_BCC_1054]
[TS₁_57r4_BCC_1097][160] [VDh_51v5_BCC_12th]
[SSS_5r3_ACC_1114]   [AsP₁_282v1_ABV_1151]
[HV₂_40v3_BCC_1172]   [SDhPS_116r1_BCC_12th]
[LTT_14v1_ACC_12th]   [STT_3v1_ACC_12th]
[DVPT_5v4_ACC_12th]   [AP_28r5_BC_12th]
[CPN_49v1_BCC_12th]   [HTT_40r6_ACC_12th]
[SS_224r5_ACC_1216]   [TS₂_47r5_BCC_13th]

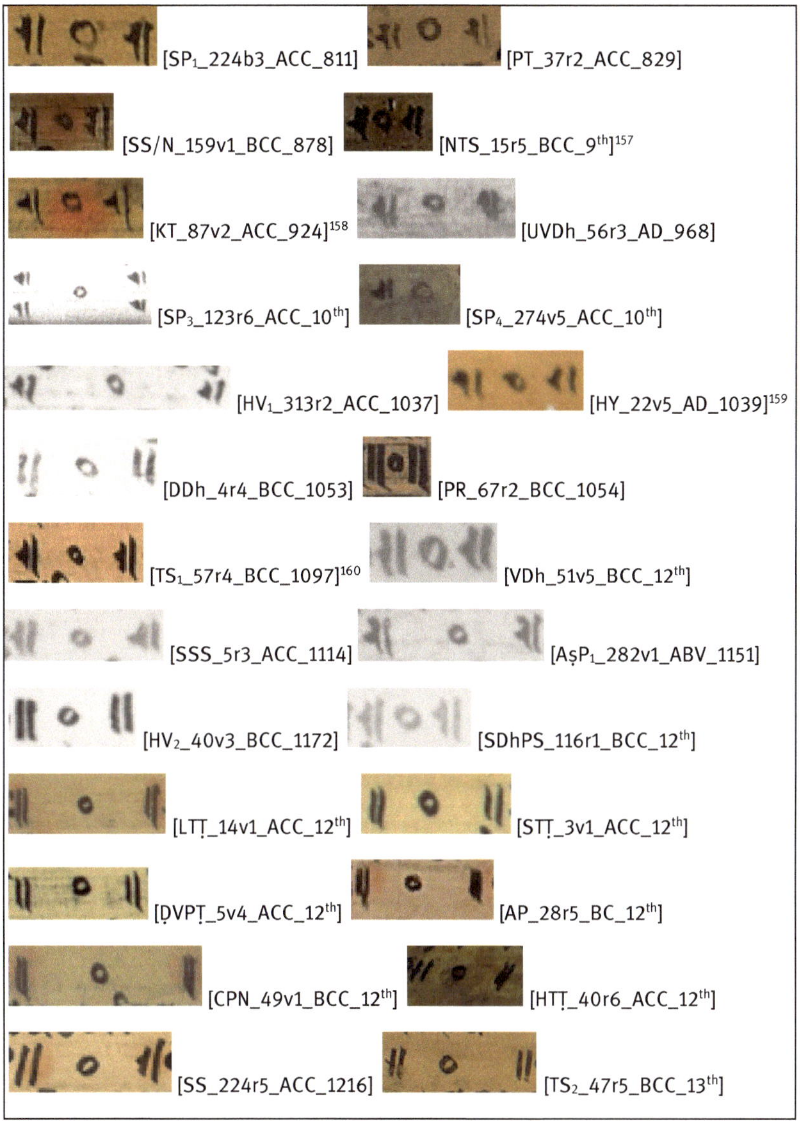

Fig. 3.4-II: Similar symbols

---

157 One circle of this manuscript has also been used by Bang 2017, 30 in Table I.4.
158 One circle of this manuscript has also been used by Bang 2017, 30 in Table I.4
159 The same circle has also been used by Bang 2017, 30 in Table I.4.
160 One circle of this manuscript has also been used by Bang 2017, 30 in Table I.4.

(3) Another type includes a symbol which looks like a 'figure-eight knot', or two small circles joined together 'horizontally'. It appears before and/or after chapter colophon etc.[161] In addition a 'figure-eight knot' also has some similarities to the (lower) part of the letters '*i*' or '*cha*'.[162] Regarding manuscripts containing Buddhist texts such as AṣP$_1$, SDhPS, one may also interpret this symbol as a representation of one of the popular Buddhist symbols *śrīvatsa* ('endless knot'). Examples can be seen in Fig. 3.4-III.

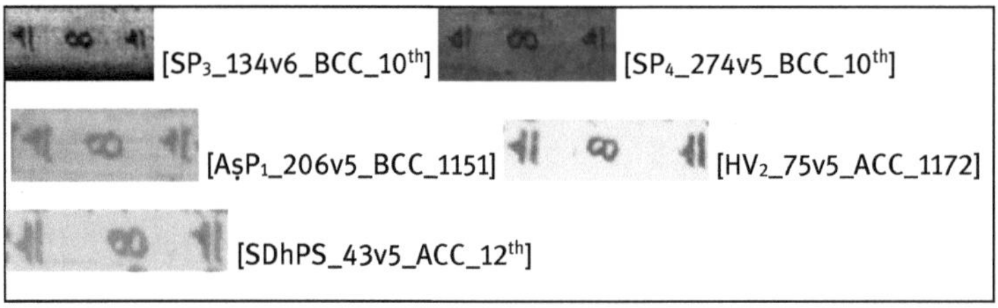

Fig. 3.4-III: Similar symbols

(4) The next type of symbol includes a nearly circle-like element embedding a slightly curved vertical-like line at its centre.[163] This symbol can be found before and/or after chapter colophons, after a particular smaller section etc. in manuscripts.[164] Examples of symbols can be seen in Fig. 3.4-IV.

161 A very similar symbol used as a sign to indicate the unwrittenable space on the folio can be found in the (birch-bark) manuscript of the *Atharvaveda* (1419 CE) (Universitätsbibliothek Tübingen) written in Śaradā script, see Einicke 2009, 171, 294 as Sar2(1419)_2.
162 For letters '*i*' and '*cha*' see Bendall 1883, Table of Letters; Bühler 1896, Tafel III, row 12, Tafel IV, row 13, Tafel V, row 16, Tafel VI, rows 3 and 21, Tafel VII, row 14.
163 This type of symbol resembles some versions of the letter-numerals '80'. For examples, see Bühler 1896, Tafel IX.
164 Similar symbols can be found in the Bhadana grant of Aparajita (ŚS 919 / 997 CE), EI 3, No. 37, Einicke 2009, 54, 284 as NagIs9(997)_1; in the manuscript of the *Viṣṇudharmaśāstra* (NS 167 / 1047 CE) (NAK 1/1002/1 / NGMPP A 1080/3), Grünendahl 1983, 14 as Ms. N6, Einicke 2009, 144, 286 as New5(1046)_1. See also Śākya 1973, 85 the first symbol in the last row.

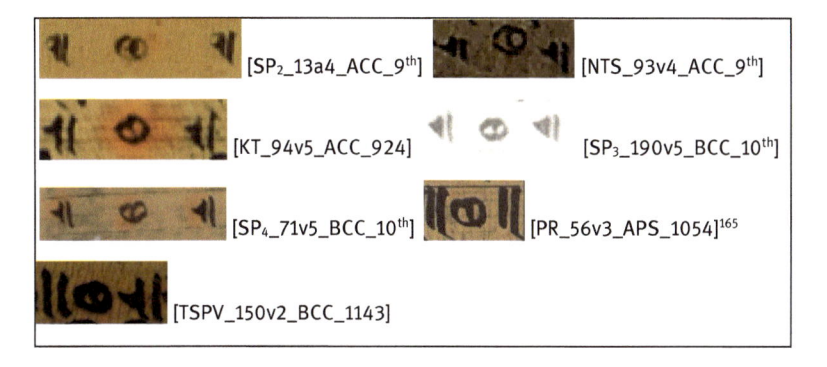

[SP_2_13a4_ACC_9^{th}]

[NTS_93v4_ACC_9^{th}]
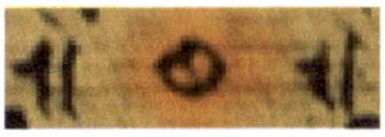
[KT_94v5_ACC_924]

[SP_3_190v5_BCC_10^{th}]

[SP_4_71v5_BCC_10^{th}]

[PR_56v3_APS_1054][165]

[TSPV_150v2_BCC_1143]

Fig. 3.4-IV: Similar symbols

(5) Very similar to the aforementioned type of symbol, is a curved vertical-like line that runs down passing through the lower part. The symbol appears to have a 'tail'.[166] The tail often continues downward and to the right. To some extent, the symbol resembles certain versions of the letter-numerals for '80'.[167] This symbol may also be interpreted as a representation of sprouting seeds.

[SP_3_147r2_BCC_10^{th}]

[NAK 1/1002/1 / NGMPP B 5/8_8r1_ACC_1047]

165 This appears after a particular verse line.

166 A similar symbol can be found in the manuscript of the *Viṣṇudharma* (NS 210 / 1090 CE) (NAK 1/1002/2 / NGMPP B 5/7), Grünendahl 1983, part 1, 10 as Ms. N3, Einicke 2009, 146, 286 as New8(1090)_6; in the manuscript of the *Sarvaprakaraṇa* (NS 277 / 1157 CE) (KL 36 / NGMPP C 4/2) on 5r4_ACC, 6r2_BCC, 8v3_ACC, 9r3_ACC, 14v1_ACC, 14v6_BCC, 16v4_BCC, 17v4_ACC, 18v5_BCC, 19v6_ACC, 20r2_ACC, 20r4_ACC, 20v2_BCC, 20v5_BCC, 23v3_ACC, 24r_ACC, 26r3_ACC; in the manuscript of the *Piṅgalāmata* (NS 294 / 1174) (NAK 3/376 / NGMPP A 42/2), Bang 2017, 30, Table I.4; in the manuscript of the *Viṣṇudharma* (NS 281 / 1161 CE) (NAK 4/1389 / NGMPP A 10/3) on 124v1_BCC, Grünendahl 1983, part 1, 12–13 as Ms. 5.

167 For the letter-numerals '80', see Bendall 1883, appendix, Letter-numerals, rows 3, 4 and 8; Bühler 1896, Tafel IX.

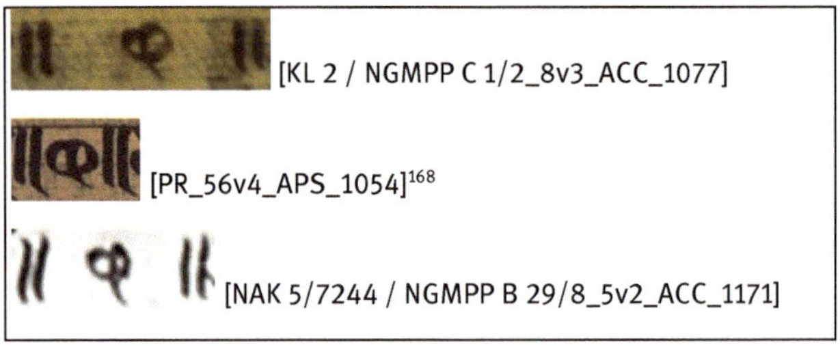

Fig. 3.4-V: Similar symbols

(6) A further type contains a symbol consisting of 'double circles'. This symbol can be found in many manuscripts.[169] Examples of symbols can be seen in Fig. 3.4-VI.

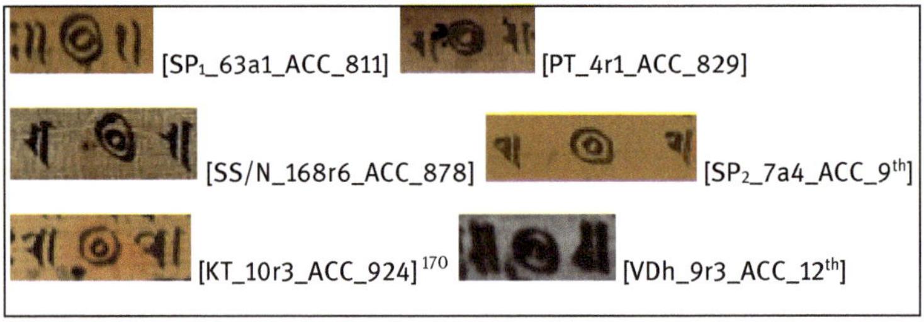

Fig. 3.4-VI: Similar symbols

168 Actually this appears after a particular verse line.

169 Examples of 'double circles' can be found in the Fragmentary Copper-Plate from Arakan (496–520), EI 37, IndoSkript, symbol, IS-Nr: 87; in the manuscript of the *Jātakamālā* (ca. 500–750 CE), IndoSkript, symbol, IS-Nr: 323; in the Kanasva Stone Inscription of Sivagana (738 CE), IndoSkript, symbol, IS-Nr: 318; in the manuscript of the *Sarvajñānottara* (ca. 9th c.) (NAK 1/1692 / A 43/12), Bang 2017, 30, Table I.4 (one double circle); in the manuscript of the *Bhairavamaṅgala* (ca. 10th/11th c.) (NAK 5/687 / NGMPP B 27/21), Bang 2017, 30, Table I.4 (one double circle); in the copper plate of the Vañapalli Grant of Sauryāditya (1020 CE), EI 35, 130–136, IndoSkript, symbol, IS-Nr: 192; in the manuscript of the *Śivadharmaśāstra* (NS 192 / 1072 CE) (NGMPP E 2787/11), IndoSkript, symbol, IS-Nr: 181; in the manuscript of the *Svacchandalalitabhairavatantra* (ca. 11th c.) (KL 68 / NGMPP C 6/5), Bang 2017, 30, Table I.4 (one double circle); see also Sarkar/Pande 1999, Fig. 15, 1 and 8.

170 One double circle of this manuscript has also been used by Bang 2017, 30 in Table I.4.

(7) Another type includes a simple symbol containing a circle at its centre surrounded by four almost semi-circular petals.[171] This symbol can be found before and/or after the chapter colophons, with the foliation etc. Regarding the symbol with foliation, it should be noted that the symbol contains only three semi-circular petals, the upper petal has most probably been replaced by the foliation number. The examples of symbol can be seen in Fig. 3.4-VII.

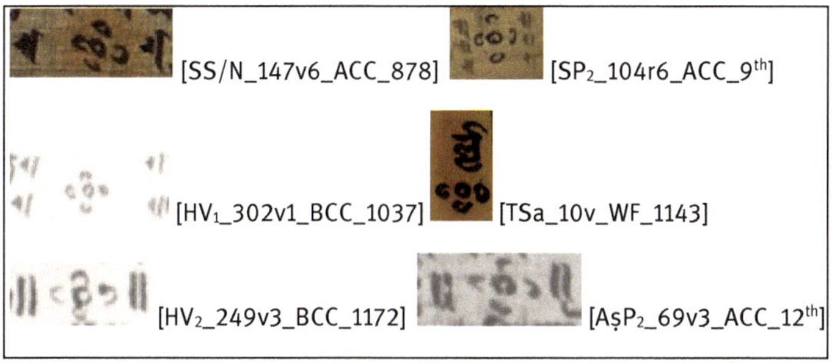

Fig. 3.4-VII: Similar symbols

(8) A stylised simple *puṣpikā* comprised of a circle surrounded by four almost semi-circular petals and four lines features frequently.[172] The symbol appears before and/or after chapter colophons or in other places with foliation, around string-holes etc. in manuscripts. Please note that in the symbol around the string-hole on the folio the hole replaces the circle. Examples can be seen in Fig. 3.4-VIII.

---

171 For example, similar symbols can be seen in the Beṇḍigānahaḷḷi Plates of Vijaya-Kṛṣṇavarman (ca. 400–450), IndoSkript, symbol, IS-Nr: 410; in the manuscript of the *Śivadharma* corpus (ca. 12th c.) (CUL Add.1694.1) on 5r5_ACC, 27r2_BCC, 27v4_ACC, 34r4_B/ACC, 123v_B/ACC.

172 Similar symbols can be seen, for instance, in the manuscript of the *Niśvāsamahātantrāntargatapratiṣṭhātantra* (NS 180 / 1060 CE) (NAK 1/279 / NGMPP A 41/15–A 42/1), Bang 2017, 30, Table I.4 (one symbol has been given); in the manuscript of the *Kubjikāmata* (NS 212 / 1092 CE) (NAK 1/1077 / NGMPP B 25/24), Bang 2017, 30, Table I.4 (one symbol has been presented); in the manuscript of the *Matasāra* (NS 317 / 1197 CE) (KL 70 / C 6/7), Bang 2017, 30, Table I.4 (one symbol has been presented); in the manuscript of the *Śivadharma* corpus (ca. 12th c.) (CUL Add.1694.1) on 118v6_B/ACC. See also Śākya 1973, 85 the second symbol in the first row.

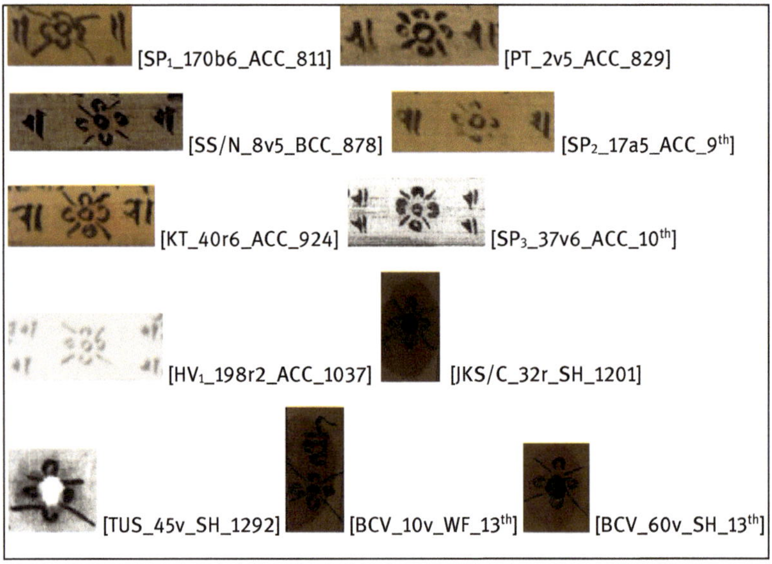

Fig. 3.4-VIII: Similar symbols

(9) Rather similar to the aforementioned type, but with a small 'line' or 'stroke' added to the outer side of four petals can also be found.[173] Examples can be seen in Fig. 3.4-IX.

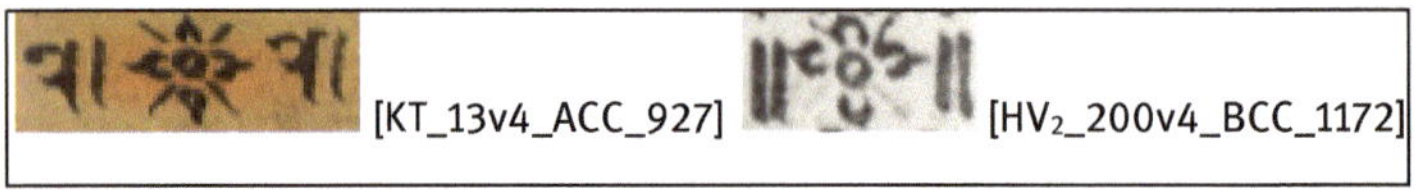

Fig. 3.4-IX: Similar symbols

173 Quite similar symbols can be found in the manuscript of the *Brahmayāmala* (NS 172 / 1052 CE) (NAK 3/370 / NGMPP A 42/6), Bang 2017, 30, Table I.4 (one symbol has been presented); in the manuscript of the *Svacchandalalitabhairavatantra* (ca. 11th c.) (KL 68 / NGMPP C 6/5) on 21r3_ACC, 61v1_ACC, 80r2_ACC, 178r1_BCC, 186v5_BCC, 189r5_BCC, 191r2_ACC; in the manuscripts of the *Viṣṇudharma* (ca. 12th c.) (KL 578 / NGMPP C 54/5), Grünendahl 1984, part 3, 6–7 as Ms. N14 on 12v3_ACC, 20r1_ACC, 21v2_ACC, 30r4_ACC, 39v5_ACC, 76v4_ACC, 181r3_BCC, 184r1–2_B/ACC, 199r3_BCC, 202r3_BCC.

(10) Another type includes a stylised *puṣpikā* similar to the previous one (see Fig. 3.4-VIII), in which, however, the semi-circular petals are facing outside.[174] This symbol can be found before and/or after chapter colophons, around string-holes (here with the hole replacing the circle), with foliation etc. (see Fig. 3.4-X below).

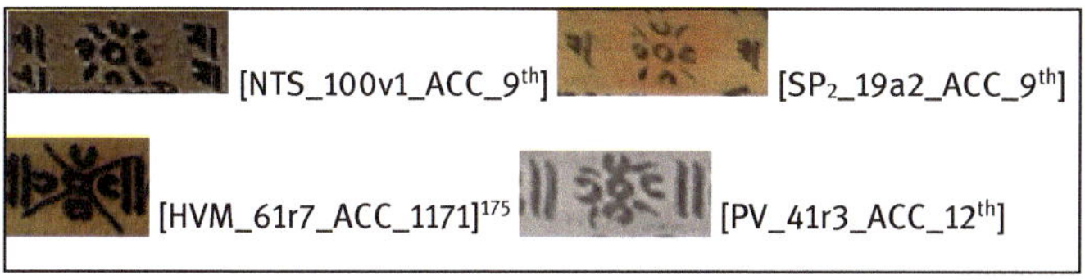

Fig. 3.4-X: Similar symbols

(11) The next type comprises a stylised *puṣpikā* containing a circle in the centre sorrounded by five thickly drawn petals. Examples of these can be seen in Fig. 3.4-XI.

Fig. 3.4-XI: Similar symbols

(12) It is possible to find a stylised *puṣpikā* containing a circle surrounded by four petals, each obtained by combining two almost semi-circular petals. This symbol appears before and/or after chapter colophon or around the string-hole

---

174 Identical symbols can be found in the Parvatiya Plates of Varnamalavarmadeva (825–875 CE), EI 92, IndoSkript, symbol, IS-Nr: 771; in the Hāoraghāṭ Plates of Balavarman III of Kāmarūpa (ca. 885–910 CE), EI 3, IndoSkript, symbol, IS-Nr: 159; in the Copper-Plate Grant of Kadamba Tribhuvanamalla (1107 CE), EI 30, IndoSkript, symbol, IS-Nr: 86; in the manuscript of the *Sārāvalī* (NS 288 / 1168 CE) (NAK 5/700 / NGMPP A 31/10) on 63v6_ACC, 117r5_ACC, 122v3_ACC, 139v2_A/BPC. See also Śākya 1973, 85 the first symbol in the fourth row from the top; Sarkar/Pande 1999, Fig. 12,1.

175 Similar symbols (without circle in the centre) appear around string-holes on nearly all folios (with a few exceptions), see section 3.5.3, Fig. 3.5.3-III below. Here the circle has been replaced by the string-hole. Additionally, a similar symbol can be found with the foliation number '80'.

(with the hole replacing the circle) etc. in manuscripts.[176] Examples can be found in Fig. 3.4-XII.

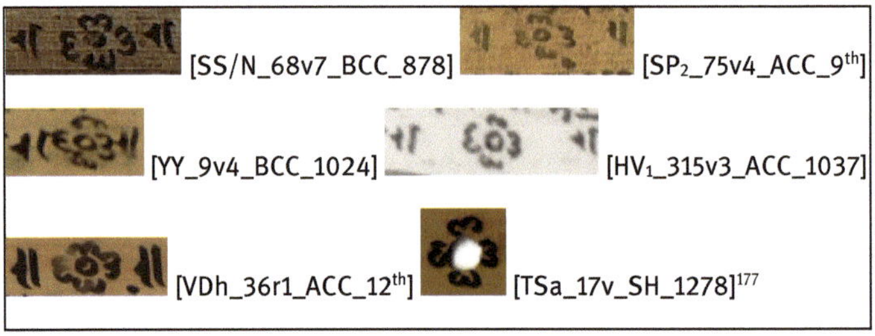

Fig. 3.4-XII: Similar symbols

(13) Another type of symbol similar to the type in no. 12, but with petals facing outward is found in manuscripts. Examples can be seen in Fig. 3.4-XIII.

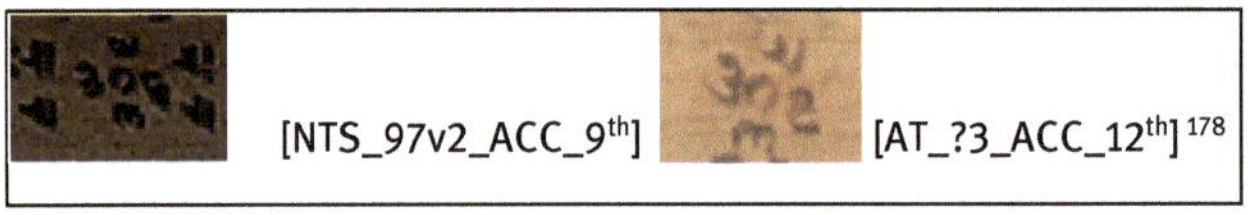

Fig. 3.4-XIII: Similar symbols

(14) The next type of stylised *puṣpikā* is one containing a circle in the centre surrounded by four lines and four petals – with the petals made by joining two semi-circles.[179] Examples can be seen in Fig. 3.4-XIV.

---

176 Similar symbols appear in the manuscript of the *Amarakoṣaṭīkā* (NS 239 / 1119 CE) (KL 560 / NGMPP C 121/1), Pant 2000, part I, 79; part II, 54, 56, IndoSkript, symbol, IS-Nr: 678.

177 This symbol appears around the string-hole on the folio and the circle is replaced by the string-hole. See also section 3.6.1, Fig. 3.6.1-I for details.

178 Regarding the specific meaning of this symbol, see section 3.6.2.1.2 and Fig. 3.6.2.1.2-II below.

179 Similar symbols appear in the manuscript of the *Bhairavamaṅgala* (ca. 10th/11th c.) (NAK 5/687 / NGMPP B 27/21), Bang 2017, 30, Table I.4 (one symbol is presented); in the manuscript of the *Svacchandalalitabhairavatantra* (ca. 11th c.) (NGMPP C 6/5) on 161r3_B/ACC; in the manuscript of the *Kalyāṇakāmadhenūvivaraṇa* (NS 224 / 1104 CE) (NAK 3/363 / NGMPP A 38/13, A 934/8) on 12r6_AC; in the manuscript of the *Amarakoṣaṭīkā* (NS 239 / 1119 CE) (KL 560 / NGMPP C 121/1), Pant 2000, part I, 78 and part II, 46, 48, 50, 143; IndoSkript, symbol, IS-Nr: 678–679; in

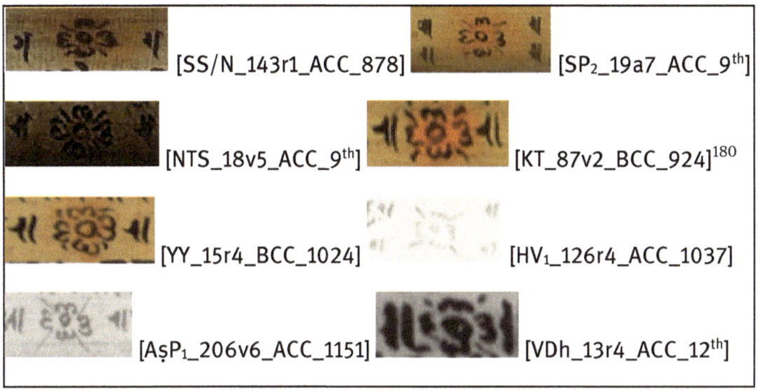

Fig. 3.4-XIV: Similar symbols

(15) Another type comprises a stylised *puṣpikā* with a circle surrounded by four petals from which a little 'stroke' or 'tail' emerges.[181] Examples can be seen in Fig. 3.4-XV.

Fig. 3.4-XV: Similar symbols

(16) Similar to the symbol of the type no. 15, but with four petals and an additional four strokes on their sides is also to be found.[183] This symbol appears before and/or

the manuscript of the *Sārāvalī* (NS 288 / 1168 CE) (NAK 5/700 / NGMPP A 31/10) on 6v5_ACC, 22r6_ACC, 70r2–3_B/ACC.

180 One similar symbol of this manuscript has also been listed by Bang 2017, 30 in Table I.4.

181 A quite similar symbol can also be found in the manuscript of the *Piṅgālamata* (NS 294 / 1174) (NAK 3/376 / NGMPP A 42/2), see Bang 2017, 30 in Table I.4.

182 Regarding the specific meaning of this symbol, see section 3.6.2.1.2 and Fig. 3.6.2.1.2-II below.

183 Quite similar symbols can be found in the manuscript of the *Viṣṇudharma* (NS 167 / 1047 CE) (NAK 1/1002/1 / NGMPP A 1080/3) on 154v3_BC, Grünendahl 1983, 14 as Ms. N6, see IndoSkript, symbol, IS-Nr: 341; in the manuscript of the *Svacchandalalitabhairavatantra* (ca. 11th c.) (NGMPP C 6/5), Bang 2017, 30, Table I.4 (one symbol is presented); in the manuscript of the

after chapter colophons, colophons or other textual parts as well as around the string-hole (with the hole replacing the circle). Examples can be seen in Fig. 3.4-XVI.

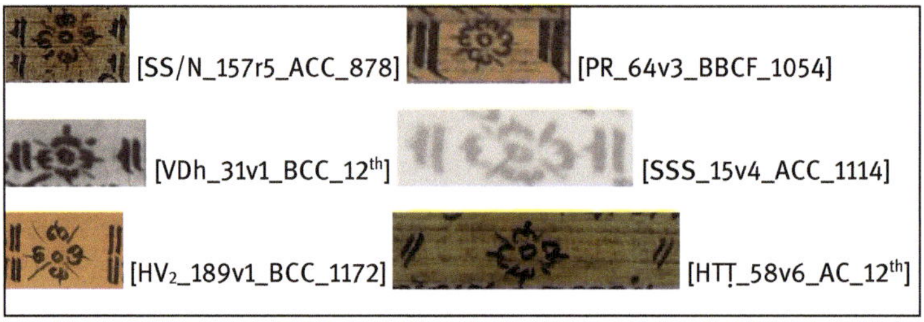

Fig. 3.4-XVI: Similar symbols

(17) Another type of symbol comprises one circle in the centre surrounded by four lines and four petals – with the petals made by joining two semi-circles. In the left and right petals one finds a further element containing a semi-circle with a stroke or a tail.

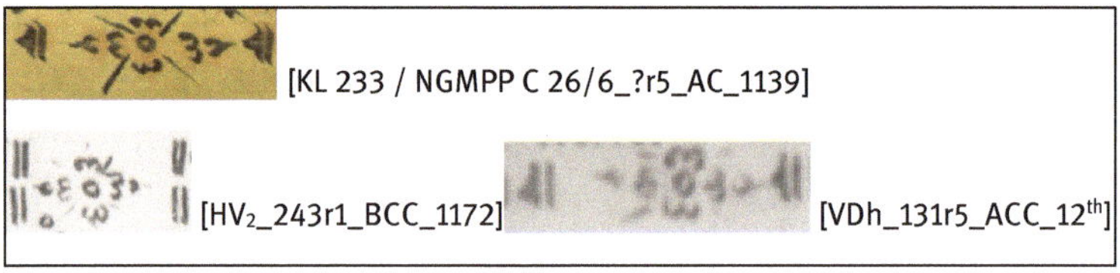

Fig. 3.4-XVII: Similar symbols

(18) A further type includes symbols containing a circle in the centre, four lines and four petals of which two petals, the right and left one, are followed by a futher petal-like elements with a 'stroke' or a 'tail'.

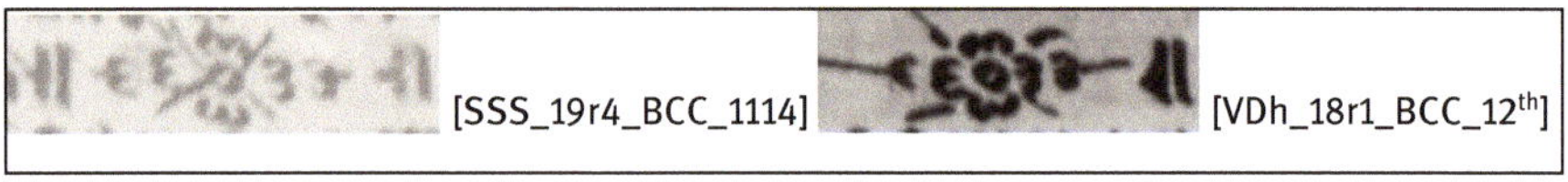

Fig. 3.4-XVIII: Similar symbols

Cāndravyākaraṇa (NS 393 / 1243 CE) (KL 17 / NGMPP C 2/9) after the colophon; Roth 1986, symbol no. 5; see also section 3.6.2.1.3 for the specific meaning of the symbol in HTṬ.

(19) The next type of symbol comprises a circle in the centre surrounded by four lines and four petals – with the petals made by joining two semi-circles followed by a semi-circular like feature and occasionally a 'stroke'.[184]

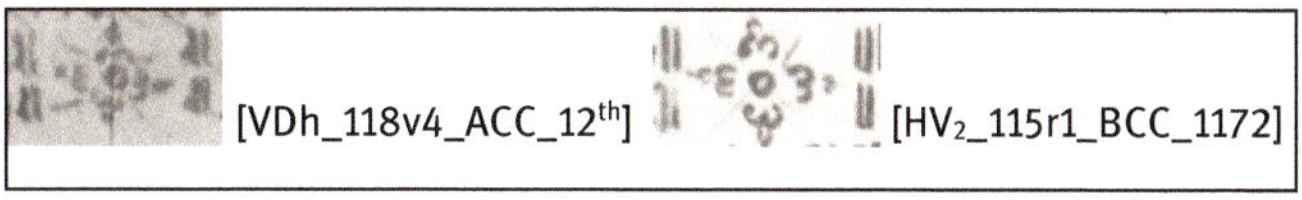

Fig. 3.4-XIX: Similar symbols

(20) Another type of stylised *puṣpikā* is comprised of a circle at the centre surrounded by more than four small semi-circular-like petals.[185] Symbols can be found before and/or after the chapter colophon and also around the string-hole where the circle is replaced by the string-hole. Examples can be seen in Fig. 3.4-XX.

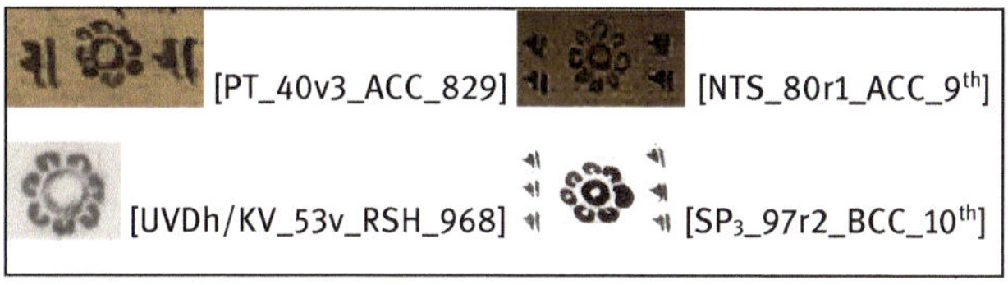

Fig. 3.4-XX: Similar symbols

(21) A further type of symbol containing 'double circles' or a circle with a 'dot' at the centre surrounded by more than four small semi-circular-like petals can be found after the chapter or colophon etc. in manuscripts (see Fig. 3.4-XXI).

---

184 A quite similar symbol appears in the manuscript of the *Amarakoṣaṭīkā* (NS 239 / 1119 CE) (KL 560 / NGMPP C 121/1), see Pant 2000, part II, 325, IndoSkript, symbol, IS-Nr: 682.

185 Almost identical symbols can be found, (3 symbols) in the manuscript of the *Śivadharmaśāstra* (NS 192 / 1072 CE) (NGMPP E 2787/11), IndoSkript, symbol, IS-Nr: 181; in the manuscript of the *Śivadharma* corpus (ca. 11th c.) (NAK 1/1261 / NGMPP A 10/5) after one of the chapter colophons (i.e. after the 16th chapter colophon of the *Vṛsasārasaṃgraha*) in line no. 1; in the manuscript of the *Hitopadeśa* (NS 604 / 1484 CE) (KL 16 / NGMPP C 2/8) on 99r4_B/ASpI, 99v3–4_B/AC.

 [SS/N_209v5_AC_878]  [SP_3_95v2_ACC_10th]

Fig. 3.4-XXI: Similar symbols

(22) Another type of symbol comprising a circle (with a dot) or double circles with eight petals is found in the manuscripts. They may appear before and/or after chapter colophons etc. One should note that the symbols look identical to some extent, but also exhibit some differences – the first symbol contains a circle with a dot at the centre,[186] the second symbol contains double circles in the centre. Furthermore, nearly all petals of the first symbol contain a kind of 'tail' or 'stroke' added to them, whereas a few petals of the second symbol do not contain a 'tail' or 'stroke'.

 [KT_78r5_ACC_924]

 [NAK 1/1261 / NGMPP A 10/5_?rv1_BCC_11th]

Fig. 3.4-XXII: Similar symbols

(23) Another type of 'almost similar' symbol comprises a symbol containing double circles at the centre and many petals is to be found in manuscripts. Please note that a few petals of the second symbol in the following Fig. look slightly different to those of the first symbol.

 [SS/N_157v4_ACC_878]  [KT_99v2_APC_924]

Fig. 3.4-XXIII: Similar symbols

186 An almost identical symbol with a circle in the centre can be found in the manuscripts of the *Khaṇḍakhādya* (NS 259 / 1139 CE) (KL 233 / NGMPP C 26/6) before the colophon.

(24) The next type of almost identical symbol can be found in some manuscripts. This symbol appears before and/or after chapter colophons, around the string-hole etc.[187] This symbol is somewhat similar in appearance to the form of symbols of the aforementioned type (Fig. 3.4-XXIII).

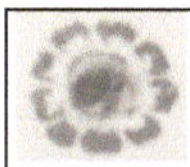
[KV/UVDh_5r_RSH_968]

[SP_3_193r5_BCC_10^{th}]

[NAK 1/1261 / NGMPP A 10/5_?rv1_BCC_11^{th}]

Fig. 3.4-XXIV: Similar symbols

(25) The next type of almost similar symbol comprises symbols made of a circle with or without a dot in the centre surrounded by a few number of dots.[188]

[SP_1_243a7_ACC_811]
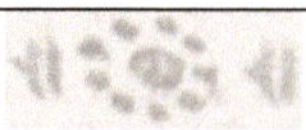
[SSS_10v6_BCC_1114]

Fig. 3.4-XXV: Similar symbols

(26) Another type of simple symbol is a symbol containing a circle in its centre surrounded by some small circles.[189] Examples can be seen in Fig. 3.4-XXVI.

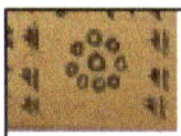
[SP_2_66v6_ACC_9^{th}]
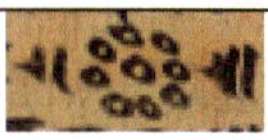
[YY_27r4_BCC_1024]

Fig. 3.4-XXVI: Similar symbols

187 A similar symbol can be found in the manuscript of the *Śivadharmaśāstra* (NS 156 / 1036 CE) (Calcutta, ASB G-4077), see IndoSkript, symbol, IS-Nr: 243.
188 A similar symbol containing a circle surrounded by seven dot-like elements can be found in the (paper) manuscript of the *Caitanyabhāgavata* (1690 CE) (Universitätsbibliothek Leipzig, Ms A 722), see IndoSkript, symbol, IS-Nr: 777.
189 A similar symbol can be found in Roth 1986, symbol no. 6.

(27) The following type of stylised *puṣpikā* can also be found in some manuscripts.[190] This symbol appears before and/or after chapter colophons, around the string-hole etc.

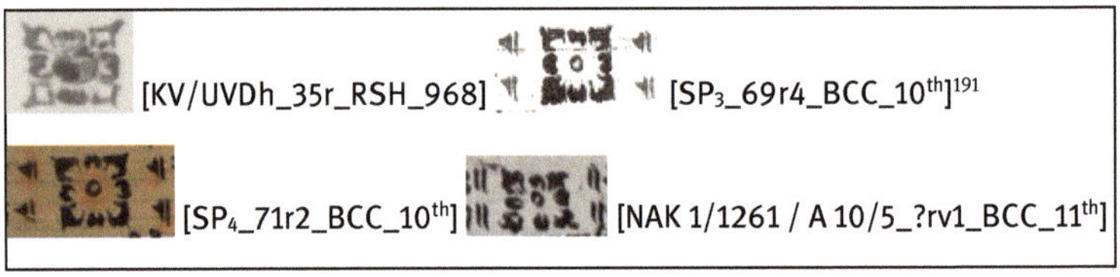

Fig. 3.4-XXVII: Similar symbols

(28) The type of symbol in the following Fig. 3.4-XXVIII can be found in manuscripts. All symbols appear before and/or after chapter colophons etc. The symbols take on the shape of a kind of 'rhombus'.

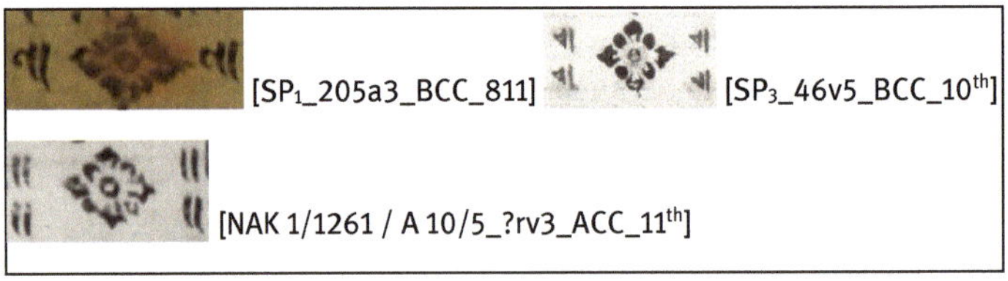

Fig. 3.4-XXVIII: Similar symbols

(29) Another type of similar symbol also has the form of a 'rhombus'.[192]

---

190 The symbol of KV/UVDh is almost identical to the symbol of SP_3, SP_4 and NAK 1/1261 / A 10/5. SP_3, SP_4 and NAK 1/1261 / A 10/5 are not dated and KV/UVDh is dated to 968 CE (see also type nos. 20 and 24). The identical symbol of the dated manuscript KV/UVDh might be helpful to approximate the date of undated manuscripts SP_3, SP_4 and NAK 1/1261 / A 10/5. Thus it is possible that SP_3, SP_4 and NAK 1/1261 / A 10/5 might have been produced a few years before or after the production of KV/UVDh. See also section 3.8.2 below.

191 In SP_3 similar symbols can be found on 26r6_BCC, 88r1_BCC, 136r4_ACC. These symbols of SP_3 and the symbol of SP_4 are discussed in section 3.8.2 below.

192 Attestations of similar symbols can also be seen in the manuscript of the *Viṣṇudharma* (1220 CE) (NAK 2/51 / NGMPP A 1163/1), Grünendahl 1989, 3–4 as N15, IndoSkript, symbol, IS-Nr: 191. See also section 3.6.2.2, Fig. 3.6.2.2-IV an almost similar symbol like this can be obtained by joining stylised 'half-like' *puṣpikā*s.

[NAK 4/1389 / NGMPP A 10/3_46r2_ACC_1161][193]

[HV$_2$_20r3_ACC_1172]

Fig. 3.4-XXIX: Similar symbols

(30) Another type of near similar stylised *puṣpikā* appears in manuscripts.[194] The symbols can be found before and/or after chapter colophons etc. There is a small difference between the two symbols – the second one contains an extra four lines.

[AṣP$_1$_169r1_ACC_1151]

[SDhPS_20r1_BCC_12th]

Fig. 3.4-XXX: Similar symbols

(31) A further type of symbol comprising a circle in the centre surrounded by eight 'sharp-formed' petals appears.[195] The symbols can be found before the chapter colophon.

[VDh_62r5_BCC_12th]

[HV$_2$_10v4_BCC_1172]

Fig. 3.4-XXXI: Similar symbols

(32) There is another type of similar symbol comprised of a symbol containing a circle with or without dot in the centre surrounded by four petal or petal-like

193 In this manuscript there are other near similar symbols before or after chapter colophons on 15vr4_BCC, 20r1_ACC.

194 I discuss the possible meanings and representations of these symbols in section 3.6.2.1.4 below.

195 A very similar symbol appears in the manuscript of the *Pañcarakṣā* (NS 596 / 1476 CE) (NAK 1/1114 / NGMPP A 47/15) on 99r_BC (see section 3.6.2.16 below).

features facing outside with a 'line' or 'stroke'.[196] In the PR it can be found before the Buddhist concluding formula (i.e. *idam avocad bhagavān* ... 'thus spoke the Bhagavān ...') and in TS$_2$ after the chapter colophon.[197]

Fig. 3.4-XXXII: Similar symbols

(33) The next near similar type of symbol has a symbol containing four almost roundish petals or petal-like elements in the centre encircled by an outer circle.

Fig. 3.4-XXXIII: Similar symbols

(34) Another near similar type of symbol can be found after chapter colophon, before the (Buddhist) opening formula etc. in manuscripts. Here the symbol is comprised of eight petals encircled by a circle. The petals are round, to a degree.

196 Near similar symbols appear in the Asoge Plates of Kadamba Jayakeśin (II) (1134 CE), EI 26, IndoSkript, symbol, IS-Nr: 438; in the manuscript of the *Kāraṇḍavyūha* (NS 478 / 1358 CE) (KL 112 / NGMPP C 12/3) before the colophon; in the manuscript of the *Mudrārākṣasa* (NS 491 / 1371 CE) (NAK 1/1692 / NGMPP A 32/6) on 28v3–4_B/ACC, 62v4_BCC, 71r3_B/ACC; in the manuscript of the *Vasundharādhāraṇī* (NS 491 / 1371 CE) (KL 114 / NGMPP C 13/2) on 18v3_AC; in the manuscript of the *Rāmāṅkanāṭikā* (NS 496 / 1376 CE) (KL 73 / NGMPP C 6/9) on 42r3_BCC, 73v1_BCC, 146v3; in the manuscript of the *Pañcarakṣā* (NS 509 / 1389 CE) (CUL Add.1701.1) on 153r1_ACC; in the manuscript of the *Cāndravyākaraṇa* (aka *Śabdalakṣaṇavyākaraṇa*) (ca. 15th c.) (NAK 1/1697 / NGMPP B 35/25) on 7r4_BCC, 15r3_BCC, 27v1_BCC, 41v2_BCC, 48r2_BCC, 51r4_BCC, 53v3_BCC. For these types of symbols, see also Sarkar/Pande 1999, 52, Fig. 12,5–6.

197 An attestation of a symbol bearing some similarities to the form of this symbol can be seen before the colophon on 422v in the Greek manuscript Biblioteca Apostolica Vaticana, Vat.gr.1626 containing Homer's *Iliad*. The manuscript was copied in 1477 CE in Rome by the famous copyist Johannes Rhosos. Use of these near similar symbols in various manuscript cultures in different regions suggests the necessity for future comparative research at an international level.

[SP_3_100r5_ACC_10th]

[DDh_9v3_ACC_1053]

[AP_1_2r3_BBOF_1151]

Fig. 3.4-XXXIV: Similar symbols

(35) Also found in manuscripts are those similar to type no. 34, but with an additional circle at the centre part. The symbols comprising eight petals and the outer part of petals are quite round.[198] All inner parts of the symbols have been encircled.

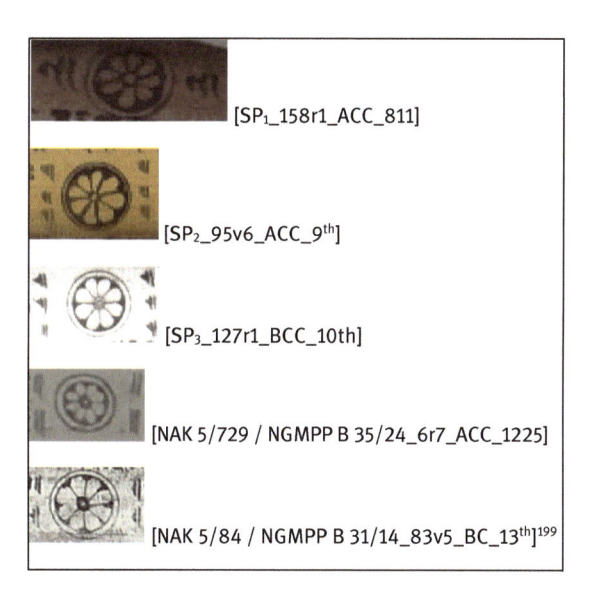

[SP_1_158r1_ACC_811]

[SP_2_95v6_ACC_9th]

[SP_3_127r1_BCC_10th]

[NAK 5/729 / NGMPP B 35/24_6r7_ACC_1225]

[NAK 5/84 / NGMPP B 31/14_83v5_BC_13th][199]

Fig. 3.4-XXXV: Similar symbols

198 Near identical symbols are in the manuscript of the *Daśabhūmikasūtra* (NAK 3/737 / NGMPP A 39/13) before the 2nd and 5th chapter colophon and after the 6th chapter colophon and the manuscript is dated from ca. 5th–7th c. (see Matsuda 1996, xvi–xviii) and ca. 6th c. (see Harimoto 2011, 93–95); in the manuscript of the *Aṣṭasāhasrikā Prajñāpāramitā* (NS 128 / 1008 CE) (CUL Add.866) on 148r2_BCC, 162r3_ACC, 168v4_ACC; in the manuscript of the *Śivadharmaśāstra* (NS 156 / 1036 CE) (ASB G-4077), see IndoSkript, symbol, IS-Nr: 243.
199 This manuscript is also microfilmed as A 1297/10.

(36) Also similar to type no. 35, but with petals of almost 'kite' shape are found in the manuscripts. Like symbols of type no. 35, the inner parts here have been encircled.

[SP_2_74v1_ACC_9^{th}]
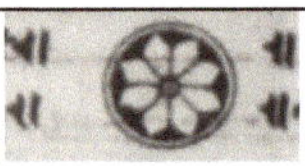
[NAK 1/1261 / A 10/5_139v5_ACC_11^{th}]

[B 35/24_19v2_ACC_1225]

Fig. 3.4-XXXVI: Similar symbols

(37) Near similar to type no. 36, but with the inner part of the symbols encircled by double circles are also found in the manuscripts.[200]

[SP_2_161b4_ACC_9^{th}]

[SP_3_19r3_ACC_10^{th}]

Fig. 3.4-XXXVII: Similar symbols

(38) Another type includes stylised *puṣpikā* comprising four virtually 'heart-shaped' petals. The petals have been encircled.[201]

[SP_1_202a2_BCC_811]

[SP_3_109v2_BCC_10^{th}]

Fig. 3.4-XXXVIII: Similar symbols

200 An identical symbol is found in the manuscript of the *Aṣṭasāhasrikā Prajñāpāramitā* (NS 128 / 1008 CE) (CUL Add.866) on 119r5_ACC.

201 An almost similar symbol is found in the manuscripts of the *Daśabhūmikasūtra* (NAK 3/737 / NGMPP A 39/13) before the 3rd chapter colophon. The manuscript can be dated ca. 5th–7th c. (see Matsuda 1996, xvi–xviii) and ca. 6th c. (see Harimoto 2011, 93–95); in the manuscript of the *Kāśikāvivaraṇapañjikā* (c. 10th/11th c.) (NAK 4/216 / NGMPP A 52/13) on 245v6_ACC.

(39) The next type includes a symbol containing eight petals of a virtual 'heart-shape'.[202] The petals have been encircled.

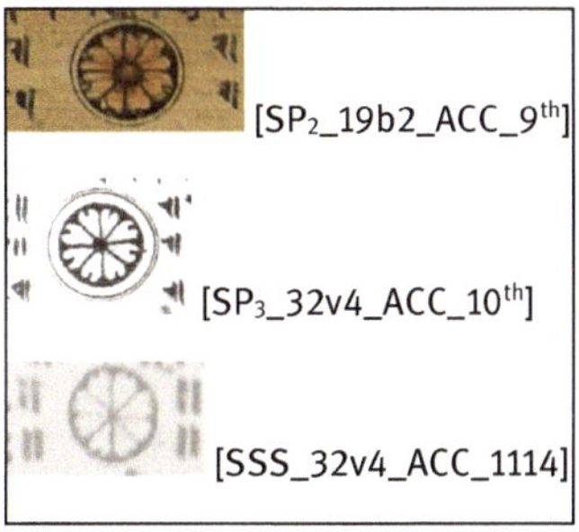

Fig. 3.4-XXXIX: Similar symbols

(40) Another type of near similar symbol comprising eight slightly curved petals running clockwise is found in manuscripts.[203]

Fig. 3.4-XL: Similar symbols

(41) To some extent similar to type no. 40, but with more than eight curved petals running clockwise direction is found in the manuscripts.[204]

202 Almost identical symbols are found in the manuscript of the *Daśabhūmikasūtra* (NAK 3/737 / NGMPP A 39/13) after the 2nd and 7th chapter colophons. The manuscript is dated ca. 5th–7th c. (see Matsuda 1996, xvi–xviii) and ca. 6th c. (see Harimoto 2011, 93–95).

203 An identical symbol is found in the manuscript of the *Aṣṭasāhasrikā Prajñāpāramitā* (NS 128 / 1008 CE) (CUL Add.866) on 38v6_ACC.

204 Almost identical symbols also appear in the manuscript of the *Aṣṭasāhasrikā Prajñāpāramitā* (NS 128 / 1008 CE) (CUL Add.866) on 13v4_ACC, 114r2_BCC.

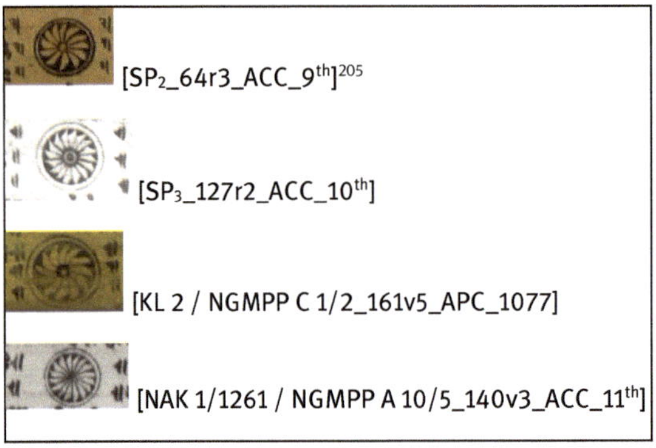

Fig. 3.4-XLI: Similar symbols

(42) Another type of symbol includes one of the types of the *siddham*[206] (henceforth, *siddham*, *siddham* symbol) which can be found in manuscripts e.g. before an invocation, benediction or before the date in the post colophonic part etc.

Fig. 3.4-XLII: Similar symbols

(43) Another type of *siddham* symbols often appear before invocations at the beginning of manuscripts.[207] These manuscripts are purported to originate from Vikra-

205 Including this symbol (type no. 41), there are a few other symbols in SP_2 and SP_3/SP_4 (with regard to the connection of SP_3 and SP_4, see section 3.8.2 below) which look quite similar in appearance e.g. type nos. 8, 35, 37, 39, 40. Furthermore, SP_2 contains two realistic *puṣpikās* (see section 3.5.1, Fig. 3.5.1-I below). Similarly, three realistic *puṣpikās* can also be found at the end of the chapters in SP_3 (see section 3.5.1, Fig. 3.5.1-II). This evidence of the use of a few almost similar symbols can imply that the scribe of SP_3/SP_4 was probably familiar with the symbols of SP_2 or that he may have consulted the SP_2 while copying the text.

206 For discussion of the term and examples of further '*siddham*' symbols, see Sander 1986, 251–261; Roth 1986, 239–249. A nearly similar *siddham* symbol can also be found in the Copper-Plate of Śivadeva (NS 221 / 1100 CE), Pant/Sharma 1977, IndoSkript, symbol, IS-Nr: 753; in the manuscript of the *Piṅgālamata* (NS 294 / 1174) (NAK 3/376 / NGMPP A 42/2) on 1v_BI, see also Bang 2017, 30, Table I.4.

207 An almost identical symbol can be found in the Nālandā Inscription of Vipulaśrīmitra (1100–1151 CE), see IndoSkript, symbol, IS-Nr: 519.

maśīla. A tiny 'dot-like' element appears added to the top-right side of most of the symbols (namely in GV, HAP, ḌVPṬ, AP, CPN). In its appearance the symbol resembles to a degree the figure-numeral '7' found in manuscripts (e.g. the foliation for 7 on the left-hand margin on 7v in AAĀ, LTṬ, ḌVPṬ, HAP, HP).[208]

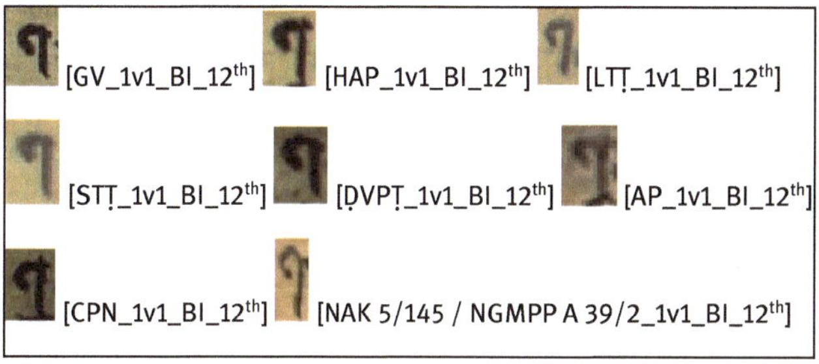

Fig. 3.4-XLIII: Similar symbols

(44) A further type of *siddham* symbol[209] can be found e.g. before the invocation, before and/or after chapter colophons etc., in manuscripts.

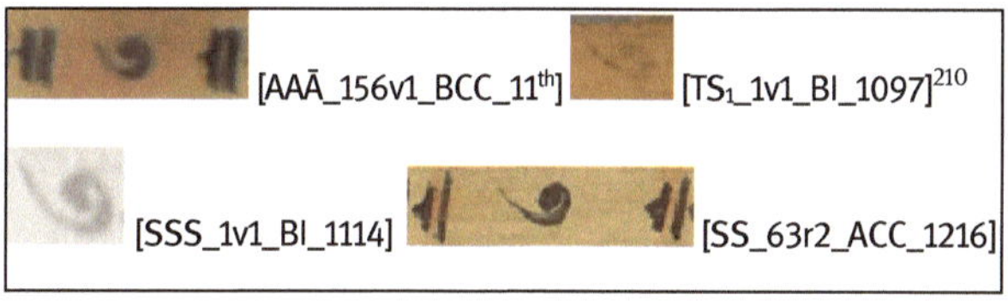

Fig. 3.4-XLIV: Similar symbols

(45) Another type of *siddham* symbol can also be found in manuscripts. Among them five may possibly originate from Vikramaśīla and the other one (i.e. AAĀ)

208 For the first numeral in the third row, numerals in the fourth and tenth rows, see Bendall 1883, appendix, Figure-numerals.

209 An almost similar symbol appears in the Taukhel Inscription of Aṃśuvarman (613 CE), see IndoSkript, symbol, IS-Nr: 604; in the manuscript of the *Bhairavamaṅgala* (ca. 10th/11th c.) (NAK 5/687 / NGMPP B 27/21) on 1v1_BI, Bang 2017, 30, Table I.4; in the manuscript of the *Kubjikāmata* (NS 212 / 1092 CE) (NAK 1/1077 / NGMPP B 25/24) on 1v_BI, Bang 2017, 30, Table I.4; in the manuscript of the *Viṣṇurahasya* (1195 CE) (NAK 3/380 / NGMPP B 29/4), see IndoSkript, symbol, IS-Nr: 208. See also Sarkar/Pande 1999, Figs. 7–10 for examples of '*siddham*'.

210 The same symbol has also been listed by Bang 2017 in 30, Table I.4.

from a nearby area.[211] Interestingly most of them have a near identical shape. Their head, slightly curved inside is followed by a curved 'tail' which always extends to the left. A tiny hook-like line or dot-like element often appears to the upper-right side of the symbol. This symbol resembles the character '*t*' also found in manuscripts (see section 3.5.2, Fig. 3.5.2-I below).

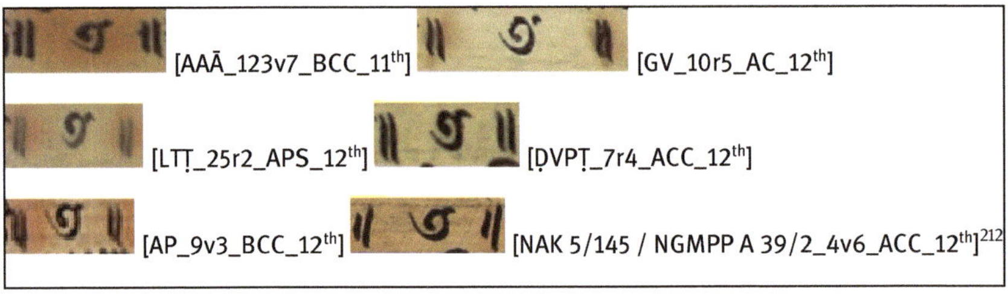

Fig. 3.4-XLV: Similar symbols

(46) Another type of symbol appears resembling the character '*tha*'[213] or the letter-numeral for '20' (henceforth '*tha*' or '*tha*' symbol).[214] This symbol can be found, before and/or after chapter colophons, before the (Buddhist) concluding formula (BCF) or before and/or after a particular text section etc.[215] In addition, a

211 An almost identical symbol appears in the manuscript of the *Abhisamācārikadharma* (1000–1100 CE), see IndoSkript, symbol, IS-Nr: 306. At least 12 almost identical symbols can be seen in the manuscript of the *Vimalakīrtinirdeśa*/*Jñānālokālaṃkāra* (1000–1300 CE), see IndoSkript, symbol, IS-Nr: 597. See also Roth 1986 and Sander 1986 for almost identical symbols of this type.

212 Further *siddham* symbols can be found on 5v7_ACC, 7r3_ACC, 10v7_B/AC.

213 For the letter '*tha*', see Bendall 1883, Table of Letters; Bühler 1896, Tafel IV, row 23 and Tafel V, row 26; Dani 1963, plate Xia; Sander 1968, Tafel 27.

214 For instance, the letter-numerals for '20', see Bendall 1883, Table of Letter-numerals; Bühler 1896, Tafel IX.

215 Further attestations of the '*tha*' are in the manuscript of the *Pālībhāṣāyaṃ Vinaya* (ca. 8th–9th c.) (NAK 3/737 / A 1151/2 and A 39/13), Einicke 2009, 138, 286 as New1(775!)_1; in the manuscript of the *Niśvāsamahātantrāntargatapratiṣṭhātantra* (NS 180 / 1060 CE) (NAK 1/279 / NGMPP A 41/15–A 42/1), Bang 2017, 30, Table I.4 (one *tha* is presented); in the manuscript of the *Śivadharmaśātra* (NS 189 / 1069 CE) (NAK 3/393 / NGMPP A 1082/3), Einicke 2009, 144, 286 as New6(1069)_1; in the manuscript of the *Aṣṭasāhasrikā Prajñāpāramitā* (ca. 12th c.) (KL 18 / NGMPP C 103/2) on 170r1_BCC; in the manuscript of the *Viṣṇudharma* (NS 281 / 1161 CE) (NAK 4/1389 / NGMPP A 10/3) on 122v1_BCC, 123r5_BCC, 124v1_ACC, 125r5_B/ACC, 126r5_B/ACC; in the manuscript of the *Śivadharma* corpus (ca. 12th c.) (CUL Add.2102) on 113r5_ACC, 319r3–4_B/ACC.

set of many '*thas*' has also been used both as line-fillers[216] or space-fillers[217] in manuscripts.

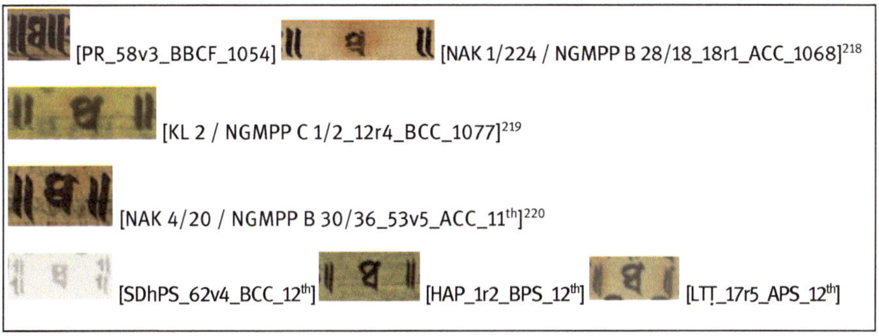
[PR_58v3_BBCF_1054]
[NAK 1/224 / NGMPP B 28/18_18r1_ACC_1068][218]
[KL 2 / NGMPP C 1/2_12r4_BCC_1077][219]
[NAK 4/20 / NGMPP B 30/36_53v5_ACC_11th][220]
[SDhPS_62v4_BCC_12th]
[HAP_1r2_BPS_12th]
[LTT_17r5_APS_12th]

Fig. 3.4-XLVI: Similar symbols

(47) Another type of symbol includes a symbol that resembles the character '*cha*'[221] (hereafter '*cha*' or '*cha*'-like symbol or '*cha*' symbol). The symbol can be found be-

216 '*Thas*' are used as line-fillers in the manuscript of the *Śivadharma* corpus (ca. 12th c.) (CUL Add.1645) on 44r1–2, 59r1, 67r1.

217 They are found as space-fillers in HV_1 on 220r5; in DDh on 46v5. In West Indian manuscripts they are used as space-fillers in TSPV on 93v7 and in TUS on 36v3.

218 Further attestations of the symbol in the manuscript can be found on 5r4–5_B/ACC, 18r1_ACC, 51v2_ACC, 74v6_ACC, 150v3_ACC, 157v4_ACC, 159v5_ACC, 162v4_B/AC; see also Bang 2017, 30, Table I.4 (one *tha* is presented).

219 Further attestations of the symbol in this manuscript can be found on 10v1_BCC, 14r5_B/ACC, 14v1_ACC, 14v3_B/ACC, 15r1_B/ACC, 16r1–2_B/ACC, 16v1_B/ACC.

220 Further attestations in the manuscript can be found on 11v5_ACC, 14v3_ACC, 50v5_B/ACC, 53v5_BCC.

221 In terms of meaning, appearance, use of the symbol I quote here some selected descriptions by scholars to help obtain an overview of it. Bühler 1896, 85: "... Da der Kreis mit einem Puncte ʘ dem alten *tha* entspricht, so werden andere, späteren *tha* ähnliche, oder gleiche Zeichen dafür gebraucht und in den modernen MSS. erscheint schliesslich das dem *tha* sehr ähnliche ថ"; Tripāṭhī 1975, 48: "'cha', 'śrī'. A portion of the Scribal Remarks consists of numerous Akṣaras of this type (cha, śrī, śrīḥ). The oldest record of the use of cha to indicate the end, which we could trace, is a 'Turfan' fragment (Kat. Nr. 816 [R4]) ... For Śrīharṣa's reference to 'cha' (in his Naiṣadhīyacarita, 10.87 and 16.98) vide Nārāyaṇa's commentary on these verses (NSP 1952, 431, and 669: grantha-lekhana-samāpti-patre samāpti-sūcakaṃ chakārādi-vartulam akṣaraṃ kriyate) and A. N. Jani, A Critical Study ... (Baroda OI, 1957), 215. ... The meaning of this sign and of other signs (whether identical with Akṣaras and figures, or not) is unknown"; Thaker 2002, 170: "At the close of the Mss, before and even after the *PRAŚASTIs*, we find such benedictions as: 'शुभं भवतु', 'कल्याणमस्तु', 'मंगलं महाश्रीः', 'लेखकपाठकयोः शुभं भवतु', etc. Similarly such symbols as '।। ठ ।।','||छ||' and '||ळ||' are placed at the close. Many a time these

fore and/or after chapter colophon, colophon etc. in manuscripts.[222] Generally the manuscripts in which we find such types of symbols come from West India.

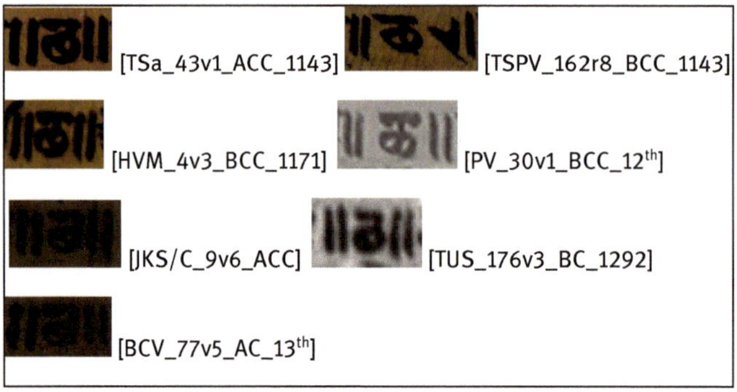

Fig. 3.4-XLVII: Similar symbols

symbols are seen at the close of sections or topics also. On observation of these symbols in a number of Mss MUNIJĪ has come to the conclusion that they represent पूर्णकुम्भ (PŪRṆAKUMBHA) or a Full JUG which is regarded as auspicious in India for all affairs. As such in Mss they indicate 'auspicious completion'. Such other symbols as '- -' and 'puṃṭa' are also found in ancient Mss. They might be picture-designs indicative of 'conclusion'. In a number of Mss certain other designs are drawn in order just to draw attention to the closure of sections or chapters. They also may be regarded similar to the same." Balbir 2006, 68 reports as follows: "The Scribal Remark generally contains syllables such as *śrī* or *cha*. The origin and the meaning of the latter ... are rather mysterious and have not been elucidated so far. Sometimes, it appears that series of such syllables, separated or not by *daṇḍas*, were written simply to finish the line (or the page) and avoid blank spaces."

222 Similar symbols can be found in the manuscript of the *Kavalayamala* (1038 CE), see Einicke 2009, 106, 285 as Nag1(1038)_1; in the manuscript of the *Śāntināthaboli* (1293 CE) (L.D. Institute, Ahmedabad ms. 8484), Einicke 2009, 107, 285 as Nag2(1293)_1; in the (paper?) manuscript of the *Jyotiṣ Ratnakośa* (1445 CE) (L.D. Institute, Ahmedabad ms. 8261), Einicke 2009, 116, 285 as NaJ1(1445)_4; in the (paper) manuscript of the *Kālakācāryakathā* (VS 1516 / 1459 CE) (L.D. Institute, Ahmadabad, ms. 419), see IndoSkript, symbol, IS-Nr: 333; in the (paper) manuscripts of the *Raghuvaṃśa* (1500 CE) (Universitätsbibliothek Leipzig, Ms A 375), Einicke 2009, 119, 285 as NaJ3(1500)_13; in the (paper?) manuscript of the *Mahāpurāṇa* (1540 CE), Einicke 2009, 109, 285 as Nag4(1540)_2; in the (paper) manuscript of the *Atharvaveda* (1550 CE) (Universitätsbibliothek Ms A 93), Einicke 2009, 121, 285 as NaJ4(1550)_10; in the (paper) manuscript of the commentary on the *Kumārasambhava* (1582 CE) (Universitätsbibliothek Leipzig Ms A 372), Einicke 2009, 128, 286 as NaJ6(1582)_21; in the (paper) manuscript of the *Abhidhānacintāmaṇi Nāmamālā* (1585 CE) (Universitätsbibliothek Leipzig Ms A 800), Einicke 2009, 129, 286 as NaJ7(1585)_3; in the (paper) manuscript of the *Grahasiddhi* (VS 1695 / 1638 CE) (L.D. Institute, Ahmadabad, ms. 8825), see IndoSkript, symbol, IS-Nr: 331; in the (paper) manuscript of the *Naiṣadhīyaprakāśa* (1650 CE) (Universitätsbibliothek Leipzig Ms A 397), Einicke 2009, 132, 286 as NaJ9(1650)_15. See also Sarkar/Pande 1999, Fig. 15, 18.

At this stage it is perhaps too early to present the above mentioned types in terms of region or exclude further possibilities of their occurrences. Certainly the list of 'similar' types of symbols may be extended. Indic manuscript culture is so vast, there are many more symbols and other elements that are not be included in this study, due to the project's limited timeframe, resources etc. I hope future studies will reveal more new insights and examples to enable an even better understanding of the use of symbols, scribal practice etc. Nonetheless, the examples presented above provide some ideas on the frequency of use of symbols in one or more areas.

We have seen a few types of 'similar' or 'near similar' symbols; from 'dots' to double circles to letter or letter-numeral-like symbols to simple stylised *puṣpikā*s and beautiful stylised *puṣpikā*s. Some stylised *puṣpikā*s are used both before and/or after chapter colophons and around string-hole(s) (e.g. type nos. 8, 12, 20, 24, 27) or before and/or after chapter colophons and with foliation numbers (type nos. 7, 8). The symbol of type no. 46 can be found before and/or after chapter colophons or other sections or as line-fillers or space-fillers.

Some symbols are used interchangeably as *akṣara*s or figure- or letter-numerals in manuscripts. Type nos. 4 and 5 can be used either as symbols or as some of the letter-numerals for '80'. The symbol of type no. 43 resembles the figure-numeral for '7'. The symbol of type no. 45 is used both as one of the types of *siddham* symbol or as an *akṣara* '*t*' (without vowel). The symbol of type no. 46 can be used both as *akṣara tha* and as the letter-numeral for '20'.

Of the 47 types of near 'identical symbols' only two (type nos. 4 and 46) appeared in manuscripts from all three areas focused on here. Of the 47, near 'identical symbols' seven (type nos. 1, 2, 5, 15, 16, 32, 44) appear mainly in Nepalese and East Indian manuscripts. Four (type nos. 7, 8, 10, 12) appear only in Nepalese and West Indian manuscripts. Thirty (type nos. 3, 6, 9, 11, 14, 17–31, 33–42) appear largely in Nepalese manuscripts. Three (type nos. 13, 43, 45) appear only in East Indian manuscripts and one (type no. 47) appears only in West Indian manuscripts.

3.5 Further types of symbols related to particular areas

Some types of symbols may have been used often or exclusively in manuscripts from one particular region. Their analysis may help locate the area where the manuscripts were (possibly) produced or the scribal practice, in combination with palaeographical evidence and the study of layout, etc.

3.5.1 Symbols in Nepalese manuscripts

As we have seen, a large variety of symbols of remarkable aesthetic value has been used in manuscripts. Nepalese manuscripts often contain unique types of symbols, as shown in the previous section (see type nos. 3, 6, 9, 11, 14, 17–31, 33–42; and see also Appendix I for other typical symbols which are not included in the list above). This section describes another type of unique symbol that I previously labeled as realistic *puṣpikā*s (see section 3.1 above), i.e. those resembling 'real flowers' with stalks and/or leaves or sepals etc. drawn.[223] I have found these in some Nepalese manuscripts. The manuscripts featuring these kinds of realistic flowers listed here date from ca. 9th to 13th c.[224] The manuscripts SP_2, SP_3 and the manuscript of the *Viṣṇudharma*[225] contain puranic texts. Whereas, HY and the manuscript of the *Kulālikāmnāyatantra*[226] contain Śaiva tantric texts. Four manuscripts (i.e. the manuscript of the *Saddharmapuṇḍarīka*;[227] the *Śatasāhasrikā Prajñāpāramitā*;[228] the *Aṣṭasāhasrikā Prajñāparamitā*[229] and $AṣP_1$) contain Buddhist Sūtras. One manuscript of the *Kalyāṇakāmadhenūvivaraṇa*[230]

223 An example of the realistic *puṣpikā* with a curved stalk and two buds can be found in the Chidivalasa plates of Devendravarman (893–895 CE), see Sarkar/Pande 1999, 8, Fig. 11, 7; at the end of the stone inscription of the time of Aśokacalladeva (Bodhgaya, Bihar) (ca. 1194 CE), EI 12, IndoSkript, symbol, IS-Nr: 731, Sarkar/Pande 1999, 89, Fig. 11,16. Here, in terms of form, the realistic *puṣpikā* resembles a 'sunflower'. Large realistic *puṣpikā*s can also be found in some (Nepalese) inscriptions. A large realistic *puṣpikā* with leaves and buds clearly resembling a lotus is in the upper part of the Inscription of Jayadeva, see Indraji 1885, No. 15, see also Sarkar/Pande 1999, 89, Fig. 26. Similarly, in the upper part of another Inscription of Śivadeva, one can find realistic *puṣpikā*s with buds etc., see Indraji 1885, No. 5.

224 Other realistic *puṣpikā*s can be found in later Nepalese manuscripts e.g. a realistic *puṣpikā* appears in the manuscript of the *Mahāsahasrapramardinī* (ca. 15th c.) (KL 252 / NGMPP C 27/11) before the chapter colophon on 108r and the colophon reads (in line nos. 1–2) as follows: '*āryamahāśītavatī nāma mahāvi*¦[2]*dyā mahānumaṃsā*(!) *samāptā*'. A *siddham* symbol is found after the colophon. Furthermore, two realistic *puṣpikā*s are found in the manuscript of the *Pañcarakṣā* (ca. 17th c.) (KL 105 / NGMPP C 11/2) on 160v. The first realistic *puṣpikā* appears after the chapter colophon in line no. 1. But the second realistic *puṣpikā* can be found around the right string-hole space. Additionally a stylised *puṣpikā* is also drawn around the left string-hole on the same folio. Two other symbols of this manuscript are presented in section 3.6.2.1.6 below. On the discussion of the possible date of this manuscript, see the footnote in section 3.6.2.1.6 below.

225 See NAK 4/766 / NGMPP A 10/1.

226 See NAK 5/877 / NGMPP A 41/3.

227 See CUL Add.2197.

228 See Royal Library, Copenhagen, Nepal 175A.

229 See KL 18 / NGMPP C 103/2.

230 See NAK 3/363 / NGMPP A 38/13.

contains a commentary on a Buddhist tantric text. One manuscript of the *Antarvyāptisamarthana*[231] contains a Buddhist work on logic, one manuscript contains a commentary on the *Nītisārapañjikā* (*Jayamaṅgalā*).[232]

All these realistic flowers appear mainly at the end of chapters or at the end of the text. Based on the frequency of examples, it seems that realistic *puṣpikā*s in Nepalese manuscripts may have been a significant element.

In SP_2 two realistic *puṣpikā*s can be found. One appears after the 45th chapter colophon on 66v2[233] and looks like a tulip in terms of appearance. The other at the end of the 6th line exactly under the right string-hole (on 207b) (see Fig. 3.5.1-I below). The height of the first *puṣpikā* corresponds to three text lines of the folio. Given the shape's level of refinement, one may speculate that both realistic *puṣpikā*s were drawn later than some of other symbols found in the same manuscript.

[SP_2_66v2_ACC_9th]

[SP_2_207b6_9th]

Fig. 3.5.1-I: Realistic *puṣpikās* after the chapter colophon and at the end of last line

In SP_3 at least three realistic *puṣpikā*s can be found on 70r1, 70v1 and 244v3. The first realistic *puṣpikā* appears before the 40th chapter colophon on 70r1.[234] Similarly, the second realistic *puṣpikā* appears before the 41st chapter colophon on 70v1 and the third one before the 136th chapter colophon on 244v3. The height of the two *puṣpikā*s on 70r1, 70v1 is approximately two text lines of the folio and the other's height on 244v3 is approximately three text lines on the folio (see Fig. 3.5.1-II).

---

231 See NAK 3/364 / NGMPP B 23/34.

232 See KL 77 / NGMPP C 6/13.

233 The chapter colophon reads *iti* || *skandapurāṇe pañca*|⊙|*catvāriṃśatimo dhyāyaḥ* ('thus, the 45th chapter in the *Skandapurāṇa* [is concluded]').

234 The chapter colophon reads *skandapurāṇe ddhyāyaḥ* | *pta* ('[thus], the chapter in the *skandapurāṇa* [is concluded]. 40.').

[SP3_70r1_BCC_10th]

[SP3_70v1_BCC_10th]

[SP3_244v3_BCC_10th]

Fig. 3.5.1-II: Realistic *puṣpikā*s before and after the chapter colophons

Additionally, one realistic *puṣpikā* can be found in the manuscript of the *Kulālikāmnāyatantra* (NAK 5/877 / NGMPP A 41/3) on 92v2. The manuscript is dated NS 158 (1037 CE).[235] The *puṣpikā* appears before the 19th chapter colophon.[236] The height of the *puṣpikā* is two lines of the folio. An example can be seen in Fig. 3.5.1-III.

[NAK 5/877 / NGMPP A 41/3_92v2_BCC_1037]

Fig. 3.5.1-III: Realistic *puṣpikā* before the chapter colophon

In HY two realistic *puṣpikā*s appear at the end of chapters.[237] The first realistic *puṣpikā* is after the 9th chapter colophon on 14r3[238] and the second realistic *puṣpikā* after another chapter colophon on 19v5.[239] The height of the *puṣpikā* on 14r3 is two text lines and on 19v5, it slightly more than one line of the folio, although it is demarcated by the one set of double *daṇḍa*. The *puṣpikā* appears in the last line on the folio. Both examples can be seen in Fig. 3.5.1-IV.

---

235 See Goudriaan and Schoterman 1988, 14. They have used the manuscript as siglum Z in their edition.

236 It reads on 92v2–3 as follows *iti laghvikāmnāye śrīmatkubjikāmatottare ṣaṭprakāre*[3] *catuṣkasya rūpe paṭalāntaraṃ ūnaviṃśatimaṃ*.

237 These two realistic *puṣpikā*s have also been used by Bang 2017, 30, Table I.4.

238 It reads *iti paramārṣasaṃhitāyām | hansaṃyā*(!) *savinirṃṇayo na⊙vamaḥ paṭala*.

239 The chapter colophon reads as follows *iti mahābhairave ha|⊙|nsayāmale pañcaviṃśatisāhasre aṃśakapaṭalaḥ*.

[HY_14r3_ACC_1039]

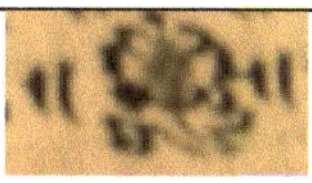
[HY_19v5_ACC_1039]

Fig. 3.5.1-IV: Realistic *puṣpikās* after the chapter colophons

In the manuscript of the *Saddharmapuṇḍarīkasūtra* (CUL Add.2197) dated from NS 185 (1065 CE), there are realistic *puṣpikās* in most of the chapter colophons. They appear after the 7th chapter colophon on 58r1, before and after the 8th chapter colophon on 62r2 and before and after the 9th chapter colophon on 64r5–6.[240] Their height is one to three lines of the folio (see Fig. 3.5.1-V). The realistic *puṣpikās* are demarcated by three sets of double *daṇḍas* of only two lines in height (on 62r2, 64r5, 77v1–2, 82r5, 94r4, 123v4, 130v3) and those demarcated by four sets of double *daṇḍas* are only three lines in height (on 120r4, 131r2). Please note that after the 24th chapter colophons on 123v4 two realistic *puṣpikās* appear. All of these realistic *puṣpikās* in this context may well be considered representations of *padmas* ('lotuses'). This manuscript is discussed for its use of other symbols and their importance later in section 3.6.2.4.2.

[CUL Add.2197_58r1_ACC_1065]

[CUL Add.2197_62r2_BCC_1065]

[CUL Add.2197_62r2_ACC_1065]

240 Further examples of realistic *puṣpikās* can be found before and after the 12th chapter colophon on 77v1–2, after the 13th chapter colophon on 82r5, before and after the 17th chapter colophon on 94r4, after the 24th chapter colophon 120r4, after the 24th chapter colophon on 123v4, before the 26th chapter colophon on 130v3 and before the 27th chapter colophon on 131v2. The chapter colophon on 120r3 and the following chapter colophon on 123v4 record the same number '24th' for the both chapters. The former one reads on 120r3 *garggadasvaraparivartto*(!) *nāma caturviṃśatimaḥ* and the latter one on 123v4 records as follows *samantamukhaparivartto nāmāvalokiteśvaravikurvanirdeśaś*(!) *caturviṅśatimaḥ*. If the name of the chapter of the first one on 120r is read correctly it should be the '*gadgadasvaraparivarta*' and therefore 23rd chapter rather than the 24th chapter. The scribe was probably confused by the writing of the chapter number.

[CUL Add.2197_64r5_BCC_1065]

[CUL Add.2197_64r6_ACC_1065]

Fig. 3.5.1-V: Realistic *puṣpikās* before and/or after the chapter colophons

In the manuscript of the *Kalyāṇakāmadhenūvivaraṇa* (NS 224 / 1104 CE) (NAK 3/363 / NGMPP A 38/13) there is a realistic *puṣpikā* before the colophon on 11r5.[241] After the colophon a stylised *puṣpikā* appears in line no. 6 similar to the symbols of the type no. 14 (see above). The height of the realistic *puṣpikā* is slightly more than one line of the folio and that of the stylised *puṣpikā* in line no. 6 is one line of the folio. Likewise, in this context, the realistic *puṣpikā* may be interpreted as a representation of a *padma* ('lotus').

[NAK 3/363 / NGMPP A 38/13_11r5_BC_1104]

Fig. 3.5.1-VI: Realistic *puṣpikā* after the colophon

In one Buddhist manuscript of the *Śatasāhasrikā Prajñāpāramitā* kept in the Royal Library, Copenhagen (Det Kongelige Bibliotek) as Nepal 175A and catalogued by Buescher (2011, 21–22, Cat. 7), one folio of which Trier (1972) presents in his appendix as plate number 111, there are two realistic *puṣpikās*. Buescher dates the manuscript NS 548 i.e. 1428 CE.[242] However, he overlooks another date mentioned in letter-numerals as NS 265 on 814v3. On palaeographical and other grounds, such as the time of the reigning king and so forth, this date should be that of the copying of the manuscript and not the date suggested by Buescher.[243]

The first realistic *puṣpikā* appears after the Buddhist verse the last part of which reads '*vamvādī mahāśramaṇaḥ*' on 814v1. The second realistic *puṣpikā* is followed

241 The line reads as follows *kalyāṇakāmadhenūvivaraṇaṃ samāptaṃ* ('[thus,] the commentary on *Kalyāṇakāmadhenū* is concluded').
242 See Buescher 2011, 21.
243 Kim 2014, 2 also suggests the original date of the manuscript to be NS 265 (1145 CE).

on the same line by a statement recording the reign of King Narendradeva.[244] From their appearance, both realistic *puṣpikā*s in this manuscript exhibit a degree of similarity to the realistic *puṣpikā*s can be found in the manuscript of the *Saddharmapuṇḍarīkasūtra* (CUL Add.2197) (see Fig. 3.5.1-V above). Once more, in this context the realistic *puṣpikā*s may be understood as representations of *padma*s ('lotuses').

[Nepal 175a_814v1_BPC_1145]

[Nepal 175a_814v1_APC_1145]

Fig. 3.5.1-VII: Realistic *puṣpikā*s before and after the post colophon (reproduced from Trier 1972, plate 111, n. 175a)

In AṣP$_1$ there are two realistic *puṣpikā*s before and after the second chapter colophon on 26v4.[245] The height of both *puṣpikā*s is only two lines of the folio, although they are demarcated by three sets of double *daṇḍa*s. The first realistic *puṣpikā* is partially highlighted in the upper part and the second one is 'fully' highlighted. In this context also both realistic *puṣpikā*s may be interpreted as representations of *padma*s ('lotuses'). Examples can be seen in Fig. 3.5.1-VIII.

[AṣP$_1$_26v4_BCC_1151]

[AṣP$_1$_26v4_ACC_1151]

Fig. 3.5.1-VIII: Realistic *puṣpikā*s before and after the chapter colophon

244 The line reads in line nos. 1–2 as follows *śrīmadrājādhirājaparameśvaraparamabhaṭṭāraka-śrīmannarendradevasya vija*[2]*yarājye* ('in the victorious kingdom of venerable Narendradeva, paramount sovereign, supreme lord, venerable king of great kings'). After the line one circle can be found between a set of double *daṇḍa*s. In this case the later double *daṇḍa*s are being used both as closing final *daṇḍa*s for the circle and one of the demarcating double *daṇḍa*s of the first realistic *puṣpikā*.

245 The colophon reads as follows *āryāṣṭasāhasrikāyāṃ prajñāpāramitāyāṃ śakra*|⊙|*parivartto nāma dvitīyaḥ* ('[thus], the second chapter, namely Śakra in the noble Perfection of Wisdom in Eight Thousand Lines is [concluded]').

On the use of symbols, the manuscript of the *Aṣṭasāhasrikā Prajñāparamitā* (ca. 12th c.)[246] (KL 18 / NGMPP C 103/2) exhibits unique examples.[247] Before the fifth chapter colophon[248] on 53v4 there is a drawing resembling a bird in full form and a head like that of a baby bird or snake which may be interpreted as a representation of a '*mayūra*' or '*mayūrī*' ('peacock' or 'peahen') and a baby peacock or peahen or snake respectively (see Fig 3.5.1-IX).[249] After the chapter colophon we find a realistic *puṣpikā* together with some floral elements surrounded on left, right and bottom sides. Regarding form and context, the realistic *puṣpikā* here may be interpreted as a *padma* ('lotus'). Both elements are lightly highlighted.

---

246 This manuscript can possibly be dated from ca. 12th c. on palaeographical grounds, although we find a date with NS 748 (1628 CE) on one of the folios. The folio seems to have been added later and the handwriting looks quite modern compared with the handwriting on other folios. The line reads: *samvat* 748 *māghaśuklaḥ*(!) *ekādaśyān tithau* ... ('the [Nepāla] era 748, on the eleventh day [of] bright fortnight of the month *māgha*'). Furthermore, we find in the same line: *taddine jīrṇṇoddhāraṇalikhita*(!) ('on that day it was written for the 'restoration' [purpose] ...'). Therefore, the date on the folio is possibly a 'restoration' date.

247 For examples and discussion of the use of further symbols, see sections 3.6.2.1.6 and 3.6.2.4.2.

248 The chapter colophon reads *āryāṣṭasāhasri*¦|⊙|*kāyāṃ prajñāpāramitāyāṃ puṇyaparyāyaparivartto nāma pañcamaḥ* ('[thus], the fifth chapter, namely the *puṇyaparyāya* in the noble Perfection of Wisdom in Eight Thousand Lines is [concluded]').

249 A feature resembling a kind of bird can be found in KT on 68v7_ACC (see section 3.6.2.2). Furthermore, attestations of drawings of birds on the upper-margin of the folio can also be found in some manuscripts. In the manuscript of the *Aṣṭasāhasrikā Prajñāpāramitā* (ca. 15th/16th c.) (NAK 4/1637 / B 22/18) we find small birds, on 151r (two birds), 156r (one bird), 157r (one bird), 170v (one bird), 191r (one bird), 193v (one bird), 194v (three birds), 195r (one bird), 201r (two birds), 201v (two birds), 208v (one bird), 211v (one bird), 214v (two birds). All these birds clearly look like peacocks. In the manuscript of the *Pañcarakṣā* (ca. 15th/16th c.) (KL 108 / NGMPP C 11/4) small birds are drawn in the centre part of the upper-margin on 43r and 46r. The bird on 43r can be found on the top of the *akṣara* '*pa*' of *patita*(!) of the text portion of '*sa klāntakāyo bhūmau patita*(!)' in the *Mahāmāyurīvidyārājñī* and the bird on 46r is drawn on the top of the *akṣara* (*trā*) of *maitrā* of '*sarvabhūteṣu me maitrā*(!) *ye kecit pṛthivī sthitā*' in the same text. In front of the beak of the bird on 43r there is a *mātrā* sign of '*au*' with two petal-like elements and in front of the beak of the bird on 46 there is a semicircle-like element and six 'dots' which possibly represent a chirping bird or perhaps a speaking godess in abstract terms. As both birds appear in the text part of the *Mahāmāyurīvidyārājñī* they can probably be interpreted in this context as a representation of the godess Mahāmāyurī.

[KL 18 / NGMPP C 103/2_53v4_BCC_12th]

[KL 18 / NGMPP C 103/2_53v4_ACC_12th]

Fig. 3.5.1-IX: Bird and realistic *puṣpikā* before and after the chapter colophon

In the manuscript of the *Viṣṇudharma*[250] (ca. 12th c.) (NAK 4/766 / NGMPP A 10/1) there are two realistic *puṣpikā*s (see Fig. 3.5.1-X). The first appears before the first chapter colophon on 3r4.[251] Following that is a stylised *puṣpikā* similar to the type no. 14. The second realistic *puṣpikā* appears after the speaker indication (*prahlāda uvāca*, 'Prahlāda said') on the right side on 98v6 (last line). The speaker indication is preceeded by a chapter colophon demarcated by the stylised *puṣpikā*s.

[NAK 4/766 / NGMPP A 10/1_3r4_BCC_12th]

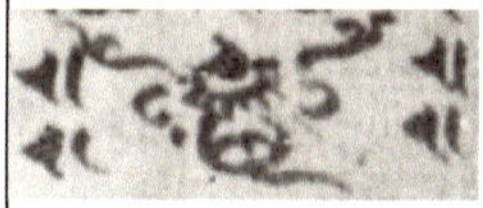
[NAK 4/766 / NGMPP A 10/1_98v6_ASpl_12th]

Fig. 3.5.1-X: Realistic *puṣpikā*s before the chapter colophon and after the speaker indication

Four realistic *puṣpikā*s are in the manuscript of the *Nītisārapañjikā* (*Jayamaṅgalā*) (KL 77 / NGMPP C 6/13) on 45v3, 81r2, 83v1. The realistic *puṣpikā* on 45v has been drawn after the 8th chapter colophon.[252] On 81v2 the realistic *puṣpikā* appears before one of the chapter colophons. The right side of the folio

250 See Grünendahl 1983, 15–16 with siglum N7.
251 The chapter colophon reads *iti vidharmopadeśe*(!) *prathamo dhyāyaḥ* ('thus, the first chapter in the instruction of the *Vi*[*ṣṇu*]*dharma* [is concluded]).
252 It reads *nītisārapañjikāyāṃ jayamaṅgalāyām aṣṭamaḥ sargaḥ* ('[thus], the eighth canto in the *Jayamaṅgalā* in the *Nītisārapañjikā* [is concluded]).

is broken, therefore, only a part of the chapter colophon has been preserved.[253] The realistic *puṣpikā*s on 83v1 appear before and after the 17th chapter colophon.[254] The height of all realistic *puṣpikā*s is two (on 81r2, 83v1) to three lines (on 45v3) of the folio. In comparison to other realistic *puṣpikā*s in this manuscript the second (on 81r2_BCC) and the last (on 83v1_ACC) *puṣpikā*s resemble, to a degree, fully-fledged *padma*s ('lotuses') and the other two realistic *puṣpikā*s (on 45v3_ACC, 83v1_BCC) look like lotuses developing towards their fully-fledged state. Examples of *puṣpikā*s can be seen in Fig. 3.5.1-XI.

[KL 77 / NGMPP C 6/13_ 45v3_ACC_12th?]

[KL 77 / NGMPP C 6/13_81r2_BCC_12th?]

[KL 77 / NGMPP C 6/13_83v1_BCC_12th?]

[KL 77 / NGMPP C 6/13_83v1_ACC_12th?]

Fig. 3.5.1-XI: Realistic *puṣpikā*s before and after the chapter colophons

One realistic *puṣpikā* appears in the manuscript of the *Antarvyāptisamarthana*[255] (NAK 3/364 / NGMPP B 23/34) before the colophon on 6r7[256] and one stylised

253 The preserved part of the colophon reads *nītisārapañjikāyāñ jayamaṅgalāya*(!)/// ('[thus, ... in the] *Jayamaṅgalā* in the *Nītisārapañjikā* [is concluded]).

254 The line reads *nītisārapañjikāyāṃ jayamaṅgalāyāṃ saptadaśaḥ sargaḥ* ('[thus], the seventeenth canto in the *Jayamaṅgalā* in the *Nītisārapañjikā* [is concluded]).

255 See Shastri 1915, Vol. II, 43. This manuscript was used by Kajiyama 1999, ix with siglum M for the edition.

256 The colophon reads *antarvyāptisamarthanaṃ samāptam iti* ('thus, the Establishment of Internal Pervasion is concluded'). Here I follow Kajiyama 1990, 130 for the English translation of the title of the work.

puṣpikā can be found after the colophon. The stylised *puṣpikā* is followed by the author line[257] and the line is again followed by another stylised *puṣpikā* (like type no. 16). The height of the realistic *puṣpikā* is slightly more than one line of the folio. Likewise the realistic *puṣpikā* may be understood as a representation of a *padma* ('lotus').

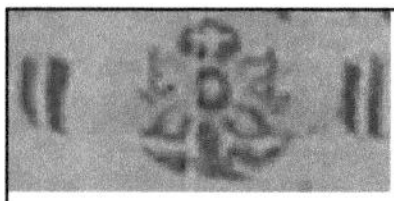

[NAK 3/364 / B 23/34_6r7_BC_13th?]

Fig. 3.5.1-XII: Realistic *puṣpikā* before the colophon

As in the case of stylised *puṣpikā*s, realistic *puṣpikā*s usually appear at the end of chapters and texts and once after the speaker indication thus marking the end of major text sections. In comparison to other symbols even within the same manuscript, they are very decorative and enhance the aesthetic value of the whole manuscript. Regarding realistic *puṣpikā*s appearing in Buddhist manuscripts the 'realistic' lotuses may be interpreted as representation of *prajñā* ('awakening aspect of wisdom').[258] Having found such realistic *puṣpikā*s in many Nepalese manuscripts,[259] I am inclined to postulate that such features could be peculiar to manuscripts produced in this area.

3.5.2 Symbols in East Indian manuscripts

In manuscripts from East India various kinds of stylised *puṣpikā*s are also found. Among them a sub-category can be singled out that includes a *siddham* symbol, used at the end of chapters, sections or whole texts. Such a symbol is found in at least six East Indian manuscripts, five possibly originating from Vikramaśīla and the other (AAĀ) from a nearby area. The *siddham* symbol has already been introduced above (see section 3.4) as type no. 45. The shape of this symbol is identical to the character '*t*' (in 'Old Bengali' script), which is the script used in the manu-

257 It reads *kṛtir iyaṃ ratnākaraśāntipādānām iti* ('thus, this work [is] of venerable Ratnākaraśānti').

258 On this topic, see also section 3.6.2.1.2 below.

259 Realistic *puṣpikā*s with leaves and buds resembling lotuses can also be found in some Nepalese Inscriptions, see e.g. Indraji 1885, Nos. 5 and 15; and Sarkar/Pande 1999, 89, Fig. 26.

scripts. An example of the character '*t*' can be seen in Fig. 3.5.2-I and compared with Fig. 3.4-XLV above.

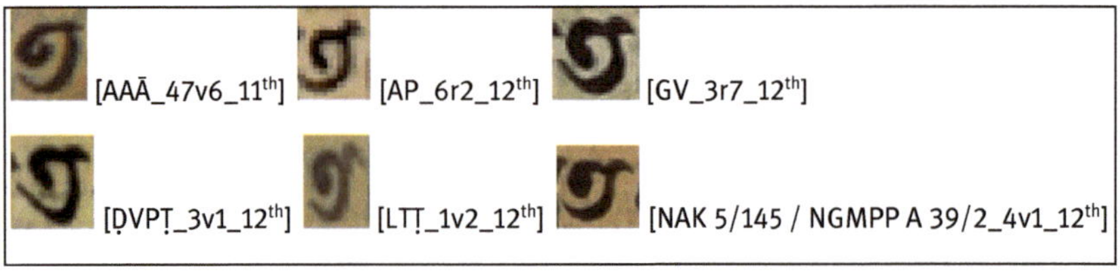

Fig. 3.5.2-I: '*t*' similar to symbols in Fig. 3.4-XLV

In the previous sections we have seen close similarities in terms of layout. Symbols in many manuscripts of this group and just above feature the writing style of '*t*' (without vowel) and are similar to one of the types of *siddham* symbols (for symbols, see section 3.4, type no. 45). In this section more observations on palaeographical evidence in the selected manuscripts of this group are presented. Aside from one manuscript (HTṬ in which Vikramaśīla has been mentioned as the copying place),[260] all manuscripts of this group contain no information on copying place or date. Therefore, it is always helpful to gather as much as information and examples of the different features they contain to enable a better understanding of their existence and group them in a more reliable manner. For this reason, some *akṣara*s, single *daṇḍa*s, double *daṇḍa*s and *visarga*s from the 'core' corpus of the East Indian manuscript group have been collected and analysed as well as another manuscript out of the 'core' corpus: the manuscript of the *Pāramitāsamāsa* (NAK 5/145 / NGMPP A 39/2) (henceforth: NAK 5/145) which could also belong to this group (on the basis of layout, symbol and paleographical evidence). For the *akṣara*s *a, i, u, ka, kha, ga, gha, ca, ja, ṭa, ṇa, ta, tha, da, dha, na, pa, bha, ma, ya, ra, la, va, śa, ṣa, sa, ha* have been selected for each manuscript (except for the CPN from which I have selected two *akṣara*s of *i*). In the following the *akṣara*s are compared for their similarities or differences in writing style.

*Akṣara*s *a* of GV, HAP, LTṬ, STṬ, ḌVPṬ, HP are identical whereas *a* of AP, CPN and NAK 5/145 have a near similar form. Furthermore, *a* of AAĀ and AT exhibit some similarities in the writing. Both contain a kind of curved line in the upper part. *I* of GV, HAP, LTT, STT, ḌVPṬ look similar but the *i* of AP and one of

260 Since PR is dated and written in another script, I have excluded it for the occasion of the palaeographical observation here.

the *i*s of CPN exhibit close similarities in the writing style. However, the second *i* of CPN, HP and NAK 5/145 are to some extent identical. *U* of GV, HAP, LTṬ, STṬ, ḌVPṬ, CPN and HP share also similarities. *Akṣara*s *u* of AAĀ and AT look somewhat similar.

Ka of GV, HAP, LTṬ, STṬ, ḌVPṬ, HP, NAK 5/145 look nearly identical. But *ka* of AAĀ and AT are near identical in form. *Kha* of GV, HAP, STṬ, ḌVPṬ, AP and CPN exhibit many similarities. *Kha* of LTṬ, HP and NAK 5/145 look similar. *Ga* of GV, HAP, LTṬ, STṬ, ḌVPṬ, AP, CPN, HP and NAK 5/145 look almost identical. However, *ga* of AAĀ, HTṬ and AT share some similarities in writing. *Gha* of GV, HAP, LTṬ, ḌVPṬ and AP share many similarities in writing. However, *gha* of HP and NAK 5/145 look nearly identical. *Gha* of HTṬ and AT are to some extent similar.

Ca of GV, HAP, LTṬ, STṬ and ḌVPṬ exhibit many similarities. *Ca* of AP and CPN look nearly similar in writing style. Furthermore, *ca* of AAĀ, HTṬ, AT and NAK 5/145 are similar if we leave the upper curved line of *ca* of HTṬ, AAĀ. *Ja* of GV, HAP, LTṬ, STṬ and ḌVPṬ are nearly identical. However, *ja* of AAĀ, AP, CPN, AT and NAK 5/145 look to some extent similar.

Ṭa of GV, HAP, LTṬ, STṬ, ḌVPṬ, AP, CPN, HP, NAK 5/145 share close similarities in writing. *Ṇa* of GV, HAP, LTṬ, STṬ, ḌVPṬ, AP, CPN, HP and NAK 5/145 exhibit many similarities. But *ṇa* of HTṬ and AT look nearly identical.

Ta of GV, HAP, LTṬ, STṬ, ḌVPṬ, AP, CPN, HP and NAK 5/145 are nearly identical. Whereas *ta* of AAĀ, HTṬ and AT contain a kind of curved stroke in the upper part. *Tha* of GV, HAP, LTṬ, STṬ, ḌVPṬ, AP, CPN and NAK 5/145 share to some extent similarities in writing style. However, *tha* of HP, HTṬ and AT exhibit slight similarities in form. *Da* of GV, HAP, LTṬ, STṬ, ḌVPṬ, AP, CPN and NAK 5/145 look identical. *Dha* of GV, HAP, STṬ, ḌVPṬ, AP, CPN and NAK 5/145 share many similarities in writing. *Dha* of AAĀ, AP look to some extent comparable in form. Furthermore, *dha* of LTṬ and CPN share to some extent similar features. *Na* of GV, HAP, LTṬ, STṬ, ḌVPṬ, AP, CPN and NAK 5/145 look similar. However, *na* of AAĀ, HTṬ and AT share some similar features if we see the writing style of the upper line of the *akṣara*s.

Pa of GV, HAP, LTṬ, STṬ, ḌVPṬ, AP, CPN and NAK 5/145 look identical. *Pa* of HAP, HP share nearly similar writing style. However, *pa* of AAĀ, HTṬ and AT look rather similar. The upper line of the *akṣara* is a bit curved and touches the (right side of) vertical stroke a bit in the lower part from the top. *Bha* of GV, HAP, LTṬ, STṬ, ḌVPṬ, AP, CPN, HP and NAK 5/145 look somewhat similar. *Bha* of AAĀ, HTṬ and AT share to some extent similar features. For instance, their upper line is slightly curved. *Ma* of GV, HAP, LTṬ, STṬ, ḌVPṬ, AP, CPN, HP and NAK 5/145 look quite similar. However, *ma* of AAĀ, HTṬ and AT share some matching features. For instance, the upper line of them is slightly curved and touches a bit of lower part of the vertical stroke from the top.

Ya of GV, HAP, LTṬ, STṬ, ḌVPṬ, AP, CPN and NAK 5/145 are nearly similar in form. Whereas *ya* of AAĀ, HTṬ and AT look to some extent similar in writing style. *Ra* of GV, HAP, LTṬ, STṬ, ḌVPṬ, AP, CPN, HP and NAK 5/145 exhibit close similarities to each other. *Ra* of AAĀ and AT share identical features. *La* of GV, HAP, LTṬ, STṬ, ḌVPṬ, AP, CPN and NAK 5/145 look similar in many cases. *Va* of GV, HAP, LTṬ, STṬ, ḌVPṬ, AP, CPN and NAK 5/145 exhibit many similarities in form. However, *va* of AAĀ, HTṬ and AT with their upper line look to some extent identical.

Śa of GV, HAP, LTṬ, STṬ, ḌVPṬ, AP, CPN, HP and NAK 5/145 are almost similar in form. But *śa* of HTṬ and AT look similar in writing style. The upper part of the right stroke is slightly curved. *Ṣa* of GV, HAP, LTṬ, STṬ, ḌVPṬ, AP, CPN and NAK 5/145 exhibit many similarities with each other. Whereas *ṣa* of AAĀ, HTṬ and AT share many identical features. Their upper line is slightly bent and the right stroke is longer. *Sa* of GV, HAP, LTṬ, STṬ, ḌVPṬ, AP, CPN, HP and NAK 5/145 are nearly identical. However, *sa* of AAĀ, HTṬ and AT share many similarities in writing. The upper line of them is curved. *Ha* of GV, HAP, LTṬ, STṬ, ḌVPṬ, AP, CPN and NAK 5/145 look rather identical. *Ha* of AAĀ share a few similarities, if we look at the writing style of the upper line.

The *visarga* sign of GV, HAP, LTṬ, STṬ, ḌVPṬ, AP and CPN are also identical. They are written with two circles. The upper circle contains a 'dot' or small curved-like 'line' on the upper right side. The *visarga* of AAĀ, HP, HTṬ and NAK 5/145 resembles the modern number '8'. However, the *visarga* of AAĀ, HP and NAK 5/145 look to some extent similar in form.

The single and double *daṇḍa*s of GV, HAP, LTṬ, STṬ, ḌVPṬ, CPN and HP are a bit similar. In the case of AAĀ the single *daṇḍa* and the first *daṇḍa* of the double *daṇḍa* contain a kind of small dot-like element on the left side in the centre of the stroke.

An important feature in this group can also be noticed in the writing of some *akṣara*s. If we look closely at some of the *akṣara*s in some manuscripts, a kind of dot-like element can be found on the top of the upper line of the *akṣara*s e.g. on the top of the upper line of *akṣara na* of GV, HAP, STṬ, AP; on the top of the upper line of *va* of GV, HAP, LTṬ, STṬ, ḌVPṬ, CPN; on the top of the upper line of *ra* of GV, LTṬ, ḌVPṬ, CPN, AP.

Furthermore, a majority of manuscripts of this group also contain an identical symbol that appears before the invocations at the beginning of the manuscripts (GV, HAP, LTṬ, STṬ, ḌVPṬ, AP, CPN and NAK 5/145) (see section 3.4, type no. 43).

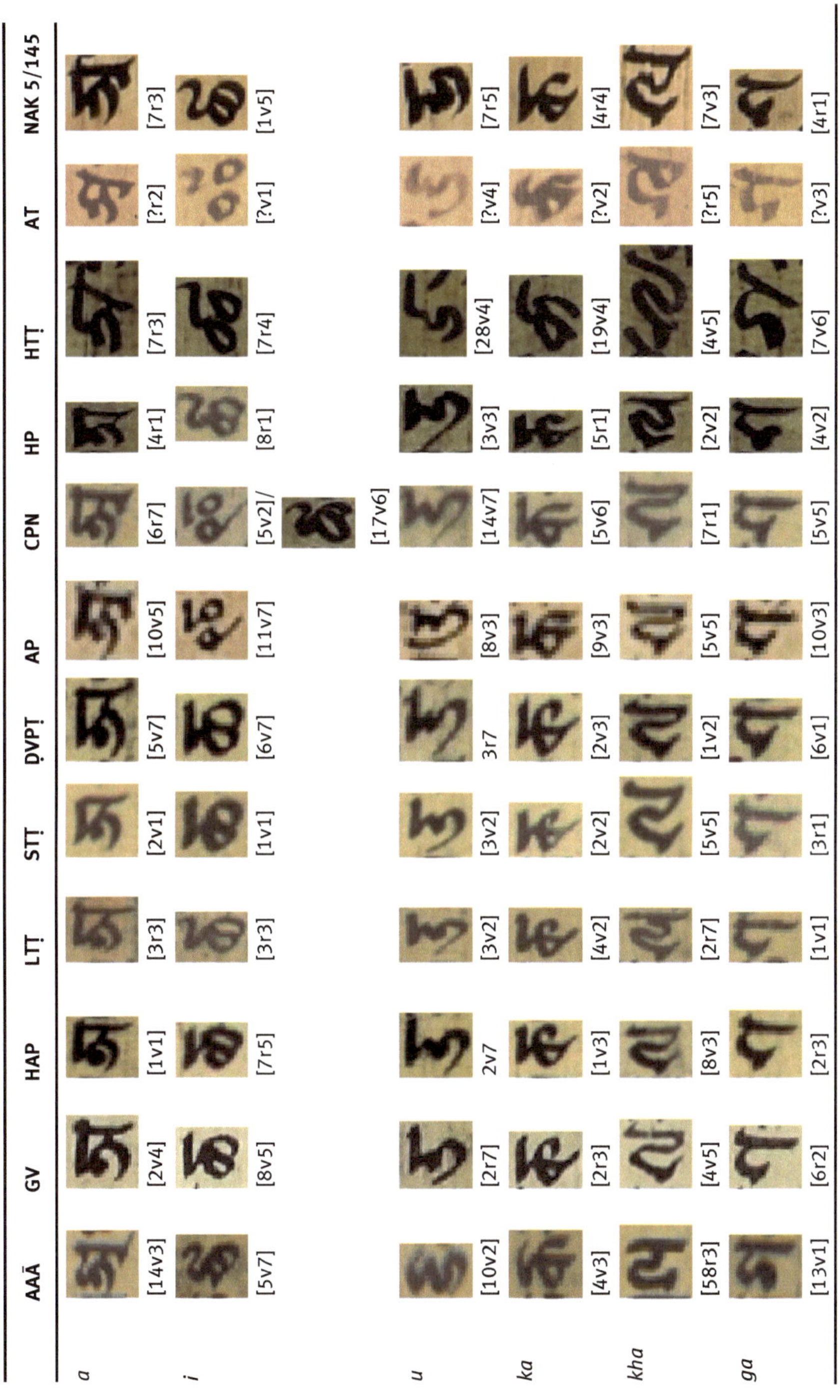

	AAĀ	GV	HAP	LTṬ	STṬ	ḌVPṬ	AP	CPN	HP	HTṬ	AT	NAK 5/145
a	[14v3]	[2v4]	[1v1]	[3r3]	[2v1]	[5v7]	[10v5]	[6r7]	[4r1]	[7r3]	[?r2]	[7r3]
i	[5v7]	[8v5]	[7r5]	[3r3]	[1v1]	[6v7]	[11v7]	[5v2]/ [17v6]	[8r1]	[7r4]	[?v1]	[1v5]
u	[10v2]	[2r7]	2v7	[3v2]	[3v2]	3r7	[8v3]	[14v7]	[3v3]	[28v4]	[?v4]	[7r5]
ka	[4v3]	[2r3]	[1v3]	[4v2]	[2v2]	[2v3]	[9v3]	[5v6]	[5r1]	[19v4]	[?v2]	[4r4]
kha	[58r3]	[4v5]	[8v3]	[2r7]	[5v5]	[1v2]	[5v5]	[7r1]	[2v2]	[4v5]	[?r5]	[7v3]
ga	[13v1]	[6r2]	[2r3]	[1v1]	[3r1]	[6v1]	[10v3]	[5v5]	[4v2]	[7v6]	[?v3]	[4r1]

	AAĀ	GV	HAP	LTṬ	STṬ	ḌVPṬ	AP	CPN	HP	HTṬ	AT	NAK 5/145
gha	[150v6]	[2v3]	[9v4]	[5v2]	[4r1]	[5v5]	[4r7]	[6r3]	[14r7]	[28v5]	[?v4]	[2v1]
ca	[11r2]	[2r4]	[3r7]	[4r5]	[10r6]	[6v5]	[10v7]	[8v6]	[6r5]	[7r2]	[?r2]	[7v3]
ja	[66r4]	[9v3]	[8v1]	[6r3]	[4r5]	[3v2]	[9r3]	[4v1]	[5r3]	[7v1]	[?v1]	[1v2]
ṭa	[14v6]	[6r1]	[1v5]	[5v7]	[7v3]	[5r5]	[7v7]	[5v1]	[3r1]	[7r2]	[?v3]	[10v2]
ṇa	[58v6]	[8v5]	[1v3]	[1v1]	[5v5]	[6v4]	[3v1]	[5v4]	[2v1]	[7r6]	[?v1]	[4r6]
ta	[11v3]	[6r4]	[9v4]	[2r4]	[5v4]	[3v5]	[9v2]	[5v2]	[3r1]	[7v3]	[?v3]	[8v6]
tha	[62r4]	[2r2]	[1v5]	[10v1]	[3r1]	[7r7]	[9v6]	[7r4]	[4r1]	[22r5]	[?r4]	[5v7]

	AAĀ	GV	HAP	LTṬ	STṬ	ḌVPṬ	AP	CPN	HP	HTṬ	AT	NAK 5/145
da	[62r5]	[9v4]	[1v6]	[4v3]	[1v1]	[5v4]	[11v3]	[5v2]	[5r2]	[21v3]	[?v4]	[2v3]
dha	[6r4]	[7v2]	[1v6]	[3r2]	[1v4]	[3v3]	[3v5]	[11v3]	[3v6]	[3r4]	[?r1]	[8v2]
na	[10v2]	[6r1]	[1v3]	[10v3]	[7v4]	[6v5]	[11v4]	[4v1]	[4r3]	[7v1]	[?v4]	[1v7]
pa	[11r4]	[1v5]	[1v5]	[14v4]	[3v1]	[3v1]	[9v3]	[4v1]	[3v3]	[7r1]	[?v1]	[7v3]
bha	[61v5]	[1v3]	[5v7]	[2v7]	[3v3]	[4v2]	[4v1]	[5v6]	[3v3]	[49v5]	[?v4]	[8v4]
ma	[5v5]	[6v4]	[1v5]	[1v1]	[3v1]	[5v4]	[14v2]	[8v5]	[5v4]	[7r1]	[?v3]	[8v3]
ya	[6r1]	[9r4]	[1v5]	[4v5]	[4r6]	7r7	[9v3]	[7r5]	[3v3]	[4v5]	[?v1]	[1v1]

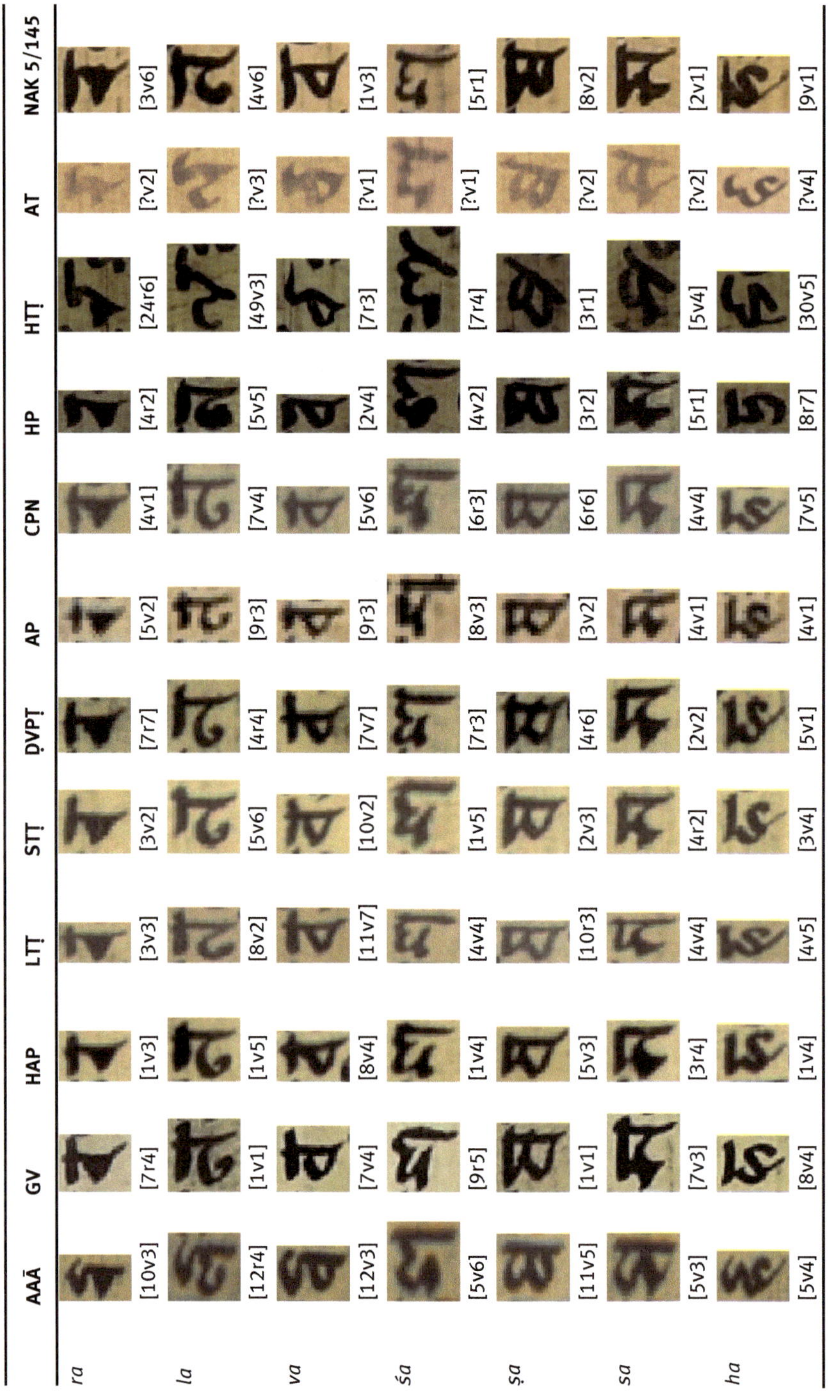

	AAĀ	GV	HAP	LTṬ	STṬ	ḌVPṬ	AP	CPN	HP	HTṬ	AT	NAK 5/145
ra	[10v3]	[7r4]	[1v3]	[3v3]	[3v2]	[7r7]	[5v2]	[4v1]	[4r2]	[24r6]	[?v2]	[3v6]
la	[12r4]	[1v1]	[1v5]	[8v2]	[5v6]	[4r4]	[9r3]	[7v4]	[5v5]	[49v3]	[?v3]	[4v6]
va	[12v3]	[7v4]	[8v4]	[11v7]	[10v2]	[7v7]	[9r3]	[5v6]	[2v4]	[7r3]	[?v1]	[1v3]
śa	[5v6]	[9r5]	[1v4]	[4v4]	[1v5]	[7r3]	[8v3]	[6r3]	[4v2]	[7r4]	[?v1]	[5r1]
ṣa	[11v5]	[1v1]	[5v3]	[10r3]	[2v3]	[4r6]	[3v2]	[6r6]	[3r2]	[3r1]	[?v2]	[8v2]
sa	[5v3]	[7v3]	[3r4]	[4v4]	[4r2]	[2v2]	[4v1]	[4v4]	[5r1]	[5v4]	[?v2]	[2v1]
ha	[5v4]	[8v4]	[1v4]	[4v5]	[3v4]	[5v1]	[4v1]	[7v5]	[8r7]	[30v5]	[?v4]	[9v1]

	AAĀ	GV	HAP	LTṬ	STṬ	ḌVPṬ	AP	CPN	HP	HTṬ	AT	NAK 5/145
visarga	[7r4]	[5r1]	[5v7]	[4v4]	[6r2]	[5v3]	[14v7]	[2v3]	[5r1]	[7v1]	[?r4]	[6v1]
Single *daṇḍa*	[6r4]	[7r5]	[7v5]	[5r5]	[6r2]	[2v4]	[11v7]	[25v3]	[14v2]	[7v1]	[?v3]	[5r4]
Double *daṇḍa*	[7v4]	[7v7]	[5v5]	[5r1]	[7v1]	[4v2]	[14r2]	[25v4]	[14v5]	[1v3]	[?v3]	[5r4]

Fig. 3.5.2-II: Table of selected *akṣaras*, *visargas* and *daṇḍas*

3.5.3 Symbols in West Indian manuscripts

In West Indian manuscripts a '*cha*' symbol can often be found at the end of smaller text units (such as simple sentences, paragraphs etc.), at the end of chapters or at the end of whole texts etc. (see Fig. 3.4-XLVII above). A few scholars have already written about this symbol, without however reaching a final interpretation of it (see 3.4, Fig. 3.4-XLVII and footnote 221).

Another variety of symbols has emerged from my analysis of West Indian manuscripts, in which the already known '*cha*' symbol is drawn together with extra surrounding elements. I categorise this type also as a stylised *puṣpikā*. The '*cha*'-like element is surrounded by *u-akṣara*-like or similar components on the left, right and bottom with or without a 'tail' added to them (see Figs. 3.5.3-I to 3.5.3-III below).[261] The upper part of the symbols often appears open (with a few exceptions). One may argue that a fourth *u-akṣara*-like part is not drawn above the symbol as its space is already taken up by the text line. Another variety of this stylised *puṣpikā* symbol contains a circle or a dot with a 'stroke' or 'tail' in the centre, instead of the '*cha*'-like element. Hereafter, I present some examples in possible chronological order.

In TSPV this type of symbols can be found at the end of chapters on 180r8, 191v6 and at the end of the text on 313v2.[262] One example can be seen in Fig. 3.5.3-I.

[TSPV_313v2_BC_1143]

Fig. 3.5.3-I: Symbol

In HVM this type of symbol can be found at least 28 times at the end of the chapters as well as at the end of the whole text. The symbol contains a '*cha*'-like element in the centre. One of the examples of the symbol can be seen in Fig. 3.5.3-II.

261 Also near similar symbols are in the manuscript of the *Kalpalatāviveka* (*Kalpapallavaśeṣa*) (VS 1205/ 1148 CE) (Jinabhadrasūri Grantha Bhaṇḍāra, Jaisalmer, no. 317) on 389r3-4_A/BCC, AC); in the manuscript of the *Upadeśapadaprakaraṇalaghuṭīkā* (VS 1212 / 1155 CE) (Jinabhadrasūri Grantha Bhaṇḍāra, Jaisalmer, no. 214/1) on 192r4_AC and 192r5_AB.); see Kapadia 1936, Plate VI, a similar symbol can be found together with the foliation '60'.
262 See section 3.6.2.4.1 below.

[HVM_4v3_ACC_1171]

Fig. 3.5.3-II: Symbol

In PV the symbol can be found twice on 10v6 and 15v1. Both symbols can be found at the end of the chapters. The symbol contains a circle in the centre (with a stroke added horizontally on top of it). In Fig. 3.5.3-III, example of the symbol can be seen.

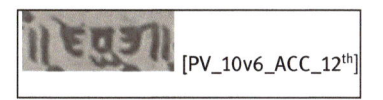

[PV_10v6_ACC_12th]

Fig. 3.5.3-III: Symbol

It can be assumed that the stylised *puṣpikā* with the '*cha*' and its simpler variations are peculiar features characterising the manuscripts from West India.

3.6 Symbols and their functions in manuscripts

As already mentioned in the previous sections (see sections 3.1 and 3.4), in most of the manuscripts of this corpus symbols appear at the end of chapters or texts. Occasionally, they are interspersed in the text to emphasise topics of particular relevance. Such symbols can be found in other parts of the manuscript. They are to be found on the margins of the folio, for instance, sometimes accompanying the foliation numbers, and around the string-holes.

Until now, very little secondary literature has addressed the issue of use of symbols in manuscripts and then only marginally, without providing a thorough analysis of their shapes, functions and possible meanings. Symbols not only demarcate texts and their sections, but may well have more than one function and can be closely related to the contents, performative usages of the text etc.

To improve our understanding of the role that some of (the florally stylised) symbols play in manuscripts, one may turn to Plofker's interpretation of the import of diagrams. While discussing diagrams appearing in astronomical paper manuscripts Plofker (2009, 5) writes:

> [...] they are occasional visual reinforcements for verbal explanations and rules, and they are generally roughly schematic rather than precisely traced.

Hereafter, I have categorised symbols according to their position on the page, shape, etc. mainly into two groups: decorative-only symbols (3.6.1) and structural and decorative symbols (3.6.2).

3.6.1 Decorative-only symbols

Decorative symbols are solely of aesthetic value. They serve no other specific function and are not linked to the tradition of the text found in the manuscript, like for instance some of the symbols drawn around the string-holes.[263]

Representation of symbols around the string-hole can be found in almost all manuscripts from Western India selected for my corpus and also, occasionally, in a few Nepalese manuscripts (see Figs. 3.6.1-VIII and 3.6.1-IX below). However, the individual shape of the symbols in both groups varies to a great degree.

It is not clear when such type of decorative elements started to appear around string-holes in West Indian manuscripts. The oldest available example is found in a Jaina manuscript containing a copy of the *Upamitibhavaprapañcā Kathā* (Bhandarkar Oriental Research Institute, Pune, Acc. no. 7a-b/1880-81) dated 906 CE.[264] Many later examples from the same area (see TSa, TSPV, HVM, PV, JKS/C, TUS and BCV in my corpus)[265] and largely from the same religious

---

263 I am not claiming that all symbols appearing around string-holes do not have any further meanings or affiliation to the contents or tradition to which the manuscripts belong. There are also cases in which we find realistic or florally stylised symbols around string-holes in manuscripts which show a close affiliation to the specific tradition. Some of them are even clear representations of ritual emblems (see section 3.6.2.6.1 below).

264 See Gopalakrishnan 2007, 30. Should the suggested date of the manuscript production by Gopalakrishnan be reliable, examples of the occurrences of such symbols in this manuscript may be the oldest of the area.

265 Stylised *puṣpikā*s can be seen around string-holes in the manuscript of the *Jayadevachandaḥ Śāstra* (VS 1190 / 1133 CE) (Jinabhadrasūri Grantha Bhaṇḍāra, Jaisalmer, no. 314/1); in the manuscript of the *Praśnottararatnamālikā* (VS 1196 / 1139 CE) (Jinabhadrasūri Grantha Bhaṇḍāra, Jaisalmer, no. 171/10); in the manuscript of the *Ṣaḍāvaśyakasūtravṛtti* (VS 1298 / 1241 CE) (Jinabhadrasūri Grantha Bhaṇḍāra, Jaisalmer, no. 136/1); in the manuscript of the *Sūtrakṛtāṅgasūtravṛtti* (VS 1200 / 1143 CE) (Jinabhadrasūri Grantha Bhaṇḍāra, Jaisalmer, no. 4); in the manuscript of the *Kalpalatāviveka* (*Kalpapallavaśeṣa*) (VS 1205 / 1148 CE) (Jinabhadrasūri Grantha Bhaṇḍāra, Jaisalmer, no. 317); in the manuscript of the *Praśnottararatnamālikā* (VS 1210 / 1153 CE) (Jinabhadrasūri Grantha Bhaṇḍāra, Jaisalmer, no. 154/13); in the manuscript of the *Upadeśapadaprakaraṇalaghuṭīkā* (VS 1212 / 1155 CE) (Jinabhadrasūri

milieu, display similar decorative elements.[266] These were also adopted in manuscripts containing texts belonging to other traditions (Hindu and Buddhist), but were never as consistently employed as the manuscripts produced by Jainas of West India.[267]

In TSa a string-hole can be found slightly more than one third space away from the left edge of the folio. Around each string-hole we find a decorative symbol made of four petals. Each petal is made by joining two almost semicircular elements on the side.[268] Furthermore, one may expect a circle in the centre part of the symbol. In this case, the circle has probably been replaced by the string-hole. Examples can be seen in Fig. 3.6.1-I.

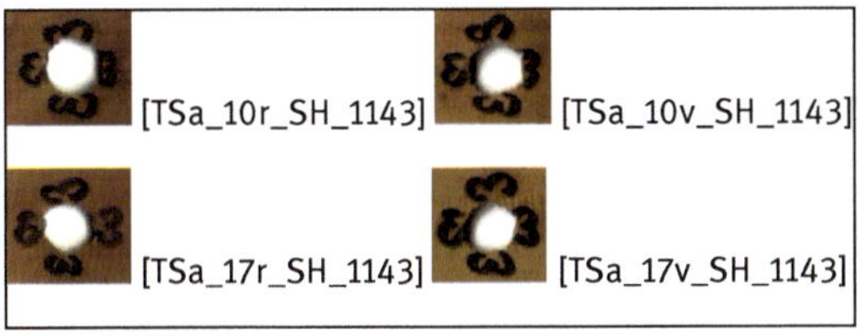

Fig. 3.6.1-I: Symbols around string-holes

In TSPV, two string-holes can be found on each folio. Symbols appear around both string-holes on the folio. At least three types of symbol can be found in the manuscript (regarding these variants see section 3.9.4 below). In these cases too, the string-hole replaces the circle at the centre part of the symbols in the manuscript. In Fig. 3.5.3-II, examples of selected symbols can be seen.

Grantha Bhaṇḍāra, Jaisalmer, no. 214/1); in the manuscript of the *Savaga Padikkamana Sutta cunni* (Sanskrit: *Śrāvakapratikramasūtracūrṇi*) (VS 1317 / 1260 CE) (Museum of Fine Arts, Boston. Denman Waldo Ross Collection, 30.1.1-229) almost on all folios, see also for symbols, the folios 1v–2r, 285v of this manuscript that are presented by Kim 2015, 68 as Fig. 14; in the manuscript of the *Sthānāṅgasūtravṛtti* (VS 1300 / 1295 CE) (Jinabhadrasūri Grantha Bhaṇḍāra, Jaisalmer, no. 6); in the manuscript of the *Praśnavyākaraṇadaśāṅgasūtravṛtti* (VS 1300 / 1295 CE) (Jinabhadrasūri Grantha Bhaṇḍāra, Jaisalmer, no. 23/3).

266 In many later Jaina paper manuscripts various kinds of symbols or elements are found at the centre or almost at the centre of the page e.g. see the manuscript containing texts of the *Kalpasūtra* and the *Kālakācārya* (1404 CE) (Royal Asiatic Society, Tod MS 34). This way of using of symbols or other elements is probably an imitation of the practise of the usage of symbols and other items often to be found around string-holes in palm-leaf manuscripts.

267 See Weber 1891, XV; Tripāṭhī 1975, 25.

268 See section 3.4, type no. 12, Fig. 3.4-XII above.

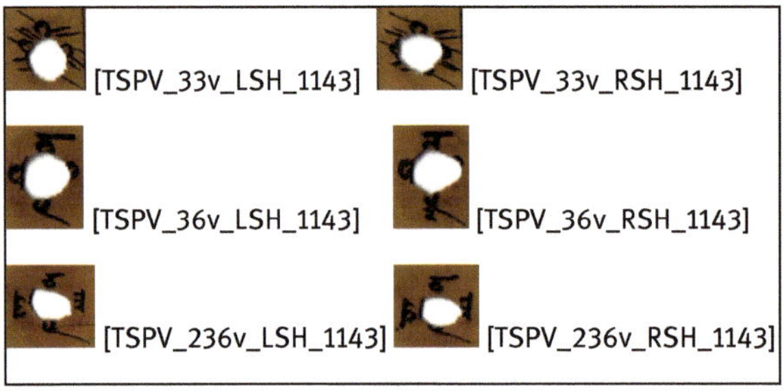

Fig. 3.6.1-II: Symbols around string-holes

In HVM, there are two string-holes on each folio. On both sides symbols can be found on all folios, except on those folios where the holes have become bigger and therefore, symbols around them have become damaged or are partially or entirely lost and their shape can no longer be seen properly. Almost only one type of symbols appears around the string-holes: it contains four lines and four semi-circular-like petals facing outside.[269] The examples of selected symbols can be seen in Fig. 3.5.3-III.

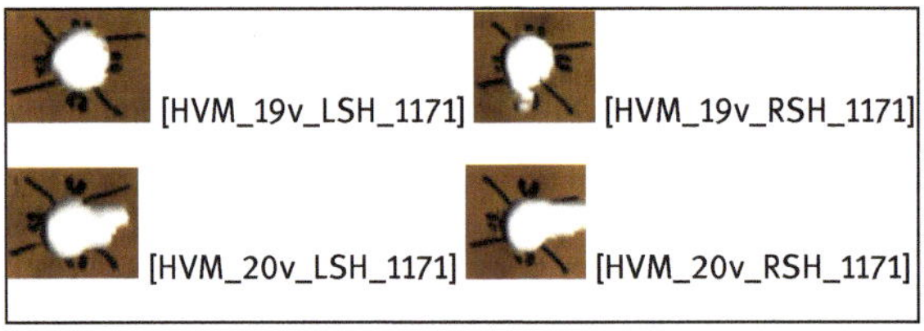

Fig. 3.6.1-III: Symbols around string-holes

In PV, one string-hole appears slightly more than one third space away from the left edge of the folio. Symbols can be found around the string-hole on each folio (with some exceptions such as on 1r, 144v and on a few very last folios). Only one type of symbol appears in the manuscript. This means all symbols contain four semi-circular-like petals and four sets of double lines. Examples of symbol can be seen in Fig. 3.6.1-IV.

269 This type of symbol has been discussed above in section 3.4, see type no. 10, Fig. 3.4-X.

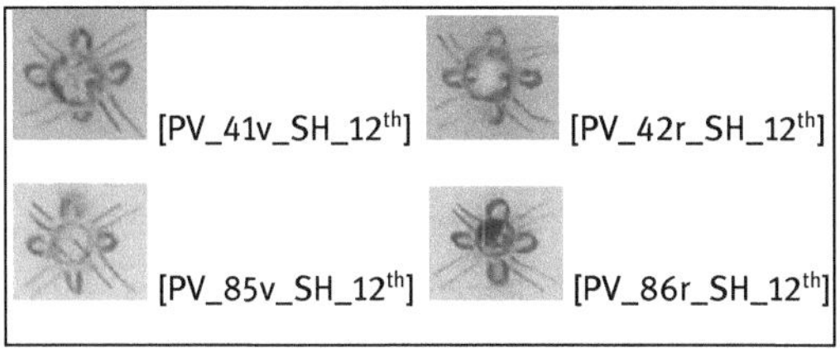

Fig. 3.6.1-IV: Symbols around string-holes

Furthermore, in JKS/C, one string-hole can be found slightly more than one third space away from the left edge of the folio. Symbols can be found around the string-hole on each folio. All symbols share an identical shape. This means all symbols contain four semi-circular petals and four lines. Examples of selected symbols can be seen in Fig. 3.6.1-V.[270]

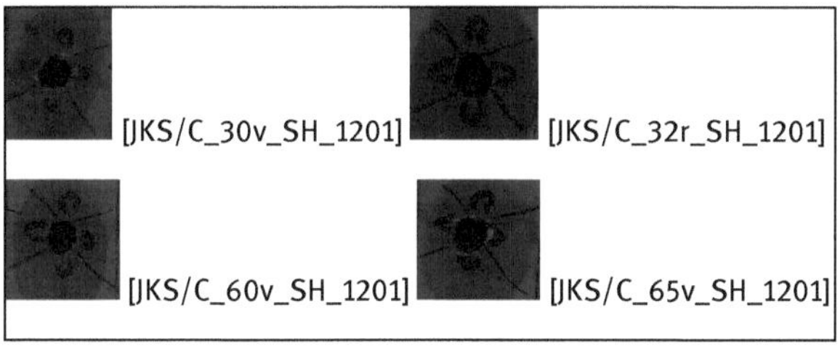

Fig. 3.6.1-V: Symbols around string-holes

In TUS, there is one string-hole slightly more than one third space away from the left edge of the folio. Symbols appear around the string-hole on each folio. Two types of symbol can be found around the string-holes in the manuscript, one containing four semi-circular petals and four lines and other one containing only four semi-circular petals whose lower petal appears with a tail added to it (regarding these variants see section 3.9.5 below). The examples of selected symbols can be seen in Fig. 3.6.1-VI.

270 Similar symbols can be found together with the foliation, see Kapadia 1936, Plates V–VI.

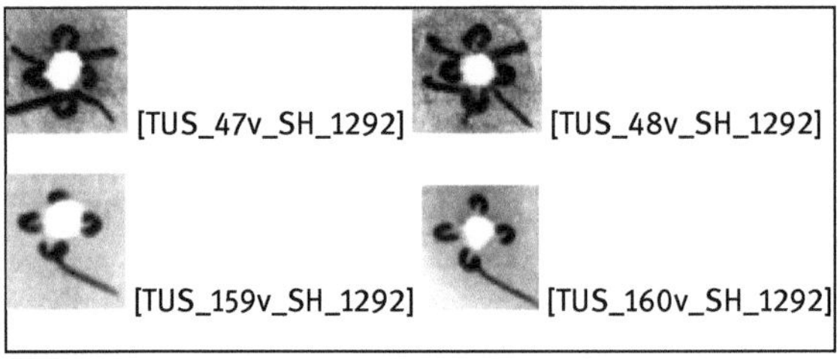

Fig. 3.6.1-VI: Symbols around string-holes

In BCV, there is one string-hole on the folio slightly more than one third space away from the left edge of the folio. Symbols appear around the string-hole on each folio. All symbols share an identical shape. That means symbol contains four almost semi-circular petals and four lines. The examples of selected symbols can be seen in Fig. 3.6.1-VII.

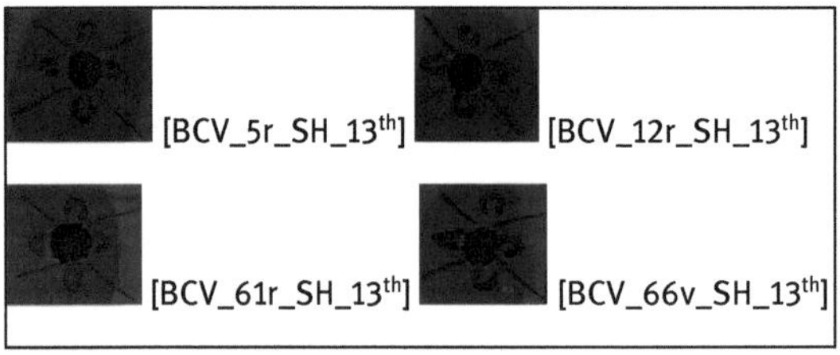

Fig. 3.6.1-VII: Symbols around string-holes

In the Nepalese manuscript KV/UVDh the folio has two string-holes. Symbols appear around both string-holes on all folios (with a few exceptions, on 1v, 44r, last folio verso where one cannot find any symbols). At least five types of symbols appear in the manuscript. In comparison to the symbols found in West Indian manuscripts, the symbols of this manuscript are drawn in a more sophisticated way. Furthermore, some symbols around the string-holes (e.g. symbols in the first and second rows in Fig. 3.6.1-VIII) and some of the symbols which appear at the end of the particular sections have an almost identical shape. This indicates that symbols at the end of smaller text units and around the string-holes have probably been drawn by the same scribe. Examples of selected symbols can be seen in Fig. 3.6.1-VIII.

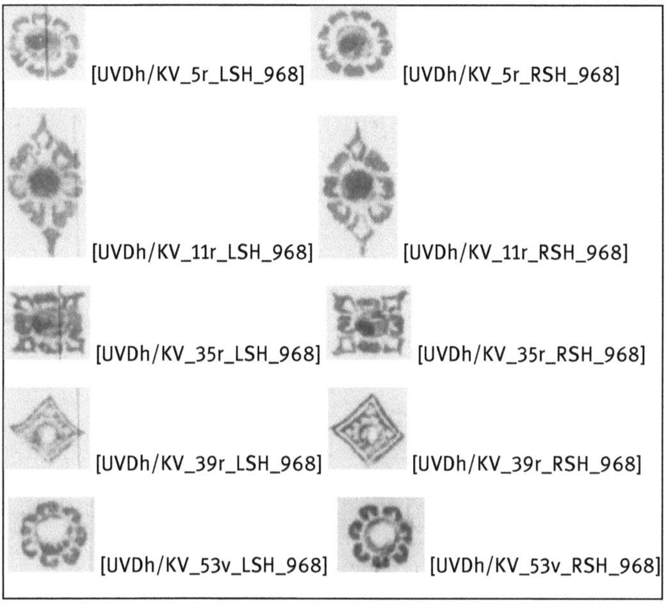

Fig. 3.6.1-VIII: Symbols around string-holes

In HV_2, two string-holes can be found on the folio. Symbols appear around both string-holes only on 53v, 68r, 204v and 310r. Furthermore, symbols around the string-holes and most of the symbols that appear at the end of the chapters are identical.[271] This indicates that symbols at the end of the chapters and around the string-holes may have been drawn by the same scribe in the manuscript. Examples of selected symbols can be seen in Fig. 3.5.3-IX.

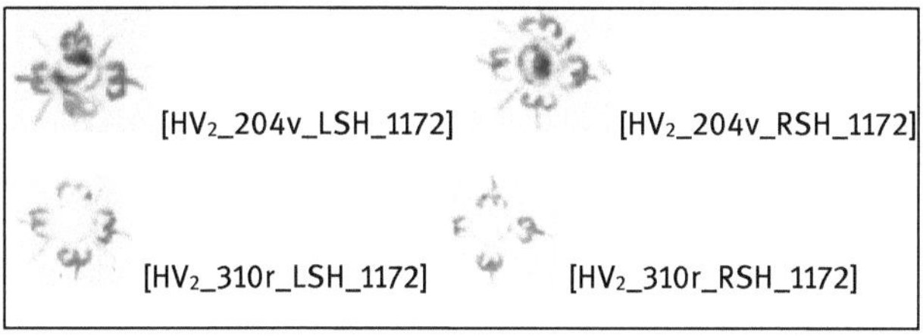

Fig. 3.6.1-IX: Symbols around string-holes

271 See type no. 16 in Fig. 3.4-XVI above.

3.6.1.1 Preliminary conclusions on decorative-only symbols

All the Western Indian manuscripts that I have used in the course of my study contain symbols around string-holes (TSa, TSPV, HVM, PV, JKS/C, TUS and BCV).[272] To some extent such symbols share nearly the same or a similar shape. Thus there are symbols containing four almost semi-circular petals and four lines around the string-holes (e.g. JKS/C, TUS and BCV). Minor variations of this pattern can also be found. For instance, symbols in PV contain four petals and four sets of double lines, whereas symbols in TSa have petals that appear to be made by joining two almost semi-circular elements on the side.

This phenomenon has not only been found in manuscripts containing texts of a specific genre (Jaina religious treatises), but from a variety of them (e.g. *kāvya*). However, it can be argued that the latter category of manuscripts was produced in a Jaina milieu, in other words by Jaina scribes most likely for a Jaina readership.

A symbol around the string-hole is to be found in only two Nepalese manuscripts of the 'core' corpus.[273] One of them (KV/UVDh) contains symbols around string-holes on almost all folios. Even within the same manuscript, symbols appear in different shapes and are beautifully drawn (see examples of selected symbol

---

272 As pointed out above, also in the manuscript of *Upamitibhavaprapañcā Kathā* (Bhandarkar Oriental Research Institute, Pune, Acc. no. 7a-b/1880-81) e.g. on some folios presented by Gopalakrishnan 2007, 30; in the manuscript of the *Jayadevachandaḥ Śāstra* (VS 1190 / 1133 CE) (Jinabhadrasūri Grantha Bhaṇḍāra, Jaisalmer, no. 314/1); in the manuscript of the *Praśnottararatnamālikā* (VS 1196 / 1139 CE) (Jinabhadrasūri Grantha Bhaṇḍāra, Jaisalmer, no. 171/10); in the manuscript of the *Ṣaḍāvaśyakasūtravṛtti* (VS 1298 / 1241 CE) (Jinabhadrasūri Grantha Bhaṇḍāra, Jaisalmer, no. 136/1); in the manuscript of the *Sūtrakṛtāṅgasūtravṛtti* (VS 1200 / 1143 CE) (Jinabhadrasūri Grantha Bhaṇḍāra, Jaisalmer, no. 4); in the manuscript of the *Kalpalatāviveka* (*Kalpapallavaśeṣa*) (VS 1205 / 1148 CE) (Jinabhadrasūri Grantha Bhaṇḍāra, Jaisalmer, no. 317); in the manuscript of the *Praśnottararatnamālikā* (VS 1210 / 1153 CE) (Jinabhadrasūri Grantha Bhaṇḍāra, Jaisalmer, no. 154/13); in the manuscript of the *Upadeśapadaprakaraṇalaghuṭīkā* (VS 1212 / 1155 CE) (Jinabhadrasūri Grantha Bhaṇḍāra, Jaisalmer, no. 214/1); in the manuscript of the *Savaga Padikkamana Sutta cunni* (Sanskrit: *Śrāvakapratikramasūtracūrṇi*) (VS 1317 / 1260 CE) (Museum of Fine Arts, Boston. Denman Waldo Ross Collection, 30.1.1-229) almost on all folios, see also for symbols, the folios 1v–2r, 285v of this manuscript that are presented by Kim 2015, 68 as Fig. 14; in the manuscript of the *Sthānāṅgasūtravṛtti* (VS 1300 / 1295 CE) (Jinabhadrasūri Grantha Bhaṇḍāra, Jaisalmer, no. 6); in the manuscript of the *Praśnavyākaraṇadaśāṅgasūtravṛtti* (VS 1300 / 1295 CE) (Jinabhadrasūri Grantha Bhaṇḍāra, Jaisalmer, no. 23/3).

273 In the manuscript of the *Aṣṭasāhasrikā Prajñāpāramitā* (NAK 4/1626 / NGMPP A 39/12) and in the manuscript of the *Haramekhalā* (NAK 1/1231 / NGMPP A 45/7) symbols can also be found around string-holes on the folio. However, in both manuscripts symbols have different shapes in comparison to the symbols found in West Indian manuscripts.

above). The other is the HV_1, in which symbols are only on one side of four folios (on 53v, 68r, 204v and 310r). These symbols are identical to most of the symbols appearing at the end of the manuscript chapters. There are no symbols around string-holes in the East Indian manuscripts of my corpus, however one may occasionally find symbols and other decorative elements in some manuscripts of this region.[274]

3.6.2 Structural and decorative symbols

All symbols appearing at the end of smaller text units, at the end of chapter or sub-chapter accompanied by sub-colophon or at the end of text with colophon or colophon-like statements etc. and divide visually units of the text, chapter, sub-chapter and text and at the same time (may) appear in decorative shape, can be understood as structural and decorative symbols in manuscripts.

Almost all symbols or features appearing at the end of chapter, sub-chapter or at the end of text in manuscripts belong to this category. The symbols appearing in other parts of the text (such as beginning or end of smaller text units) that play visual structural role can also be understood as structural and decorative components.

In the following section, some symbols are presented that appear at the beginning of smaller text units, at the end of chapter, at the end of text or within a part of the text, are analysed for how they give special indication of the text contents or exhibit specific importance for the text, tradition or ritual aspects.

274 Decorated string-hole spaces and margins with various motifs can be found e.g. in the manuscript of the *Aṣṭasāhasrikā Prajñāpāramitā* (Nālandā, Bihar, ca. 1041 CE) (Los Angeles County Museum of Art, M72.20a-b), see Weissenborn 2012, 192 as Abbildung 59 the first, last folios and other two folios, Kim 2013, 51 as Figure 2–3 the first and last folios; in another manuscript containing the same text (Nālandā, Bihar, 1058/1140 CE) (Asia Society, New York Mr. and Mrs John D. Rockefeller 3rd Acquisitions Fund, 1987.1) on 1v, 2r, 299v, 300r, Weissenborn 2012, 193 as Abbildung 61, Kim 2013, 44 as Figure 2-1; in another manuscript of the same text (Nālandā, Bihar, ca. 1039–1069 CE) (Wellcome Library, Sansk ε I.) on 101v and 102r, Kim 2013, 84, Figure 3–4; in another manuscript containing the same text (Nālandā, Bihar, ca. 1114 CE) (Tibet Museum, Lhasa) on a few folios along with beginning and end, Weissenborn 2012, 202 as Abbildung 77; in another manuscript of the same text (Vikramaśīla, ca. 1147 CE) (British Library, London, Or. 6902) on 163v and 164r, Kim 2013, 114 as Figure 4–1; in the manuscript of the *Pañcarakṣā* (ca. 1177 CE) (NAK 5/83) on 57r, 58v, Kim 2015, 59 as Fig. I; in the manuscript of the *Aṣṭasāhasrikā Prajñāpāramitā* (ca. 1191 CE) on 109v, 110r, 216v, 217r, Kim 2015, 67 as Fig. 12; in the manuscript containing the same text (ca. 12th c.) (NAK 5/196), Kim 2013, 4 as Figure 0–2; in the manuscript of the same text (Nālandā, Bihar, ca. 12th c.) (Royal Asiatic Society, London, Hodgson 1) on a few folios presented by Weissenborn 2012 as Abbildung 1.

3.6.2.1 Examples of symbols with a particular meaning

At times, the shape of certain symbols clearly represents ritual items relevant to a specific religious or performative tradition. At other times, symbols of a similar relevance can be drawn in a more abstract form. In this instance, the symbols should not be understood as mere decorations, but be evaluated for other, possible, cultural significances. Moreover, the symbols may also bear a close relation to the scribal activity, indicating that the scribes may have been especially aware of the kind of text they were copying.

3.6.2.1.1 A particular floral symbol in the *Suśrutanighaṇṭu* of SS/N

Manuscript SS/N contains copies of the *Suśrutasaṃhitā*, a medical treatise, and of the *Suśrutanighaṇṭu*, a thesaurus listing the synonyms of various plants' names. The entire manuscript presents a plethora of symbols: a few dots (type no. 1), simple circles (type no. 2), double circles (type no. 6) and small stylised *puṣpikā*s (circles surrounded by almost semi-circular petals with or without four lines, such as type nos. 7 and 8). All these kinds of symbols are found in the section of the manuscript containing the *Suśrutasaṃhitā*, whereas the section containing the *Suśrutanighaṇṭu*[275] presents only simple circles and double circles (placed after the title at the beginning of each section), with the exception of three stylised *puspikā*s.

Among them, two stylised small *puṣpikā*s of no special aesthetic value are found at the beginning of the sections '*sālasāra* ...' ('Śāl tree') and '*elā pippaly ādau* ...' ('Cardamom [and] pepper etc.'). Furthermore, a more refined stylised *puṣpikā* placed between double *daṇḍa*s is found on 217r (line no. 2 above the left string-hole) at the beginning of the section on water-lilies (or lotuses).[276] Here, there is no title heading of the section, only the symbol, which appears to have been in place of the title. For the symbol and the transliteration of the relevant section see below.

275 The text has been 'edited' by Suvedī/Tivārī 2002 with the title *Sauśrutanighaṇṭuḥ*.
276 On water-lilies, see Hanneder 2002, 295–308.

Fig. 3.6.2.1.1-l: Symbol at the beginning of a particular section, fol. 217r © KL

[217r2–3]  *utpalaṃ kandajaṃ nīlaṃ ślakṣṇanālaṃ jalodbhavaṃ* ␣ | ␣
śībharaṃ śītavīryaṃ ca sūryabodhi śaśiprabhaṃ ␣ || ␣
raktotpalaṃ raktanālaṃ śrīniketaṃ|⊙| *manoramaṃ* ␣ |
viśālaṃ raktakumudaṃ bhramareṣṭaṃ varodbhavaṃ ␣ ||
kumuda(!) śvetavarṇaś ca śaṣmagardabhakaṃ +///[3] *tam* ␣ |
- - - *ttañ ca vijñeyaṃ śyāmavṛttam athāpi ca* ␣ || ␣
saugandhikaṃ raktanīlaṃ karṇapūraṃ varotpa|⊙|*laṃ* ␣ |
jātyutpalañ ca paṭhitaṃ vṛttendīvaram eva ca ␣ ||
kuvalayaṃ kuḍmalañ caiva kālajaṃ kākaḍmalam(!) ␣ | ␣
kākotpalañ ca paṭhitaṃ kā|⊙|*kaloḍḍyam(!) athāpi ca* ␣ || ␣[277]

This symbol may have been drawn by the same person or scribe who copied this part of the text.[278] This is because the double *daṇḍa*s that demarcate the symbol look similar to the double *daṇḍa*s that appear on the same folio (i.e. the double *daṇḍa*s demarcating the double circles in the first line). We can assume the scribe was familiar with (i.e. understood) the content of the text he was copying. As there is no heading for the lotus/water-lily section, we may assume that the scribe drew an abstract representation of a water-lily to provide the reader with a visual clue of that particular section's topic or to give a particular emphasis to that section more generally.

277 I have transcribed the text here as it appears in the manuscript. For the 'edition', see Suvedī/Tivārī 2002, 97, verses 265–269.

278 On suggestions for the identification of the scribe, see Klebanov 2010, 65–66; Klebanov (forthcoming).

3.6.2.1.2 Symbols in AT

The manuscript AT is of a particularly interesting visual organisation. It is an MTM belonging to Vajrayāna Buddhism. Here one 'dot' or circle-like symbol and four stylised *puṣpikās* can be found at the end of the texts.

Symbols at the end of mainly one of the texts,[279] *Satsukhāvabodhana*, appear to have a special significance. In line no. 3, before the colophon (see transcription and translation below), there is a 'dot-like' symbol placed between a set of double *daṇḍas*. After the colophon there is a series of three stylised simple *puṣpikās*, each of which is also placed between a set of double *daṇḍas*. Although they look rather plain, they form a unique set (see Fig. 3.6.2.1.2-II).

The first symbol (i.e. stylised *puṣpikā*) is made of a circle surrounded by four petals facing inwards; it can be understood as a representation of a *padma* ('lotus'), which at a more abstract level represents *prajñā*, i.e. the wisdom-aspect of awakening and the female deity or practitioner.[280] Keeping this in mind, the second symbol, composed of a circle surrounded by four petals facing outwards, may be interpreted as a *vajra* ('thunderbolt'); a representation of *karuṇā* or *upāya* ('compassion'), i.e. the compassion-aspect of awakening and the male deity or practitioner.[281] These interpretations find support in the shape of the third symbol. This can be understood as a *samāyoga*/*saṃyoga* ('combination', 'union') of the first two symbols and, thus, a representation of the union of *padma* and *vajra*.[282] Such a combination is graphically expressed by the petals of the third symbol, which are obtained by drawing together the petals of the first two symbols (for Illustration of symbols, see Fig. 3.6.2.1.2-II below).

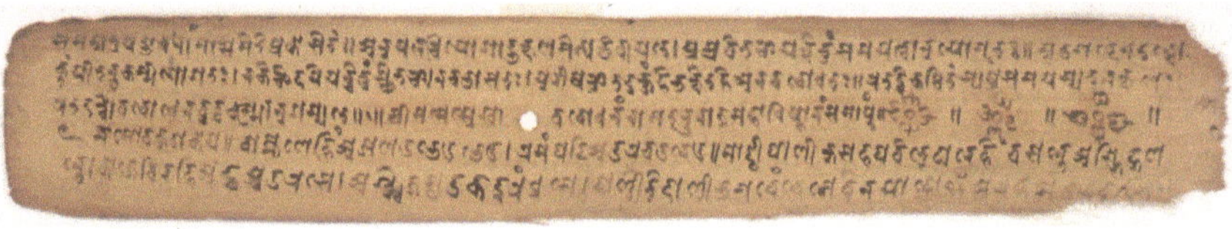

Fig. 3.6.2.1.2-I: Symbols after the chapter colophon, fol. ?v © General Library, University of Tokyo

---

279 There is a statement on one of the folios in line no. 3 in this manuscript which reads mentioning a work *Dohākoṣa* of Sarahapāda as follows *kṛtir iyaṃ dohākoṣasarahapādānām*.

280 See Snellgrove 1959, Part I, 27 and 137.

281 Ibid. 140.

282 See Pal 1978, Part II, 83: "Many of the later Vajrayāna sects believe that *Bodhicitta* can be achieved by the combination of right knowledge (*prajñā*) with right method (*upāya*), usually regarded as compassion (*karuṇā*). In visual terms the male of the pair represents method or compassion while the female symbolizes knowledge or wisdom."

[?v3]  *śrīmatsatsukhā⊙vabodhanaṃ nāma tantrarājamahādhiṣṭhānaṃ*

samāptaṃ 

'[Thus], the great Tantra of great power called the glorious awakening true bliss is concluded.'

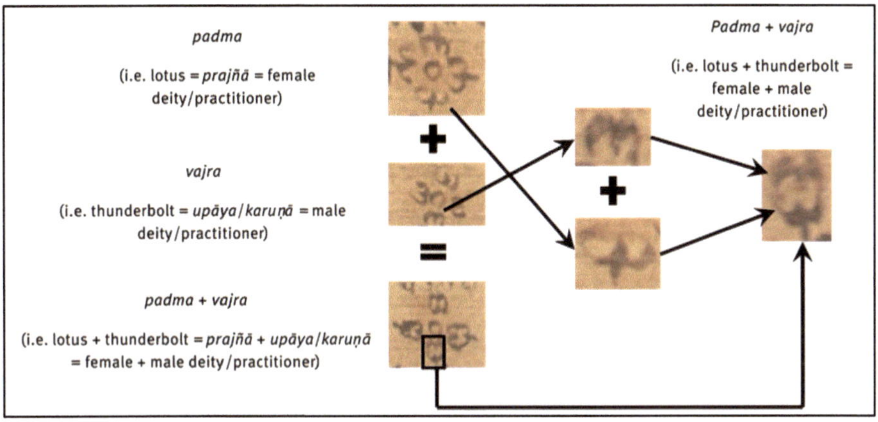

Fig. 3.6.2.1.2-II: Illustration of symbols

From the appearance of these symbols, one can assume that they have probably been drawn by the same scribe who copied the text: the double *daṇḍa*s at the sides of the symbols are similar to the *daṇḍa*s found in the text written on the same folio (for instance double *daṇḍa*s in the first line). We can assume the scribe knew what kind of text he was copying and to which particular school of thought it belonged. Otherwise it would be difficult to justify the occurrence of such a sophisticated set of symbols.

3.6.2.1.3 Symbols in HTṬ

This is a particularly interesting manuscript as its post-colophon (on 59r depicted in Fig. 3.6.2.1.3-I) tells us it was copied in Vikramaśīla, one of the greatest

Buddhist monastic universities of Eastern India.[283] The scribe records that a Buddhist called Viśuddhirakṣita had had the manuscript copied. Such a formulation may be an indication that the manuscript was an official copy for the library of the monastery.[284] This manuscript contains two circles (on 40r6, 51v3 like type no. 2), three symbols (on 20v1, 40r2, 59r6) that resemble some similarities to type no. 4, two stylised *puṣpikā*s (on 51v3 like type no. 15; on 59r5 like type no. 16) and two florally stylised *vajra*s (on 48r6, 59r4).[285]

One of the two stylised *puṣpikā* together with one of the two florally stylised *vajra*s appears at the end of the text accompanying the colophon (on 59r). It is not certain if they have a specific meaning or are merely decorative. As in the example described in 3.6.2.1.2, here too the two symbols may be understood as representing the combination of a *vajra* (in line no. 4), depicted here in a florally stylised form, and a *padma* (in line no. 5), drawn in the shape of stylised *puṣpikā*, i.e. a stylised simple flower. Both symbols have been highlighted.

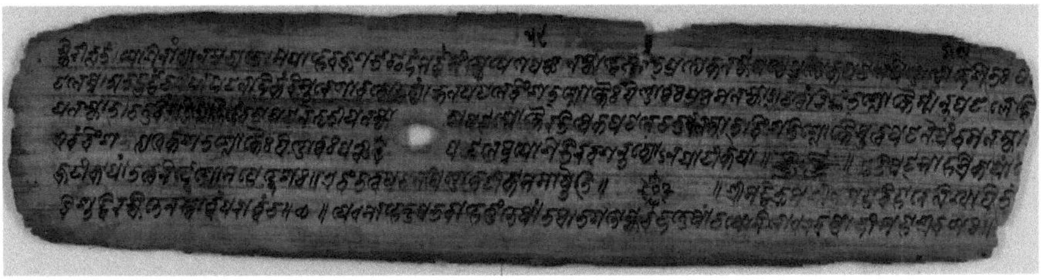

Fig. 3.6.2.1.3-I: Symbols before and after colophon, fol. 59r © KL

283 See the Manuscript of the Month from 04.2012 at: <http://www.manuscript-cultures.uni-hamburg.de/mom/2012_04_mom_e.html> (last accessed on 05.11.2018).

284 This and other manuscripts probably copied in Vikramaśīla have also been studied by Dr Martin Delhey at the Centre for the Study of Manuscript Cultures (CSMC), Hamburg, in the sub-project C01 titled 'A Twelfth-Century East Indian Monastic Library and its Fate', see Delhey et al. 2015.

285 Examples of nicely drawn realistic *vajras* can be found (on both string-hole spaces) in the manuscript of the *Aṣṭasāhasrikā Prajñāparamitā* (NS 135 / 1015 CE) (CUL Add.1643) on 2v, 5v, 8v, 11v, 113v, 14r, 20v, 40v, 44r, 86r, 89r, 99v, 120r, 123v, 127r, 133r, 139r, 147r, 151r, 157v, 164v, 169r, 176v, 179v, 181rv, 182v, 183rv, 184r, 185rv–188rv, 193r, 214v, 216v, 218v, 220v, 221r, 222v, see Losty 1982, 31. Among other symbols, I also present below some florally stylised *vajra*s and 'realistic' *vajra*s that we find in other Buddhist manuscripts. See Kim 2013, 24, Figure I-1 in which a Buddhist priest, with a manuscript in front of him, uses a *vajra* ritual implement to invoke the Goddess Prajñāpāramitā during the *Prajñāpāramitā pūjā*. Among other things, florally stylised *vajra*s in some manuscripts contain the text of the *Prajñāpāramitā* or *Aṣṭasāhasrikā Prajñāparamitā* (see section 3.6.2.1.6).

[59r4–6]  *iti ṣaṭsāhasrikāyāṃ ///++[5]jraṭīkāyāṃ tatvanirddeśo mahoddeśaḥ || evaṃ tatvapaṭalapiṇḍārthaṭīkā samāpteti*  *śrīmadvikramaśīlamahāvihāre likhāpitaṃ[6] viśuddhirakṣitena svārthaṃ parārthaṃ ca* 

'Thus, [this is] the *Mahoddeśa* [called] the instruction of truth in the *Ṣaṭsāhasrikā*, in the commentary on the [Heva]jra. Thus, the commentary [called] *Tatvapaṭalapiṇḍārtha* is concluded. Viśuddhirakṣita had had [this] copied in the glorious great Vikramaśīla monastery for himself and others.'

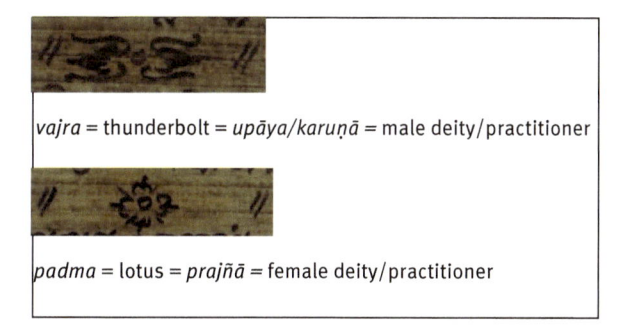

vajra = thunderbolt = *upāya/karuṇā* = male deity/practitioner

padma = lotus = *prajñā* = female deity/practitioner

Fig. 3.6.2.1.3-II: Symbols with a particular meaning

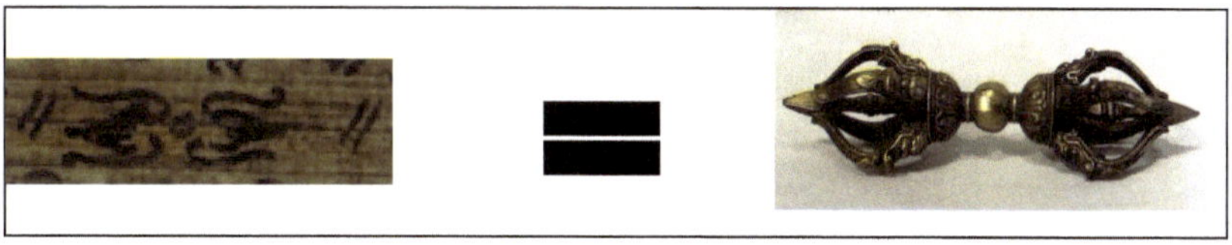

Fig. 3.6.2.1.3-III: Comparison between a florally stylised *vajra* and a modern one

It seems that both symbols were probably drawn by the person who copied the text. This is evidenced by the double *daṇḍa*s that delimit the symbols being similar to the *daṇḍa*s appearing in other parts of the text (e.g. see double *daṇḍa*s in the fifth line on the same folio). The scribe was probably familiar with the text he was copying and the tradition to which the text belonged. The assumption is supported by the scribe's name given as Viśuddhirakṣita, possibly a Buddhist name.

3.6.2.1.4 Symbols in AṣP$_1$

This manuscript belongs to Mahāyāna Buddhism. The manuscript exhibits significant examples of symbols. Among which,[286] we find florally stylised simple symbols. Eight (e.g. on 54v5_ACC, 149r5_ACC, 160v5_B/ACC, 169r1_ACC, 200v2_B/ACC) share an almost similar shape (those in Fig. 3.6.2.1.4-I) (see type no. 30). All these symbols appear at the end of chapters.

It is possible to understand these florally stylised symbols as *viśvavajra*s ('double *vajras*'),[287] one of the essential ritual emblems in Buddhism, also associated with Amoghasiddhi ('Unfailing Accomplishment') one of the five Buddhas,[288] symbolising the principle of absolute stability. These florally stylised double *vajra*s are quite similar in shape to double *vajra*s found in later manuscripts from Nepal or on the piller of *stūpa*s (e.g. Figs. 3.6.2.1.6-XXX and 3.6.2.1.6-XXXI below) etc.

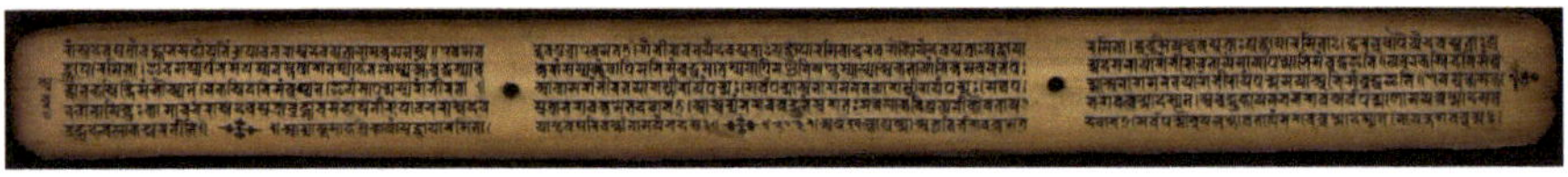

Fig. 3.6.2.1.4-I: Symbols before and after the chapter colophon, fol. 160v © NAK

---

286 This manuscript also contains two realistic *puṣpikā*s on 26v4 (see section 3.5.1), two nicely drawn stylised *puṣpikā*s on 2r3_BBOF, 17v4_B/ACC, stylised simple *puṣpikā*s on 54v5_BCC, 149r5_BCC, 206v6_ACC, circles on 92r4, 282v1–2 and four 'figure-eight knot' symbols on 54v5_ACC, 72v5_BCC, 132v5_BCC, 206v6_BCC (probably these symbols can be interpreted as 'endless knot' in this context).

287 While describing the *maṇḍala* Johnston 2000, Vol. 2, 808 provides an explanation of the *viśvavajra* symbol as follows: "The *viśvavajra* is a complex device and a symbol of the absolute, adamantine nature of enlightenment. At the very core of the *viśvavajra* is a single point that represents the unconditioned potentiality from which all phenomena arise. The structural components of the *viśvavajra* that appear to radiate out of this infinitesimal core symbolize all aspects of phenomenal existence. Specifically each of the prongs and the centre of the *viśvavajra* represent one of five *jina*, or victor, Buddhas. Each of these Buddhas presides over a *kula*, or family, to which all living creatures in the Buddhist world system belong."

288 The five Buddha families has been given in the *Hevajratantra*, chapter 5.5-7 in Snellgrove 1959, Part II, 16 as follows: "Vajra Padma tathā Karma Tathāgata Ratnaiva ca | kulāni pañcavidhāny āhur uttamāni mahākṛpa || Vajre Ḍombī bhaven mudrā Padme Nartī tathaiva ca | Karmaṇi Rajaky ākhyata Brāhmaṇī ca Tathāgate || Ratne Caṇḍālinī jñeyā pañcamudrā viniścitāḥ | tathāgatakulaṃ caitat saṃkṣepenābhidhīyate ||" and its translation can be seen in Snellgrove 1959, Part I, 61 as follows: "Vajra, Padma, Karma, Tathāgata, Ratna; these are known as the Five Families supreme, O thou of great compassion. These then are their five Mudrā: Ḍombī for Vajra, Nartī for Padma, Rajakī for Karma, Brāhmaṇī for Tathāgata, and Caṇḍālinī for Ratna. For shortness they are called the families of the *tathāgata*s."

[160v5]  *āryāṣṭasāhasrikāyāṃ prajñāpāramitā|⊙|yān devapa-rivartto nāma paṃcadaśamaḥ* 

'[Thus], the fifteenth chapter, namely the *deva* [ends] in the noble Perfection of Wisdom in Eight Thousand Lines.'[289]

3.6.2.1.5 Symbols in SDhPS

This manuscript also belongs to Mahāyāna Buddhism and contains an influential Sūtra text. In terms of symbols, this manuscript is of a particular interest. Among others,[290] at least seventeen stylised *puṣpikā*s are to be found at the end of the chapters. Fourteen of them[291] share an almost identical shape (such as symbols depicted on 20r in Fig. 3.6.2.1.5-I below) and two other symbols (on 31v4 and 69r1) have a similar shape. Like the symbols described in AṣP$_1$ above, the symbol in this manuscript can also be understood as *viśvavajra*s.

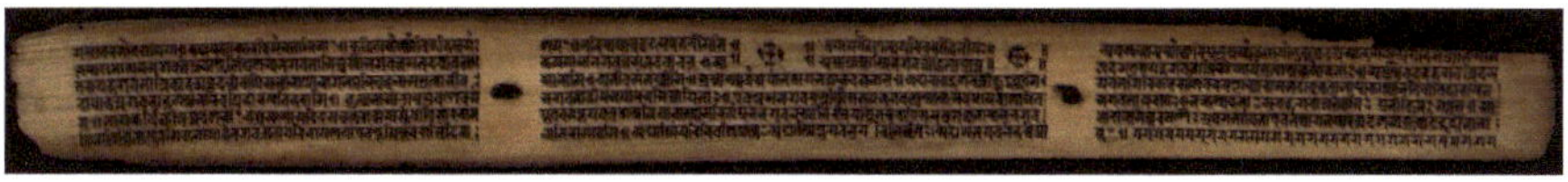

Fig. 3.6.2.1.5-I: Symbols at the end of the chapter, fol. 20r © NAK

[20r1]  *upāyakauśalyaparivartto dvitīyaḥ* 

'[Thus], the second chapter, [namely] the *upāyakauśalya* ('skill in means') [is concluded]'.

289 For the translation of the title of the work I refer here to Conze 1973.
290 Such as 'figure-eight knot-like' symbols on 43v5_ACC (probably this symbol can be interpreted as 'endless knot' in this context), circles 100v6_ACC, 106v_ACC, 116r1_BCC, '*tha*' symbols on 46v6_ACC, 58v2_BCC, 62v4_B/ACC, 79r3_ACC, 84v3_ACC, 89v6_BCC, 93v2_ACC, 100v5_BCC, 110r5_ACC, 113v5_ACC, 134v4_B/ACC and a series of three large symbols on 138v, 139rv (see section 3.6.2.2.2 below) can be found in the manuscript.
291 For instance, the symbols on 11r1_BCC, 20r1_B/ACC, 31v4_ACC, 36v6_B/ACC, 43v4_BCC, 65r2_ACC, 69r1_ACC, 77r3_ACC, 79r3_ACC, 89v6_ACC, 106v5_BCC, 113v5_BCC.

This manuscript will be discussed further below in sections 3.6.2.4.1 and 3.6.2.4.2. In fact, it contains a set of three more large symbols on 138v (the penultimate folio of the manuscript), and on 139rv (the last folio of the manuscript). The symbol in the middle part on 139v has a stylised *puṣpikā* at its centre that shares the same shape of the other stylised *puṣpikā*s (as on 20r1 in this manuscript and symbols such as appear on 160v5 in AṣP$_1$) found in this manuscript. The examples of symbols presented in the following chapter may support my interpretation of this type of florally stylised symbols (in this manuscript and in AṣP$_1$) as *viśvavajras* (see section 3.6.2.1.6 below) and other symbols.

3.6.2.1.6 Symbols in some selected Buddhist manuscripts

In the following, I present some selected florally stylised or near realistic symbols we find in the Buddhist manuscripts datable as ca. 12th to 19th c. In so doing, we will see the practice and development of usage of symbols in manuscripts (written on palm-leaf and paper) as well as in other places such as on the pillars of a religious site. The examples will also support the interpretation or identification of some of the aforementioned florally stylised symbols, such as *vajra* (in HTṬ), *viśvavajras* (in AṣP$_1$, SDhPS) presented above.

MTM of the *Bodhicaryāvatāra*, *Āryavalokiteśvarastotra* etc. (KL 127 / NGMPP C 14/5)

In the MTM (NS 337 / 1217 CE) (KL 127 / NGMPP C 14/5) containing a few Buddhist texts (e.g. part of the *Bodhicaryāvatāra*, *Āryavalokiteśvarastotra* etc.) we find two *vajras*.[292] The manuscript is damaged and some folios are in a fragmentary condition. The foliation has not been preserved. One of the *vajras* can be found in the part of the text of the *Āryavalokiteśvarastotra* before the colophon in line no. 5 and the other one appears in the part of text of the *Bodhicaryāvatāra* after the donor phrase (*deyadharmo* [']*yam* ... 'this [is] a pious gift ...') in line no. 7 (see Fig. 3.6.2.1.6-I). After the second *vajra* we find the date written in letter-numerals.[293]

292 One should note that there are at least two different hands clearly visible in this manuscript.

293 It reads as follows *samvat* () *ā la grā āśāḍhaśukladvitīyāyāṃ*(!) ('the [Nepāla] era 337, on the 2nd lunar day of bright fortnight of [the month] *āṣāḍha*'). The lower part of most of the *akṣaras* of °*śukladvitīyāyāṃ* is lost due to the damaged condition of the folio.

The year should be the NS 337 corresponding to 1217 CE.[294] From the appearance, the first *vajra* looks to some extent realistic one and the second one more like florally stylised one. Both are drawn vertically and their height corresponds to one line of the folio. A stylised *puṣpikā* can be found after the author line (*kṛtir ācāryaśāntidevasya* ... 'the work of preceptor Śāntideva ...') in line no. 5 and before the verse '*ye dharmā* ...' In this case, the stylised *puṣpikā* can probably be interpreted as a representation of a *padma* ('lotus') pairing the *vajra*.

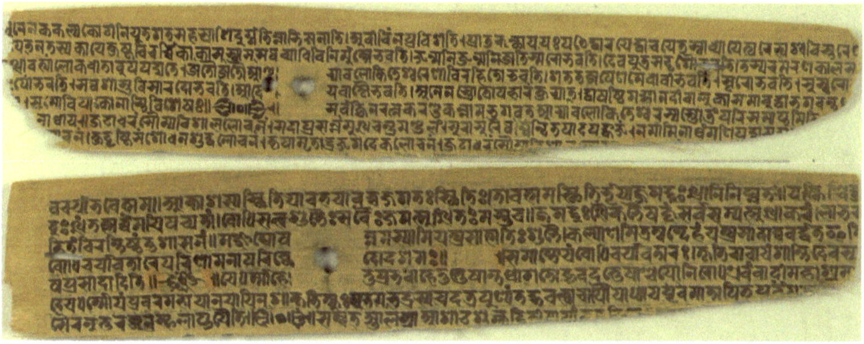

Fig. 3.6.2.1.6-I: Realistic and stylised *vajra*s after the chapter colophon and colophon, fol.? © KL

	[KL 127 / NGMPP C 14/5_?5_BCC_1217][295]
	[KL 127 / NGMPP C 14/5_?7_BD_1217][296]

Fig. 3.6.2.1.6-II: Realistic and stylised *vajra*s after the colophon and chapter colophon

294 Working on one of the texts of this MTM, Szántó 2017 recently suggested the date for the part of the MTM as NS 237 corresponding to 1117 CE. It seems he might have also read the same date that we find in the part of the text of the *Bodhicaryāvatāra* and confused with the first letter-numeral of the year (). He probably read it by mistakenly as the letter-numeral for '200'. However, this first letter-numeral probably stands here for '300', see for the letter-numeral for '300', Bendall 1883, Letter-numerals, note; see also Bühler 1896, Tafel IX, column XX, row for the letter-numeral '300'. In this case the year should, therefore, probably be the NS 337 corresponding to 1217 CE.

295 In the text of the *Āryavalokiteśvarastotra*.

296 In the text of the *Bodhicaryāvatāra*.

Manuscript of the *Aṣṭasāhasrikā Prajñāparamitā* (KL 18 / NGMPP C 103/2)

As stated, the manuscript of the *Aṣṭasāhasrikā Prajñāparamitā* (ca. 12th c.) (KL 18 / NGMPP C 103/2) contains significant items of symbols (see sections 3.5.1 above and 3.6.2.4.2 below). Among others, we find before the 14th chapter colophon on 112r6 a stylised *puṣpikā* and after the chapter colophon a florally stylised *vajra*. The *vajra* looks very similar to the *vajra*s that we have seen in the aforementioned MTM of the *Bodhicaryāvatāra*, *Āryavalokiteśvarastotra* etc. (KL 127 / NGMPP C 14/5). Also in this context the stylised *puṣpikā* can probably be interpreted as a representation of a *padma* ('lotus') that pairs the *vajra*.

Fig. 3.6.2.1.6-III: Stylised *puṣpikā* and stylised *vajra* before and after chapter colophon, fol. 112r © KL

[KL 18 / NGMPP C 103/2_112r6_BCC_12th]

[KL 18 / NGMPP C 103/2_112r6_ACC_12th]

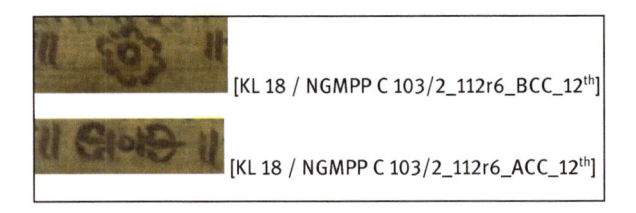

Fig. 3.6.2.1.6-IV: Stylised *puṣpikā* and florally stylised *vajra* before and after the chapter colophon

Manuscript of the *Aṣṭasāhasrikā Prajñāparamitā* (NAK 3/359 / NGMPP A 35/11)

The manuscript of the *Aṣṭasāhasrikā Prajñāparamitā*[297] (ca. 12th c.) (NAK 3/359 / NGMPP A 35/11) displays further remarkable instances with regard to symbols. Before a chapter colophon on line no. 1 there is a stylised *puṣpikā* on the floral

297 The manuscript contains 68 folios and is in incomplete state. Many folios seem to be missing or perhaps they are misplaced in bundles of other manuscripts. Among available folios, some are broken on the margins (such as the folio in Fig. 3.6.2.1.6-V) and one folio is already in fragmentary condition. There is no date on the available folios. The proposed approximate date for this manuscript is based on the palaeographical ground.

type of pedestal[298] and after the chapter colophon a florally stylised *vajra* in line no. 2 drawn vertically, on a lotus-like element. Additionally the *vajra* contains further elements on the left and right sides. Both symbols are drawn in 'red' ink. Most part of the chapter colophon is lost due to the damaged condition of the leaf, however, one can still read some part of it.[299] In this case this should clearly be the second chapter colophon (see note below).

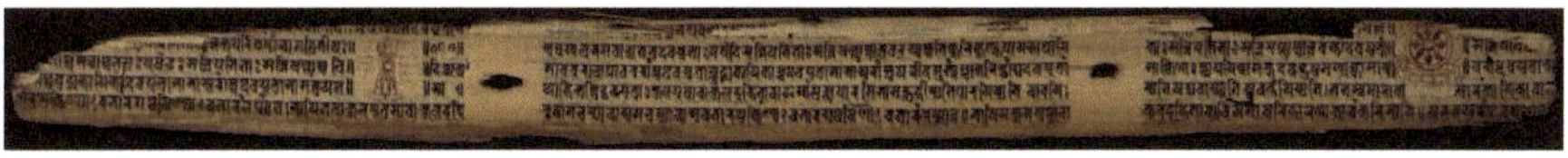

Fig. 3.6.2.1.6-V: Stylised *puṣpikā* and florally stylised *vajra* before and after the chapter colophon, fol.? © NAK

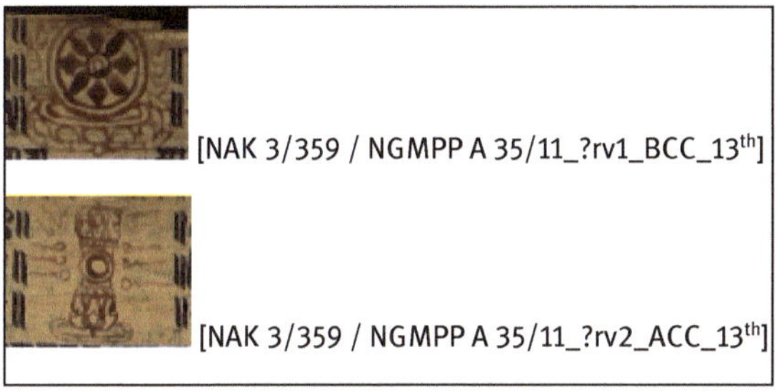

Fig. 3.6.2.1.6-VI: Stylised *puṣpikā* and florally stylised *vajra* before and after the chapter colophon

Manuscript of the *Sādhanamālā* (NAK 3/387 / NGMPP B 24/11)

In the manuscript of the *Sādhanamālā*[300] ('Garland of Realisation') (ca. 13th c.) (NAK 3/387 / NGMPP B 24/11) we find a *viśvavajra* on 146v2 and it appears after the line (*āryamārīcīdhāriṇīpāṭhopadeśa*(!) ||).[301] After the symbol we find invoca-

298 Some scholars have interpreted similar types of symbols as *dharmacakra*, e.g. Mevissen 1997, 43, Tafel 8. In the example the symbol appears at the very end of the text in one Mongolian block print containing the *Pañcarakṣā*.
299 The remaining part can be read *śakraparivartto nāma dvitīyaḥ* ('... the second chapter, namely the Śakra ...').
300 See Shastri 1915, 83; Bhattacharyya 1925, xii with siglum N.
301 Its translation as follows 'the teaching lesson on the *Dhāriṇī* of *Āryamārīcī*'.

tions.[302] The symbol looks like an almost realistic one. Generally the height of the symbol is supposed to be three lines of the folio. However, the folio contains only two lines of the 'main text' in the upper part and a content list which is written in column-like structure in the lower part on the folio. The content list seems to have been written later with the different hand.

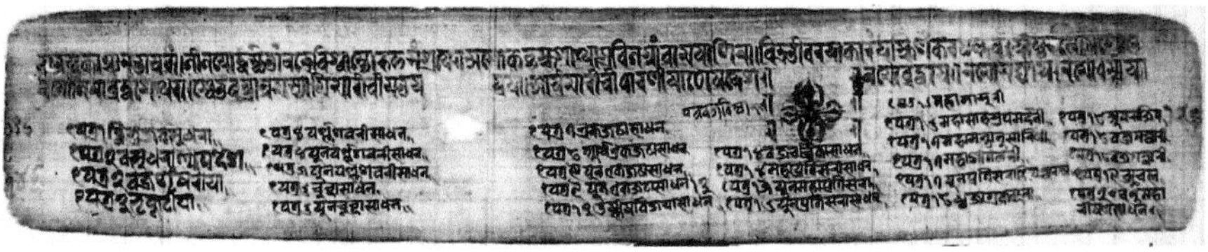

Fig. 3.6.2.1.6-VII: Nearly realistic *viśvavajra* after the colophon, fol. 146v © NAK

[NAK 3/387 / NGMPP B 24/11_146v2_AC_13th]

Fig. 3.6.2.1.6-VIII: Nearly realistic *viśvavajra* after the colophon

MTM of the *Bālārkastutiṭīkā, Daśakrodhāgnisalokasaṅgraha, Pañcatathāgatastuti* (KL 45 / NGMPP C 4/11)

In the MTM containing texts of the *Bālārkastutiṭīkā*, *Daśakrodhāgnisalokasaṅgraha*, *Pañcatathāgatastuti* (NS 545 / 1415 CE) (KL 45 / NGMPP C 4/11) there is also a symbol before the colophon in the part of the *Daśakrodhāgnisalokasaṅgraha* on 37v5 possibly to be understood as a florally stylised *vajra* (see Fig. 3.6.2.1.6-XXVIII below). The symbol contains a circle in the centre, two leaf-like elements on the left and right sides and the leaves are divided almost in half

302 They read *namo buddhāya* || *namo*(!) *saṅghāya* | *namo dharmaya*(!) || ('homage to Buddha, bow to Saṅgha, bow to Dharma'). For the translation, minor errors have been read in the most possible correct way.

by a line. Following which everything is enclosed by an outer line giving the symbol a kind of floral shape.[303]

After the colophon we find a stylised *puṣpikā* which may be interpreted here as a *padma*. As mentioned above, the symbols (i.e. the florally stylised *vajra* and stylised *puṣpikā*) may also be understood as representations of the male and female deities or practitioners corresponding to the *upāya* and *prajñā* respectively.

The manuscript contains two dates. The first can be found after the colophon of the *Bālārkastutiṭīkā* on 37r5[304] and corresponds to 1415 CE. The second date is written on the bottom margin on 37v[305] and looks rather modern compared to the hand of the aforementioned first date. It was probably added later. The line of date is preceded by a *siddham* symbol.

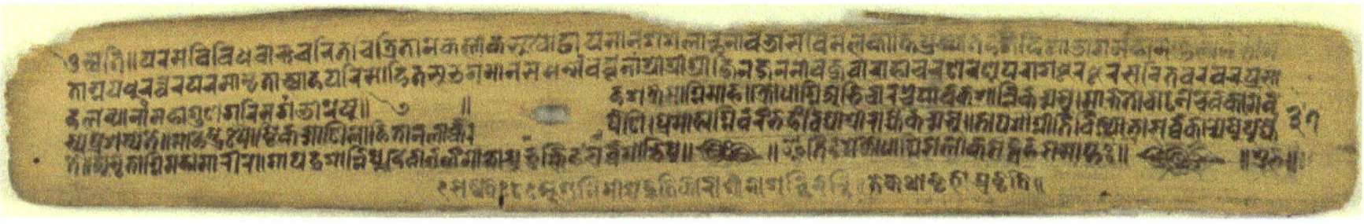

Fig. 3.6.2.1.6-IX: Florally stylised *vajra* before the colophon, fol. 37v © KL

[KL 45 / NGMPP C 4/113_7v5_BCC_1425]

Fig. 3.6.2.1.6-X: Florally stylised *vajra* before the colophon

303 An almost similar type of florally stylised *vajra*s, however, without outer line also appear in later paper manuscripts e.g. in the manuscript of the *Laṅkāvatāra* (NS 910 / 1790 CE) (NAK 3/610 / B 88/2) on 13v3; in the manuscript of the *Samādhirājasūtra* (NS 960 / 1840 CE) (NAK 3/611 / NGMPP B 94/1) on 87v3; in the manuscript of the *Gaṇḍavyūha* (ca. 19th c.) (NAK 3/258 / NGMPP A 110/4) on 101v5, 137v3.

304 It reads *nepālikābde* 545 *pauṣe* | *śubhaṃ* || ('in the Nepāla era 545 [and] in the [mongh of] *pauṣa*. Auspiciousness')

305 It reads *samvat* 585 ... ('the [Nepāla] era 585 ...).

Manuscript of the *Pañcarakṣā* (NAK 1/1114 / NGMPP A 47/15)

An example of an almost fully-fledged realistic *viśvavajra* can be found in the manuscript of the *Pañcarakṣā* ('Five Protections') (NS 596 / 1476 CE) (NAK 1/1114 / NGMPP A 47/15) on the left string-hole space on 99r. In this case the string-hole replaces the centre core of the *viśvavajra*. On the same folio there are four stylised *puṣpikā*s where one finds the colophon[306] and other colophonic features. In addition, a florally stylised *viśvavajra* is to be found on the left string-hole space in another manuscript (ca. 15th/16th c.) (KL 108 / C 11/4) which contains the same text (see below).

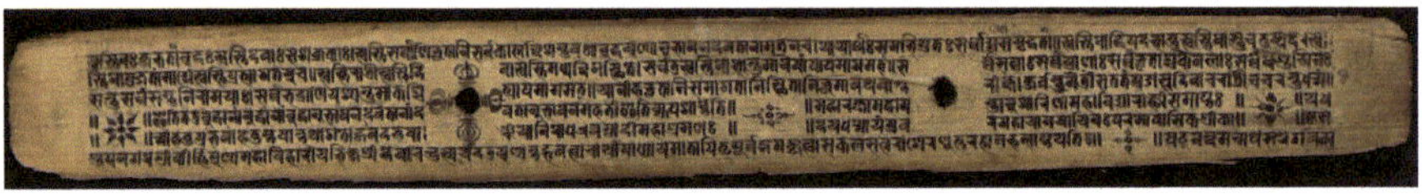

Fig. 3.6.2.1.6-XI: Realistic *viśvavajra* around the string-hole, fol. 99r © NAK

[NAK 1/1114 / NGNPP A 47/15_99r_LSH_1476]

Fig. 3.6.2.1.6-XII: Realistic *viśvavajra* around the string-hole

Manuscript of the *Pañcarakṣā* (KL 108 / NGMPP C 11/4)

We also find, one florally stylised *viśvavajra* in another manuscript of the *Pañcarakṣā* (ca. 15th/16th c.) (KL 108 / NGMPP C 11/4) around the left string-hole space and one stylised *puṣpikā* around the right string-hole space on 63v. The stylised *puṣpikā* can probably be understood in this context as a *padma* pairing the stylised *viśvavajra*. As with the aforementioned example, the string-hole replaces the centre core of the *viśvavajra* and the centre part (i.e. circle) of the stylised *puṣpikā*. Furthermore, we find four petal-like elements in the *viśvavajra* which may be understood as pointing of the four directions.

306 The colophon on 99r4 reads *mahārakṣā mahāmantrānuśāriṇī mahāvidyārājñī samāptaḥ*(!) || ('[thus], the great protection, the *Mahāmantrānuśāriṇī*, the queen of great wisdom is concluded').

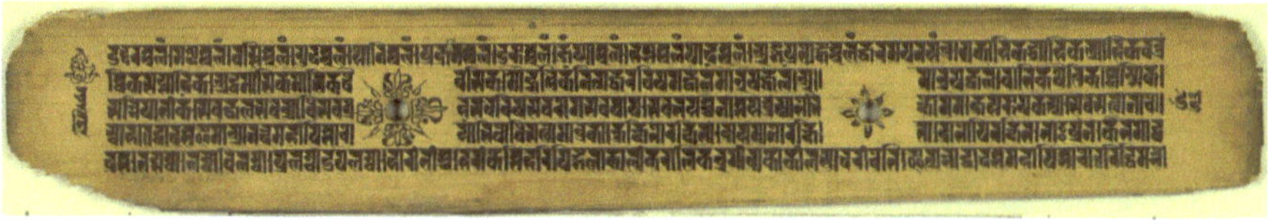

Fig. 3.6.2.1.6-XIII: Florally stylised *viśvavajra* and stylised *puṣpikā* around the string-holes, fol. 63v © KL

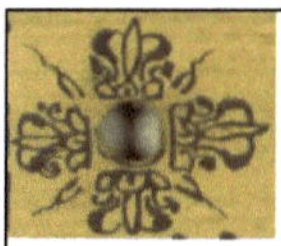

[KL 108 / NGMPP C 11/4_63v_LSH_15th/16th]

[KL 108 / NGMPP C 11/4_63v_RSH_15th/16th]

Fig. 3.6.2.1.6-XIV: Florally stylised *viśvavajra* and stylised *puṣpikā* around the string-holes

Manuscript of the *Pañcarakṣā* (KL 105 / NGMPP C 11/2)

In another manuscript (ca. 17th c.)[307] (KL 105 / NGMPP C 11/2) containing the same text as the aforementioned manuscript there is one stylised simple

---

307 We do not find the date on the existing folios in the manuscript. The penultimate folio (168rv) is in fragmentary condition and most of the lower part of the folio is broken. Furthermore, the majority of the text in the fragmentary folio is also faded. In the colophonic part we find mentioning of the name of country and name of a King. It reads on 167v5–168r1 as follows *svastiḥ śrīnepālaviṣaye rājadhirājapa*[168r1]*meśvaraśrīkusaratnamalladevasya*(!) *vijayajye*(!) ('heil! The glorious Nepāla kingdom of the venerable king of great kings, supreme lord, Kusaratnamalladeva'). Before and after the line we find blank spaces. Many parts of the *akṣara*s on 168r1 are faded. Therefore, some part of the text is illegible. A King called Kusaratnamalla can roughly be read but we know little about him and his period of reign. The last folio (rv) is mainly blank excluding a short line on recto. The line seems to have been written later in a different hand. It reads mentioning a name of another King: *svati*(!) *śrīmatviṣayarājādhirājapala*(!)*meśvaraparamabhaṭṭāraka śrī* 3 *lakṣakṣminalasiṃhamalladevasya vijayalāryya*(!) ('hail! In the victorious [kingdom] of triple venerable Lakṣakṣminalasiṃhamalladeva, paramount sovereign, supreme lord, king of great kings of glorious kingdom). In this case the King should probably be Laṣmīnarasiṃhamalla, although it reads the name as 'Lakṣakṣminalasiṃhamalla'. Actually

puṣpikā on 167v1 before the colophon which might be understood as a *padma* in this context and after the colophon a florally stylised *viśvavajra* on 167v2.[308] After the *viśvavajra* is the verse *'ye dharmā ...'* can be found. The height of the *puṣpikā* is one line of the folio and the height of the *viśvavajra* two lines of the folio. Additionally, the *viśvavajra* contains four lines which may be understood as pointing out the four directions.

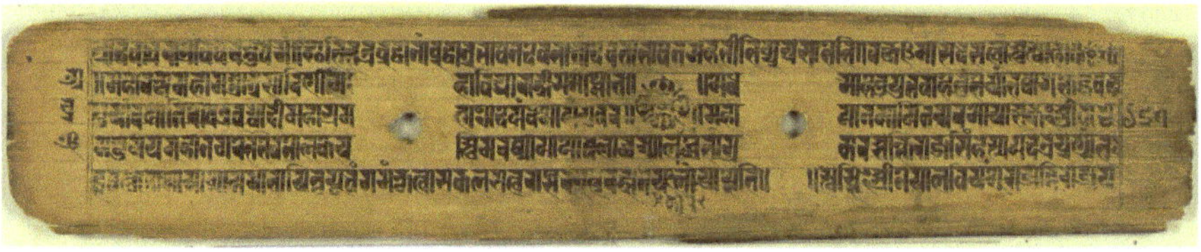

Fig. 3.6.2.1.6-XV: Stylised *puṣpikā* and florally stylised *viśvavajra* before and after the colophon, fol. 167v © KL

[KL 105 / NGMPP C 11/2_167v1_BC_17th]

[KL 105 / NGMPP C 11/2_167v2_AC_17th]

Fig. 3.6.2.1.6-XVI: Stylised *puṣpikā* and florally stylised *viśvavajra* before and after the colophon

MTM of the *Sugatāvadāna, Vasudhārādevīvratakathā* (NAK 5/235 / NGMPP B 102/5)

In the MTM (NAK 5/235 / NGMPP B 102/5) containing two texts i.e. the *Sugatāvadāna* (on 1r–80r) and the *Vasudhārādevīvratakathā* (on 81v–96) there is a great variety of symbols before and/or after the chapter colophons and at the

King Laṣmīnarasiṃhamalla reigned in Kathmandu ca. 1620–1641 CE (see Regmi 1966, 55–60). With this we could probably date this manuscript to no later than ca. 17th c.

308 The colophon reads *mahārakṣā mahāmantrānusāriṇi ma¦⊡mahāvidyārājñī(!) samāptati(!)* ('thus, the great protection, the *Mahāmantrānusāriṇi*, the queen of great wisdom is completed').

end of particular sections etc. The manuscript is written in *nīlapatra* ('black paper') and can probably be dated ca. 18th c.[309]

There are circles (type no. 2),[310] *siddham* symbols[311] and various stylised *puṣpikās*[312] some of which can probably be understood as *padma* according to the context (e.g. see Fig. 3.6.2.1.6-XVII for selected stylised *puṣpikās* on 39r1, 69v1, 75v4 below).

There are also six florally stylised *vajra*s on 6v4, 38r5, 58v4, 66r3, 69v2 and 77v5 (see Fig. 3.6.2.1.6-XVII). As seen below all *vajra*s are drawn differently to some degree. Several contain additional elements such as lines or petals and others are drawn simply. The height of all *vajra*s is one line of the folio. We also find florally stylised *viśvavajra*s on 26v2, 39r1 and 78r1. The first two *viśvavajra*s (on 26v2, 39r1) appear before the chapter colophons and their height is two lines of the folio. The latter *viśvavajra* (on 78r1) appears after the chapter colophon and its height is one line of the folio.

Additionally, two florally stylised *śrīvatsa*s ('endless knot') are on 70r2 and 75v4. The second *śrīvatsa* contains dots in the inner part. The height of the first *śrīvatsa* is one line of the folio whereas the height of the second is two lines (see also *śrīvatsa* and other symbols in the manuscript of the *Sugatāvadānādisaṅgraha* (NS 1006 / 1886 CE) (NAK 4/1381 / NGMPP A 126/4) below). There is also a florally stylised *śaṇkha* ('conch-shell') on 66r1.

[26v2_BCC_17th/18th]

[38r5_APS_17th/18th]

[39r1_BCC_17th/18th]

[39r1_ACC_17th/18th]

309 The date is suggested on the basis of the similarities of the overall layout, symbols and palaeographical evidence that can be seen in the dated (*nīlapatra*) manuscript containing the *Aparimitāyurdhāraṇīsūtra* and *Sarvadurgatipariśodhana* (NS 820 / 1700 CE) (CUL Add.1623).

310 On 4r1, 7r1, 14r1, 16r2, 16r5, 20v5, 21v3, 26v3, 28r1, 35v5, 37r5, 46v1, 47r3, 50v2, 60v5, 61v4, 63r4, 65r4, 70v4, 71v3, 72v1, 72v3, 72v5, 73r1, 73r5, 73v1, 73v2, 73v5, 74r1, 74r2, 74r4, 74v1, 74v3, 74v5, 75r3, 78v5, 79r1, 80r5, 80v1.

311 On 28r3, 36v5, 65r4, 71r1, 78r5, 78v3, 79r3, 79v1, 80r4.

312 See 4v1, 6v5, 11v4, 16r4, 22v2–3, 24r2, 28r3, 29r5, 30v1, 34r1, 35r1, 35r3, 36v3, 39r1, 39v4, 45r1, 45r4–5, 48r1, 57v2, 58v2, 58v5, 62v1, 64v3, 65r5, 65v2–3, 66r1, 68v2, 69r4, 69v1, 71r1, 71r3, 75r4, 75v3, 78v1, 79r2, 79v4, 80r1, 80r4, 80v1.

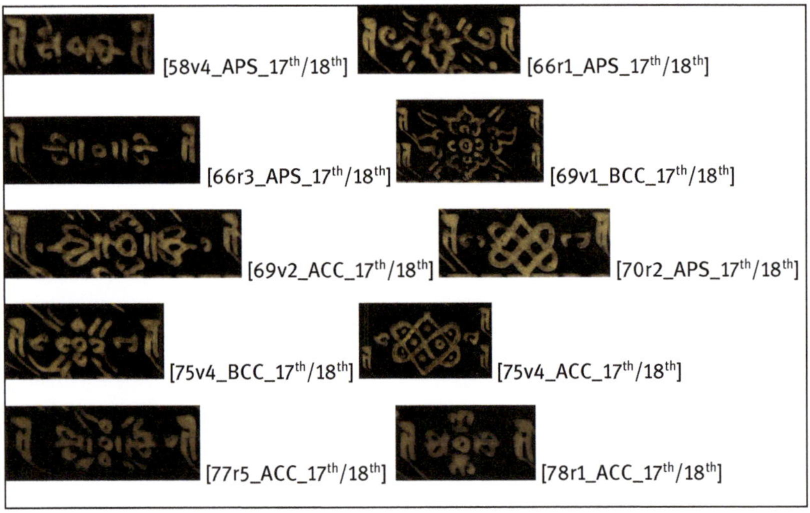

Fig. 3.6.2.1.6-XVII: Various symbols

Manuscript of the *Lalitavistara* (NAK 4/9 / NGMPP B 99/5)

In the (paper) manuscript of the *Lalitavistara* ('the Play in Full') (NS 829 / 1709 CE) (NAK 4/9 / NGMPP B 99/5) there are various kinds of symbols, such as circles, a variety of stylised *puṣpikā*s (such as on 192v6), a realistic simple *puṣpikā* with a stalk, a florally stylised *vajra* and a realistic *viśvavajra*. The realistic *puṣpikā* appears before the 21st chapter colophon on 232v,[313] and in this context may be interpreted as a *padma*. After the same chapter colophon on the same line no. 6 we find a florally stylised *vajra*. The *vajra* comprises two leaf-like elements on the left and right with a vertical line at their centre, one circle and two sets of three dots in the centre. An almost realistic *viśvavajra* is drawn after the colophon on 299r3.[314]

313 The chapter colophon reads on 232v6 *māragharṣaṇaparivartto nāmaikaviṃśatimaḥ* ([thus], the 21st chapter, namely the *māragharṣaṇa* [is concluded]).

314 The colophon reads on 299r2–3 *samāptaṃ cedaṃ sarvabodhisatvacaryāprasthānam iti* || *lalitavistaro*(!) *nāma mahāyānasūtraṃ parisamāptaṃ* ('thus, the path of deeds of all Bodhisattvas is also entirely completed. The *Mahāyānasūtra* called the Play in Full is entirely concluded').

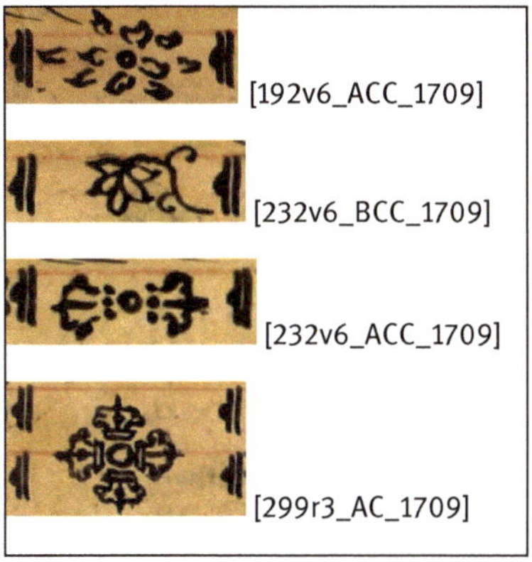

Fig. 3.6.2.1.6-XVIII: Stylised and realistic *puṣpikā*s, stylised *vajra* and realistic *viśvavajra*

Manuscript of the *Laṅkāvatāra* (NAK 3/610 / NGMPP B 88/2)

In terms of symbols, the (paper) manuscript of the *Laṅkāvatāra* ('the Descent into *Laṅkā*') (NS 910 / 1790 CE) (NAK 3/610 / NGMPP B 88/2) exhibits further noteworthy examples. In the manuscript we find, among others, two symbols that may be understood as florally stylised *vajra*s. The first florally stylised *vajra* appears after the 1st chapter colophon on 13v3 here drawn vertically with its height corresponding to two lines of the folio. A nearly similar *vajra* can also be found after the chapter colophon in the manuscript of the *Samādhirājasūtra* (NS 960 / 1840 CE) on 87v3 (see below).[315]

The second florally stylised *vajra* comprises two petal-like elements with a line its centre and appears before the 9th chapter colophon on 162v6. Near similar symbols can also be found e.g. in the MTM of the *Bālārkastutiṭīkā*, *Daśakrodhāgnisalokasaṅgraha*, *Pañcatathāgatastuti* on 37v (see Fig. 3.6.2.1.6-IX above);[316] in the manuscript of the *Gaṇḍavyūha* on 101v5, 137v3 (see below).[317]

Furthermore, some of the stylised *puṣpikā*s of this manuscript (such as on 13v2) share close similarities in appearance to symbols featuring in a few other manuscripts.[318]

---

315 See NAK 3/611 / NGMPP B 94/1.
316 See KL 45 / NGMPP C 4/11.
317 See NAK 3/258 / NGMPP A 110/4.
318 See the manuscript of the *Samādhirājasūtra* (NS 960 / 1840 CE) (NAK 3/611 / NGMPP B 94/1) on 66v3, 87v3; in the manuscript of the *Prajñāpāramitā* (NS 961 / 1841 CE) (NAK 4/215 / NGMPP B 90/2) on 55r1; in the manuscript of the *Saddharmapuṇḍarīkasūtra* (NS 962 / 1842 CE) (NAK 4/217 / NGMPP

 [13v2_BCC_1790]  [13v3_ACC_1790]

 [162v6_BCC_1790]

Fig. 3.6.2.1.6-XX: Stylised *puṣpikā* and florally stylised *vajra*s

Manuscript of the *Samādhirājasūtra* (NAK 3/611 / NGMPP B 94/1)

Additionally, the (paper) manuscript of the *Samādhirājasūtra* ('the King of *Samādhi*') (NS 960 / 1840 CE) (NAK 3/611 / NGMPP B 94/1) displays some striking symbols. Of the various stylised *puṣpikā*s before and/or after the chapter colophons (such as on 66v3), we find two florally stylised *vajra*s and a few florally stylised *viśvavajra*s in this manuscript.

The first *vajra* appears after the 20th chapter colophon on 87v3 and is drawn vertically at a height of nearly two lines of the folio. The second florally stylised *vajra* can be found before the 35th chapter colophon on 172v7. However, other additional elements such as 'curved lines' or 'half circles' with dot(s) appear around it. After that a florally stylised *viśvavajra* containing an additional element appears after the chapter colophon on 173r1, the height of the *viśvavajra* is two lines of the folio.

There are florally stylised symbols on 66v4 that may be interpreted as florally stylised *viśvavajra*. The symbol contains a circle at the centre, four leaf-like elements on four sides divided nearly in half by a line. After that it is enclosed by an outer line giving the whole symbol a kind of floral form. In this context one may speculative the use of the extra line is as a protective element for the *viśvavajra*. On the left and right sides of the *viśvavajra* we find elements with a 'half-circle' or a 'curved line' facing outside containing a 'dot' or 'line'. Almost similar symbols can also be found in other manuscripts.[319] Furthermore, some of the stylised *puṣpikā*s of this manuscript (such as on 66v3) display close similarities in appearance to symbols found in other manuscripts.[320]

A 128/20) on 126r2; in the manuscript of the *Gaṇḍavyūha* (NS 966 / 1846 CE) (NAK 3/284 / NGMPP A 110/1) on 223v3; in the manuscript of the *Gaṇḍavyūha* (NS 972 / 1852 CE) (NAK 5/75 / NGMPP A 110/3) on 130v2; in the manuscript of the *Gaṇḍavyūha* (ca. 19th c.) (NAK 3/258 / NGMPP A 110/4) on 53r2.

319 E.g. in the manuscript of the *Prajñāpāramitā* (1841 CE) (NAK 4/215 / NGMPP B 90/2) on 132r5; in the manuscript of the *Saddharmapuṇḍarīkasūtra* (NS 962 / 1842 CE) (NAK 4/217 / NGMPP A 128/20) on 33v3; in the manuscript of the *Gaṇḍavyūha* (1852 CE) (NAK 5/75 / NGMPP A 110/3) on 38r8 (without outer line); in the manuscript of the *Gaṇḍavyūha* (ca. 19th c.) (NAK 3/258 / NGMPP A 110/4) on 56v3, 177r6 (without outer line).

320 E.g. in the manuscript of the *Laṅkāvatāra* (NS 910 / 1790 CE) (NAK 3/610 / NGMPP B 88/2) on 13v2 (see above); in the manuscript of the *Prajñāpāramitā* (NS 961 / 1841 CE) (NAK 4/215 / B

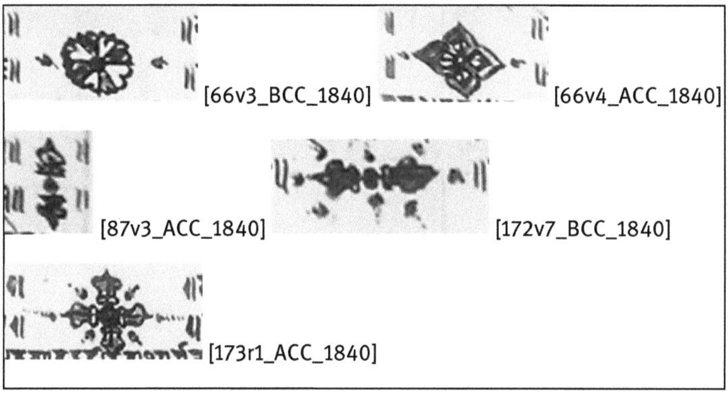

Fig. 3.6.2.1.6-XXI: Stylised *puṣpikā*, florally stylised *vajra*s and *viśvavajra*s

Manuscript of the *Prajñāpāramitā* (NAK 4/215 / NGMPP B 90/2)

In the (paper) manuscript of the *Prajñāpāramitā* (NS 961 / 1841 CE) (NAK 4/215 / NGMPP B 90/2) among various kinds of stylised *puṣpikā*s (such as on 55r1) and *siddham* symbols, there are some florally stylised *viśvavajra*s (e.g. on 132r5). The appearance of the *viśvavajra*s in this manuscript closely resemble florally stylised *viśvavajra*s found in other manuscripts.[321] The appearance of the stylised *puṣpikā*s in this manuscript (e.g. 55r1) display close similarities to symbols found in other manuscripts.[322]

90/2) on 55r1; in the manuscript of the *Saddharmapuṇḍarīkasūtra* (NS 962 / 1842 CE) (NAK 4/217 / NGMPP A 128/20) on 126r2; in the manuscript of the *Gaṇḍavyūha* (NS 966 / 1846 CE) (NAK 3/284 / NGMPP A 110/1) on 223v3; in the manuscript of the *Gaṇḍavyūha* (NS 972 / 1852 CE) (NAK 5/75 / NGMPP A 110/3) on 130v2; in the manuscript of the *Gaṇḍavyūha* (ca. 19th c.) (NAK 3/258 / NGMPP A 110/4) on 53r2.

321 See the manuscript of the *Samādhirājasūtra* (NS 960 / 1840 CE) (NAK 3/611 / NGMPP B 94/1) on 66v4; in the manuscript of the *Saddharmapuṇḍarīkasūtra* (NS 962 / 1842 CE) (NAK 4/217 / NGMPP A 128/20) on 33v3; in the manuscript of the *Gaṇḍavyūha* (1852 CE) (NAK 5/75 / NGMPP A 110/3) on 38r8 (without outer line); in the manuscript of the *Gaṇḍavyūha* (ca. 19th c.) (NAK 3/258 / NGMPP A 110/4) on 56v3, 177r6 (without outer line).

322 For instance, in the manuscript of the *Laṅkāvatāra* (NS 910 / 1790 CE) (NAK 3/610 / NGMPP B 88/2) on 13v2; in the manuscript of the *Samādhirājasūtra* (NS 960 / 1840 CE) (NAK 3/611 / NGMPP B 94/1) on 66v3, 87v3; in the manuscript of the *Saddharmapuṇḍarīkasūtra* (NS 962 / 1842 CE) (NAK 4/217 / NGMPP A 128/20) on 126r2; in the manuscript of the *Gaṇḍavyūha* (NS 966 / 1846 CE) (NAK 3/284 / NGMPP A 110/1) on 223v3; in the manuscript of the *Gaṇḍavyūha* (NS 972 / 1852 CE) (NAK 5/75 / NGMPP A 110/3) on 130v2; in the manuscript of the *Gaṇḍavyūha* (ca. 19th c.) (NAK 3/258 / NGMPP A 110/4) on 53r2.

Fig. 3.6.2.1.6-XXII: Stylised *puṣpikā* and florally stylised *viśvavajra*

Manuscript of the *Saddharmapuṇḍarīkasūtra* (NAK 4/217 / NGMPP A 128/20)

The (paper) manuscript of the *Saddharmapuṇḍarīkasūtra* (NS 962 / 1842 CE) (NAK 4/217 / NGMPP A 128/20) also exhibits remarkable examples of symbols. Among various kinds of stylised *puṣpikā*s the manuscript contains, two *siddham* symbols, one florally stylised *vajra*, one florally stylised *ṣaṭkoṇa* ('six-angled') symbol, and many florally stylised *viśvavajra*s such as the one after the chapter colophon on 33v3 (see Fig. 3.6.2.1.6-XXIII).

Many of the stylised *puṣpikā*s (see 126r2) in this manuscript are quite similar to stylised *puṣpikā*s in other manuscripts.[323] The florally stylised *vajra* before the chapter colophon on 183v4 in this manuscript is another striking example in terms of form. The symbol is drawn vertically containing additional elements such as two 'curved lines' and one semi-circle with a dot on left and right sides. After the same chapter colophon there is a *ṣaṭkoṇa* symbol demarcated by an outer line. Furthermore, the florally stylised *viśvavajra* in this manuscript are almost identical in form to symbols in other manuscripts.[324]

---

323 For instance, in the manuscript of the *Laṅkāvatāra* (NS 910 / 1790 CE) (NAK 3/610 / NGMPP B 88/2) on 13v2; in the manuscript of the *Samādhirājasūtra* (NS 960 / 1840 CE) (NAK 3/611 / NGMPP B 94/1) on 66v3, 87v3; in the manuscript of the *Prajñāpāramitā* (NS 961 / 1841 CE) (NAK 4/215 / B 90/2) on 55r1; in the manuscript of the *Gaṇḍavyūha* (NS 966 / 1846 CE) (NAK 3/284 / NGMPP A 110/1) on 223v3; in the manuscript of the *Gaṇḍavyūha* (NS 972 / 1852 CE) (NAK 5/75 / NGMPP A 110/3) on 130v2; in the manuscript of the *Gaṇḍavyūha* (ca. 19th c.) (NAK 3/258 / NGMPP A 110/4) on 53r2.

324 For instance, in the manuscript of the *Samādhirājasūtra* (NS 960 / 1840 CE) (NAK 3/611 / NGMPP B 94/1) on 66v4; in the manuscript of the *Prajñāpāramitā* (1841 CE) (NAK 4/215 / NGMPP B 90/2) on 132r5; in the manuscript of the *Gaṇḍavyūha* (1852 CE) (NAK 5/75 / NGMPP A 110/3) on 38r8 (without outer line); in the manuscript of the *Gaṇḍavyūha* (ca. 19th c.) (NAK 3/258 / NGMPP A 110/4) on 56v3.

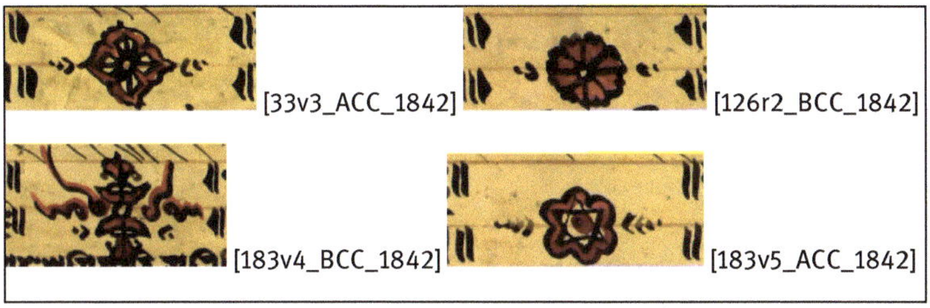

Fig. 3.6.2.1.6-XXIII: Stylised *puṣpikā*, florally stylised *vajra* and *viśvavajra*

Manuscript of the *Gaṇḍavyūha* (NAK 3/284 / NGMPP A 110/1)

The (paper) manuscript of the *Gaṇḍavyūha* ('the Array of Flowers') (NS 966 / 1846 CE) (NAK 3/284 / NGMPP A 110/1) includes, among various kinds of stylised *puṣpikās* and *siddham* symbols, a few florally stylised symbols which and their appearance, can most probably be understood as *viśvavajra* such as on 324r5. Like florally stylised *viśvavajras* in other manuscripts,[325] the *viśvavajra* is here are also comprised of four leaf-like elements in which a line touches the centre core or circle and the line parts the four leafy elements almost in half. In addition, the symbol contains an outer line which encloses its inner parts. Furthermore, some of the stylised *puṣpikās* (such as on 223v3) are identical to the stylised *puṣpikā* found in other manuscripts.[326]

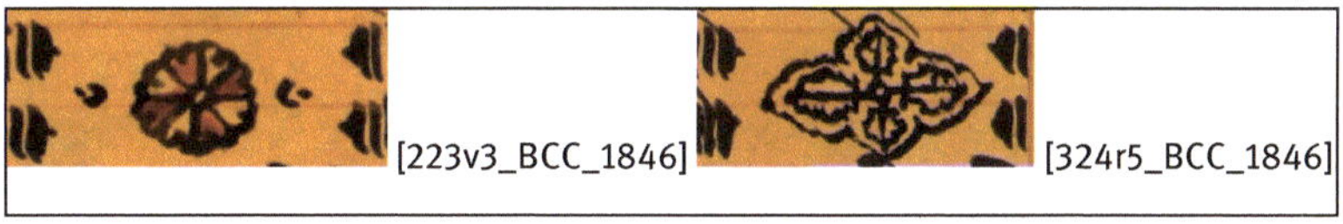

Fig. 3.6.2.1.6-XXIV: Stylised *puṣpikā* and florally stylised *viśvavajra*

325 See the manuscript of the *Samādhirājasūtra* (NS 960 / 1840 CE) (NAK 3/611 / NGMPP B 94/1) on 66v4; the manuscript of the *Prajñāpāramitā* (NS 961 / 1841 CE) (NAK 4/215 / NGMPP B 90/2) on 132r5; the manuscript of the *Saddharmapuṇḍarīkasūtra* (NS 962 / 1842 CE) (NAK 4/217 / NGMPP A 128/20) on 33v3 (see above); the manuscript of the *Gaṇḍavyūha* (1852 CE) (NAK 5/75 / NGMPP A 110/3) on 38r8 (without outer line); in the manuscript of the *Gaṇḍavyūha* (ca. 19th c.) (NAK 3/258 / NGMPP A 110/4) on 56v3.

326 See the manuscript of the *Laṅkāvatāra* (NS 910 / 1790 CE) (NAK 3/610 / NGMPP B 88/2) on 13v2; in the manuscript of the *Samādhirājasūtra* (NS 960 / 1840 CE) (NAK 3/611 / NGMPP B 94/1) on 66v3, 87v3; *Prajñāpāramitā* (NS 961 / 1841 CE) (NAK 4/215 / B 90/2) on 55r1; in the manuscript of the *Saddharmapuṇḍarīkasūtra* (NS 962 / 1842 CE) (NAK 4/217 / NGMPP A 128/20) on 126r2 (see above); in the manuscript of the *Gaṇḍavyūha* (NS 972 / 1852 CE) (NAK 5/75 / NGMPP A 110/3) on 130v2; in the manuscript of the *Gaṇḍavyūha* (ca. 19th c.) (NAK 3/258 / NGMPP A 110/4) on 53r2.

Manuscript of the *Gaṇḍavyūha* (NAK 5/75 / NGMPP A 110/3)

Another (paper) manuscript of the *Gaṇḍavyūha* (NS 972 / 1852 CE) (NAK 5/75 / NGMPP A 110/3) shows interesting examples of symbols. Among them are *siddham* symbols, various kinds of stylised *puṣpikā*s, a few florally stylised *vajra*s one florally stylised *viśvavajra* and a florally stylised *chattra* ('parasol'). Of these, one of the stylised *puṣpikā*s (see 130v2) is similar in appearance to symbols in other manuscripts.[327]

The florally stylised *vajra*s on 160v4, 167v4, 289v4 appear identical. The stylised *vajra* on 288v4 also displays many similarities to the aforementioned *vajra*s but here it is drawn vertically and contains an additional element hanging down on the left and right sides. This additional element may be understood as an offering like a 'piece of cloth' or 'scarf' or 'shawl' perhaps intended to pay homage to *vajra* i.e. a male practitioner or deity.

Additionally, there is a florally stylised *viśvavajra* on 38r8, the centre part of which looks similar to the florally stylised *viśvavajra*s of a few other manuscripts.[328] Here, the symbol is not enclosed by an outer line. However, on six sides of the *viśvavajra* there are elements with a 'semi-circle' or a 'curved line' facing outside containing a dot. There is also a florally stylised symbol on 289v4 possibly to be understood as *chattra*.

---

327 See the manuscript of the *Laṅkāvatāra* (NS 910 / 1790 CE) (NAK 3/610 / NGMPP B 88/2) on 13v2; in the manuscript of the *Samādhirājasūtra* (NS 960 / 1840 CE) (NAK 3/611 / NGMPP B 94/1) on 66v3, 87v3; in the manuscript of the *Prajñāpāramitā* (NS 961 / 1841 CE) (NAK 4/215 / B 90/2) on 55r1; in the manuscript of the *Saddharmapuṇḍarīkasūtra* (NS 962 / 1842 CE) (NAK 4/217 / NGMPP A 128/20) on 126r2; in the manuscript of the *Gaṇḍavyūha* (NS 966 / 1846 CE) (NAK 3/284 / NGMPP A 110/1) on 223v3; in the manuscript of the *Gaṇḍavyūha* (ca. 19th c.) (NAK 3/258 / NGMPP A 110/4) on 53r2.
328 For instance, in the manuscript of the *Samādhirājasūtra* (NS 960 / 1840 CE) (NAK 3/611 / NGMPP B 94/1) (see above); in the manuscript of the *Saddharmapuṇḍarīkasūtra* (NS 962 / 1842 CE) (NAK 4/217 / NGMPP A 128/20) on 33v3; in the manuscript of the *Gaṇḍavyūha* (ca. 19th c.) (NAK 3/258 / NGMPP A 110/4) on 56v3.

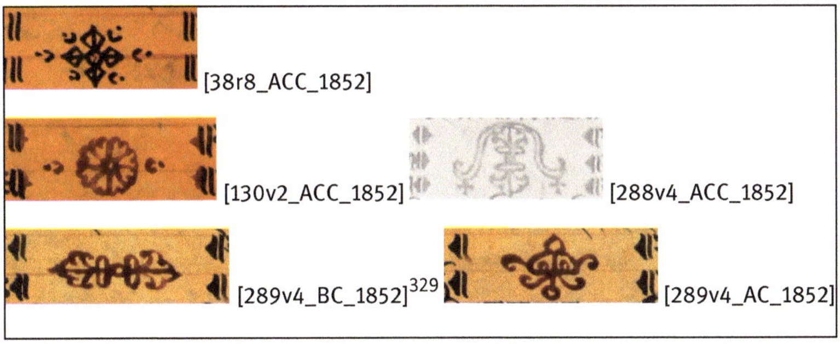

Fig. 3.6.2.1.6-XXV: Stylised *puṣpikā* and florally stylised *chattra*, *vajra*s and *viśvavajra*

Manuscript of the *Gaṇḍavyūha* (NAK 3/258 / NGMPP A 110/4)

Another (paper) manuscript of the *Gaṇḍavyūha* (19th c.) (NAK 3/258 / NGMPP A 110/4) exhibits further striking examples of symbols. These are some floral symbols e.g. on 101v5, 137v3, 326v2, 333v2 that may be interpreted as florally stylised *vajra*s.

The florally stylised *vajra*s on 101v5, 137v3 are composed of two leaf-like elements and one circle in the centre. Both leaf-like elements contain a line dividing them in half. They are drawn horizontally. However, the symbols on 137v3 and on 326v2 are drawn vertically containing lines that touch the top of the symbol and hang down on left and right sides. These lines may be interpreted as an offering object like a 'piece of cloth' or 'scarf' or 'shawl' as has just been seen on the top of the symbol in the manuscript of the *Gaṇḍavyūha* (NS 972 / 1852 CE) on 288v4.[330] The florally stylised *vajra*s (on 101v5, 333v2) look almost similar to symbols of other manuscripts.[331] Florally stylised *viśvavajra*s such as on 56v3, 177r6 (without an outer line) seem identical to symbols in other manuscripts.[332] Other stylised *puṣpikā*s such

329 Similar symbols can be found on 160v4_ACC, 167v4_ACC.
330 See NAK 5/75 / NGMPP A 110/3.
331 See the MTM of the *Bālārkastutiṭīkā*, *Daśakrodhāgnisalokasaṅgraha*, *Pañcatathāgatastuti* (NS 545 / 1415 CE) (KL 45 / NGMPP C 4/11) on 37v; in the manuscript of the *Laṅkāvatāra* (NS 910 / 1790 CE) (NAK 3/610 / B 88/2) on 13v3; in the manuscript of the *Samādhirājasūtra* (NS 960 / 1840 CE) (NAK 3/611 / NGMPP B 94/1) on 87v3.
332 E.g. in the manuscript of the *Samādhirājasūtra* (NS 960 / 1840 CE) (NAK 3/611 / NGMPP B 94/1) on 66v4; in the manuscript of the *Prajñāpāramitā* (1841 CE) (NAK 4/215 / NGMPP B 90/2) on 132r5; in the manuscript of the *Saddharmapuṇḍarīkasūtra* (NS 962 / 1842 CE) (NAK 4/217 / NGMPP A 128/20) on 33v3; in the manuscript of the *Gaṇḍavyūha* (1852 CE) (NAK 5/75 / NGMPP A 110/3) on 38r8 (without outer line), 399v1.

as on 53r2 in this manuscript appear identical to stylised *puṣpikā*s seen in the aforementioned manuscripts.[333]

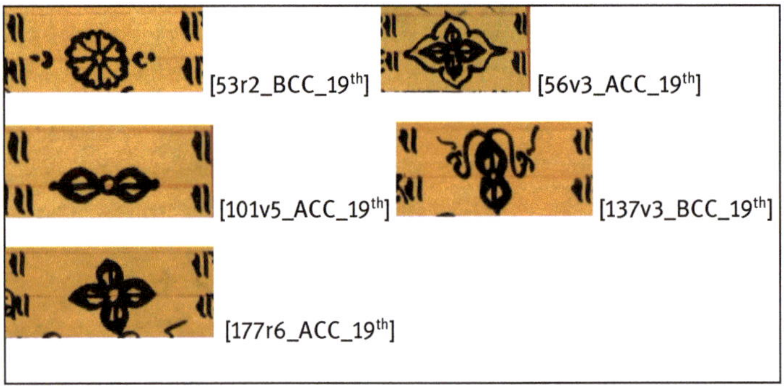

Fig. 3.6.2.1.6-XXVI: Stylised *puṣpikā*, florally stylised *vajra*s and *viśvavajra*s

MTM of the *Sugatāvadānādisaṅgraha* (NAK 4/1381 / NGMPP A 126/4)

The (paper) MTM containing Buddhist texts (NS 1006 / 1886 CE) (NAK 4/1381 / NGMPP A 126/4) exhibits unique examples on the use of symbols. Alongside *siddham* and stylised *puṣpika*s, a florally stylised *śrīvatsa* ('endless knot') in line no. 2, a *śaṅkha* ('conch shell') in line no. 2, a stylised *puṣpika* in line no. 5 which in this context is obviously to be interpreted as *padma*, a *chattra* ('parasol') in line no. 5, a *vajra* in line no. 7, a *dhvaja* ('banner') in line no. 9, a *matsyayugma* ('a pair fish') in line no. 9 here depicted in 'white' and 'red' pigment, a *kalaśa* ('vase', 'water pot') in line no. 12 and a *cāmarayugma* ('a pair fly-whisks') in line no. 12 almost at the end of the text on 74v[334] in the manuscript.[335]

---

333 See in the manuscript of the *Laṅkāvatāra* (NS 910 / 1790 CE) (NAK 3/610 / NGMPP B 88/2) on 13v2; in the manuscript of the *Samādhirājasūtra* (NS 960 / 1840 CE) (NAK 3/611 / NGMPP B 94/1) on 66v3, 87v3; in the manuscript of the *Prajñāpāramitā* (NS 961 / 1841 CE) (NAK 4/215 / B 90/2) on 55r1; in the manuscript of the *Saddharmapuṇḍarīkasūtra* (NS 962 / 1842 CE) (NAK 4/217 / NGMPP A 128/20) on 126r2; in the manuscript of the *Gaṇḍavyūha* (NS 966 / 1846 CE) (NAK 3/284 / NGMPP A 110/1) on 223v3; in the manuscript of the *Gaṇḍavyūha* (NS 972 / 1852 CE) (NAK 5/75 / NGMPP A 110/3) on 130v2.

334 We do not have a running foliation from the beginning to the end in the manuscript (save for the modern example on the bottom left margin of the folio). A new foliation number is found for each new text beginning with '1' on the upper left and bottom right margins of the manuscript.

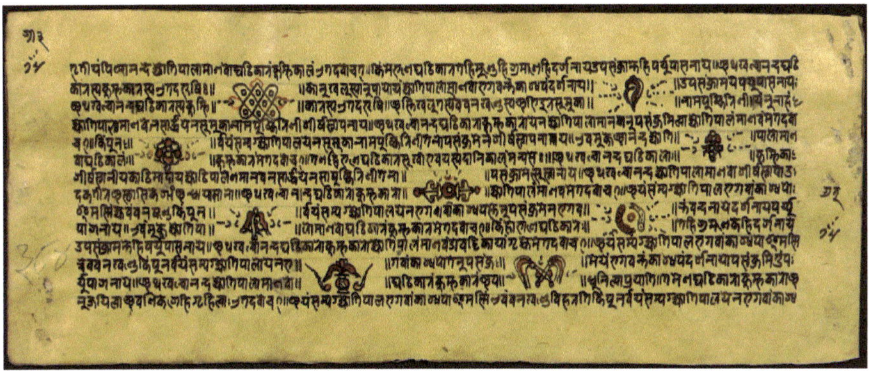

Fig. 3.6.2.1.6-XXVII: Various stylised symbols, fol. 74v © NAK

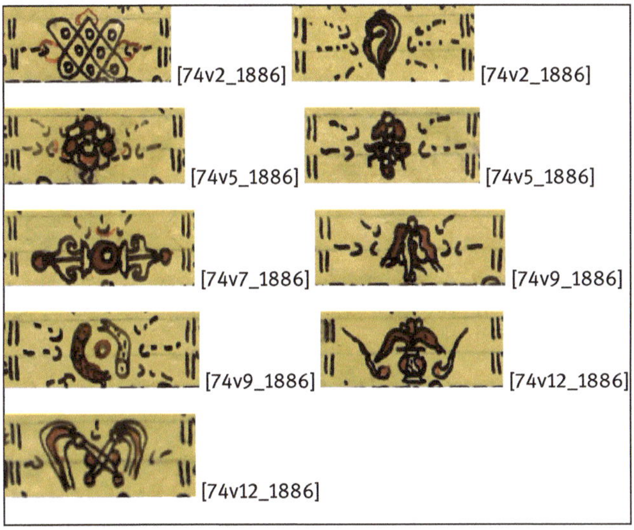

Fig. 3.6.2.1.6-XXVIII: Various florally stylised symbols

335 Here one would normally expect *aṣṭamaṅgala* symbols ('eight auspicious symbols') such as *chattra*, *matsyayugma*, *kalaśa*, *padma*, *śaṅkha*, *śrivatsa*, *dhvaja*, *dharmacakra* that have been of popular use in the Buddhist tradition in various areas of the sub-continent and beyond in diverse places and objects. Here we have a set of nine symbols. The *dharmacakra* is missing. *Cāmarayugma* and *vajra* have been added to the group.

There are two florally stylised *vajra*s on 1v in line no. 1 at the beginning of one of the texts (i.e. *Vajrasattvakāya*) in the same manuscript after the invocation[336] and after the first half of a verse. Both *vajra*s have been drawn vertically containing additional elements on the left and right sides and their height corresponds to two lines of the folio. Furthermore, it is noteworthy that in the near centre of the folio there is a miniature of the Vajrasattva holding a *vajra* in his right hand. In this context one may deduce the scribe was probably aware of the textual content he was copying which is why he drew the florally stylised *vajra*s that appear after the invocation and the first half of a verse on the folio.

Preliminary conclusions

Attestations of the use of similar types of florally stylised symbols and other new examples in the MTM containing the texts of the *Bālārkastutiṭīkā*, *Daśakrodhāgnisalokasaṅgraha*, *Pañcatathāgatastuti* (KL 45 / NGMPP C 4/11) before the colophon of the *Daśakrodhāgnisalokasaṅgraha* on 37v5, and near similar florally stylised symbols are in other manuscripts.[337] There is a near similar symbol on the upper part of the pillar of one of the *stūpas*[338] at Swayambhunath, Kathmandu (see Figs. 3.6.2.1.6-XXIX and 3.6.2.1.6-XXXI (left)) which is most likely a representation of a *vajra*.[339] We may assume here that the florally stylised symbols of the aforementioned manuscripts are florally stylised *vajra*s.

Attestations of florally stylised symbols seen in the aforementioned manuscripts[340] are also be found e.g. on the upper part of the other side of the pillar of the

336 It reads *oṃ namaḥ guruvajrasattvāyaḥ*(!) ('oṃ, homage to the preceptor Vajrasattva').

337 See the manuscript of the *Laṅkāvatāra* (NS 910 / 1790 CE) (NAK 3/610 / B 88/2) on 13v3; in the manuscript of the *Samādhirājasūtra* (NS 960 / 1840 CE) (NAK 3/611 / NGMPP B 94/1) on 87v3; in the manuscript of the *Gaṇḍavyūha* (ca. 19th c.) (NAK 3/258 NGMPP A 110/4) on 101v5, 137v3.

338 This *stūpa* is located in the western part of the premises of Swayambhunath near the entrance to the main *stūpa*.

339 Dr Costantino Moretti (École française d'Extrême-Orient, Paris) tells of the use of quite similar types of *vajra*s can also be found in some manuscripts from Dunhuang, for instance, in manuscript Pelliot chinois 2105 verso (Bibliothèque nationale de France, Paris), which contains a ritual text, entitled *Jin'gangding yuqie niansong guiyi* corresponding to sections of two texts ascribed to Amoghavajra. This manuscript may date back to the 10th c. Attestations of such symbols in different manuscript cultures of different areas suggest there is a need for comparative transcultural research on this topic in the future.

340 See the manuscript of the *Prajñāpāramitā* (NS 961 / 1841 CE) (NAK 4/215 / NGMPP B 90/2) on 132r5; and that of the *Saddharmapuṇḍarīkasūtra* (NS 962 / 1842 CE) (NAK 4/217 / NGMPP A 128/20) on 33v3; the *Gaṇḍavyūha* (NS 972 / 1852 CE) (NAK 5/75 / NGMPP A 110/3) on 38r8 (without outer line); the *Gaṇḍavyūha* (ca. 19th c.) (NAK 3/258 NGMPP A 110/4) on 56v3.

same *stūpa* at the Swayambhunath, Kathmandu (see Figs. 3.6.2.1.6-XXX and 3.6.2.1.6-XXXI (right)). The florally stylised symbol on the pillar is most likely a representation of a *viśvavajra*. Here we can deduce that these florally stylised symbols appearing in the aforementioned manuscripts may be interpreted as florally stylised *viśvavajras*.

These florally stylised *viśvavajra*s of the above (paper) manuscripts, permit the assumption that the florally stylised symbols in the AṣP$_1$,[341] and in the SDhPS[342] are also florally stylised *viśvavajra*s (see Fig. 3.6.2.1.6-XXX below). These and the above examples of *vajra*s suggest a long and significant tradition of the use of such symbols in manuscripts as well at religious sites and other places.

On the position of realistic or florally stylised *vajra*s and *viśvavajra*s, of the preceding examples above, they may appear at the end of the chapter, text and even smaller text units or around the string-holes of the manuscripts.

[KL 45 / NGMPP C 4/11_37v5_BCC_1425]

[NAK 4/9 / NGMPP B 99/5_162v6_BCC_1790]

[NAK 3/611 / NGMPP B 94_187v3_ACC_1840]

[NAK 3/258 NGMPP A 110/4_101v5_ACC_19th]

[NAK 3/258 NGMPP A 110/4_137v3_BCC_19th]

on the piller of one of the *stūpa*s at Swayambhunath, Kathmandu

Fig. 3.6.2.1.6-XXIX: Comparison of florally stylised *vajra*s

341 See 54v5_ACC, 149r5_ACC, 160v5_B/ACC, 169r1_ACC, 200v2_B/ACC.

342 See 11r1_BCC, 20r1_B/ACC, 31v4_ACC, 36v6_B/ACC, 43v4_BCC, 65r2_ACC, 69r1_ACC, 77r3_ACC, 79r3_ACC, 89v6_ACC, 106v5_BCC, 113v5_BCC.

 [AṣP$_1$_160v5_ACC_1151]  [NAK 4/215 / B 90/2_132r5_BCC_1841]  [NAK 3/258 NGMPP A 110/4_177r6_ACC_19th]	 on the piller of one of the *stūpa*s at Swayambhunath, Kathmandu

Fig. 3.6.2.1.6-XXX: Comparison of florally stylised *viśvavajra*s

Fig. 3.6.2.1.6-XXXI: Florally stylised *vajra* (left) and *viśvavajra* (right) on the pillar of one of the *stūpa*s at Swayambhunath, Kathmandu (image by author 2018)

As mentioned elsewhere, when focusing on the study of palaeography in his book Śākya (1973, 85) also presents some symbols in the table. At the top of the table, Śākya informs us that the symbols presented in his table have been 'adapted' from manuscripts, however, he does not tell us from which manuscripts they were adapted. In the second last row of his table there are three florally stylised symbols (Fig. 3.6.2.1.6-XXXII) most likely florally stylised *vajra*s. They are quite similar to the florally stylised *vajra*s in the Buddhist manuscripts presented above. The first symbol of the last three symbols in the second last row in Śākya's table (Fig. 3.6.2.1.6-XXXII) have similarities to the symbols in the manuscript of the *Laṅkāvatāra*,[343] on 13v3, 162v6 (see Fig. 3.6.2.1.6-XX) and in the manuscript of the *Samādhirājasūtra*,[344] on 87v3 (see Fig. 3.6.2.1.6-XXI). The last two symbols in the second last row in Śākya's table are quite similar to symbols found in the manuscript of the *Gaṇḍavyūha*,[345] on 288v4, 289v4 (see Fig. 3.6.2.1.6-XXV).

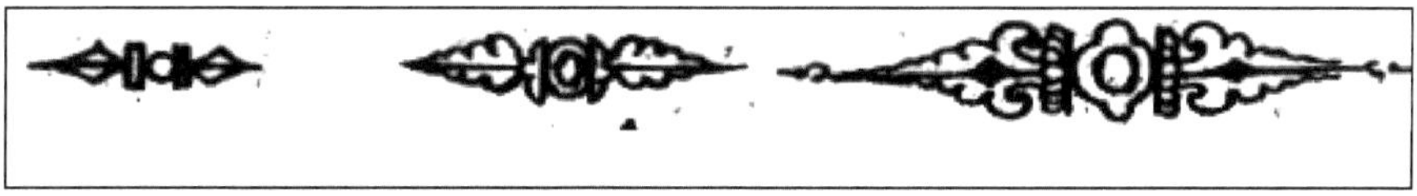

Fig. 3.6.2.1.6-XXXII: Extracted last three symbols from the second last row from the table of Śākya (reproduced from Śākya 1973, 85)

The last three symbols in the last row of the same table of Śākya (1973, 85), appear to be floral types. These symbols may be interpreted as representations of florally stylised *dhvaja* or *chattra* for these kinds of symbols appear in paper Buddhist manuscripts, similar to the manuscript of the *Gaṇḍavyūha*[346] on 289v4 (see Fig. 3.6.2.1.6-XXV) and in an MTM containing Buddhist texts[347] on 74v5, 74v9 (see Fig. 3.6.2.1.6-XXVIII). Thus, we can assume Śākya probably adapted these florally stylised symbols and the aforementioned florally stylised *vajra*s from the Buddhist manuscripts too.

Fig. 3.6.2.1.6-XXXIII: Extracted symbols from the last row of Śākya's table (reproduced from Śākya 1973, 85)

343 See NAK 3/610 / NGMPP B 88/2.
344 See NAK 3/611 / NGMPP B 94/1.
345 See NAK 5/75 / NGMPP A 110/3.
346 See NAK 5/75 / NGMPP A 110/3.
347 See NAK 4/1381 / NGMPP A 126/4.

3.6.2.1.7 Symbol in PV

PV is kept in the NAK. There is no further information about the place of copying and scribal activities mentioned in the manuscript. On the possibilities of place of production, one may assume that it may have been copied by a 'Jaina' scribe in a certain place in the Gujarat or Rajasthan regions and later brought to Nepal. It is also possible a 'Jaina' scribe copied the text in Nepal,[348] or a Nepalese scribe familiar with Jaina writing customs, copied the text in Nepal or in the Gujarat or Rajasthan regions after which the manuscript was brought to Nepal. Based on palaeographical grounds and according to layout- and symbol-related evidence I have grouped this manuscript for the present book in Western India.

In this manuscript at the chapters's end we find (and also at the end of some smaller text units) mostly '*cha*' symbols[349] (type no. 47) and, occasionally, some stylised *puṣpikās*[350] (see Appendix below). Stylised *puṣpikā*s also appear around string-holes on almost all folios (see section 3.6.1 above for more detail).

On the first line of 89v is a simple *svastika*[351] symbol which seems to be of a particular importance. Here it is a *vāmāvarta svastika* ('a left-facing *svastika*'). The symbol appears in the middle of a sentence in the 26th chapter, about the *nandyāvartakakaraṇa*, on the '*Nandyāvartaka* measure (for query analysis)'.[352] As we know, the *nandyāvarta* symbol is one of the eight auspicious symbols in Jainism,[353] belonging particularly to the Śvetāmbara ('white-clad') tradition. In PV the *svastika* is integrated into the text and is situated within the explanation on the shape of the *nandyāvarta* symbol. It is followed by the *svastikavad bhavati* | (see the part of the transcribed text before and after the *svastika* below).

348 On this topic, see Acharya 2007, 4.

349 For instance, on 10r4_B/ACC, 10v5_BCC, 14r5_BCC, 18r4–5_B/ACC, 18v5_B/ACC, 24v2_BCC, 30v1–2_B/ACC, 36r3–4_B/ACC, 39r2_B/ACC, 41v1_ACC, 48r3–4_B/ACC, 50v5–51r1–2_B/ACC, 52r3–4_B/ACC, 64r1_ACC, 64r5–6_ACC, 65r1–2_ACC, 66r4–5_B/ACC, 66v3–4_ACC, 67r_ACC, 67v2_ACC, 71v1–2_B/ACC, 74r5_B/ACC, 75v2–3_B/ACC, 80v3–4_B/ACC, 87r5_B/ACC, 105v1–2_B/ACC, 115r4–5_B/ACC, 117r2_B/ACC, 120v2–3_B/ACC, 131r3_B/ACC, 136v3–4_B/ACC, 137r5_B/ACC, 138v3–4_B/ACC, 147r5_B/ACC, 149r3_AC, 149r3_AAL, 149v3_BI.

350 Namely on 10v6_ACC, 14r5_ACC, 24v2_ACC, 41r3_ACC, 44r2_ACC.

351 The *Svastika* can be used as insertion sign in manuscripts (Thaker 2000, 146). In some of the manuscripts in my corpus, the *svatika* is also used as an insertion mark e.g. on 147v in SS/N, on 105r6 in NTS, on 83v4 in AṣP$_2$. In SP$_4$ the *svastika* was used one time as an indicator sign for the deletion on 10v5 and as an insertion mark on 11r in line 1 and 4; see also Roth 1986, plate 1, 21, 23 for *svastika* symbols.

352 See Acharya 2007, 8.

353 See Moeller 1979, 149–154; on eight auspicious symbols, see also at: <http://www.jainpedia.org/themes/principles/holy-symbols/eight-auspicious-symbols.html> (last accessed on 06.10.2018).

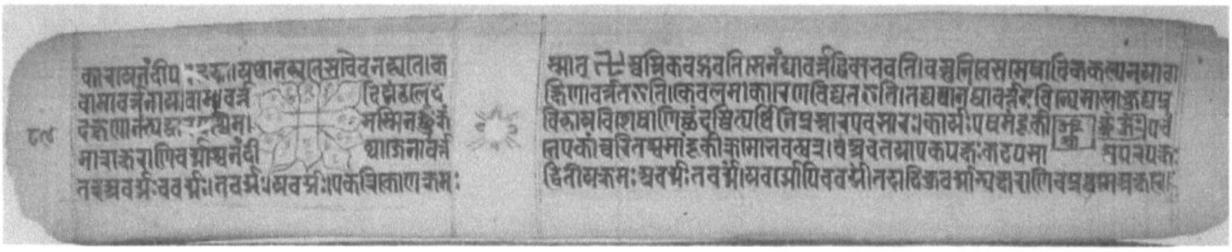

Fig. 3.6.2.1.7-I: *Svastika* in a particular place, fol. 89v © NAK

[89v1] *ka*||⊙||*smāt*  *svastikavad bhavati* | *sa naṃdyāvartta*(!) *dvidhā bhavati* |

‘How can it be like a *svastika*? The *naṃdyāvartta* is twofold.’

Palaeography and its appearance indicate the *svastika* symbol could have been drawn by the same scribe who copied the text. It is safe to assume the scribe had knowledge of what he was writing with the *svastika* symbol appearing just before the expression ‘*svastikavad*’. The scribe may have drawn the *svastika* deliberately to visually reinforce textual explanation.

3.6.2.2 Selected examples of puzzling symbols in manuscripts

Some manuscripts contain symbols interesting in appearance which at the same time are puzzling for their drawing effect. This section presents a few symbols from selected manuscripts.

KT

Among other symbols,[354] in KT, there are those with an interesting and puzzling appearance. On 78r7 before and after the chapter colophon there are symbols like a ‘leaf’ or leaf-like element (see Fig. 3.6.2.2-I). Both symbols have a dot at their centre. Before the chapter colophon on 68v7 and after the chapter colophon on 69v5 other puzzling types of symbols with an ‘eye’ or eye-like features. After the chapter colophon on 68v7 the symbol looks like a ‘bird’ or bird-like element. Here it may be a representation of a *Garuḍa* because after the symbol there is a speaker indication as follows: *garuḍa uvāca* (‘*Garuḍa* said’). All of these symbols are lightly highlighted. Some other symbols and features of this manuscript have been discussed above in section 3.6.2.4.1 and below in section 3.9.3.

354 For instance, circles (type no. 2), double circles (type no. 6), some stylised *puṣpikā*s (type nos. 8, 9, 14, 22, 23).

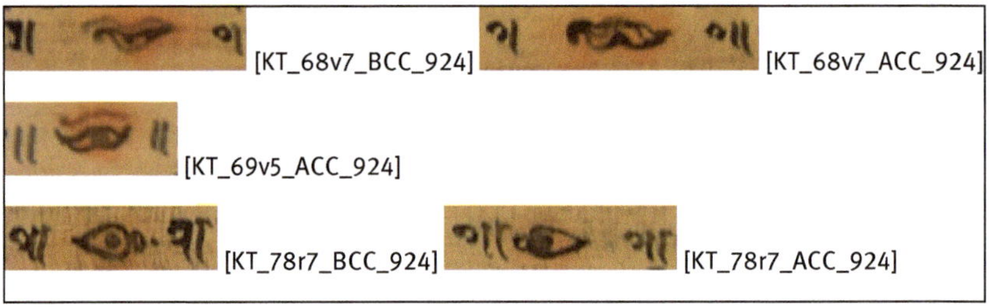

Fig. 3.6.2.2-I: Puzzling symbols before and/or after the chapter colophons

PR

Among other symbols,[355] in PR we find stylised 'half-like' *puṣpikā*s on 15r5, 16r5, 19r5, 45r5 that appear after and/or before the chapter colophon or before the concluding Buddhist formula, or before the invocation etc.[356] Some of them are a little over half-size (as with 19r5), but look to be precisely 'half'. These symbols fulfil similar functions to the full type of symbols in the manuscript. In the inner part of one of the stylised 'half' *puṣpikā*s that appears after the concluding formula on 19r5 there is a kind of realistic *puṣpikā* with buds, on the left and right side, at the sprouting stage. The inner part of the symbol could be interpreted to be a *padma* representation.[357] Another puzzling type of symbol appears before the chapter colophon on 19v1. This symbol consists of an arrow-like element at the centre part and two elements resembling one of the letter-numerals for

355 For example, stylised full *puṣpikā*s on 19v1, 20v1, 64v3–5, 67r2, 70r3, one stylised simple *puṣpikā* on 64v3 (type no. 16), one circle on 67r2 (type no. 2), circle with curved line in the centre part on 54r2, 54r3, 56v3, 56v4, 56v5, 57r1, 57r2, 57r4, 61v1, 70r6 (type nos. 4 and 5), spiral-like symbols on 55r1, 55r2, 61v3, 61v4, 62r1, 63r2, 63r3, 63r4, 63v1, 63v3, 64r5) and *tha*s on 54r3, 55r1, 56v3, 58r1, 58v3, 61v5, 62v3 (type no. 46) can be found at the end of the chapter, beginning of smaller text units, *mantra*s and invocations in the manuscript.

356 Similar types of stylised 'half-like' *puṣpikā*s can also be found before or after the chapter colophons on 18r7, 26v6, 77v7, 98v7, 144r7, 158r7 in the Nepalese manuscript of the *Aṣṭasahasrikā Prajñāpāramitā* (NS 268 / 1148 CE) (Museum für Asiatische Kunst, Berlin, I 5410 & I 5411 and Asiatic Society, Calcutta, G.4203), see Melzer /Allinger 2010, 6–7. Furthermore, one half-like stylized *puṣpikā* appears after the chapter colophon in the manuscript of the *Tiṅbheda* (NAK 4/257 / NGMPP B 36/2) on 48r2.

357 Also in the inner part of one example of 'full' symbol in the manuscript of the *Aṣṭasahasrikā Prajñāpāramitā* (ca. 11th c.) (Bodleian Library, Oxford, Ms Sansk. a 7(R)) at the end of the 11th chapter one can observe a realistic type of *puṣpikā*, see Weissenborn 2012, 198, Abbildung 70(c). This realistic type of *puṣpikā* may also be understood as a *padma*. However, with its somewhat open petals the *puṣpikā* here appears fully-fledged.

'50'[358] with an extra small stroke on the upper and lower sides. In this context the symbol is perhaps an abstract representation of the *vajra* or similar item.

[PR_19r5_BCF_1054]

[PR_19r5_ACF_1054]

[PR_19v1_BCC_1054]

Fig. 3.6.2.2-II: Puzzling symbols

Manuscript of the *Ratnakaraṇḍikā* (KL 522 / NGMPP C 49/1)

In the manuscript of the *Ratnakaraṇḍikā* (NS 299 / 1179 CE) (KL 522 / NGMPP C 49/1), there are two finely formed symbols exhibiting a puzzling effect of drawing skills. One of the symbols appears before the chapter colophon on 81v1 and the other after a chapter colophon on 165r3 (see Fig. 3.6.2.2-III). Both symbols are quite uniquely drawn. They contain four 'half-like' stylised *puṣpikā*s on the upper, lower, left and right side.[359] But if we combine the lower element with the upper element or the other way round we get a 'full' stylised *puṣpikā* (see the first row of the second column in Fig. 3.6.2.2-IV). Similarly if we combine the left element with the right element or the other way round we get another full stylised *puṣpikā* (see second row of the second column in Fig. 3.6.2.2-IV).[360] Furthermore, if we look closely at the both symbols on 81v1 and 165r3 there is something interesting at their centre. There is a stylised *puṣpikā* containing four petals or leaf-like elements in both symbols. This is expressed graphically by leaving the undrawn space at the centre of the symbols.

358 For the letter-numeral '80', see Bendall 1883, Table of Letter-numerals, row 5.

359 For instance, attestations of nearly identical 'half-like' symbols similar to this facing side up can be found in the manuscript of the *Viṣṇudharma* (1161 CE) (NAK 4/1389 / NGMPP A 10/3) on 20r1_B/ACC, 53r5_ACC, 88r5_BCC, 106r6_BCC, 133r6_ACC; in another manuscript of the *Viṣṇudharma* (1220 CE) (NAK 2/51 / NGMPP A 1163/1), IndoSkript, symbol, IS-Nr: 191.

360 After joining the left and right elements we get near similar symbols listed in type no. 29 above.

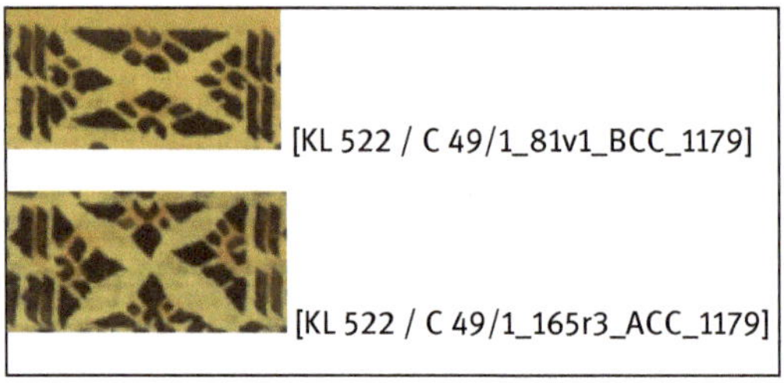

Fig. 3.6.2.2-III: Puzzling symbols before and after the chapter colophons

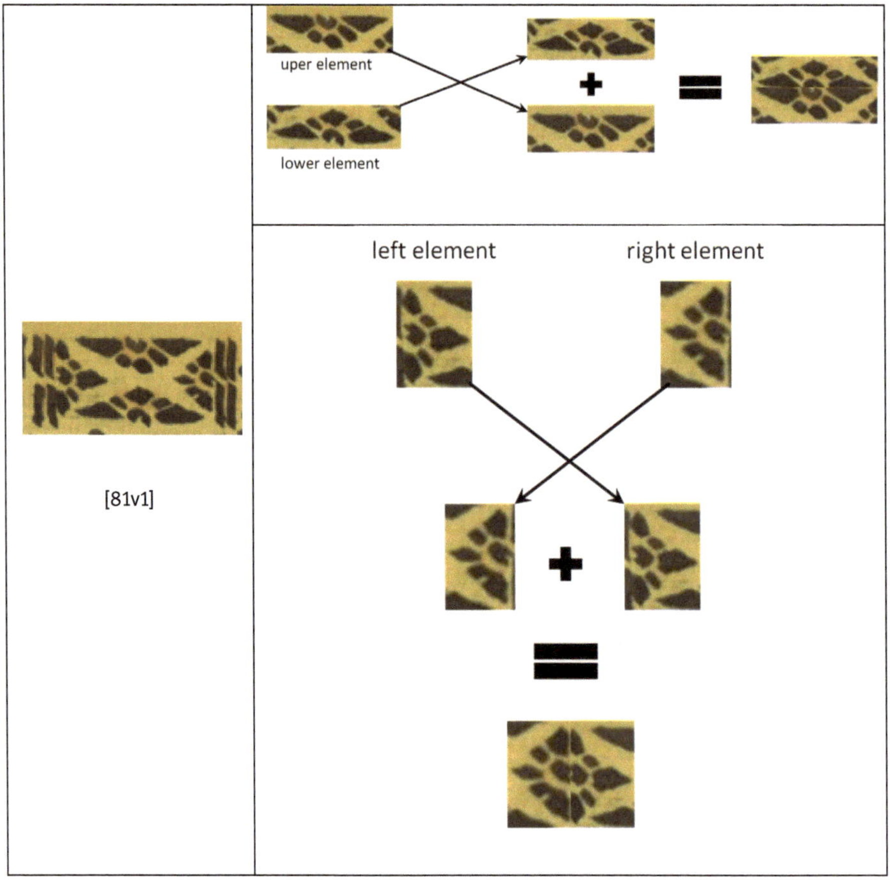

Fig. 3.6.2.2-IV: Illustration of puzzling symbol, on fol. 81v1

VDh

In VDh there are different kinds of symbols.[361] Some exhibit puzzling features, see 19v5, 140v3 and 140v4. After the chapter colophon on 19v there is a puzzling style of symbol with appearance of a kind of hook. At the centre of this symbol is a circle. Two symbols before and after the chapter colophon on 140v, the second[362] looks like a kind of 'larval stage of butterfly' or 'moth-like insect' and the first has other elements on its sides like the form of butterfly or a later development of the larval stage from the previous symbol.

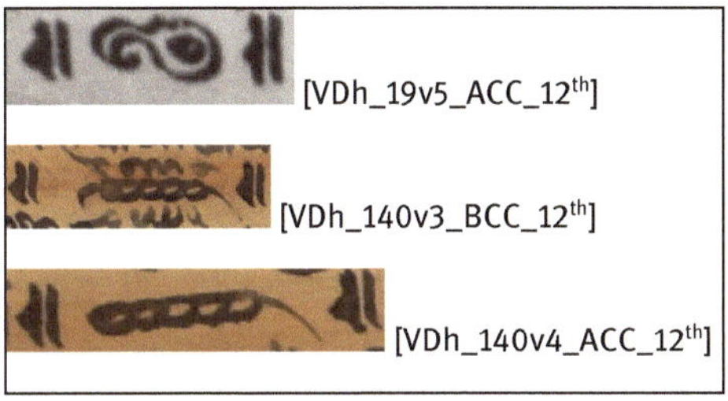

Fig. 3.6.2.2-V: Puzzling symbols before and/or after chapter colophons

STṬ

Circles predominate after chapter colophons in STṬ save for one symbol on 5v7. The symbol on 5v consists of '*u*-like' two elements placed together and both contain a tail-like line. Yet another component is to be seen between the '*u*-like' elements.

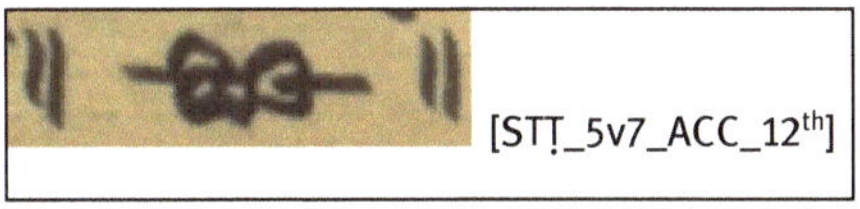

Fig. 3.6.2.2-VI: A puzzling symbol after the chapter colophon

---

361 See the three circles on 20v3_ACC, 51v5_BCC, 122r2_ACC (type no. 2), a variety of stylised simple *puṣpikā*s such as type nos. 6, 12, 14, 16, 17, 18, 19, 31, some beautifully drawn stylised *puṣpikā*s (see section 3.6.2.4.1). For other symbols see Appendix.

362 Similar symbols appear before and/or after chapter colophons on 138r3, 139v2, 143r2, 143r2, 150v5. This type of symbol is also used as space-filler in the manuscript, as at the bottom of 139v5, 140r5.

3.6.2.3 An observation: Creation of symbols in SP_3

By making use of or re-using a certain symbol more than once a scribe could well be demonstrating his drawing skills and practice through his manner of implementing symbols in a manuscript. While doing so he may introduce new symbols, forms or varieties of symbols lending them a more sophisticated and elegant appearance. To this end he may use or reuse a particular symbol repeatedly adding other elements to the symbol or utilising a specific symbol as part of a new symbol. This section presents selected symbols of SP_3 and discusses how, when drawing symbols in the manuscripts a scribe may use his craftsmanship innovatively.

In Fig. 3.6.2.3-I the first symbol has a circle at its centre surrounded by four petals and four lines (on 44r6).[363] However, the second symbol is comprised of the first symbol with three additional petal-like elements on the left and right sides (on 106r6).

[SP_3_44r6_BCC_10th]

[SP_3_106r6_BCC_10th]

Fig. 3.6.2.3-I: Use and reuse of symbols

The first symbol consists of one circle at its centre and five petal-like elements at the sides (on 83v6).[364] The second symbol, however, is composed of a near similar symbol to the first, placed at the centre with additional circles and petal-like elements (on 171v2).

[SP_3_83v6_ACC_10th]

[SP_3_171v2_BCC_10th]

Fig. 3.6.2.3-II: Use and reuse of symbols

363 More near identical symbols appear in the manuscript on 31r1_ACC, 37v_ACC, 106r6_ACC, 123r6_BCC, 125v2_ACC.

364 A near identical symbol appears in the manuscript on 164r3_ACC. See type no. 11 in section 3.4 above.

The first symbol consists of one circle at its centre and a few petal-like elements on the sides (on 18r5).[365] But the second (on 165v1) and third symbols (on 171v2) are near similar to the first including a quite attractive use of concentric circles and other additional features.

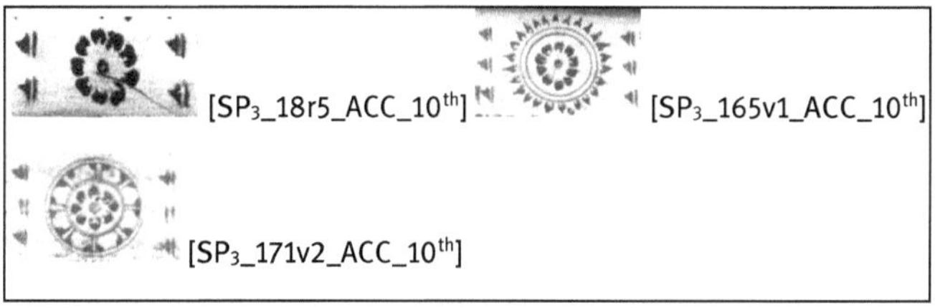

Fig. 3.6.2.3-III: Use and reuse of symbols

The first symbol consists of double circles at the centre surrounded by a few petal-like features (on 193r5).[366] The second symbol, however, is made out of the first symbol adding three petal-like elements on the left and right sides (on 24v5).[367] Following this the third symbol is made up of the first symbol with many other additional petal-like elements on its outer sides (on 69r4). The symbol has the shape of a kind of 'rhombus'. The fourth symbol is composed of the first with additional petal-like features resembling a kind of 'square box' (on 146r4). The next symbol consists of the first with more petal-like elements added to each of its four corners (on 176v3). Likewise, the symbol afterward is composed of the first with double circles and other features added (on 166v1).

365 Other near similar symbols can be found in the manuscript on 18r5_ACC, 46v5_ACC, 60r6_BCC, 198r4_BCC.

366 Other near similar symbols appear in this manuscript on 138r5_BCC, 159r3_ACC, 186r1_ACC, 193r5_BCC, 198r5_ACC, 244v3_ACC, 246r1_BCC. See type no. 24 in section 3.4 above.

367 An almost identical symbol is also drawn on 168v5_BCC.

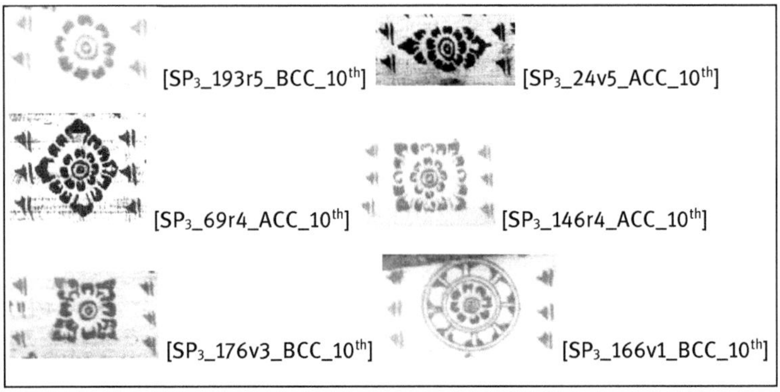

Fig. 3.6.2.3-III: Use and reuse of symbols

The first symbol contains a circle at its centre surrounded by some petal-like features (on 46v5).[368] It has a kind of 'rhombus' shape. The second symbol is composed of the first using with other elements, e.g. double circles and many petal-like features on the outer side (on 180r1).

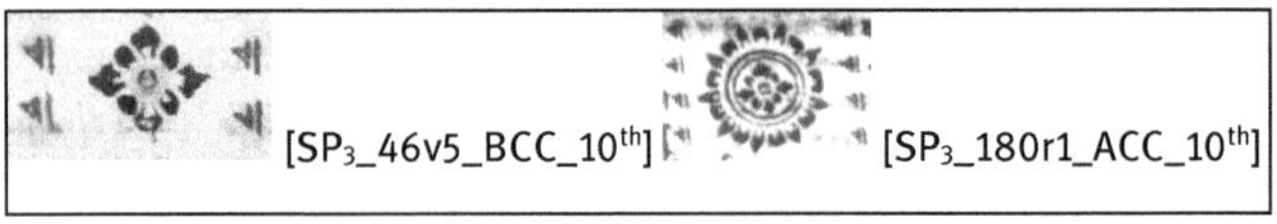

Fig. 3.6.2.3-IV: Use and reuse of symbols

The first symbol is made of double circles and more petal-like elements on the outer side (on 20v3). The second symbol, however, is composed out of the first symbol with the addition of small petal-like elements between the 'main petals' (on 54v4).[369] The third symbol is somewhat similar to the second, but encircled by concentric circles (on 162r2).

---

368 See type no. 28 in section 3.4 above.

369 Other almost identical symbols appear in the manuscript on 24v5_BCC, 27r5_ACC, 44r6_ACC, 56v4_ACC, 148v4_BCC, 150v5_ACC, 168v5_ACC, 200v4_ACC. An identical symbol can also be found in the manuscript of the *Śivadharmaśāstra* (1037 CE) (Calcutta, ASB G-4077), IndoSkript, symbol, IS-Nr: 243.

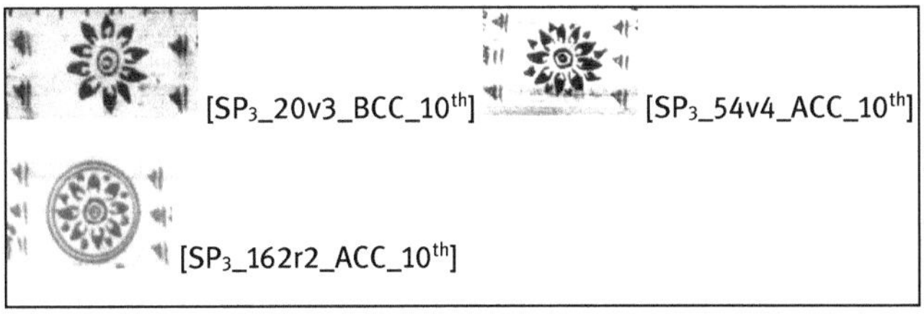

Fig. 3.6.2.3-V: Use and reuse of symbols

The first symbol contains eight petals with dark shadow-like elements at its centre resembling additional petals or petals of two different colours (on 76r2).[370] They are encircled. The second symbol is made of the first symbol or a few elements of the first with other additional features and circles outside (on 133v4).

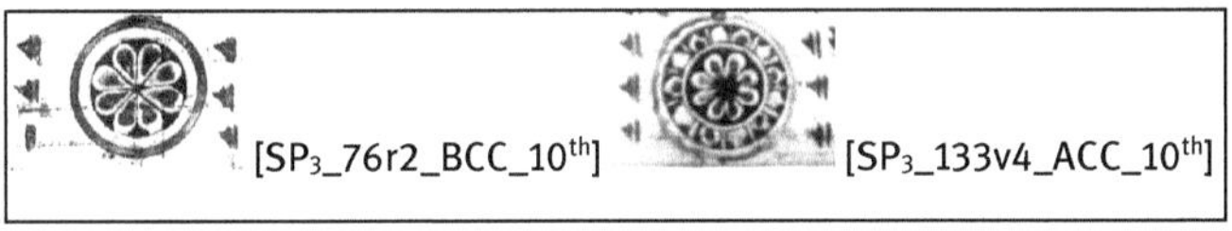

Fig. 3.6.2.3-VI: Use and reuse of symbols

The first symbol is made of eight petals, double circles and a circle on its outer side (on 147v4). The inner parts of the second (on 23r1) and third symbol (on 145r4) are composed of the near similar symbol to the first with other elements added to the outer side.

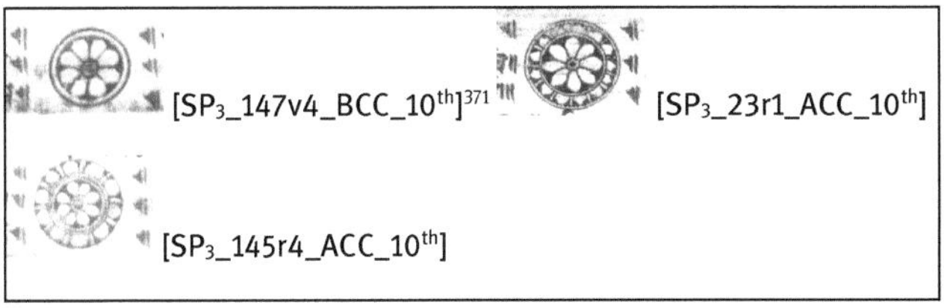

Fig. 3.6.2.3-VII: Use and reuse of symbols

370 Three other almost similar symbols appear in the manuscript on 74v2_B/ACC, 76r2_ACC.
371 A few similar symbols appear in the manuscript, see 112v2_BCC, 127r1_BCC, 147v4_BCC, 165v1_BCC and in SP$_4$ on 5r1_ACC.

The first symbol has double circles in the centre, twelve petals and outer circles (on 60v1). Compared to the petals of preceding symbols (see Fig. 3.6.2.3-VII), the symbol's petals are thinner, and their outer edges are slightly sharper. The second symbol uses nearly the same symbol to the first with additional elements on its outer side (on 114r4).

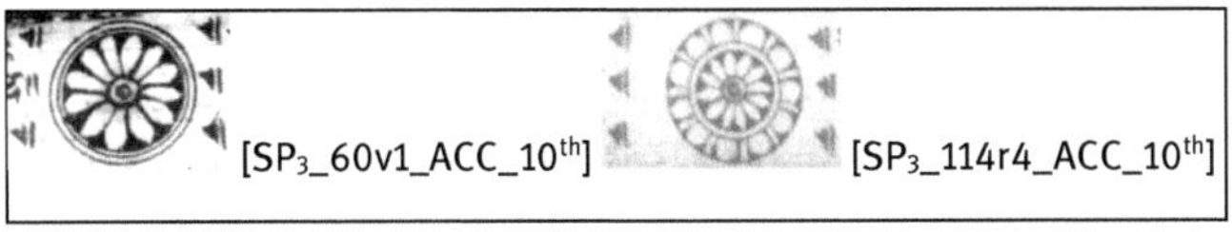

Fig. 3.6.2.3-VII: Use and reuse of symbols

The first symbol has double circles at its centre with four lines and four petals on its sides (on 147v4). The petals have additional elements at the centre. They may have been used to represent the different colours or blemishes found in the petals of real flowers. The second symbol is composed of the almost identical petals to those in the first symbol (on 133v4).

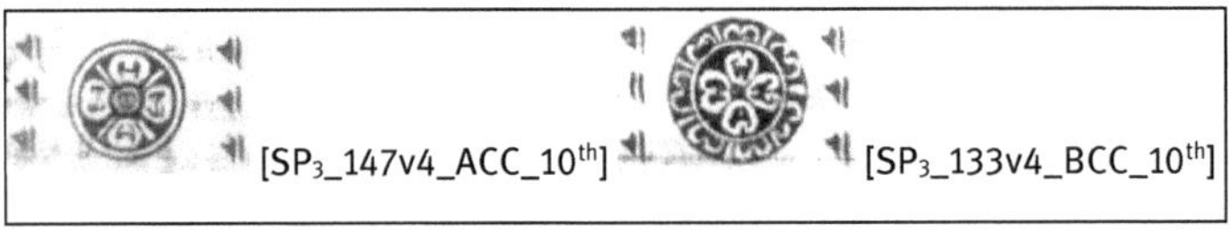

Fig. 3.6.2.3-VIII: Use and reuse of symbols

The first symbol has four 'heart-shaped' petals and circles at its outer side (on 109v2).[372] The second has four similar types of heart-shaped petals, but with additional features at its outer side (on 103v1).

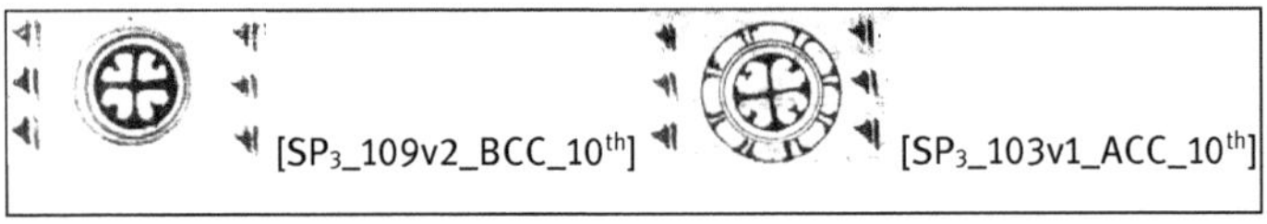

Fig. 3.6.2.3-IX: Use and reuse of symbols

372 See type no. 38 in section 3.4 above.

The first symbol consists of eight heart-shaped petals and concentric circles at its outer side (on 32v4). The second symbol is almost similar symbol to the first, but with additional elements at its outer side (on 32v3).

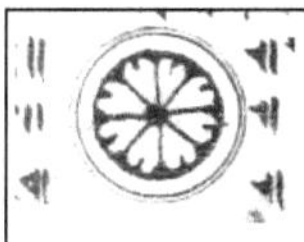
[SP3_32v4_ACC_10th]

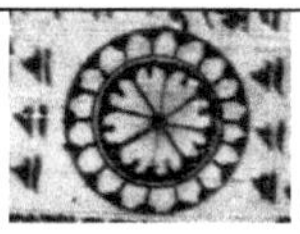
[SP3_32v3_BCC_10th]

Fig. 3.6.2.3-IX: Use and reuse of symbols

3.6.2.4 Symbols used to mark hierarchies in texts

As mentioned above, some manuscripts contain a great variety of symbols. Some symbols are of a very decorative style, whereas others are quite simple. The size is of particular importance as a symbol may occupy the equivalent to a single line or be the height of the entire written section of a folio from top to bottom. For their complexity and quality the distribution of these symbols may occasionally indicate the various hierarchical levels of the sections of a text.

The frequency of symbols on the folio can also be relevant. Symbols occur before and/or after a chapter colophon. However, at the end of a particular text, there may be a series of many symbols.

3.6.2.4.1 Shape, size and distribution: Symbols at the end of chapters and at the end of the text in selected manuscripts

This section indicates the pattern characterizing the shape, size and distribution of symbols largely featuring at the end of chapters and the entire text.

KT

There are various kinds of symbols at the end of the chapters in KT, circles (type no. 2), double circles (type no. 6), stylised *puṣpikā*s (with a circle, four petals and four lines) (see, type nos. 8, 9, 14, 22, 23) and some, still rather puzzling symbols (see section 3.9.3). All symbols occupy the space of one line only on the folio (e.g. the symbols at the end of the 7th chapter on 13v4 and the 54th chapter on 82r2). However, at the end of KT on 99r2–3 after the colophon, there are two slightly larger symbols that differ in shape from those appearing at the end of chapters.

The size of the first symbol (on 99r2) occurring after the statement providing the date of the manuscript's copying, is an area of two lines of the folio. The symbol is followed by a benediction phrase followed by a statement providing the donor's name (Udayapālasoma) and place of copying (Bhaktapur). Compared to the symbols at the end of the chapters, both symbols are of a clearly different form, but appear like a later addition or redrawing. The first symbol (on 99r2) has double circles in the middle part surrounded by a few petal-like elements.[373] The second symbol (on 99v3) also contains double circles at the centre but the circles are surrounded by wavy petal-like elements, drawn in a quite different shape. Regarding the latter it may be that the symbol consisted originally of only double circles and the additional elements were added later.

[13v4] | *iti kiraṇākhye tantre*|⊙| *saptamaḥ paṭalaḥ* 

[82r2] || *iti kiraṇākhye mahātantre catuḥpañcāśat paṭalaḥ* || *ślokā* 71 

Fig. 3.6.2.4.1-I: Symbols at the end of the chapters

[99r1–4]  *iti kiraṇākhye mahātantre catuḥṣaṣṭiḥ paṭalaḥ* 

ślokā 21 || *samāpta*[2]*ñ cedaṃ kiraṇākhyaṃ mahātantraṃ saptatyadhikadvisahasram iti*

 *samvat* 44 \44/ *jeṣṭhamāse likhitam idam iti*  *śubham astu* ||

[3]*śrībhaktapurādhivāsino bhaṭṭapaṇḍitācāryaśrīudayapālasomasya pustakam idaṃ*

 [4]*granthapramāṇa sahasra 2 śata 7*[374]

Fig. 3.6.2.4.1-II: Symbols at the end of the 64th chapter and end of the text

373 See section 3.4, type no. 24 above.
374 For this textual part, see also Shastri 1915, 99; Goodall 1998, lxxxiv.

VDh

In VDh there are various kinds of symbols at the end of the chapters. The height of the symbols is one to two lines of the folio (e.g. symbols at the end of one of the chapters on 36r1 occupy an area of one line and at the end of one of the chapters on 62r5 symbols occupy two).

However, at the end in VDh on 160v, there are four nicely drawn symbols. Of these, two symbols accompanied by the colophon are much larger, their height is over half that (top to bottom) of the folio. Both symbols are of a far more attractive form to the other symbols at the end of the chapters.

[36r1]  |⊙| *iti viṣṇudharmmeṣv anarakadvādaśīvratan*(!) *nāma*[375] 

[62r5]  *iti viṣṇudharmmeṣu vipramāhātmyaṃ*[376] 

Fig. 3.6.2.4.1-III: Symbols at the end of the chapters

[160v3]  *iti viṣṇudharmeṣu śāstramāhātmyam parāmṛtat*(!)
dha¦⊙*rmottamaṃ samāpta*(!)  *oṃ namo ṇārāyaṇāya*(!) *namaḥ* |
viṣṇudharmeṣv amī vṛttāntāḥ[377]  ⊙ *kriyāyogapravṛttiḥ* | *acyutām-*
barīṣasamvādaḥ  *śukraprasarasamvādaḥ* | *śugati*(!)

Fig. 3.6.2.4.1-IV: Symbols at the end of the text

375 Grünendahl 1983, 144 reads the line as *iti viṣṇudharmeṣu narakadvādaśī nāma*.

376 For the line, see also Grünendahl 1984, 78.

377 For this textual part, see also Grünendahl 1983, 16.

AAĀ

There are almost no stylised *puṣpikā*s at the end of the chapters in this manuscript save for one simple stylised *puṣpikā* at the end of the 32nd chapter (on 164v5) and some *siddham* symbols (e.g. on 84v5).[378] The symbol at the end of the 32nd chapter has one circle at its centre surrounded by larger circles; the height of the symbol is two lines of the folio. Aside from these, 'blank spaces' feature usually at the end of chapters.[379]

However, at the end in AAĀ on 165v, there are two nicely drawn stylised *puṣpikā*s. The folio features only four lines thus most of the lower part of the folio is blank, save for the remaining part of the space that has the two symbols in line no. 3. Originally both symbols were accompanied by a line providing the name of the author (Haribhadra). However, before the author line, the colophon (see below) has been added by means of an insertion mark. The handwriting of the other lines on the folio, appears to be different to the handwriting of the colophon. Both symbols appear larger, at more than half of the height (top to bottom) of the folio and have been placed between five sets of double *daṇḍa*s. Their shape and size are identical. After the second symbol, the verse '*ye dharmā* ...' can be found (in line nos. 3–4) followed by a *siddham* symbol.

378 On 35r3_BCC, 48v4_BCC, 61r_BCC, 79r7_B/ACC, 83r3_BCC, 84v5_BCC, 93v2, 96r4_BCC, 104_B/ACC, 123v7_BCC, 127r6_BCC, 132r2_BCC, 134r4_BCC, 135v6_BCC, 144r1_B/ACC, 156v1_BCC, 165v4_ABV) (type nos. 44, 45). See also section 3.4, Fig. 3.4-XLIV and section 3.5.2 above.

379 On 35r3_ACC, 48v4_ACC, 61r3_ACC, 64r1_ACC, 66v4_ACC, 74r5–6_B/ACC, 78r2_B/ACC, 83r3_ACC, 84v5_ACC, 88r5_B/ACC, 93v2_ACC, 96r4_ACC, 102r2_B/ACC, 103v2–3_B/ACC, 108r2_B/ACC, 119r3_B/ACC, 123v7_ACC, 127r6_ACC, 132r2_ACC, 134r4_ACC, 135v6_ACC, 139r3_ACC, 141r5_ACC, 147v7_ACC, 156v2_ACC, 159r7_ACC, 164r2_ACC. See also section 4.1.2 below.

[78r2]  *abhisamayālaṅkārālokāyāṃ prajñāpāramitāvyākhyāyāṃ niraya-parivarto nāma saptamaḥ*[380] 

[84v5]  ⊡*abhisamayālaṅkārālokāyāṃ prajñāpāramitāvyākhyāyāṃ sarvvajñatāparicchedas tṛtīyaḥ*[381] 

[164v5] *abhisamayālaṅkārālokāyāṃ prajñāpā¦⊡ramitāvyākhyāyāṃ parīndanāparivartto nāma dvātriṃśattamaḥ*[382] 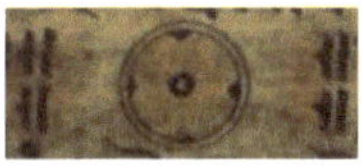

Fig. 3.6.2.4.1-V: Symbols and blank spaces at the end of the chapter

[165v3–4]  *\abhisamayālaṅkārālo⊡kā++ṣṭasahasrikāprajñāpāramitavyākhyā samāptā ||/ kṛtir iyam ācāryaha⊡ribhadrapādāṇāṃ*  *ye dharmmā hetuprab-havā hetuṃ teṣāṃ tathāgato hy avadat | teṣāṃ ca yo¦[4] nirodha evamvādī mahāśramaṇaḥ*[383] 

Fig. 3.6.2.4.1-VI: Symbols at the end of the text

380 For the line, see also Tucci 1932, 261.
381 For the line, Ibid. 285, footnote 1.
382 For the line, Ibid. 562.
383 For some part of the textual part, Ibid. 564.

TSPV

There are ‘*cha*’ symbols at the end of the chapters in TSPV (type no. 47, mostly before chapter colophons) and some stylised *puṣpikā*s (always after chapter colophons) which are simple in shape (see 253?v8). However, at the end of the text on 313v2 stylised *puṣpikā*s appear which, compared to the symbols appearing at the end of the chapters (e.g. on 150v2 and 253?v8), are significantly more attractive in shape and their distribution sequence is different. The symbols at the end are always surrounded by *cha* symbols. The first, second and third stylised *puṣpikā*s are placed between *cha* symbols. After the second stylised *puṣpikā*, a benediction statement (*maṅgalaṃ mahāśrīḥ*, ‘auspiciousness [and] great prosperity’) is followed again by another stylised *puṣpikā* placed between the *cha* symbols. This too is followed by a statement of benediction (*śubhaṃ bhavatu*, ‘may there be auspiciousness’) and two stylised *puṣpikā*s have been placed between the three *cha* symbols.

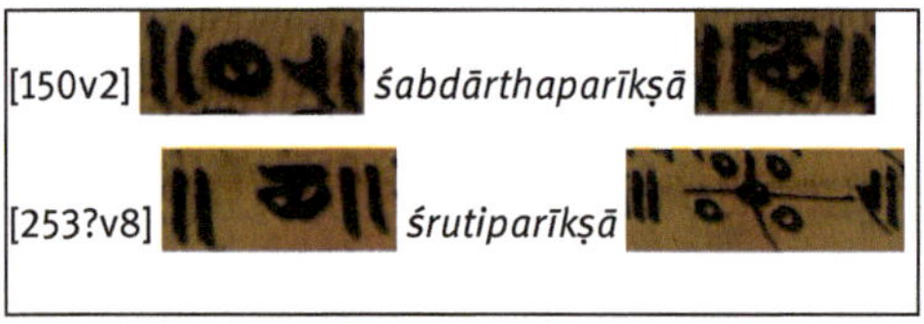
[150v2] śabdārthaparīkṣā
[253?v8] śrutiparīkṣā

Fig. 3.6.2.4.1-VII: Symbols at the end of the chapter

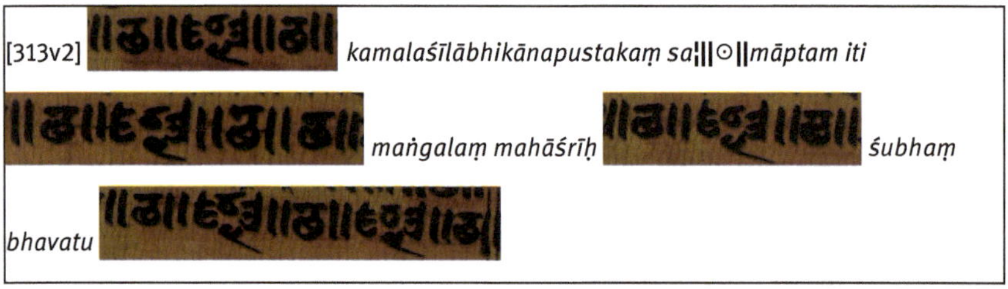
[313v2] kamalaśīlābhikānapustakaṃ sa¦||⊙||māptam iti
maṅgalaṃ mahāśrīḥ
śubhaṃ
bhavatu

Fig. 3.6.2.4.1-VIII: Symbols at the end of the text

SDhPS

There are a few circles,[384] '*tha*' symbols[385] (e.g., on 58v2), a 'figure-eight knot' symbol (on 43v5_ACC), and some simple and beautiful stylised *puṣpikās* (e.g., on 79r3) (which could be understood as double *vajra*)[386] in the manuscript. All of the symbols at the end of the chapters are a height of one to three lines of the folio.

However, almost at the end of the text on 138v, 139r and 139v there are a series of three nicely drawn large symbols[387] (see the three symbols on the last folio on 139v). Each of the three symbols appears at the centre of every text-section. All symbols are almost the entire height of the folio (top to bottom). Compared to the symbols at the end of chapters, the symbols on 138v, 139r and 139v are far larger and have a sophisticated form. It is also interesting to note that the symbol at the centre part of the second text-section on 139v (see below) contains a florally stylised double *vajra* at its centre.

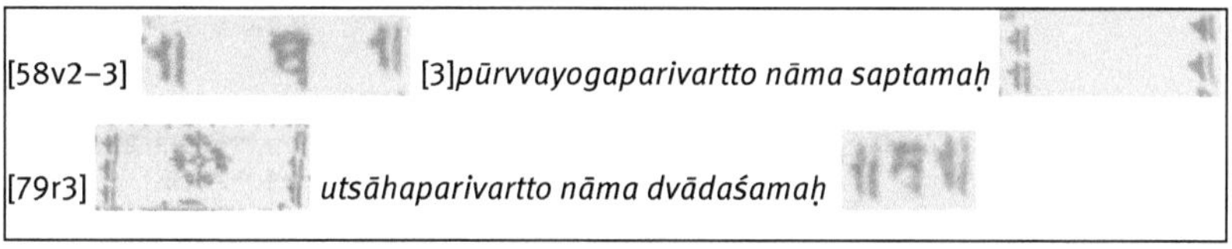
[58v2–3]
[3]*pūrvvayogaparivartto nāma saptamaḥ*
[79r3]
utsāhaparivartto nāma dvādaśamaḥ

Fig. 3.6.2.4.1-IX: Symbols at the end of chapters

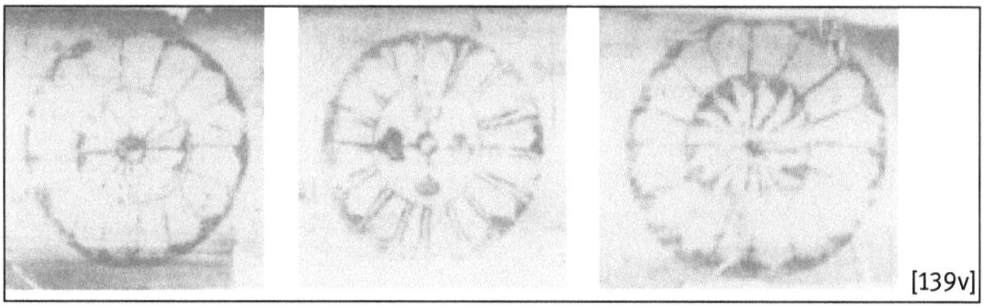
[139v]

Fig. 3.6.2.4.1-X: Symbols at the very end of text

384 On 100v5_ACC, 106v5_ACC, 116r1_BCC (type no. 2).

385 On 46v6_ACC, 58v2_BCC, 62v4_B/ACC, 79r3_ACC, 84v2_ACC, 89v6_BCC, 93v2_ACC, 100v5_BCC, 113v5_ACC, 134v4_B/ACC (type no. 46).

386 See section 3.6.2.1.5 above.

387 These symbols are discussed below. See section 3.6.2.2.3.

It can be assumed from the way in which symbols change in terms of size, distribution and decorative value they may be understood as an important visual marker indicating the hierarchy of different parts of a text.

3.6.2.4.2 Set of symbols at the (very) end of texts in Buddhist manuscripts

As seen above (in section 3.6.2.4.1) the SDhPS features a series of three large symbols at the (very) end of its text. An almost similar pattern is to be seen in other manuscripts where symbols may or may not be accompanied by a colophon or colophon-like statements.

To the best of my knowledge, one of the oldest existing evidence of this type of distribution is at the end of a birch-bark manuscript of the *Dīrghāgama* from Gilgit on 454v (see Fig. 3.6.2.2.3-I below).[388] The manuscript is in *pothī* format and thought to date approximately from the second half of the 8th c.[389] The manuscript bears one of the crucial texts related to the Mūlasarvāstivāda tradition of one of the schools of non-mahāyānic Buddhism.

A series of three symbols appear at the end of the text at more than half the height (top to bottom) of the folio. All symbols appear identical in size and are not placed between series of double *daṇḍa*s or long vertical lines. Some elements of the symbols look similar e.g. the inner circles or outer concentric circles. The gaps between these circles seem to be identical in size. Of the three symbols, the first symbol appears a few centimetres from the left edge and the second appears almost at the centre of the folio and the third is a few centimetres off the right edge (see examples in Fig. 3.6.2.4.2-I).[390] The part of the fifth and sixth lines on the folio on which the three symbols appear, read as follows: [5]*samā*[6]*ptaś ca␣ dī␣rghā+ma␣ḥ* ||[391] ('[thus], the *Dīrghā*[*ga*]*ma* is also concluded') and indicate the end of the text.

388 See Melzer 2014, 229.

389 For the date, Ibid. 227 and 229.

390 Losty 1982, 29 understands these three symbols as *dharmacakra*s noting 'the Buddhist Wheel of the Law'. As other elements also feature in the inner part of such kinds of symbols, e.g. florally stylised *double vajra* in a later manuscript from Nepal (see Figs. 3.6.2.4.2-VII and 3.6.2.4.1-X) which also contain a similar way of distributing the three symbols at the end, however, the interpretation of such symbols as *dharmacakra*s remains at the moment unclear.

391 Clearly visible gaps between *akṣara*s are marked using a ␣ sign in the transliteration.

Fig. 3.6.2.4.2-I: A series of three large symbols at the end of the text in the manuscript of the *Dīrghāgama*, fol. 454v (reproduced from Melzer 2014, 232, Fig. 2)

Fig. 3.6.2.4.2-II: Enlarged symbols (reproduced from Melzer 2014, 232, Fig. 2)

Likewise a series of three beautifully drawn large symbols appears at the end of the text in the manuscript of the *Vinayavastvāgama* on the last folio 523r (GBM 1050).[392] This manuscript is purported to originate from Gilgit, dated from approximately the same period (i.e. ca. second half of the 8th c.)[393] as the aforementioned manuscript of the *Dīrghāgama*. The manuscript contains one of the popular and influential texts relating to the Mūlasarvāstivāda tradition of Buddhism.

Of the three symbols, the first symbol is almost on the left-hand margin, the second symbol in the centre and the third appears on the right margin of the folio. Similar to the symbols in the aforementioned manuscript, the symbols in this manuscript are not placed between series of double *daṇḍa*s or long vertical lines. The part of the last line (no. 6) on 523r on which the three symbols appear, can be read as follows: *vi␣na␣ya␣sa␣ṅgha␣bhe␣da␣va␣stu␣sa␣mā␣pta␣ḥ* || ('[thus], the *Vinayasaṅghabhedavastu* is completed') and indicates the end of the text.

392 See Melzer 2014, 233.
393 For the date, Ibid., 234.

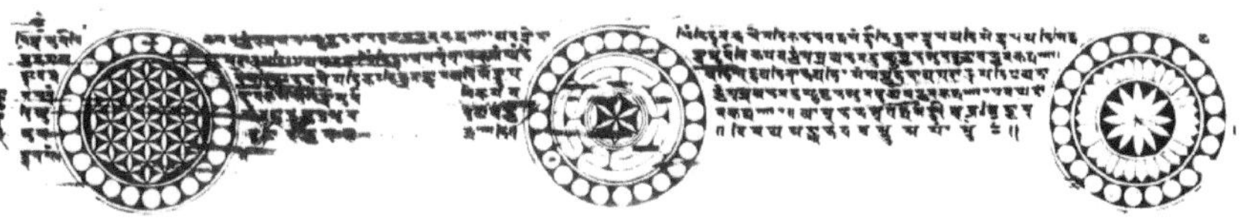

Fig. 3.6.2.4.2-III: A series of three large symbols at the end of the text in the manuscript of the *Vinayavastvāgama*, fol. 523r (reproduced from Melzer 2014, 233, Fig. 3)

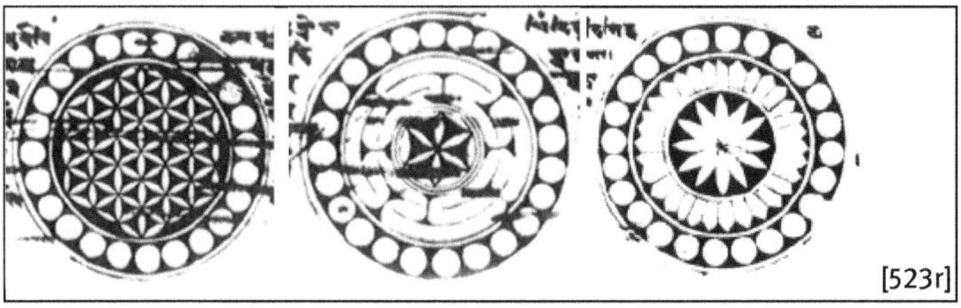

Fig. 3.6.2.4.2-IV: Enlarged symbols (reproduced from Melzer 2014, 233, Fig. 3)

A set of three large and beautifully drawn symbols also appears near the end of the text on 202r in the Nepalese manuscript of the *Aṣṭasāhasrikā Prajñāparamitā* (CUL Add.866).[394] This manuscript is dated NS 128 (1008 CE) and contains a Sūtra text belonging to the Mahāyāna Buddhism.

The folio has two string-holes and the text is divided into three text-sections. Among the three symbols, the first and third symbols appear almost at the centre of the first and third text-sections. However, the second symbol appears immediately after the left string-hole, at the left side of the second text-section. All three symbols have been placed between seven sets of double *daṇḍa*s vertically arranged on the folio, with the exception of six sets of double *daṇḍa*s after the last symbol. In this instance, the first *daṇḍa*s have been lost due to the damaged condition of the leaf. Part of the second line on 202r contains the 32nd chapter colophon and is followed by the colophon indicating the end of the text (line no. 3).[395]

394 See Bendall 1883, 1–4 and plate I. 3.

395 The sub-colophon and colophon read on 202r2–3 *āryāṣṭasāhasrikāyāṃ prajñāpāramitā*¦|⊙|*yāṃ parīndanāparivartto*(!) *nāma dvātriṅśatimaḥ* || 39 || [3] *samāptā ceyam bhagavaty āryāṣṭasahasrikā*(!) *prajñāpāra*¦|⊙|*mitā sarvatathāgatajananī sarvabodhisatvapratyekajinaśrāvakā*¦|⊙|*ṇāṃ ca mātā* ... ('[thus], the 32nd chapter, namely, the parīndanā in the noble Perfection of Wisdom in Eight Thou-

Fig. 3.6.2.4.2-V: A series of three large symbols at the end of the text of the *Aṣṭasāhasrikā Prajñāparamitā*, fol. 202r © CUL

Fig. 3.6.2.4.2-VI: Enlarged symbols

When returning to examine the SDhPS, a near similar style of distribution of the symbols presents itself. It also contains one of the influential Sūtra texts of the Mahāyāna tradition.

Simple circles feature at the end of chapters in the manuscript,[396] one 'figure-eight knot' symbol,[397] florally stylised *viśvavajras* (see section 3.6.2.1.5),[398] '*tha*' symbols[399] and blank spaces.[400] All these symbols are a height of one to three lines of the folio. However, a set of three symbols can be found on 138v (the penultimate folio of the manuscript), and on 139r and 139v (the last folio of the manuscript).[401] All nine symbols are so large they are almost the entire height (top to bottom) of the folio. Two string-holes can be found on the folio and the text has been divided into three

sand Lines is concluded. 39. The Goddess, the Perfection of Wisdom in Eight Thousand Lines, the mother of all the Tathāgatas, all Bodhisattvas, each Jina and Śrāvaka is also concluded ...').

396 Namely on 100v5_ACC, 106v5_ACC, 116r1_BCC (type no. 2).

397 Namely on 43v5_ACC (type no. 3).

398 For instance, on 11r1_B/ACC, 20r1_B/ACC.

399 Namely on 46v6_ACC, 58v2_BCC, 62v4_B/ACC, 79r3_ACC, 84v2_ACC, 89v6_BCC, 93v2_ACC, 100v5_BCC, 113v5_ACC, 134v4_B/ACC (type no. 46).

400 Namely on 46v5_BCC, 58v3_ACC, 77r2_BCC, 84v2_BCC, 93v2_BCC, 98r3_B/ACC, 110r4_BCC, 116r1_ACC, 125v3–4_B/ACC, 130r4_B/ACC, 138r2_B/ACC.

401 In October 2018 I had the opportunity to see some part of this manuscript at the NAK including folios 138v, 139rv and received the digitised colour images of them and a few other folios. It seems folio 139 has deteriorated considerably since the manuscript was microfilmed. The upper and lower parts of the symbols on the folio (rv) are even more damaged. The folio has been repaired recently using supportive paper.

text-section. All symbols near the end of the text appear at the centre part of each text-section and have been placed between a series of double parallel vertical ruling-lines. Please note that the second symbol on 139v contains a florally stylised *viśvavajra* at its centre (see section 3.6.2.1.5). Moreover, the left and right symbols on 139r look similar.

Part of the first line on 139v contains the 27th chapter colophon.[402] It is also the last chapter of the work in the manuscript. The chapter colophon is followed by a short statement and the verse '*ye dharmā* ...' on the second line of the folio. A part of the left side of the folio 139rv has been damaged so a section of the text on the left has also been lost. In addition, folio 139v contains only one and almost a half of the text lines.

Fig. 3.6.2.4.2-VII: Three series of three large symbols at the end of the text in SDhPS, fols. 138v, 139rv © NAK

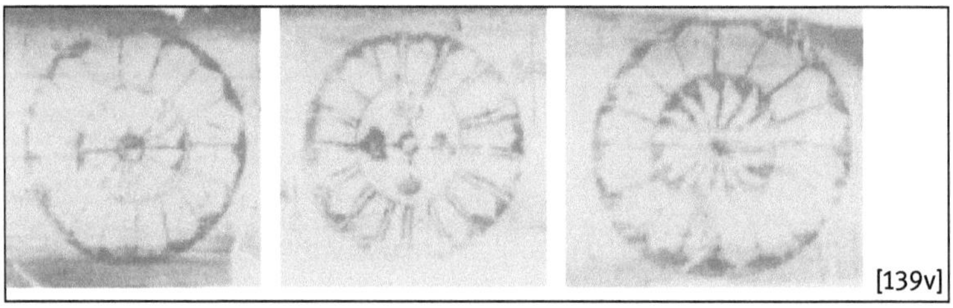

Fig. 3.6.2.4.2-VIII: Enlarged symbols

402 The chapter colophon reads *saddharmapuṇḍarīke dharmaparyā*||⊙||*ye saptāviṁśatimaḥ*(!) *parivartaḥ* ... ('[thus], the 27th chapter called the *dharmaparyāya* in the Lotus of the True Law [is concluded]').

Almost the same pattern with three symbols appears at the end of the text in another Nepalese manuscript of the *Saddharmapuṇḍarīka* on 132r (CUL Add.2197). The manuscript has been dated NS 185 (1065 CE). By contrast with the symbols found in other manuscripts[403] described above and in manuscripts[404] presented in this section below, symbols in Add.2197 are far smaller in size with only a height of four text lines. Aside from their size, the symbols have almost the same features as the other examples collected in this section. All three symbols appear almost at the centre of each text-section and are situated between three sets of vertical lines. They also appear at the near end of the 27th chapter and are slightly larger than the other symbols found at the end of other chapters in the manuscript.

The other side of the folio (i.e. 132v) contains the 27th chapter colophon and is followed by the manuscript production date, as well as other information such as the copying place, name of scribe etc. Before and after the chapter colophon, there are blank spaces and their height is one line of the folio. After the second blank space a *siddham* symbol appears followed by the date.[405] It should be noted that the inner part (i.e. petals) of the first symbol looks somewhat similar to the inner element of the right symbol on 139v in SDhPS. The centre part of the centre symbol of the manuscript also exhibits some similarities to the middle part of the first symbol on 138v in SDhPS.

Fig. 3.6.2.4.2-IX: Symbols at the end of the text, fol. 132r(?) © CUL

403 Such as in the manuscript of the *Dīrghāgama*; in the manuscript of the *Vinayavastvāgama*; in the manuscript of the *Aṣṭasāhasrikā Prajñāparamitā* (CUL Add.866), SDhPS).
404 For instance, in the *Aṣṭasāhasrikā Prajñāparamitā* (NGMPP E 2122/7); in the manuscript of the *Aṣṭasāhasrikā Prajñāparamitā* (KL 18 / NGMPP C 103/2).
405 The 27th chapter colophon and dating line read on 132v1  *saddharmapuṇḍarīke*|⊙| *dharmaparyāye anuparīndanāparivartaḥ saptāviṃśatimaḥ*(!)   *samvat* 185 *māghakṛṣṇadivādaśa*|⊙|*myā budhadine* | ('[thus], the 27th chapter called the *anuparīndanā* in the *dharmaparyāya* in the Lotus of the True Law [is concluded]. The [Nepāla] era 185 (1065 CE), on Wednesday, the 12th of dark fortnight of the month *māgha*').

Fig. 3.6.2.4.2-X: Enlarged symbols

There is a series of three large symbols near the end of the text in the manuscript of the *Aṣṭasāhasrikā Prajñāparamitā* (NGMPP E 2122/7) on 186?r. On palaeographical grounds the manuscript can probably be dated 11th c. As seen below, the margins of the folio are damaged, therefore, a part of the first symbol and a small part at the bottom of the second and third symbol has been lost. The symbols have placed between sets of vertical lines and their height is almost that of the entire height of the folio.

Part of the chapter colophon can be found in line nos. 4–5 on the folio, but part of it has been lost due to damage on the left and right margins. Here we can assume that it is most probably the 32nd chapter colophon, because after the stylised *puṣpikā*, the number '39' is also present after the 32nd chapter colophon in the manuscript containing the same text (e.g., in the manuscript of the *Aṣṭasāhasrikā Prajñāparamitā* (CUL Add.866) on 201r2). Before and after the chapter colophon there are stylised *puṣpikā*s (lines nos. 4 and 5). A final statement indicating the end of the text appears after the chapter colophon and the verse number.[406]

Fig. 3.6.2.4.2-XI: Symbols at the end of the text, fol. 186?r © NAK

406 The part of the chapter colophon and the colophon on 186?r4–5 read  ||◯||*āryāṣṭasāhasrikāyām pra[j]ñāpārami///*[5]*///ttamaḥ*  39 || ||◯||*samāptā ceyaṃ bhagavaty āryāṣṭasāhasrikāyaṃ prajñāpā*||◯||*ramitā sarvatathāgatajananī sarvabodhi///* ('[thus], [the 32nd chapter] in the noble Perfection of Wisdom in Eight Thousand Lines [is concluded]. 39. The Goddess, the Perfection of Wisdom in Eight Thousand Lines, the mother of all the Tathāgatas, all Bodhi[sattvas]').

Fig. 3.6.2.4.2-XII: Enlarged symbols

Near the end of the text in another manuscript of the *Aṣṭasāhasrikā Prajñāparamitā* (ca. 12th c.) (KL 18 / NGMPP C 103/2) a similar type of distribution of symbols occurs on 196v. As is evident, the folio is already in a fragmentary condition and, significantly, most of the left side of the folio is broken. On the left side there may have been a similar type of symbol to that in the second and third text-sections. The remaining two symbols have been placed between vertical lines and their height is almost the entire whole height of the folio. On 196r6 we can read *āryāṣṭasāha///* which is most probably the preserved part of the 32nd chapter colophon of which the most part is now lost, and on 196v there are the symbols and part of the colophon in the first line.[407] Here we can assume that the beginning part of the colophon (i.e. *samāptā ceyaṃ bhagavaty āryāṣṭasāhasrikāyaṃ*) found after the 32nd chapter colophon on 201r3 in the manuscript of the *Aṣṭasāhasrikā Prajñāparamitā* (CUL Add.866) and also after the 32nd chapter colophon in the manuscript of the *Aṣṭasāhasrikā Prajñāparamitā* (NGMPP E 2122/7) on 186?r4–5 (that has just been seen above) has been lost.

Fig. 3.6.2.4.2-XIII: Symbols at the end of the text, fol. 196v © KL

407 It reads *prajñāpāramitā sarvatathāgatajananī bodhisatvapratyekajinaśrāvakānāñ*(!) *ca mātā* ... ('[the Goddess], the Perfection of Wisdom [in Eight Thousand Lines], the mother of all the Tathāgatas, all Bodhisattvas, each Jina and Śrāvaka [is also concluded ...]').

Fig. 3.6.2.4.2-XIV: Enlarged symbols

To verify the occurrence of such symbols at the end or near end of the text in the manuscripts seen above, attention is turned to the blank spaces present in some Buddhist manuscripts. Attestations of a series of three large blank spaces at the nearly end of the text appear in a few other manuscripts. Bearing this in mind, we can assume the blank spaces were supposed to be filled with sets of three large symbols or similar items seen in the manuscripts mentioned above.[408] In the following, three manuscripts are presented featuring large blank spaces at the end.

In the manuscript of the *Bodhisattvabhūmi* (CUL Add.1702)[409] a series of three large blank spaces can be found at the nearly end of the text on 144v. The first blank space is on the left, the second almost in the middle section and the third appears at the right section of the folio. The folio contains five lines and the part of the fifth line of the text is the ending line.[410] It is possible the three blank spaces here were to feature three large symbols as seen in the manuscripts above.

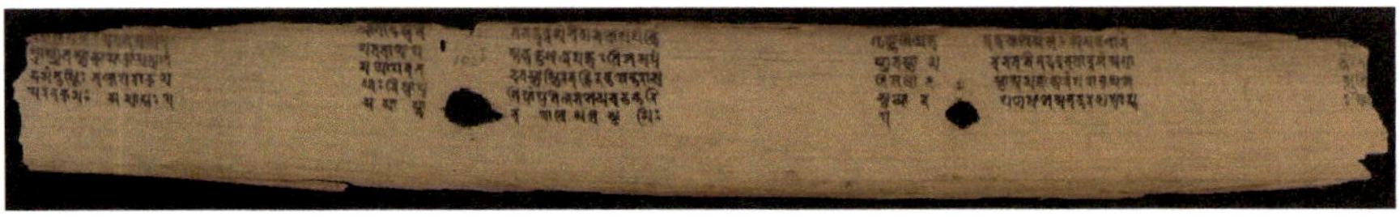

Fig. 3.6.2.4.2-XV: Large blank spaces at the end of the text, fol. 144v © CUL

408 For instance, in the manuscript of the *Dīrghāgama*; in the manuscript of the *Vinayavastvāgama*; in the manuscript of the *Aṣṭasāhasrikā Prajñāparamitā* (CUL Add.866); SDhPS; in the manuscript of the *Saddharmapuṇḍarīka* (CUL Add.2197); in the manuscript of the *Aṣṭasāhasrikā Prajñāparamitā* (NGMPP E 2122/7); in the manuscript of the *Aṣṭasāhasrikā Prajñāparamitā* (KL 18 / NGMPP C 103/2).

409 The manuscript is undated. Bendall 1883, XXXIX and 191–196 dates the manuscript from the 9th c., whereas Harimoto 2017, 355–376 recently suggested it could possibly be mid-8th c.

410 It reads *sa␣mā␣ptā*|⊙| *ca␣ bodhi␣satva␣bhū␣miḥ* || ('[thus], the Bodhisatva path is concluded') (the second blank space appears between *miḥ* and the double *daṇḍa*).

Furthermore, an attestation of three large blank spaces can also be observed in the manuscript of the *Sarvakulatattvasiddhividhivistaratantra* (KL 143 / NGMPP C 14/20).[411] Some part of the text can be seen at the top of the folio. It is likely it was to have been the first line of the folio but most of the line is now lost.[412] Additionally, the remaining parts of the two stylised *puṣpikās*[413] and double *daṇḍa*s in the first line are visible (see note below). The second line ends with a reading[414] before the uppermost double *daṇḍa*s of the first blank space (left). An invocation[415] is on the bottom left part of the folio under the first blank space, preceded by a *siddham*. Compared with the handwriting of the text on other folios, both seem to have been written by another hand. Aside from them, sets of double *daṇḍa*s can be found on the left, middle and right part of the folio. It is possible the blank spaces between the sets of double *daṇḍas* were to be filled with similar types of large symbols as evidenced by the manuscripts in the above section.

Fig. 3.6.2.4.2-XVI: Large blank spaces at the end of the text, fol.? © KL

In the manuscript of the *Aṣṭasāhasrikā Prajñāpāramitā* (NAK 5/76 / NGMPP A 37/11–A 38/1) a series of three large blank spaces can be found on 195v. They appear in the part of the colophon and post colophon. Each appears almost at the centre of the text-section. The 32nd chapter colophon, the verse number and part of the colophon is on 195r6 and the remaining part of the colophon on

411 This manuscript is not dated. However, on paleographical grounds it may be dated ca. 9th c. It should be noted that this manuscript shares a degree of similarities with the manuscript of the *Bodhisattvabhūmi* (CUL Add.1702) for the size of its writing support, layout and a bit of its palaeography.

412 The preserved part of the line reads *ca* +++ *[bha]gavato bhaṣitam␣m abhyanandann iti* .

413 Parts of these symbols look like type no. 12 (see above).

414 The remaining part reads [... *tan]traṃ samāptam*' ('[... tan]tra is concluded').

415 It reads *oṃ namo buddhāyaḥ*(!) || ('oṃ, homage to Buddha').

195v1.[416] A small part of the colophon '*mitā sarvatathāgatajananī sarvabo*' that was written exactly in the upper part of the left blank space (see Fig. 3.6.2.4.2-XVIII) and '*kāṇa*' on the left side of the upper part of the middle blank space on 195v, seem to have been deleted intentionally to keep the upper part fully open as there are no text lines at the top and bottom of the right blank space. The part of the colophon '*mitā sarvatathāgatajananī sarvabo*' and '*kāṇa*' which were originally written in the upper part of the first and second blank spaces, were probably deleted to keep the blank space open and the same parts were then written again after the blank spaces.

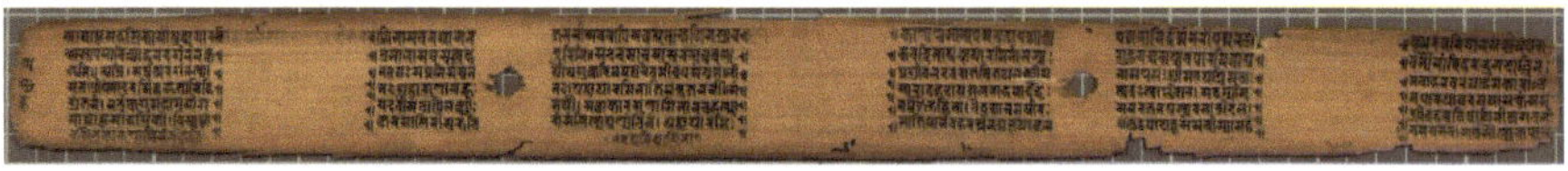

Fig. 3.6.2.4.2-XVII: Large blank spaces at the end of the text in the manuscript of the *Aṣṭasāhasrikā Prajñāpāramitā*, fol. 195v © NAK

Fig. 3.6.2.4.2-XVIII: Enlarged left blank space in which some part of the first line of the text is erased to keep the space free

416 It reads *āryāṣṭasāhasrikāyāṃ|⊙| prajñāpāramitāyāṃ parīnda+parivartto nāma dvātriṅśattamaḥ || 39 || samāptā ceyaṃ bhaga+* [195v1]*ty āryāṣṭasahasrikāyā* (!) *prajñāpāra* \||/ <<*mitā sarvatathāgatajananī sarvabo*>> \||/ *mitā sarvatathāgata|⊙|jananī sarvabodhisatvapratyekajinaśrāva*<<*kāṇa*>>\||/ *kāṇāñ ca mātā* ... ('[thus], the 32nd chapter, namely, the parīnda[na] in the noble Perfection of Wisdom in Eight Thousand Lines is concluded. 39. [The Goddess], the Perfection of Wisdom in Eight Thousand Lines, the mother of all the Tathāgatas, all Bodhisattvas, each Jina and Śrāvaka is also concluded ...').

It is important to stress here that all seven manuscripts featuring such large symbols at the end or near end of the texts, such as the manuscript of the *Dīrghāgama, Vinayavastvāgama* (GBM 1050), *Aṣṭasāhāsrikā Prajñāparamitā* (CUL Add.866), SDhPS, *Saddharmapuṇḍarīka* (CUL Add.2197), *Aṣṭasāhasrikā Prajñāparamitā* (NGMPP E 2122/7) and *Aṣṭasāhasrikā Prajñāparamitā* (KL 18 / NGMPP C 103/2) contain Buddhist texts.

Similarly, the three manuscripts, that of the *Bodhisattvabhūmi* (CUL Add.1702), *Sarvakulatattvasiddhividhivistaratantra* (KL 143 / NGMPP C 14/20) and *Aṣṭasāhasrikā Prajñāpāramitā* (NAK 5/76 / NGMPP A 37/11–A 38/1) that feature a series of three large blank spaces at the end or near end of the text, also contain Buddhist texts. One of the manuscripts even contains the same text (i.e. *Aṣṭasāhasrikā Prajñāpāramitā*) as three manuscripts; the *Aṣṭasāhasrikā Prajñāparamitā* (CUL Add.866), *Aṣṭasāhasrikā Prajñāparamitā* (NGMPP E 2122/7) and *Aṣṭasāhasrikā Prajñāparamitā* (KL 18 / NGMPP C 103/2) which feature a series of large symbols at the end. It is likely the blank spaces in the three manuscripts were left free for the similar series of three large symbols contained in the other manuscripts described in the section above.

The occurrence and distribution of such large symbols at the end of the texts in the manuscripts from Gilgit and Nepal display a significant relation regarding their development and use in the two areas. There is only one visible difference apparent between the symbols in both manuscripts which lies in the symbols in the Gilgit manuscripts (such as the manuscripts of the *Dīrghāgama* and *Vinayavastvāgama* (GBM 1050)) not being placed between sets of double *daṇḍa*s or long vertical lines. The symbols in the Nepalese manuscripts e.g., the manuscript of the *Aṣṭasāhāsrikā Prajñāparamitā* (CUL Add.866), SDhPS, *Saddharmapuṇḍarīka* (CUL Add.2197), *Aṣṭasāhasrikā Prajñāparamitā* (NGMPP E 2122/7) and *Aṣṭasāhasrikā Prajñāparamitā* (KL 18 / NGMPP C 103/2) appear either between sets of double *daṇḍa*s or long vertical lines. This latter phenomenon can be seen in the case of the large blank spaces at the end or near end of the texts in the Nepal manuscripts such as the manuscript of the *Bodhisattvabhūmi* (CUL Add.1702), *Sarvakulatattvasiddhividhivistaratantra* (KL 143 / NGMPP C 14/20) and *Aṣṭasāhasrikā Prajñāpāramitā* (NAK 5/76 / NGMPP A 37/11–A 38/1).

Thus far, I have not seen a similar pattern of symbols in manuscripts containing other texts, whether medical, poetic, puranic, or otherwise. Thus, it may be assumed that this phenomenon may have been a feature both proper and in keeping with Buddhist manuscript tradition.

3.7 Symbols occurring together with foliation numbers

In some manuscripts of my corpus, small and stylised simple *puṣpikā*s occur together with foliation numbers. These can be understood as decorations and as some sort of structural element in the manuscript where they appear at regular intervals. Regarding the latter, it is difficult to say whether or not this kind of information was of any help to the actual user of the manuscript.

In manuscripts from West India, a small stylised *puṣpikā* occurs every ten folio numbers (e.g. folio number 10, 20, 30, etc.).[417] Such symbols appear frequently under the letter-numerals[418] on the left-hand margin of the folio. These symbols are presented below with the foliation number accompanying them, and the (figure-numerical) foliation, without symbol, on the right-hand margin of the same folio.

TSa

TSa is made up of 187 folios. The letter-numerical foliation can be found on the left-hand margin and figure-numerical foliation on the right-hand margin on the verso. With every tenth foliation a small stylised *puṣpikā* appears on the left-hand margin. This is placed exactly under the letter-numeral. All symbols look identical (except for number 100, which appears with the additional upper elements such as the circle and two semi-circular petals on the left and right sides and number 130, which only features a circle): they contain a central circle or a dot surrounded by the three almost semi-circular petals on the left, right and lower sides. The use of additional elements for number 100 may be to emphasize the number '100'. All symbols with foliation can be seen in Fig. 3.7.1-I.

417 For the study of the foliation of Jaina manuscripts, see Kapadia 1973, 171–186. Small stylised *puṣpikā*s can be found together with most of the tenth foliation in Plates V–VII.
418 For the label 'letter-numerals', see Bendall 1883, liii; Kapadia 1973, 171–186; Balbir et al. 2006, 61–62.

	Left-hand margin	Right-hand margin
10		
20		
30		
40		
50		
60		
70		
80		
90		
100		

110		
120		
130	 [419]	
140		
150		
160		
170		

419 In this case there is just a circle. This may have been drawn for a centre part of the stylised *puṣpikā* or similar symbol.

180		

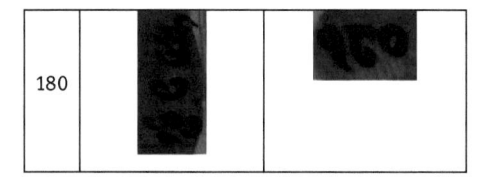

Fig. 3.7-I: Symbols with foliation numbers

TSPV

TSPV consists of 309 folios. Letter-numerical foliation can be found on the left-hand margin and figure-numerical foliation on the right-hand margin of the verso. In most of TSPV every tenth letter-numerical foliation is accompanied by a small stylised *puṣpikā* (between 130–300, there are no symbols with foliation). There appears to have been more than one scribe involved in the manuscript's production; it may be that one of the scribes simply did not draw symbols with foliation, explaining why no symbols appear in some parts of the manuscript (see section 3.9.4 for more details below). Symbols appear exactly under the letter-numerals on the left-hand margin on the folio. Most of the symbols look almost identical (except for 100, 140 and 310). Each symbol contains one circle and on the top of the circle a line or a stroke has been added horizontally. The circle appears surrounded by three almost semi-circular petals on the left, right and bottom sides. However, regarding the symbol with the number 100, there is an additional circle almost similar to the centre part of other symbols with a horizontal line or a stroke at the top, and two semi-circular petals at its left and right sides. Similar to the symbol in the aforementioned manuscript, the use of the additional elements with the stylised *puṣpikā* for the foliation number 100 is perhaps to emphasize the number '100'. The foliation number 140 contains only a circle beneath it and the symbol with number 300 is slightly different and more attractive with its differing petals on the right and left sides. All symbols with foliation can be seen in Fig. 3.7.1-II.

	Left-hand margin	Right-hand margin
40		
50		
60		
70		
80		
90		
100		
110		

120		
130		
140		
300		?
310		?

Fig. 3.7-II: Symbol with foliation

HVM

HVM consists of 107 folios. Letter-numerical foliation can be found on the left-hand margin and figure-numerical foliation on the right-hand margin on the verso. As in the aforementioned manuscripts, every tenth letter-numerical foliation in this manuscript also appears with a small stylised *puṣpikā*. The symbol is exactly under the letter-numerals on the left-hand margin of the folio. Most of the symbols are identical. The symbols on 10, 20, 30, 50, 70 and 90 look similar. The symbols contain one circle in the centre surrounded by three almost semi-circular petals and two lines. Each of its petals faces the outside. The symbol with 40 also contains one circle at its centre and two lines and three near semi-circular petals, however, each of its petals faces inside and one 'tail' has been added to each petal. The symbol with 60 consists of one circle at the centre surrounded by two almost semi-circular petals (on the left and right), two lines and one circle on the bottom. The symbol with 80 contains one circle at its centre surrounded by four lines and four near semi-circular petals.[420] Like the above-mentioned examples, each petal faces the outside. The symbol with 100 is made of one circle at the centre surrounded by two near semi-circular petals facing inside, one circle at the bottom and two lines. Both petals (left and right) and the circle contain a tail. All symbols with foliation can be seen in Fig. 3.7-III.

	Left-hand margin	Right-hand margin
10		
20		
30		
40		
50		
60		

420 See section 3.4, type no. 10 above.

70		
80		
90		
100		

Fig. 3.7-III: Symbol with foliation

BCV

BCV consist of 78 folios. Similar to other manuscripts, letter-numerical foliation can be found on the left-hand margin and figure-numerical foliation on the right-hand margin on the verso. However, an exception is that only the tenth foliation in the manuscript is accompanied by small stylised *puṣpikā*. A symbol can be found under the letter-numerical foliation on the left hand-margin on the folio. It contains one circle in the centre surrounded by four almost semi-circular petals and four lines.[421] The symbol with foliation can be seen in Fig. 3.7-IV.

421 Identical symbols with foliations can be found, see Kapadia 1936, Plate V, with foliation 30, column 3, Plate VI, with foliation 50, column 3, with foliation 60, column 3, with foliation 70, column 2, with foliation 80, column 2, with foliation 90, column 3. See section 3.4, type no. 8 above.

	Left-hand margin	Right-hand margin
10		

Fig. 3.7-IV: Symbol with foliation

3.7.1 Preliminary conclusions

Manuscripts HVM, TSa, TSPV and BCV, purported to originate from West India, contain symbols every ten folios in a remarkable number of cases.[422] The symbols are small and simple in shape, but quite well drawn. To the best of my knowledge, such a feature is uncommon in manuscripts from the regions of Nepal and East India; thus it may be assumed it occurs only in West Indian manuscripts. These symbols are clearly decorative, but also structure the bundle, dividing it into well-defined units. Whether this was their intended function remains uncertain. They cannot be compared to the numbers (or symbols, etc.) used to order the quires of a codex manuscript as the ten folio units are not bound together.

422 Also in the manuscript of the *Tilakamañjarī* (VS 1130 / 1073 CE) (Jinabhadrasūri Grantha Bhaṇḍāra, Jaisalmer, no. 402) with foliation 110, 150; in the manuscript of the *Udbhaṭakāvyālaṅkāralaghuvṛtti* (VS 1160 / 1103 CE) (Jinabhadrasūri Grantha Bhaṇḍāra, Jaisalmer, no. 329) with foliation 10; in the manuscript of the *Upadeśapadaprakaraṇalaghuṭīkā* (VS 1193 / 1136 CE) (Jinabhadrasūri Grantha Bhaṇḍāra, Jaisalmer, no. 215) with foliation 170, 190, 200, 210, 290; in the manuscript of the *Savaga Padikkamana Sutta cunni* (*Śrāvakapratikramasūtra-cūrṇi*) (VS 1317 / 1260 CE) (Museum of Fine Arts, Boston. Denman Waldo Ross Collection, 30.1.1-229) with foliation 10, 30, 40, 50, 60, 70, 80, 90, 100, 120, 130, 150 (only with circle), 160 (only with circle), 170 (only with circle), 180, 200 (with two circles), 220, 240(?), 250, 270. The lower element that appears with foliation 110 is hard to identify as some part of it is faded. The folios 20, 190, 230, 260, 280 seem to be missing; also in the manuscript of the *Sthānāṅgasūtravṛtti* (VS 1300 / 1295 CE) (Jinabhadrasūri Grantha Bhaṇḍāra, Jaisalmer, no. 6) with foliation 10, 20, 30, 40, 50, 60, 70, 80, 90, 160, 170, 180, 240, 250, 280, 310, 330 (partly lost), 340. Furthermore, many of the tenth foliations that are presented by Kapadia 1936 they also appear with stylised small *puṣpikās*, for instance, Plate I, with foliations 10, 20, 30, 40, Plate II, foliation with 50, 60, 70, 80, 90, 100, 110, 200, 260, 290, 300, 400, Plate V, foliation with 10, 20, 30, 40, Plate VI, foliation with 50, 60, 70, 80, 90, Plate VII, foliation with 100, 200, 300, 400. These attestations of symbols mainly with the tenth foliation in West Indian manuscripts suggest a distinct practice.

3.8 Symbols and other features as a means to connect separated parts of the manuscript

Palm-leaf manuscripts are bundles of leaves held mainly together by a piece of string (*sūtra* or *nāḍī*) threaded through pre-bored holes. The front and back folios of the bundle are usually protected by wooden covers (*paṭa* or *paṭalī*).[423]

As the strings are loosened or strings and wooden covers removed when the manuscript texts are read, it may easily occur – intentionally or not – that unrelated or stray folios find their way in the bundle when it is restrung, or folios are not placed back in their original position and have been left out of the bundle to which they belong. Regarding the latter, different parts of the manuscript can end up in libraries and archives quite distant from one another. Alongside palaeographical and layout-related features, symbols assist in reconstructing manuscripts by reconnecting the dismembered parts. Here I will present two relevant examples.

3.8.1 An observation: Symbols and other features on folio in SP_1 and one of the folios in A 38/5

In the NAK, one of the bundles of MS 3/737 contains many folios from different manuscripts. This information has been reiterated by other scholars[424] and by the relevant entry in the NGMCP online catalogue.[425] The manuscript was photographed by the NGMPP on reel no. A 38/5 and later retaken under various nos., namely A 39/19, A 934/20, A, 1166/5, A 1169/3 and A 1170 (henceforth, I call it A 38/5). Among the scholars who delved into the fragmentary folios of this manuscript, I would like to mention the recent study of Harimoto (2011, 93, note 7), who informs us that the bundle contains one folio belonging to SP_1.

SP_1 is also kept in the same archive in Kathmandu as MS no. 2/229 and has been photographed by the NGMPP on reel no. B 11/4. The manuscript is damaged in many places and the foliation is almost completely lost. It has been used by Bhaṭṭarāī (1988) with siglum ‘*kha*’ and by Adriaensen et al. (1998) with siglum ‘SP_1’ for their editions. In this study I too call it SP_1 and compare the features of the folio

423 For instance, see Bühler 1896, 93; Losty 1982, 7.

424 Such as, Matsuda 1996; Harimoto 2011.

425 See NGMCP entry at: <http://ngmcp.fdm.uni-hamburg.de/mediawiki/index.php/A_38-5_Saddharmapu%E1%B9%87%E1%B8%8Dar%C4%ABka(s%C5%ABtra)> (last accessed on 10.10.2018).

from bundle of A 38/5 and features from folios of SP_1. I also discuss the features of SP_1 in sections 3.9.1 and 4.2.2.1 below.

All symbols in SP_1 are only the height of one text line (see Appendix below). Similarly, the symbol on the folio from A 38/5 also has the same height on the folio. The shape of the symbols is similar to some extent (see Fig. 3.8.1-I below). Furthermore, the double *daṇḍa*s demarcating the symbols (and that are also placed after *śloka*s) are similar in both cases: a hook-like line has been added horizontally on the left side of the first of the two *daṇḍas*[426] (see Fig. 3.8.1-I and section 3.9.1 below).

Symbol in SP_1	**Symbol on one of the folios which is in A 38/5**
 [221a4_ACC_9th]	 [?3_ACC_9th]

Fig. 3.8.1-I: Symbol on one of the folios in SP_1 and on one folio in A 38/5

Space-fillers provide further evidence as they are of almost identical shape. They have a hooked 'head' followed by a wavy 'tail' that becomes a straight line at the end (e.g., see Fig. 3.8.1-II).

Selected space-filler on one folio in SP_1	**Space-filler on one of the folios which is in A 38/5**
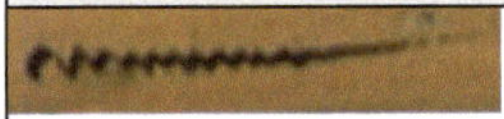 [220b_?rv5_9th]	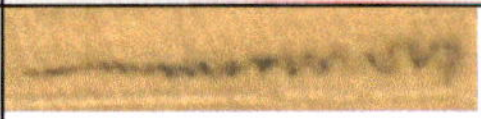 [?rv5_9th]

Fig. 3.8.1-II: Space-filler on one of the folios of SP_1 and on one folio in A 38/5

The overall layout is almost identical in both cases. There are two string-holes[427] on each folio and the text is divided into three text-sections, each with five lines of text. Another similar feature is how the *śloka*s are divided in a similar style: most of the first and second halves of each *śloka* has been divided by means of small gaps in

426 See Bühler 1896, 84: 'Vom Ende des 8. Jahrh. bis zum 13. Jahr. erhält der erste Strich auch einen Haken in der Mitte links ...' ('from the end of the 8th c. until 13th c. the first stroke contains a hook in the middle left') (the translation is mine).

427 One should not be confused here as string-hole with the damaged part at the near centre on the folio in A 38/5.

each text-section (e.g., see Fig. 3.8.1-III and 3.8.1-IV). When the arrangement of lines of *ślokas* is done in this manner, each line of the folio usually contains three *ślokas*.

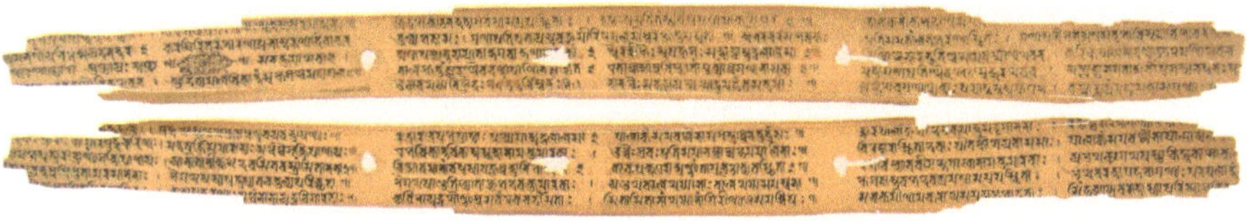

Fig. 3.8.1-III: Overall layout, the folio which is now in the bundle of A 38/5 © NAK

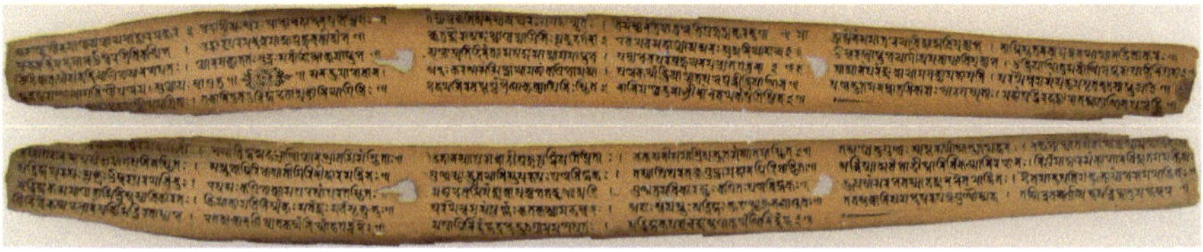

Fig. 3.8.1-IV: Overall layout, one of the folios (220b/221a) of SP_1 © NAK

Based on the blatant similarities of the shape of symbols, *daṇḍas*, space-fillers and overall layout, the assumption can be made that the folio from A 38/5 belongs to SP_1.

3.8.2 An observation: Symbols and other features in SP_3 and SP_4

In the Bodleian Library, Oxford, one manuscript of the *Skandapurāṇa* has been kept under MS Sansk a 14 (R). This manuscript has been designated by Adriaensen et al. (1998) with the siglum 'SP_3' for their edition. I use the same siglum for this study.

There are 22 fragments of the *Skandapurāṇa* collected under manuscript 4/2260 in the NAK, that have been photographed by the NGMPP on reel B 12/2 (later retake as A 1084/7). This manuscript is designated by Bhaṭṭarāī (1988) with the siglum '*ga*' and by Adriaensen et al. (1998) with the siglum 'SP_4'. In the present work I also refer to this manuscript as SP_4.

Adriaensen et al. have already pointed out the close connection between SP_3 and SP_4, which, according to them, once formed a single bundle, although they are now kept in different libraries. In addition to other factors, such as palaeographical evidence, layout, etc.,[428] the editors based their assumption on the fact that the symbols of both manuscripts are of near identical shape.

Hereafter, I will focus on the symbols appearing in both SP_3 and SP_4, and I will also examine the use of colour, although I only had the opportunity to see but a few colour images[429] of SP_3 for the preparation of this book.

The first set of similar symbols contains double circles surrounded by eight petals, in turn enclosed by double concentric circles (see Fig. 3.8.2-I).[430] They can be found on 5r1 in SP_4 and on 112v2, 127r1, 147v4, 165v1 in SP_3. The symbols in both manuscripts occupy an area of three lines on the folio. The double *daṇḍa*s that enclose the symbols in both manuscripts are identical: the first *daṇḍa* of the two often have a sharp hooked element.

Symbol in SP_4, Nepal	**Symbols in SP_3, Bodleian**	
 [5r1_ACC_10th]	 [147v4_BCC_10th]	 [165v1_BCC_10th]

Fig. 3.8.2-I: Similar symbols in SP_3 and SP_4

The second set of identical symbols appears on 71r2 in SP_4 and on 26r6, 69r4, 88r1, 136r4 in SP_3 (e.g., see Fig. 3.8.2-II below).[431] The height of all symbols is two lines of the folio and consists of one circle and eight petals. Double *daṇḍa*s enclosing symbols in both manuscripts are also identical.

Symbol in SP_4, Nepal	**Symbols in SP_3, Bodleian**	
 [71r2_BCC_10th]	 [26r6_BCC]	 [69r4_BCC_10th]
	 [88r1_BCC_10th]	 [136r4_ACC_10th]

Fig. 3.8.2-II: Similar symbols in SP_3 and SP_4

428 See Adriaensen et al. 1998, 34.

429 Here I thank my friend Dr Camillo Formigatti (Oxford Library) who was so kind and checked some folios of this manuscript for me at the library during the preparation of the present book.

430 See section, 3.4, type no. 35 above.

431 See section 3.4, type no. 27 above.

The third set of identical symbols is found on 71r2, 71v1 in SP$_4$ and 3v5, 70r1, 139r4, 193r5 in SP$_3$ (see Fig. 3.8.2-III). Some of the left part of the symbol on 3v5 in SP$_3$ has been lost, however, its right part is still visible, and looks similar to the part of other symbols presented here. The symbols consist of circle surrounded by eight petals and their height is two lines of the folio. Here the double *daṇḍa*s that enclose the symbols are almost identical.

Symbol in SP$_4$, Nepal	**Symbols in SP$_3$, Bodleian**
 [71r2_ACC_10th]	 [3v5_ACC_10th]  [70r1_ACC_10th]
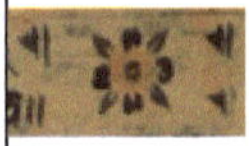 [71v1_ACC_10th]	 [139r4_BCC_10th]  [193r5_ACC_10th]

Fig. 3.8.2-III: Similar symbols in SP$_3$ and SP$_4$

The fourth type of 'near' similar symbols can be found on 68v3 in SP$_4$ and on 21v1, 196v1 in SP$_3$ (see Fig. 3.8.2-IV). The symbol has at its centre, double circles surrounded by eight petals. To some extent, the symbols have a 'rhombus'-like appearance. The height of the symbols in both manuscripts is that of two lines of the folio. The double *daṇḍa*s that demarcate the symbols in both manuscripts are identical.

Symbol in SP$_4$, Nepal	**Symbol in SP$_3$, Bodleian**
 [68v3_BCC_10th]	 [21v1_BCC_10th]  [196v1_BCC_10th]

Fig. 3.8.2-IV: Similar symbols in SP$_3$ and SP$_4$

Another set of identical symbols found in both manuscripts features a symbol containing one curved-like line at its centre (see Fig. 3.8.2-V).[432] As already mentioned above in section 3.4 (Fig. 3.4-IV), this symbol has similarities with some of the letter-numerals '80'. This symbol can be found on 71v5 in SP$_4$ and many times (such as the right column in Fig. 3.8.2-V) in SP$_3$ and its height is often just

432 See also section 3.4, type no. 4 above.

one line of the folio. Furthermore, double *daṇḍa*s that enclose symbols in both manuscripts are also identical.

Symbol in SP₄, Nepal	Symbols in SP₃, Bodleian
 [71v5_BCC_10th]	 [29r3_BCC_10th]  [141r1_ACC_10th]  [100r_BCC_10th]  [147r2_BCC_10th]  [147r2_ACC_10th]  [150v5_BCC_10th]  [158r2_BCC_10th]  [158r2_ACC_10th]  [190v5_BCC_10th]  [191r6_ACC_10th]  [236v4_BCC_10th]  [236v5_ACC_10th]  [240r5_BCC_10th]  [240r5_ACC_10th]

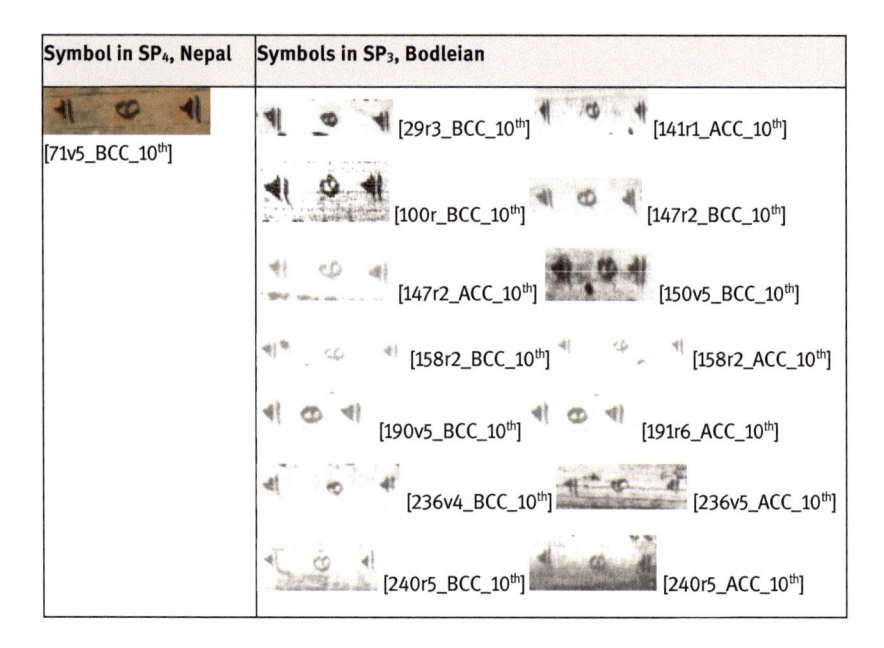

Fig. 3.8.2-V: Similar symbols in SP_3 and SP_4

The sixth set includes the symbol that looks like a 'figure-eight knot', or two small circles joined together horizontally (see Fig. 3.8.2-VI below).[433] They appear on 247v5 in SP_4 and on folios (such as right column in Fig. 3.8.2-VI) in SP_3. In both manuscripts they are a height of one text-line of the folio. The double *daṇḍa*s that demarcate symbols in both manuscripts are identical.

Symbol in SP₄, Nepal	Symbols in SP₃, Bodleian
 [247v5_BCC_10th]	 [21v1_ACC_10th]  [84v6_BCC_10th] 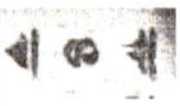 [88r1_ACC_10th]  [132r4_BCC_10th]

433 See section 3.4, type no. 3 above.

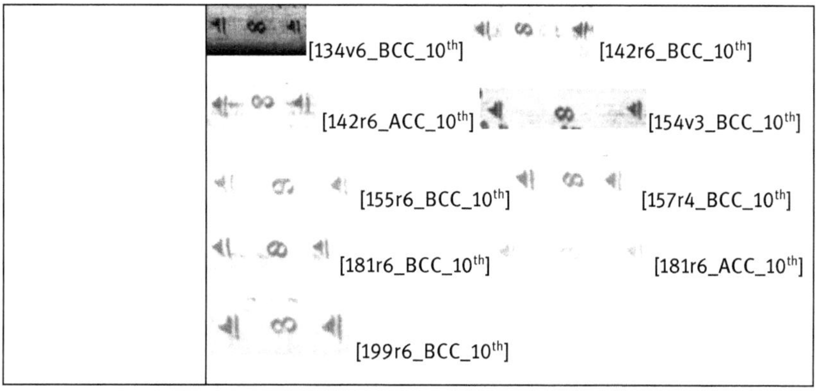
[134v6_BCC_10th]
[142r6_BCC_10th]
[142r6_ACC_10th]
[154v3_BCC_10th]
[155r6_BCC_10th]
[157r4_BCC_10th]
[181r6_BCC_10th]
[181r6_ACC_10th]
[199r6_BCC_10th]

Fig. 3.8.2-VI: Similar symbols in SP_3 and SP_4

Another set of identical symbols includes a simple circle (see Fig. 3.8.2-VII).[434] They are on 274v5 in SP_4 and on folios (as seen in the right column in Fig. 3.8.2-VII) in SP_3 and occupy only one line on the folio. Similar to the examples above, the double *daṇḍa*s that enclose the symbols in both manuscripts are identical.

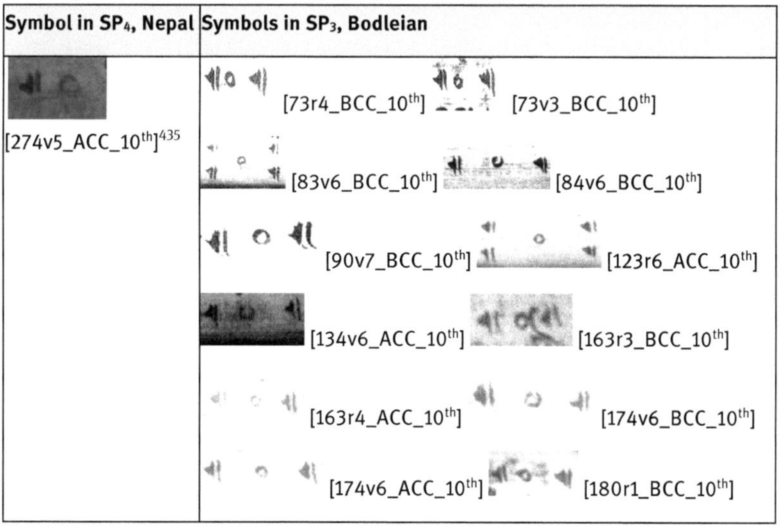
Symbol in SP4, Nepal
Symbols in SP3, Bodleian
[274v5_ACC_10th]435
[73r4_BCC_10th]
[73v3_BCC_10th]
[83v6_BCC_10th]
[84v6_BCC_10th]
[90v7_BCC_10th]
[123r6_ACC_10th]
[134v6_ACC_10th]
[163r3_BCC_10th]
[163r4_ACC_10th]
[174v6_BCC_10th]
[174v6_ACC_10th]
[180r1_BCC_10th]

434 See section 3.4, type no. 2 above.

435 This symbol appears right before the right string-hole space and the second set of double *daṇḍa*s appears after the string-hole space.

	 [187v3_ACC_10th]  [199r6_ACC_10th]  [234v1_ACC_10th]

Fig. 3.8.2-VII: Similar symbols in SP_3 and SP_4

The use of colour could also be helpful in establishing a connection between SP_3 and SP_4. In the latter, *daṇḍa*s or around the spaces of *daṇḍa*s appearing before and after almost all speaker indications (e.g., *sana*[*tkumāra*] *u*[*vāca*] 'Sanatkumara said') are highlighted (see also section 5.1 below). As mentioned above, there was only the opportunity to see a few colour images of SP_3. The presence of colour can also be seen on *daṇḍa*s or around the spaces of *daṇḍa*s that appear before and after speaker indications (Fig. 3.8.2-IX).

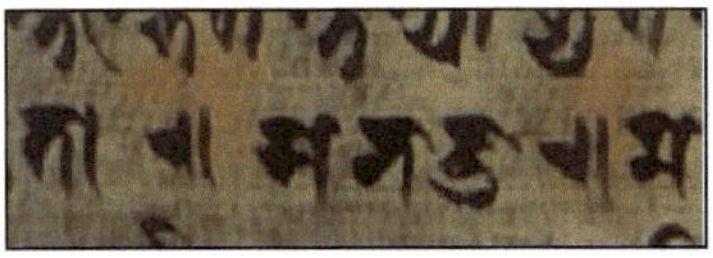

Fig. 3.8.2-VIII: Highlighted *daṇḍa*s or around the spaces of *daṇḍa*s before and after the speaker indication (extracted part from 62r4 of SP_4)

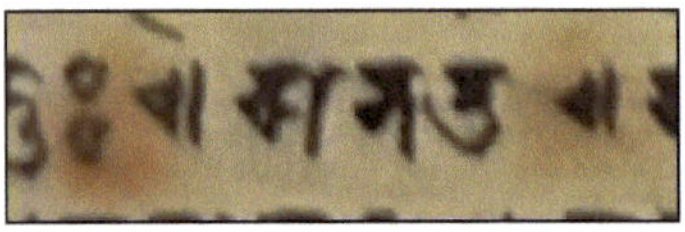

Fig. 3.8.2-IX: Highlighted *daṇḍa*s or around the spaces of *daṇḍa*s before and after the speaker indication (extracted part from 48r3 of SP_3)

A few identical or near identical symbols appearing at the end of the chapters in SP_3 and SP_4 have already been seen. Most of the *daṇḍa*s that appear at the end of *śloka*s or that enclose symbols are identical in both manuscripts. In addition, one can also see a similar use of colour on certain *daṇḍa*s or spaces around the *daṇḍa*s. Alongside other evidence, this example shows how symbols and other visual features can be used to reconstruct dismembered parts of a manuscript.

3.9 Symbols and other features as a means to identify a change of scribe

If more than one scribe were involved in the course of the production of a manuscript, symbols and other features (such as palaeographical evidence, space-fillers and the overall layout of the page) may be helpful in determining the number of scribes involved on that particular manuscript. In the following, a few selected examples taken from five manuscripts of my corpus will be presented to demonstrate how such features can help identify differing scribal hands in one manuscript.

3.9.1 Symbols and other features in SP_1

As already mentioned in the previous chapter, manuscript SP_1 is kept in the NAK under MS no. 2/229 and has been photographed by the NGMPP on reel no. B 11/4. The manuscript is damaged in many parts and most of the foliation has not been preserved (with a few exceptions). Bhaṭṭarāī (1988) has used it with siglum '*kha*' in his edition and Adriaensen et al. (1998) with siglum 'SP_1'.

In the considerably disordered folios of SP_1, one finds a few folios on the recension of the *Pārameśvara(tantra)* and a few folios of SP_1 bear near similar handwriting to the folios of the recension of the *Pārameśvara(tantra)*. Here I limit myself to the majority of the folios that contain the copy of the *Skandapurāṇa* which were 'probably' copied by two different scribes. This is evidenced by noticeable differences in the symbols, palaeographical features and the overall layout. Hereafter, the two scribes are labelled A and B.

Both A and B scribes draw symbols at the end of the chapters and place them between double *daṇḍas*. Scribe A draws only double circles aside from three small and stylised simple *puṣpikās*. These three stylised *puṣpikās* contain a circle or dot surrounded by four almost semi-circular petals and four lines (see the first column in Fig. 3.9.1-I). Conversely, scribe B draws a large variety of beautiful symbols (see the second column in Fig. 3.9.1-I). Furthermore, clear differences are to be seen in the double *daṇḍas* written by scribe A or B (see below).

Scribe A	Scribe B
 [42b4_BCC_9^{th}]	 [77a4_BCC_9^{th}]
 [52b5_ACC_9^{th}]	 [84a4_BCC_9^{th}]
 [165b5_ACC_9^{th}]	 [105b3_ACC_9^{th}]
 [260b5_ACC_9^{th}]	 [203a1_ACC_9^{th}]

Fig. 3.9.1-I: Symbols by scribes A and B

Both scribes write *daṇḍa*s before and after the chapter colophons or around their symbols. Scribe A, however rarely uses double *daṇḍa*s to demarcate verses, or before and after speaker indications.[436] Instead, he uses single *daṇḍa*s that are more or less straight (see the first row in the first column in Fig. 3.9.1-II), where the first of the two *daṇḍa*s are shorter than the second one (see the first column in the second row in Fig. 3.9.1-II). On the other hand, scribe B's single *daṇḍa*s written in various places within the manuscript are slightly curved or slanted (see the second column in the first row in Fig. 3.9.1-II). Scribe B writes double *daṇḍa*s at the end of *śloka*s that differ to those of scribe A writes before and after chapter colophons. As stated in the previous chapter, the first of the two *daṇḍa*s has a hook-like component added horizontally at its centre (see the second column in the second row in Fig. 3.9.1-II). It is also important to note that scribe A's *daṇḍa*s are slightly thicker than scribe B's *daṇḍa*s.

436 A portion of the transcription of the text from (131a4): *pitara uvāca | tatas te suraśārdūlāḥ |⊙|prapracchaḥ svāṃ sutāṃ tadā | prāyaścittāni dharmāñ ca vedāṃ sāṃgāṃ savistarāṃ | te ca tebhyas tadā putrā |⊙|ācakṣuḥ prayatā subhāḥ |* ...

	Scribe A	**Scribe B**
Single *daṇḍa*	 [42b3_9th]  [42b4_9th]  [70a115v3_9th]	 [74a3_9th]  [74a4_9th]  [74a5_9th]
Double *daṇḍa*	 [48b4_9th]  [57a4_9th]  [63a1_9th]	 [74a3_9th]  [74a4_9th]  [74a5_9th]

Fig. 3.9.1-II: Single and double *daṇḍa*s by scribes A and B

Differences appear in the way scribe A and B write *akṣara*s. Here are two examples of each of the selected *akṣara*s, namely *ka*, *ga*, *thā* and *hā* (see Fig. 3.9.1-III).

	Scribe A	**Scribe B**
ka	 [121a4_9th]  [121a5_9th]	 [318a1_9th]  [318b4_9th]
ga	 [109b6_9th]  [111b3_9th]	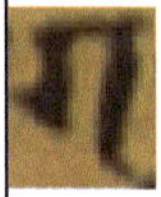 [317a4_9th]  [318a4_9th]
thā	 [109b1_9th]  [121a2]	 [317b1_9th]  [317b3_9th]
hā	 [104a1_9th]  [104b2_9th]	 [314a1_9th]  [314a4_9th]

Fig. 3.9.1-III: *Akṣara*s by scribes A and B

Space-fillers also indicate the work of at least two different scribes. Scribe A draws space-fillers with a hooked head followed by a more or less straight line. Space-fillers are always drawn from left to right (see the first column in Fig. 3.9.1-IV). Scribe B also draws space-fillers with a hooked head, but the following 'tail' is rather wavy at first and then becomes straight. The direction scribe B draws the filler is both left to right and right to left (see the second column in Fig. 3.9.1-IV).

Scribe A	Scribe B
 [11b7_9th]	 [80b116r6_9th]
 [165a78r7_9th]	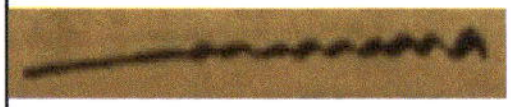 [78a193v6_9th]

Fig. 3.9.1-IV: Space-fillers by scribes A and B

In addition to the different symbols and palaeographical evidence that reveal information on the number of scribes involved in the production of SP_1, elements of the overall layout should also be taken into consideration. There are two string-holes on each folio and the text has been divided into three text-sections. Scribe A writes most of the text without any further division. This means there are no clear gaps between the first and second half of the *śloka* (see Fig. 3.9.1-V). However, scribe B divides the *śloka*s by leaving gaps between their first and second halves on many folios (see Fig. 3.9.1-VI).[437]

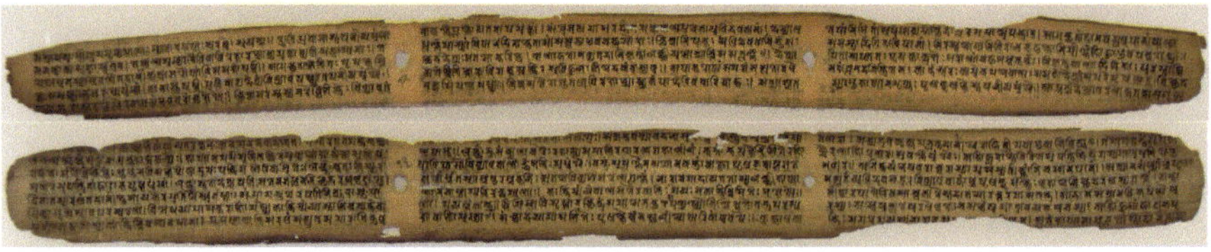

Fig. 3.9.1-V: Overall layout by scribe A (61ab) © NAK

437 I discuss the use of gaps and layout features further in section 4.2.2.1 below.

Fig. 3.9.1-VI: Overall layout by scribe B (74ab) © NAK

This significantly large amount of evidence clearly indicates that at least two scribes have been involved in the production of SP_1.[438]

3.9.2 Symbols and other features in SP_2

Features in another manuscript of the *Skandapurāṇa* tells of the involvement of at least two scribes in its production. This manuscript has been kept in the NAK, under the MS no. 1/831 and has been photographed by the NGMPP on reel B 12/3 (and retaken as A 1086/2?). This manuscript was designated by Bhaṭṭarāī (1988) with siglum '*ka*' and by Adriaensen et al. (1998) with 'SP_2' in their editions. Here it is referred to as SP_2.

From the appearance of the symbols at the end of the chapters and other palaeographic and layout-related evidence, it is safe to assume there were at least two scribes involved in the manuscript production.[439] Here, are presented several selected symbols, *daṇḍa*s, *akṣara*s, space-fillers and layout features that are possible to be attributed to one or the other of the two scribes. The two scribes are dubbed A and B.

Scribes A and B both draw symbols at the end of chapters. Scribe A draws a variety of symbols from simple double circles to two realistic *puṣpikās*[440] (see left column in Fig. 3.9.2-I). It should be noted that most of his symbols appear after chapter colophons. At times he leaves blank spaces at the end of chapters, where one would expect symbols. His symbols vary enormously in shape, size and artistic value. Their height is of one to three lines of the folio. Whereas, scribe B draws only simple double circles encompassing only one line of the folio (see the right column in Fig. 3.9.2-I).

438 Only if we exclude the other hand that appears similar to the handwriting of PT etc.

439 Save for one folio on which a content list with numbers arranged in columns placed between vertical lines. Most of these numbers have no writing accompanying them. But a few of these numbers contain 'titles' from a few chapters. It is likely the numbers unaccompanied by writing were to be filled by 'chapter titles'. However, the handwriting of these items looks modern by comparison with the hands of the text of other folios.

440 Both realistic *puṣpikā*s have been discussed in section 3.5.1 above. See also Fig. 3.5.1-I.

Scribe A	Scribe B
 [5a6_ACC_9th]	 [187b3_BCC_9th]
 [19a7_ACC_9th]	 [187b3_ACC_9th]
 [19b2_ACC_9th]	 [198a3_ACC_9th]
 [63v5_ACC_9th]	 [192a3_ACC_9th]
 [66v2_ACC_9th]	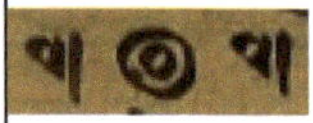 [198a3_ACC_9th]

Fig. 3.9.2-I: Symbols by scribes A and B

Regarding the *daṇḍa*s, A writes two types of single *daṇḍa*s; his first type of single *daṇḍa* is slanted and the second type more or less straight but with a hook-like element added horizontally to its centre (see the left column in the first row in Fig. 3.9.2-II), but scribe B's, single *daṇḍa*s are predominantly straight (see the right column in the first row in Fig. 3.9.2-II).

Both scribes use double *daṇḍa*s. A uses at least two types of double *daṇḍa*s. A's first *daṇḍa* of the first double *daṇḍa*s includes a hook-like element at its near centre; and the line at the top curves to the left. However, the first *daṇḍa* of his second type of double *daṇḍa*s only features a hook-like element.

B draws at least three types of double *daṇḍa*s. The first *daṇḍa* of his first type of double *daṇḍa*s has no additional element and is slightly shorter than the second (see the left column in the second row in Fig. 3.9.2-II). This type of double *daṇḍa*s often appear after the second half of the *śloka*s.

The first *daṇḍa* of his second type of double *daṇḍa*s contains only a hook-like element (see the right column in the third row in Fig. 3.9.2-II), however, the first *daṇḍa* of his third type of double *daṇḍa*s has a remarkable curved line on its upper side (see the right column in the fourth row in Fig. 3.9.2-II). The left part looks significantly thicker. Both types of double *daṇḍa*s appear before and after the symbols at the end of the chapters.

	Scribe A	Scribe B
Single *daṇḍa*	 [14a5_9th]  [28b3_9th]	 [198b3_9th]  [203a5_9th]
Double *daṇḍa*	 [5a3_9th]  [13a4_9th]	 [198b3_9th]  [203a5_9th]
		 [185a3_9th]  [185a3_9th]
	 [171b2_9th]  [174a3_9th]	 [189a3_9th]  [189a3_9th]

Fig. 3.9.2-II: Single and double *daṇḍa*s by scribe A and B

Differences can also be seen in the way the *akṣara*s are written. I have gathered some selected *akṣara*s here, namely *a* and *ka*. Upon close examination, it is barely possible to make out whether A or B wrote them (see Fig. 3.9.2-III).

	Scribe A	Scribe B
a	 [14b6_9th]  [19a3_9th]	 [203b6_9th]  [205b2_9th]
ka	 [19a3_9th]  [23a6_9th]	 [205b4_9th]  [208a3_9th]

Fig. 3.9.2-III: *Akṣara*s by scribes A and B

Space-fillers provided other important evidence. Scribe A's space-fillers look like a tight coil with a slanted 'tail'. The head of the space-fillers is often bent down (see the left column in Fig. 3.9.2-IV below). However, most of scribe B's space-fillers look like a kind of stretched coil followed by a nearly straight 'tail' (see the lower three examples in right column). Their heads are on both the upper and lower sides (see the right column in Fig. 3.9.2-IV).

Scribe A	Scribe B
 [7b7_9^{th}]	 [190b7_9^{th}]
 [15b7_9^{th}]	 [191a1_9^{th}]
 [56a1_9^{th}]	 [203b1_9^{th}]
 [169a1_9^{th}]	 [208a6_9^{th}]

Fig. 3.9.2-IV: Space-fillers by scribes A and B

In terms of layout is concerned, there are two string-holes on each folio and the text has been divided into three text-sections. On many folios scribe A uses small gaps between the first and second half of the *śloka*s (see the lower folio in Fig. 3.9.2-V). On at least one folio such small gaps are justified in text-sections (see the upper folio in Fig. 3.9.2-V). Scribe B often writes the text in a dense way without clear, visible gaps between the first and second halves of *śloka*s or lines (see in Fig. 3.9.2-VI).[441]

Fig. 3.9.2-V: Overall layout by scribe A, fols.(?) (5ab) © NAK

441 I discuss the use of gaps and layout features of this manuscript further in section 4.2.2.2 below.

Fig. 3.9.2-VI: Overall layout by scribe B, fols.(?) (205ab) © NAK

Based on the differences in the characteristics of the symbols, *daṇḍa*s, *akṣara*s, space-fillers, the overall layout and how they are written and designed, it is safe to assume at least two scribes, working on the manuscript production either together or one after the other.

3.9.3 Symbols and other features in KT

Another relevant example is the manuscript copy of the *Kiraṇatantra*. The manuscript is kept in the NAK under NAK no. 5/893 and has been microfilmed by the NGMPP on reel A 40/3. The manuscript contains an important śaiva trantric text. Goodall (1998) used the manuscript in his edition with the siglum 'N_1'.[442] Here I call it KT.

Apart from a portion of the text (a part of the second line and third and fourth lines) on the folio 99r and the last two folios there is a table of contents of probably added later. Here it can be assumed there were at least three scribes involved in the manuscript production. The three scribes are denoted as A, B and C.

All three scribes draw symbols at the end of chapters. Scribe A largely draws symbols containing circles surrounded by four petals and four lines. He also draws a few double circles (see left column in Fig. 3.9.3-I).

Scribe B also draws symbols at the end of chapters. But his symbols have different stylised *puṣpikā*s, double circles and some puzzling symbols (see the middle column in Fig. 3.9.3-I).[443] Please note that some of his symbols appear to have been drawn over previously made symbols. In symbol on 50r4, four lines of the previous symbol remain visible.

442 See Goodall 1998, lxxxiv–lxxxv.

443 I have discussed this manuscript and some of its features in section 3.6.2.2 and 3.6.2.4.1 above.

Scribe C also draws symbols at the end of chapters. However, he usually draws stylised *puṣpikās* consisting of a circle surrounded by four petals and four lines. Each petal of the symbol appears to have been made by joining two almost semi-circular elements on the side. He also draws several circles, one with a curved line at its centre, one with a curved line surrounded by a circle and a double circle (see right column in Fig. 3.9.3-I below). Compared to the symbols of scribe A and B, his are quite different in shape. One can also see a few differences between the *daṇḍa*s of scribe A, B and C demarcating the symbols.

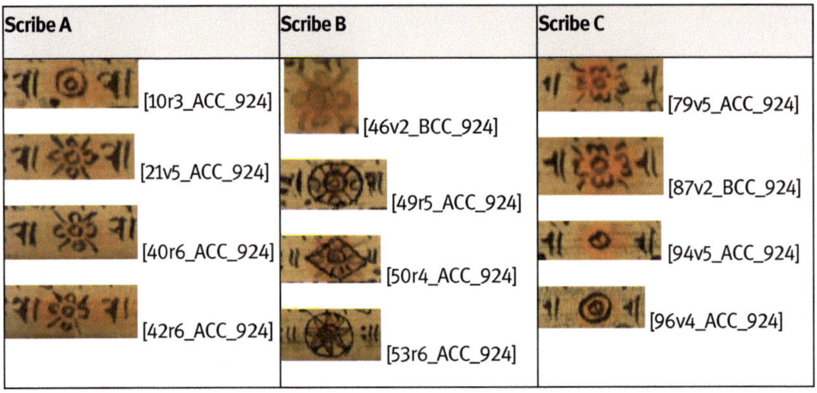
Scribe A
Scribe B
Scribe C
[10r3_ACC_924]
[21v5_ACC_924]
[40r6_ACC_924]
[42r6_ACC_924]
[46v2_BCC_924]
[49r5_ACC_924]
[50r4_ACC_924]
[53r6_ACC_924]
[79v5_ACC_924]
[87v2_BCC_924]
[94v5_ACC_924]
[96v4_ACC_924]

Fig. 3.9.3-I: Symbols by scribes A, B and C

The manner in which the *akṣara*s are written also differs significantly. The following figure shows the differences characterising some selected *akṣara*s (i.e. *i*, *ṇā* and *ma*).

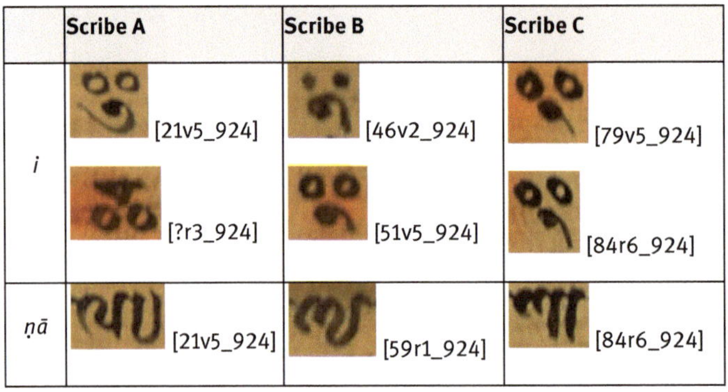
Scribe A
Scribe B
Scribe C
i
[21v5_924]
[?r3_924]
[46v2_924]
[51v5_924]
[79v5_924]
[84r6_924]
ṇā
[21v5_924]
[59r1_924]
[84r6_924]

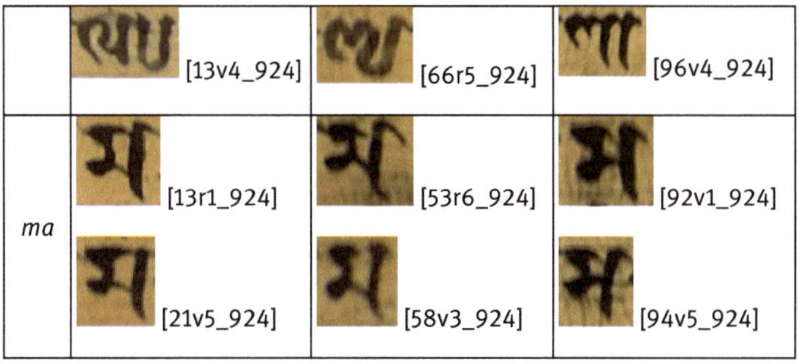
[13v4_924]
[66r5_924]
[96v4_924]
ma
[13r1_924]
[53r6_924]
[92v1_924]
[21v5_924]
[58v3_924]
[94v5_924]

Fig. 3.9.3-II: *Akṣara*s by scribes A, B and C

Regarding the space-fillers, the wavy lines drawn by scribe A are far denser than those of scribe B and C (see the left column in Fig. 3.9.3-III). The front part of space-fillers of B always starts from the right (see the middle column in Fig. 3.9.3-III). The beginning part of C's space-fillers commences with a hooked head, followed sometimes by a short wavy line ending in a more or less straight line (see the right column in Fig. 3.9.3-III).

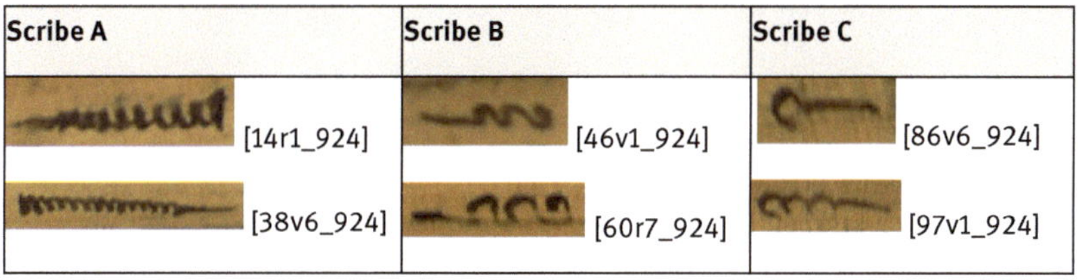
Scribe A
Scribe B
Scribe C
[14r1_924]
[46v1_924]
[86v6_924]
[38v6_924]
[60r7_924]
[97v1_924]

Fig. 3.9.3-III: Space-fillers by scribes A, B and C

In terms of layout, there are two string-holes on each folio. Scribe A divides the text into three text-sections determined by the string-holes. However, scribe B and C divide the text into two text-sections only. Compared with scribes B and C, scribe A's handwriting is more attractive and the *akṣara*s appear slightly larger (see Figs. 3.9.3-IV and 3.9.3-VI). Furthermore, scribe A has left generous free spaces on the left and right margins and the text has been more carefully arranged than those on the folios of scribes B and C.

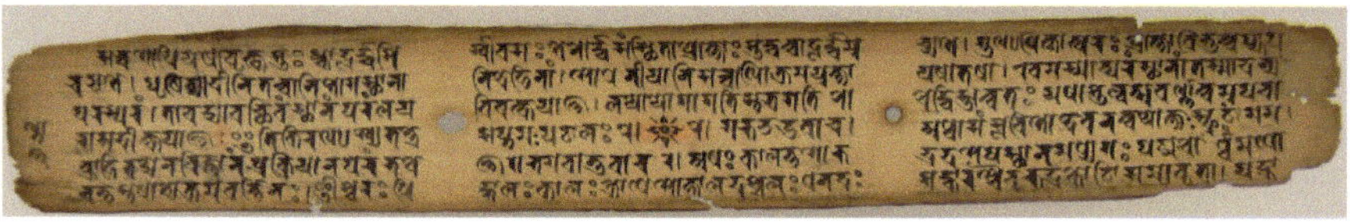

Fig. 3.9.3-IV: Overall layout by scribe A, fol. 13v © NAK

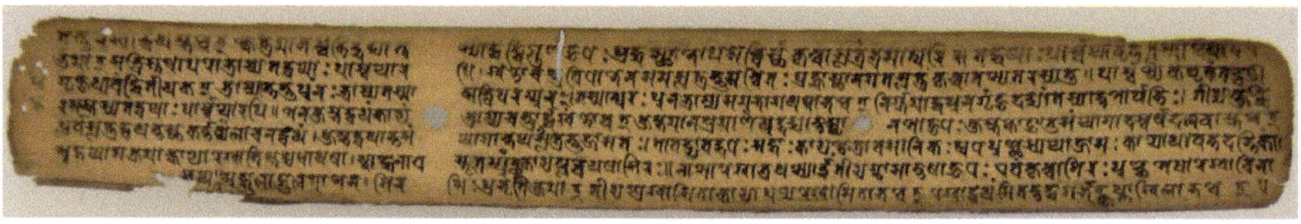

Fig. 3.9.3-V: Overall layout by scribe B, fol. 44v © NAK

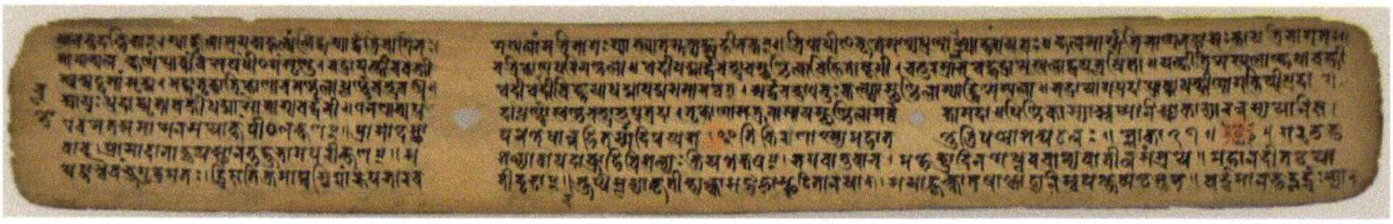

Fig. 3.9.3-VI: Overall layout by scribe C, fol. 79v © NAK

Such clear differences in the drawing of the symbols, writing the *akṣaras*, making space-fillers and the overall layout make it safe to assume that at least three scribes have worked on the manuscript production.

3.9.4 Symbols and other features in TSPV

Here attention is turned to manuscript TSPV which is in possession of Jinabhadrasūri Grantha Bhaṇḍāra, Jaisalmer under MS no. 378 and dated ca. 1143 c.[444]

The analysis of symbols, space-fillers and overall layout suggest that at least four scribes have been involved in the production of the manuscript. Here, identified as scribes A, B, C and D.

With the exception of scribe C, all scribes draw symbols around the string-holes. These symbols present clear differences. Scribe A's symbols appear to be

444 See Jambuvijay 2000, 40.

comprised of largely strokes or lines (see the left column in Fig. 3.9.4-I). Compared to B and D; A's symbols are less sophisticated.

Scribe B's symbols contain four almost semi-circular petals. One line seems to have been added horizontally to the upper part of the semi-circular petal. A 'tail' has been added to the lower part of the lower semi-circular petal and the 'tail' hangs downward to the right (see second column from left in Fig. 3.9.4-I).

D's symbols are slightly similar to those of B. One horizontal line is added to the upper element of the symbol and a tail to its lower part. However, the left and right elements of D's symbols are clearly differently drawn to those of both A and B. The petals are made by joining two semi-circular elements on the side (see right column in Fig. 3.9.4-I). As the examples show, parts of D's symbols are frequently missing due by the part of the folio around the string-holes being missing.

Scribe A	Scribe B	Scribe C	Scribe D
 [29v_LSH_1143]	 [35v_LSH_1143]	-	 [200r?_LSH_1143]
 [29v_RSH_1143]	 [35v_RSH_1143]		 [200r?_RSH_1143]
 [33v_LSH_1143]	 [36v_LSH_1143]		 [200v?_LSH_1143]
 [33v_RSH_1143]	 [36v_RSH_1143]		 [200r?_RSH_1143]

Fig. 3.9.4-I: Symbols by scribes A, B and D

Scribes A, B, C and D all use space-fillers, but of different shapes. Scribe A draws semi-circle-like space-fillers with the upper left part bending inward and touching the inner part. The upper right part, however, is simply bent inwards (see the left column in Fig. 3.9.4-II). B largely draws coil-like space-fillers followed by a slanted line (see the second column from the left in Fig. 3.9.4-II). With a few exceptions C usually draws two types of space-fillers. The first type has a hooked head followed by a slanted line. The second looks like a semi-circle with its upper left and right lines bent inwards (see the third column from the left in Fig. 3.9.4-II). Notably, the second type seems to be a variation of the letter-numeral ‘80’.[445]

Space-fillers of D are almost similar to the second type of space-fillers written by C, but their upper right part is followed by a sort of tail (see right column in Fig. 3.9.4-II).

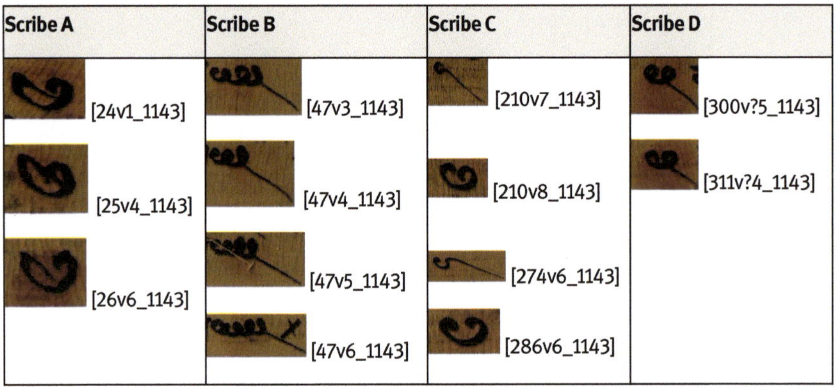
Scribe A
Scribe B
Scribe C
Scribe D
[24v1_1143]
[25v4_1143]
[26v6_1143]
[47v3_1143]
[47v4_1143]
[47v5_1143]
[47v6_1143]
[210v7_1143]
[210v8_1143]
[274v6_1143]
[286v6_1143]
[300v?5_1143]
[311v?4_1143]

Fig. 3.9.4-II: Space-fillers by scribes A, B, C and D

Differences can also be seen all the four scribes’ overall layout. There are two string-holes on each folio and the text is divided into three text-sections. All scribes use ruling-lines except for C.

A’s ruling-lines consist of sets of parallel vertical lines, which demarcate each text-section on the folio (see Fig. 3.9.4-III). A clear gap can be seen between those vertical lines. Scribes B and D largely use a set of two parallel vertical lines. Scribes A, B and D write the text more or less in straight lines and their handwriting is tidy. However, C’s handwriting is less neat to that of A, B and D and the lines are often not particularly straight.

445 See Bendall 1883, Table of Letter-numerals; Kapadia 1936, Plate II, VI.

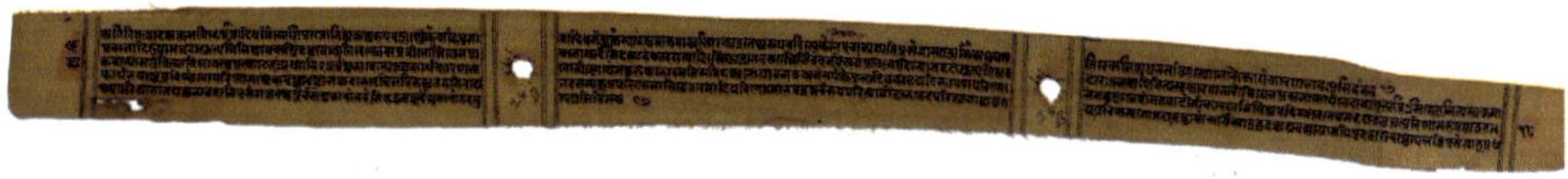

Fig. 3.9.4-III: Overall layout by scribe A, fol. 18v © Jinabhadrasūri Grantha Bhaṇḍāra, Jaisalmer

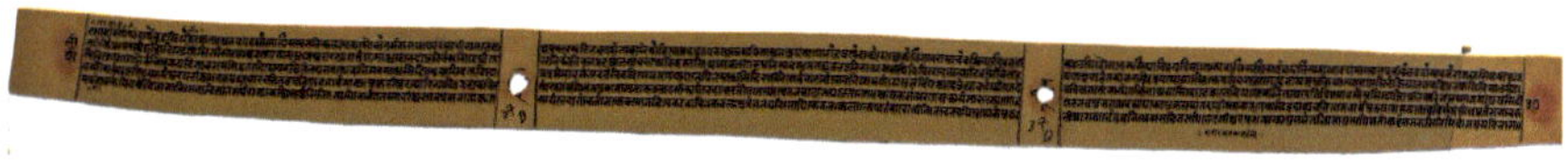

Fig. 3.9.4-IV: Overall layout by scribe B, fol. 37v ©-Jinabhadrasūri Grantha Bhaṇḍāra, Jaisalmer

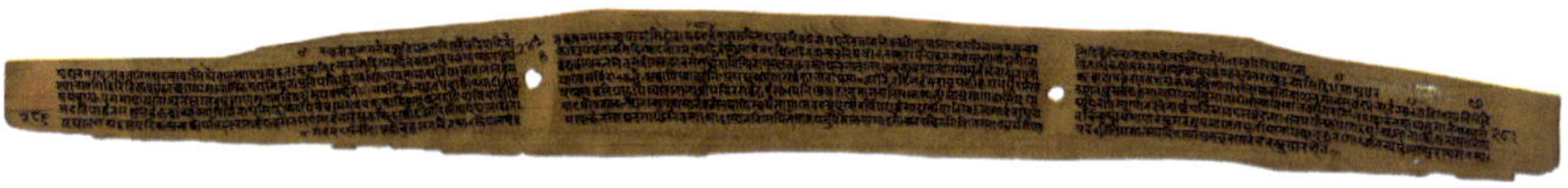

Fig. 3.9.4-V: Overall layout by scribe C, fol. 281v/286v? © Jinabhadrasūri Grantha Bhaṇḍāra, Jaisalmer

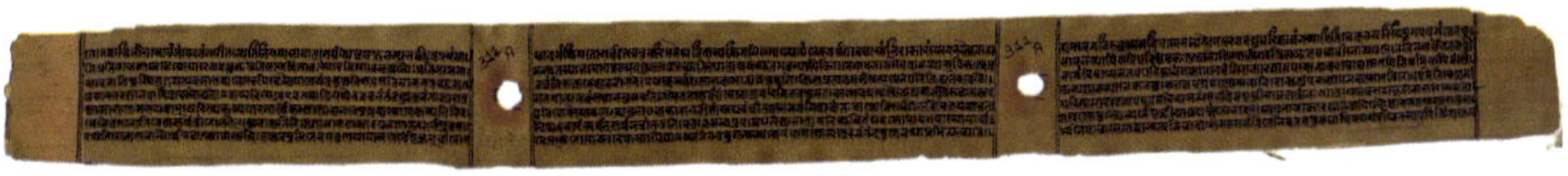

Fig. 3.9.4-VI: Overall layout by scribe A, fol. 312v © © Jinabhadrasūri Grantha Bhaṇḍāra, Jaisalmer

3.9.5 Symbols and other features in TUS

The last example in this section is the manuscript kept in the Sanghavinā pādāno bhanḍāra under MS no. 168 (2) and dated VS 1349 (corresponding to ca. 1292 CE). The manuscript was used by Sanghavi and Rasiklal (1987) in their edition. The manuscript contains an important text of the Lokāyata tradition.

Aside from '*cha*' symbols, stylised *puṣpikās* can be found around the string-holes on the folio. From the appearance of the symbols and the overall layout, we may assume at least two scribes were involved in the manuscript production. To demonstrate this a few observations on selected symbols around the string-holes and on the overall layout will be presented. The scribes are referred to as A and B.

Both A and B draw symbols around string-holes. A often makes symbols containing four almost semi-circular petals and four lines (see the left column in Fig. 3.9.5-I).[446] B's symbols also contain four almost semi-circular petals; however, they do not contain the four lines. Their lower petal is followed by a 'tail' added to its lower part. This tail frequently runs downward to the right (see right column in Fig. 3.9.5-I).

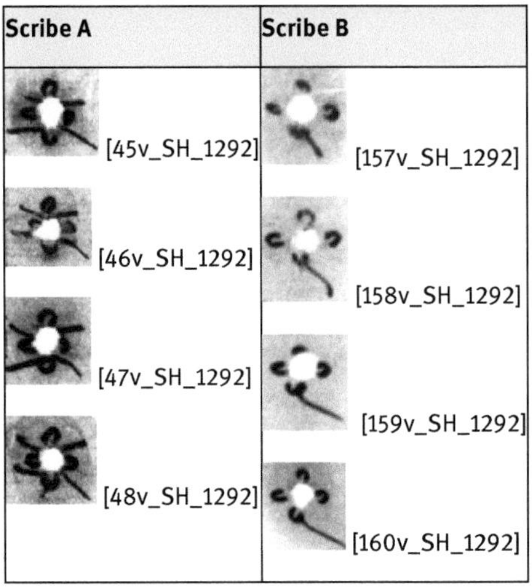
Scribe A
Scribe B
[45v_SH_1292]
[157v_SH_1292]
[46v_SH_1292]
[158v_SH_1292]
[47v_SH_1292]
[159v_SH_1292]
[48v_SH_1292]
[160v_SH_1292]

Fig. 3.9.5-I: Symbols by scribes A and B

Regarding the manuscript layout, both scribes write the text in two text-sections with each text-section demarcated by vertical ruling-lines. Some gaps between the text-lines can be seen on the folios written by B (see in Fig. 3.9.5-III), but the same gaps are not as clearly visible on A's folios (see in Fig. 3.9.5-II). The size of A's characters is bigger than those of B's characters. B's writing is more attractive and regular than that of A.

446 Most of the symbols found around string-holes in the manuscript of the *Savaga Padikkamana Sutta cunni* (*Śrāvakapratikramasūtra-cūrṇi*) (VS 1317 / 1260 CE) (Museum of Fine Arts, Boston. Denman Waldo Ross Collection, 30.1.1-229) appear to some extent like this type.

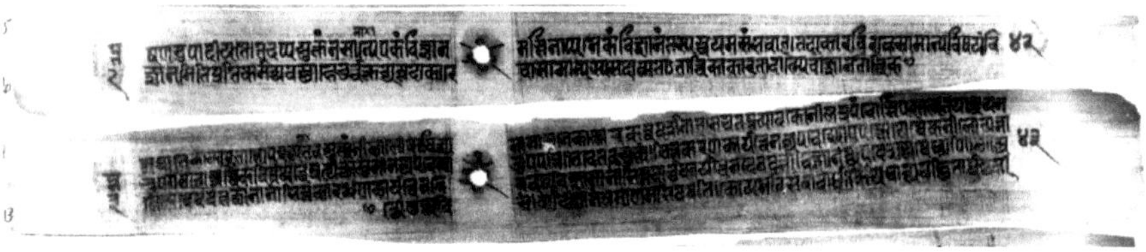

Fig. 3.9.5-II: Overall layout by scribe A, fols. 42v, 43v © Hemacandrācārya Jaina Jñānamandir, Patan

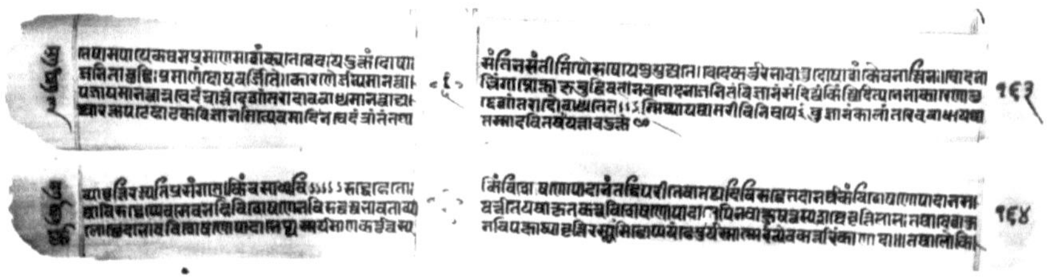

Fig. 3.9.5-III: Overall layout by scribe B, fols. 163v, 164v © Hemacandrācārya Jaina Jñānamandir, Patan

3.9.6 Symbols and other features as means to identify a change of scribes – Preliminary conclusions

In Nepalese manuscripts SP_1, SP_2 (ca. 9th c.) and KT (924 CE) remarkable changes in terms of symbols, space-fillers, *akṣara*s, and the overall layout, occur, the instant there is a change of scribe. In the 12th c. West Indian manuscript TSPV and the 13th c. manuscript TUS, there is clear evidence of changes affecting symbols drawn around string-holes. Alongside other features these examples show that (e.g. palaeographical and layout related ones), symbols serve as one of the essential components enabling us to understand if a manuscript has been copied by more than one scribe and whether the symbols have been drawn by the scribes themselves.

3.10 Some preliminary conclusions on use of symbols

In my corpus symbols can be found in almost all manuscripts from all areas. On the whole, symbols serve both to structure the texts and decorate the manuscript.

In terms of the regional occurrence and distribution of symbols, in most of the manuscripts of the three areas under scrutiny here, they often appear at the end of chapters or whole texts. However, stylised *puṣpikās* often appear around string-holes or together with folio numbers in manuscripts from Western India. Only occasionally, in a few Nepalese manuscripts, is the same practice observed and their occurrence is not even consistent within the same manuscript.

Compared to manuscripts from East and West India, Nepalese manuscripts are characterised by an extremely large variety of symbols. Their size varies to a large extent, ranging from an area of one line to the almost the whole height of the folio's written area. The aesthetic value of Nepalese symbols is noteworthy compared with the symbols used in the manuscripts from the other two areas here under investigation. In manuscripts from Nepal we find symbols drawn in a vivid and realistic style, representing real flowers with petals, stalks and leaves (see section 3.5.1). It may be noted that changes in size or quality of symbols in the same manuscript may serve to represent the hierarchical levels of the text.

A variety of symbols are to be found in East Indian manuscripts. They are largely at the end of chapters or whole texts and appear in different shape and size. Conversely, West Indian manuscripts comprise a smaller variety of symbols. Their size is small, usually occupying one text line of the folio. An important custom for this region is for all manuscripts (with but a few exceptions) to include symbols around the string-holes. The available data suggests the drawing of stylised *puṣpikā* with four petals, with or without four lines or similar features could well have been a widespread convention for manuscripts produced in this area. Only manuscripts from West India, feature small symbols like stylised *puṣpikās* appearing every ten pages together with the folio number on the left margin.

As already mentioned in section 3.6.2.1, some symbols may be drawn in a manner reflecting the religious and ritualistic aspects of the text or the whole manuscript in which they are found e.g. the series of three symbols on the folio at the end or the final conclusion of Buddhist manuscripts (see section 3.6.2.2.3).

Combined with several other features (such as palaeographical peculiarities, layout, etc.), symbols can also help understand whether more than one scribe was involved in the production of a specific manuscript (see section 3.9). Likewise, symbols may to some extent help with the possible dating of hitherto undated manuscripts and reassemble different parts of a currently dismembered manuscript (see section 3.8).

4 Use of space

Here the use of 'blank spaces' and 'gaps' (see below for the definitions of these two terms) used to structure and delimit the various sections or units of a text within the frame of a text-section on the pages of the manuscript will be investigated. Blank spaces and gaps can be considered features of the overall page layout regarding the use of those parts of the page largely not containing writing or symbols.

4.1 Blank space

The label 'blank space' serves to indicate an empty space appearing within the frame or pre-planned frame of text-section on the page at the end of smaller text units, chapters or even whole texts, and is delimited by a set of double *daṇḍa*s. Regarding blank spaces occupying more than one text line and appearing at one or both sides of chapter colophons or colophons, the text of the chapter colophon or colophon is only written on the first text line. Such blank spaces can often accompany and highlight the chapter colophons or colophonic statements. Otherwise they appear at a particular location in the manuscript text, thus serving as a reader's aid to navigation. So they are to be understood as features structuring the various parts of a text.

To the best of my knowledge, to the present day only few studies have dealt with such blank spaces, e.g. Einicke (2009, 344–345). In her study she presents examples from one inscription and a few manuscripts.[447] Aside from the inscription, her examples are from manuscripts dated from the fifteenth to twentieth c.

Their presence in modern transcriptions is often completely omitted; if reported at all, they are usually represented by symbols or signs that give little much information on their appearance.

On the reason for the existence of blank spaces, it should always be kept in mind that some blank spaces may not have been intended, and serve as a sign that the scribe may have intended to fill them with symbols or have someone place sym-

---

447 Such blank spaces are labeled by Einicke 2009, 344 as 'Zwei Doppeldaṇḍas ohne Zwischenelement'. All of her examples (see 344–345; SarIs(1002)_1, Ben2(1446)_41, Bir2(1834)_1, Bir3(1874)_22, Bir4.1(1884)_23, Bir4.2(1884)_21, Bir4.2(1884)_22, Bir5(1902)_19, Naj6(1582)_20, New16(1826)_3) from both inscription and manuscripts are demarcated by only a set of double *daṇḍa*s, therefore, it can be assumed that these examples are probably only one line in height.

https://doi.org/10.1515/9783110543087-004

bols or similar items there (see section 3.6.2.4.2 where a set of three large 'blank spaces' from three manuscripts appear at the end or near end of the texts).

In most manuscripts, the presence of a chapter colophon or colophon-like phrase is highlighted by symbols or blank spaces. If the former ones have not been used, blank spaces often appear and the reader may use them as means of navigation through the manuscript. Flipping through densely written folios, blank spaces easily catch the attention of the eye. In the following sections examples largely from Nepalese and East Indian manuscripts from my 'core' corpus will be presented.

4.1.1 Blank spaces in Nepalese manuscripts

SP$_1$

In SP$_1$, one of the oldest dated manuscripts of the corpus, there is at least one blank space at the end of one chapter. The blank space is just one line of the folio. Aside from the blank space, a variety of symbols are found at the end of the chapters in this manuscript.[448] The blank space can be found before the chapter colophon and is followed by double circles (see Fig. 4.1.1-I).

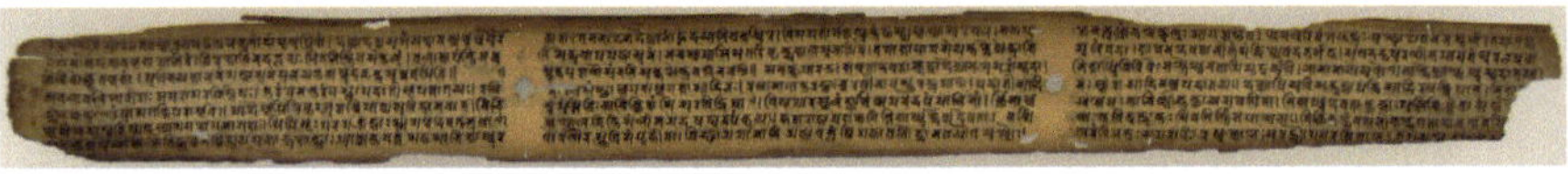

Fig. 4.1.1-I: Blank space before the chapter colophon and symbol after the chapter colophon, fol. 64a3 © NAK

[64a3]  |⊙|*skandapurāṇe suṃbhanisumbhasaindravarṇṇanaḥ*(?)[449] 

'[Thus], the description of Sumbha and Nisumbhasa ... in the *Skandapurāṇa* [is concluded].'

---

448 For symbols, see section 3.9.1 and Appendix below.
449 Bhaṭṭarāī 1988, 373 reads this line without any remarks as follows *iti skandapurāṇe śumbhaniśumbhayuddhe sainyavarṇanaṃ nāma catuḥṣaṣṭitamodhyāyaḥ*. Furthermore, Yokochi 2013, 299 in the critical edition reads the line *iti skandapurāṇe catuḥṣaṣṭo 'dhyāyaḥ*.

SP$_2$

In SP$_2$ various kinds of simple or beautifully drawn symbols feature at the end of the chapters.[450] Nonetheless there are at least 41 blank spaces in the same manuscript.[451] They all appear at the end of the chapters. Most of the blank spaces in the manuscript are three lines in height. However, some blank spaces are one to two text lines of the folio. The height of a few blank spaces is only two lines on the folio, though they are delimited by three sets of double *daṇḍa*s. See one of the blank spaces that appears after the chapter colophon in Fig 4.1.1-II.

Fig. 4.1.1-II: Blank space after the chapter colophon, fol. 164a3 © NAK

[164a3] *skandapurāṇe aṣṭatriṃ*|⊙|*śottaraśato*(!) *dhyāyaḥ*[452] 

'[Thus], the 138th chapter in the *Skandapurāṇa* [is concluded].'

SP$_3$

In SP$_3$ there is a large number of beautifully drawn symbols, of which three fully fledged *puṣpikā*s, feature at the end of the chapters.[453] However, at least eleven

---

450 For instance, circles with curved-like line in the centre (type no. 4), double circles (type no. 6), a variety of different kinds of stylised *puṣpikā*s (such as type nos. 7, 8, 10, 12, 14, 26, 35, 37, 39, 40, 41), one realistic *puṣpikā* at the end of the chapter and one realistic *puṣpikā* under the right string-hole on one folio. For discussion and examples of symbols, see sections 3.4, 3.5.1, 3.9.1 and Appendix.
451 Note that in a few blank spaces figure-numerals added later feature in the upper part, most correspond to chapter numbers written in word in chapter colophons (such as 26, 42, 132, 153, 162). Furthermore, in two blank spaces the speaker name '*vyāsa*' has been written normally to be expected after the first set of double *daṇḍa* of the blank spaces.
452 Bhaṭṭarāī 1988, 749 reads the line as *iti skandapurāṇe gaṇayuddhe jambhavadhe aṣṭatriśaduttaraśatatamodhyāyaḥ*.
453 See sections 3.4, 3.5.1 and Appendix below.

blank spaces appear at the end of the chapters.[454] Blank spaces in this manuscript are a size of one to three text lines. See the two blank spaces demarcating one of the chapter colophons in Fig. 4.1.1-III.

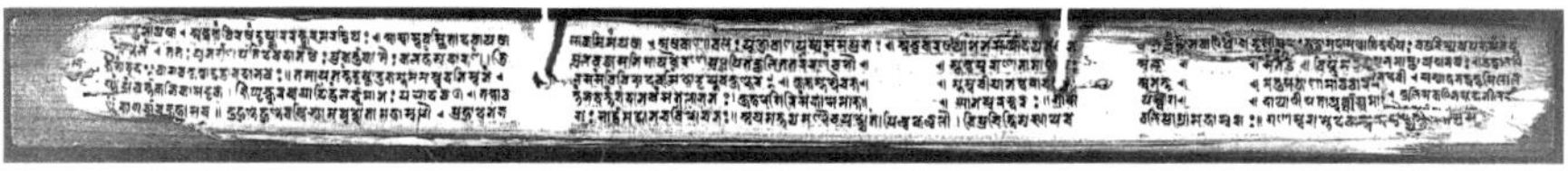

Fig. 4.1.1-III: Blank spaces before and after the chapter colophon, fol. 232v © Bodleian Library, Oxford

[232v2] *skandapurāṇe nāmādhyāyaḥ*|⊙|'130'

'[Thus], namely, the chapter 130 in the *Skandapurāṇa* [is concluded].'

HV₁

In HV₁ a few circles, some simple stylised symbols and a few well drawn stylised symbols can be found at the end of some chapters. However, blank spaces usually feature at the end of the chapters.[455] There are also two blank spaces after

454 Blank spaces appear on 153r1–2_B/ACC, 154v3_ACC, 157r4_ACC, 160v1_ACC, 164r3_BCC, 168r1_ACC, 198v5_B/ACC, 232v2_B/ACC.

455 Further blank spaces can be found on 4v4_ACC, 9r3_ACC, 10r2_ACC, 15v2_ACC, 17r5_ACC, 21r1_ACC, 25r5_ACC, 26v4_ACC, 29v1_ACC, 48v3_ACC, 51r1_ACC, 53v4–5_B/ACC, 61v2_ACC, 62v5_BCC, 65v3_ACC, 72r4_ACC, 75r1_ACC, 75v5_B/ACC, 79r3_ACC, 80r5_B/ACC, 85v4_ACC, 87v1_ACC, 91r5_BCC, 93r3_ACC, 94r3_ACC, 95r4_ACC, 96v2_ACC, 97v4_BCC, 100r5_B/ACC, 102r4_BCC, 103v5_B/ACC, 104v4_ACC, 106v3_ACC, 107r4_ACC, 108v4_ACC, 110r2_ACC, 111r4_ACC, 115v3_ACC, 117v3_ACC, 121r3_B/ACC, 122v1_ACC, 125r1_ACC, 128v3_ACC, 132v2_ACC, 134r2_ACC, 139r3_ACC, 140v5_ACC, 143r2_ACC, 149v4_ACC, 151r5_ACC, 154r4_BCC, 155v3_BCC, 157v1_BCC, 160r1_ACC, 171r2–3_B/ACC, 173v5_ACC, 176r5_BCC, 178r1_ACC, 179v5_B/ACC, 179v5_ASI, 180v2_BCC, 182v3_ACC, 184v4_ACC, 187r2_ACC, 191r2_ACC, 193r5_ACC, 199v3_ACC, 200v4_ACC, 201v3_ACC, 205r2_ACC, 212r5_ACC, 218r2_ACC, 224r1_BCC, 228r2_ACC, 230v3_ACC, 232v1_BCC, 234v1_ACC, 236r2_BCC, 237v2_ACC, 239r4_ACC, 242v3_ACC, 244r2_B/ACC, 245r2_BCC, 246r2_BCC, 249v2_ACC, 250r3_BCC, 251r4_B/ACC, 252v2_ACC, 256v2_ACC, 266v5_B/ACC, 268v1_ACC, 285r4_BCC, 287v4_ACC, 289r5_ACC, 292v1_B/ACC, 293v5_B/ACC, 294v4–5_B/ACC, 295v1_B/ACC, 296r3_B/ACC, 297v3_B/ACC, 298v2_BCC, 300v2_B/ACC, 304r4_B/ACC, 307r3_ACC, 309v2_ACC, 311r4_ACC, 319r3_ACC, 321r3_B/ACC, 324v3_BCC, 326v5_ACC.

speaker indications.[456] The blank spaces are one to three lines of the folio in height. Most of the blank spaces are a size of two lines of the folio. See the blank space in Fig. 4.1.1-IV after the chapter colophon.

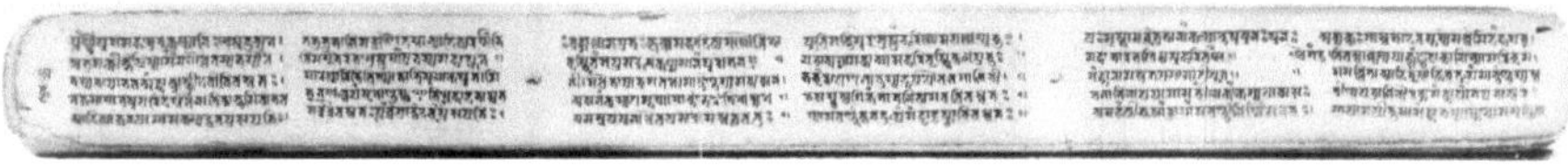

Fig. 4.1.1-IV: Blank space after the chapter colophon, fol. 15v © NAK

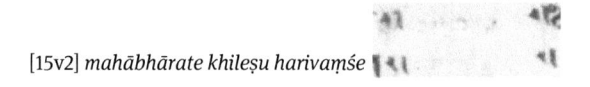

[15v2] *mahābhārate khileṣu harivaṃśe* 

'[Thus, the chapter] in the supplementary *Harivaṃśa* in the *Mahābhārata* [is concluded].'

DDh

Though five simple circles and the majority of attractively drawn stylised *puṣpikā*s are at the end of the chapters in DDh, blank spaces appear at least four times at the end of chapters.[457] They are a height of one to two lines of the folio. An example of the blank space appears after the chapter colophon in Fig. 4.1.1-V. It is surrounded by three sets of double *daṇḍa*s, though it occupies only two lines on the folio.

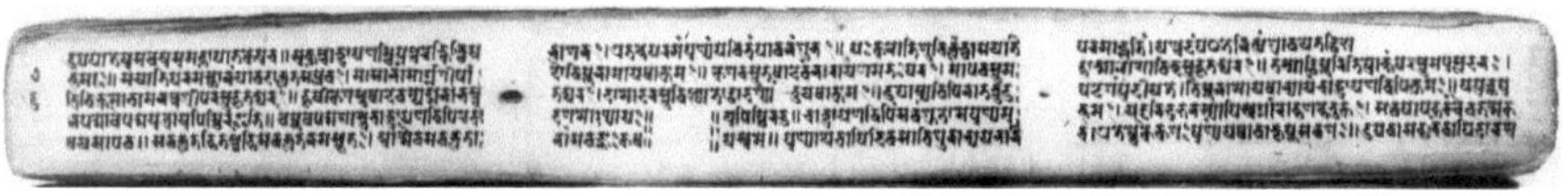

Fig. 4.1.1-V: Blank space after the chapter colophon, fol. 58v © NAK

[58v4] *vaiṣṇave dharmaśāstre cāndrāyaṇavidhir ekā*|○|*daśamo* '*dhyāyaḥ* 

'[Thus], the eleventh chapter, the instruction on *cāndrāyaṇa* in the Vaiṣṇava treatise on *dharma* [is concluded].'

456 Namely on 17r5_ASpI, 80r5_ASpI.
457 On 57r2_ACC, 58v4_ACC, 63r4_ACC, 68r5_ACC.

TS1

In TS1 blank spaces feature at the end of most chapters,[458] except at the end of the 13th chapter that contains stylised *puṣpikā*[459] and circles.[460] The height of blank spaces in this manuscript is two to four lines of the folio. See the blank spaces before and after the chapter colophon in Fig. 4.1.1-VI. The height of both blank spaces is two lines of the folio, even though the second blank space appears surrounded by three sets of double *daṇḍa*s.

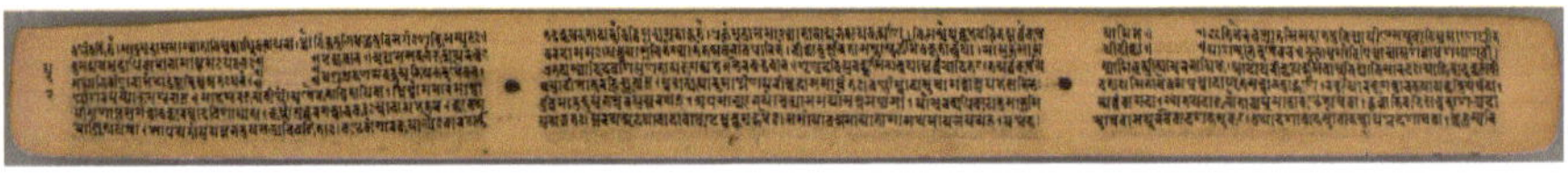

Fig. 4.1.1-VI: Blank spaces before and after the chapter colophon, fol. 42v © NAK

[42v1–2]  *iti bhairavasrotasi mahātantre vidyāpīṭhe saptakoṭipramāṇe*

śrīta[2]*ntrasadbhāve mudrādhikāro nāmāṣṭamaḥ paṭalaḥ* 

458 Namely on 14r2_B/ACC, 18r5_B/ACC, 24r3_ACC, 25v6_BCC, 26r1_ACC, 28r6_B/ACC, 35r4_B/ACC, 39v4_ACC, 42v1–2_B/ACC, 57r5_ACC, 90r5_B/ACC, 95r4_B/ACC, 96v6_B/ACC, 104r3_B/ACC, 108r3_B/ACC, 118r1_B/ACC, 121v5_BCC, 123r4_B/ACC, 127v2–3_B/ACC, 139r3–4_B/ACC, 148r1_B/ACC, 149r2_ACC, 161v4–5_B/ACC, 171r1_B/ACC, 179v5–6_B/ACC, 181v4–5_B/ACC, 182v5–6_B/ACC, 186r1–2_B/ACC, 186r2_AC.

459 On 99r3_BCC.

460 On 24r2_BCC, 39v3_BCC, 57r4_BCC, 99r3_ACC, 121v5_BCC, 149r1_BCC. Please note that circles are also frequently used before opening phrases (such as on 21v4 *sāṃpratam mad samuddhāraṃ kathayāmi tava priye* | on 24v1 *ataḥ paraṃ pravakṣāmi parāyāvidhim uttāmam* | etc.) on 4v3, 5r2, 5r5, 5v2, 6v4, 16v5, 21v4, 21v5, 22r5, 23r2, 23v5, 24v1, 30r6, 37v1, 41r3, 49r6, 49v2, 49v6, 50r3, 50v1, 50v2, 50v1, 50v2, 50v5, 51v2, 52r2, 62v3, 67v3, 70r3, 70r4, 77r2, 77v5, 78r2, 78v4, 80r1, 84v5, 85v5, 86r1, 106r4, 107v2, 112r5, 112v4, 113r1, 114v4, 124v2, 124v5, 124v6, 125r1, 129r5, 130r4, 130v5, 132r1, 132r6, 132v6, 134r1, 134r5, 134v2, 134v4, 135r2, 135r3, 135r6, 136v6, 137r3, 138r5, 138v4, 141v1, 141v4, 142r3, 142r4, 142v, 143r3, 167v2, 171v4, 175v1, 176v4, 177v6, 178v6, 185r1. A few dots can be found before opening phrases on 25r2, 66v2, 79v3, 167v5, 184v4. One dot is used before a *mantra* on 52r4 and circles are also used before some *mantra*s on 52r5, 52r6. Circles can also be found after some of particular sections on 53r4, 55v5. Two sets of circles have been drawn placing horizontally after a few invocations (for instance, on 172v5 *oṃ vṛṣavāhanāya namaḥ* ) on 172v5–6, 173r1–3.

'Thus, the eighth chapter, namely the section on *mudrā* in the *vidyāpīṭha* in the glorious *Tantrasadbhāva* measuring seven thousand [lines] in the great Tantra in the Bhairava branch [is concluded].'

AṣP₁

In AṣP₁ many blank spaces feature before and/or after chapter colophons, before the concluding Buddhist formula and after the colophon,[461] however, there are also two attractively drawn realistic *puṣpikā*s, various kinds of florally stylised symbols and a dot-like symbol, some 'figure-eight knot' symbols and a simple circle. Blank spaces in the manuscript are a height of one to three lines of the folio. The height of most of the blank spaces is two lines of the folio, even though they appear surrounded by three sets of double *daṇḍa*s. See the blank spaces before and after the chapter colophon in Fig. 4.1.1-VII.

Fig. 4.1.1-VII: Blank spaces before and after the chapter colophon, fol. 184r © NAK

[184r2]  *āryāṣṭa*¦|⊙|*sāhasrikāyāṃ prajñāpāramitāyāṃ śūnyatāparivart-*

to nāmāṣṭādaśaḥ 

'[Thus], the eighteenth chapter, namely the *śūnyatā* in the noble Perfection of Wisdom in Eight Thousand Lines [is concluded].'

461 On 50v2–3_B/ACC, 92r3_BCC, 99v4_B/ACC, 106r3–4_B/ACC, 110r2_ACC, 122r4_B/ACC, 145v3_B/ACC, 178v1_BCC, 184r2_B/ACC, 192r3_B/ACC, 222r5_BCC, 222v1_ACC, 225r1–2_B/ACC, 228v3_B/ACC, 234r2_B/ACC, 238v4–5_B/ACC, 244r5_ACC, 254r4_B/ACC, 257r2–3_B/ACC, 263r5_BCC, 263v1_ACC, 280v5_B/ACC, 282r2_ABCF, 282r2–3_B/ACC, 282r5_AC.

HV_2

In HV_2 mostly symbols can be found at the end of the chapters, however, there are also a few blank spaces at the end of some chapters.[462] The blank spaces are two lines of the folio in height. But most of the blank spaces measure one line of the folio. See the blank spaces in Fig. 4.1.1-VIII.

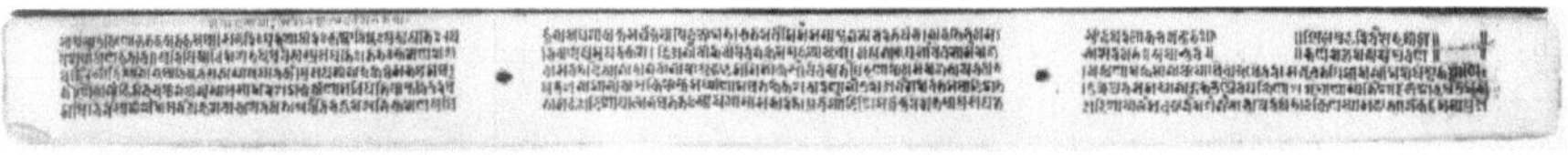

Fig. 4.1.1-VIII: Blank spaces before and after the chapter colophon, fol. 8r1

[8r1] || *khileṣu harivaṃśe tṛtīya*(!) ||

'[Thus], the third [chapter] in the supplementary *Harivaṃśa* [is completed].'

SDhPS

Blank spaces feature at the end of some chapters in SDhPS.[463] Blank spaces in the manuscript are two to four lines of the folio in height. Aside from blank spaces; circles, stylised *puṣpikā*s and '*tha*' symbols feature at the end of chapters. Furthermore, a series of three beautifully drawn large symbols are on the last folios (on 138v, 139r, 139v) at the end or near end of the text in the manuscript (see section 3.6.2.4.2 above). See the blank spaces in Fig. 4.1.1-IX. The blank spaces measure three lines of the folio in height, although they appear surrounded by four sets of double *daṇḍa*s.

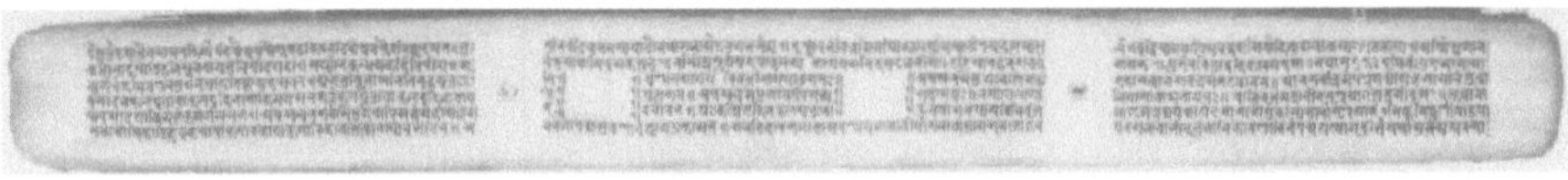

Fig. 4.1.1-IX: Blank spaces before and after the chapter colophon © NAK

462 On 8r1_B/ACC, 69r1–2_B/ACC, 95r5_BCC, 133r5–133v1_B/ACC, 149r5_BCC, 154r5_B/ACC, 179v5_BCC, 186v5_BCC, 243v1_BCC, 256r1_ACC, 265r5_BCC, 267r4_BCC, 273r5_BCC, 351r5_B/ACC.
463 On 46v5_BCC, 58v3_ACC, 77r2_BCC, 84v2_BCC, 93v2_BCC, 98r3_B/ACC, 110r4_BCC, 116r1_ACC, 125v3–4_B/ACC, 130r4_B/ACC, 138r2_B/ACC.

[98r3]  *puṇyaparyāyaparivartto nāma ṣoḍaśamaḥ* 

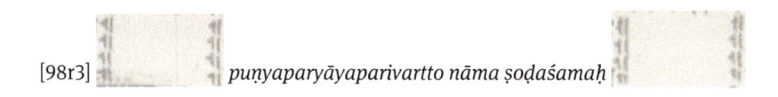

'[Thus], the sixteenth chapter, namely the *puṇyaparyāya* [is completed].'

AṣP₂

In AṣP₂ the majority of beautifully drawn symbols are at the end of the chapters. However, four blank spaces have also been used before and after two chapter colophons, on 44r4–5_B/ACC and 145r3_B/ACC. Blank spaces in the manuscript measure one to two text lines of the folio in height. Examples of blank space can be seen in Fig. 4.1.1-X.

Fig. 4.1.1-X: Blank spaces before and after the chapter colophon, fol. 145r © NAK

[145r3]  *āryāṣṭasā|○|hasrikāyām prajñāpāramitāyāṃ mupāyakauśalyam-īmānsāparivartto*(!) *nāma viṃśatimaḥ* 

'[Thus], the twentieth chapter, namely the *upāyakauśalyamīmānsā* in the noble Perfection of Wisdom in Eight Thousand Lines [is completed].'

Aṣṭasāhasrikā Prajñāpāramitā (NAK 5/76 / NGMPP A 37/11–A 38/1)

In the manuscript of the *Aṣṭasāhasrikā Prajñāpāramitā* (NAK 5/76 / NGMPP A 37/11–A 38/1) a series of three large blank spaces can be found on 195v. Each blank space appears almost at the centre of the text-section. Blank spaces feature in the part of the colophon and post colophonic parts. The examples have also been presented in section 3.6.2.4.2 above and discussed in detail.

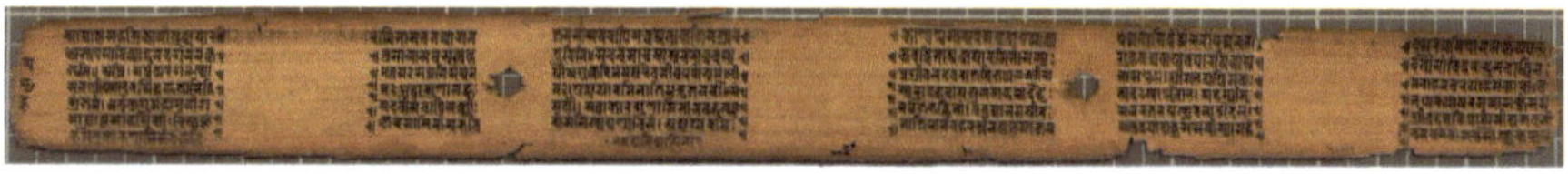

Fig. 4.1.1-XI: A series of three large blank spaces at the end of the text © NAK

SS

Save for a few circles[464] and a majority of *siddham* (like type no. 44), only blank spaces feature before and/or after chapter colophons or before and/or after author lines, after the *mantra* and after the donor phrase) in SS on 1v7, 2r1, 2r5, 2r5, 3r1, 3r2, 3r4, 3v1, 3v2, 3v3, 3v4, 4v6, 6v5, 9v5, 11r2–3, 12r2, 15r5, 24v7, 34v6, 115v4–5 etc. In this manuscript nearly all blank spaces measure one text line on the folio (except the blank spaces on 6v5_ACC, 6v5_AAL, 7v4_AAL, 73v3_AAL, 89v2_ACC that are two text lines in height). See the blank space in Fig. 4.1.1-XII.

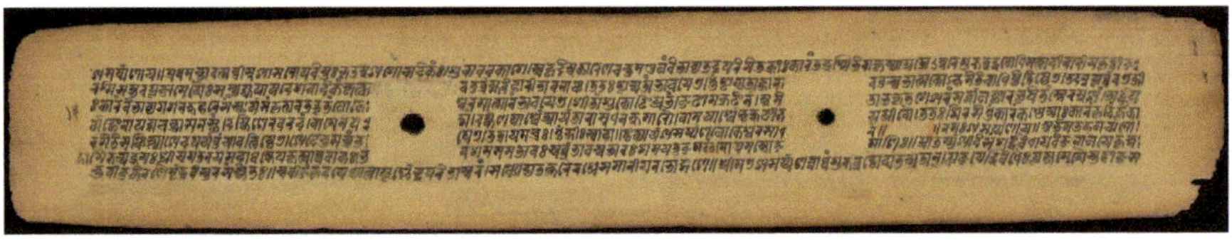

Fig. 4.1.1-XII: Blank space at the end of a text, 13v © CUL

[13v5] *ity āryakhasarppaṇalokeśvarasādha*☐*naṃ* 

'Thus, the *Sādhana* on the noble Khasarppaṇalokeśvara [is completed].'

In Nepalese manuscripts containing various kinds of text, blank spaces can be found. In most of the manuscripts of this corpus, blank spaces appear at the end of a chapter before and after the chapter colophon. However, in some manuscripts, blank spaces feature only before or after the chapter colophon. The size of the blank space varies even within a manuscript or from manuscript to manuscript. They measure from one line to almost the entire height of the folio.

4.1.2 Blank spaces in East Indian manuscripts

The use of blank space is also attested in many East Indian manuscripts that have investigated in the course of this study. In the following section a few examples have been selected to illustrate how blank spaces appear.

464 For instance, on 49v4, 49v7, 223r4, 224r2, 224r4, 224r5, 225r2, 225v2, 226r2, 226v1 (type no. 2).

AAĀ

In AAĀ, aside from the *siddham* and three stylised *puṣpikā*s (see section 3.6.2.4.1 above), blank spaces feature at the end of most of the chapters.[465] Most of the blank spaces measure two text lines of the folio in height. Only two blank spaces measure one line, namely on 147v7, 159r7. Furthermore, in the majority of cases, blank spaces appear after chapter colophons (see note below). See Fig. 4.1.2-I.

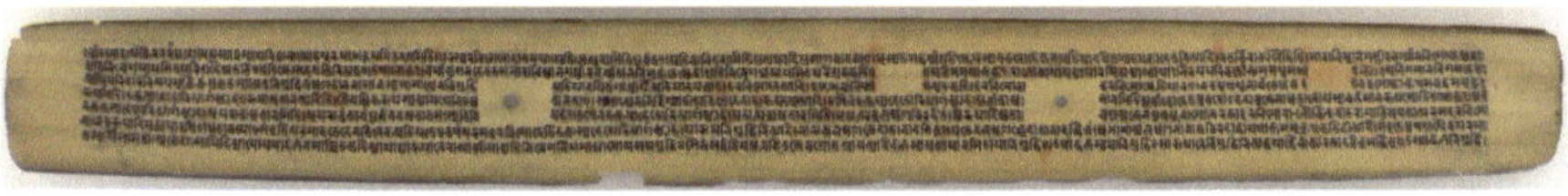

Fig. 4.1.2-I: Blank spaces before and after the chapter colophon, fol. 78r © NAK

[78r2]  *abhisamayālaṅkārālokāyāṃ prajñāpāramitāvyākhyāyāṃ ni-*
rayaparivarto nāma saptamaḥ[466] 

'[Thus], the seventh chapter, namely the *niraya* in the commentary on the *Prajñāpāramitā* in the *Abhisamayālaṅkārālokā* [is completed].'

GV

In GV numerals indicating the chapter number are placed between double *daṇḍa*s (on 6v4, 8v6), aside from this, one *siddham* (on 10r6) (type no. 45) at the end of two chapters and one blank space features before the last chapter colophon (on 10r5). In this instance, the blank space appears precisely under the right string-hole. See Fig. 4.1.2-II.

---

465 On 35r3_ACC, 48v4_ACC, 61r3_ACC, 64r1_ACC, 66v4_ACC, 74r5–6_B/ACC, 78r2_B/ACC, 83r3_ACC, 84v5_ACC, 88r5_B/ACC, 93v2_ACC, 96r4_ACC, 102r2_B/ACC, 103r2–3_B/ACC, 108r2_B/ACC, 119r3_B/ACC, 123v7_ACC, 127r6_ACC, 132r2_ACC, 134r4_ACC, 135v6_ACC, 139r3_ACC, 141r5_ACC, 147v7_ACC, 156v2_ACC, 159r7_ACC, 164r2_ACC.

466 For the line, see also Tucci 1932, 261.

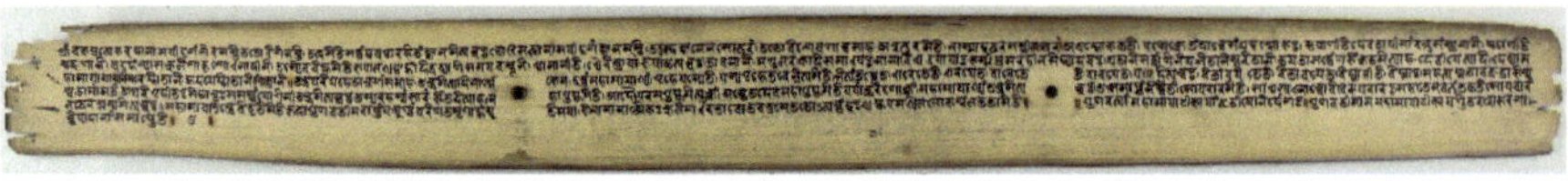

Fig. 4.1.2-II: Blank space at the end of the text, fol. 10r © KL

[10r5]  *guṇavatyāṃ mahāmāyāṭīkāyāṃ tṛtīyo nirdeśaḥ* ||

'[Thus], the third instruction in the commentary [called] *Mahāmāyā* on the *Guṇavati* [is completed].'

HP

In HP, aside from two symbols (on 4v7, 23r1), blank spaces appear at the end of sub-chapters and chapters.[467] With the exception of one blank space before the colophon, all blank spaces appear after the sub-colophons and measure one text line of the folio. An example of the blank space can be seen in Fig. 4.1.2-III.

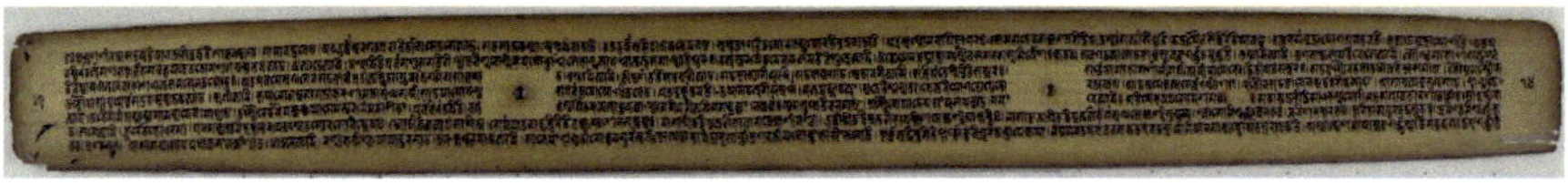

Fig. 4.1.2-III: Blank space after the chapter colophon, fol. 14v © KL

[14v5] *abhiṣekapaṭalo daśamaḥ* 

'[Thus], the tenth *abhiṣeka* chapter [is completed].'

467 On 5v4_ACC, 6v3_ACC, 6v5_ACC, 8r5_ACC, 9r1_ACC, 9v2_ACC, 13r3_ACC, 14r2_ACC, 14v5, 15r1_ACC, 15r3_ACC, 17r1_ACC, 18r1_ACC, 21r4_ACC, 22r3_ACC, 22r4_ACC, 22r5_ACC, 22r7_ACC, 22v4_ACC, 22v6_ACC, 23r1_BC.

HAP

In HAP, only blank spaces have been used at the end of the chapters.[468] Blank spaces in the manuscript measure one to two lines in height on the folio. See Fig. 4.1.2-IV.

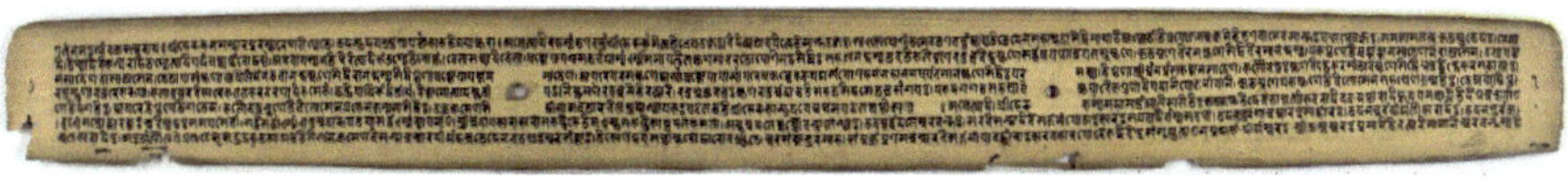

Fig. 4.1.2-IV: Blank space after the chapter colophon, fol. 1v © KL

[1v5] ... *iti śrīherukābhyudaye prathamapaṭalapañjikā*<<y>> 

'... Thus, the *pañjikā* of the first chapter in the glorious *Herukābhyudaya* [is completed].'

LTṬ

In LTṬ predominantly '*tha*' symbols,[469] three *siddham*[470] and a few circles[471] feature at the end of smaller text units and chapters. However, at the very end of the colophon a blank space appears on 30v1. After which the folio is largely blank. See Fig. 4.1.2-V.

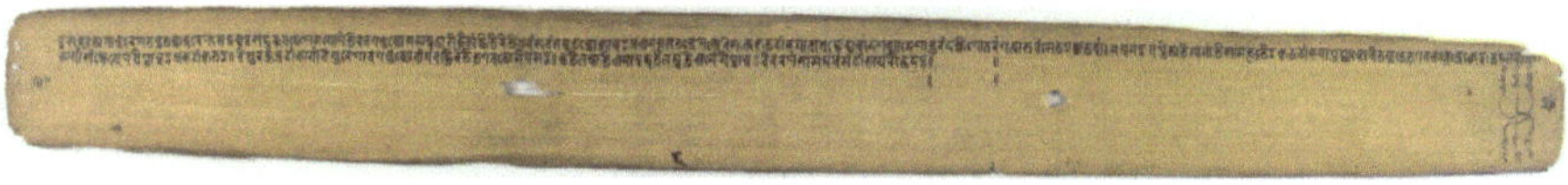

Fig. 4.1.2-V: Blank space at the end of the colophon, fol. 30v © KL

468 On 1v5_ACC, 10r2_AC, 10r3_APC.
469 On 5r6, 6r2, 6r3, 6r5, 6v1, 6v4, 6v6, 7v2, 7v5, 8r2, 8v5, 8v6, 11r3, 15r3, 15r7, 15v3, 16v2, 16v7, 17r2, 17r5, 19r2, 19r5, 19v1, 19v4, 20r2 (type no. 46).
470 On 17v2, 25r2, 25r4 (type no. 45).
471 On 3r3, 4v2, 9v5, 14v1, 15v7, 16r4, 17v7, 27r6, 30r1) (type no. 2).

[30v2] *iti lakṣābhidhānād uddhṛte laghvabhidhāne piṇḍārtha<<ḥ>>vivaraṇaṃ nāma prathamaṭīkāparicchedaḥ*[472] 

'Thus, the first chapter of the commentary called *Piṇḍārthavivaraṇa* in the *Laghvavidhāna* selected from the *Lakṣābhidhāna* [is completed].'

CPN

In CPN at the end of the sub-chapters and chapters, only blank spaces have been used (with the exception of one circle at the end of one of the chapters on 49v1).[473] The majority of blank spaces measure two lines in height on the folio. The height of four blank spaces is one line of the folio (on 13v7, 33r7, 49v1, 52v7). Save for the blank spaces before and after the colophon, all blank spaces appear after the chapter colophons in this manuscript. An example of the blank space can be seen in Fig. 4.1.2-VI.

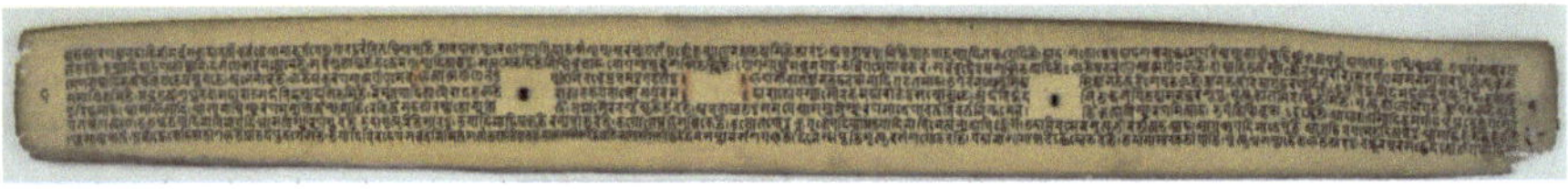

Fig. 4.1.2-VI: Blank space after the chapter colophon, fol. 7v © KL

[7v1] *ity ātmapīṭhe catu⊡ṣpīṭhanibandhe prathamaḥ paṭalaḥ* 

'Thus, the first chapter in the *ātmapīṭha* in the *Catuṣpīṭhanibandha* [is completed].'

STṬ

In STṬ a puzzling symbol (on 5v7),[474] a symbol resembling a kind of syllable-like element (on 6r1) and a majority of circles[475] appear at the end of sub-chapters,

472 For the line, see also Cicuzza 2001, 26.
473 On 7v1_ACC, 12v4_ACC, 13v7_ACC, 19v4_ACC, 25v4_ACC, 31r1_ACC, 32r7_ACC, 33r7_ACC, 48r2_ACC, 49v1, 50v4, 52v7_ACC, 53v6_B/ACC.
474 See section 3.6.2.2 above for more details.

chapters and smaller text units in the manuscript. Aside from which, two blank spaces appear at the end of the chapters (e.g. on 2v1, 6r3). Please note that all these elements can be found after the sub-colophons. See Fig. 4.1.2-VII.

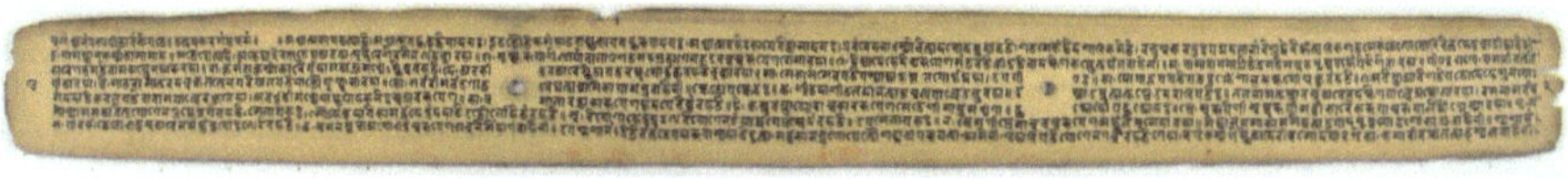

Fig. 4.1.2-VII: Blank space after the chapter colophon, fol. 2v © KL

[2v1] *tatvaprakaraṇaṃ prathamaṃ* 

'[Thus], the first *Tatvaprakaraṇa* [is completed].'

AP

Aside from one circle and *siddham*,[476] blank spaces appear in AP at the end of many chapters.[477] All blank spaces measure only one line in height on the folio (except for one of the blank spaces on 38r2 which measures two lines on the folio). See Fig. 4.1.2-VIII.

Fig. 4.1.2-VIII: Blank spaces before and after the chapter colophon, 37r © NAK

475 On 2v1, 3r1, 3v6, 4r3, 4r6, 4v5, 5r1, 6r2, 6r3, 6r6, 6v2, 6v5, 7r1, 7r2, 8v3, 8v6, 9r1, 9r3, 9r6, 9r7, 9v1, 9v3, 10r4, 10r6, 10r7, 10v1, 11r6, 11r7, 11v1, 11v3, 11v4, 11v5, 11v6, 11v7) (type no. 2)

476 For example, one circle on 28r5 (type no. 2) and *siddham* symbols on 7v7_B/ACC, 9v3_B/ACC, 13v3_B/ACC, 14r5_ACC, 21v6_ACC, 28r5_AAL) (type no. 45).

477 On 21r7-21v1_B/ACC, 22r3_ACC, 22v7_ACC, 23r2_ACC, 23v2_ACC, 37v7_B/ACC, 38r2_B/ACC, 38r5_AC.

[37r7]  *paṇḍitābhayākaraguptakṛtāyām abhayapaddhatyāṃ*

śrībuddhakapālamahātantraṭīkāyāṃ trayodaśaḥ paṭalaḥ 

'[Thus], the thirteen chapter in the commentary, the glorious *Buddhakapālamahātantra* in the *Abhayapaddhati* written by Paṇḍita Abhayākaragupta [is completed].'

To summarize, in most East Indian manuscripts of this corpus, blank spaces are partly or entirely at the end of the chapters, sub-chapters, and occasionally at the end of the text before and/or after colophon or in the part of the post colophon. In most of the manuscripts, blank spaces appear only after the text-line of sub-colophons. Furthermore, blank spaces are one to two lines in height on the folio.

4.1.3 Blank spaces in West Indian manuscripts

Unlike Nepalese and East Indian manuscripts, blank spaces are not used at the end of chapters or sub-chapters in the West Indian manuscripts of the 'core' corpus. As already mentioned in the section on layout, West Indian manuscripts texts are generally written in a very dense and compact way. This results in hardly any free spaces occurring between simple sentences, *śloka*s, or at the end of chapters.

Of the possible reasons for such a peculiarity, one may assume that the practice of leaving a blank space at the end of chapters or whole texts may not have been seen as a dividing device for the text in the manuscript from this region.

One may speculate that another reason may be closely related to aesthetic principles guiding the hands of the scribes. Blank spaces could have been seen as breaks interrupting the evenness of the page layout, causing irregularities in the way in which lines appear on the folio.

4.1.4 Blank space – Overall conclusions

In manuscripts of the corpus blank spaces appear mainly in manuscripts from Nepal and East India, but not from West India.

In Nepalese manuscripts blank spaces range from one line to the entire height of the folio. However, in almost all East Indian manuscripts (mostly from Vikramaśīla) blank spaces occupy just one to two text lines of the folio. In some

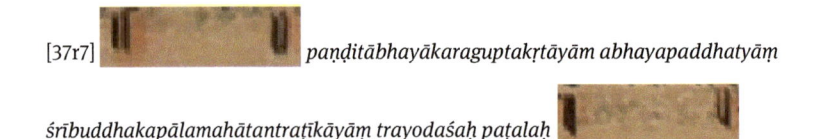

manuscripts from both areas there are virtually only blank spaces at the end of the chapters; e.g. in TS$_1$ (save for two symbols), CPN (with the exception of one circle) and HP (save for two symbols). Such blank spaces can also occur in manuscripts where symbols have been attractively drawn (e.g., in SP$_1$, SP$_2$, KV/UVDh, SP$_3$, HV$_1$, DDh, AṣP$_1$, HV$_2$, SDhPS, AṣP$_2$, AAĀ, etc.).

Quite frequently the number of sets of double *daṇḍa*s delimiting a blank space corresponds to the number of text lines the blank space occupies on the page. However, examples of blank spaces are also present where the number of sets of double *daṇḍa*s does not correspond to the lines on the page. In this instance, if a blank space is delimited by three sets of double *daṇḍa*s, the actual height of the blank may only be that of two text lines of the folio or if there are four sets of doble *daṇḍa*s, the height may be just three lines of the folio (see SP$_2$, DDh, TS$_1$, AṣP$_1$, SDhPS) etc. Moreover, in the case of blank spaces of more than one text line in size and appearing at one or both sides of chapter colophons or colophons, the text of (sub-)chapter colophon or colophon is often only written on the first text line.

The use of blank spaces in manuscripts can be understood as one of the main means to visually indicate the end of a chapter, sub-chapter or of a whole text etc.

4.2 Gaps

I label ‘gap’ a small but conspicuous space left largely unwritten on the folio used to separate smaller text units, such as sentences, *pāda*s or half *śloka*s.[478] Bühler (1896, p. 84) made a short remark on gaps (he calls them ‘ein grösserer Zwischenraum’ a larger gap) used to divide smaller text units such as *pāda*s or half verses with regard to inscriptions:

> In den sorgfältig geschriebenen metrischen Inschriften der späteren Zeit folgt mitunter ein grösserer Zwischenraum am Ende der Pāda oder der Halbverse und die Zeilen enthalten oft je einen Halbvers oder Vers.

478 In some manuscripts we also occasionally find small gaps between *akṣara*s in lines or in the last line on the folio. In the latter case, such gaps are mainly used between *akṣara*s to fill the free space on the folio and to show the regularity of the line e.g. in the manuscript of the *Vinayavastvāgama* (GBM 1050) on the last folio 523r in the last line (see section 3.6.2.4.2); in the manuscript of the *Bodhisattvabhūmi* (CUL Add.1702) on 144v in the last line (see section 3.6.2.4.2); in the manuscript of the *Viṣṇudharma* (NAK 4/1389 / NGMPP A 10/3) on one of the folios (NGMPP exposure 144) in the last line.

> In the carefully written metrical inscriptions from the later period a large free space occurs occasionally at the end of the Pāda or the half verses and the lines contain often a half verse or a verse.[479]

In this chapter, examples of manuscripts emerge showing the gaps can be divided into two main categories according to how they appear on the page: (a) those simply occurring within the text line, and (b) those that are integrated into the text-section of the page.

4.2.1 Gaps: type (a)

To show the first kind of gaps seen in manuscripts examples are provided from manuscripts of my corpus, and an example from a manuscript preserved in the University Library of Cambridge.[480]

4.2.1.1 Gaps used to divide *pāda*s in NTS

In NTS every *pāda* is divided by small gaps, only in the first folios of the manuscript (folios 1–4). Almost always, a single *daṇḍa* is placed after the first half of each *śloka*, and a double *daṇḍa* is placed after its second half (see Fig. 4.2.1.1-I from an extracted and enlarged part of the folio Fig. 4.2.1.1-II). However, no *daṇḍa* occurs between the first and second *pāda*s or between the third and the fourth.

Sometimes, the last *halanta* (i.e. a consonant without vowel) of a *pāda* is written after the gaps at the beginning of the following *pāda* (e.g., in line no 2: *tena pṛcchāmi bhagava␣n yena vetsi mataṅga tvam* ||).

Here is the transcription of a part of the text from folio 1v in which gaps are indicated by the sign ␣. To illustrate the way in which gaps appear on this folio, the left part has been extracted and enlarged; I have marked the gaps with a small rhombus (◊) (see Fig. 4.2.1.1-II below).

479 The translation is mine.

480 It is significant that on some folios of the manuscript (NAK 3/737 / NGMPP A 38/5) written in Bamiyan/Gilgit Type 1 (see Sander 1968), smaller text units such as sentences are divided by small gaps. Furthermore, the use of gaps between smaller text units is also in many folios in the manuscript of the *Śatasāhasrikā Prajñāpāramitā* (NAK 5/197 / NGMPP A 36/2), e.g., on 29v.

Fig. 4.2.1.1-I: Gaps between *pāda*s on the folio, fol. 1v © NAK

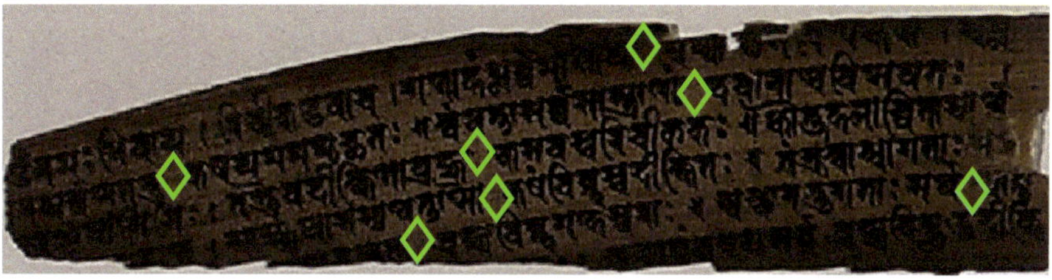

Fig. 4.2.1.1-II: Extracted and enlarged part from folio 1v?

[1v1–2] *oṃ namaḥ śivāya | ricīka uvāca |*
gato haṃ pūrvvam āśāyāṃ ␣ puṣpā++++dhes[481] *tathā |*
apū|⊙|rvvadṛṣṭam āścarya ␣n tan dṛṣṭvā kautukānvitaḥ ||
aṣṭā++saha[482]*///*[483]
[2] *///++van sarvvam etat tu ␣ kathaya mama pṛcchataḥ ||*
tvaṃ vettā sarvvaśāstrāṇāṃ ␣ devānāñ ca viśeṣataḥ ||⊙|
tena pṛcchāmi bhagava ␣n yena vetsi mataṅga tvam ||
mataṅga uvāca |
śṛṇu vatsa samāsena ␣ pravakṣyā|⊙|mi tavākhilam |
naimiṣe vasamānais tu ␣ śrutaṃ[484]*///++++++*[485]
...

One may wonder why this type of *śloka* division appears only on folios 1–4 and not throughout the entire manuscript. Tentatively it could be argued this style was implemented to emphasise the very beginning of the text and was later dropped as it required too much time and effort to maintain consistency.

481 Most parts of the *akṣara*s have been lost.
482 After which something has been stuck on the folio, making the *akṣara*s illegible. The element was possibly used for 'restoration' purposes on the leaf.
483 The upper part of the folio is damaged. Only some lower parts or strokes or *akṣaras* are visible.
484 After which only a small part of one *akṣara* is visible.
485 The text has been transcribed as faithfully as possible. Even the apparent scribal errors and other grammatical mistakes have not been considered here. This text is critically edited and translated in Kafle 2015, 99–100 and 195–196.

4.2.1.2 Gaps used to divide *pāda*s in SS/N

This manuscript is of particular importance for its visual organisation. It is assumed more than one scribe was involved in the manuscript production which, however is not a subject of discussion here.[486]

Small gaps are found on many folios between the first and second half of *śloka*s (e.g., on 110rv, 112rv–121rv, 125rv–131rv, 133rv–139rv, 141rv–176rv, 187rv–209rv, 213rv–217rv, 219rv). In many cases, *daṇḍa*s appear in the middle of the gaps. I have selected one folio (198r) from SS/N (see Fig. 4.2.1.2-I below) and transcribed a part of the text marking the position of each gap.[487] To show the gaps on the folio more clearly, part of folio 198r has been extracted and enlarged. Small circles highlight the position of the gaps in the extracted part (○) (see Fig. 4.2.1.2-II below).

Fig. 4.1.2-I: Use of gaps, fol. 198r © KL

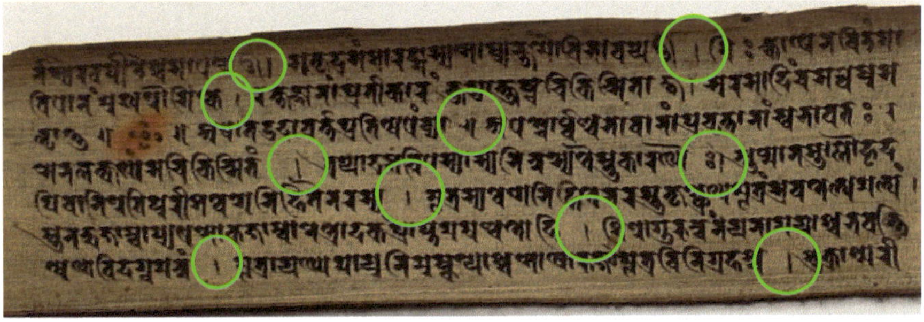

Fig. 4.2.1.2-II: Extracted and enlarged part from fol. 198r

486 According to the symbols, space-fillers and paleographical evidence it seems safe to assume at least five scribes worked on the manuscript production. See also Klebanov 2010, 61–63.
487 The text portion given below is the part of the chapters *krimiroga* ('disease caused by worms') the *Kāyacikitsā* ('General medicine') section. Here I have transcribed the text from the manuscript as faithfully as possible.

[198r1–2] *rnasyair avapīḍaiś ca sādhayet* |␣
śakṛdrasaṃ sāraṅgasya soṣya bhūmau vibhāvayet␣ | ␣
niḥkvāthena(!) *viḍaṃgā*|⊙|*nāṃ cūrṇṇaṃ pradhamanan tu tat*␣ | ␣
ayaścūrṇṇāny anenaiva vidhinā yojayīta ca␣ | ␣
sakāṃsanīlaṃ tailaṃ ca nasyaṃ syāt surasādike␣ | ␣
indraluptavidhiś cāpi vidhe|⊙|*yo romarājiṣu*␣ | ␣
dantajānāṃ samuddiṣṭaṃ∽[2] *vidhānaṃ mukharogike*␣ | ␣
raktajānāṃ pratīkāraṃ kuryāt kuṣṭhacikitsitāt | ␣
surasādiṃ ca sarveṣu sa|⊙|*rvathaivopayojayet*␣|␣
pravyaktatiktakaṭukaṃ bhojanaṃ ca hitaṃ sadā␣|␣
kulattharasasaṃyuktaṃ kṣārapānañ ca pūjitaṃ␣|␣
kṣīrāṇi māṃsāni ghṛtāni caiva|⊙| *dadhīni śākāni ca parṇṇavanti*␣|␣
māṣānato mlāṃ madhurāṃ rasāṃś ca krimīṃ jighāṃsuḥ parivarjayīta ||[488]

It may be interesting to know why scribe(s) used gaps on many folios in the manuscript. As stated in the previous chapter, leaving small gaps in the writing may be related to the scribe's own habits or practice, perhaps even the oral transmission of the text. Nonetheless, to a degree these text divisions visually demarcate smaller text units in the manuscript. The gaps appear not only between the first and second half of the *śloka*, but also between the first and second half of other stanzas in the manuscript.

4.2.1.3 Gaps used to divide *pādas* in the *Śivadharma* corpus (CUL Add.1645)

Furthermore, in the copy of the *Śivadharma* corpus[489] (CUL Add.1645), dated NS 259 (1139 CE), the first and second half of the verses are divided on many folios (e.g., 2rv–5rv, 9v, 10rv, 13rv–14rv, 21rv–24rv, 26rv–33rv) by small gaps. These small gaps usually appear before and after the *daṇḍa*s. I have selected two folios in which visible gaps can be found. This example reveals another interesting phenomenon: as the gaps appear to be aligned in blank diagonal lines, their distribution renders the folio a sort of striped layout (e.g. 23r). The effect may be intentional.

A part of the text from 22v has been transcribed with the designated mark for gaps. The text portion is part of one of the chapters of the *Śivadharmaśāstra* ('Treatise on Śaiva Religion')[490] of the *Śivadharma* corpus. To show the occurrence of gaps, I have extracted and enlarged the middle part of 22v and put circles around gaps (see Fig. 4.2.1.4-II below).

488 For part of the section of the text with reading variations and its translation see, Sharma 2001, Vol. III, 544–545. Please note this manuscript was not consulted for his study.
489 On the study of Nepalese manuscripts of the *Śivadharma* corpus, see De Simini 2016, 233–286.
490 On the translation of the title, Ibid. 238.

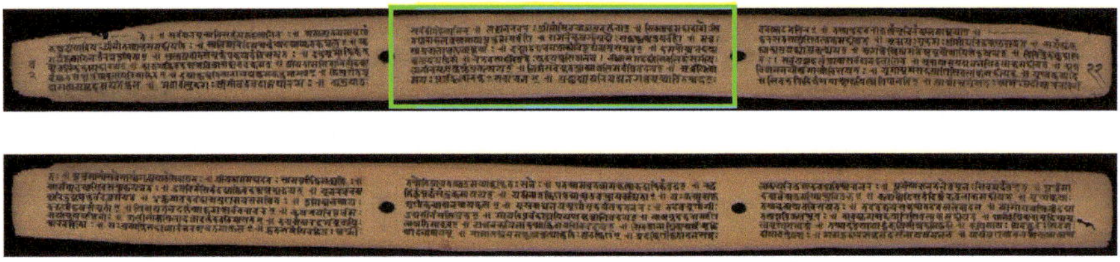

Fig. 4.2.1.4-I: Use of gaps, fols. 22v, 23r © CUL

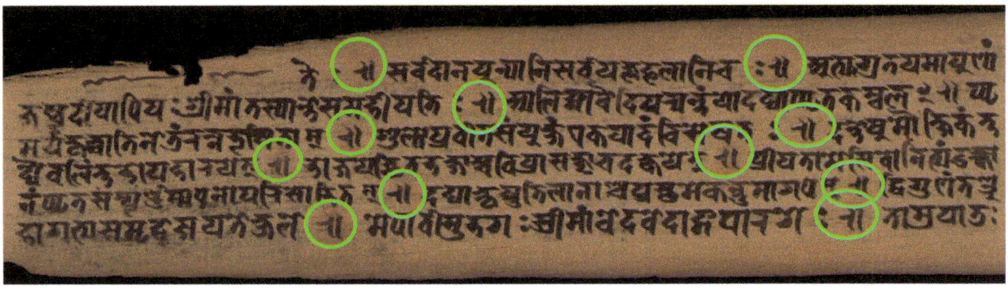

Fig. 4.2.1.4-II: Extracted and enlarged part from fol. 22v

[22v1–2] ∽∽ *taiḥ* ␣ ||
sarvadānapunyāni(!) *sarvayajñaphalāni ca*␣*ḥ*(!) || ␣
aty ugratayamāpuṇyaṃ|⊙|*sarvatīrthaphalāni ca* ␣ || ␣
labdhānaravaraḥ śrīmāṃśivayātrāpravarttanāt ␣ || ␣
śivaloke mahābhogaiḥ śi|⊙|*vavat*(!) *modate ciram* ␣ || ␣
tasyān te devarājatvaṃ sūciraṃ kālam āpnuyāt ␣ || ␣ ∽
[2]*japadīpādhipaḥ śrīmāṃ tasyān te sa mahīpatiḥ* ␣ || ␣
ālijñāvaidiparyantaṃ(!) *yo dadhyāghṛtakambalam* ␣ || ␣
ghṛ|⊙|*tadhārāphalan tasya māghapūrṇami parvvaṇi* ␣ || ␣
...

4.2.2 Gaps: type (b)

Another style of text division occurring in only a few manuscripts integrates gaps into the text-section layout of the page. Here each text-section looks as if it has been divided into two halves by the gaps. In the many cases in which a text is composed in *śloka* verses, this visual arrangement corresponds to the separation of the first half from the second one.

Bühler (1896, 84) briefly mentioned that this occurs in some Indian inscriptions,[491] while appreciating the care taking in its realization, one may confidently assume that scribes writing in such a style may have known the structure of the text and took care in its writing. Near similar type of usage of gaps between the *pāda*s can also be found in some early Gandharan Buddhist scrolls dating from ca. 1st c.[492] and also in some other inscriptions from other areas such as South-East Asia[493] (N.B. the scope and framework of this study prevents going into any detail here).

I have found a near similar kind of text division in at least three Nepalese manuscripts of this corpus so far. In SP_1, and SP_2 some verses are separated by gaps, whereas in the third HV_1, most of the text is divided by such gaps.

4.2.2.1 Gaps used to divide *ślokas* in SP_1

This puranic manuscript displays many significant aspects in its visual text-organisation. There are two string-holes on the folio and the text appears divided into three text-sections. As already mentioned in the previous chapter (see 4.2.1.1 above), there may have been at least two scribes involved on the manuscript production (excluding the folios on which similar hand writing can be found as in the *Pārameśvaratantra*). Only one of the two scribes writes the text dividing the *śloka*s by means of gaps. At least on '134' of the extant folios, the text may have been written by this scribe (e.g., on 73a–155a, 181b–189a, 191a–205a, 213a–224a, 230a–256a).[494] In general, one may assume the consistent style of puranic texts, mostly composed in *śloka*s, may have helped the scribe write in this particular layout.

491 See section 4.2 above.

492 Attestations of usage of gaps to divide parts of verses can also be observed in early Buddhist scrolls, for instance, in the Rhinocers sūtra scroll (ca. 1st c.) (British Library Kharoṣṭhī Fragment 5B) (see Salomon 2000, Pl. 1–2); in the Khotan Dharmapada scroll (ca. 2nd c.) (Bibliothèque nationale de France, Paris/Institute for the Eastern Manuscripts of the Russian Academy of Sciences, St. Petersburg) (see Baums 2014).

493 Examples of usage of gaps can be seen in the stone inscription from Văt Ph'u, Basăk, Laos datable to the 6th to 7th c. The text is in Sanskrit and composed in *śārdūlavikrīḍita* (stanzas 1, 3–5) and *sragdharā* (stanza 2) metres. The stanzas are clearly divided by small gaps between every first and second *pāda*, and also between every third and fourth *pāda*, see Salomon 1998, 282–283, Fig. 19; in the Stela from Mỹ Sơn (19 May 687) (Corpus of the Inscriptions of Campā, C. 87); in the Pedestal at Mỹ Sơn (ca. 7th c.) (Corpus of the Inscriptions of Campā, C. 79); in the Pedastal at Mỹ Sơn (ca. 7th c.) (Corpus of the Inscriptions of Campā, C. 97); in the 8th c. inscription from Combodia (K. 1236), see Goodall 2013, Fig. 5. See also Salomon 1998, 66. For the Corpus of the Inscription of Campā: <http://isaw.nyu.edu/publications/inscriptions/campa/inscriptions/index.html>) (last accessed on 25.05.2018).

494 The digital colour images were produced in 2010.

On many of these folios, gaps are used to divide text-section in two halves (e.g., on 74ab–76ab, 77a, 80a, 81b, 83ab–85ab, 86, 87, 94ab–96ab, 97a, 98ab, 100ab, 101b, 102b, 103ab–104ab, 105a, 106ab–107ab, 110b, 111a, 112a, 113ab, 114b, 115ab–119ab, 120a, 121a, 122ab–144ab, 145a, 147ab, 148ab–150ab, 151a, 152b, 153a, 155a, 181b, 182ab–183ab, 184a, 185a, 186a, 191, 194ab(?), 195b–196ab, 197a, 199ab, 201b, 202b, 204ab, 205a, 213a, 214ab–223ab, 224a, 230a, 231ab–248ab, 249a, 250b, 251ab–255ab, 256a, 278b).

The regular distribution of gaps has been dropped should additional elements e.g. sub-colophon, speaker indication, symbols etc. occur, or if the text has verses composed in other metres than *śloka*. In the latter, text-sections are not regularly divided into two halves (e.g., on 73a, 77b, 78ab–79ab, 80b, 81a, 82ab, 88ab–93ab, 97b, 99ab, 101a, 102a, 105b, 108ab, 109ab, 110a, 114a, 118b, 139b, 146, 151b, 152a, 153b, 154ab, 186b, 187ab, 188ab, 189b, 192ab–193ab, 195a, 197b, 198ab, 200ab, 201a, 202a, 249b, 250a, 279a, 287b, 288a). See Fig. 3.9.2-V for an image of one folio of similar case (lower ones).

Fig. 4.2.2.1-I, provides two examples where the first and second half of *ślokas* are divided by gaps within each text-section. Some portion of the text of the upper folio of Fig. 4.2.2.1-I has been transcribed with the designated mark for gaps. The central part of the upper folio of Fig. 4.2.2.1-I has been extracted and enlarged to show the occurrence of gaps in text-sections more clearly (see Fig. 4.2.2.1-II below). One box has been added to emphasize the occurrence of gaps.

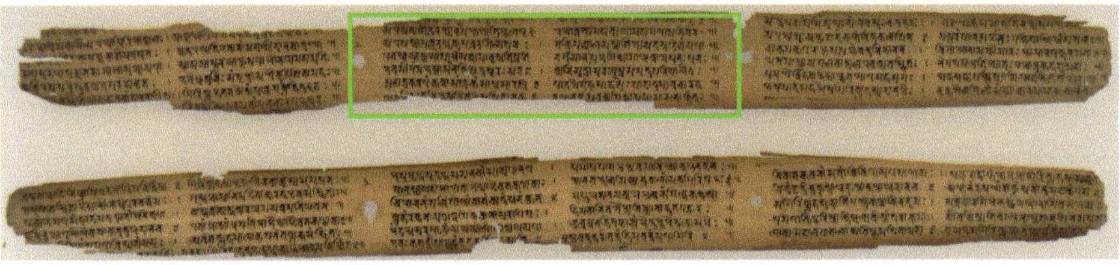

Fig. 4.2.2.1-I: Use of gaps; fols.?, 74ab © NAK

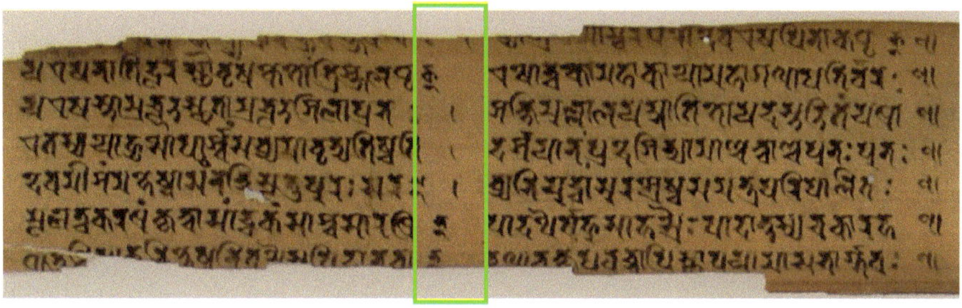

Fig. 4.2.2.1-II: Extracted and enlarged part from fol.?, 74a © NAK

[74a1–2] *///mbaradharo deva eṣa pinākadhṛk* |||⊙|
yas tv eṣa kapisiṃhāsyo nīlavastraḥ(!) *caturbhujaḥ*␣|␣
taruṇārkkasamo bhāti nandy eṣa gaṇanāya+
[2]*///++rucco gnisaṃkāśo ya eṣo gnir ivojjvalaḥ*␣|␣
brāhmaṇādhipa+++ha+ca+++++␣|||⊙|
ya eṣa nātidūrastho vṛṣaketo(!) *triśūladhṛk*␣
eṣo ndhako mahākāyo mahāgaṇapatir varaḥ |||⊙|
ya eṣo(!) *sthāya*(!) *kūjantaṃ bhāti citrakalāpina*␣*m*␣
mayūraṃ bālasūryabhaḥ(!) *śaktipāṇir mmahābalaḥ*(!) ||[495]
...

4.2.2.2 Gaps used to divide *śloka*s in SP_2

This puranic manuscript exhibits further examples in terms of layout. As mentioned in chapter 3.9.2, there may have been at least two scribes involved in the manuscript production. One of the two scribes makes use of type (a) gaps, i.e. adds gaps between the various parts of the *śloka*s without arranging them more precisely within the text-sections.

Gaps are used largely on 4, 5b, 6ab–12ab, 15ab, 17ab–20ab, 22ab–34ab, 37ab–40ab, 45ab–46ab, 83ab, 91ab–95ab, 72ab, 73ab, 106ab–108a, 110ab, 112ab–115ab, 119ab–120ab, 122ab–123ab, 128ab–136ab, 138ab–141ab, 144ab–149ab, 151ab–152ab, 155ab–156ab, 158ab, 163ab, 165a, 167ab, 166b, 168ab–169ab, 215b, 216a.[496]

Gaps are used only at times on 13ab–14ab, 16ab, 21ab, 35ab, 36ab, 41ab–44ab, 47ab–71ab, 74ab–82ab, 84ab–90ab, 96ab–105ab, 108b, 109ab, 111ab, 116ab–118ab, 121ab, 124ab–127ab, 137ab, 142ab–143ab, 150ab, 153ab–154ab, 157ab, 159ab–161ab, 162a, 164ab, 165b, 166a, 170ab–182ab, 183a.

495 Please note I have transcribed the text from the manuscript as faithfully as possible. For the 'edition', see Bhaṭṭarāī 1988, Ch. 132.9–13.
496 The digital colour images were produced in 2010.

Furthermore, the same scribe also uses type (b) gaps, arranging *śloka*s in text-sections at least on two folios (on 5a, 162b). However, there are some exceptions to this pattern. In case of image 5a (shown in Fig. 4.2.2.2-II), in the fifth line on the folio, a chapter colophon appears together with double circles, followed by the (partly) abbreviated speaker indication (*sanatku*[*māra*] *u*[*vāca*]). Although these elements do respect the metrical structure of the main text, they have been adjusted to the style of the layout. However, the justification of the text-sections has been lost as the extra gaps have not been added between single *akṣara*s. After the speaker indication, *śloka*s start again, but here there is not enough space to accommodate one *pāda* in each half of the text-sections: as a result the final part of the *pāda* slips into the first half on the immediate right, as shown in Fig. 4.2.2.2-I.

Fig. 4.2.2.2-I: Extracted part from fol. 2v

Fig. 4.2.2.2-II, shows where most of the first and second half of *śloka*s has been divided by gaps within each text-section. A part of the text has been transcribed with the designated mark for gaps. The right part of the folio has been extracted and enlarged to show the occurrence of gaps in text-sections more clearly (see Fig. 4.2.2.2-III below). One box has been added to emphasize the occurrence of gaps.

Fig. 4.2.2.2-II: Use of gaps; fol. 2v? (5a) © NAK

Fig. 4.2.2.2-III: Extracted and enlarged part from fol. 2v? (5a)

[2v1–2] ///+++++++++*dānam athāpi ca*␣|␣
andhakasya tathotpattiḥ pṛthivyāś caiva bandhanam |||⊙|
hiraṇyākṣavadhaś caiva hiraṇyakaśipos tathā␣|␣
balaśayamanaṃ(!) *caiva devyāḥ samaya eva ca*␣|||⊙|
devānā(!) *gamanañ caiva a*+++++++␣
+++++++++*krasya ca visa*///++
[2]///+*tasya ca tathotpattir devyāś cāndhakadarśanaṃ*␣|␣
śailādidaityasammarddo devyāś ca śatarūpatā |||⊙|
āryāvara<<*da*>>*pradānañ ca śailādis tava eva ca*␣|␣
devasyāgamanañ caiva vṛttasya kathanan tathā|||⊙|
pativratāyāś cākhyānaṃ guruśuśrūṣaṇasya ca␣|␣
ākhyānaṃ pañcacūḍāyās tejasaś cāpy adhṛṣyatā///[497]
...

The editors of SP_1,[498] maintain that manuscript SP_1 is a slightly older copy than SP_2 (the same can be said of the two versions of the same text they contain; the *Skandapurāṇa*). Both manuscripts feature the same kind of layout, in which type (a) and type (b) gaps have been implemented. It is possible to hypothesise that the scribe(s) of SP_2 may not only have consulted SP_1, but were also influenced by the latter's layout.

4.2.2.3 Gaps used to divide *śloka*s in HV_1

This manuscript shows significant features with in terms of its visual text-organisation. There are two string-holes on the folio. According to the string-holes the text appears to have been divided into three text-sections. In most parts of the manuscript *śloka*s have been divided by gaps on almost all the folios (with exceptions where no *śloka* division by gaps can be seen, e.g., on 1v, 307v–308rv).

In the majority of the folios, the first and second half of the *śloka*s have been divided by means of precise gaps in each text-section (e.g., on 2rv–267rv, 268v, 269rv–276rv, 278rv–290r, 291rv–293rv, 296rv–297rv, 300rv–302rv, 305rv, 309rv, 310rv, 311v, 312rv, 313rv, 314v, 325rv–326rv, 329rv).

Two examples in Fig. 4.2.2.3-I, show where the first and second half of *śloka*s have been divided by gaps within each text-section. The centre part of the folio 39v of Fig. 4.2.2.3-I has been extracted and enlarged to illustrate in detail the use

---

497 Here I transcribe the text from the manuscript as faithfully as possible. For the edition, see Bhaṭṭarāī 1988, Ch. 2.15–23 and for the critical edition, see Adriaensen et al. 1998, Ch. 2.14cd–23ab.
498 See Adriaensen et al. 1998, 32–33.

of gaps by means of a box in the area of gaps (see Fig. 4.2.2.3-II). A part of the text of the upper folio 39v of Fig. 4.2.2.3-I has been transcribed with a mark designating the use of gaps on the folio.

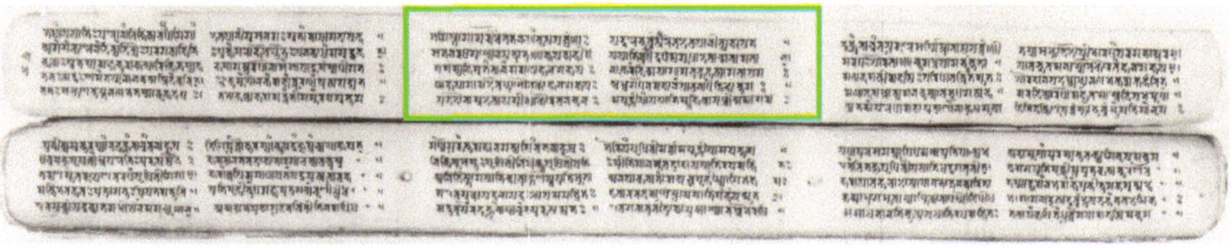

Fig. 4.2.2.3-I: Use of gaps; fols. 39v, 40r © NAK

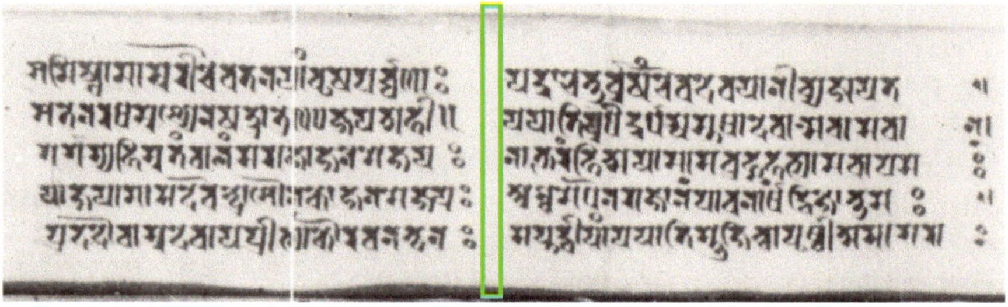

Fig. 4.2.2.3-II: Enlarged and extracted part from fol. 39v

[39v1–2] *teṣāṃ yayātiḥ pañcānāṃ vijitya va\su/dhām imāṃ* ␣
devayānīm uśanasaḥ sutāṃ bhāryām avāpa ha ␣ |||⊙|
śarmiṣṭhām āśurī(!) *caiva tanayāṃ vṛṣaparvvaṇaḥ* ␣
yaduñ ca turvuṣaṃ caiva devayānī vyajāyata ␣ |||⊙|
druhyuṃ cānuṃ ca pūrūñ ca śarmmiṣṭhā vārṣaparvvaṇī ␣
tasya śakro dadau prīto rathaṃ paramabhāsvaram |
[2]*asaṃgaṃ kāñcanaṃ divyaṃ divyaiḥ paramavājibhi* ␣
ḥ yuktaṃ manojavai(!) *śubhraiḥ yena kāryaṃ samudvaha* ␣ *t* ||⊙|
sa tena rathamukhyena ṣaḍrātreṇājayan mahī(!) || ␣
yayāti(!) *yudhi*(!) *durdharṣas tathā devān savāsavā*␣*n*||⊙|
sa rathaḥ pauravāṇān tu sarvveṣām abha\va/t tadā || ␣
yāvat tava sanāmno(!) *vai kauravaṃ janamejayam* |
...

4.2.3 Gaps – Preliminary conclusion

Gaps can be understood as a crucial dividing device in terms of the visual demarcation of smaller text units in the manuscript. They can be found between sentences or parts of *śloka*s (as described in Gaps: type (a) and Gaps: type (b)).

Gaps have been found largely in the Nepalese manuscripts of my corpus. Three manuscripts, where precisely the first and second half of the *śloka*s have been (partially or almost entirely) divided by gaps within text-section (like Gaps: type (b)) contain puranic texts (SP_1, SP_2) and an epic text (HV_1).

We can assume that the presence of gaps reflects the work of a skilful scribe, who took care and great effort in producing the manuscript and implemented a well-planned layout strategy.[499] The scribe was probably familiar with the metrical structure of the text he was writing down. Regarding the use of manuscripts exhibiting such kinds of features, the division of smaller text units may have helped readers orient themselves in the text. It can also be said that gaps can be understood as a reader-friendly layout.

499 This openly contradicts the statement of Al-Beruni. For the English translation of his statement, see Sachau 1910, Vol. I, 18 "... the Indian scribes are careless, and do not take pains to produce correct and well-collated copies". It may not bear out that the scribes did not pay sufficient attention to the production of manuscripts, when we observe the use of various kinds of symbols, the arrangement of smaller text units in manuscripts or the overall layout of East Indian manuscripts where text lines have been written with remarkable regularity (see section 2.4.2 above).

5 Use of colour

In a way not too dissimilar from that of European manuscripts,[500] coloured inks (especially red ink) are used for writing symbols, individual words, various kinds of statements or even lengthy portions of a text within Indic manuscript cultures. In this respect, Jaina paper manuscripts feature the use of coloured ink more prominently.[501] Colours, particular in the form of powders or pastes, are used to delete or correct texts or part of them.[502]

In this chapter, however, I will neither investigate the use of inks, nor the use of coloured powders and pastes for emending texts, but instead study the use of powders and/or pastes used to highlight various elements in manuscripts (such as individual words, portions of a text, numbers, *daṇḍa*s, symbols etc.) that are usually a 'yellowish-red' or 'yellowish-brown'.[503] As will be demonstrated later, almost all highlighted elements in many manuscripts of the 'core' corpus of the present study appear not to have been highlighted for the purpose of corrections or deletions.[504] Highlighting helps readers orient themselves in texts and, at the same time, emphasises important parts or elements of what they are reading. Here the application of colour can be understood as another means for structuring texts in manuscripts.

For highlighting in manuscripts, the colour is lightly applied on the script or on other element once it has been written or drawn, it is possible, however, that the colour may have faded since its original application. The Sanskrit term *lepa*, which, among other things, means literally, 'the act of smearing or anything smeared on',[505] might possibly be the term for describing the method of colour application, as the highlighted features appear to have been highlighted without the use of a brush or stylus (the sharp edges that can be seen in the letters and symbols themselves, written in black ink, cannot be detected in the

500 See Jacobi-Mirwald 2008, 47; Schneider 2009, 153–158.

501 See Bühler 1896, 92; Tripāṭhī 1975, 29. For many colourful examples of Jaina paper manuscripts, see JAINpedia at: <http://www.jainpedia.org/manuscripts/browse.html> (last accessed on 19.11.2018).

502 See below in this chapter for some selected relevant quotations from Bühler 1896, 86; Thaker 2002, 143; Einicke 2009, 35.

503 See section 5.2 regarding the colour compositions in some manuscripts of my corpus which was carried out during the Nepal field trip to Nepal. In particular, the colouring agent could possibly be 'ochre'.

504 For instance, symbols around string-holes or at the end of the chapters or *daṇḍa*s before and/or after textual parts etc. could not be highlighted for corrections etc.

505 See Monier-Williams 1872, 902 s.v. *lepa*.

https://doi.org/10.1515/9783110543087-005

application of colour). Instead, the scribe or reader may have either used his fingers,[506] a small piece of cloth or similar items for smearing the pigment.

Frequently, there is little accuracy in the highlighting, and some of the highlighted parts go beyond the *akṣara*s or symbols or other elements that should perhaps not have been highlighted (see Fig 5.1-IV below where the sign for the *visarga* is highlighted together with the *daṇḍa*). At times the colour is applied only lightly and partly on parts of the *akṣara*s or other elements (see the lightly highlighted *mantra* in Fig. 5.1-XXIII and partly highlighted symbols in Fig. 5.1-XII below). In these cases, we should understand which was most likely intended for highlighting.

Thus far, only a few studies have dealt with the topic, and they assert the use of colours in manuscripts is to correct texts or delete part of them (whereby the material nature of the pigments is briefly mentioned). Bühler (1896, 86) argues the use of colour as follows:

> Dieselben Zeichen finden sich gleichfalls in MSS., wo in später Zeit die Delenda auch durch gelbe Farbe verdeckt werden.
>
> 'The same signs can also be found in MSS., where in later periods the Delenda are also covered by the yellow colour.'[507]

Tripāṭhī (1975, 29) in his Jaina manuscripts catalogue briefly mentions colours and their purpose thusly:

> Yellow or white colours. Very often incorrect akṣaras or parts thereof are covered over with yellow colour ("haratāla")[508] or white colour ("saphedo", from saphed = white).

In his study, largely based on the study of West Indian ('Jaina') manuscripts, Thaker (2002) describes three different cases of highlighting. Firstly, Thaker (p. 138) talks of colours being used for highlighting different features in the written part of manuscripts as follows:

> Scholars applied *GERU* i.e. Ochre to important notable words, phrases, sentences etc. which would then naturally attract the reader's attention.

---

506 See Thaker 2002, 143 uses 'thumb marks' as he describes the colour application on the foliation and string-holes of palm-leaf manuscripts from West India. It can also be possible that finger or similar items might have been used for highlighting not only the foliation, but also other features in manuscripts.

507 The translation is mine.

508 Probably Tripāṭhī 1975 was referring to the Sanskrit term '*haritāla*' ('yellow orpiment', see Apte 1957, 1749, s.v. *haritāla*) instead of 'haratāla'.

Then (p. 143) he mentions:

> Some-times thumb marks were made with vermilion at the places of numbering and also of cutting hole.[509]

Finally, he (p. 146) gives the reason by mentioning another material:

> Still later on the more decent method of covering the delenda with turmeric or a yellow pigment was adopted for Mss.

More recently, Einicke (2009, 35) has mentioned the use of colours for corrections:

> Die Abschriften konnten im Anschluss vom Schreiber selbst oder von einer anderen Person noch einmal mit der Vorlage abgeglichen und korrigiert werden, was zu interlinearen, späteren Einfügungen führte. Häufig wurde bei Korrekturen wohl auch eine andere Farbe verwendet, so dass sich verschiedene zeitliche Korrekturschichten evtl. schon dadurch voneinander trennen lassen.
>
> 'The copies can be subsequently compared and corrected once again by the scribe himself or by another person with the master copy, which resulted in later, interlinear insertions. Often, it seems, another colour was also used for the corrections, so that this alone may enable us to distinguish different chronological layers.'[510]

In this chapter, I will try to understand which among the many textual and pictorial elements found in manuscript folios are singled out for the readers' attention. As in the previous chapters, I will match peculiar features with specific areas of manuscript production. In what follows I present the use of colours as text-related features.[511]

---

509 At least in JKS/C and BCV, the colour which has been used for other features such as symbols and *daṇḍa*s does not seem to be different to the colour used for highlighting foliation and symbols on the string-hole spaces.

510 The translation is mine.

511 The use of coloured paste and/or power can also be found on covers in manuscripts which I do not investigate in detail in the present study. This can possibly be categorised as colours as ritual-related features. As it has been reported and studied by scholars (see Gellner 1996; Kim 2013) some manuscripts might have significant value as ritual objects or cultic meaning in some particular traditions or were considered to be a representation of particular deities etc. and were used in rites, one can find traces of coloured pastes, powders, etc. that were also used in the rites. Traces of colour paste or powder and sometimes other substances (such as sandalwood paste, bundle of threads or lights) can be seen in several manuscripts. In the following I give a preliminary list of manuscripts in which one can find such traces, e.g. red and yellow mixed colours are smeared on the outer part of the front cover in SP_2; eight spots made of a reddish-like power/paste on the outer part of the back cover of PR; on the outer part of the front cover of the manuscript of the *Pañcarakṣā* (NS 183 / 1063 CE) (NAK 3/688 / NGMPP B 30/45 and B 31/1); on the outer part of the front cover of the manuscript of the *Prajñāpāramitāstotra, Aṣṭasāhasrikā Prajñāpāramitā* and *Vajradhvajapariṇāmanā* (ca. 11th c.) (CUL Add.1643) with five spots; on the outer part of the back cover of the manuscript of the *Aṣṭasāhasrikā Prajñāpāramitā* (ca. 11th c.) (CUL Add.2190); on the outer part of the front cover of the manuscript of the *Śivadharma* corpus (NS 259 / 1139 CE) (CUL Add.1645) with three spots; on the outer part of the back cover of the manuscript of the *Rāmāyaṇa* (ŚS 1076 / 1154 CE) (NAK 1/934 / NGMPP A 25/2); on the outer part of the back cover of the manuscript of the *Aṣṭasāhasrikā Prajñāpāramitā* (ca. 12th c.) (CUL Add.1544); on the outer part of the front cover of the manuscript of the *Pañcarakṣā* (NS 325 / 1205 CE) (CUL Add.1644); on the outer part of the front cover of the manuscript of the *Bṛhannāradīyapurāṇa* (LS 395 / 1275 CE) (NAK 5/748 / NGMPP B 5/5); on the outer part of the back cover of the manuscript of the *Kriyākāṇḍakramāvalī* (ca. 14th–15th c.) (CUL Add.1406); on both outer parts of the front and back covers of the manuscripts of the *Kāraṇḍavyūha* (ca. 14th–15th c.) (CUL Add.1267); on the outer part of the front cover of the manuscript of the *Pañcarakṣā* (ca. 15th–16th c.) (NAK 5/7457 / NGMPP B 31/17) including a big bundle of lights on the right side; on the outer part of the front cover of the manuscript of the *Devīmāhatmya* (ca. 15th–16th c.) (KL 20 / NGMPP C 3/1) containing basically seven big spots; on the outer part of the back cover of the manuscript of the *Pañcarakṣā* (NS 655 / 1535 CE) (NAK 4/21 / NGMPP B 30/29); on the outer part of the back cover of the MTM of the *Upākarmasnānavidhi* and *Ṣaḍaṅgarudrī* (NS 667 / 1547 CE) (NAK 1/1534 / NGMPP A 1156/27) containing five big spots; on the outer part of the front cover of the manuscript of the *Sphuṭārthā Abhidharmakoṣavyākhyā* (NS 671 / 1551 CE) (CUL Add.1041) with five big spots and a small bunches of curd on the left and right sides; on the outer part of the front cover containing five big spots and also on the outer part of the back cover of the manuscript of the *Bhāgavatapurāṇa* (NS 694 / 1574 CE) (KL 90 / NGMPP C 7/1); on the outer part of the front cover of the manuscript of the *Itihāsasamuccaya* (ca. 16th c.) (KL 510 / NGMPP C 48/1); on the most part of the outer part of the front cover of the (ca. 16th–17th c.) (*nīlapatra*) manuscript of the *Pañcarakṣā* (NAK 5/7633 / NGMPP A 139/2) including butter-lights bound on the left side; on the most part of the outer part of the front cover of the (*nīlapatra*) manuscript of the *Aṣṭasāhasrikā Prajñāpāramitā* (NS 774 / 1654 CE); on the most part of the outer part of the back cover of the *Kāraṇḍavyūha* (NS 788 / 1668 CE) (NAK 3/286 / A 109/6) including a kind of strip bound on the right side; on the outer part of the front cover of the (paper) manuscript of the *Devīpurāṇa* (NS 805 / 1685 CE) (NAK 1/885 / NGMPP B 208/4); on the outer part of the front cover of the (*nīlapatra*) manuscript of the *Pañcarakṣā* (NS 815 / 1695 CE) (CUL Or.2258); intensively on the outer part of the back cover and some on the outer part of the front cover of the (*nīlapatra*) manuscript of the *Aparimitāyurdhāraṇīsūtra* and *Sarvadurgatipariśodhana* (NS 820 / 1700 CE) (CUL Add.1623); intensively on the outer part of the front cover and some on the outer part of the back cover of the (paper) manuscript of the *Pañcarakṣā* (ca. 17th c.) (CUL Add.1164.1); on the outer part of the front cover and also on the outer back cover of the (paper) manuscript of the *Dhāraṇīsaṅgraha* (NS 839 / 1719 CE) (CUL Add.1326); on the outer part of the front cover of the (paper) manuscript of the *Aparimitāyurdhāraṇīsūtra* (ca. 17th–18th c.) (CUL Add.1277); on the outer part of the front cover of the (paper) manuscript of the *Suvarṇaprabhāsasasūtra* (NS 960 / 1840 CE) (NAK 3/612 / NGMPP B 94/8); on the most part of the outer part of the front cover of the (paper) manuscript

5.1 Colours as text-related feature

Thaker (2002, 138) stated that "important notable words, phrases, sentences etc." may appear highlighted. However, he does not provide examples of such highlighting so we are left to ponder what kind of elements are important, and what kind of functions such highlighted features might have in relation to the text or the manuscript. These highlighted features do automatically draw the readers' attention, but they could also play a crucial role in the text structure and be used to emphasize different levels of the text. In some cases highlighted features appear as a substitution for a particular item, one would usually expect to find in the manuscript (see the highlighted *daṇḍa*s etc. before and after the chapter colophon below).

There are many features highlighted in the manuscripts of this corpus e.g. invocation, *daṇḍa*s, various kinds of symbols, blank spaces, individual words, quotation formulas, *mantra*s, colophons, foliation numbers, etc.

(1) Invocation

At the very beginning of the text in a manuscript it is a common convention that (or at the beginning of a particular text in MTMs), for a statement with or without auspicious symbols[512] to appear for the purpose of showing respect to particular deities and ensure its completion and preservation. Occasionally, such statements also appear (partly or entirely) highlighted in some of manuscripts of the corpus.[513]

A few manuscripts of the corpus contain highlighted invocations. At the beginning of the *Suśrutanighaṇṭu* part in SS/N the invocation appears highlighted

of the *Saddharmapuṇḍarīkasūtra* (NS 962 / 1842 CE) (NAK 4/217 / NGMPP A 128/20); on the outer part of the front cover of the (paper) manuscript of the *Samādhirājasūtra* (NS 964 / 1844 CE) (NAK 3/279 / NGMPP B 94/6); on the outer part of the front cover of the (paper) manuscript of the *Lalitavistara* (NS 964 / 1844 CE) (NAK 3/278 / NGMPP B 100/3); on the most part of the outer part of the front cover of the (paper) manuscript of the *Guhyasamādhi* (NS 967 / 1847 CE) (NAK 3/283 / NGMPP A 111/5).

512 For detailed studies and discussions on 'auspicious symbols' and terms for the types of symbols, see Roth 1986, 239–249; Sander 1986, 252–261; Bhattacharya 1995, 201–228.

513 For highlighted invocations, see in AṣP$_1$ (NS 271 / 1151 CE) (NAK 5/195 / NGMPP A 36/4) on 1v1; in the manuscript of the *Sarvaprakaraṇasaṅgraha* (NS 277 / 1157 CE) (KL 36 / NGMPP C 4/2) on 1v1; in the manuscript of the *Cāndradhātupāṭha* (NS 476 / 1356 CE) (CUL Add.1162) on 1v1; in the manuscript of the *Hitopadeśa* (ca. 15th c.) (CUL Add.1407) on 1v1; in the (paper) manuscript of the *Dhāraṇīsaṅgraha* (CUL Add.1326) (NS 839 / 1719 CE) on 1v1.

on 200v1. *Siddham* can be found before the invocation. The transcription of the highlighted invocation can be seen in red along with the *siddham* symbol in Fig 5.1-I.

[200v1]  *namaḥ sarvajñāyānuttaravaidyarājāya ||*

Fig. 5.1-I: Highlighted invocation

In the Śaiva tantric manuscript TS$_2$, the invocation appears partly highlighted on 1v. The *Siddham* appears before it. The transcription of the highlighted invocation is written in red along with the *siddham* symbol in Fig. 5.1-II.

[1v1]  *namo mahābhairavāya digdevatādibhyo gurubhyaḥ ||*

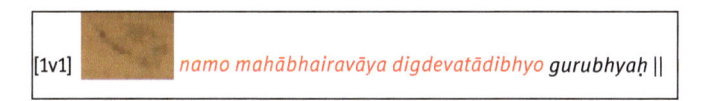

Fig. 5.1-II: Highlighted invocation

In the Buddhist manuscript SS containing *sādhana*s, the invocation has been highlighted, on 1v. The *Siddham* appears before the scribe invocation. The highlighted invocation has been given in red along with the *siddham* in Fig. 5.1-III.

[1v1]  *namaḥ sarvabuddhabodhisatvebhyaḥ ||*

Fig. 5.1-III: Highlighted invocation

(2) *Daṇḍa*(s)

*Daṇḍa*s can appear partially or almost entirely highlighted in some manuscripts. In the following some selected examples of *daṇḍa*s that appear in different parts in manuscripts are presented.

(a) Highlighted *daṇḍa*s marking the end of a verse or part of a verse

In the *Suśrutanighaṇṭu* part of the SS/N most of the double *daṇḍa*s appear highlighted, on 210rv–217rv, 219rv. To see the colour application, a part of the text from 210r1–2 has been transcribed and highlighted *daṇḍa*s have been used in red (see the transcription below).

> [210r1–2] *śatāvarī sūkṣmapatrā pīvarīndīvarī ca sā* |
> *abherū bahumūlā ca jāṭāūlā ca śabditā* || |⊙|
> *śarivā gopavalyā ca tathā cotpalaśārivā* |
> *sugandhamūlabhadrā ca kṛṣṇavaly api cocyate* ||
> *jīvakaḥ priyanāmā ca dīrghāyuḥ kūrcaśīrṣakaḥ* ||⊙|
> *maṅgalyanāmadheyaś ca prāyaḥ svāṅgaś ca kīrtitaḥ* ||
> *ṛṣabhaḥ kakudī śrīmāṃ vikarṇī gopa*[2]*tis tathā* |
> *dhūrdharo bandhuro vīraḥ pṛthivīpatir eva ca* ||
> *mahāsahā mahāparṇṇī siṃhavinnā tathai*|⊙|*va ca* |
> *pāṇḍuromaśaparṇṇī ca haṃsamāsā ca śabditā* ||
> *kṣudrasahā mudgaparṇṇī sūryaparṇṇī tathaiva ca* |
> *svanumārjāragandhā ca kākamu*|⊙|*dgā ca kīrtitā* ||[514]
> ...

(b) Highlighted *daṇḍa*s before and after the speaker indication

In SP_4, double *daṇḍa*s before and after the (partly) abbreviated speaker indications appear highlighted on almost all available folios, namely on 6v, 9r, 9v, 10r, 10v, 11r1, 61v, 62r, 62v, 63r, 63v, 65r, 67r.[515] In what follows, some part of the text has been given in transcription;[516] the highlighted *daṇḍa*s are marked in red:

> [6v5] ///*mahādevaṃ svalokaṃ pratyapadyataḥ*[517] || *vāyur u* ||[518]
> [9r4] *paśyatām eva sarveṣāṃ tatraivāntaradhīyata*[519] || *sana u* ||

---

514 Here I transcribe the text as it appears in the manuscript. For the edition, see Suvedī/Tivārī 2000, 55–56.

515 Although I had the opportunity to see only a few colour images of SP_3 and I have used mainly b/w images in the course of my study, if one zooms the b/w images in, a greyish shade which most probably indicates the presence of colour can also be seen on *daṇḍa*s that appear before and after almost all speaker indications. See also chapter 3.8.2 above.

516 Here I transcribe the text portions from the manuscript as faithfully as possible. For the 'edition', see Bhaṭṭarāī 1988 and for the critical edition, see Adriaensen et al. 1998.

517 For the edition, see Bhaṭṭarāī 1988, Ch. 5.72 cd and for the critical edition, see Adriaensen et al. 1998, Ch. 5.65cd.

518 The free space between '*vā*' and *daṇda*, '*ru*' and *daṇḍa* is also highlighted.

[9v1] *vicareyaṃ sukhaṃ deva sarvāṃ lokān namas tava*[520] || *brahma u* ||
[9v3] *tena coktaṃ*|⊙|*sthito smīti sthāṇus tena tataḥ smṛtaḥ*[521] || *devadeva u* ||
[9v6] ///*na u* || *tataḥ sā krodhadīptāsyā na jagrāhāti ko*|⊙|*pitā*[522] |

We can assume that the presence of colour on double *daṇḍa*s before and after the speaker indications helps the reader to single out parts of the text to easily attribute them to the right speaker.

(c) Highlighted *daṇḍa*s before and/or after sub-colophons

Symbols and blank spaces can be often delimited by *daṇḍa*s and they appear before and/or after the (sub-)chapter colophon. At times the chapter number may appear after the (sub-)chapter colophon delimited by double *daṇḍa*s. *Daṇḍa*s may be highlighted together with the symbols, blank spaces and chapter numbers themselves.

The distribution of all these elements can appear mainly in two specific configurations: (a) single or double highlighted *daṇḍa*s are placed at the *beginning* of a (sub-)chapter colophon, followed by a blank space or a symbol or chapter number surrounded by highlighted or without highlighted *daṇḍa*s; and (b) single or double highlighted *daṇḍa*s are placed at the *end* of a (sub-)chapter colophon, preceded by a blank space or a symbol surrounded by highlighted or without highlighted *daṇḍa*s.

In KT, for instance, the symbols are mostly before and after the chapter colophons. However, in a few cases, there are no symbols either before or after the chapter colophons. In these cases, the first '*i*' of the word '*iti*' or the *daṇḍa* following the last statement of the chapter or the *daṇḍa* after the chapter colophon are highlighted. In Fig. 5.1-IV the *visarga* and the *daṇḍa* after the chapter colophon on 70v4 and the '*i*' of *iti* on 76r1 are highlighted.

519 Bhaṭṭarāī 1988, Ch. 9.32cd; Adriaensen et al. 1998, Ch. 9.30cd.
520 Ibid. Ch. 10.3cd; Ch. 10.3cd.
521 Ibid. Ch. 10.10cd; Ch. 10.10cd.
522 Ibid. Ch. 10.20ab; Ch. 10.20ab.

[70r4]  *iti kiraṇākhye tantre aṣṭacatvāriṃśatimaḥ*⊙ *paṭalaḥ* |

[76r1-2] *iti kiraṇākhye tantre*⌒[2] *ekapañcāśakaṃ paṭalam*(!) 

Fig. 5.1-IV: Highlighted *daṇḍa* and *akṣara* after and before the chapter colophons

In GV, highlighted double *daṇḍa*s delimit the first two chapter numbers of the first two chapter colophons and one blank space before the last chapter colophon. Furthermore, double *daṇḍa*s before the chapter colophon or colophon can also be highlighted, e.g., on 6v4, 8v6 and 10r5. See Fig. 5.1-V for an example of the highlighted double *daṇḍa*s before the chapter colophon and highlighted double *daṇḍa*s after the chapter colophon.

[6v4] || *guṇavatyāṃ śrīmahāmāyāṭīkāyāṃ prathamo*⊡ *nirdeśaḥ* 

Fig. 5.1-V: Highlighted *daṇḍa*s before and after the chapter colophon

In HTP, almost all double *daṇḍa*s accompanying blank spaces or symbols at the end of (sub-)chapters appear highlighted. At the beginning of (sub-)chapter colophons there are no symbols or blank spaces. Single or double *daṇḍa*s appear before the chapter colophons and are, in the main, highlighted. See Fig. 5.1-VI for two examples of the (sub-)chapter colophons.

[5v4] || *mantrapaṭalo dvitīyaḥ* 

[6v3] || *devatāpaṭalas tṛtīyaḥ* 

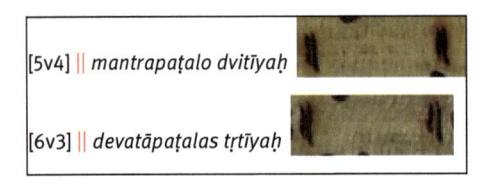

Fig. 5.1-VI: Highlighted *daṇḍa*s before and after chapter colophons

A similar configuration is in CPN.[523] There are no symbols or blank spaces before the (sub-)chapter colophons. But blank spaces appear after the (sub-)chapter colophons and are surrounded by one or two sets of highlighted double *daṇḍa*s. See Fig. 5.1-VII for two examples of (sub-)chapter colophons.

[7v1] | *ity ātmapīṭhe catu□ṣpīṭhanibandhe prathamaḥ paṭalaḥ*

[25v4] || *iti parapīṭhe catuṣpīṭhanibandhe tṛtīyaḥ paṭalaḥ*

Fig. 5.1-VII: Highlighted *daṇḍa* before the chapter colophons

These examples make it possible to assume that highlighted *daṇḍa*s and part of the *akṣara*s or *akṣara*s fulfil the same structural function as the symbols and blank spaces appearing before and/or after the (sub-)chapter colophon and colophons.

(3) Symbols

Symbols appearing at the end of a particular chapter, section or text are partly or entirely highlighted in some of the manuscripts of my corpus. Furthermore, in West Indian manuscripts symbols appearing around string-holes or with foliations are frequently highlighted.

(a) Highlighted symbols at the end of chapters

Highlighting symbols can have a structuring value used to indicate clearly where an important section of a text, such as a (sub-)chapter or a particular section, ends.

523 Similar style of highlighting of *daṇḍa*s (single or double) before the chapter colophons (if there are no symbols or blank spaces before the chapter colophons) appear in a few manuscripts of the area, e.g. in AP on 14r5_BCC, 21v6_BCC, 22r3_BCC, 22v7_BCC, 23r2_BCC, 23v2_BCC; in the manuscript of the *Ḍākinīvajrapañjarapañjikā* (NAK 5/20 / NGMPP A 47/17(1)) (preserved in Nepal) on 6r1_BCC, 6v2_BCC, 11r5_BCC, 11v5_BCC, 12r3_BCC, 12r6_BCC.

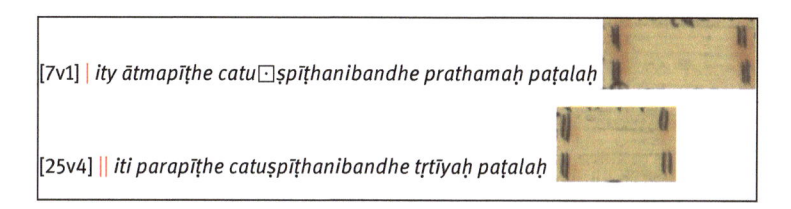

In SP_1, some symbols in the part written by scribe B are highlighted (scribe A doesn't use colour at all).[524] All highlighted symbols are placed at the end of chapters. See Fig. 5.1-VIII for some selected highlighted symbols.

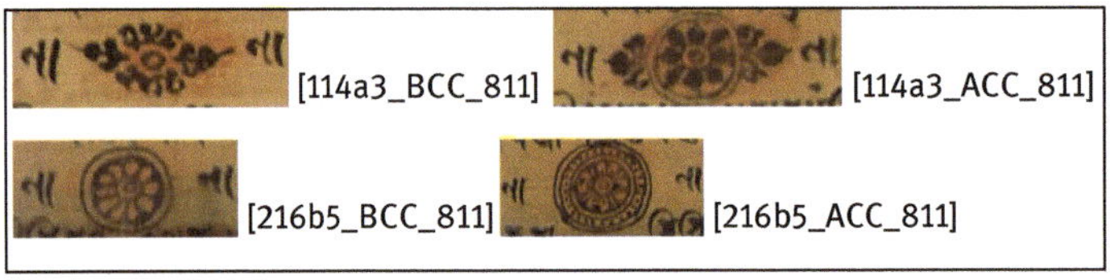

Fig. 5.1-VIII: Highlighted symbols

In SP_2 a few symbols are highlighted. All of the highlighted symbols appear in the part by scribe B in the manuscript. Fig. 5.1-IX shows two examples of highlighted symbols.

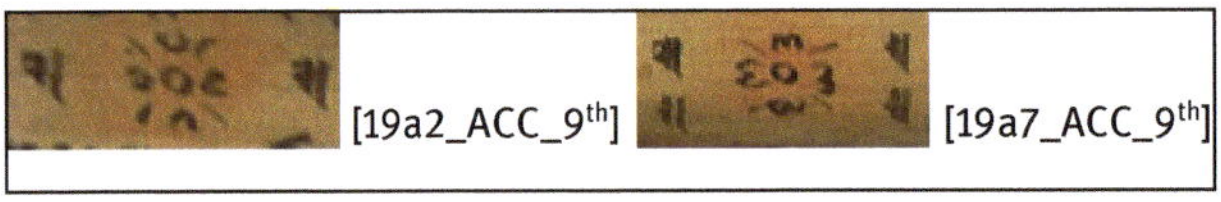

Fig. 5.1-IX: Highlighted symbols

In SS/N, most of the symbols appear highlighted. Fig. 5.1-X shows two examples of highlighted symbols.

Fig. 5.1-X: Highlighted symbols

In KT, all symbols are highlighted. All symbols can be found at the end of the chapters. Fig. 5.1-XI shows examples of highlighted symbols.

524 Concerning the possible number of involvement of scribes, see section 3.9.1 and 4.2.21 above.

 [25v1_ACC_924]  [87v2_BCC_924]

Fig. 5.1-XI: Highlighted symbols

In SP_4, all symbols appear partly highlighted (except for symbols on 6v6_BCC,[525] 274v5_ACC[526]). The double *daṇḍa*s that delimit the symbols are also partly highlighted. In the majority of cases, the colour has been lightly applied to the centre part of the symbols. All symbols appear at the end of the chapters. Fig. 5.1-XII shows two partly highlighted symbols.

 [68v3_ACC_10th]  [71r2_BCC_10th]

Fig. 5.1-XII: Highlighted symbols

In YYS, apart from the symbols (on 9v4_B/ACC, 11r6_B/ACC),[527] all symbols appearing at the end of the chapter before and/or after chapter colophons have been highlighted partially. Furthermore, the symbols before and after the colophon are also highlighted. Fig. 5.1-XIII shows two examples of highlighted symbols.

 [15r4_BCC_1024]  [38r4_ACC_1024]

Fig. 5.1-XIII: Highlighted symbols

In AAĀ, all *siddham* (on 35r3_BCC, 48v4_BCC, 61r2_BCC, 79r7–79v1_B/ACC, 83r3_BCC, 84v5_BCC, 96r4_BCC, 104v2_B/ACC, 123v7_BCC, 127r6_BCC, 132r2_BCC, 134r4_BCC, 135v6, 144r1_B/ACC, 156v1_BCC, 165v3_ABV) and stylised *puṣpikā*s (on 164v5_ACC, 165v3_B/AC) appear at the end of the chapters and at the end of the text they are highlighted. Fig. 5.1-XIV features two selected highlighted symbols.

525 This symbol seems to be a later addition.
526 This is just a circle.
527 These four symbols appear before and after the first two chapter colophons.

[144r1_BCC_11th]
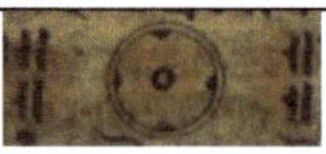
[164v5_ACC_11th]

Fig. 5.1-XIV: Highlighted symbols

In HTṬ, excluding some symbols (on 40r6_ACC, 51v3_BCC, 58v6_APC), all symbols that appear at the end of the chapters are highlighted. Fig. 5.1-XV shows two selected highlighted symbols.

[48r6_ACC_12th]

[51v3_ACC_12th]

Fig. 5.1-XV: Highlighted symbol

(b) Highlighted symbols around string-holes

Highlighted symbols are not only used to single out various parts of a text, but are also used outside the text-sections on the page and their highlighting may exhibit a degree of aesthetic value.

In TSa one string-hole can be found on each folio. On all folios, symbols have been drawn around the string-holes. The majority of symbols are highlighted. Fig. 5.1-XVI shows examples of highlighted symbols.

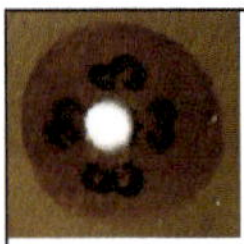
[TSa_37r_SH_1143]
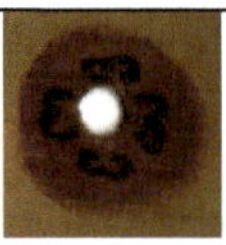
[TSa_38r_SH_1143]

Fig. 5.1-XVI: Highlighted symbols around string-holes

In HVM there are two string-holes on each folio and symbols appear around both string-holes. Almost all symbols are highlighted. Fig. 5.1-XVII shows examples of highlighted symbols.

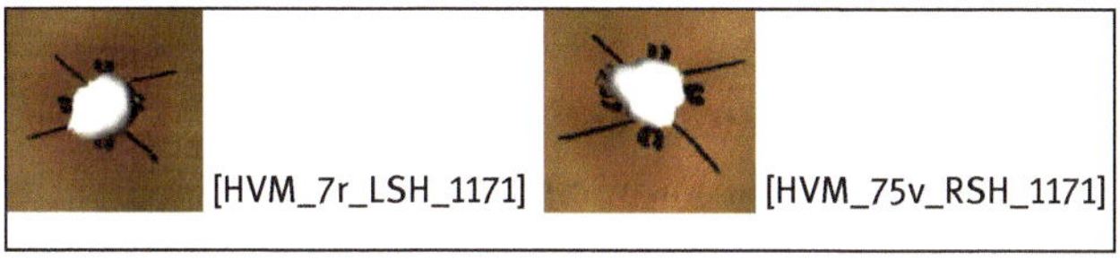

Fig. 5.1-XVII: Highlighted symbols around string-holes

In JKS/C one string-hole can be found on each folio and symbols have been drawn around almost all string-holes (except on 1r).[528] All symbols have been highlighted intensively. Fig. 5.1-XVIII shows two highlighted symbols.

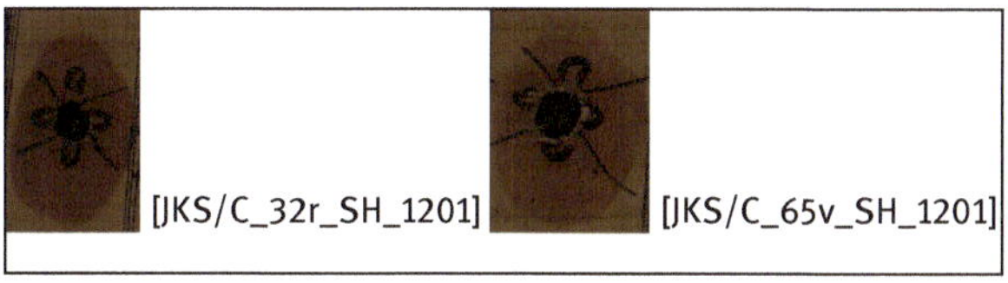

Fig. 5.1-XVIII: Highlighted symbols around string-holes

Likewise, in TUS one string-hole can be found on each folio and symbols have been drawn around string-holes on almost all folios. Although only having access to b/w images of this manuscript for the preparation of this book, traces of colour application on the symbols can clearly be noticed. Fig. 5.1-XIX shows examples of highlighted symbols.

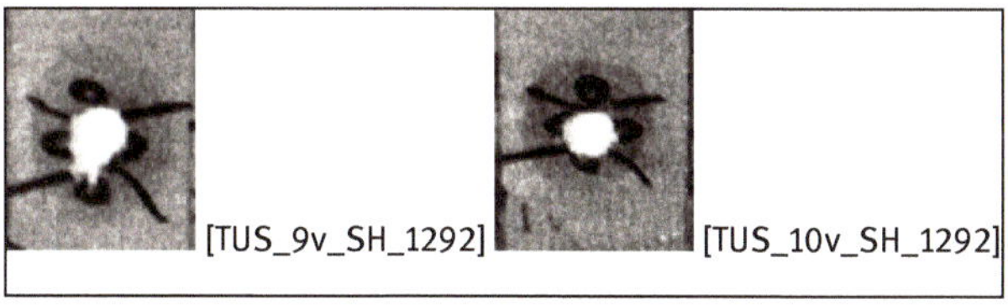

Fig. 5.1-XIX: Highlighted symbols around string-holes

528 Please note that, among symbols around the string-holes, also many other elements appear highlighted in the manuscript, for instance, nearly all '*cha*' symbols (see Appendix below), many space-fillers such as on 31v1, 31v2, 32v3, 47r4, 47r5, 51v4, 62v1, most of the *daṇḍa*s (single or double *daṇḍa*s), the '*sūtra*' numbers.

In BCV there is one string-hole on each folio. Symbols have been drawn around the string-holes on almost all folios (except on 1r and 78v).[529] All symbols have been intensely highlighted.[530] Fig. 5.1-XX shows two highlighted symbols.

[BCV_60v_SH_13th]
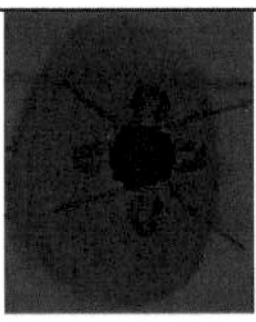
[BCV_61r_SH_13th]

Fig. 5.1-XX: Highlighted symbols around string-holes

(4) Quotation formulas

Among others, quotation phrases or formulas also appear highlighted in manuscripts. In AAĀ *'tathā coktam ... iti'*,[531] *'yathoktam'* and *'etad uktam'* are often lightly highlighted.[532] Hereafter, I limit my observation to the formula *'tathā coktam ... iti'*, which is the most frequently used in the manuscript.[533]

529 Please note that, among symbols around the string-holes, almost all '*cha*' symbols (see Appendix below), many space-fillers (e.g. on 3r6, 10r5, 64r5, 66v5) and many *daṇḍa*s (single or double *daṇḍa*s) are also highlighted in the manuscript.

530 Also most of the symbols around string-holes are highlighted in the manuscript of the *Ṣaḍāvaśyakasūtravṛtti* (VS 1298 / 1241 CE) (Jinabhadrasūri Grantha Bhaṇḍāra, Jaisalmer, no. 136/1); in the manuscript of the *Sthānāṅgasūtravṛtti* (VS 1300 / 1295 CE) (Jinabhadrasūri Grantha Bhaṇḍāra, Jaisalmer, no. 6); in the manuscript of the *Praśnavyākaraṇadaśāṅgasūtravṛtti* (VS 1300 / 1295 CE) (Jinabhadrasūri Grantha Bhaṇḍāra, Jaisalmer, no. 23/3).

531 See Tubb/Boose 2007, 200–201: "The word *iti* is normally placed immediately after the word or words that are quoted by it. Thus *iti* marks the end of a quotation, but in most cases the beginning must be determined on the basis of context."

532 According to personal communication of Prof. Harunaga Isaacson, other formulae such as '*tad āhuḥ*', '*yad āhuḥ*' may also be used in the text.

533 This can be found on 7r1–2, 7r6, 7v4–5, 7v7–8r1, 8r3–4, 8r6–7, 8v1, 8v2, 8v6, 10r5, 11r2, 13v1–2, 14r6, 16v2–3, 18r5, 19r3–4, 19v7, 20v7–21r1, 21v7, 22r6–7, 23r2, 23r5, 23v3–4, 24v3–4, 25r4, 25v1–2, 29r1–2, 29r3, 29r5, 29r6–7, 29v1–2, 29v3, 30r4–5, 30r6–7, 30v1–2, 30v6–7, 35r2, 37r6, 38r1–2, 38r3, 38r6, 38v2, 40v2, 41v1, 42r4, 42r6, 44r5, 44r7, 44v2, 44v4, 44v6, 45r5, 63v6, 66v3, 73v3–4, 74r5, 76r6, 76v6, 78r2, 78v1, 78v6, 79v2–3, 80r1–2, 80r6, 80v2, 80v5–6, 81r3–4, 81r5, 81r6, 81v5–6, 82v5–6, 83r1, 83r4, 84v2, 84v6, 85v4–5, 88r3, 88r7, 88v1, 91r4, 93v2, 1006–7, 101r6–7, 102r1–2, 104v7–105r1, 106r7, 116v4–5, 117r1, 117r3–4, 117r6, 118v2, 118v3, 118v4, 118v5, 121r4–6, 121r6–121v1, 123v4–6, 124v3–4, 124v5–6, 126r5–6, 126v6, 127r3, 127r4, 128r3, 129v1, 129v5, 131r3–4, 131r6, 133v2–3, 136v2–3, 137r2–3, 137r7, 139v3–4, 140r1, 140r6–7, 141r4–5, 142r1,

Within this formula, '*tathā coktam*' appears always (entirely) highlighted and occasionally '*iti*' appears entirely highlighted. However, in many cases either part of the '*iti*' and the following *daṇḍa* appear highlighted or only the *daṇḍa* is highlighted. Verses can often be found between '*tathā coktam*' and '*iti*'. To illustrate the style of highlighted features I have selected part of the text and transcribed as they appear in the manuscript from 29r below. For the highlighted part, red colour is used in the transcription (see below). In addition, highlighted portions of '*tathā coktam* ... *iti*' from 29r have been extracted and enlarged (see Fig. 5.1-XXII).

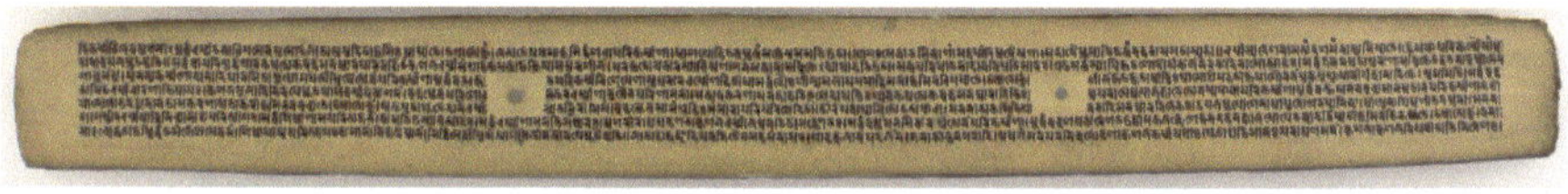

Fig. 5.1-XXI: Highlighted quotation formulae, fol. 29r

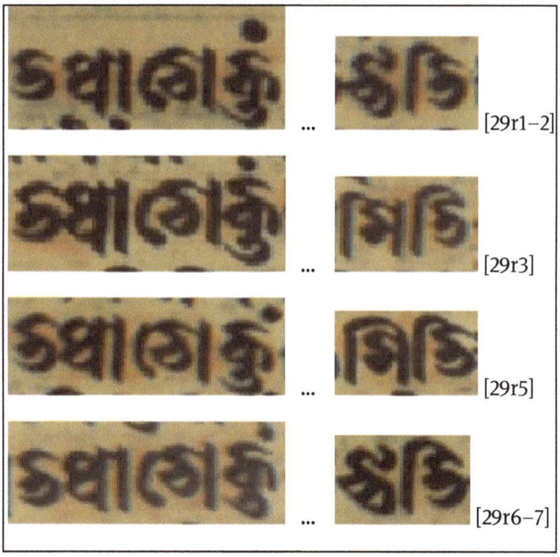

Fig. 5.1-XXII: Extracted and enlarged quotation formulae from 29r

142v6, 143v1–2, 144v5, 145v1, 146r3–4, 146v1, 146v2, 146v5, 147v2–3, 149r7–149v1, 150r1–2, 150r4–5, 150r6–7, 150r7–150v1, 151r6–7, 150r7–150v1, 151r6–7, 151v3, 151v6, 151v7, 152r1, 152r3, 152r4, 153r3–4, 153v3, 153v4, 153v7–154r1, 154r2, 154v1–2, 155v3, 155v7, 156r6, 164r6, 164v1.

[29r1–2] *tathā coktaṃ* |
labhyate prathamā bhūmir ddaśadhā parikarmaṇā |
āśayo hitavastutvaṃ sattveṣu samacittatā |
tyāgaḥ sevā ca mitrāṇāṃ saddharmmālambanaiṣaṇā |
sadā naiṣkramyacittatvaṃ buddhakāyagatā spṛhā ||
dharmasya deśanā satyaṃ daśamaṃ vākyam iṣyate |
jñeyañ ca parikarmaiṣāṃ sva[2]*bhāvānupalambhata iti* ||
[29r3] *tathā coktam* |⊡
śīlaṃ kṛtajñatā kṣāntiḥ prāmodyaṃ mahatī kṛpā
gauravaṃ guruśuśrūṣā vīryaṃ dānādike 'ṣṭamam iti |
[29r5] *tathā coktaṃ* |
atṛptatā śrute dānaṃ dharmma¦⊡*sya ca nirāmiṣaṃ* |
buddhakṣetrasya saṃśuddhiḥ saṃsārāparikheditā |
hrīr apatrāpyam ity etat pañcadhā mananātmakam iti
śrā⊡*vakādimanaskāravivekaḥ* |
[29r6–7] *tathā coktaṃ* |
vanā¦[7]*śā 'lpecchatā tuṣṭir dhūtasaṃlekhasevanaṃ* |
śikṣāyā aparityāgaḥ kāmānāṃ vijugupsanaṃ |
nirvvit sarvvāstisaṃtyāgo 'valīnatvānapekṣate iti ||[534]

One may wonder why such elements such as '*tathā coktam* ... *iti*' frequently appear highlighted in the manuscript, but one may be assume the highlighted features serve to provide visual hints on the passages quoted in the text. Here, colour application on these elements may be used to differentiate between the main text and the commentary. Thus, this way of applying the colour can be understood as a device used to divide the text.

(5) *Mantras*

In SS many *daṇḍa*s are highlighted. However, aside from *daṇḍa*s, a few *mantras*[535] appear partly or entirely highlighted; on 17v1–7, 18r6, 85v6, 85v7, 86r2–3, 86v1, 92r1, 94r5, 95r6, 114r2 and 131v1. Occasionally, even the *daṇḍa*s before and after the *mantra*s are highlighted, e.g. on 34v1–6. To illustrate the style of highlighting, highlighted *mantra*s have been transcribed into red below. Two partly highlighted *mantra*s have been extracted and enlarged from folios 18r1 and 95r6 (see Fig. 5.1-XXIII). In this case the colour is lightly applied on some of the *akṣara*s.

534 Here I transcribe the text from the manuscript as faithfully as possible. For the edition, see Tucci 1932, 95–97.
535 For the studies on *mantra*, see Padoux 2011; Goodall/Isaacson 2016, 4–9.

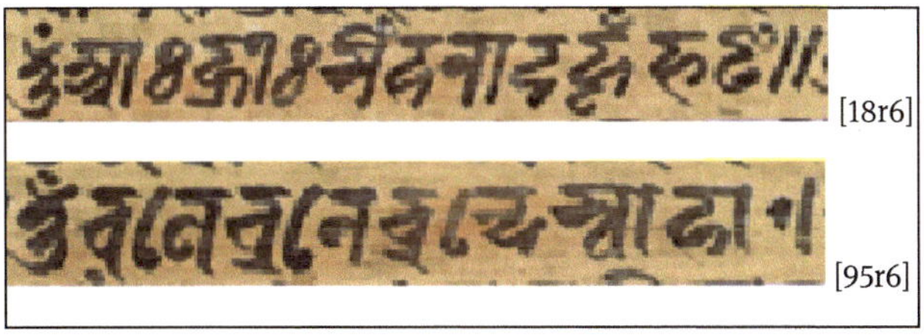

Fig. 5.1-XXIII: Extracted and enlarged part of the highlighted *mantra*s

> [17v1] *atra mantraḥ* | *oṃ hrīḥ svāhā* || *iti lokanāthasādhanaṃ samāptaṃ* ||
> [17v6–7] *japamantraḥ* || *oṃ āḥ hrīḥ siṃhanāda huṃ phaṭ* || *i*[7]*ti siṃhanādasādhanaṃ* ||
> *tad yathā oṃ akaṭe vikaṭe nikaṭe kaṭaṅkaṭe karoṭe karoṭe vīrye svāhā* ||
> [18r6] *japyamantraḥ* ||⊡ *oṃ āḥ hrīḥ siṃhanāda huṃ phaṭ* || *tadanantaraṃ dhāriṇī* (!) *bhavati* ||
> [85v6] *tāṃkāraḥ sa evaṃvidhaḥ* || *oṃ tāṃ tāṃ tāṃ*¦⊡*tāṃ tāṃ iti*[536] | *anena sarvvaśatrūn stambhayati* |
> [85v7] *oṃ trāṃ trāṃ trāṃ trāṃ trāṃ punaḥ*[537] | *tāṃkāraṃ lakṣaṃ japet grāmaśataṃ labhate* | *oṃ truṃ truṃ truṃ truṃ anena sarvvarakṣā kṛtā bhavati* ||
> [95r6] *iyañ cundāyā mudrā* | *mantraś cā*⊡*yaṃ* | *oṃ cale cule cunde svāhā* | *cundāsādhanaṃ* ||

This is an MTM and contains various influential *sādhana* texts related to the Buddhist tantric tradition. As it is believed *mantra*s contain 'magical' power and efficacy, and some of them even appear highlighted, it appears safe to assume the colour application on the *mantra*s is employed to emphasise their importance and occurrence in the manuscript.

(6) (Sub-)chapter colophons or colophons

In a few manuscripts of my corpus, some (sub-)chapter- or final-colophons are highlighted. In the following, some partially or entirely highlighted chapter colophons from selected manuscripts are presented.[538]

---

536 This appears partially highlighted.
537 This appears partially highlighted.
538 In the manuscript of the *Kāśikāvivaraṇapañjikā* (ca. 10th/11th c.) (NAK 4/216 / NGMPP A 52/13) nearly all chapter colophons are partially or entirely highlighted, e.g., on 146v1–2, 164v4, 173r4, 204r6–7, 245v6, 301r3, 372r4–5, 389v4–5. See for the manuscript information at: <http://ngmcp.fdm.uni-hamburg.de/mediawiki/index.php/A_52-13_K%C4%81%C5%9Bik%C4%81v%E1%B9%9Btti> (last accessed on 03.09.2018).

SP$_2$

In SP$_2$, some chapter colophons are partly, and other chapter colophons are entirely highlighted. The 4th, 38th, 53rd chapter colophons appear partly highlighted and the 27th, 51st, 113th, 119th chapter colophons are entirely highlighted. Fig. 5.1-XXIV shows examples of partly or entirely highlighted chapter colophons.

[63v4–5] *skandapurāṇe a*[5]*ṣṭatriṃśatimo dhyāyaḥ*
[160?v4] *skandapurāṇe trayodaśottaraśato dhyāyaḥ*

Fig. 5.1-XXIV: Partly and entirely highlighted chapter colophon

SS/N

Among many features (such as symbols, *daṇḍa*s etc.), at least one (sub-)chapter colophon appears highlighted in the manuscript. Fig. 5.1-XXV shows the partly highlighted section colophon.

[68v7]
... *samāptan nidānasthānam*

Fig. 5.1-XXV: Highlighted section colophon

TS$_1$

In TS$_1$ among a few highlighted features, the first chapter colophon appears lightly highlighted. Fig. 5.1-XXVI shows the highlighted chapter colophon.

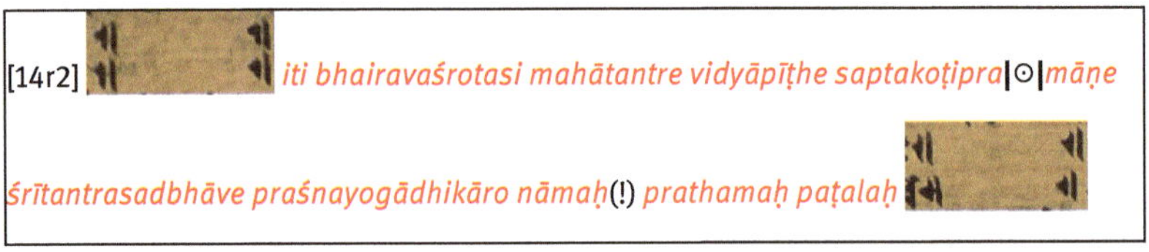
[14r2] *iti bhairavaśrotasi mahātantre vidyāpīṭhe saptakoṭipra*|⊙|*māṇe*
śrītantrasadbhāve praśnayogādhikāro nāmaḥ(!) *prathamaḥ paṭalaḥ*

Fig. 5.1-XXVI: Highlighted chapter colophon

AAĀ

In AAĀ all chapter colophons are partially highlighted except the 32nd chapter colophon. Thus some characters of each chapter colophon are highlighted. Fig. 5.1-XXVII shows two examples of chapter colophon. In colophons *akṣara*s seem to have been randomly highlighted (see examples below).

[48v4] 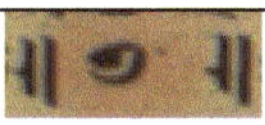 *abhisamayālaṅkārālokāyāṃ prajñāpāramitāvyākhyāyāṃ*

śakra¦⊡*parivartto nāma dvitīyaḥ* 

[61r2–3] 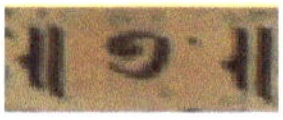 *abhisamayālaṅkārālokāyāṃ prajñāpāramitāvyākhyāyāṃ*

apra[3]*meyaguṇadhāraṇapāramitāstūpasatkāraparivartto nāma tṛtīyaḥ* 

Fig. 5.1-XXVII: Partly highlighted chapter colophons

AṣP₁

In AṣP₁ some chapter colophons seem to have been highlighted e.g. the 3rd, 9th, 13th, 19th, 23rd, 25th, 26th, 29th, 30th, 31st. Although, only having viewed a part of the manuscript where highlighting was present, and only a few digitised colour images of folios of this manuscript before the preparation of the book, traces of the use of colour are visible (i.e. greyish spot) in many chapter colophons of the b/w images. Fig. 5.1-XXVIII shows one of the examples of highlighted chapter colophon.

[50v2–3] 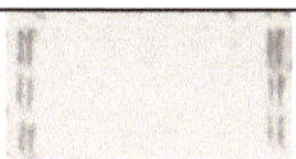 *āryāṣṭasāhasri*[3]*kāyām*(!) *prajñāpāramitāyām aprameyaguṇad-*

hāraṇapāramistūpasatkāraparivartas(!) *tṛtī*|⊙|*yaḥ* 

Fig. 5.1-XXVIII: Highlighted chapter colophon

Manuscript of the *Sarvaprakaraṇasaṅgraha* (KL 36 / NGMPP C 4/2)

In the manuscript of the *Sarvaprakaraṇasaṅgraha* (NS 277 / 1157 CE) (KL 36 / NGMPP C 4/2), among others, all chapter colophons are highlighted (on 1v2, 2v6, 4v4, 5r4, 6r2, 8v3, 9r3, 10r4, 11r1, 11r5, 14v1, 14v5–6, 16v4, 17v5, 18v5, 19r3, 19v6, 20r2, 20r4, 20v2, 20v4, 21r3, 21v4, 23v3, 24r6, 25r6, 26r3, 26v1, 27v1, 28r1–2, 29r4, 29v2, 30r6–30v1, 30v4, 31r6, 33v2, 34r1–2, 34r6, 34v6, 36v4, 37r2, 38r1, 40r3, 40v4, 42r5, 43v2, 44r5, 45r1, 45v6).

Fig. 5.1-XXIX: Highlighted chapter colophon

(7) Foliation

In some manuscripts of the corpus, foliation numbers appear partially or entirely highlighted. The highlighting is present occasionally in only a few Nepalese and East Indian manuscripts. However, foliations appear highlighted in almost all West Indian manuscripts of my corpus. Below are some selected examples.

SS

Of this corpus foliation appears highlighted only in SS from Nepal. There is only figure-numerical foliation on the left-hand margin on the folio. Among other features (such as highlighted *daṇḍa*s, *mantra*s etc.), foliation appears lightly highlighted. Fig. 5.1-XXX features examples of the highlighted foliation in the manuscript.

	Left-hand margin
2	
222	

Fig. 5.1-XXX: Highlighted foliation

AAĀ

In AAĀ all foliation numbers appear highlighted. The foliation is in figure-numerals and appears on the left-hand margin on the folio. Fig. 5.1-XXXI features examples of highlighted foliation.

	Left-hand margin
27	
44	

Fig. 5.1-XXXI: Highlighted foliation

Please note that in almost all manuscripts from West India of the corpus foliation,[539] letter-numerals on the left-hand margin and figure-numerals on the right-hand margin appear intensely highlighted on both sides. It seems that highlighting foliation in West Indian manuscripts may well have been a kind of prevailing custom.

The highlighted spots with letter-numerals and figure-numerals look slightly different. It is conspicuous from the start that the numbers expressed in letter-numerals are written vertically, while those of figure-numerals horizontally. This style probably affected the way in which the highlighting colour is applied. The shape of the highlighted spot over the letter-numerals on the left margin looks often rather lean and long.[540] Whereas, the shape of the highlighted spot applied over the figure-numerals on the right margin is of an almost round form (see Figs. 5.1-XXXII–5.1-XXXV below). This pattern, also appears with single letter-numerals, where it would not be strictly necessary to give a long, lean shape to the highlighting. These features may be understood as coordinates, to help the reader position the manuscript in the appropriate way when holding it up. In the following, examples of the highlighted foliation in West Indian manuscripts of my corpus are presented.

TSa

Almost all foliations on both sides are highlighted in TSa, e.g., on 110v, 111v and 142v in Fig. 5.1-XXXII. The spots of the highlighted foliation on the left looks long and lean and on the right-hand margin almost round in shape.

539 On the use of colour particularly in paper manuscripts from the same area, Losty 1982, 43 notes the following: "The reverse also has an additional red roundel in each of the outer margins; these occur also in palm-leaf manuscripts and are the places where the foliation is marked, the letter system in the left margin, and the numeral one in the right". Similarly, Thaker 2002, 143 also expresses about the use of colour on foliation and string-holes in palm-leaf manuscripts thusly: "Some-times thumb marks were made with vermilion at the places of numbering and also of cutting holes." However, it seems that neither Losty nor Thaker have noticed the differences in highlighted spots in palm-leaf manuscripts from this area.

540 From the appearance and size of the highlighted spots of the left and right foliations in West Indian manuscripts, it is possible to think the left foliation may have been highlighted using the thumb whereas the right foliation was either an index or other fingers but not the thumb (see examples below).

	Left-hand margin	Right-hand margin
110		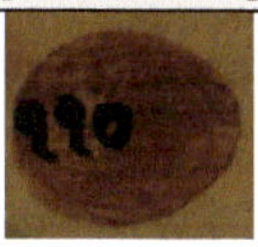
111		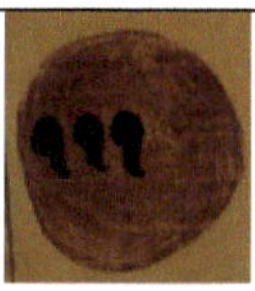
142		

Fig. 5.1-XXXII: Highlighted foliations

JKS/C

In JKS/C the foliations on both margins have been highlighted. As we can see, the highlighted spot of the foliation on the left-hand margin is long and lean and the spot on the right-hand margin appears almost round in shape. Fig. 5.1-XXXIII shows examples of highlighted foliations on both sides on 30v and 65v.

	Left-hand margin	Right-hand margin
30		
65		

Fig. 5.1-XXXIII: Highlighted foliations

TUS

In TUS, foliations also seem to have been highlighted on both sides. As mentioned above, even only viewing b/w images of the manuscript, traces of colour on foliations on both margins are visible e.g. on 9v and 10v. As in the aforementioned manuscripts from West India, the spots of highlighted foliation on the left look long and lean and on the right-hand margin quite round. Fig. 5.1-XXXIII shows examples of highlighted foliations.

	Left-hand margin	Right-hand margin
9	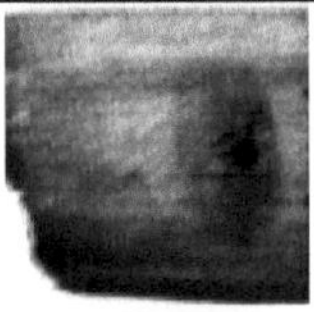	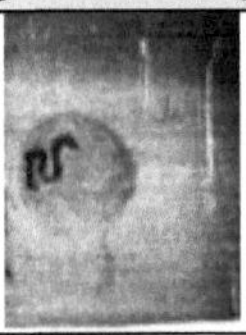
10	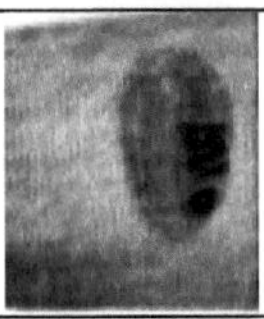	

Fig. 5.1-XXXIV: Highlighted foliations

BCV

In BCV, foliations on both margins have been highlighted. Similar to the aforementioned manuscripts from this region, the spots of highlighted foliation on the left look long and lean and on the right-hand margin almost round. Fig. 5.1-XXXV shows examples of highlighted foliations.

	Left-hand margin	Right-hand margin
17		

20		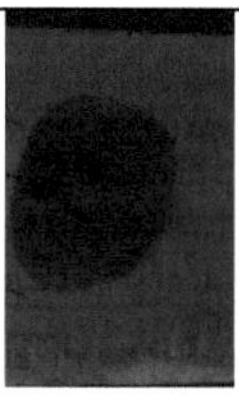

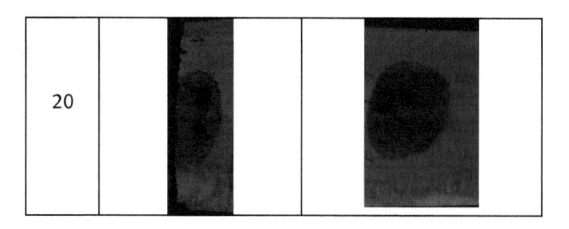

Fig. 5.1-XXXV: Highlighted foliations

Preliminary conclusions on highlighted foliations

We have seen examples of some different styles of highlighting foliations in one Nepalese and one East Indian manuscript of this corpus. Among West Indian manuscripts we have seen highlighted foliation in JKS/C, TS, TUS and BCV.[541]

Differences in the manner of highlighting between West Indian manuscripts and Nepalese and East India manuscript are evident. In West Indian manuscripts, both foliations on the left and right margins appear intensely and consistently highlighted with a vivid colour, and their highlighted spots (on the left and right foliations) look clearly different in shape. Although in one manuscript of the core corpus from Nepal and East India featuring highlighted foliation, the colour is very pale. In both manuscripts from Nepal and East India foliation can be found only on the left-hand margin.

5.1.1 Overall conclusions on use of colours

Colours can be found in manuscripts of almost all regions. They are applied in various shapes and used for different purposes. On the style of colour application, a close similarity exists between Nepalese and East Indian manuscripts. The manner of colour application in West Indian manuscripts bears some similarities to the Nepalese and East Indian manuscripts, but is generally applied in a more vivid way.

541 Highlighted foliations can also be seen in the manuscript of the *Upamitibhavaprapañcā Kathā* (Bhandarkar Oriental Research Institute, Pune, Acc. no. 7a-b/1880-81) on some folios that are presented by Gopalakrishnan 2007, 30; in the manuscript of the *Ṣaḍāvaśyakasūtravṛtti* (VS 1298 / 1241 CE) (Jinabhadrasūri Grantha Bhaṇḍāra, Jaisalmer, no. 136/1); in the manuscript of the *Sthānāṅgasūtravṛtti* (VS 1300 / 1295 CE) (Jinabhadrasūri Grantha Bhaṇḍāra, Jaisalmer, no. 6); in the manuscript of the *Savaga Padikkamana Sutta cunni* (*Śrāvakapratikramasūtra-cūrṇi*) (VS 1317 / 1260 CE) (Museum of Fine Arts, Boston. Denman Waldo Ross Collection, 30.1.1-229).

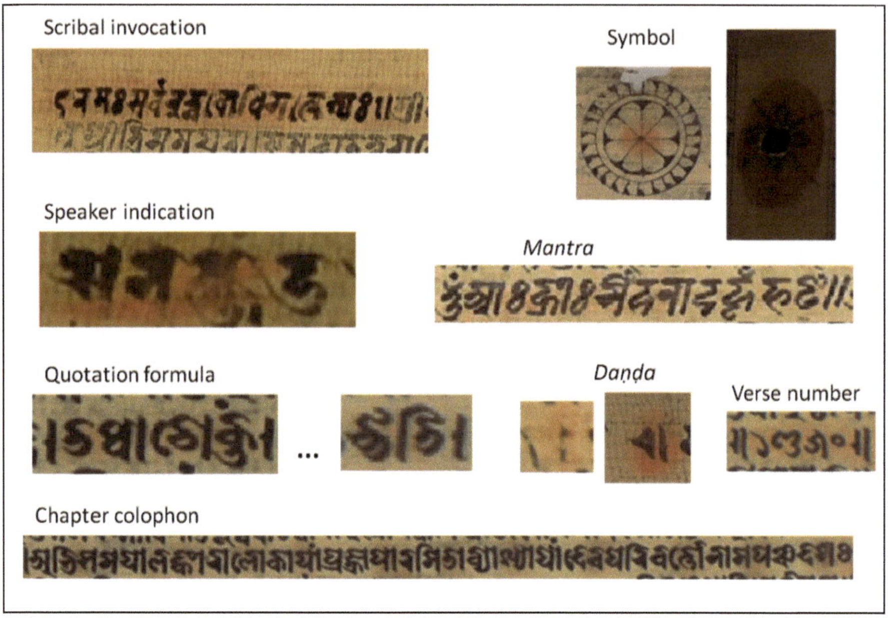

Fig. 5.1.1-I: An overall overview of various highlighted features in manuscripts

Examples of partly or entirely highlighted invocations have been seen (e.g., in SS/N, TS_1, $AṣP_1$, SS). And examples of *daṇḍa*s highlighted after the *pāda*s or the full *śloka*s (e.g., in SS/N), before and after the speaker indication (e.g., in SP_4), or before and after chapter colophons when there is no symbol (e.g., in KT, GV, HTP and CPN). Furthermore, examples of highlighted symbols at the end of chapters (e.g., in SP_1, SP_2, SS/N, KT, SP_4, YYS, AAĀ and HTṬ) and around string-holes (e.g., in HVM, JKS/C, TUS, BCV and TSa) have also featured.

In one of the manuscripts of this corpus we have seen quotation formulas highlighted (e.g., AAĀ) and a few *mantra*s highlighted in another manuscript (e.g., SS). Partly or entirely highlighted chapter colophons in various manuscripts (e.g., in SP_2, SS/N, AAĀ, $AṣP_1$ and TS_1) have also been viewed. Furthermore, highlighted foliations (e.g., in SS, AAĀ, JKS/C, TSa, TUS and BCV) have also been found.

There are other highlighted features I have not included in my discussion above, appearing in the manuscripts of this corpus (see Fig 5.1.1-I). They are, *śloka* numbers (e.g., in AAĀ) and blank spaces at the end of chapters (e.g., in AAĀ).

All these examples clearly show that colour in manuscripts cannot have been used purely for marking corrections or deletions. Some highlighted elements are undoubtedly serving a structuring function too; in other words, the use of colour can be understood as another device for organising texts in manuscripts.

5.2 Scientific examination of manuscripts

This section deals with some preliminary findings of the material analysis carried out in March 2013 on palm-leaf manuscripts kept in the KL and the NAK. As a group of researchers affiliated to the CSMC, we went to Kathmandu in March 2013 to examine the manuscripts scientifically.[542] The assessment took place in cooperation with scientists[543] (Project Area Z) employing mobile and non-destructive equipment to examine the composition of the writing materials in manuscripts.

The scientific examination carried out in Kathmandu, was in conjunction with two Sanskrit-related projects i.e. the sub-project B04 (the results of which are included in this section here), and C01 titled 'A Twelfth-Century East Indian Monastic Library and its Fate'. The results of the scientific examination of the latter sub-project can be seen in Delhey et al. (2015, 119–152). For the study of the latter project, manuscripts were selected mainly from what is purported to be Eastern India, or more specifically, Vikramaśīla one of its famous monasteries. They analysed the composition of ink, substances used in the writing support (i.e. palm-leaf) during the production process or at a later time. I have also used some of the manuscripts the other authors used for the study of the visual organisation of text (e.g. layout, symbols, use of colours and also for palaeographical analysis) during the project period of 2011–2015 e.g., the manuscript of the *Hevajrapañjikā* (HP); the manuscript of the *Abhayapaddhati* (AP); the manuscript of *Catuṣpīṭhanibandha* (CPN); the manuscript of *Laghutantraṭīkā* (LTṬ); the manuscript of the *Hevajratantraṭīkā* (HTṬ). Taking their results into account as well as the outcome of my study on layout, use of symbols, use of colours and palaeographical evidence, we may say that most of these manuscripts build a group pertaining to a similar place of origin (for a detailed examination of the layout of these manuscripts, see chapter 2; for a detailed analysis of symbols, chapter 3; for a detailed study of the use of blank spaces, chapter 4; and a study of use of colours, section 5.1 in this chapter).

As we have seen in previous sections (3 and 5.1 above), symbols and colours are crucial devices for structuring the texts in manuscripts. To this end, the colourants used for highlighting different features and symbols (discussed in the previous section 5.1), were examined for the project during the field research in Nepal.

---

542 The research group comprised of Dr Orna Almogi, Dr Martin Delhey, Prof. Dr Oliver Hahn, Prof. Dr Harunaga Isaacson, Emanuel Kindzorra, Claire McDonald, Boryana Pouvkova and Prof. Dr Ira Rabin.

543 Prof. Dr Oliver Hahn, Emanuel Kindzorra and Prof. Dr Ira Rabin in particular took on the task of scientific examination during the field research for my project and helped me explore possible answers to the research questions. This section is mainly based on their examination.

The key questions on the use of colourants in manuscript, were – whether or not the same colouring agent was used for highlighting in different (selected) manuscripts? And whether the same colouring agent was applied in various parts of a single manuscript (*daṇḍa*s, foliation numbers and symbols, etc.)? These research questions are crucial, for the identification of either the same or different colourants could provide valuable information on the production process of manuscripts about their origin and the number of persons or scriptoriums involved.

What is interesting about the symbols is that they can be drawn in various ways even within the same manuscript (as seen in the above examples in sections of chapter 3). Thus it was crucial to test how they (particularly the symbols featuring a very decorative form with 'accurate' roundish circles) were produced and what items were used to draw them. Thus, one of the typical symbols was analysed.

Selected scholars' remarks on the colouring agents

As already presented in the previous section (see section 5.1 above), many features in the manuscripts appear highlighted. To the best of my knowledge, there are no natural scientific studies on the material composition of colours used in Indic manuscripts (or even in Indic palm-leaf manuscripts) used in features such as symbols, foliations etc.[544] The tests carried out during the Nepal research trip are the first on-site examination attempts of their kind on such documents and materials.[545]

Scholars have expressed a number of opinions on the materials used for highlighting various features in manuscripts, which I have quoted and discussed in previous section (see section 5.1). Bühler (1896, 86) talks of the 'yellow colour' being used for deletion in manuscripts. We do not know about the content of colouring materials. Tripāṭhī (1975, 29) gives concise information on the colouring materials in his catalogue of Jaina manuscripts for corrections of *akṣara*s as 'yellow ("haratāla") or white colours ("saphedo", from saphed = white).' As Tripāṭhī describes only manuscripts from Western India (Jaina paper manuscripts) in his catalogue, it is possible that the colouring substance used for highlighting in that region contains just *haratāla*. The expression he suggests may be a Sanskrit term or a term derived from Sanskrit '*haritāla*' and its

---

544 For the results of the sub-project C01 called 'A Twelfth-Century East Indian Monastic Library and its Fate', see Delhey et al. 2015, 119–152.

545 Trier (1972) is one of the important studies on the material aspects of examination. His study was mostly based on Nepalese paper, but he has also investigated some palm-leaf manuscripts during his examination, however, not the colouring agent and symbol.

use may possibly be found in that region. The Sanskrit word *haritāla* means, among other things, 'yellow orpiment' or 'sulphuret of arsenic'.[546] In AAĀ which is thought to originate from East India, we found traces of orpiment only once on the highlighted foliation (see below). However, in other places no use of orpiment could be found. Another substance mentioned by Tripāṭhī is 'saphedo' (white colour). No 'white colour' was found in the manuscripts examined. It is possible that this colouring material was used in Western Indian manuscripts only. Thaker (2002) should also be mentioned with regard to colours. In his study, he mentions three different colouring agents used for highlighting in three different places.[547] Firstly, he (p. 138) notes that 'ochre' is applied on "important notable words, phrases, sentences etc.", and (p. 143) 'vermilion' for highlighting foliation numbers and symbols around the string-holes. Lastly (p. 146) he talks generally of 'turmeric' or 'a yellow pigment' for the delenda which seems to stem from Bühler's observations. Thaker's study was based on Western Indian manuscripts in particular which were not included for scrutiny in the above Nepal. However, in the course of the material a colouring agent was found in all four Nepalese and East Indian manuscripts (see below) which could well be 'red ochre' (see below for the term). On the other hand, no traces of vermilion or turmeric were found in the examined manuscripts.

Red ochre

The term 'ochre' is derived from Greek *ōkhrós*, meaning 'pale yellow', and 'pale'. Ochre is a natural iron oxide pigment which appears in a number of compositions and structures, and therefore can vary in colour from yellow to brown.[548] Red ochre contains hematite or dehydrated iron oxide. The Sanskrit term '*gairika*' ('red chalk')[549] may be equivalent to 'red ochre'. In modern Indic languages such as Hindi and Nepali, the term '*geru*' (most probably derived from Sanskrit) exists for 'red ochre'.[550] In prehistorical times it was used for cave paintings etc. It is still in use today in paint houses, walls, pots, etc. (in Nepal, certainly).

---

546 See Monier-Williams 1872, 1167 s.v. *haritāla*. See also section 5 above.

547 See chapter 5 above.

548 See Jokobi-Mirwald 2008, 112–113.

549 See Monier-Williams 1872, 296 s.v. *gairika*.

550 See Caturbedi 1970, 182 s.v. *geru*; Paṇḍeya 2000, 391 s.v. *geru*.

The manuscripts selected for scientific examination

Four palm-leaf manuscripts of the 'core' corpus have been selected for scientific examination.[551] According to various palaeographical features and the analysis of layout, symbols and colophonic statements, the manuscripts have been divided into two groups. The first group includes two Nepalese manuscripts, one containing a medical text (SS/N) and another containing a puranic text (SP_4). The second group features two manuscripts, the first containing a commentary text of the Mahāyānic tradition (AAĀ) and the other[552] (HTṬ) one of Vajrayāna Buddhism. One of them (HTṬ), according to its colophon, originated from Vikramaśīla and the other (AAĀ) is thought to come from somewhere in East India. Regarding the period of their production, an approximate production period is from the 9th to the 12th c. (see below). The manuscripts of each group have been presented and analysed in possible chronological order.

SS/N

As mentioned elsewhere, nearly all symbols in this manuscript, and at times *daṇḍa*s and other features appear highlighted (see section 5.1). Aside from a few exceptions, almost all symbols are generally to be found at the end of the chapters or sub-chapters (see also sections 3.6.2.1.1 and 3.6.2.2.1).

SP_4

As stated elsewhere, this manuscript is thought to date from 10th c. and contains an influential puranic text. It is now in poor condition and consists of 22 fragments. Well drawn symbols can be found in the manuscript (see Appendix below). All symbols appear at the end of the chapters. The *daṇḍa*s and symbols are partially or entirely highlighted (see section 5.1 above).

AAĀ

The manuscript is thought to date from ca. 11th c. It consists of 162 folios (for the manuscript description, see section 1.2 above). In this manuscript the use of col-

---

551 The analysis of two of these manuscripts is also briefly mentioned in Delhey et al. 2015, unfortunately, the reasons for the selection of these manuscripts has not been sufficiently described (see p. 146 and footnote 40).

552 This manuscript was analysed for my study and also for the study of the sub-project C01.

our is on many features such as *daṇḍa*s, symbols, quotation formulas, chapter colophons, foliation etc. (see section 5.1).

HTṬ

The manuscript is thought to date from ca. 12th c.[553] There are 33 folios extant (for the manuscript description, see section 1.2 below). From the post-colophon it can be seen that it had been copied by a certain Viśuddhirakṣita in Vikramaśīla an important monastery in East India (see section 3.6.2.1.3 where it has been discussed in detail). Almost all symbols, a few parts of sentences, chapter colophons are partially or entirely highlighted (see section 5.1 for more detail).

Scientific equipment and analysis

Mobile and non-destructive techniques were used for the material analysis. X-ray fluorescence analysis (XRF) was used for elemental analysis, visible spectroscopy (VIS) for the determination of colorants and UV-VIS-NIR-microscopy.[554]

Results of the material examination

To indicate the measuring spot and the method, we used the following notation (see Fig. 5.2-I):

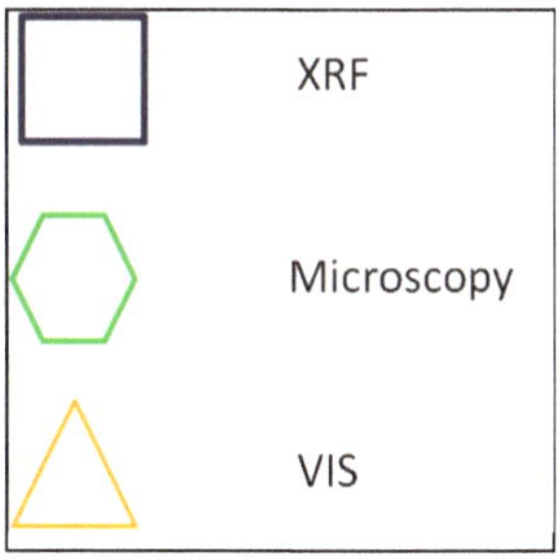

Fig. 5.2-I: Notation used to document the experiments

553 See Sferra 2009, 436.

554 I am grateful to Prof. Dr Oliver Hahn and Prof. Dr Ira Rabin for their suggestions concerning the technical parts and for checking the draft of this chapter. My thanks also go to Dr Sebastian Bosch who checked this chapter at the final stage of this book providing me with many valuable suggestions.

SS/N

The colouring agents analysed on 188v of SS/N are found on the highlighted symbols appearing at the end of the fourth sub-chapter (on 188v1) and at the end of the fifth sub-chapter of the *Kāyacikitsā* ('General medicine')[555] section (on 188v6). The analysis indicated that the colouring agent used for highlighting is most probably red ochre, as the XRF results clearly show a significant increase in the iron (Fe) signal at 6.4 keV compared to the reference measured on pure palm-leaf (see Fig. 5.2-II).

Fig. 5.2-II: Colour examination on fol. 188v © KL

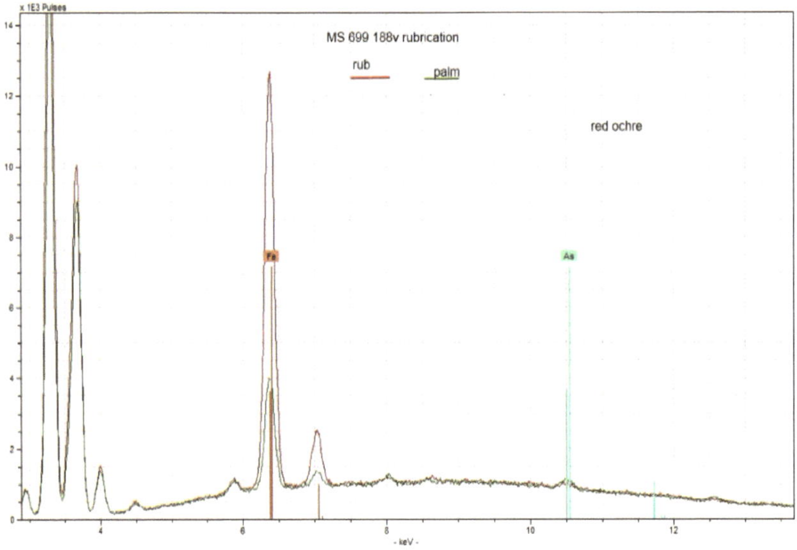

Fig. 5.2-III: XRF-spectra from fol. 188v

555 See Sharma 2001, 313.

The highlighted symbol on 205v2 has been examined using microscopy and visible spectroscopy (see Fig. 5.2-IV below). The symbol appears at the end of the sub-chapter (i.e. 27th sub-chapter) of the *Kāyacikitsā*. Again, the analysis indicated that the colouring agent used for highlighting is most probably red ochre.

Fig. 5.2-IV: Examination on fol. 205v © KL

SP$_4$

Some selected features have been analysed on two folios, namely 65r and 68v, of SP$_4$. The partially highlighted symbol that appears at the end of the chapter on 65r (in line 5 and 6) was examined using microscopy (see upper folio in Fig. 5.2-V).

On 68v (lower folio in Fig. 5.2-V), highlighted *daṇḍa*s and symbol appearing after the chapter colophon were analysed using microscopy and XRF. Furthermore, the spot near the highlighted double *daṇḍa*s (line no. 4) on the lower left side of the first symbol before the chapter colophon was examined with microscopy and XRF. In addition, the highlighted double *daṇḍa*s after the abbreviated speaker indication (i.e. *suśarma u*) in the third line has been analysed by XRF. In all cases, the colourant used for highlighting features seems to be red ochre.

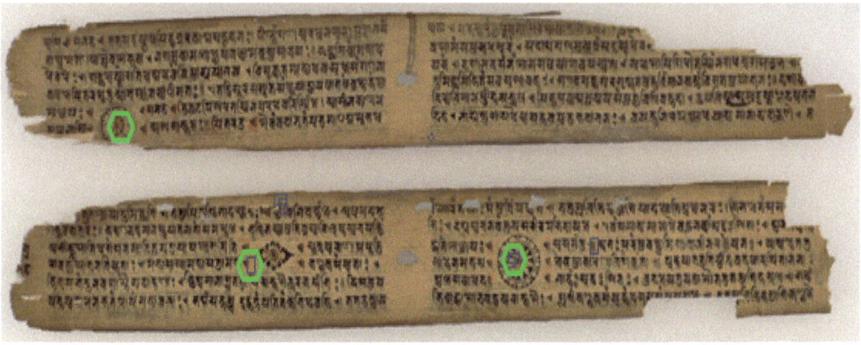

Fig. 5.2-V: Examination on fols. 65r, 68v © NAK

Production of the symbol in SP_4

As evidenced in chapter 3, the symbols are crucial dividing devices and can appear different even within a single manuscript. Some symbols in manuscripts may have been drawn just using a stylus and no other additional tools. In other cases, one may assume the symbols were drawn using extra tools, as the circles in some symbols are almost perfectly round, in stark contrast to symbols thought to be drawn with a stylus or free hand.

Thus far, little is known of the making process or utensils used to draw symbols in manuscripts. It is crucial to learn more about how they are produced and what tools might have been implemented for drawing symbols. Here, one beautifully drawn symbol on 10v (see Fig. 5.2-VI) appearing at the end of the chapter in SP_4 was selected for examination (see arrow pointing the symbol).

The image was produced using a Canon SX200 IS camera, shows there is a hole at the centre of the symbol (see arrow pointing the broken part in Fig. 5.2-VI). This could have been caused by a compass, or a similar instrument when drawing the symbol.

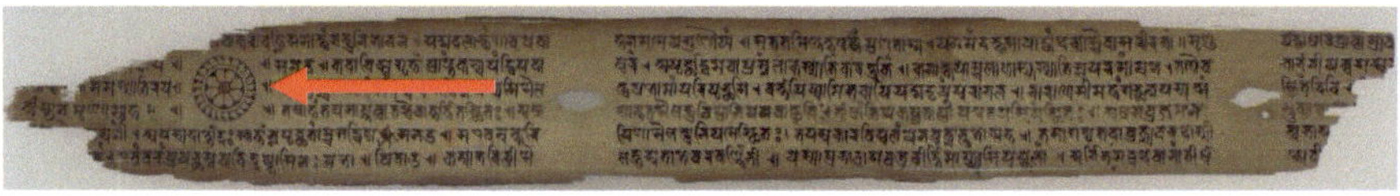

Fig. 5.2-VI: Examination on symbol on the fragment of fol. 10v © NAK

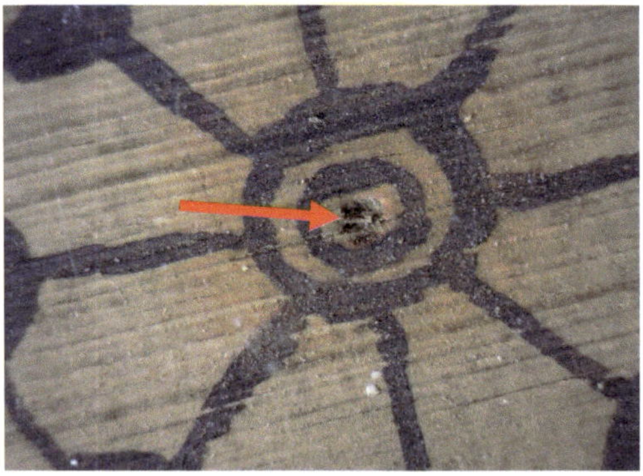

Fig. 5.2-VII: Point where the sharp part of the compass or similar item may have been placed

While checking the Cambridge manuscript collection online, I found a similar type of hole at the centre of one of the symbols (right ones) in Add.866, on 202r (see Fig. 5.2-VIII).[556] The symbol has been drawn beautifully and it is the whole height of the folio (see also chapter 3.6.2.2.3 above). If we look closely at the symbol, it contains many circles.

When we zoom in on the image of the folio, there is a hole exactly at the centre of the symbol (see arrow pointing the hole in left excerpt in Fig. 5.2-IX). This may have been created by a compass, or a similar item, in the process of drawing (like the symbol of SP_4 mentioned above). In addition, on 202v (i.e. the other side of the same folio) one can also see the other side of the hole (see arrow pointing the hole in right excerpt in Fig. 5.2-IX). Furthermore, traces of the coloured ink used to draw the symbol on the recto of the folio are still visible on the verso side, too.

Fig. 5.2-VIII: Extracted and enlarged part from fol. 202r

Fig. 5.2-IX: Extracted and enlarged part of the symbol from fol. 202r and part of the back side of the symbol from fol. 202v

556 See Bendall 1883, plate I, 3.

AAĀ

In AAĀ, various features have been analysed on 22v, 44v and 165r. On 22v the highlighted foliation, the ink of the *akṣara* appearing above the left string-hole space on the first line and a highlighted *akṣara* appearing before the left string-hole space on the fifth line have been examined using XRF (see Fig. 5.2-X). The examination also indicated that the colouring substance used for highlighting the foliation and the *akṣara* on the fifth line could be red ochre (see Fig. 5.2-XI). One many assume that whoever highlighted the foliation may have also highlighted other elements of the text on the same folio.

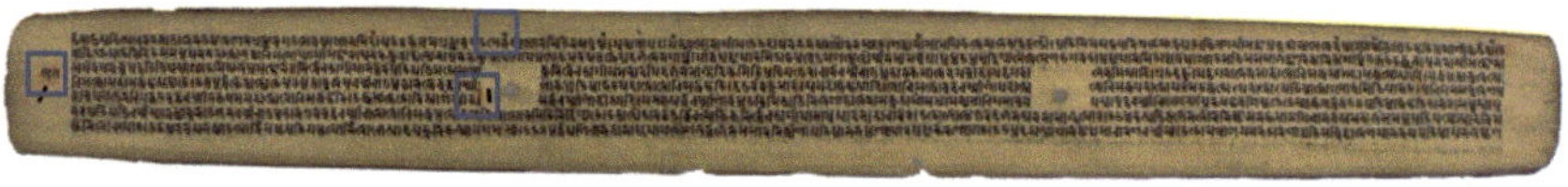

Fig. 5.2-X: Examined features on fol. 22v © NAK

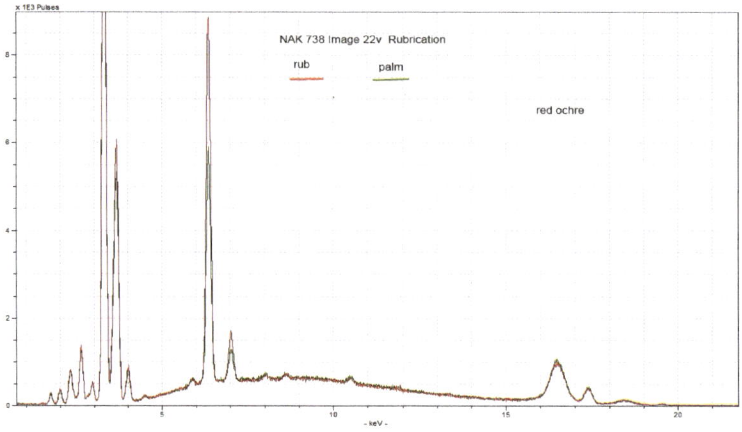

Fig. 5.2-XI: XRF-spectra from fol. 22v

On 44v highlighted foliation was analysed by XRF reveals that the colouring agent used for highlighting could also be red ochre (see Fig. 5.2-XII).

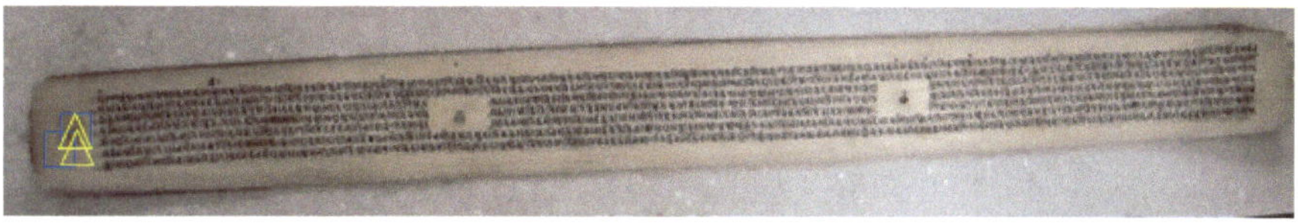

Fig. 5.2-XII: Examined features on fol. 44v © NAK

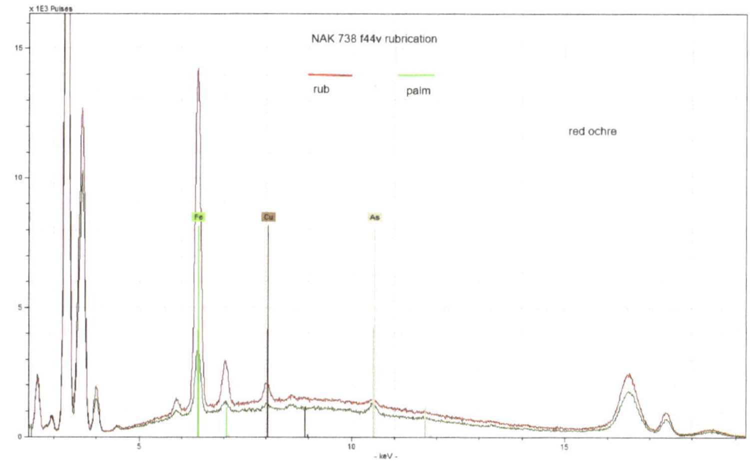

Fig. 5.2-XIII: XRF-spectra from foliation on fol. 44v

The colour used for highlighted symbols (on the third line) and the ink used for the symbols and the text were also examined by microscopy and XRF on 165r (see Fig. 5.2-XIV). Symbols appear at the end of the text and demarcate the colophon, partially written by a second hand. The second symbol is followed by the popular Buddhist verse '*ye dharmā* ...'.

As the colour used for highlighting symbols is extremely weak, it was difficult to ascertain the composition of the colouring substance used. However, analysis shows that the ink of the text and that used for drawing the symbols is the same.

Fig. 5.2-XIV: Examined features on fol. 165r © NAK

HTṬ

The highlighted symbol (line no. 3) on 51v in HTṬ has been examined by XRF (see Fig. 5.2-XV). The highlighting colorant seems to be red ochre.

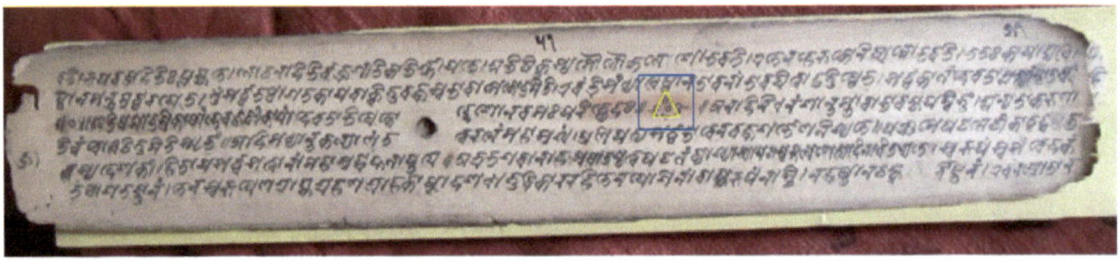

Fig. 5.2-XV: Examined feature on fol. 51v © KL

5.2.1 Preliminary conclusions on scientific examination of manuscripts

The examination confirmed that the main substance used to highlight various elements such as foliation numbers, *daṇḍa*s and symbols, on all four manuscripts (SS/N, SP$_4$, AAĀ and HTṬ) was red ochre. These results are a humble first attempt at categorising colouring substances used in manuscripts from Nepal and East India. Further data certainly needs to be checked against these preliminary results before any generalisation can be drawn.

Concerning the ink; analysis confirmed the substance used to draw symbols and that used to write the text in AAĀ are identical (ink of symbol on 165r and text on the same folio). This indicates that it is possible whoever copied the text may have also drawn the symbols using the same ink.

Compared with the vast number of Indic manuscripts, the number of manuscripts from the areas analysed during our study is quite limited. However, it is hoped this is a useful first step towards a better understanding of the materials used for the production of Indic manuscripts and it will trigger further investigations on the topic. Collaborative studies (like this section) comprising researchers from the fields of the natural sciences and indological studies will certainly help in the future to gain more insights into the production process of manuscripts, scribal practices and their use.

6 Conclusions

Due to the project's limitations of time, resources, framework and so forth, only selected corpora of the manuscripts from the East and West India, and Nepal have been dealt with in the present study. Therefore, the conclusion drawn here on the basis of the analysis of the selected manuscripts may not be universally applicable for the rest of the corpora of the respective regions. Nonetheless, the present study can argue with a degree of confidence that the analysis made here is certainly applicable, to a great extent, to manuscripts contemporaneous to the period of the present study. As mentioned elsewhere in chapter 1, the present study, with a few exceptions,[557] is an initial scientific step towards the study of the largely unexplored manuscript-culture of the regions. It is hoped that this will foster further scientific research on the topic.

As far as Nepalese manuscripts are concerned, (although exceptions also exist here) the manuscripts produced between the 9th c. and 13th c. show that in the course of time, to some extent, a more and more standardised layout was used (see section 2.4.1, Figs. 2.4.1-I–2.4.1-XXII). These manuscripts exhibit overall layouts for arranging the text on a folio, including, at times, the use of two or three text-sections. Gaps can be found between parts of verses (see sections 4.2.1 and 4.2.2). Ruling-lines can be also found occasionally. Of the manuscripts originating from East India or, more precisely, from Vikramaśīla, the text seems to have been organised with 'delicate care'. Most of the manuscripts produced there contain seven lines per folio (see section 2.4.2, Figs. 2.4.2-III–2.4.2-X). The lines are written rather more consistently than those of the Nepalese and West Indian manuscripts. The number of letters (*akṣaras*) per line does not differ as much from one manuscript to the other. Space-fillers are not used in the manuscripts. No text-sections are found. In most of the manuscripts square-shaped free spaces appear around both string-holes on the folio. Three lines have been left clear to create a free space around the string-holes in height on the folios. Furthermore, ample free space appears on the margins of the folio in the majority of the manuscripts. Clear visible gaps—like those that between parts of the *śloka*s in some Nepalese manuscripts—are not to be found in the manuscripts from this area. Furthermore, with regard to text genres, all manuscripts contain Buddhist texts. In the West Indian manuscripts, texts are generally organised in two to three text-sections. Although ruling-lines are only occasionally found in

557 Such as Śākya 1973; Roth 1986; Sander 1986; Bhattacharya 1995; Sarkar/Pande 1995; Einicke 2009; IndroSkript etc.

https://doi.org/10.1515/9783110543087-006

some of the Nepalese and East Indian manuscripts, they are present in all of the West Indian manuscripts of my corpus (see section 2.4.3, Figs. 2.4.3-I–2.4.3-VII). Each text-section appears demarcated by vertical ruling-lines. Ample free space on the left and right-hand margins can also be found in the West Indian manuscripts. Hardly any gaps can be observed between smaller text units.

Symbols, appear in manuscripts of this corpus from all areas (see sections 3.4, 3.5.1, 3.5.2, 3.5.3). They appear predominantly at the end of the subchapters, chapters or text in the manuscript. However, in the manuscripts from the Western India, stylised *puṣpikā*s frequently appear around the string-hole or together with the foliation numbers on the left-hand margin of the verso (see sections 3.6.1, 3.7). A large variety of symbols can be found in the Nepalese manuscripts. In terms of their aesthetic value, some of the symbols exhibit the highest level of sophistication of all the symbols in the corpus (e.g. see section 3.4). Furthermore, even realistic types of representation of *puṣpikā*s with stalks, leaves and sepals ('realistic *puṣpikā*s') have been found in a few Nepalese manuscripts (see section 3.5.1, Figs. 3.5.1-I–3.5.1-XII). Varieties of the use of symbols are also found in the East Indian manuscripts of the corpus. Symbols in the East Indian manuscripts appear in different shapes and sizes. A smaller variety of symbols can be traced in the West Indian manuscripts (the occurrence of beautifully drawn colourful symbols and other elements in later paper manuscripts from the area is well known to this researcher). They are drawn in a small size and form and are a height of one text line on the folio (see section 3.4, Fig. 3.4-XLVII and section 3.5.3, Figs. 3.5.3-I–3.5.3-III). In this region an important custom is for all manuscripts (with only few exceptions) to contain symbols around the string-holes (see section 3.6.1, Figs. 3.6.1-I–3.6.1-VII). Manuscripts from this region also frequently feature small, stylised *puṣpikā*s together with every tenth foliation number on the left-hand margin verso (see section 3.7, Figs. 3.7-I–3.7-IV).

In terms of the appearance of symbols, some precisely drawn, representing elements clearly related to the specific religious affiliation to which the manuscript belongs or the text the manuscript contains. But some symbols appear in simple sketch-like forms or even in more abstract forms. Here the idea of the drawing can only be pieced together in connection with the content of the text or only with prior knowledge of its relation to a particular school of thought to which it is obviously referring. In some cases, a few symbols can clearly be linked to the performative aspects of knowledge, i.e. to the rites in which the manuscripts can be employed.

Furthermore, a particular type of use of symbols and their way of distribution on the folios may also point out a specific tradition or be closely related to manuscripts containing a text of a specific religious affiliation (see section

3.6.2.4.2). Moreover, among other features (such as palaeography, layout etc.), they may also help to identify various scribal hands in a manuscript (see sections 3.9.1–3.9.5). Symbols may be interpreted as means to help approximate the date of production of a manuscript and also be used to reconstruct the dismembered parts of a single manuscript (see sections 3.8.1–3.8.2). According to their appearance and possible functions, they should be understood as decorative or structuring devices.

Blank spaces can be found in manuscripts from both the Nepalese and East India regions of my corpus, but not in the corpus of manuscripts from the West India. For whatever reason, blank spaces have been left in the manuscripts, it appears that during the course of time, leaving a free space at the end of a subchapter, chapter or text may have developed into a kind of convention and used as a dividing device (see section 4.1). Use of such blank spaces in a manuscript can be understood as one of the main devices to visually indicate the end of a chapter, sub-chapter or text. At times changes in the size of blank spaces in the manuscript may also be taken as hints regarding the endings at different levels of the text.

Gaps have been left in some of the Nepalese manuscripts within this corpus. They can be found between sentences or parts of a verse either within the text line or integrated into the text-section layout of the page in manuscripts (see sections 4.2.1, 4.2.2). Gaps can be understood as a crucial dividing device in terms of visual demarcation for smaller text units. A careful effort, a planned strategy and also a detailed knowledge of the structure of the text may be all the necessary requirements for a scribe who intended to insert gaps while working in a particular manuscript.

Colours are used in the manuscripts from all the regions in this corpus (see section 5.1). As for the style of colour application, a close similarity can be observed between the Nepalese and East Indian manuscripts. The method of colour application in the West Indian manuscripts has similarities with the Nepalese and East Indian manuscripts. However, the use of colour in the West Indian manuscript is generally intense (see the highlighted foliations and symbols around string-holes in section 5.1). It is not only used to indicate text deletions and corrections, but also as an important visual text dividing device. Colours applied over specific elements on the folio offer some sort of structural function for the text. In some cases, colour application on manuscript covers can show a close connection to the ritual performances for which the manuscripts were quite probably employed.

Regarding the materials used for highlighting foliation numbers, *daṇḍa*s, symbols, etc., the examination confirmed that the colouring agent was probably the red ochre in some of the manuscripts from Nepal and East India (see section 5.2). Additionally, the analysis confirmed that the ink used for writing the text and drawing symbols could be similar in one manuscript. This may indicate that the person who wrote down the text may have also drawn the symbols using the same ink. Furthermore, symbols made of precise circles were most probably drawn with compasses or a similar instrument (see Figs. 5.2-VII, 5.2-IX).

As we have seen, the topic of visual text-organisation is vast in terms of the variety of elements used in the manuscripts. However, it is hoped that these results will contribute to the studies and towards a better understanding of the visual organisation of texts in Indic manuscripts. Many topics and questions have yet to be addressed and many subjects require further study. Therefore, this book draws to a close in the hope that its outcome will foster further research in the field, to answer those questions remaining unanswered while simultaneously raising new ones.

Appendices

I. List of selected symbols and blank spaces in Nepalese manuscripts

Manuscript SP_1 (811 CE)

Symbols and blank spaces

[38a5_ACC][558]

[42b4_BCC]

[64a3_BCC]

[73a4_BCC]

[73a5_ACC]

[75a6_BCC]

[75b1_ACC]

[75b6_BCC]

[75b6_ACC]

[76b1_BCC]

[76b1_ACC]

[77a4_BCC]

[77a4_ACC]

[79a2_BCC][559]

[79a2_ACC]

558 Further double circles can be found on 41a3_BCC, 41a4_ACC, 41b3_BCC, 42a7_BCC, 42a7_ACC, 42b4_BCC, 43b4_BCC, 43b4_ACC, 48a2_BCC, 48a2_ACC, 48b4_BCC, 48b4_ACC, 49b2_BCC, 49b2_ACC, 52a4_BCC, 52b5_BCC, 52b5_ACC, 54a5_BCC, 54a5_ACC, 57a4_BCC, 58b7_BCC, 63a1_BCC, 63a1_ACC, 64b1_ACC, 64a3_ACC, 66a1_BCC, 66a1_ACC, 67b7_BCC, 68a1_ACC, 69b2_ACC, 88b1_BCC, 93b2_BCC, 99a2_ACC, 102a4_BCC, 104a166v3?_BCC, 106a7_BCC (168v?), 105b3_BCC, 110b4_BCC, 157b5_BCC, 157b5_ACC, 158b6_BCC, 158b6_BCC, 58b6_ACC, 160b6_ACC, 161b6_ACC, 163b3_ACC, 164b7_ACC, 165b1_ACC, 165b5_ACC, 166b2_ACC, 166b6_ACC, 167a2_ACC, 167b4_ACC, 168a7_ACC, 168b7_ACC, 167b5_ACC, 169a7_ACC, 169b5_ACC, 170a3_ACC, 173b3_BCC, 173b3_ACC, 173b3_ACC, 176a1_BCC, 176a1_ACC, 176b4_ACC, 179b1_BCC, 179b1_ACC, 208a6_BCC, 208a6_ACC, 209a6_BCC, 209a6_ACC, 210a3_BCC, 210a4_ACC, 210b6_BCC, 210b6_ACC, 211b1_ACC, 224b3_BCC, 226b6_ACC, 241b3_ACC, 259a2_BCC, 259a3_ACC, 260a1_ACC, 260b5_ACC, 261b2_BCC, 260b5_ACC, 264b1_ACC, 266a7_ACC, 267a5_BCC, 267a6_ACC, 268a4_ACC, 270b4_ACC, 271b4_BCC, 271b4_ACC, 288b1_BCC, 288b1_ACC, 289b5_ACC, 292a5_ACC.

559 Possibly folio 114v.

https://doi.org/10.1515/9783110543087-007

 [79b3_BCC]  [79b3_ACC]  [81a3 _ACC][560]

 [81b3_BCC]  [82a6_BCC]  [82a7_ACC]

 [83b3_BCC][561] 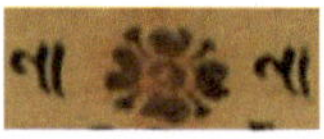 [83b_ACC]  [84a4_BCC]

 [84a4_ACC]  [85a2_BCC]  [85a3_ACC]

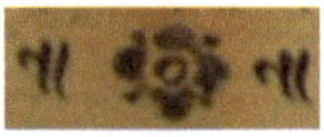 [85b5_BCC]  [85b5_ACC]  [85a3_BCC]

 [85a3_ACC]  [88a1_BCC]  [88a1_ACC]

 [88b1_ACC]  [89b3_BCC]  [89b3_ACC]

 [92b4_BCC]  [92b4_ACC][562]  [93b2_ACC]

 [95b3_BCC][563]  [96b1_BCC][564]  [96b_ACC]

 [97b3_BCC][565]  [97b_ACC]  [99b4_BCC]

 [99b4_ACC]  [100b5_BCC]  [100b5_ACC]

 [102a4_ACC]  [103a1_BCC]  [103a1_ACC]

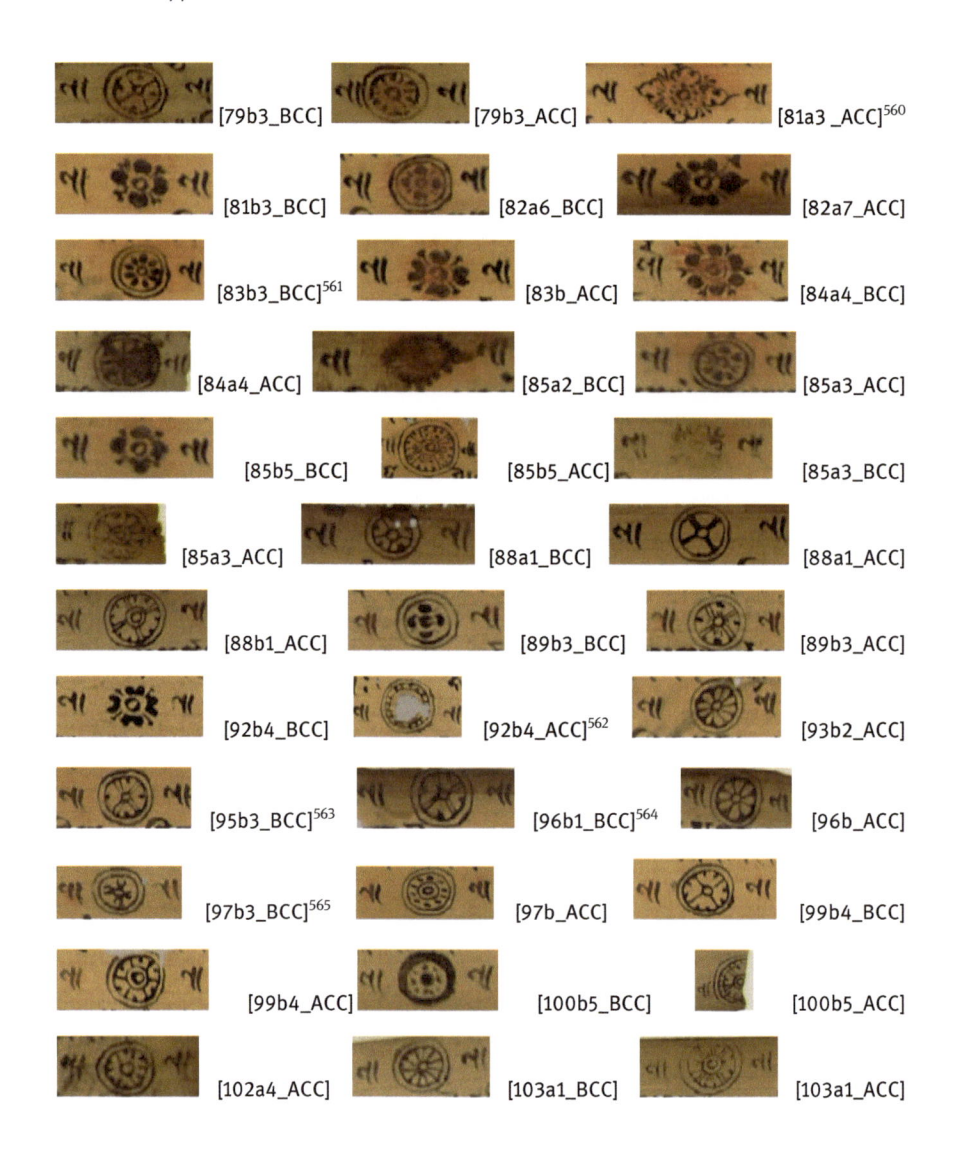

560 Possibly folio 116v.
561 Possibly folio 118v.
562 This symbol has been placed exactly around the right string-hole on the folio.
563 Possibly folio 157r.
564 Possibly folio 158r.
565 Possibly folio 159r.

[105b3_ACC] [106a7_ACC][566] [106b4_BCC]

[106b4_ACC] [108a4_BCC] [108a4_ACC]

[108b4_BCC] [108b4_ACC] [110a1_BCC]

[110a1_ACC] [110b4_BCC] [111a1_BCC]

[111a1_ACC] [114a3_BCC] [114a3_ACC]

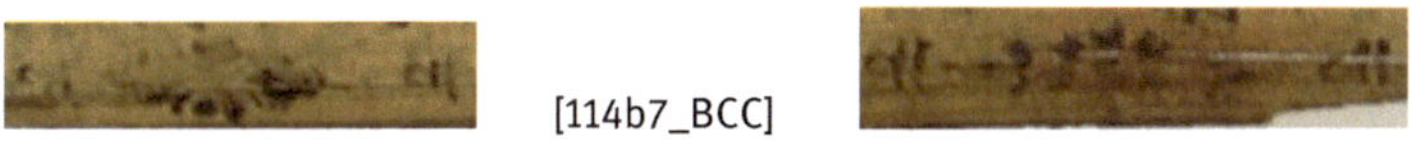
[114b7_BCC] [114b7_ACC]

[117a4_BCC] [117a4_ACC] [117b6_BCC]

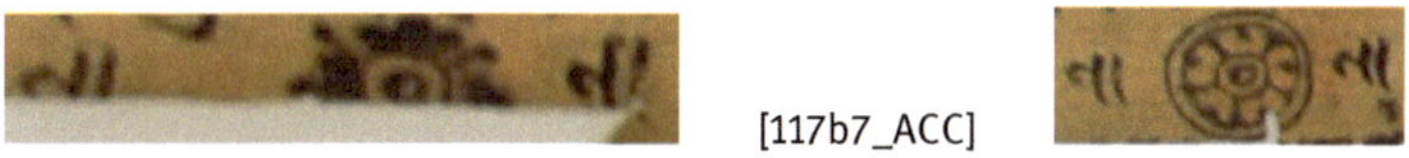
[117b7_ACC] [118b5_BCC]

[118b5_ACC] [146a3_BCC] [146a4_ACC]

[149a1_BCC] [149a1_ACC] [150a2_BCC]

[150a2_ACC] [153a7_BCC] [154a3_BCC]

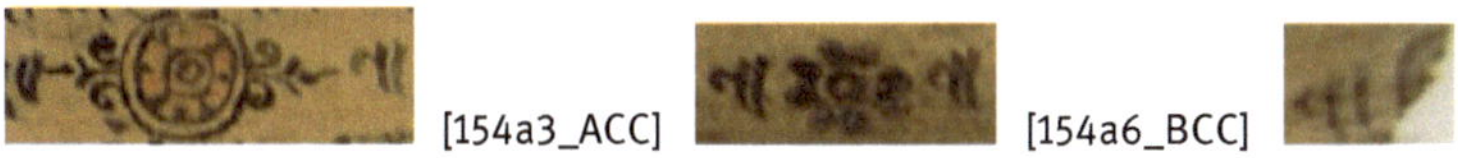
[154a3_ACC] [154a6_BCC] [154a6_ACC]

[170b6_ACC] [181b3_BCC] [181b3_ACC]

[183a3_BCC] [183a3_ACC] [183b3_BCC]

566 Possibly folio 168v.

[183b3_ACC] [189b3_BC][567] [192a3_BCC]
[192a3_ACC] [193a1_BCC] [193a1_ACC][568]
[193b6_BCC] [193b6_ACC] [197a7_BCC]
[197a7_ACC] [198b7_BCC] [198b7_ACC]
[200a6_BCC] [200a6_ACC] [202a2_BCC]
[203a1_BCC] [203a1_ACC] [205a3_BCC]
[214a2_BCC] [214a2_ACC] [215a1_BCC]
[215a1_ACC] [216b5_BCC] [216b5_ACC]
[218a3_ACC] [219a6_ACC] [220a5_BCC]
[220a5_ACC] [221a4_BCC] [221a4_ACC]
[221b3_BCC] [221b4_ACC] [224a5_BCC]
[224a5_ACC] [232b5_BCC] [232b5_ACC]
[233a5_BCC] [233a5_ACC] [234b5_BCC]
[234b6_ACC] [237b5_BCC] [237b5_ACC]

567 Further circles can be found on 189b4_AC, 224a5_ACC.
568 A nearly similar style of symbol appears in KT on 99v3.

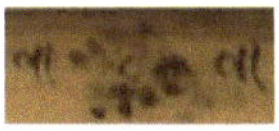 [239b1_BCC]  [239b1_ACC] 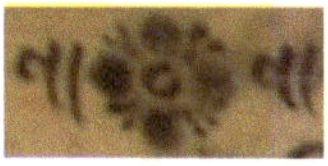 [240a2_ACC]

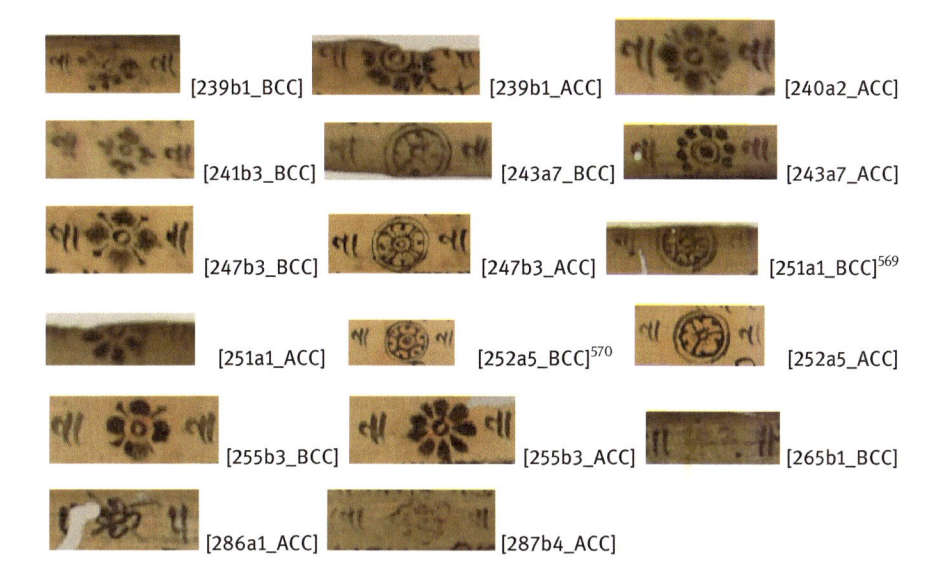

 [241b3_BCC]  [243a7_BCC]  [243a7_ACC]

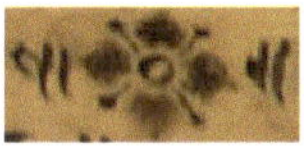 [247b3_BCC]  [247b3_ACC]  [251a1_BCC][569]

 [251a1_ACC]  [252a5_BCC][570]  [252a5_ACC]

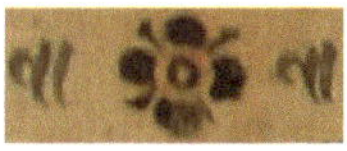 [255b3_BCC] 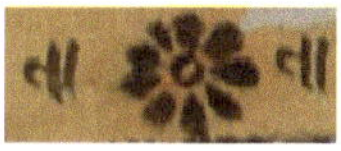 [255b3_ACC]  [265b1_BCC]

 [286a1_ACC]  [287b4_ACC]

Manuscript PT (829 CE)

Symbols

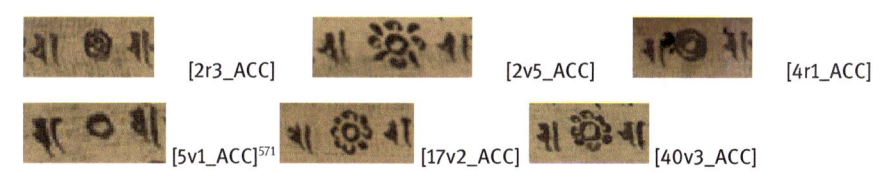

 [2r3_ACC]  [2v5_ACC]  [4r1_ACC]

 [5v1_ACC][571]  [17v2_ACC]  [40v3_ACC]

569 Possibly folio 181v.

570 Possibly folio 182v.

571 Further circles can be found on 2r2 (before invocation), 6v3_ACC, 20r1_ACC, 22r1_ACC, 23v1_ACC, 24r3_ACC, 35v5_ACC, 36r2_ACC, 37r2_ACC, 38v1_ACC, 42v1_ACC.

Manuscript SS/N (878 CE)

Symbols

Suśrutasaṃhitā

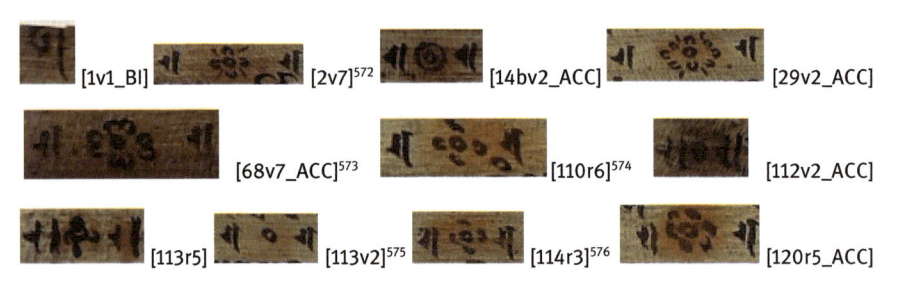

 [1v1_BI]  [2v7][572]  [14bv2_ACC]  [29v2_ACC]

 [68v7_ACC][573]  [110r6][574]  [112v2_ACC]

 [113r5]  [113v2][575]  [114r3][576]  [120r5_ACC]

---

572 This symbol appears after the first sub-chapter and there is no number for the sub-chapter. Normally we find numbers at the end of most of the sub-chapters in the *Nidāna* section. Further identical symbols appear on 3r7_ACC, 5r2_BCC, 6r1_BCC, 7r3_BCC, 7v7_BCC, 8v2_BCC, 8v5_BCC, 9r3_BCC, 9r3 (after the versified lines with the list of names of the first tenth chapters (1–10) in the *Nidāna* section), 11r3_BCC, 13r_BCC, 14r6_ACC, 15v5_ACC, 17v_ACC, 21r6_ACC, 21v8_ACC, 23v1_ACC, 24v3_ACC, 26r4_ACC, 26v3_ACC, 28r7_ACC, 28v6–7 (before and after the versified lines with the list of names of the third tenth sub-chapters (21–30) in the *Nidāna* section), 90r2 (at the end of the chapter), 90r5 (at the end of the chapter).

573 There is a similar symbol after the ending line for the *Nidāna* section on 68v7.

574 Similar symbols appear, for instance, on 116v3_ACC, 121r7_ACC, 125v2_ACC, 128r7_ACC, 129r5_ACC, 130v5_ACC, 137v_ACC, 139v1_ACC, 144v6_ACC, 147v6_ACC, 153v5_ACC, 158v1_BCC, 165r4_ACC, 171r2_ACC, 173r1_ACC, 174v1_ACC, 175v3_ACC, 175v7_ACC, 185r6_ACC, 193r4_ACC, 199r3_ACC, 198r3_ACC, 203v3_ACC, 205v2_ACC.

575 Further circles can be found, for instance, on 114r3_BCC, 114r3_ACC, 117r7_ACC, 142v7_ACC, 153r1_ACC, 158v5_BCC, 159v1_BCC, 159v5_BCC, 159v7_BCC, 160v2_BCC, 162r3_ACC, 162v3_ACC, 163v2_ACC, 164v4_ACC, 166r3_ACC, 173v4_ACC, 175v1_ACC, 175r2_ACC, 175v5_ACC, 176r2_ACC, 176r4_ACC, 176r6_ACC, 176v6_ACC, 188v1_ACC, 188v6_ACC, 189v4_ACC, 190v2_ACC, 191r2_ACC, 193r4_BCC, 195r2_ACC, 195v5_ACC, 197v1_ACC, 199v4_ACC, 201v6_ACC, 200r3_ACC, 204r3_ACC, 208r3_ACC, 209r6_ACC.

576 This symbol appears after the versified lines with the list of the names of the second tenth sub-chapters (11–20) in the *Cikitsā* section.

 [126v6][577]  [132v7_ACC][578]  [133v6_ACC

 [143r1][579]  [143r1][580]  [150r1_ACC]

 [151v3_ACC]  [157r4][581]  [157r5][582]  [161v4_BCC]

 [163r2_ACC]  [165v7_ACC]  [168r6_ACC]

 [170r2_ACC]  [171v1_ACC]  [172r7][583]

 [173r5_ACC]  [174v2][584]  [175r6_ACC]

 [176v1_ACC]  [176v7][585]

 [176v7][586]  [177v3_ACC]

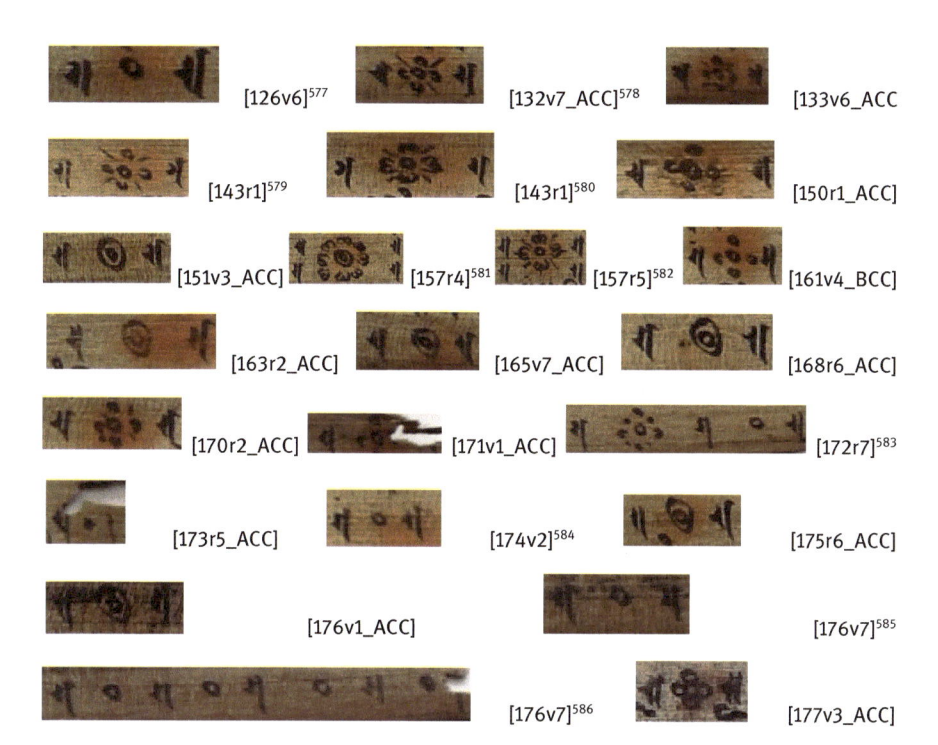

577 This symbol can be found after the versified lines for the third tenth sub-chapters (21–30) in the *Cikitsā* section.
578 Similar symbol appears on 135r7_ACC, 146r7_ACC, 196v4_ACC, 197r1_ACC, 201r1_ACC, 202v1_ACC, 208r3_BCC.
579 This symbol appears after the versified lines with the list of the names of the fourth tenth sub-chapters (31–40) in the *Cikitsā* section.
580 This symbol can be found after the ending line for the *Cikitsā* section.
581 This symbol appears before the versified lines with the list of the names of eight sub-chapters (1–8) in the *Kalpa* section.
582 This symbol can be found after the ending line for the *Kalpa* section.
583 This symbol appears after the versified lines with the list of the names of the second tenth sub-chapters (11–20) in the *Śālakya* section.
584 This symbol can be found after the ending line for the *Śālakya* section.
585 This symbol appears after the versified lines with the list of the names of the first tenth sub-chapters (1–10) in the *Kumārabhṛtya* section.
586 These circles can be found after the ending line for the *Kumārabhṛtya* section. A similar style of distribution of a series of four circles placed between double *daṇḍa*s can also be found in SSS at the very end after the verse of asking for the book protection '*udakānala* ...' on 54v6.

[177v4_ACC][587]

[177v5][588]

[192r2_ACC]

[192v4_ACC]

[193v6][589]

[193v6][590]

[199r3_BCC]

[200r4][591]

[200v1_BI]

[209v4][592]

[209v5][593]

[209v5][594]

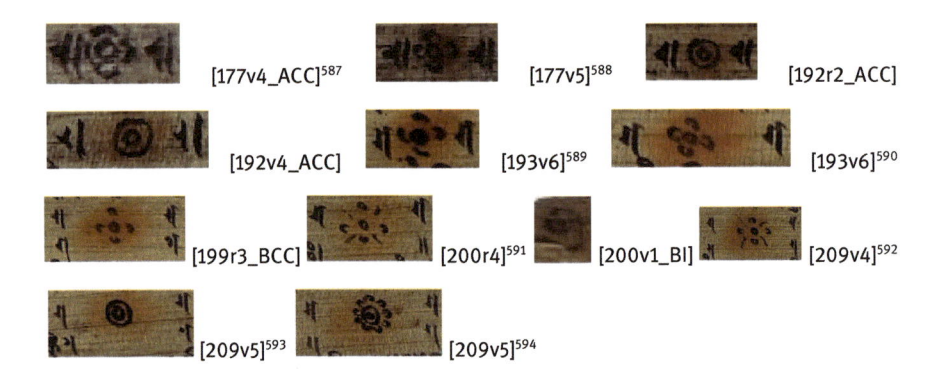

587 This symbol appears after the versified lines with the list of the names for the first tenth sub-chapters (1–10) in the *Kumārabhṛtya* section. This is a later added folio, therefore, this contains the same as on 176v.
588 This symbol appears after the ending line for the *Śālakya* section.
589 This symbol appears before the versified lines with the list of the names of the first tenth sub-chapters (1–10) in the *Kāyacikitsā* section.
590 This symbol can be found after the versified lines with the list of the names of the first tenth sub-chapters (1–10) in the *Kāyacikitsā* section.
591 This symbol appears after the versified lines with the list of the names for the second tenth sub-chapters (11–20) in the *Kāyacikitsā* section.
592 This symbol appears before the versified lines with the list of the names of the chapters sub-chapters (21–30) in the *Kāyacikitsā* section.
593 This symbol is before the ending line for the *Suśrutasaṃhitā*.
594 This symbol can be found after the ending line for the *Suśrutasaṃhitā*.

Suśrutanighaṇṭu

[210r5][595]

[210v5][596]

[213r6][597]

[213v6][598]

[217r2][599]

[219v6][600]

[219v6][601]

Manuscript SP₂ (ca. 9th c.)

Symbols and blank spaces

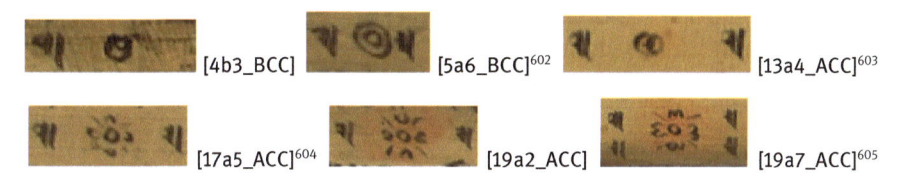

[4b3_BCC]

[5a6_BCC][602]

[13a4_ACC][603]

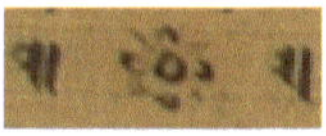
[17a5_ACC][604]

[19a2_ACC]

[19a7_ACC][605]

595 Similar circles can be found for other sections on 211r5, 212r5, 213r3, 215r4, 215r5, 215v5, 215v6, 216r6, 217r4, 217r6. All these circles appear before particular sections.
596 This symbol can be found before a particular section.
597 Further double circles appear on 214v2, 214v3, 215r3, 215v3, 216r4, 216v2, 217r1, 217r6, 217v2, 217v3.
598 This symbol can be found before a particular section.
599 On the significant of this symbol, see section 3.6.2.1.1 above.
600 This symbol can be found before the ending line for the *Nighaṇṭu*.
601 These circles can be found after the ending line for the *Nighaṇṭu*.
602 Further double circles can be found on 5a6_ACC, 7a4_ACC, 185a2_BCC, 185a3_ACC, 186a7_BCC, 183b5_BCC, 183b6_ACC, 187a2_BCC, 187a2_ACC, 187b3_BCC, 187b3_ACC, 198a3_BCC, 198a3_ACC, 190a4_BCC, 198a3_ACC, 191a1_BCC, 191a2_ACC, 192a3_BCC, 192a3_ACC, 193a2_BCC, 194a5_ACC, 195a5_ACC, 196a3_ACC, 199b1_BCC, 215a5_ACC, 220a2_ACC, 199b1_ACC.
603 Nearly identical symbols are on 10a3_ACC, 18a2_ACC, 141b5_ACC, 178a4_ACC.
604 Similar symbols appear on 6a3_BCC, 172a5_ACC.
605 Similar symbols are on 6a3_ACC, 64r7_ACC, 66r2_ACC.

 [19b2_ACC]  [20b2_ACC][606]  [23b7_BCC][607]

 [52r6_ACC]  [55v4_ACC]  [59r1_ACC][608]

 [60r2_ACC]  [63v5_ACC]  [64r3_ACC]

 [64v7_ACC]  [64v7_ACC]  [65v5_ACC]

 [66v2_ACC][609] 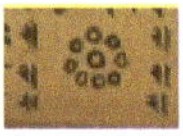 [66v6_ACC]  [67v3_ACC]  [68r6_ACC]

 [69v3_ACC]  [70v6_ACC][610]  [74v1_ACC]

 [75v4_ACC]  [78r1_ACC] 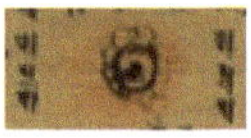 [83v3_ACC]

 [84v1_ACC]  [88r4_ACC]  [89v4_BCC]

 [89v5_ACC]  [94v2_ACC]  [95v6_ACC]

 [98v1_ACC] 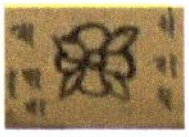 [99v5_ACC] 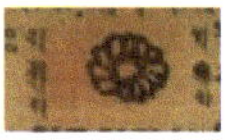 [100v2_ACC]  [104r6_ACC]

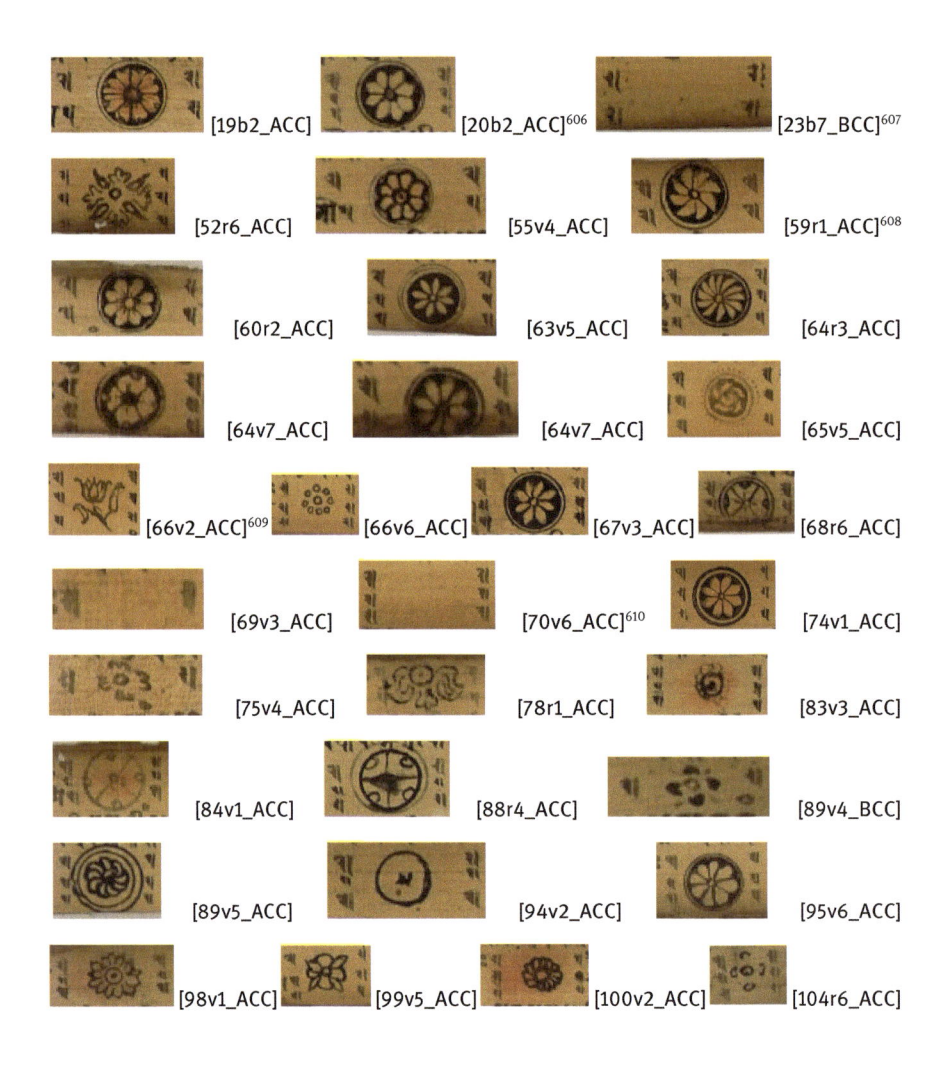

606 Almost all symbols and blank spaces occupy only two lines in height on the folio, although they are surrounded by three sets of double *daṇḍa*s.
607 Further blank spaces occupying an area of two lines in height appear on 25b1_ACC, 27a4_ACC, 28a6_ACC, 30a3_ACC, 109b5_ACC, 150r5_ACC, 171b2_ACC.
608 Three identical symbols can be found on 22a6_ACC, 63r4_ACC, 84v6_ACC.
609 See section 3.5.1 above.
610 Further blank spaces can be found on 92v7_ACC, 117v6_ACC, 111b3_ACC, 152r5_ACC, 153r4_ACC, 116a3_ACC, 160v4_ACC, 167v3_ACC, 177v5_ACC, 139b1_ACC, 134b1_ACC, 159a3_ACC, 164a3_ACC, 164b4_ACC, 166a4_ACC, 167a200v4_ACC, 168a3_ACC, 202r4_ACC, 202v3_ACC, 169b6_ACC, 171a4_ACC, 173a5_ACC, 174a3_ACC, 175b2_ACC, 176a2_ACC, 177a1_ACC, 179b2_ACC, 181a3_ACC, 183a3_ACC, 216b2?_ACC.

 [105v7_ACC]  [107v4_ACC]  [111v3_ACC]

 [114v1_ACC] 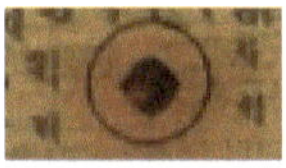 [115r4_ACC]  [116v1_ACC]

 [163v6_ACC]  [165r2_ACC]  [129a2_ACC]

 [130b2_ACC]  [133a5_ACC]  [134a5_ACC]

 [135b1_ACC]  [136b6_ACC]  [138b1_ACC]

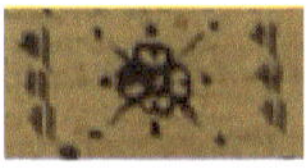 [138a5_ACC]  [142a5_ACC]  [140b5_ACC]

 [160a2_ACC]  [161a2_ACC]  [161b4_ACC]

 [163a5_ACC]  [186a7_ACC]

Manuscript NTS (ca. 9th c.)

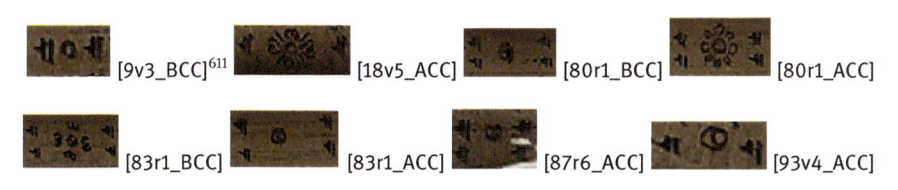

Symbols

 [9v3_BCC][611]  [18v5_ACC]  [80r1_BCC]  [80r1_ACC]

 [83r1_BCC]  [83r1_ACC]  [87r6_ACC]  [93v4_ACC]

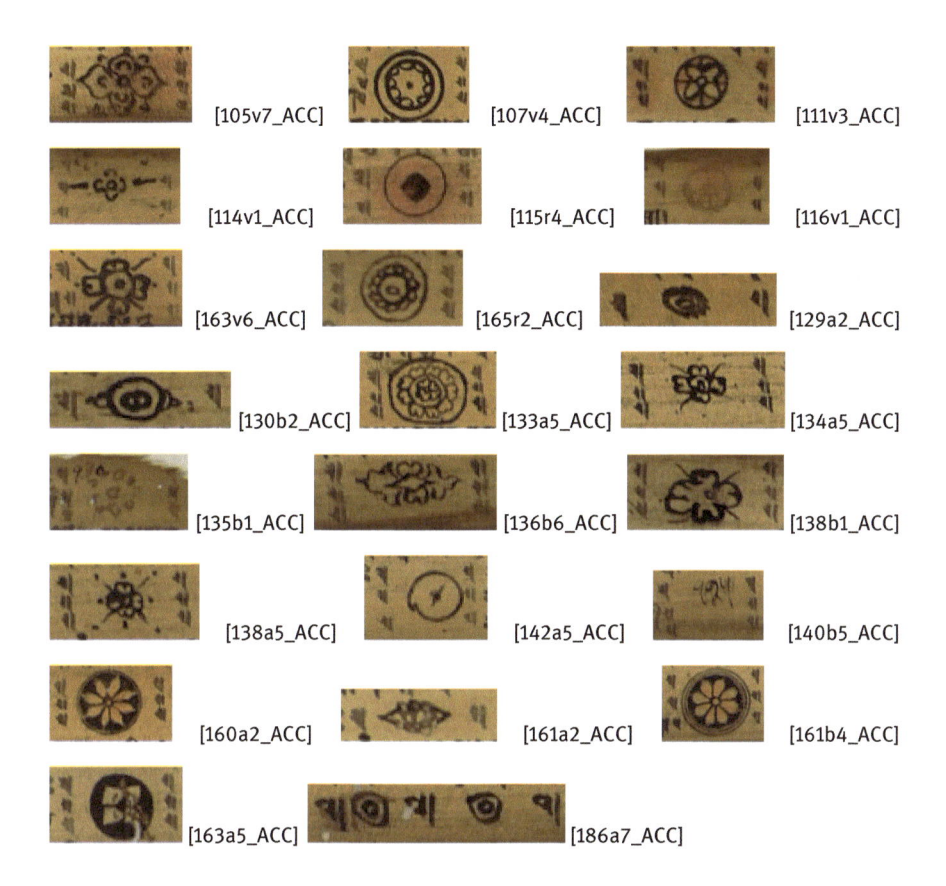

611 Further circles can be found, for instance, on 9v3_ACC, 9v4_ACC, 15r5_BCC, 15r5_ACC, 18v5_BCC, 18v5_ACC, 19v1_BCC, 19v1_ACC, 19v4_ACC, 19v4_ACC, 20r4_BCC, 20r4_ACC, 20v4_BCC, 20v4_ACC, 21r6_BCC, 21r6_ACC, 22r3_BCC, 22r3_ACC, 22v6_BCC, 22v6_ACC, 23v1_BCC, 23v1_ACC,

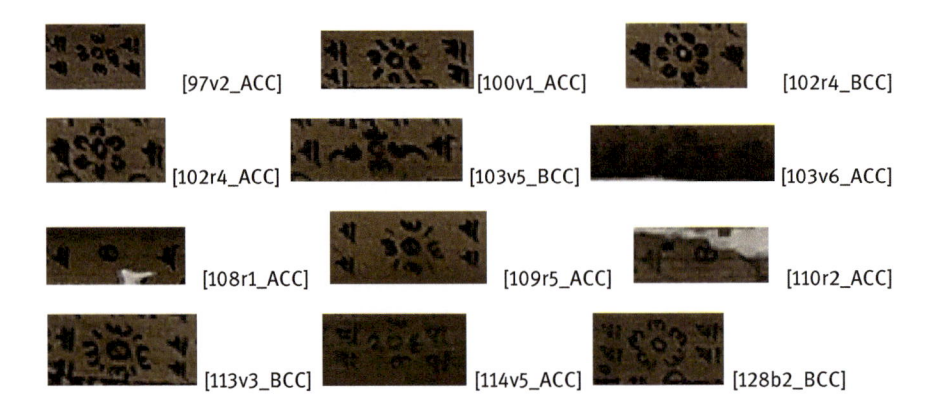

 [97v2_ACC]  [100v1_ACC]  [102r4_BCC]

 [102r4_ACC]  [103v5_BCC]  [103v6_ACC]

 [108r1_ACC]  [109r5_ACC]  [110r2_ACC]

 [113v3_BCC]  [114v5_ACC]  [128b2_BCC]

Manuscript KT (924 CE)

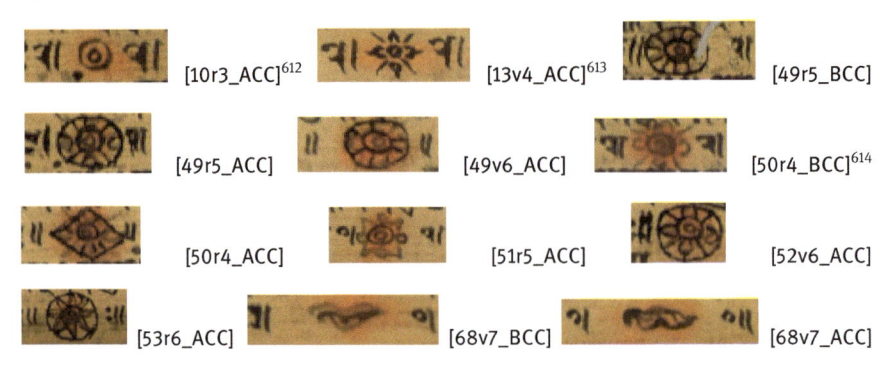

Symbols

 [10r3_ACC][612]  [13v4_ACC][613]  [49r5_BCC]

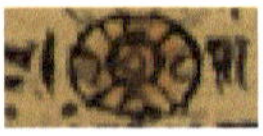 [49r5_ACC] 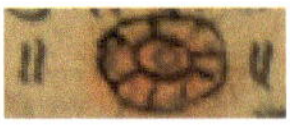 [49v6_ACC]  [50r4_BCC][614]

 [50r4_ACC]  [51r5_ACC]  [52v6_ACC]

 [53r6_ACC]  [68v7_BCC]  [68v7_ACC]

24v3_BCC, 24v3_ACC, 25v4_BCC, 25v5_ACC, 26v1_BCC, 26v1_ACC, 29r5_BCC, 29r5_ACC, 32r3_BCC, 32r4_ACC, 34v4_BCC, 36v3_BCC, 36v4_ACC, 36v4_ACC, 41r4_BCC, 41r4_ACC, 41r4_ACC, 44v4_BCC, 48r4_BCC, 48r4_ACC, 51r3_BCC, 51r3_ACC, 54v5_BCC, 54v5_ACC, 57v3_BCC, 57v3_ACC, 61v3_BCC, 61v3_ACC, 69r4_BCC, 69r4_ACC, 72v3_BCC, 72v3_ACC, 89r1_BCC, 96v3_BCC, 96v3_ACC, 130a6_ACC, 130a_ACC, 89r1_ACC, 101v2_ACC, 112r1_BCC, 112r2_ACC.

612 Further double circles can be found on 22v6_ACC, 30r4_ACC, 34r3_ACC, 35v3_ACC, 51v6_ACC, 60r4_BCC, 63v3_BCC, 63v3_ACC, 64r5, 65r5_ACC, 66r5_ACC, 72v2_ACC, 76r2_ACC, 99v2_AC.

613 Identical symbols appear on 12r1_ACC, 21v5_ACC, 24v5_ACC, 25r6_BCC, 25v1_ACC, 26v1_ACC, 27v3_BCC, 27v3_ACC, 31r2_ACC, 38r1_ACC, 40r6_ACC, 42r6_ACC.

614 Nearly similar symbols are on 46v2_BCC, 46v2_ACC, 54r3_ACC, 55r6_BCC, 55r6_ACC, 57r3_BCC, 57r3_ACC, 57v4_BCC, 57v4_ACC, 58r3_BCC, 58r4_ACC, 58v3_BCC, 58v3_ACC, 59r1_BCC, 59r2_ACC, 59v4_BCC, 60v6_BCC, 60v6_ACC, 70v4_BCC, 71r2_ACC.

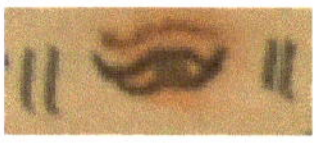 [69v5_ACC]  [77r1_ACC]  [78r7_BCC]

 [78r7_ACC]  [78r5_BCC]  [78r5_ACC]

 [79v6_ACC][615] 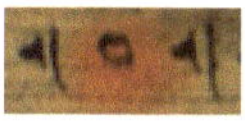 [87v2_ACC][616]  [93v6_ACC][617]

 [94v5_ACC]  [96v4_ACC]  [99v2_AD]

 [99v3][618]

Manuscript KV/UVDh (968 CE)

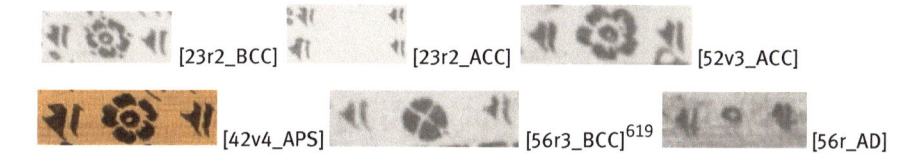

Symbols and blank spaces

 [23r2_BCC]  [23r2_ACC] 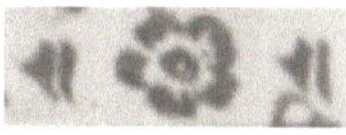 [52v3_ACC]

 [42v4_APS]  [56r3_BCC][619]  [56r_AD]

615 Further identical symbols can be found on 82r2_ACC, 84r6_ACC, 87v2_BCC, 88r1_ACC, 92r5_ACC, 97v1_ACC, 99v1_BCC.

616 A circle can be found on 99v1_ACC.

617 These symbols appear at the end of the last line (no. 6) on the right side.

618 This symbol can be found after the line in which the name of the donor and place is mentioned.

619 This symbol appears at the end of the text of the UVDh.

Symbols around string-holes

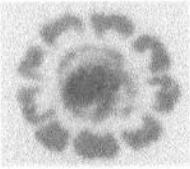 [5r_RSH] 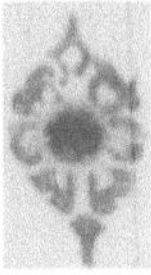 [11r_LSH]  [35r_RSH]

 [39r_RSH] 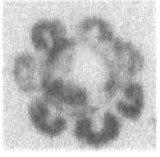 [43r_LSH]

Manuscript SP$_3$ (ca. 10th c.)

Symbols and blank spaces

 [12v1_BCC]  [14r4_BCC] 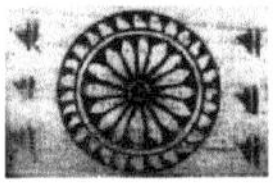 [14r4_ACC]

 [18r5_ACC][620]  [19r3_BCC][621]  [19r3_ACC]

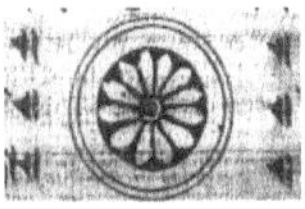 [20r4_BCC]  [20r4_ACC]  [20v3_BCC]

 [20v3_ACC]  [21v1_BCC][622]  [21v1_ACC][623]

620 Nearly identical symbols appear on 18r5_BCC, 27r5_BCC, 46v5_ACC, 60r6_BCC, 198r4_BCC. Similar symbols can also be found around string-holes in KV/UVDh, for instance, 5r_LSH, 5r_RSH.

621 Nearly similar symbols are in DDh, for instance, on 25v2.

622 A nearly identical symbol appears on 196v1_BCC.

623 Similar symbols are on 84v6_BCC, 88r1_ACC, 132r4_BCC, 134v6_BCC, 142r6_BCC, 142r6_ACC, 154v3_BCC, 155r6_BCC, 157r4_BCC, 181r6_BCC, 181r6_ACC, 185r3_B/ACC, 199r6_BCC.

 [22r4_BCC]  [22r4_ACC]  [23r1_ACC]

 [24v5_ACC]  [26r6_ACC][624] 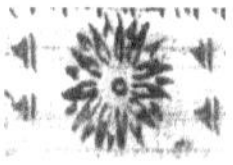 [27r5_ACC]

 [29r3_BCC][625]  [29r3_ACC] 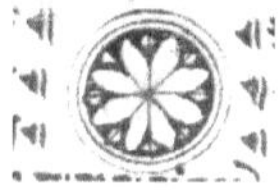 [31r1_BCC]

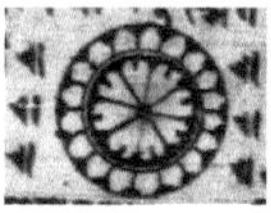 [32v3_BCC] 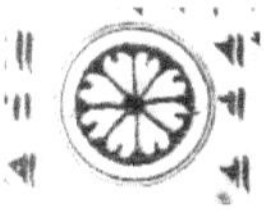 [32v4_ACC]  [34v2_BCC]

 [34v2_ACC]  [35v5_BCC]  [35v5_ACC]

 [37v6_BCC]  [37v6_ACC][626]  [46v5_BCC]

 [50r2_BCC]  [50r2_ACC][627]  [56v4_ACC][628]

 [60v1_ACC] 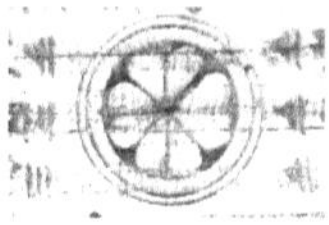 [64r2_BCC]  [70r1_BCC]

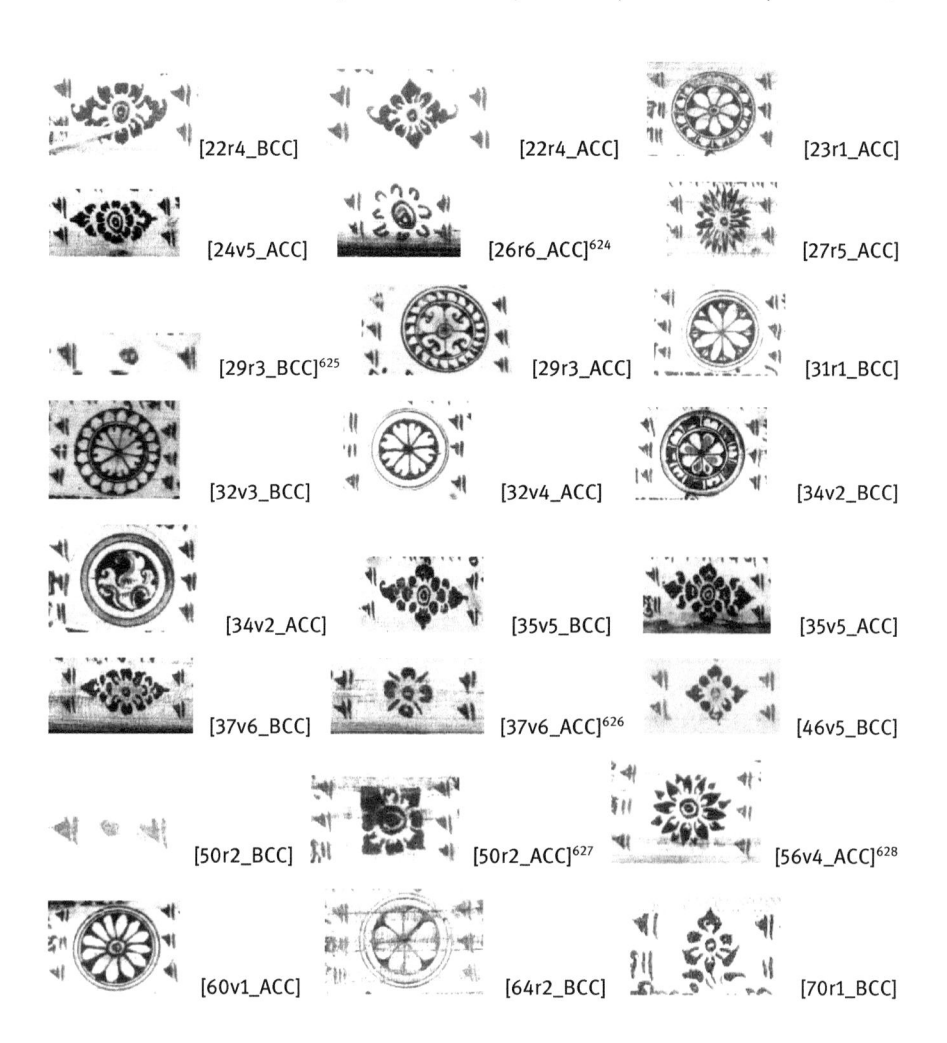

624 From its outlook, it was possibly drawn later.
625 This type of symbols can be found on 100r4_BCC, 141r1_ACC, 143r6_ACC, 147r2_BCC, 147r2_ACC, 149v6_BCC, 150v5_BCC, 158r2_BCC, 158r2_B/ACC, 160v1_BCC, 167v6_BCC, 190v5_BCC, 191r6_ACC, 236v4_BCC, 236v5_ACC, 240r5_B/ACC.
626 Nearly identical symbols appear on 31r1_ACC, 44r6_BCC, 106r6_ACC, 123r6_BCC, 125v2_ACC, 235r2_BCC.
627 Nearly identical symbols can be found on 138r5_ACC, 159r3_BCC, 200v4_BCC.
628 Almost similar symbols are on 24v5_BCC, 44r6_ACC, 148v4_BCC, 150v5_ACC, 168v5_ACC, 200v4_ACC.

[70r1_ACC][629]

[69r4_BCC][630]

[69r4_ACC]

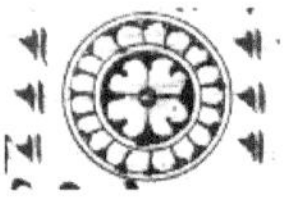
[69v3_BCC]

[69v3_ACC]

[70v1_BCC]

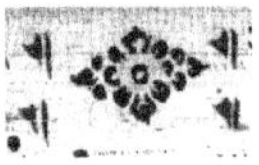
[70v1_ACC]

[72r6_BCC]

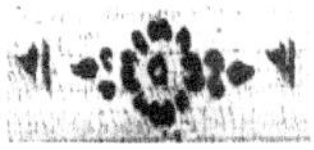
[72r6_ACC]

[72v4_BCC]

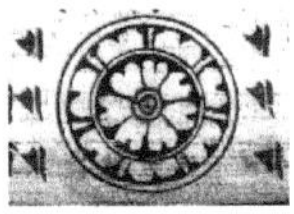
[72v4_ACC]

[73r4_BCC][631]

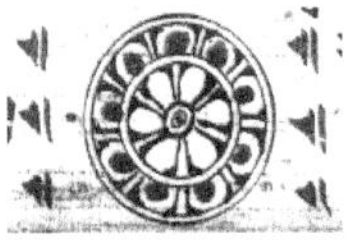
[73r4_ACC]

[73v3_ACC]

[74v2_BCC][632]

[81r4_BCC]

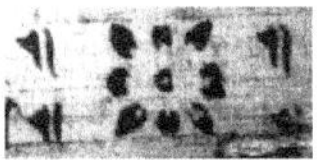
[81r4_ACC]

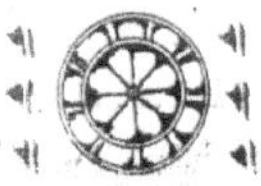
[82v4_BCC]

[82v4_ACC]

[83v6_ACC]

[90v7_ACC][633]

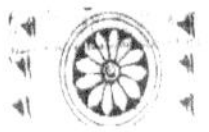
[92r3_BCC]

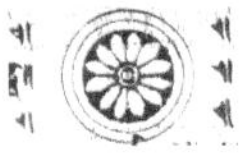
[92r3_ACC]

[95v1_BCC]

[95v2_ACC]

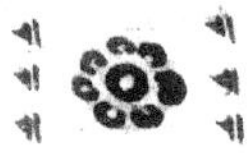
[97r2_BCC]

[97r2_ACC]

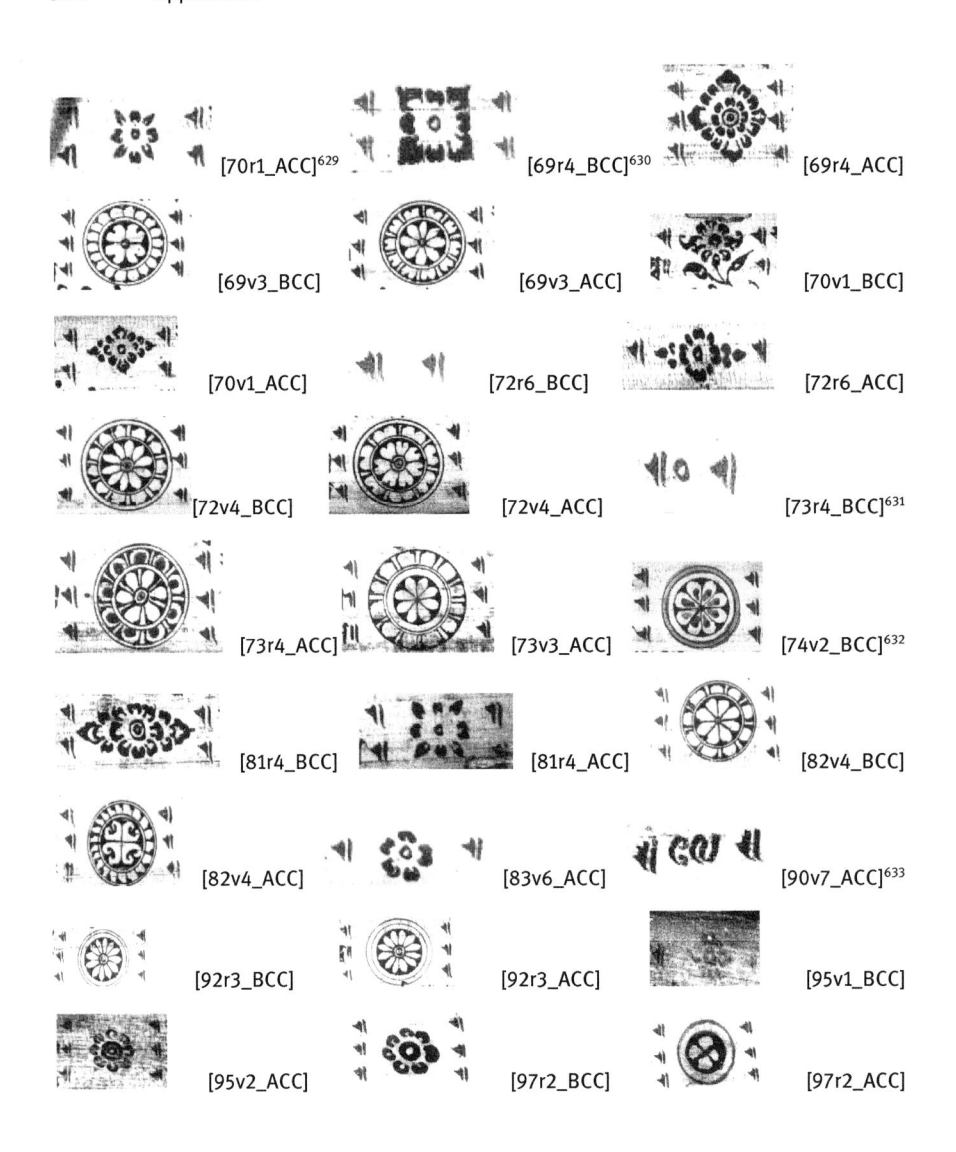

629 Similar symbols can be found on 3v5_ACC, 139r4_BCC, 193r5_ACC.
630 Nearly similar symbols appear on 26r6_BCC, 88r1_BCC, 136r4_ACC.
631 Further circles appear on 83v6_BCC, 84v6_ACC, 90v7_BCC, 123r6_ACC, 134v6_ACC, 163r3_BCC, 163r4_ACC, 174v6_BCC, 174v6_ACC, 180r1_BCC, 187v3_ACC, 199r6_ACC, 234v1_ACC.
632 Three similar symbols can be found on 74v2_ACC, 76r2_B/ACC.
633 This is the letter-numerals 57 for the chapter number.

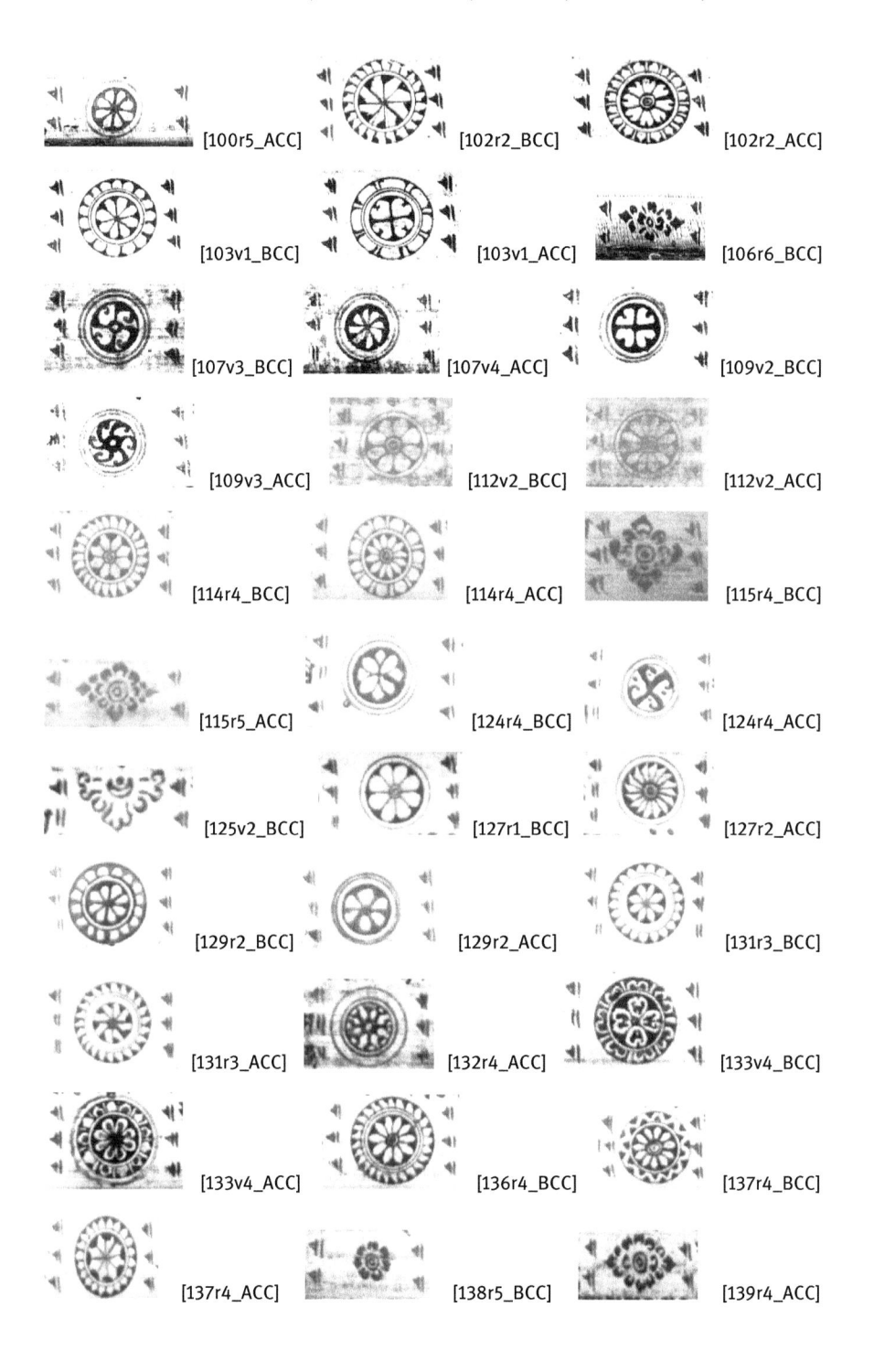

[100r5_ACC]
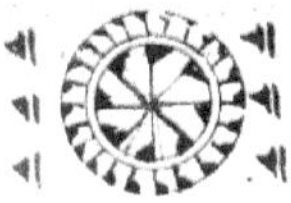
[102r2_BCC]
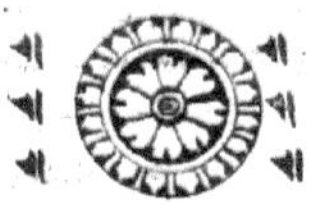
[102r2_ACC]

[103v1_BCC]

[103v1_ACC]

[106r6_BCC]

[107v3_BCC]

[107v4_ACC]

[109v2_BCC]

[109v3_ACC]

[112v2_BCC]

[112v2_ACC]

[114r4_BCC]

[114r4_ACC]

[115r4_BCC]

[115r5_ACC]

[124r4_BCC]

[124r4_ACC]

[125v2_BCC]

[127r1_BCC]
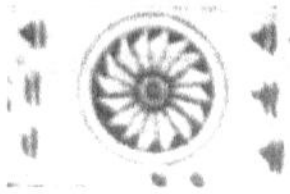
[127r2_ACC]

[129r2_BCC]

[129r2_ACC]

[131r3_BCC]

[131r3_ACC]

[132r4_ACC]

[133v4_BCC]
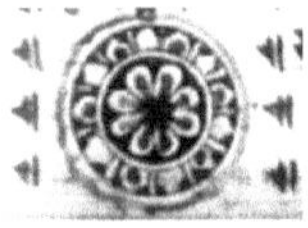
[133v4_ACC]
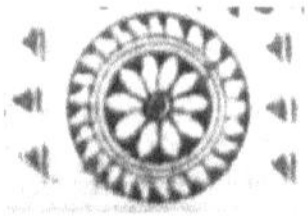
[136r4_BCC]

[137r4_BCC]
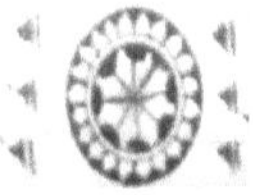
[137r4_ACC]

[138r5_BCC]
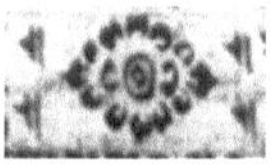
[139r4_ACC]

 [141r1_BCC]
 [143r5_BCC]
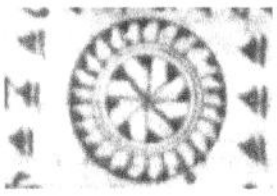 [145r3_BCC]

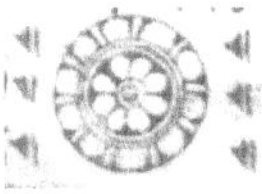 [145r4_ACC]
 [146r4_BCC]
 [146r4_ACC]

 [147v4_BCC]
 [147v4_ACC][634]
 [148v4_ACC]

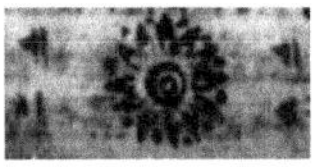 [150v5_ACC]
 [151v5_ACC]
 [153r1_BCC][635]

 [155r6_ACC]
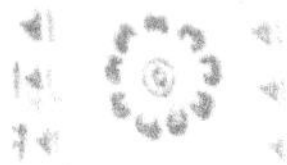 [159r3_ACC]
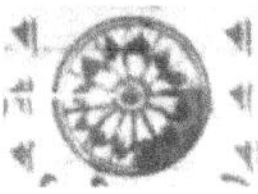 [162r2_BCC]

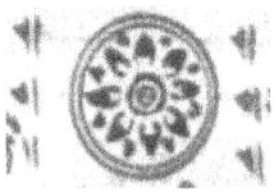 [162r2_ACC]
 [164r3_ACC]
 [165v1_BCC]

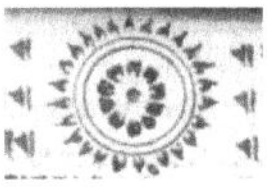 [165v1_ACC
 [166v1_BCC]
 [166v1_ACC]

 [168r1_ACC]
 [168v5_BCC]
 [171v2_BCC]

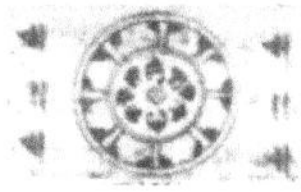 [171v2_ACC]
 [176v3_BCC]
 [176v3_ACC]

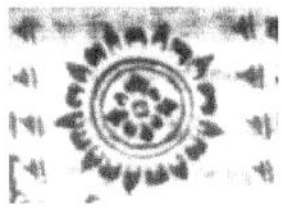 [180r1_ACC]
 [186r1_BCC]
 [186r1_ACC][636]

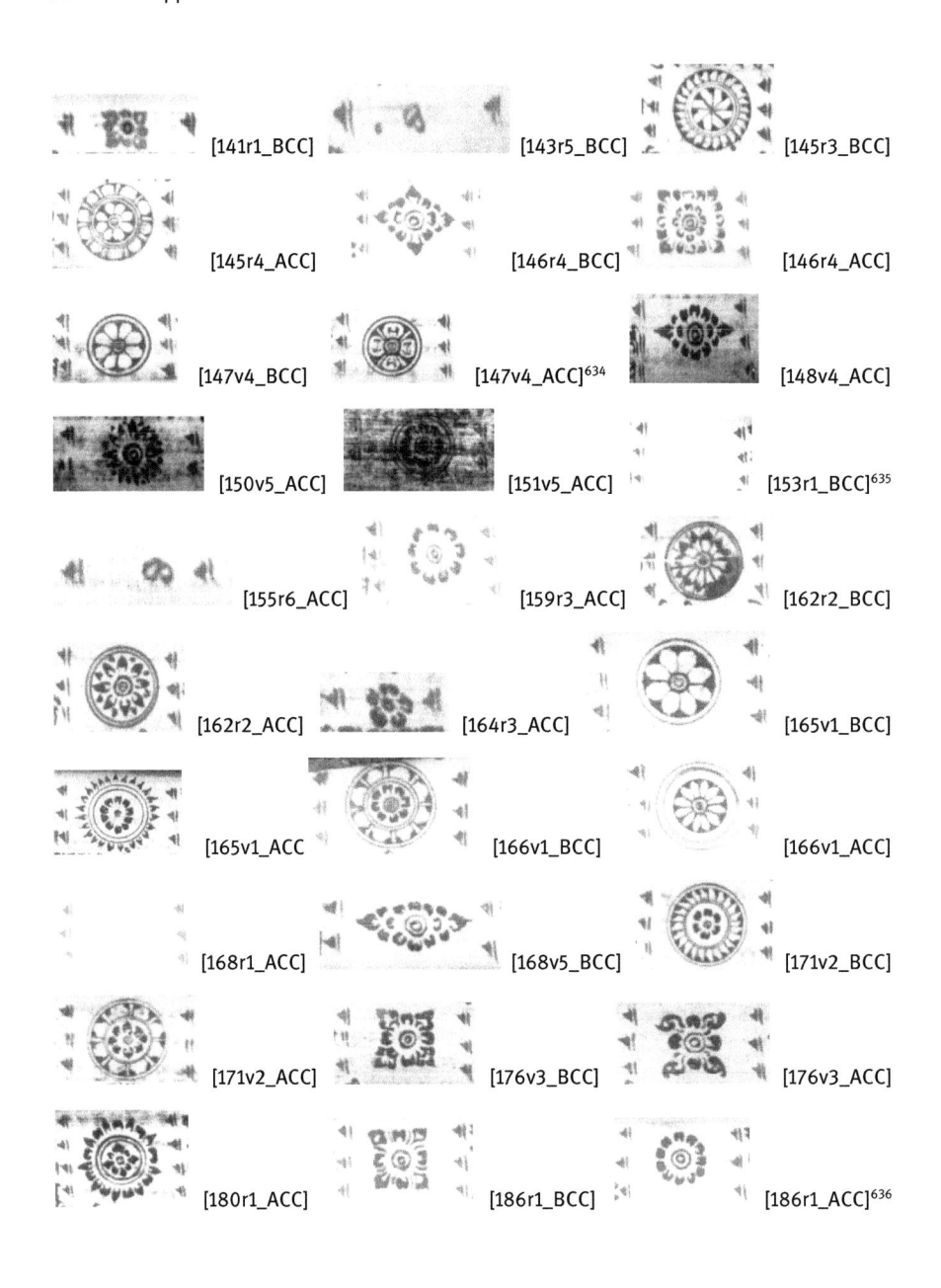

634 Almost similar type of symbol can be found in DDh on 4r4.

635 Further blank spaces can be found on 153r2_ACC, 154v3_ACC, 157r4_ACC, 160v1_ACC, 164r3_BCC, 168r1_ACC, 232v2_BCC, 232v2_ACC.

636 Nearly identical symbols can be found on 244v3_ACC, 246r1_BCC.

 [190v5_ACC]  [193r5_BCC] 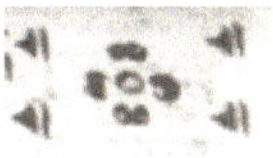 [196v1_ACC]

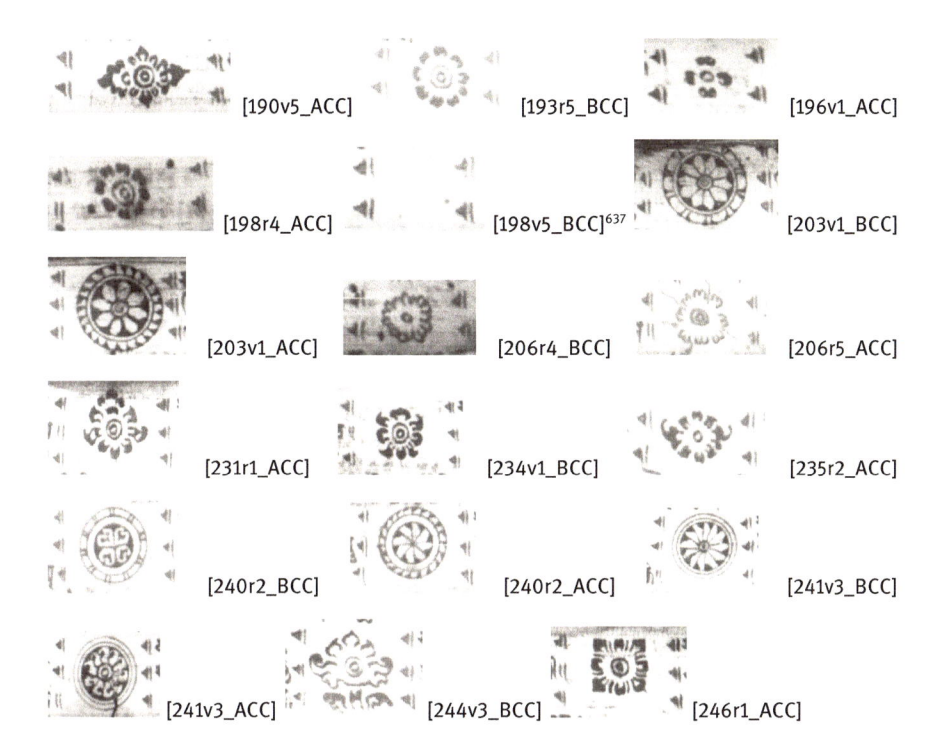

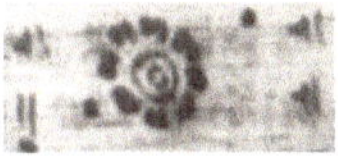 [198r4_ACC]  [198v5_BCC][637]  [203v1_BCC]

 [203v1_ACC]  [206r4_BCC]  [206r5_ACC]

 [231r1_ACC]  [234v1_BCC]  [235r2_ACC]

 [240r2_BCC]  [240r2_ACC]  [241v3_BCC]

 [241v3_ACC]  [244v3_BCC]  [246r1_ACC]

Manuscript SP4 (ca. 10th c.)

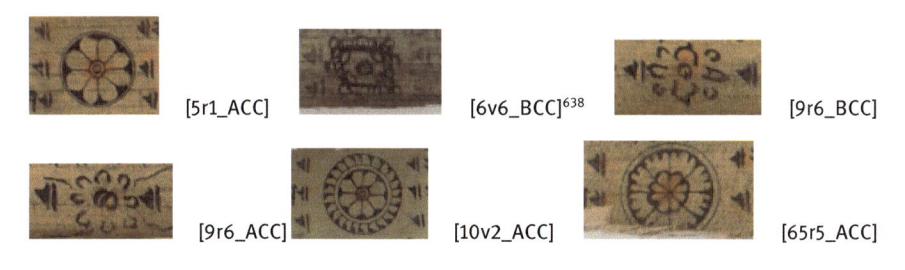

Symbols

 [5r1_ACC]  [6v6_BCC][638]  [9r6_BCC]

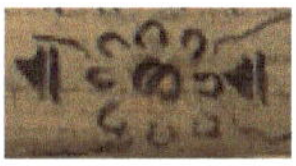 [9r6_ACC]  [10v2_ACC]  [65r5_ACC]

637 A similar size of blank space appears on 198v5_ACC.

638 In comparison to other symbols, this symbol and symbols on 9r6 seem to have been drawn later.

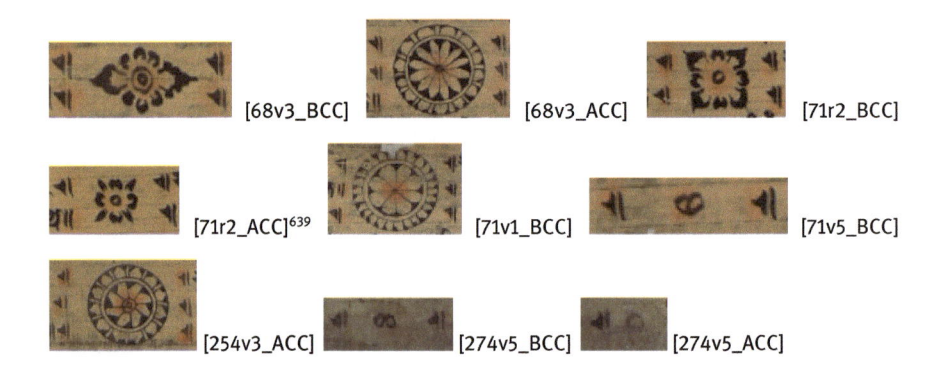

 [68v3_BCC]  [68v3_ACC]  [71r2_BCC]

 [71r2_ACC][639]  [71v1_BCC]  [71v5_BCC]

 [254v3_ACC]  [274v5_BCC]  [274v5_ACC]

Manuscript YY (1024 CE)

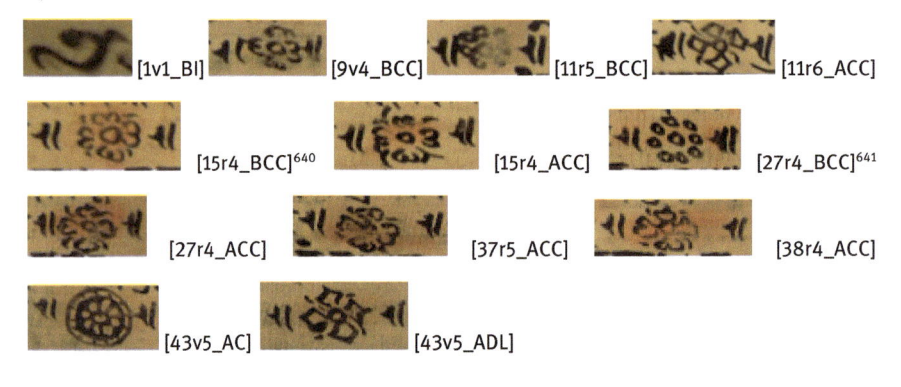

Symbols

 [1v1_BI]  [9v4_BCC]  [11r5_BCC]  [11r6_ACC]

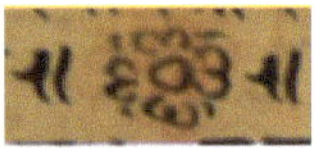 [15r4_BCC][640]  [15r4_ACC]  [27r4_BCC][641]

 [27r4_ACC]  [37r5_ACC]  [38r4_ACC]

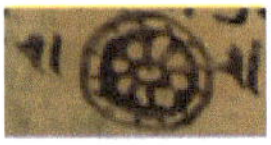 [43v5_AC]  [43v5_ADL]

639 An identical symbol appears on 71v1_ACC.
640 Nearly similar symbols appear on 9v4_ACC, 23v6_BCC, 43v4_BC.
641 Further nearly identical symbols can be found on 23v6_ACC, 37r5_BCC.

Manuscript HV_1 (1036 CE)

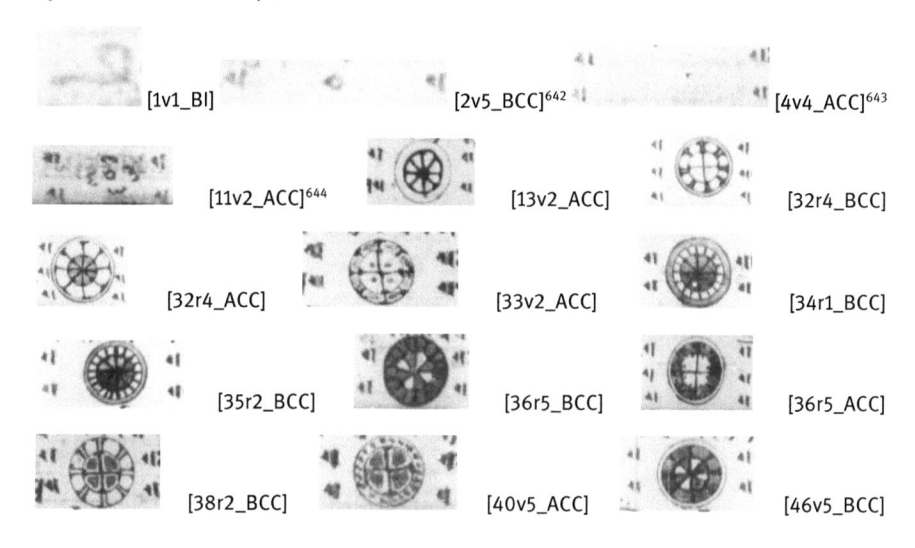

Symbols and blank spaces

[1v1_BI]

[2v5_BCC][642]

[4v4_ACC][643]

[11v2_ACC][644]

[13v2_ACC]

[32r4_BCC]
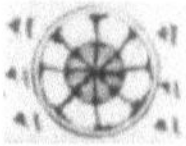
[32r4_ACC]
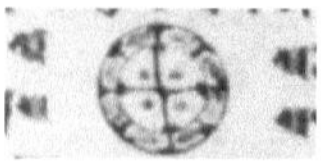
[33v2_ACC]
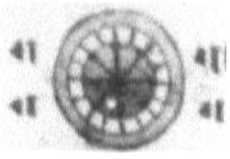
[34r1_BCC]

[35r2_BCC]

[36r5_BCC]
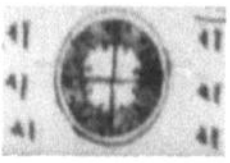
[36r5_ACC]
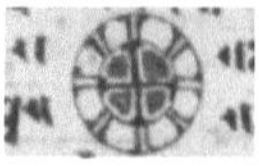
[38r2_BCC]
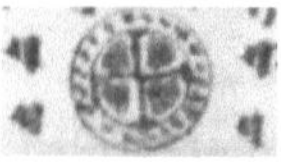
[40v5_ACC]

[46v5_BCC]

---

642 A few circles can be found on 2v5_ACC, 13v2_ASpI, 313r2_ACC.

643 This blank space seems to have been used in order to maintain the division of the verse within the text-section. Further blank spaces occupying an area of two lines in height can be found on 9r3_ACC, 10r2_ACC, 15v2_ACC, 17r5_ACC, 17r5_ASpI, 21r1_ACC, 25r5_ACC, 26v4_ACC, 29v1_ACC, 48v3_ACC, 53v4_BCC, 53v5_ACC, 61v2_ACC, 62v5_BCC, 65v3_ACC, 72r4_ACC, 75r1_ACC, 75v5_BCC, 75v5_ACC, 79r3_ACC, 80r5_BCC, 80r5_ACC, 80r5_ASpI 85v4_ACC, 87v1_ACC, 91r5_BCC, 93r3_ACC, 94r3_ACC, 95r4_ACC, 96v2_ACC, 97v4_BCC, 100r5_BCC, 100r5_ACC, 102r4_BCC, 103v5_BCC, 103v5_ACC, 104v4_ACC, 106v3_ACC, 107r4_ACC 108v4_ACC, 110r2_ACC, 111r4_ACC, 115v3_ACC, 117v3_ACC, 121r3_BCC, 121r3_ACC, 122v1_ACC, 125r1_ACC, 128v3_ACC, 132v2_ACC, 134r2_ACC, 139r3_ACC, 140v5_ACC, 143r2_ACC, 149v4_ACC, 155v3_BCC, 157v1_BCC, 160r1_ACC, 171r2_BCC, 171r3_ACC, 173v5_ACC, 176r5_BCC, 178r1_ACC, 179v5_BCC, 179v5_ACC, 179v5_ASpI, 180v2_BCC, 182v3_ACC, 184v4_ACC, 187r2_ACC, 191r2_ACC, 193r5_ACC, 199v3_ACC, 200v4_ACC, 201v3_ACC, 205r2_ACC, 218r2_ACC, 228r2_ACC, 230v3_ACC, 232v1_BCC, 234v1_ACC, 236r2_BCC, 237v2_ACC, 239r4_ACC, 244r2_BCC, 244r2_ACC, 245r2_BCC, 246r2_BCC, 249v2_ACC, 250r3_BCC, 251r4_BCC, 251r4_ACC, 252v2_ACC, 268v1_ACC, 285r4_BCC, 287v4_ACC, 292v1_BCC, 292v1_ACC, 293v5_BCC, 293v5_ACC, 294v4_BCC, 294v5_ACC, 295v1_BCC, 295v1_ACC, 296r3_ACC, 297v3_ACC, 298v2_BCC, 300v2_ACC, 304r4_BCC, 304r4_ACC, 307r3_ACC, 309v2_ACC, 311r4_ACC, 319r3_ACC, 321r3_ACC, 321r3_BCC, 324v3_BCC, 326v5_ACC.

644 Nearly identical symbols can be found on 260r5_ACC, 281v4_ACC, 298v3_ACC, 305v3_BCC, 315v3_ACC.

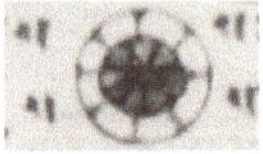 [46v5_ACC] 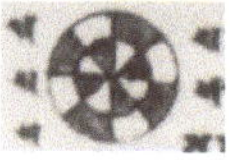 [48r1_BCC][645]  [51r1_ACC][646]

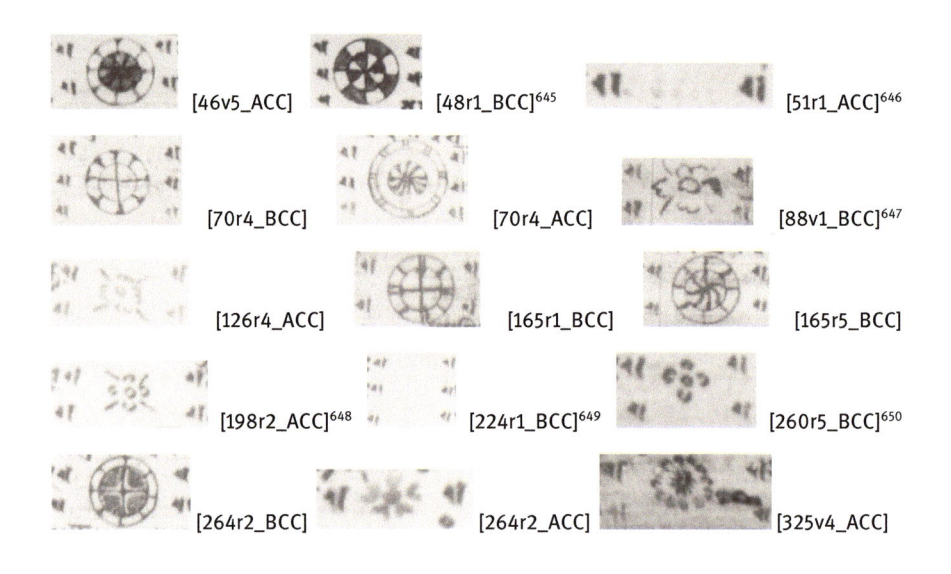

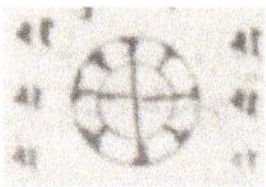 [70r4_BCC]  [70r4_ACC]  [88v1_BCC][647]

 [126r4_ACC] 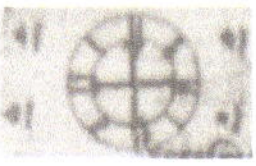 [165r1_BCC]  [165r5_BCC]

 [198r2_ACC][648] 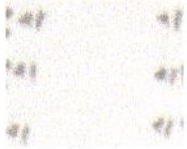 [224r1_BCC][649] 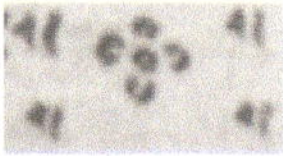 [260r5_BCC][650]

 [264r2_BCC]  [264r2_ACC] 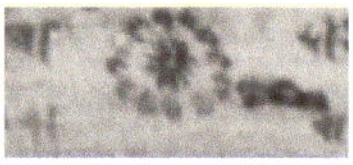 [325v4_ACC]

Manuscript HY (1039 CE)

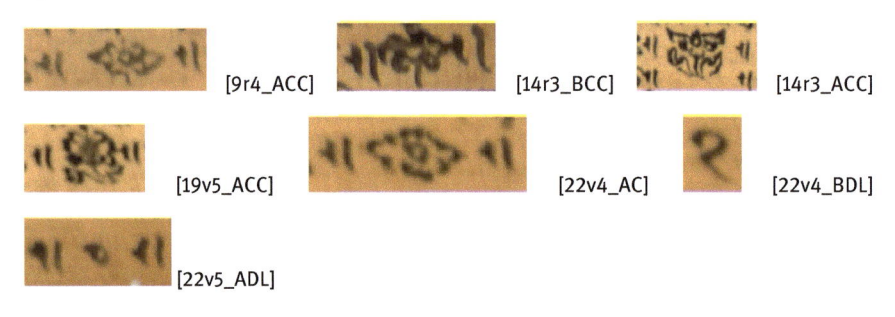

Symbols

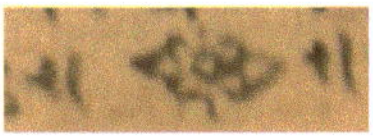 [9r4_ACC] 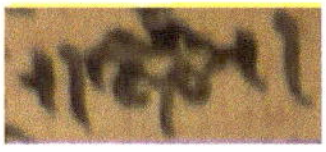 [14r3_BCC]  [14r3_ACC]

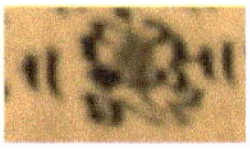 [19v5_ACC] 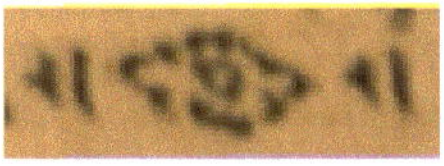 [22v4_AC]  [22v4_BDL]

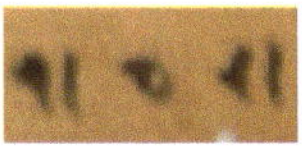 [22v5_ADL]

645 This symbol appears in the gap between the first and second half of the verse.
646 Blank spaces occupying an area of one line in heigt on folios can be found on 151r5_ACC, 154r4_BCC, 212r5_ACC, 242v3_ACC, 256v2_ACC, 266v5_BCC, 266v5_ACC, 289r5_ACC, 297v3_BCC, 300v2_BCC.
647 This symbol has been drawn exactly in the gap between the first and second half of the verse.
648 A few identical symbols appear on 225v2_BCC, 229r4_ACC, 241v1_ACC, 257v2_BCC.
649 Another blank space occupying an area of 3 lines can be found on 296r3_BCC.
650 Further symbols appear on 302v1_BCC, 302v1_ACC, 315v2_BCC.

Manuscript DDh (1039 CE)

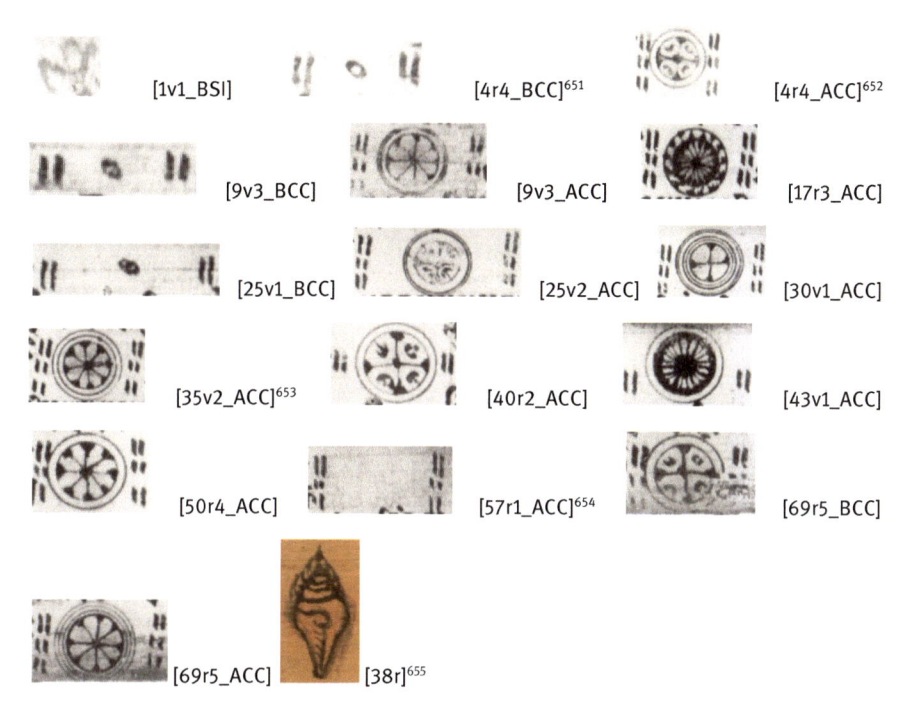

Symbols and blank spaces

 [1v1_BSI]  [4r4_BCC][651]  [4r4_ACC][652]

 [9v3_BCC]  [9v3_ACC] 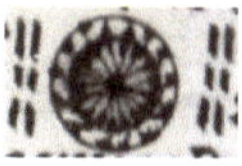 [17r3_ACC]

 [25v1_BCC]  [25v2_ACC] 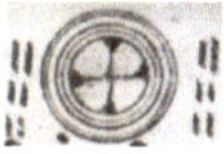 [30v1_ACC]

 [35v2_ACC][653]  [40r2_ACC] 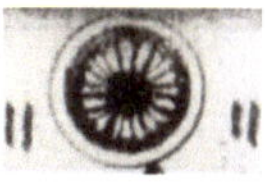 [43v1_ACC]

 [50r4_ACC]  [57r1_ACC][654]  [69r5_BCC]

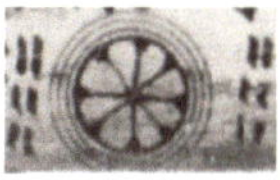 [69r5_ACC]  [38r][655]

651 Further circles can be found on 17r3_BCC, 69r5_ADL.
652 Most of the symbols and blank spaces are demarcated by three sets of double *daṇḍa*s, even though they occupy only two text lines in height of the folio.
653 An almost identical symbol can also be found in the manuscript of the *Aṣṭasāhasrikā Prajñāpāramitā* (CUL, Add.866) on 98v5.
654 For similar blank spaces, see 58v4_ACC, 63r4_ACC, 68r5_ACC.
655 This symbol appears on the left-hand margin on the folio.

Manuscript TS₁ (1097 CE)

Symbols and blank spaces

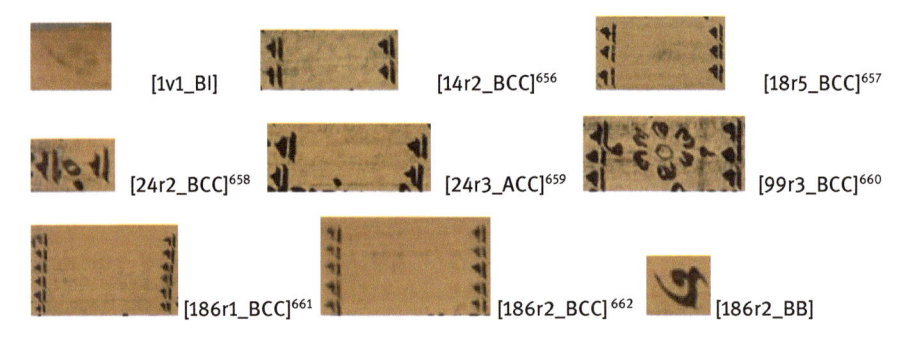

[1v1_BI]

[14r2_BCC][656]

[18r5_BCC][657]

[24r2_BCC][658]

[24r3_ACC][659]

[99r3_BCC][660]

[186r1_BCC][661]

[186r2_BCC][662]

[186r2_BB]

---

656 Further blank spaces occupying an area of two lines in height can be found on 14r2_ACC, 25v6_BCC, 28r6_BCC, 35r4_BCC, 35r4_ACC, 39v4_ACC, 42v1_BCC, 96v6_BCC, 96v6_ACC, 104r3_BCC, 104r3_ACC, 118r1_BCC, 127v3_ACC, 139r4_ACC, 148r1_ACC, 179v6_ACC.

657 Further blank spaces appear on 18r5_ACC, 26r1_ACC, 28r6_ACC, 42v2_ACC, 57r5_ACC, 90r5_B/ACC, 95r4_BCC, 95r4_ACC, 108r3_B/ACC, 118r1_ACC, 121v5_BCC, 123r4_B/ACC, 127v2_BCC, 139r3_BCC, 148r1_BCC, 149r2_ACC, 161v4_BCC, 161v5_ACC, 171r1_B/ACC, 179v5_BCC, 181v4_BCC, 181v5_ACC, 182v6_B/ACC, 186r2_AC. All these blank spaces occupy an area of two lines in height of the folio, although they are demarcated by three sets of double *daṇḍa*s (except for the blank space on 28r6_ACC of which the lower sets of two double *daṇḍa*s are on the free space of the bottom margin).

658 Further circles can be found, for instance, on 39v3_BCC, 57r4_BCC, 99r3_ACC, 121v5_ACC, 149r1_BCC.

659 This blank space occupies only an area of one text line in height on the folio, even though it is demarcated by two sets of double *daṇḍas*.

660 This symbol occupies an area of only two text lines in height on the folio.

661 This blank space occupies an area of only four lines in height, although it is demarcated by six sets of double double *daṇḍas*.

662 This blank space occupies an area of only three lines in height, although it is demarcated by five sets of double double *daṇḍas*.

Manuscript VDh (ca. 12th c.)

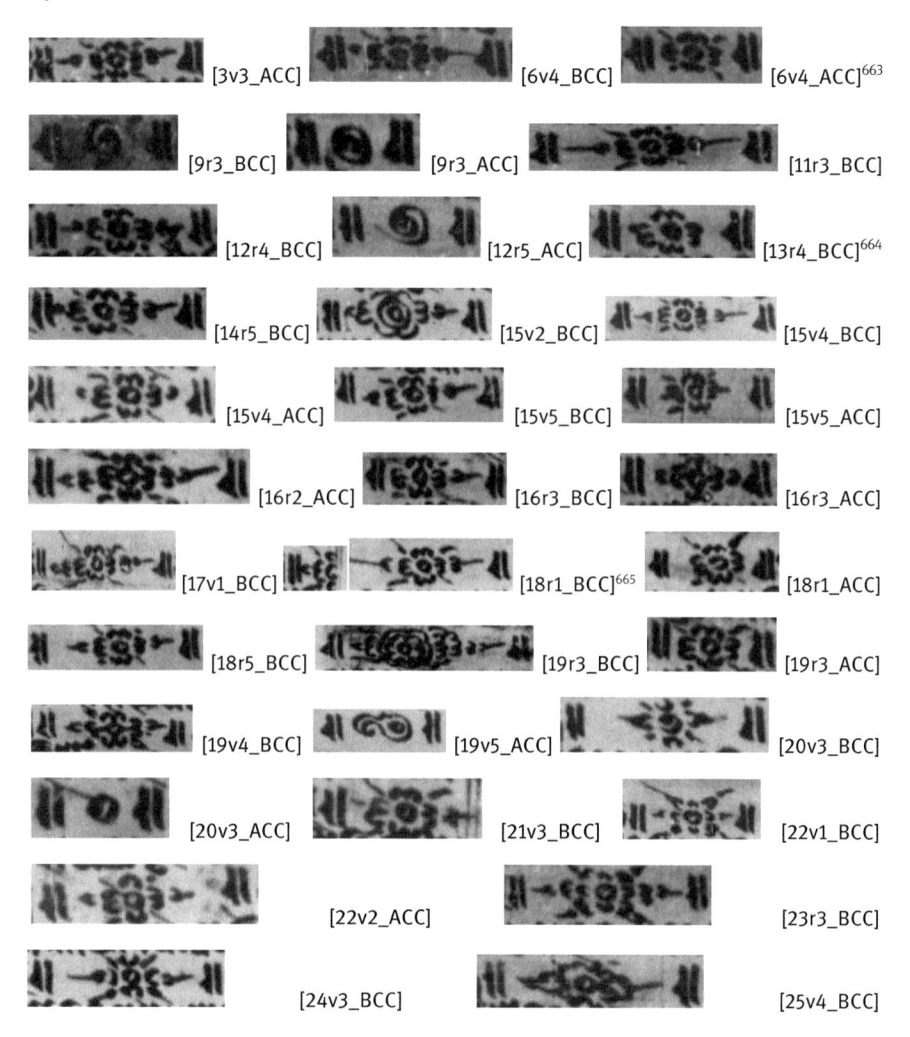

Symbols

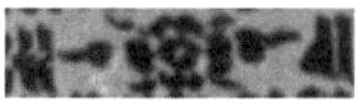 [3v3_ACC] 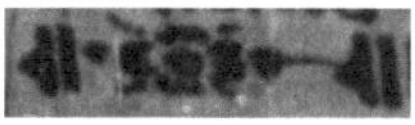 [6v4_BCC] 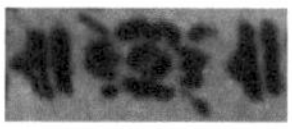 [6v4_ACC][663]

 [9r3_BCC]  [9r3_ACC]  [11r3_BCC]

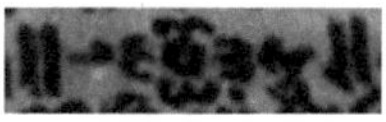 [12r4_BCC] 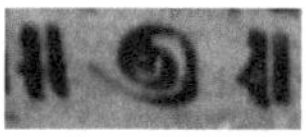 [12r5_ACC] 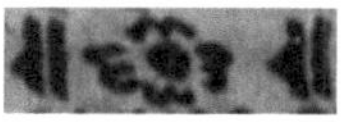 [13r4_BCC][664]

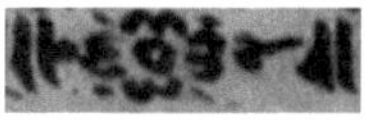 [14r5_BCC]  [15v2_BCC]  [15v4_BCC]

 [15v4_ACC]  [15v5_BCC] 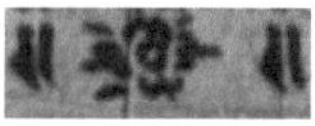 [15v5_ACC]

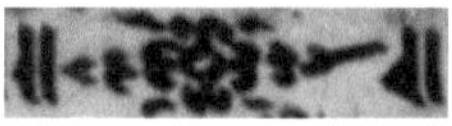 [16r2_ACC]  [16r3_BCC] 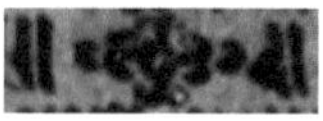 [16r3_ACC]

 [17v1_BCC]  [18r1_BCC][665] 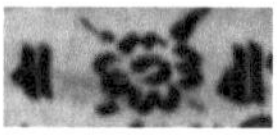 [18r1_ACC]

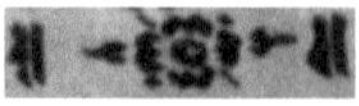 [18r5_BCC]  [19r3_BCC] 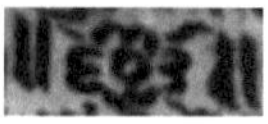 [19r3_ACC]

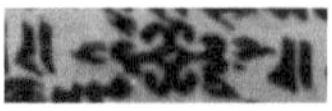 [19v4_BCC]  [19v5_ACC] 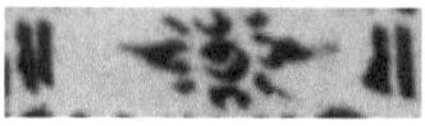 [20v3_BCC]

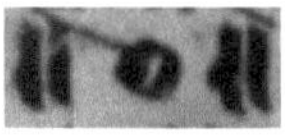 [20v3_ACC]  [21v3_BCC] 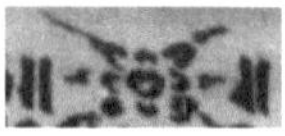 [22v1_BCC]

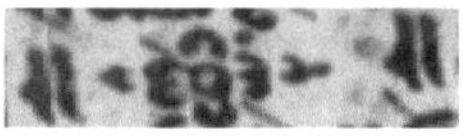 [22v2_ACC] 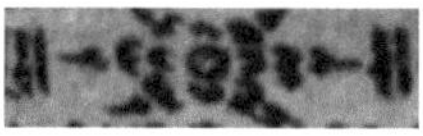 [23r3_BCC]

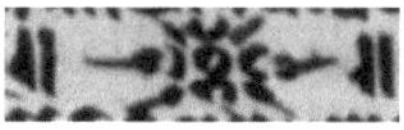 [24v3_BCC] 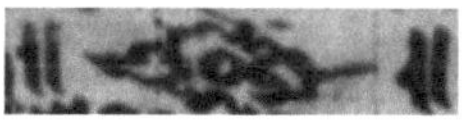 [25v4_BCC]

663 Identical symbols can be found on 11r4_ACC, 13r4_ACC.

664 Nearly similar symbols appear on 14r5_ACC, 17v2_ACC, 18r5_ACC, 21v4_ACC, 23r4_ACC, 24v3_ACC, 27r2_ACC, 36r1_ACC, 40r2_BCC, 40v2_ACC, 49v1_ACC

665 The 'half-like' symbol before it appears exactly before the left string-hole space and this symbol can be found after the left string-hole space.

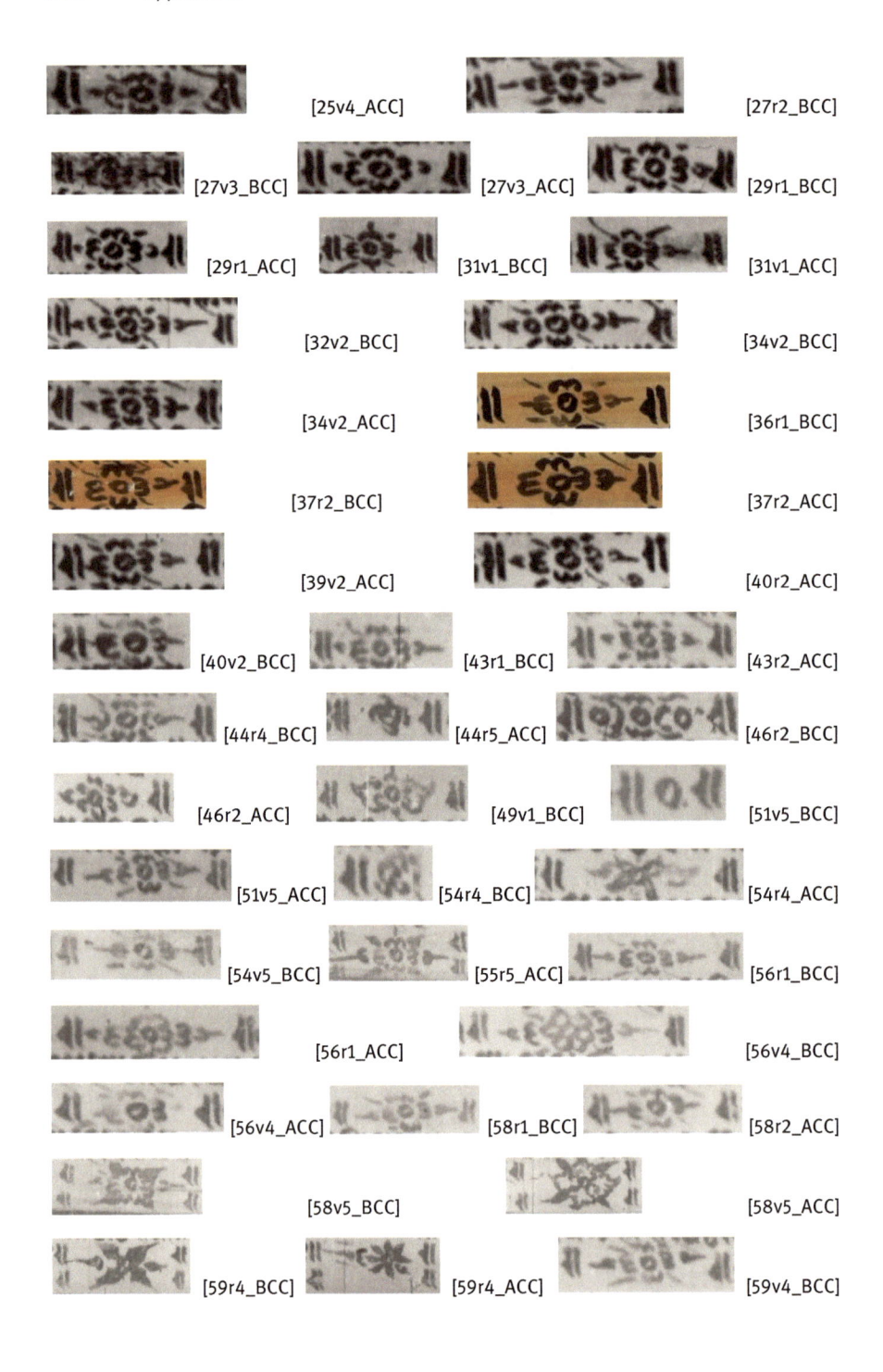

[25v4_ACC]

[27r2_BCC]

[27v3_BCC]

[27v3_ACC]
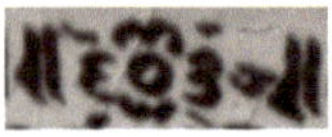
[29r1_BCC]

[29r1_ACC]
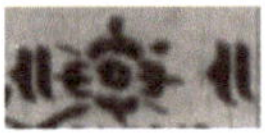
[31v1_BCC]

[31v1_ACC]

[32v2_BCC]

[34v2_BCC]

[34v2_ACC]

[36r1_BCC]

[37r2_BCC]

[37r2_ACC]

[39v2_ACC]
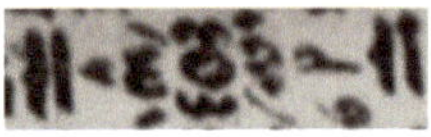
[40r2_ACC]

[40v2_BCC]

[43r1_BCC]

[43r2_ACC]

[44r4_BCC]

[44r5_ACC]

[46r2_BCC]

[46r2_ACC]

[49v1_BCC]

[51v5_BCC]

[51v5_ACC]

[54r4_BCC]

[54r4_ACC]

[54v5_BCC]

[55r5_ACC]

[56r1_BCC]

[56r1_ACC]

[56v4_BCC]

[56v4_ACC]

[58r1_BCC]

[58r2_ACC]

[58v5_BCC]

[58v5_ACC]
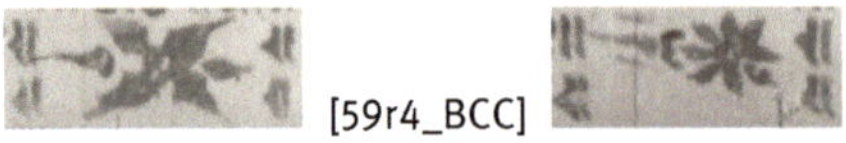
[59r4_BCC]
[59r4_ACC]

[59v4_BCC]

 [60r1_ACC]  [60r5_BCC]  [60r5_ACC]

 [61r3_BCC]  [61r3_ACC]

 [61v2_BCC]  [61v2_ACC]  [62r5_BCC]

 [62r5_ACC]  [63r1_BCC]  [63r1_ACC]

 [63r5_BCC]  [63r5_ACC]  [64r2_BCC]

 [64r2_ACC]  [65r5_BCC] 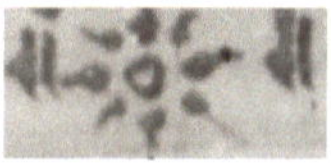 [65r5_ACC]

 [66r3_BCC]  [66r3_ACC]  [66v1_BCC]

 [66v1_ACC]  [68r1_BCC]  [68r1_ACC]

 [69r2_BCC]  [69r2_ACC]  [70r1_BCC]

 [70r1_ACC]  [71r2_BCC]  [71r3_ACC]

 [73r3_BCC] 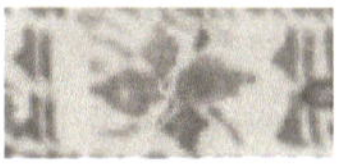 [73r3_ACC] 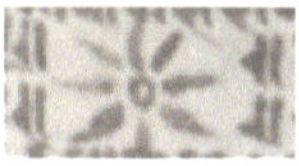 [75v3_BCC]

 [75v3_ACC]  [76v4_ACC]  [79v5_BCC]

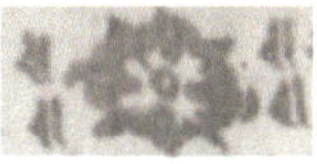 [80r1_ACC]  [83r1_BCC]  [83r1_ACC]

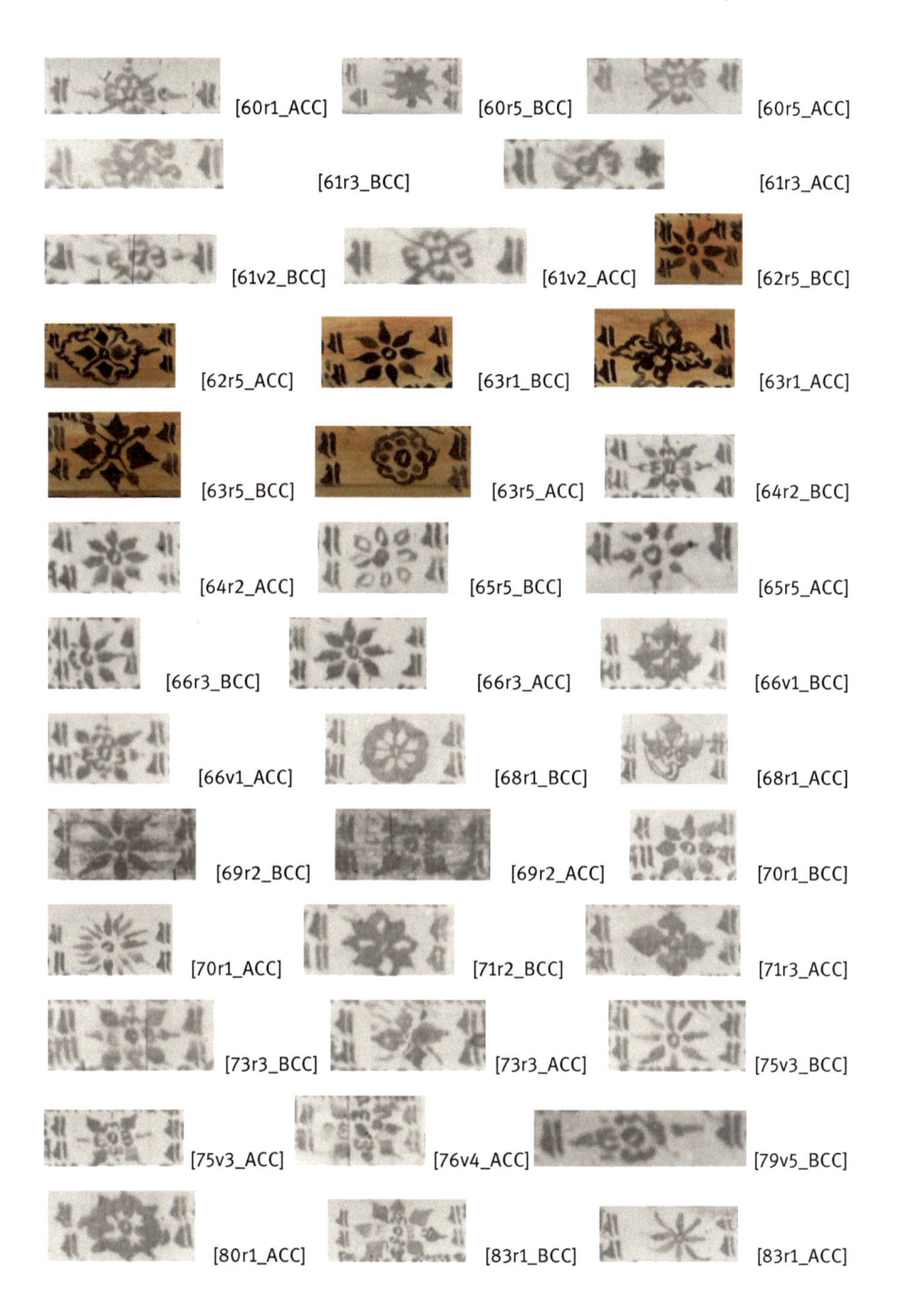

 [84v4_BCC]  [84v5_ACC] 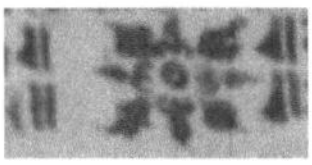 [85v4_BCC]

 [85v4_ACC] 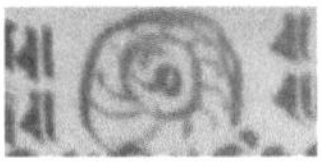 [89r1_BCC] 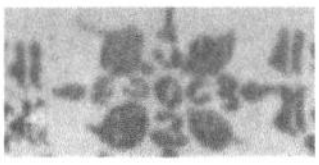 [89r1_ACC]

 [89r5_BCC]  [89r5_ACC] 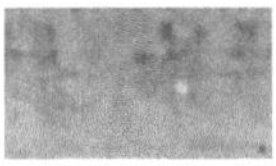 [93r5_BCC][666]

 [93r5_ACC] 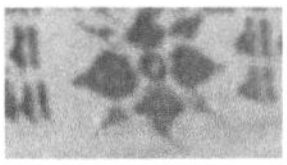 [95r4_BCC] 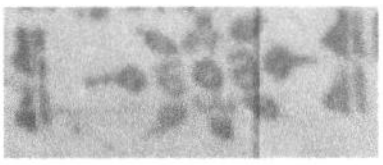 [95r5_ACC]

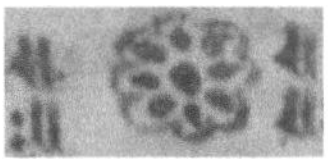 [96v1_BCC] 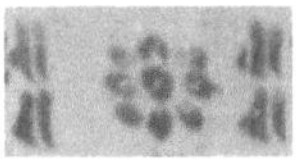 [96v1_ACC] 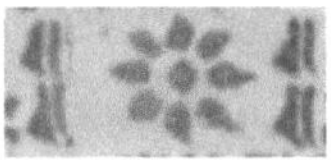 [98r3_BCC]

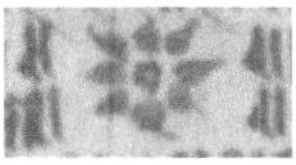 [98r3_ACC] 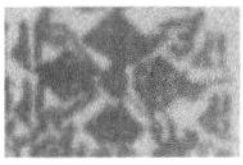 [102r3_BCC] 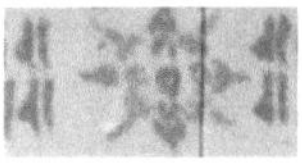 [102r4_ACC]

 [105r5_BCC] 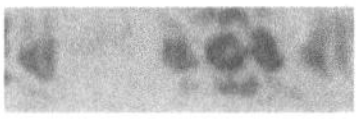 [105r5_ACC] 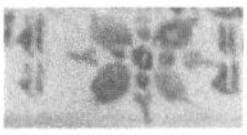 [107v5_BCC]

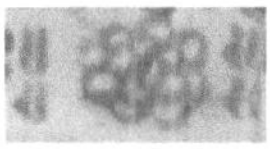 [107v5_ACC] 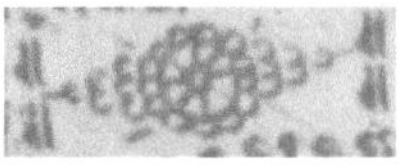 [112v3_BCC] 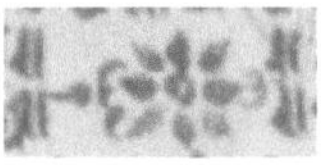 [112v3_ACC]

 [114r2_BCC] 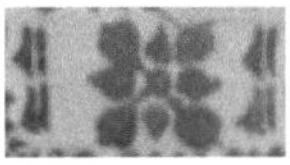 [114r2_ACC] 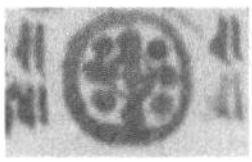 [115r4_BCC]

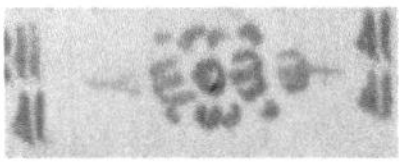 [115r5_ACC] 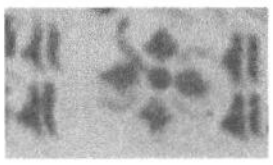 [118v4_BCC] 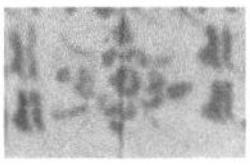 [118v4_ACC]

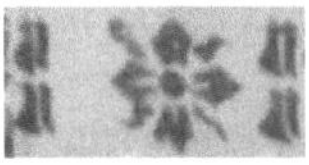 [119v2_BCC] 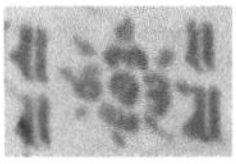 [119v2_ACC] 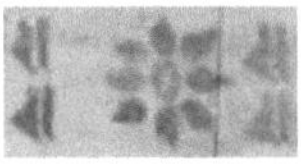 [121r1_BCC]

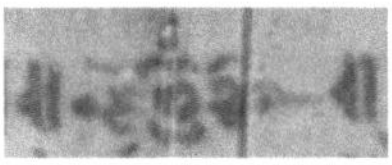 [121r1_ACC]  [121v1_BCC] 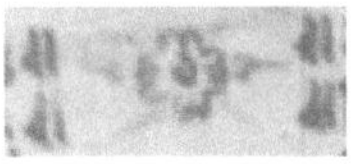 [121v1_ACC]

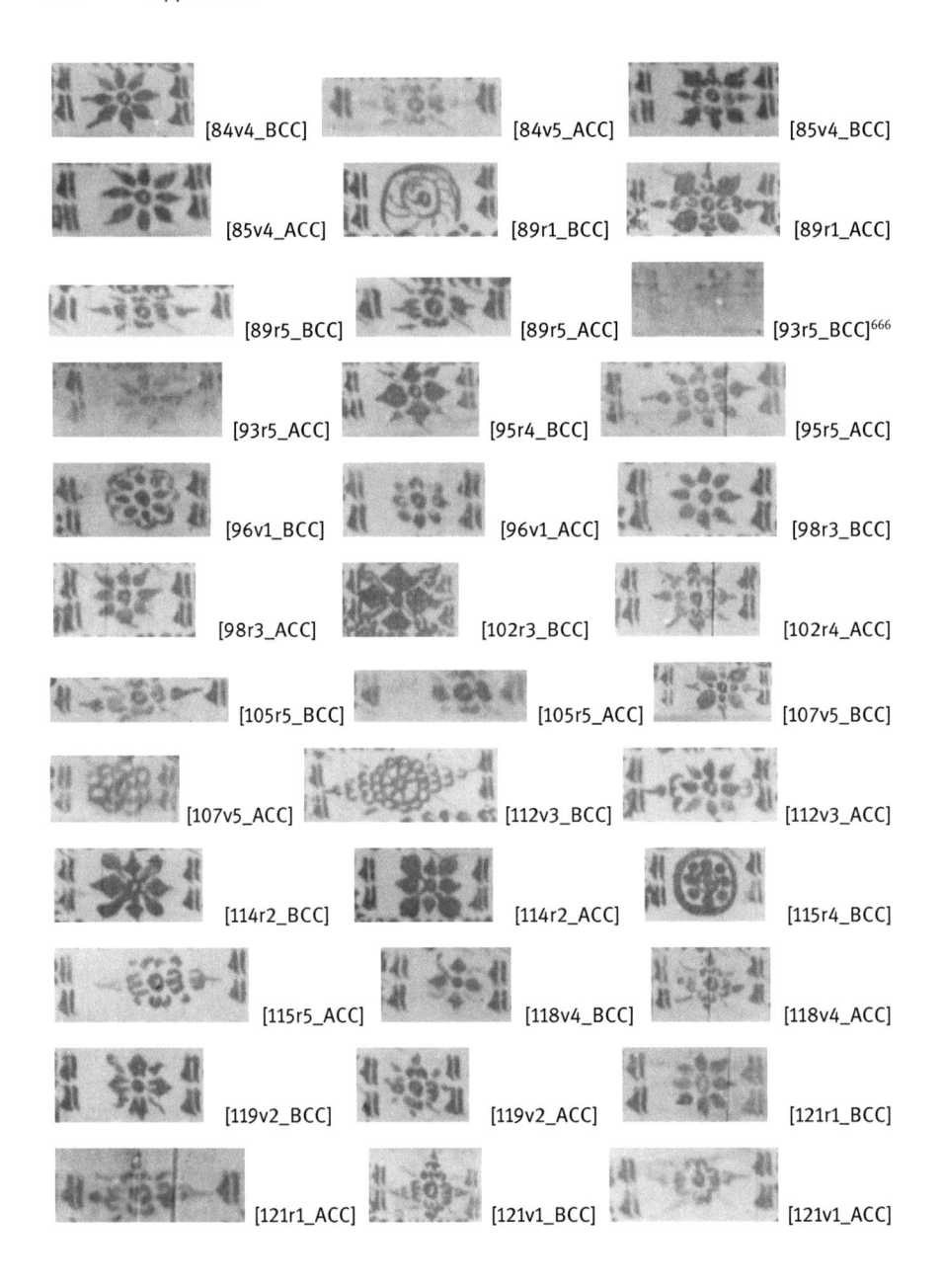

666 The writing on the folio is faded.

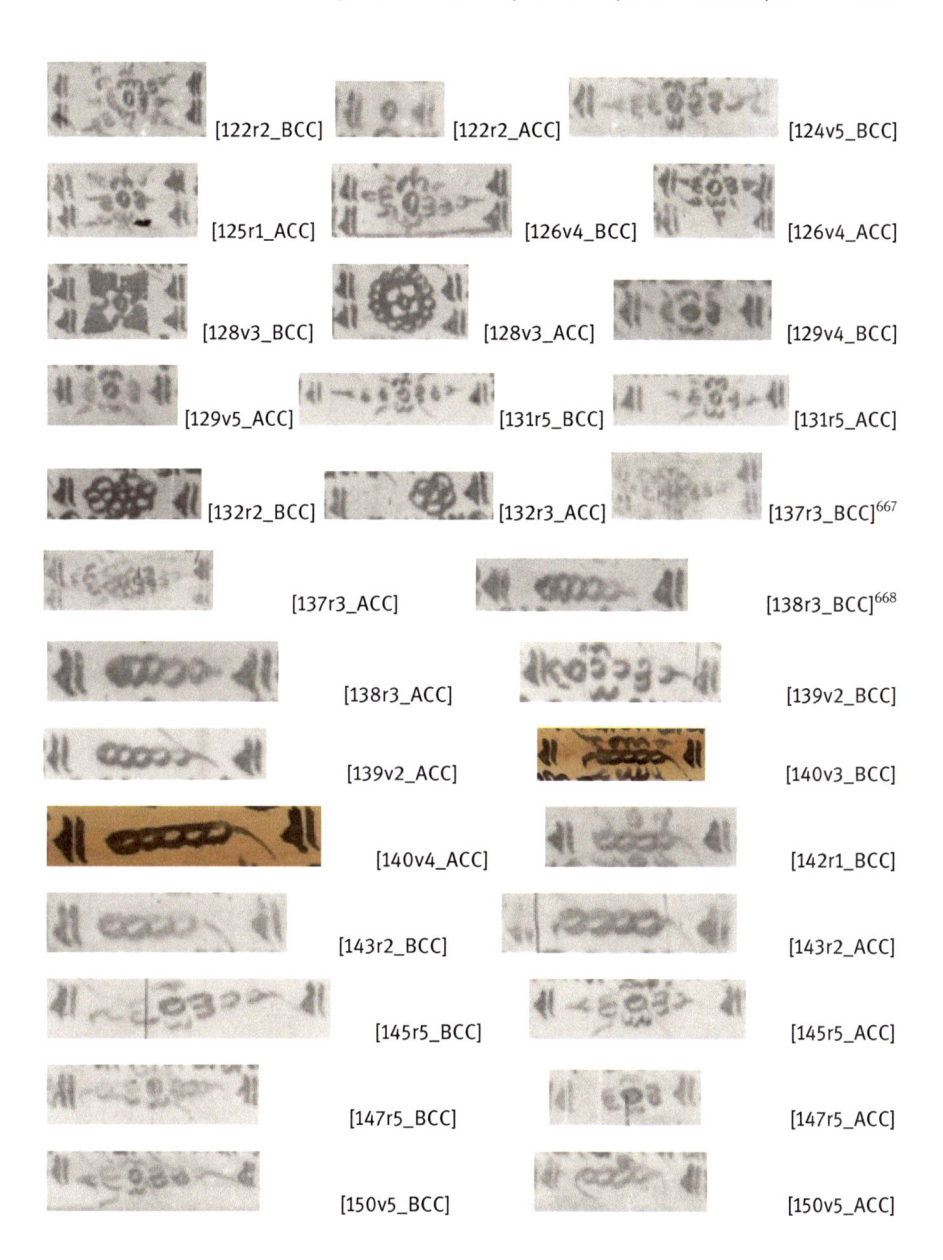

 [122r2_BCC]  [122r2_ACC]  [124v5_BCC]

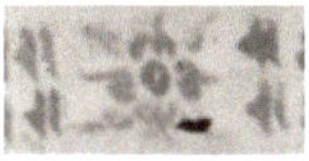 [125r1_ACC]  [126v4_BCC]  [126v4_ACC]

 [128v3_BCC] 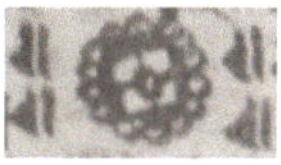 [128v3_ACC]  [129v4_BCC]

 [129v5_ACC]  [131r5_BCC]  [131r5_ACC]

 [132r2_BCC]  [132r3_ACC]  [137r3_BCC][667]

 [137r3_ACC]  [138r3_BCC][668]

 [138r3_ACC]  [139v2_BCC]

 [139v2_ACC]  [140v3_BCC]

 [140v4_ACC]  [142r1_BCC]

 [143r2_BCC]  [143r2_ACC]

 [145r5_BCC]  [145r5_ACC]

 [147r5_BCC]  [147r5_ACC]

 [150v5_BCC]  [150v5_ACC]

---

667 The writing on the folio is faded.

668 This type of symbol is also used as space-fillers in the manuscript, for example, on the bottom of 139v5, 140r5.

 [153v4_BCC]  [153v4_ACC]  [155v3_BCC]

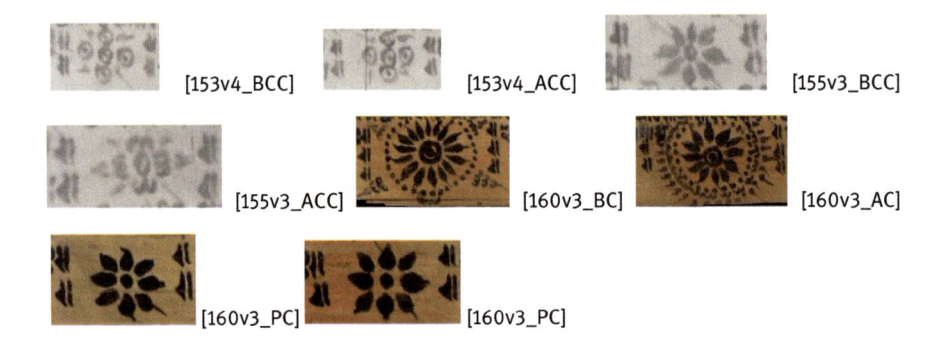

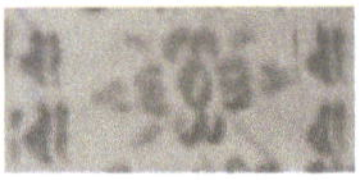 [155v3_ACC]  [160v3_BC]  [160v3_AC]

 [160v3_PC]  [160v3_PC]

Manuscript SSS (1114 CE)

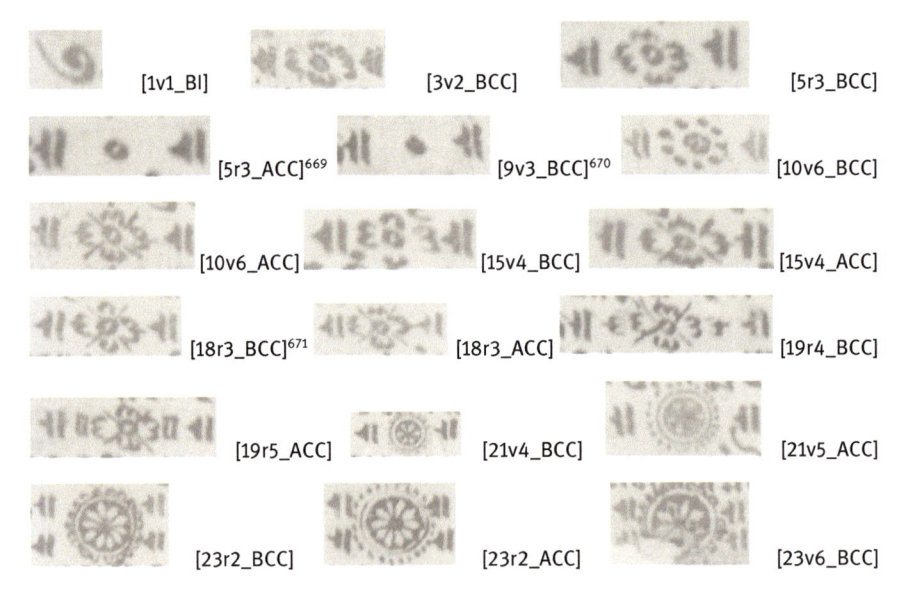

Symbols

 [1v1_BI]  [3v2_BCC] 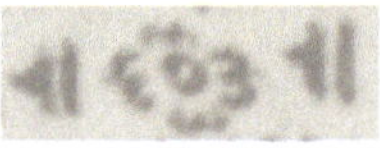 [5r3_BCC]

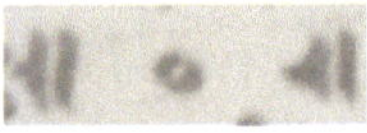 [5r3_ACC][669]  [9v3_BCC][670]  [10v6_BCC]

 [10v6_ACC]  [15v4_BCC]  [15v4_ACC]

 [18r3_BCC][671]  [18r3_ACC]  [19r4_BCC]

 [19r5_ACC]  [21v4_BCC] 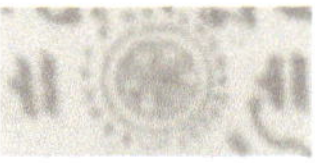 [21v5_ACC]

 [23r2_BCC]  [23r2_ACC] 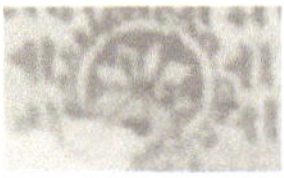 [23v6_BCC]

669 Further circles are on 9v4_ACC, 30r5_BCC, 29v4_BCC, 30v6_BCC, 37r3_BCC, 37r4_ACC.
670 A dot can also be found on 3v2_ACC.
671 Two similar symbols are on 20r5_BCC, 20r5_ACC.

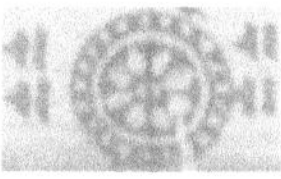 [23v6_ACC] 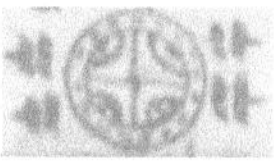 [25v6_BCC] 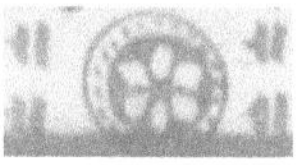 [25v6_ACC]

 [28r3_BCC]  [28r4_ACC] 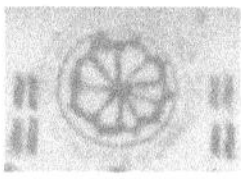 [29r1_BCC]

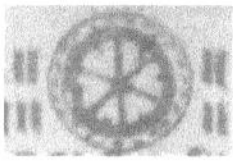 [29r1_ACC] 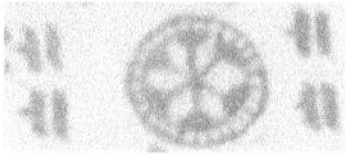 [29v4_ACC] 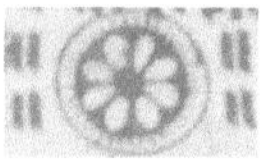 [30r5_ACC][672]

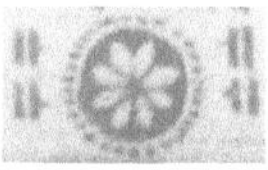 [30v6_ACC]  [31v6_BCC] 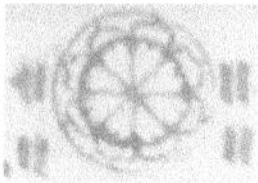 [32r1_ACC]

 [32v4_BCC] 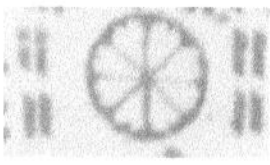 [32v4_ACC][673] 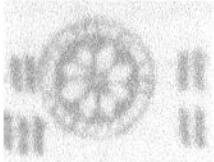 [33v1_BCC]

 [33v1_ACC] 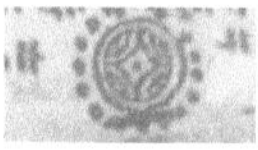 [34v6_BCC]  [35r1_ACC]

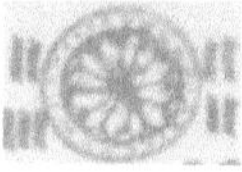 [36r1_BCC] 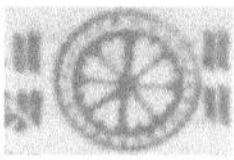 [36r1_ACC] 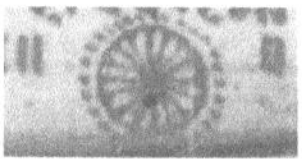 [36v6_ACC]

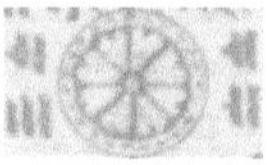 [41v3_ACC] 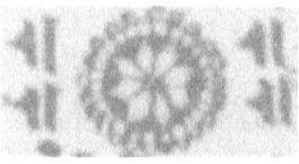 [43r4_ACC] 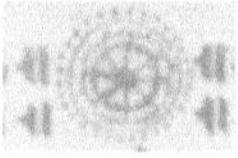 [44r1_ACC]

 [45v3_ACC] 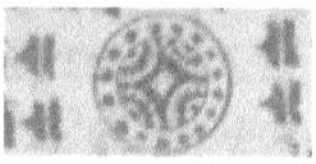 [47r5_ACC]  [48r6][674]

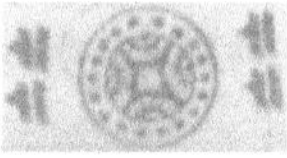 [48r6][675] 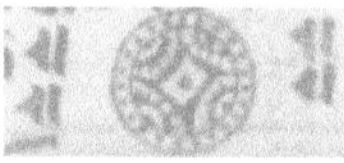 [51r6][676] 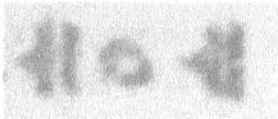 [51r6][677]

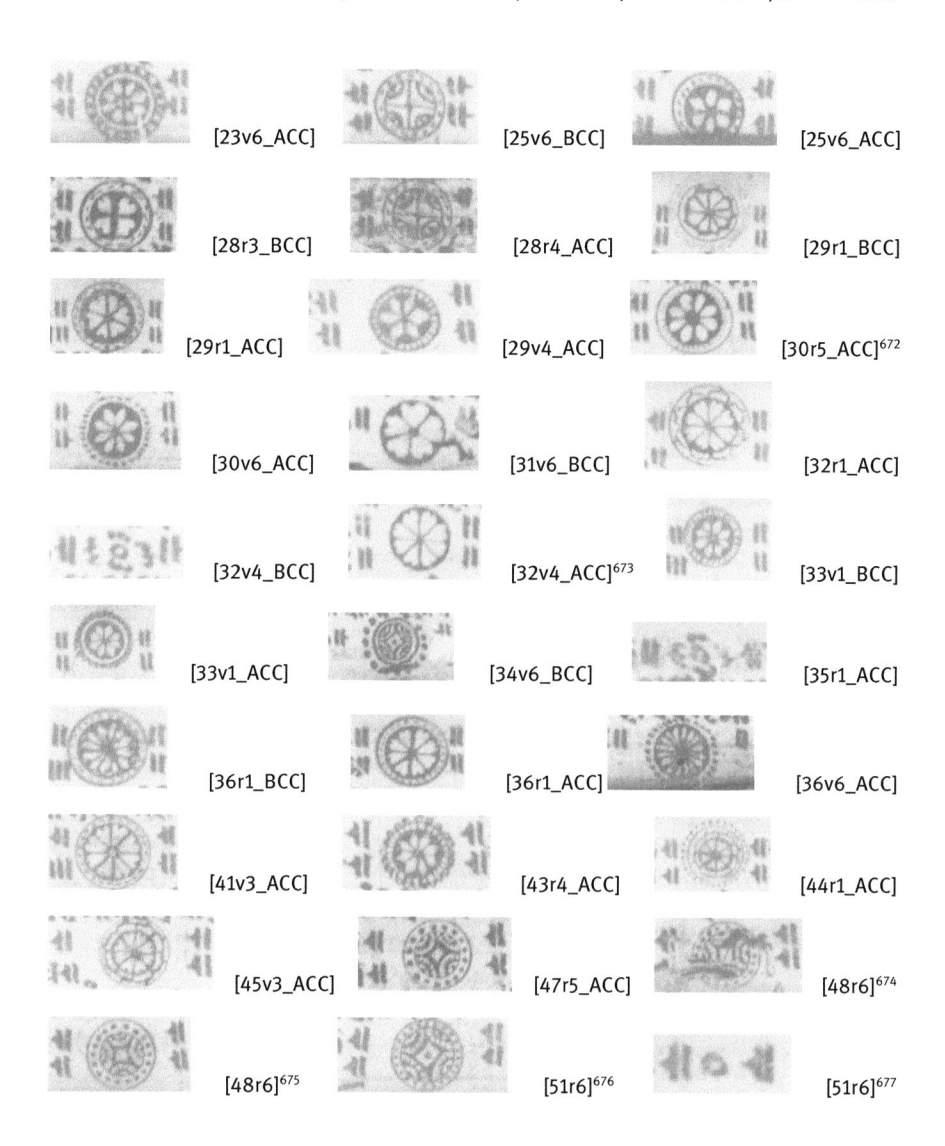

672 A nearly identical symbol with dots can also be found in the manuscript of the *Aṣṭasāhasrikā Prajñāpāramitā* (CUL, Add.866) on 69v5.
673 A nearly similar symbol is on 37v6_ACC.
674 This appears after the author line.
675 This can be found after the 'colophonic line' for the *Siddhasārasaṃhitā*.
676 This symbol is drawn before the colophonic line for both *Siddhasārasaṃhitā* and *Nighaṇṭu*.
677 This appears after the colophonic line for both *Siddhasārasaṃhitā* and *Nighaṇṭu*.

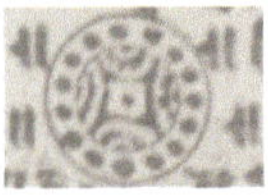
[54v4][678]

[54v4][679]

[54v6][680]

[54v6][681]

Manuscript AṣP₁ (1151 CE)

Symbols and blank spaces

[17v4_BCC][682]

[17v4_ACC]

[26v4_BCC]

[26v4_ACC]

[50v2_BCC][683]

[54v5_BCC][684]

[54v5_ACC][685]

[92r3_BCC][686]

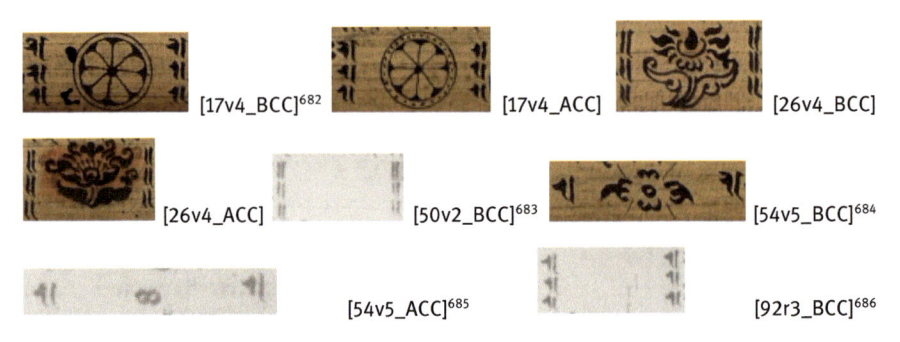

678 This can be found before the ('second') colophonic line for the *Nighaṇṭu*.

679 This is after the (second) colophonic line for the *Nighaṇṭu*.

680 It appears before the verse of asking for the book protection.

681 These circles appear after the verse of asking for the book protection. Similar way of distribution of four sets of circles placed between double *daṇḍa*s can also be found in SS/N after the *Kumārabhṛtya* section on 176v7.

682 A similar symbol is on 2r3_BBOF.

683 Most of the blank spaces in this manuscript are demarcated by three sets of double *daṇḍa*s, even though they occupy only two text lines in height of the folio.

684 A similar symbol appears on 149r5_BCC.

685 A few nearly identical symbols appear on 72v5_BCC, 132v5_BCC, 206v6_BCC.

686 Further blank spaces can be found on 99v4_BCC, 99v4_ACC, 50v3_ACC, 106r3_BCC, 106r4_ACC, 110r2_ACC, 122r4_BCC, 122r4_ACC, 145v3_BCC, 145v3_ACC, 178v1_BCC, 184r2_BCC, 184r2_ACC, 192r3_BCC, 192r3_ACC, 228v3_BCC, 228v3_ACC, 234r2_BCC, 234r2_ACC, 222v1_ACC, 225r1_BCC, 238v4_BCC, 254r4_BCC, 254r4_ACC, 263v1_ACC, 282r2_BBCF, 282r2_BCC, 282r2_ACC.

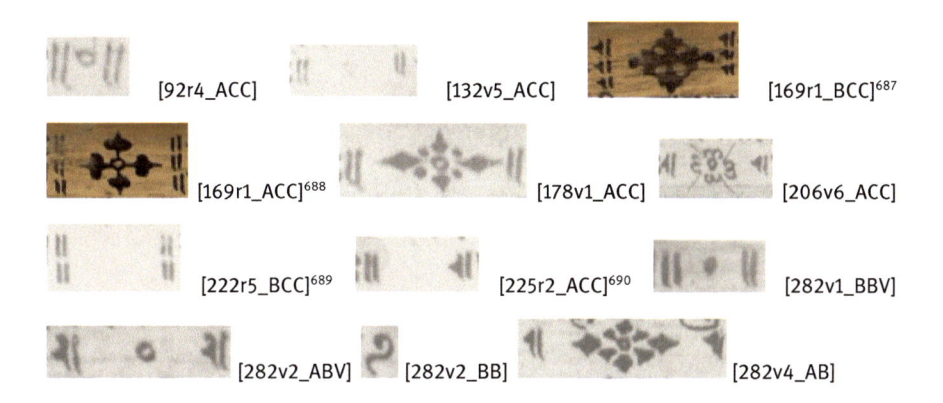

 [92r4_ACC]  [132v5_ACC]  [169r1_BCC][687]

 [169r1_ACC][688]  [178v1_ACC]  [206v6_ACC]

 [222r5_BCC][689]  [225r2_ACC][690]  [282v1_BBV]

 [282v2_ABV]  [282v2_BB]  [282v4_AB]

687 This symbol and the symbol after chapter colophon are surrounded by three sets of double *daṇḍa*s, even though they occupy only two text lines in height on the folio.
688 Identical symbols appear on 54v5_ACC, 149r5_ACC, 160v5_BCC, 160v5_ACC, 200v2_BCC, 200v2_ACC.
689 Further blank spaces can be found on 238v5_ACC, 244r5_ACC, 263r5_BCC, 280v5_BCC, 280v5_ACC.
690 Two blank spaces are on 257r2_BCC, 257r3_ACC.

Manuscript HV_2 (1172 CE)

Symbols and blank spaces

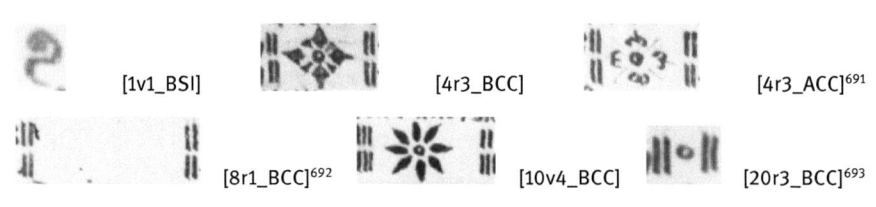

 [1v1_BSI]  [4r3_BCC] 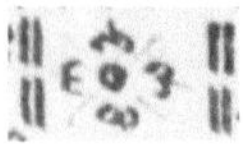 [4r3_ACC][691]

 [8r1_BCC][692]  [10v4_BCC] 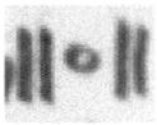 [20r3_BCC][693]

---

691 Nearly similar symbols can be found on 10v4_ACC, 12v1_BCC, 12v1_ACC, 14v3_BCC, 14v3_ACC, 16v1_BCC, 24v2_BCC, 26r2_BCC, 26r2_ACC, 28v5_BCC, 28v5_ACC, 29r5_BCC, 29r5_ACC, 33v1_BCC, 34v3_ACC, 36r1_ACC, 37v4_ACC, 40v3_ACC, 46v4_BCC, 46v4_ACC, 48r2_ACC, 48v3_BCC, 48v4_ACC, 49v4_ACC, 50v4_ACC, 52r5_BCC, 52r5_ACC, 53v4_BCC, 53v4_ACC, 55v4_BCC, 55v4_ACC, 61r5_BCC, 61r5_ACC, 62v3_ACC, 65v2_BCC, 65v3_ACC, 68r2_BCC, 68r2_ACC, 72r2_BCC, 72r2_ACC, 74v5_BCC, 77v1_ACC, 78r5_BCC, 78r5_ACC, 80r3_BCC, 80r3_ACC, 82v5_BCC, 85v3_ACC, 87r5_BCC, 87r5_ACC, 88v1_BCC, 90r5_BCC, 90r5_ACC, 93r4_BCC, 93r4_ACC, 94r3_BCC, 96v3_BCC, 96v3_ACC, 99r4_BCC, 99r4_ACC, 101r4_BCC, 101r5_ACC, 103r1_BCC, 103r1_ACC, 103v5_BCC, 103v5_ACC, 105v4_BCC, 105v5_ACC, 108r1_ACC, 109r4_BCC, 109r4_ACC, 111v3_ACC, 115r1_ACC, 116r3_BCC, 116r3_ACC, 116v5_BCC, 117r1_ACC, 120r5_BCC, 120r5_ACC, 121v3_BCC, 121v3_ACC, 124r4_BCC, 124r5_ACC 125v3_BCC, 125v3_ACC, 128r1_BCC, 128r1_ACC, 129v5_ACC, 132r1_BCC, 132r2_ACC, 136v1_ACC, 138v2_BCC, 138v2_ACC, 140r4_ACC, 141v2_BCC, 141v2_ACC, 143r1_BCC, 143r1_ACC, 145r4_ACC, 147v5_BCC, 147v5_ACC, 149v1_ACC, 151v2_ACC, 157v3_BCC, 157v3_ACC, 159v2_BCC, 159v3_ACC, 160r4_BCC, 160r4_ACC, 161r2_BCC, 161r2_ACC, 164v4_BCC 164v4_ACC, 165v5_BCC, 165v5_ACC, 168v5_BCC, 168v5_ACC, 170r2_BCC, 170r2_ACC, 172v2_BCC, 172v2_ACC, 175v1_BCC, 175v1_ACC, 178r5_BCC, 178r5_ACC, 180r1_ACC, 181v4_BCC, 181v4_ACC, 182v1_BCC, 182v1_ACC, 183v2_BCC, 183v2_ACC, 184v2_BCC, 184v2_ACC, 191r3_ACC, 189v1_BCC, 189v1_ACC, 190v2_ACC, 193v2_BCC, 193v2_ACC, 195r2_BCC, 195r2_ACC, 196r1_BCC, 196r1_ACC, 197v3_BCC, 197v3_ACC, 200v4_ACC, 203v4_BCC, 203v4_ACC, 204v1_BCC, 204v1_ACC, 205r4_BCC, 205r4_ACC, 206r5_BCC, 206r5_ACC, 207r4_BCC, 207r4_ACC, 208r1_BCC, 208r1_ACC, 209r3_BCC, 209r3_ACC, 210r5_BCC, 221r1_BCC, 236v3_BCC, 236v3_ACC, 243r1_BCC, 243v2_ACC, 245r2_ACC, 246v1_BCC, 246v1_ACC, 248r4_BCC, 249v3_ACC, 251r3_BCC, 251r3_ACC, 252v5_BCC, 252v5_ACC, 255r4_BCC, 255r4_ACC, 255v5_BCC, 256v2_BCC, 257v2_BCC, 257v2_ACC, 259v5_BCC, 259v5_ACC, 264r3_BCC, 264r3_ACC, 269r4_BCC, 269r4_ACC, 270r2_BCC, 270r2_ACC, 271r3_ACC, 272v5_BCC, 272v5_ACC, 273r5_ACC, 273v5_BCC, 273v5_ACC, 275v2_BCC, 275v2_ACC, 276r1_BCC, 276r1_ACC, 279r2_BCC, 279r2_ACC, 279v4_BCC, 279v4_ACC, 281r4_BCC, 283r5_ACC, 284v5_BCC, 284v5_ACC, 286r2_BCC, 286r2_ACC, 287v4_BCC, 289v2_BCC, 289v2_ACC, 290v3_BCC, 290v3_ACC, 291v5_BCC, 291v5_ACC, 292v2_BCC, 292v2_ACC, 293r4_BCC, 293r4_ACC, 296r3_BCC, 296r3_ACC, 297v2_BCC, 297v2_ACC, 301r4_BCC, 301r4_ACC, 302r4_BCC, 302r4_ACC, 304r1_BCC, 304r2_ACC, 307v1_BCC, 307v1_ACC, 310r3_BCC, 310r3_ACC, 323v2_BCC, 326v5_BCC, 326v5_ACC, 330r4_BCC, 330r4_ACC, 332v3_BCC, 332v3_ACC, 333v5_BCC, 333v5_ACC, 334r3_BCC, 334r3_ACC, 335v4_BCC, 335v4_ACC, 336v1_BCC, 336v1_ACC, 337r2_BCC, 337r2_ACC, 338v1_BCC, 338v1_ACC, 339r5_BCC, 339r5_ACC, 340r3_BCC, 340r3_ACC,

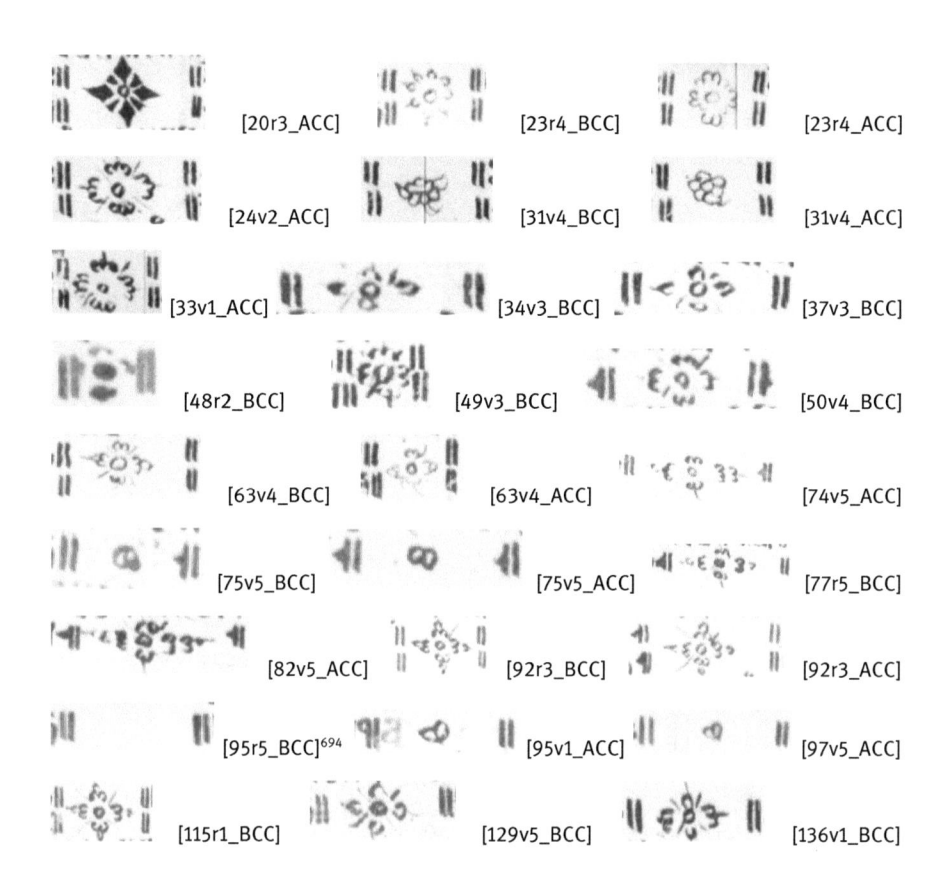

[20r3_ACC]

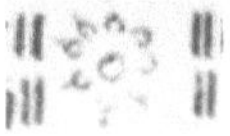
[23r4_BCC]

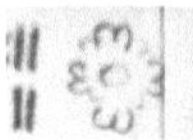
[23r4_ACC]

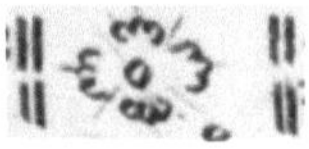
[24v2_ACC]

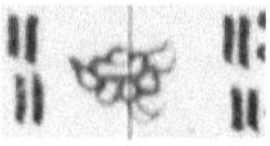
[31v4_BCC]

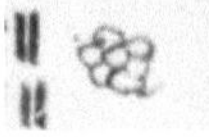
[31v4_ACC]

[33v1_ACC]

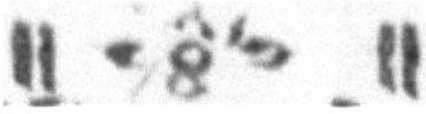
[34v3_BCC]

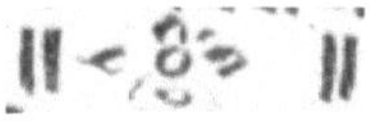
[37v3_BCC]

[48r2_BCC]

[49v3_BCC]

[50v4_BCC]

[63v4_BCC]

[63v4_ACC]

[74v5_ACC]

[75v5_BCC]

[75v5_ACC]

[77r5_BCC]

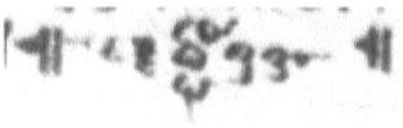
[82v5_ACC]

[92r3_BCC]

[92r3_ACC]

[95r5_BCC][694]

[95v1_ACC]

[97v5_ACC]

[115r1_BCC]

[129v5_BCC]

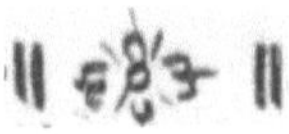
[136v1_BCC]

340v4_BCC, 340v4_ACC, 342r4_BCC, 342r4_ACC, 343r4_BCC, 343r4_ACC, 345r4_BCC, 345r5_ACC, 347r2_BCC, 347r3_ACC, 349r1_ACC, 352v2_BCC, 352v3_ACC, 355r1_BCC, 355r1_ACC, 356v4_BCC, 356v4_ACC, 358v1_BCC, 358v1_ACC, 361r3_BCC, 361r3_ACC, 365v4_BCC, 365v4_ACC, 367v4_BCC, 367v4_ACC, 370r2_BCC, 370r3_ACC, 371r5_BCC, 372r5_BCC, 372r5_ACC, 373v2_BCC, 376r3_BCC, 376r3_ACC, 379v1_BCC, 379v1_ACC, 380v3_BCC, 380v4_ACC, 382v4_BCC, 382v4_ACC, 385r4_BCC, 385r4_ACC, 388r3_BCC, 388r3_ACC, 389r5_BCC, 389v1_ACC, 390v5_BCC, 390v5_ACC, 393v5_BCC, 398r3_BCC, 398r3_ACC, 401r2_BCC, 401r2_ACC, 403r1_BCC, 403r2_ACC, 405r5_BCC, 405r5_ACC, 407v2_BCC, 407v2_ACC, 409v2_ACC, 411v1_BCC, 411v2_ACC.

692 Blank spaces occupying an area of two lines in height on folio can be found on 8r1_ACC, 69r1_BCC, 69r2_ACC, 133v1_ACC, 256r1_ACC.

693 A few circles appear on 40v3_BCC, 62v3_BCC, 108r1_BCC, 111v3_BCC, 190v1_BCC, 256v2_ACC, 260r4_BCC, 260r4_ACC, 261v5_BCC, 261v5_ACC, 305r2_BCC, 371r5_ACC, 373v2_ACC, 393v5_ACC.

694 A few blank spaces occupying an area of one line in height on folio can be found on 85v3_BCC, 133r5_BCC, 149r5_BCC, 151v2_BCC, 154r5_BCC, 154r5_ACC, 179v5_BCC, 186v5_BCC, 243v1_BCC, 265r5_BCC, 267r4_BCC, 273r5_BCC, 351r5_BCC, 351r5_ACC.

 [140r4_BCC] 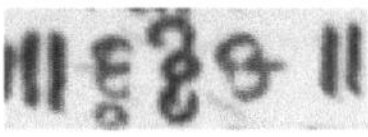 [145r4_BCC] 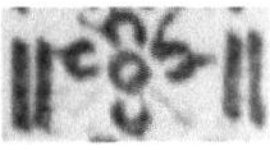 [200v4_BCC]

 [210r5_ACC] 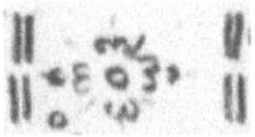 [243r1_ACC]

 [249v3_BCC]  [271r3_BCC]  [281r4_ACC]

 [283r4_BCC]  [287v4_ACC] 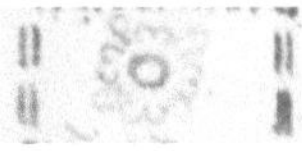 [305r2_ACC]

 [416r1_PC][695]  [416r1_PC] 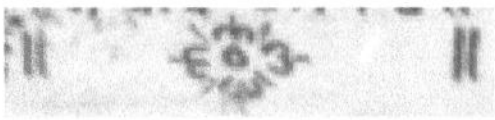 [416r5_ADL]

Symbols around string-holes

 [204v_LSH]  [204v_RSH]

695 This symbol and the following *siddham* appear in the post colophonic part.

Manuscript SDhPS (ca. 12th c.)

Symbols and blank spaces

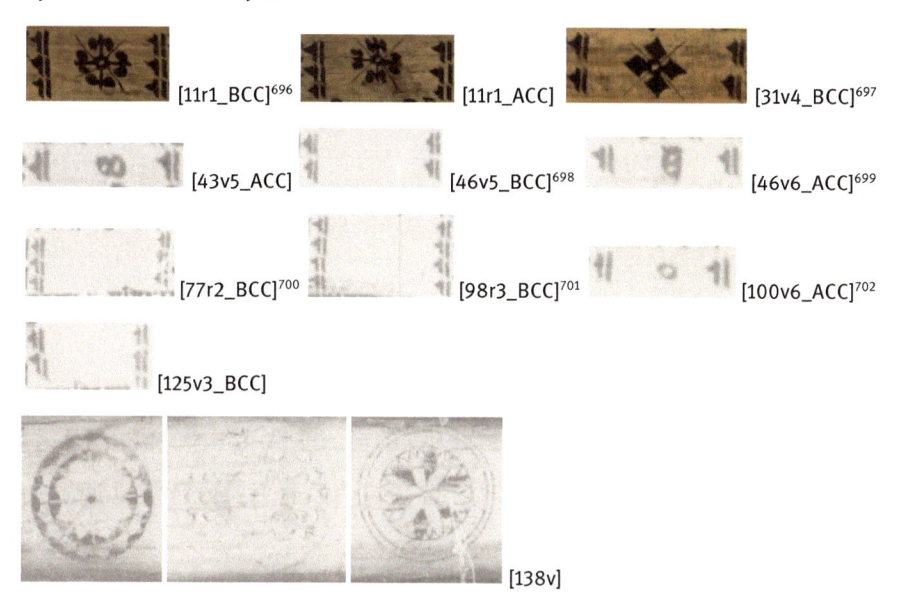

[11r1_BCC][696]

[11r1_ACC]

[31v4_BCC][697]

[43v5_ACC]

[46v5_BCC][698]

[46v6_ACC][699]

[77r2_BCC][700]

[98r3_BCC][701]

[100v6_ACC][702]

[125v3_BCC]

[138v]

696 Nearly similar symbols can be found on 20r1_BCC, 20r1_ACC, 31v4_ACC, 36v6_BCC, 36v6_ACC, 43v4_BCC, 65r2_ACC, 69r1_ACC, 77r3_ACC, 79r3_BCC, 89v6_ACC, 106v5_BCC, 113v5_BCC.
697 A similar symbol appears on 69r1_BCC.
698 Similar blank spaces occupying an area of two lines in height are on 58v3_ACC, 93v2_BCC.
699 Further *tha* symbols can be found on 58v2_BCC, 62v4_BCC, 62v4_ACC, 79r3_ACC, 84v2_ACC, 89v6_BCC, 93v2_ACC, 100v5_BCC, 110r5_ACC, 113v5_ACC, 134v4_BCC, 134v4_ACC.
700 See blank spaces on 84v2_BCC, 125v3_BCC, 130r4_ACC. These blank spaces occupy an area of only two lines in height, although they are demarcated by three sets of the double *daṇḍa*s in height on folios.
701 Further blank spaces are on 98r3_ACC, 110r4_BCC, 116r1_ACC, 125v3_ACC, 130r4_BCC, 138r2_BCC, 138r2_ACC. These blank spaces occupy an area of only three lines in height, although they are demarcated by four sets of the double *daṇḍa*s on folios.
702 Further circles appear on 106v5_ACC, 116r1_BCC.

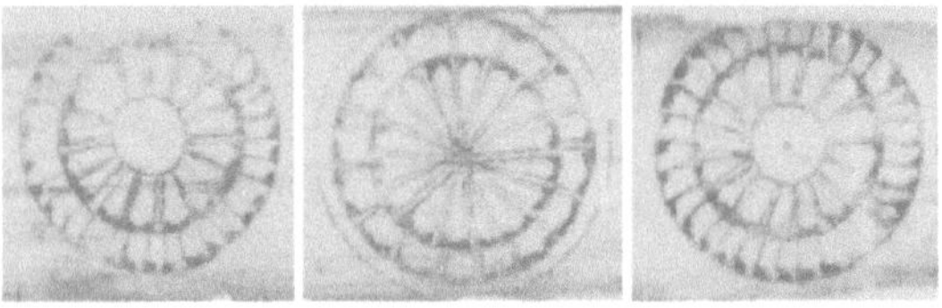

[139r]

[139v]

Manuscript AṣP$_2$ (ca. 12th c.)

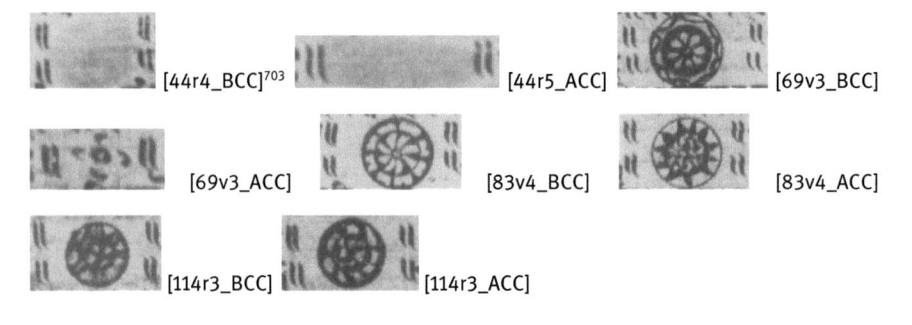

Symbols and blank spaces

 [44r4_BCC][703]  [44r5_ACC] 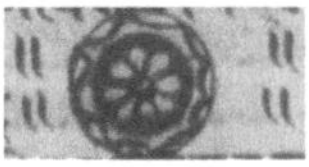 [69v3_BCC]

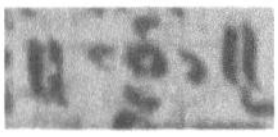 [69v3_ACC] 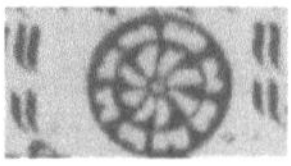 [83v4_BCC] 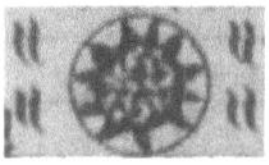 [83v4_ACC]

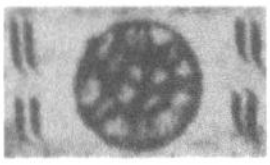 [114r3_BCC] 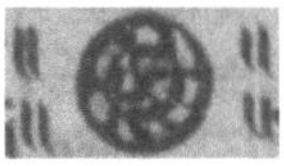 [114r3_ACC]

703 Blank spaces occupying an area of two lines in height appear on 145r3_BCC, 145r3_ACC. Both blank spaces on this folio and on 145r3 seem to have been highlighted.

Manuscript SS (1216 CE)

Symbols and blank spaces

 [1v1_SI]  [6v5_ACC][704]  [8v5_ACC][705]

 [30v4_ACC][706]  [43v5_ACC][707]  [99r3_ACC]

---

704 Further blank spaces occupying an area of two lines in height on folios can be found on 6v5_AAL, 7v4_AAL, 73v3_AAL, 89v2_ACC.

705 A majority of blank spaces occupying an area of one line in height appear on 11r2_ACC, 12r3_ACC, 12r5_ACC, 12v6_ACC, 13v5_ACC, 15r5_ACC, 15r5_AAL, 16v1_ACC, 17r4_ACC, 17r5_AAL, 17v1_ACC, 17v3_ACC, 17v7_ACC, 18r2_ACC, 18v2_ACC, 21v2_ACC, 21v2_BAL, 21v3_BAL, 22r4_ACC, 22v5_ACC, 23r2_ACC, 24r4_ACC, 24v4_ACC, 24v7_ACC, 25r2_ACC, 25v5_ACC, 26v1_ACC, 27v1_ACC, 27v6_ACC, 28v3_ACC, 29v1_ACC, 29v1_ACC, 31r5_ACC, 31v7_ACC, 33r3_ACC, 33r3_AAL, 34v6_ACC, 35r4_ACC, 35v2 (before mantra), 35v3_ACC, 36v6_ACC, 37r4_ACC, 37r7_AAL, 38r4_ACC, 39r2_ACC, 42v7_ACC, 44r5_ACC, 45r2_ACC, 46v2_ACC, 49v2_ACC, 54r2_ACC, 59r1_ACC, 61r3_ACC, 63v1_ACC, 100v3_ACC, 109v1_ACC, 113r3_ACC, 115v4_ACC, 115v4_AAL, 115v5_ACC, 117r5_ACC, 126r4_ACC, 126v1_ACC, 127r3_ACC, 182v1_ACC, 192r6_AAL, 193v7_ACC, 194v7_ACC, 203v3_ACC, 205r3_ACC, 207r1_AAL, 208v5_AAL, 209r1_ACC, 209v1_ACC, 210r6_ACC, 211r1_ACC, 212r1_ACC, 212v1_ACC, 213r2_ACC, 213v7_ACC, 214r5_AAC, 214v4_ACC, 215r6_ACC, 216r5_ACC, 216v6_ACC, 218r5_ACC, 218r7_ACC, 219r3_ACC, 219v6_ACC, 220v2_ACC, 221r6_ACC, 223r2_AAL, 228r4_ACC, 228r4_AAL, 228r5 (after the donor phrase '*deyadharmo* …').

706 Similar *siddham* symbols appear on 40r1_ACC, 41r5_ACC, 41v7_ACC, 44v1_ACC, 47v1_ACC, 50r2_ACC, 51r4_ACC, 51v2_ACC, 52v3_ACC, 53r3_BAL, 53r3_AAL, 53r4_ACC, 53r7_ACC, 53v1_ACC, 53v6_ACC, 55r4_ACC, 56r1_ACC, 57r1_ACC, 59v7_ACC, 60v6_ACC, 62v3_ACC, 62v6_ACC, 63r2_ACC, 63r6_ACC, 65v1_ACC, 67v3_ACC, 68r7_ACC, 68r7_AAL, 70v3_AAL, 73v1_ACC, 74r3_ACC, 74r6_ACC, 75r4_ACC, 75v1_ACC, 76r1_ACC, 76r6_BCC, 76r6_ACC, 76v3_ACC, 77r2_ACC, 78r3_ACC, 78r7_ACC, 83v2_ACC, 83v2_AAL, 84r2_ACC, 84v4_BCC, 84v4_ACC, 85r1_ACC, 85r7_ACC, 86v3_ACC, 87r2_ACC, 87r5_ACC, 87v1_ACC, 88v1_ACC, 89r1_ACC, 89v3_ACC, 90v4_ACC, 92r6_ACC, 93r6_ACC, 94r2_ACC, 94r6_ACC, 94v6_ACC, 94v6_AAL, 95r6_ACC, 95v3_ACC, 95v7_ACC, 96v2_ACC, 96r6_ACC, 97v7_ACC, 98v4_ACC, 100r4_ACC, 101r4_ACC, 102r1_ACC, 102r7_ACC, 105r3_AAL, 105v1_ACC, 105r6_ACC, 107v3_ACC, 108v1_ACC, 108v7_ACC, 109r5_ACC, 110r2_ACC, 110v1_ACC, 110v1_ACC, 111r1_ACC, 111r7_ACC, 113v3_ACC, 114r2_ACC, 116v2_ACC, 117v1_ACC, 119r6_ACC, 119v2_ACC, 120r7_ACC, 120v5_ACC, 120v7_ACC, 122v1_ACC, 123v6_ACC, 124r7_ACC, 125r5_AAL, 125v3_ACC, 133r1_ACC, 136v1_ACC, 137v1_ACC, 139r5_ACC, 139r5_AAL, 139v4_ACC, 140v7_ACC, 140v7_AAL, 141v1_ACC, 143r2_ACC, 143v2_ACC, 143v6_ACC, 144r3_ACC, 144r7_ACC, 144v5_ACC, 145v1_ACC, 146r1_ACC, 146r3_ACC, 146r7_ACC, 146v1_ACC, 146v2_ACC, 147r2_ACC, 152r4_ACC, 152r7_ACC, 152v5_ACC, 153v6_ACC, 153v6_AAL, 154v5_ACC, 155v3_ACC, 157r1_ACC, 157r4_ACC, 157r7_ACC, 157v3_ACC, 158v6_ACC, 158v6_AAL, 162r4_ACC, 164v2_ACC, 165v1_ACC, 166r1_ACC, 168v2_ACC, 169r1_ACC, 169r4_ACC,

Manuscript TS$_2$ (ca. 13th c.)

Symbols

 [1v1_BI]  [25r5_BCC][708]  [25r6_ACC][709]

169r7_AAL, 170r3_ACC, 170v2_ACC, 171r1_ACC, 171v3_ACC, 175v1_BCC, 175v1_ACC, 176v4_ACC, 176v5_AAL, 177r7_ACC, 178r7_ACC, 178v5_ACC, 178v6_ACC, 179r2_ACC, 180v1_ACC, 184r5_ACC, 184r7_ACC, 185v1_ACC, 188v1_ACC, 188v1_AAL, 189v1_ACC, 189v1_AAL, 190v3_ACC, 190v3_AAL, 192r1_ACC, 193r4_ACC, 193r7_BCC, 193r7_ACC, 194r6_ACC, 194v2_ACC, 195v5_ACC, 196r3_ACC, 200v3_ACC, 201r5_AAL, 201v5_ACC, 203v4_ACC.

707 A few circles can be found on 49v4_ACC, 49v7_ACC, 223r4_ACC, 224r2_ACC, 224r4_ACC, 224r5_ACC, 225r2_ACC, 225v2_ACC, 226r2_ACC, 226v1_ACC.

708 Further circles can be found on 47r5_BCC, 51v2_BCC, 73r6_ACC, 78v5_ACC, 106r4_BCC.

709 Identical symbols appear on 33r4_B/ACC (the chapter colophon starts after the upper double *daṇḍa* of the symbol in line no. 4 and ends exactly in the lower double double *daṇḍa* in line no. 5 of the same symbol, therefore there is no other symbol after the chapter colophon), 43v6_BCC, 44r1_ACC, 47r5_ACC, 51v3_ACC, 64v1_ACC, 73r5_BCC, 78v4_BCC, 106r5_ACC.

II. List of selected symbols and blank spaces in East Indian manuscripts

Manuscript PR (1054 CE)

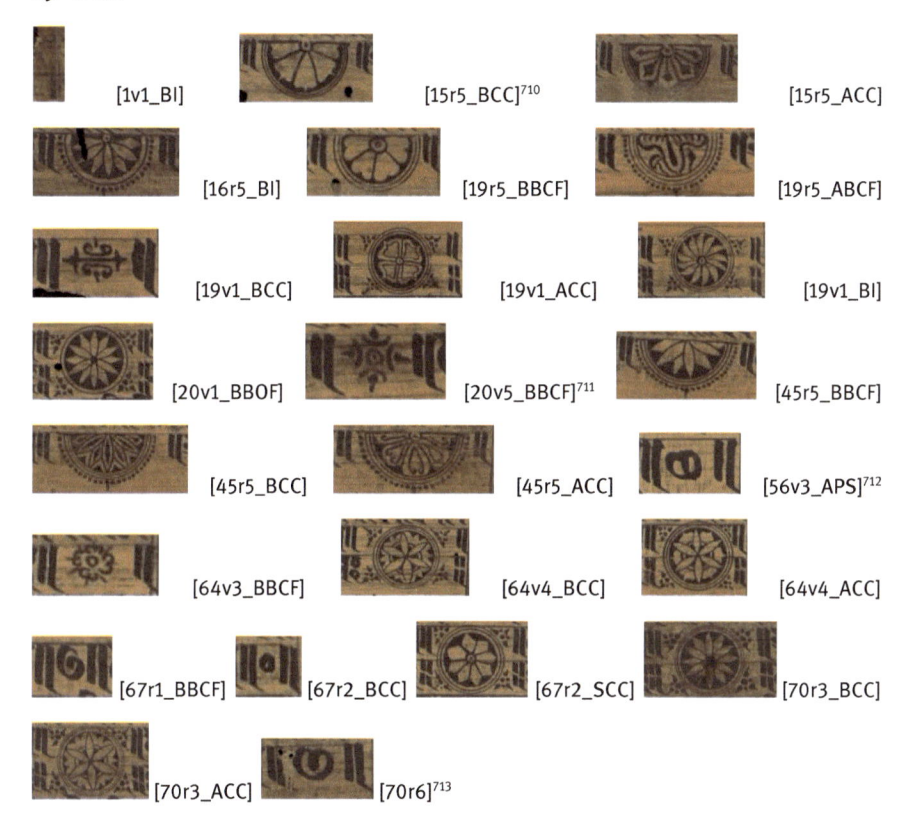

Symbols

 [1v1_BI]
 [15r5_BCC][710]
 [15r5_ACC]

 [16r5_BI]
 [19r5_BBCF]
 [19r5_ABCF]

 [19v1_BCC]
 [19v1_ACC]
 [19v1_BI]

 [20v1_BBOF]
 [20v5_BBCF][711]
 [45r5_BBCF]

 [45r5_BCC]
 [45r5_ACC]
 [56v3_APS][712]

 [64v3_BBCF]
 [64v4_BCC]
 [64v4_ACC]

 [67r1_BBCF]
 [67r2_BCC]
 [67r2_SCC]
 [70r3_BCC]

 [70r3_ACC]
 [70r6][713]

710 Similar types of stylised 'half' *puṣpikās* can be found on 18r7, 26v6, 77v7, 98v7, 144r7, 158r7 in the Nepalese manuscript of the *Aṣṭasahasrikā Prajñāpāramitā* (NS 268 / 1148 CE) (Museum für Asiatische Kunst, Berlin, I 5410 & I 5411 and Asiatic Society, Calcutta, G.4203), see Melzer/Allinger 2010, 6–7.
711 Nearly identical symbols appear in TS₂.
712 Symbols like this appear after verse lines in this manuscript.
713 This symbol appears after the Buddhist donor phrase.

Manuscript AAĀ (ca. 11th c.)

Symbols and blank spaces

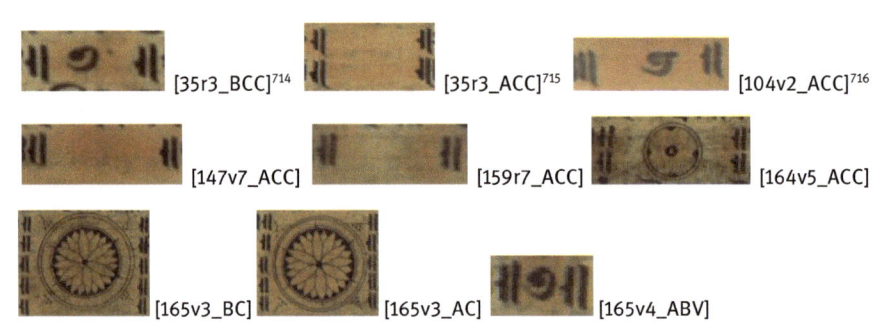

 [35r3_BCC][714]  [35r3_ACC][715]  [104v2_ACC][716]

 [147v7_ACC]  [159r7_ACC]  [164v5_ACC]

 [165v3_BC]  [165v3_AC]  [165v4_ABV]

Manuscript GV (ca. 12th c.)

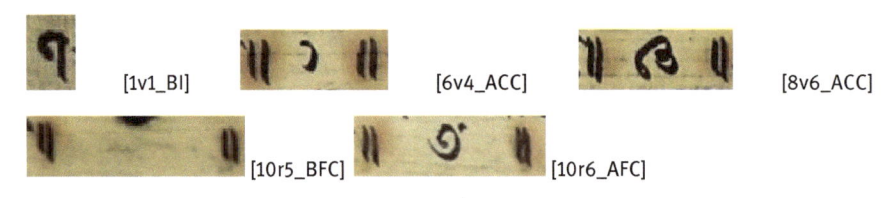

Symbols and blank space

 [1v1_BI]  [6v4_ACC]  [8v6_ACC]

 [10r5_BFC]  [10r6_AFC]

714 Further nearly similar symbols can be found on 48v4_BCC, 61r2_BCC, 83r3_BCC, 84v5_BCC, 93v2_BCC, 96r4_BCC, 104v2_BCC, 127r6_BCC, 132r2_BCC, 134r4_BCC, 135v6_BCC, 144r1_BCC, 156v1_BCC, 165v4_ABV.

715 See further blank spaces on 48v4_ACC, 61r3_ACC, 64r1_ACC, 66v4_ACC, 74r5_BCC, 74r6_ACC, 78r2_BCC, 78r2_ACC, 83r3_ACC, 84v5_ACC, 88r5_BCC, 88r5_ACC, 93v2_ACC, 96r4_ACC, 102r2_BCC 102r2_ACC, 103r2_BCC, 103r3_ACC, 108r2_BCC, 108r2_ACC, 119r3_BCC, 119r3_ACC, 123v7_ACC, 127r6_ACC, 132r2_ACC, 134r4_ACC, 135v6_ACC, 139r3_ACC, 141r5_ACC, 156v2_ACC, 164r2_ACC.

716 Similar symbols can be found on 79r7_BCC, 123v7_BCC, 144r1_ACC.

Manuscript HAP (ca. 12th c.)

Symbols and blank spaces

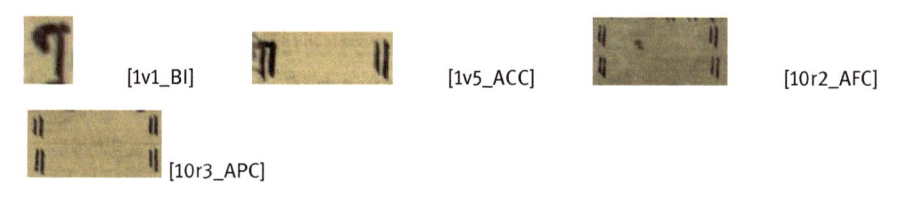

 [1v1_BI]  [1v5_ACC]  [10r2_AFC]

 [10r3_APC]

Manuscript LTṬ (ca. 12th c.)

Symbols and blank spaces

 [1v1_BI]  [3r3_ACC][717]  [5r6_APS]

 [30v2_AC]

Manuscript STṬ (ca. 12th c.)

Symbols and blank spaces

 [1v1_BI]  [2v1_ACC][718]  [3r1_ACC][719]

 [5v7_ACC]  [6r1_ACC] 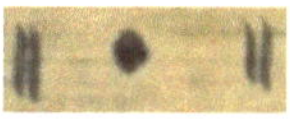 [7r2_ACC]

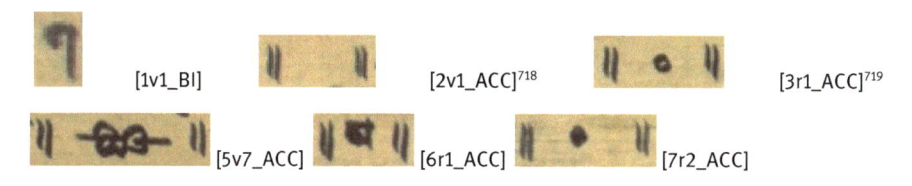

717 Further circles appear on 4v2_APS, 14v1_ACC.
718 The other blank space appears on 6r3_ACC.
719 Further circles can be found on 3v1_ACC, 3v6_ACC, 4r3_ACC, 4r6_ACC, 4v5_ACC, 5r1_ACC, 5r1_ACC, 6r2_ACC, 6r2_ACC, 6r3_ACC, 6r6_ACC, 6r6_ACC, 6v2_ACC, 6v5_ACC, 6v5_ACC, 7r1_ACC, 9v1_ACC, 9v3_ACC, 10r4_ACC, 10r6_ACC, 10r7_ACC, 10v1_ACC, 11r6_ACC, 11r7_ACC, 11v1_ACC, 11v3_ACC, 11v4_ACC, 11v5_ACC, 11v6_ACC, 11v7_ACC, 11v7_ACC.

Manuscript ḌVPṬ (ca. 12th c.)

Symbols

 [1v1_BI]  [2v5_ACC][720]  [6r1_ACC]

 [7r4_ACC]

Manuscript AP (ca. 12th c.)

Symbols and blank spaces

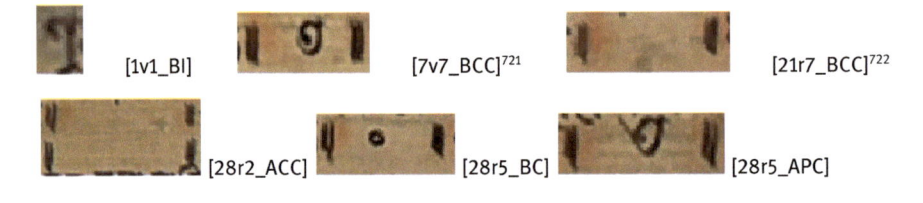

 [1v1_BI]  [7v7_BCC][721]  [21r7_BCC][722]

 [28r2_ACC] 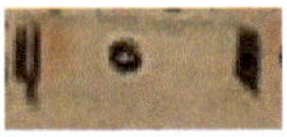 [28r5_BC]  [28r5_APC]

720 Further circles can be found on 3r4_ACC, 3r6_ACC, 5r5_ACC, 5v4_ACC, 6v1_ACC, 6v6_ACC, 7r4_ACC, 7r6_ACC, 7v1_ACC, 7v2_ACC, 8v2_ACC, 8v3_ACC.

721 Similar symbols appear on 7v7_ACC, 9v3_BCC, 9v3_ACC, 13v3_BCC, 13v3_ACC, 14r5_ACC, 21v6_ACC.

722 Further blank spaces occupying an area of one line can be found on 21v1_ACC, 22r3_ACC, 22v7_ACC, 23r2_ACC, 23v2_ACC, 27v7_B/ACC, 28r2_BCC, 28r5_AC.

Manuscript CPN (ca. 12th c.)

Symbols and blank spaces

[1v1_BI]

[7v1_ACC][723]

[13v7_ACC][724]
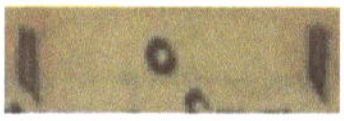
[49v1_BCC]

Manuscript HP (ca. 12th c.)

Symbols and blank spaces

[1v1_BI]

[4v7_ACC]

[5v4_ACC][725]

[23r1_AC]

723 Further blank spaces occupying an area of two lines in height can be found on 12v4_ACC, 19v4_ACC, 19v4_ACC, 25v4_ACC, 31r1_ACC, 32r7_ACC, 48r2_ACC, 50v4_ACC, 53v6_BCC, 53v6_ACC.

724 See on 33r7_ACC, 49v1_ACC, 52v7_ACC.

725 Further blank spaces occupying an area of one line in height appear on 6v3_ACC, 6v5_ACC, 8r5_ACC, 9r1_ACC, 9v2_ACC, 13r3_ACC, 14r2_ACC, 14v5_ACC, 15r1_ACC, 15r3_ACC, 17r1_ACC, 18r1_ACC, 21r4_ACC, 22r3_ACC, 22r4_ACC, 22r5_ACC, 22r7_ACC, 22v4_ACC, 22v6_ACC, 23r1_BC.

Manuscript HTṬ (ca. 12th c.)

Symbols

 [20v1_ACC]  [40r6_ACC][726]  [48r6_ACC]

 [51v3_ACC]  [58v4_BFC]  [58v5_AC]

 [58v6_APC]

Manuscript AT (ca. 12th c.)

Symbols

 [?v3_BCC]  [?v3_ACC]  [?v3_BI]

 [?v2_ACC]

726 One circle can be found on 51v3_BCC.

III. List of selected symbols in West Indian manuscripts

Manuscript TSa (1143 CE)

Symbols

 [1v1_BI]  [3r6_ACC][727]  [187v5_ACC]

Symbols around string-holes

 [10r_SH]  [10v_SH]

Symbols with foliations

 [10v_WF]  [20v_WF]

727 Further *cha* symbols appear on 5v2_BCC, 5v2_ACC, 7r3_BCC, 7r4_ACC, 8v2_ACC, 11v2_BCC, 11v3_ACC, 12r5_BCC, 12r5_ACC, 14v2_BCC, 14v2_ACC, 15v4_BCC, 15v5_ACC, 16v3_ACC, 17r2_ACC, 17v3_ACC, 27v3_ACC, 31v6_ACC, 34v5_ACC, 35v3_ACC, 43v1_ACC, 83r3_ACC, 99v6_ACC, 144v3_ACC, 159v5_BCC, 159v6_ACC, 187v5_BC, 187v5_AC, 187v5_B/AB.

Manuscript TSPV (1143 CE)

Symbols

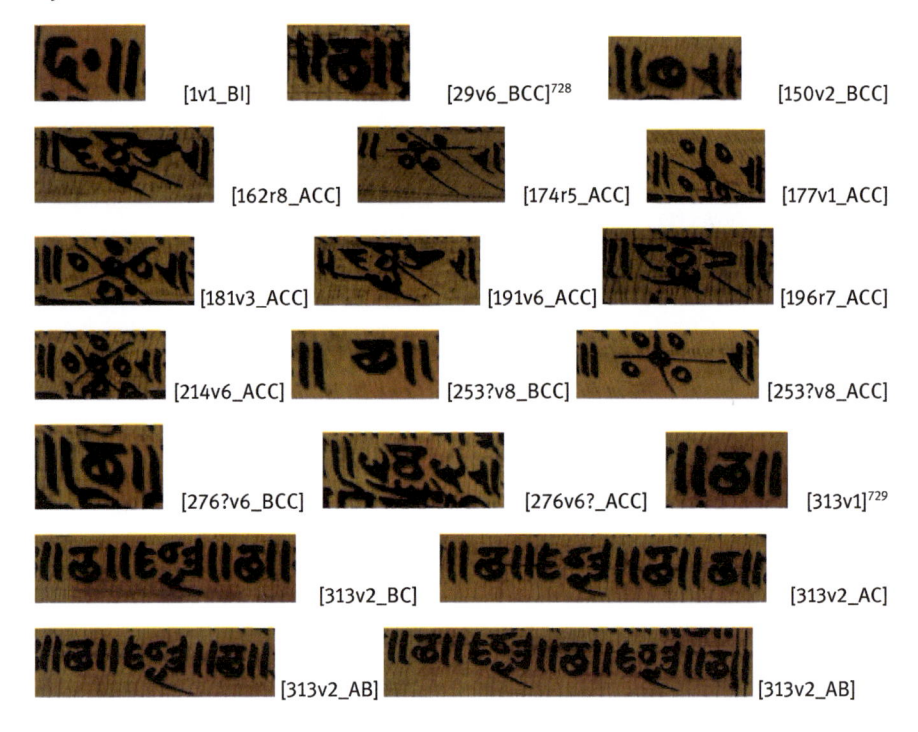

 [1v1_BI]  [29v6_BCC][728]  [150v2_BCC]

 [162r8_ACC]  [174r5_ACC]  [177v1_ACC]

 [181v3_ACC]  [191v6_ACC]  [196r7_ACC]

 [214v6_ACC]  [253?v8_BCC] 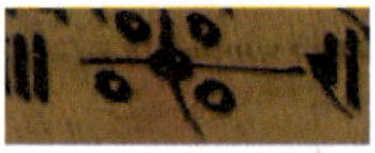 [253?v8_ACC]

 [276?v6_BCC]  [276v6?_ACC]  [313v1][729]

 [313v2_BC]  [313v2_AC]

 [313v2_AB]  [313v2_AB]

Symbols around string-holes

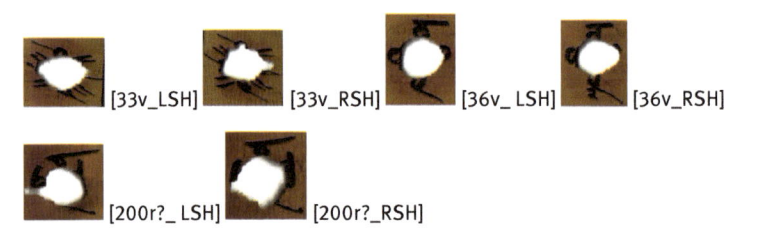

 [33v_LSH]  [33v_RSH]  [36v_ LSH]  [36v_RSH]

 [200r?_ LSH]  [200r?_RSH]

728 Further *cha* symbols can be found on 29v6_ACC, 80r8_BCC, 118r4_BCC, 118r4_ACC, 150v2_ACC, 181v3_BCC, 191v6_BCC, 196r7_BCC, 205v2_BCC, 205v2_ACC, 214v6_BCC.

729 This appears before a particular verse at the end.

Symbols with foliations

 [40v_WF]  [90v_WF]

Manuscript HVM (1171 CE)

Symbols

 [1v1_BI]  [3r2_BCC][730]  [3r2_ACC][731]

 [6v2_ACC][732]  [7v4_ACC][733]  [24v1_ACC]

 [31v4_ACC][734]  [36v7_ACC]  [38v4_ACC]

 [61r7_ACC][735]

---

730 Similar symbols can be found on 4v3_BCC, 7v3_BCC, 10v7_BCC, 15r5_BCC, 16v4_BCC, 18r2_BCC, 19v1_BCC, 22v2_BCC, 24v1_BCC, 26v5_BCC, 29v4_BCC, 31v4_BCC, 34v1_BCC, 36v7_BCC, 38v4_BCC, 41r2_BCC, 42v5_BCC, 44v3_BCC, 46v3_BCC, 47v4_BCC, 49r2_BCC, 53r1_BCC, 54v2_BCC, 57r6_BCC, 58v7_BCC, 61r7_BCC, 63r2_BCC, 64v6_BCC, 66r5_BCC, 68r4_BCC, 69v5_BCC, 71r4_BCC, 73r1_BCC, 75r2_BCC, 76v3_BCC, 78v2_BCC, 80v4_BCC, 82r2_BCC, 88v3_BCC, 90v4_BCC, 92v1_BCC, 94r7_BCC, 102v2_BCC, 104r2_BCC, 106v2_BCC.

731 Similar symbols appear on 4v3_ACC, 11r1_ACC, 15r5_ACC, 16v5_ACC, 22v3_ACC, 26v5_ACC, 41r2_ACC, 47v4_ACC, 54v2_ACC, 57r6_ACC, 68r4_ACC, 69v5_ACC, 71r4_BCC, 73r1_ACC, 78v2_ACC, 80v4_ACC, 82r2_ACC, 88v3_ACC, 106v2_ACC, 107v1_AC, 107v1_ADL.

732 A similar set of symbols can be found on 66r5_ACC, 102v3_ACC, 107v1_BC, 107v1_AB.

733 A similar set of symbols appears on 29v4_ACC, 42v5_ACC, 46v3_ACC, 53r1_ACC, 63r2_ACC, 64v6_ACC, 76v4_ACC, 90v4_ACC, 94r7_ACC, 104r2_ACC.

734 Similar symbols appear on 34v1_ACC, 44v4_ACC, 92v1_ACC.

735 Similar sets of symbols can be found on 18r2_ACC, 49r2_ACC, 75r3_ACC.

Symbols around string-holes

 [20v_LSH]  [20v_RSH]

Symbols with foliations

 [10v_WF]  [80v_WF]

Manuscript PV (12th c.)

Symbols

 [10r4_BCC][736]  [10v6_ACC]  [15v1_ACC]

 [24v2_ACC]  [41r3_ACC]  [44r2_ACC]

Symbols around string-holes

 [41v_SH]  [42r_SH]

736 Nearly similar symbols appear on 10r4_ACC, 10v5_BCC, 14r5_BCC, 18r4_BCC, 18r4_ACC, 18v5_BCC, 18v5_ACC, 24v2_BCC, 30v1_BCC, 30v2_ACC, 36r3_BCC, 36r3_ACC, 39r2_BCC, 39r2_ACC, 41v1_ACC, 48r3_BCC, 48r3_ACC, 50v5_BCC, 51r1_ACC, 52r3_BCC, 52r4_ACC, 54r1_ACC, 54r5_ACC, 55r2_ACC, 55v3_ACC, 56r4_BCC, 56r4_ACC, 56v3_ACC, 57r4_ACC, 57v2_ACC, 60r5_ACC, 66r1_ACC, 71v1_BCC, 71v1_ACC, 74r5_BCC, 74r5_ACC, 75v2_BCC, 75v3_ACC, 80v3_BCC, 80v4_ACC, 87r5_BCC, 87r5_ACC, 105v1_BCC, 105v2_ACC, 115r4_BCC, 115r5_ACC, 117r2_BCC, 117r2_ACC, 120v2_BCC, 120v3_ACC, 131r3_BCC, 131r3_ACC, 135v4_ACC, 135v3_BCC, 137r5_BCC, 137r5_ACC, 138v3_BCC, 138v3_ACC, 147r5_BCC, 147r5_ACC, 148v5_BC, 148v5_AC, 149r3_AC (second additional colophon), 149r3_AAL, 149v1_AI, 149v3_BI.

Manuscript JKS/C (1201 CE)

Symbols

 [9v6_ACC][737]  [67v1][738]

Symbols around string-holes

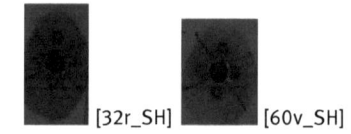

 [32r_SH]  [60v_SH]

Manuscript TUS (1292 CE)

Symbols

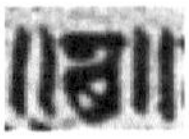 [33v2][739]  [176v3][740]

Symbols around string-holes

 [48v_SH] 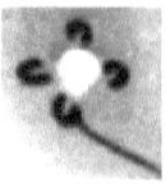 [160v_SH]

---

737 Further *cha* symbols can be found after smaller text units, at the end of the chapters etc. in the manuscript, for instance, on 2r2, 2r3, 5r2, 5r4, 7r2, 7r4, 9r1, 9r2, 9r5, 13r1, 18r1, 21r1, 21v1, 22r4, 23v4, 24r1, 27r5, 30v3, 31v4, 32r1, 32v5, 32v6, 33v1, 33v3, 33v4, 34r2, 34r3, 34r4, 34v4, 34v5, 35r2, 35v2, 36r1, 36v5, 37r1, 37r3, 37r4, 37r5, 37v2, 37v3, 37v4, 38v1, 39r1, 39v4, 40v3, 40v4, 42r2, 42r5, 43v6, 44v3, 45r4, 45v4, 46r6, 46v3, 48v3, 50r1, 50v3, 51r2, 52r5, 55v4, 56r4, 56v4, 57r2, 57v3, 58r3, 58v1, 58v3, 59r2, 60v5, 61r2, 61r4, 61v3, 62r1, 62r2, 62v4, 62v6, 63v5, 64r1, 65r1, 65r4, 65v4, 65v5, 66r3, 66v1, 66v5, 66v6, 67r5, 67v2 (type no. 47).

738 This can be found before the line of the date.

739 This symbol appears after a smaller text unit.

740 This symbol appears before the line of the date.

Manuscript BCV (ca. 13th c.)

Symbols

 [1v1_BI]  [77v5_AC][741]  [78r6_BB]

 [78r6_BB]

Symbols around string-holes

 [5r_SH]  [12r_SH]

Symbol with the foliation

 [10v_WF]

741 Further *cha* symbols can be found after smaller text units, at the end of the chapters etc. in the manuscript, for instance, on 1v7, 2r2, 2r3, 2v3, 2v6, 3v3, 3v5, 4r2, 4r3, 4r4, 7r4, 8v1, 8v2, 19r5, 20r1, 22r2, 33v2, 34v1, 34v2, 34v4, 35v2, 36v2, 37v4, 38r2, 39r3, 40v3, 41v1, 42r2, 43r5, 43v2, 43v5, 46v5, 48r3, 48r5, 48v2, 49r1, 49r2, 50r1, 50r6, 54v3, 55r3, 56r1, 56r3, 56v3, 57r2, 58r3, 58r6, 58v4, 59r2, 62v3, 63v6, 64v5, 65r2, 65r3, 65r5, 68r3, 68v3, 76r3, 76v1, 76v3, 77v5, 78r6) (type no. 47).

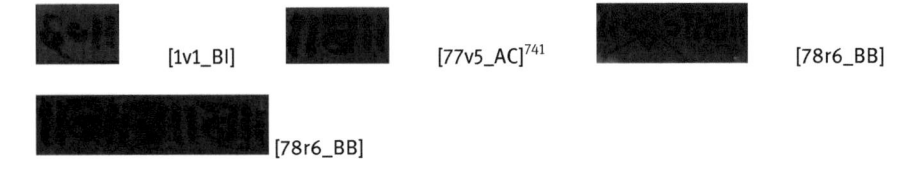

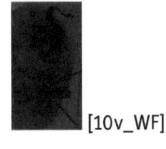

References

Acharya, Diwakar (2007), 'The Original Paṇhavāyaraṇa/Praśnavyākaraṇa Discovered', in *International Journal of Jain Studies*. Vol. 3, No. 6, 1–10.

Adriaensen, R., H.T. Bakker and H. Isaacson (eds) (1998), *The Skandapurāṇa. Volume I. Adhyāyas 1–25. Critically Edited with Prolegomena*. Groningen: Egbert Forsten.

Apte, V.S. (1957), *The Practical Sanskrit-English Dictionary*. Poona: Prasad Prakashan. (revised and enlarged edition).

Balbir, Nalini et al. (2006), *Catalogue of the Jain Manuscripts of the British Library*. Vols I–II. London: The British Library & The Institute of Jainology.

Bang, Jung-Lan (2017), *Selected Chapters from the* Tantrasadbhāva. *Based on the tradition of llth century Śaiva Sanskrit Manuscript in Nepal*. Hamburg: Universität Hamburg. (unpublished PhD dissertation).

Baums, Stefan (2014), 'Gandhāran Scrolls: Rediscovering an Ancient Manuscript Type', In Quenzer, Jörg B. et al. (eds), *Manuscript Cultures: Mapping the Field*. Studies in Manuscript Cultures 1. Berlin: De Gruyter, 183–225.

Bendall, Cecil (1883), *Catalogue of the Buddhist Sanskrit Manuscripts in the University Library*, Cambridge. Cambridge: University Press.

Bhattacharyya, Benoytosh (1925), *Sādhanamālā*. Vol. 1. Baroda: Central Library.

Bhattacharya, Gouriswar (1995), 'The bhale symbol of the Jainas', in *Berliner Indologische Studien* 8, 201–228.

Bhaṭṭarāī, Kṛṣṇaprasāda (ed.) (1988), *Skandapurāṇasya Ambikākhaṇḍaḥ*. Mahendraratnagranthamālā 2. Dang: Mahendra Sanskrit University.

Boucher, Daniel (1991), 'The Pratītyasamutpādagāthā and Its Role in the Medieval Cult of the Relics', in *Journal of the International Associationof Buddhist Studies* 14.1, 1–27.

Braarvig, Jens and Fredrik Liland (2010), *Traces of Gandhāran Buddhism. An Exhibition of Ancient Buddhist Manuscripts in the Schøyen Collection*. Oslo: Hermes Publishing.

Buescher, Hartmut (2011), *Catalogue of Sanskrit Manuscripts*. Copenhagen: NIAS Press.

Bühler, G. (1896), *Indische Palaeographie: von circa 350 A. Chr. circa 1300 P. Chr.* Strassburg: Trübner.

Caturvedi, Mahendra (1970), *A Practical Hindi-English Dictionary*. Delhi: National Publishing House.

Cicuzza, Claudio (ed.) (2001), *The Laghutantraṭīkā by Vajrapāṇi: A Critical Edition of the Sanskrit Text*. Serie Orientale Roma 86. Roma: Istituto Italiano per l'Oriente.

Conze, Edward (trans.) (1973), *The Perfection of Wisdom in Eight Thousand Lines & Its Verse Summary*. Delhi: Sri Satguru Publication. (Indian Repr.).

Das, JP (2007), *Chitra-pothi. Illustrated Palm-leaf Manuscripts from Orissa*. New Delhi: Niyogi Books.

Dani, Ahmad Hasan (1963), *Indian Palaeography*. Oxford: Clarendon Press.

Delhey, Martin et al. (2015), 'The Library at the East Indian Buddhist Monastery Vikramaśīla: An Attempt to Identify its Himalayan Remains', In *Manuscript Cultures*, 8: 2–24.

Delhey, Martin et al. (2015), 'Material Analysis of Sanskrit Palm-leaf Manuscripts Preserved in Nepal', in *Journal of the International Association of Buddhist Studies*, 36: 119–152.

Dimitrov, Dragomir (2016), *The Legacy of the Jewel Mind. On the Sanskrit, Pali, and Sinhalese Works by Ratnamati. A Philological Chronicle (Phullalocanavaṃśa)*. Series Minor LXXXII. Napoli: Università degli studi di Napoli "L'Orientale".

https://doi.org/10.1515/9783110543087-008

Einicke, Katrin (2009), *Korrektur, Differenzierung und Abkürzung in indischen Inschriften und Handschriften*. Abhandlungen für die Kunde des Morgenlandes 68. Wiesbaden: Harrassowitz.

Emmerick, R.E. (ed.) (1980), *The Siddhasāra of Ravigupta. Volume 1: The Sanskrit Text*. Verzeichnis der orientalischen Handschriften in Deutschland. Supplementband 23,1. Wiesbaden: Franz Steiner Verlag.

Formigatti, Camillo Alessio (2015), Sanskrit *Annotated Manuscripts from Northern India and Nepal*. Hamburg: University of Hamburg.

Friedrich, Michael and Cosima Schwarke (eds) (2016), *One-Volume Libraries: Composite and Multiple-Text Manuscripts*. Studies in Manuscript Cultures 9. Berlin: De Gruyter.

Gellner, David (1996), '"The Perfection of Wisdom": A Text and Its Uses in Kwā Bahā, Lalitpur', In Lienhard, S. (ed.), *Change and Continuity. Studies in the Nepalese Culture of the Kathmandu Valley*. Alessandria: Ed. dell'Orso, 223–240.

Godakumbura, Charles E. (1980), *Catalogue of Ceylonese manuscripts*. Copenhagen: Royal Library.

Goodall, Dominic (ed.) (1998), *Bhaṭṭa Rāmakaṇṭha's Commentary on the Kiraṇatantra. Critical Edition and Annotated Translation*. Pondichéry: Institut Français de Pondichéry.

Goodall, Dominic (2013), 'Les influences littéraires indiennes dans les inscriptions du Cambodge: l'exemple d'un chef-d'œuvre inédit du VIIIe siècle (K. 1236)', in *Comptes Rendus des séances de l'année 2012 (janvier-mars) de l'Académie des Inscriptions et Belles-Lettres*, 345–357.

Goodall, Dominic (2015), *The Niśvāsatattvasaṃhitā. The Earliest Surviving Śaiva Tantra. Volume 1. A Critical Edition & Annotated Translation of the Mūlasūtra, Uttarasūtra & Nayasūtra*. Edited by Dominic Goodall in collaboration with Alexis Sanderson & Harunaga Isaacson, with contribution of Nirajan Kafle, Diwakar Acharya & others. Collection Indologie 128. Early Tantra Series 1. Pondicherry: Institut Français de Pondichéry; Paris: École Française d'Extrême-Orient; Hamburg: Asien-Afrika-Institut, Universität Hamburg.

Goodall, Dominic and Harunaga Isaacson (2016), *Tantric Studies. Fruits of A Franco-German Collaboration on Early Tantra*. Collection Indologie 131. Early Tantra Series 4. Pondicherry: Institut Français de Pondichéry; Paris: École Française d'Extrême-Orient; Hamburg: Asien-Afrika-Institut, Universität Hamburg.

Gopalakrishnan, Sudha (2007), *Vijñānanidhi*: *Manuscript Treasures of India*. New Delhi: The National Mission for Manuscripts.

Goswamy, B.N. (2006), *The Word is Sacred, Sacred is the Word: The Indian Manuscript Tradition*. Delhi: Niyogi Books.

Goudriaan, T. and J.A. Schoterman (1988), *The Kubikāmatatantra: Kulālikāmnāya Version*. Critical Edition. Leiden: Brill.

Grierson, George (1916), 'On the Sarada Alphabet', in *Journal of the Royal Asiatic Society* XVII, 677–708.

Grünendahl, Reinhold (ed.) (1983–1989), *Viṣṇudharmāḥ. Precepts for the Worship of Viṣṇu*. Part 1–3. Wiesbaden: Harrassowitz.

Hanneder, Jürgen (2002), 'The Blue Lotus: Oriental Research between Philology, Botany and Poetics?' in *Zeitschriften der Deutschen Morgenländischen Gesellschaft*. Bd. 152, 295–306.

Harimoto, Kengo (2011), 'In Search of the Oldest Nepalese Manuscript', In Freschi, E. et al. (eds), *Rivista degli studi oriental, Nuova Serie*, LXXXIV, 1/4, 85–106.

Harimoto, Kengo (2014), 'Nepalese Manuscripts of the *Suśrutasaṃhitā*', in *Journal of Indian and Buddhist Studies*, 62, 3: 1087–1093.
Harimoto, Kengo (2017), 'The Dating of the Cambridge *Bodhisattvabhūmi* Manuscript Add.1702', In Vergiani, V. et al. (eds), *Indic Manuscript Cultures through the Ages: Material, Textual and Historical Investigations*. Studies in Manuscript Cultures 14. Berlin: De Gruyter.
Hartmann, Jens-Uwe (1998), 'The Rañjanā Script', In Kretschmar, Andreas (ed.), *The Fifth Seal: Calligraphic-Icons / Kalligraphikons; the Radheshyam Saraf Art Collection*. Kathmandu: Art Network International. 37–39.
Hoernle, A.F.R. (1900), 'An Epigraphical Note on Palm-leaf, Paper and Birch-bark', in *Journal of the Royal Asiatic Society of Bengal I* (69, 2), 93–134.
Indraji, Bhagwanlal (1885), *Twenty-three Inscriptions from Nepal*. Bombay.
Jakobi-Mirwald, Christine (2008), *Buchmalerei: Terminologie in der Kunstgeschichte*. Berlin: Dietrich Reimer Verlag. (Dritte, überarb. und erw. Aufl. unter Mitarb. von Martin Roland).
Jambuvijay, Muni (ed.) (2000), *Jaisalamera ke prācīna Jaina granthabhāndārom kī sūcī* [A Catalogue of Manuscripts in Jaisalmer Jain Bhandaras]. Delhi: Motilal Banarsidass. (1st Edition).
Janert, Klaus Ludwig (1995), *Bibliographie mit den Berichten über die mündliche und schriftliche Textweitergabe sowie die Schreibmaterialien in Indien*. Sarasvati Series 13. Bonn: VGH Wissenschaftverlag GMBH.
Johnston, William M. (2000), *Encyclopedia of Monasticism*. Vol. 2. Chicago: Fitzroy Dearborn.
Kafle, Nirajan (2015), *The Niśvāsamukha, the Introductory Book of the Niśvāsatattvasaṃhitā*. Critical Edition, with an Introduction, Annotated Translation Appended by Śivadharmasaṅgraha 5–9. Leiden: Universiteit Leiden.
Kajiyama, Yūichi (ed.) (1999), *The Antarvyāptisamarthana of Ratnākaraśānti*. Tokyo: The International Research Institute for Advanced Buddhology, Soka University.
Kapadia, H.R. (1936), 'Foliation of Jaina Manuscripts and Letter-numerals', in *Annals of the Bhandarkar Oriental Research Institute*, Vol. XVIII, 171–186.
Katre, S.M. (1954), *Introduction to Indian Textual Criticism*. Deccan College Hand-Book Series 5. Poona: Deccan College.
Kim, Jinah (2013), *Receptacle of the Sacred: Illustrated Manuscripts and the Buddhist Book Cult in South Asia. Berkeley*: University of California Press.
Kim, Jinah (2014), 'Review of Buescher, Hartmut, Catalogue of Sanskrit Manuscripts: Early Acquisitions and the Nepal Collection', in *H-Asia, H-Net Reviews*, 1–5.
Kim, Jinah (2015), 'Painted Palm-Leaf Manuscripts and the Art of the Book in Medieval South Asia', in *Archives of Asian Art*, 65.2: 57–86.
Klebanov, Andrey (2010), *The *Nepalese Version of the Suśrutasaṃhitā and its Interrelation with Buddhism and the Buddhists*. Hamburg: Universität Hamburg. (unpublished Magisterarbeit).
Klebanov, Andrey (forthcoming), 'Textual history of the *Suśrutasaṃhitā* (1): Study of 3 Nepalese Manuscripts', In Preisendanz, K. et al. (eds), *Proceeding of the Panel "The Transmission of Sanskrit Medical Texts"*. (special issue of *eJIM* – electronic Journal of Indian Medicine).
Losty, Jeremiah P. (1982), *Art of the Book in India*. London: The British Library.
Matsuda, Kazunobu (1996), *Two Sanskrit Manuscripts of the Daśabhūmikasūtra Preserved at The National Archives, Kathmandu*. Bibliotheca Codicum Asiaticorum 10. Tokyo: The Centre for East Asian Cultural Studies for Unesco.
Matsuda, Kazunobu (2000), '*Śrīmālādevīsiṃhanādanirdeśa*' In Braarvig, J. (ed.), *Buddhist Manuscripts in the Schøyen Collection*. Vol. I, 63–76. (Plate III,2).

Melzer, Gudrun and Eva Allinger (2010), 'Eine nepalesische Palmblatthandschrift der *Aṣṭasahasrikā Prajñāpāramitā* aus dem Jahr NS 268 (1148 AD), Teil I"; in *Indo-Asiatische Zeitschrift*, 14: 3–21.
Melzer, Gudrun (2014), 'A Paleographic Study of a Buddhist Manuscript from the Gilgit Region: A Glimpse into a Scribes' Workshop', In Quenzer, Jörg B. et al. (eds), *Manuscript Cultures: Mapping the Field.* Studies in Manuscript Cultures 1. Berlin: De Gruyter, 227–275.
Mevissen, Gerd J.R. (1992), 'Transmission of Iconographic Traditions: Pañcaraksā Heading North', in *South Asian Archaeology*, 1989: 415–424.
Mevissen, Gerd J.R. (1997), 'Mongolische Pañcarakṣā-Blockdrucke in Berliner Sammlungen', in *Indo-Asiatische Zeitschrift*, 1: 24–43.
Moeller, Volker (1979), 'Das Nandyāvarta-Symbol?', in *Zeitschriften der Deutschen Morgenländischen Gesellschaft.* Bd. 129, 149–154.
Monier-Williams, M. (1872), *A Sanskrit-English Dictionary: Etymologically and philologically arranged with special reference to Cognate indo-european languages.* Oxford: The Clarendon Press.
Moriguchi, Mitutoshi (1989), *A Catalogue of the Buddhist Tantric Manuscripts in the National Archives of Nepal and Kesar Library.* Tokyo: Sankibou Busshorin.
Padoux, André (2011), *Tantric Mantras. Studies on mantrasastra.* London: Routledge.
Pal, Pratapaditya (1978), *The Arts of Nepal: Painting.* Part II: Leiden: Brill.
Pant, Mahes Raj and Aishvarya Dhar Sharma (1977), *The Two Earliest Copper-plate Inscriptions from Nepal.* Nepal Research Centre Miscellaneous Papers No. 12. Kathmandu: Nepal Research Centre.
Pant, Mahes Raj (2000), *Jātarūpa's Commentary on the Amarakoṣa.* Part I–II. Delhi: Motilal Banarsidass.
Pāṇḍeya, Phaṇīndraprasāda (2000): *Saṃkṛta-Nepālī Bṛhat Śabdakośa.* Mahendra Saṃskṛta Viśvavidyālaya Granthamālā 51. Dang: Mahendra Sanskrit University.
Petech, Luciano (1984), *Medieval History of Nepal (c. 750–1482).* Serie Orientale Roma LIV. Roma: Instituto Italliano per il Medio ed Estremo Orientale. (2nd, thoroughly rev. edn.).
Pingree, David (2003), 'The logic of non-Western science: mathematical discoveries in medieval India', in *Daedalus*, 132.4: 45–54.
Plofker, Kim (2009), 'Spoken Text and Written Symbol: The Use of Layout and Notation in Sanskrit Scientific Manuscripts', in *Digital Proceedings of the Lawrence J. Schoenberg Symposium on Manuscript Studies in the Digital Age*, Vol. 1.
Pollock, Sheldon (2006), *The Language of the Gods in the World of Men.* Berkeley: University of California Press.
Rajbanshi, Shankar Man (1974), 'The Evolution of Devanagari Script', in *Kailash – A Journal of Himalayan Studies.* Vol. 2, nos 1–2, 23–120.
Regmi, D.R. (1965/66), *Medieval Nepal. Early Mediaval Period. Part I; A History of the Three Kingdoms 1520 A.D. to 1768 A.D.* Part II. Calcutta: Mukhopadhyay.
Roth, Gustav (1986), 'Mangala-Symbols in Buddhist Sanskrit Manuscripts and Inscriptions', In Bhattacharya, Gouriswar (ed.), *Deyadharma: Studies in Memory of Dr. D.C. Sircar* 20. Delhi: Sri Satguru Publications, 239–249.
Roth, Gustav (ed.) (1970), *Bhikṣuṇī-Vinaya: Including Bhikṣuṇī-Prakīrṇaka and a Summary of the Bhikṣuṇī-Prakīrṇaka of the Ārya-Mahāsāṃghika-Lokottaravādin.* Tibetan Sanskrit Works Series 12. Patna: K.P. Jayaswal Research Institute.
Sachau, Edward C. (1910), *Alberuni's India. An account of the religion, philosophy, literature, geography, chronology, astronomy, customs, laws and astrology of India about A.D. 1030.* London. Vol. 1. (reprint).

Śākya, Hemarāja (1973), *Nepāla lipi-prakāśa*. Kaṭhamāṇḍauṃ: Nepālarājakīyaprajñā-pratiṣṭhāna.
Salomon, Richard (1998), *Indian Epigraphy. A Guide to the Study of Inscriptions in Sanskrit, Prakrit, and other Indo-Aryan Languages*. New York: Oxford University Press.
Salomon, Richard (2000), *A Gāndhārī Version of the Rhinoceros Sūtra: British Library Kharoṣṭhī Fragment 5B*. With a contribution by Andrew Glass. Gandhāran Buddhist Texts, Vol. 1. Seattle: University of Washington Press.
Sander, Lore (1968), *Paläographisches zu den Sanskrithandschriften der Berliner Turfansammlung*. Mit 40 Alphabettafeln. Wiesbaden: Steiner.
Sander, Lore (1986), 'Om or Siddham – Remarkes on Openings of Buddhist Manuscripts and Inscription from Gilgit and Central Asia', in Bhattacharya, Gouriswar (ed.), *Deyadharma: Studies in Memory of Dr. D.C. Sircar* 20. Delhi: Sri Satguru Publications, 251–261.
Sanderson, Alexis (2009), 'The Śaiva Age: The Rise and Dominance of Śaivism during the Early Medieval Period', in Einoo, Shingo (ed.), *Genesis and Development of Tantrism*. Institute of Oriental Culture Special Series 23. Tokyo: University of Tokyo, 41–350.
Sanghavi, Pandit Sukhlalji and Parikh C. Rasiklal (eds) (1987), *Tattvopaplavasimha of Shri Jayarasi Bhatta: Edited with an introduction and indices*. Bauddha Bharati Series 20. Varanasi: Bauddha Bharati. (1st edition).
Sarkar, H. and B. M. Pande (1999), *Symbols and Graphic Representations in Indian Inscriptions*. New Delhi: Aryan Books International.
Sarma, K.V. (1992), 'Scribes in Indian Tradition', in *The Adyar Library Bulletin*, 56: 31–46.
Schneider, Karin (2009), *Paläographie und Handschriftenkunde für Germanisten: Eine Einführung*. Tübingen: Max Niemeyer Verlag. (2. überab. Aufl.).
Sferra, Francesco (2009), 'The Laud of the Chosen Deity, the First Chapter of the Hevajratantrapiṇḍārthaṭīkā by Vajragarbha', In Einoo, Shingo (ed.), *Genesis and Development of Tantrism*. Institute of Oriental Culture Special Series 23. Tokyo: University of Tokyo, 435–468.
Shastri, Haraprasad (1905–15), *A Catalogue of Palm-Leaf and Selected Paper Mss. Belonging to the Durbar Library, Nepal*. Vol. 1–2. Calcutta: The Baptist Mission Press.
De Simini, Florinda (2016), *Of Gods and Books: Cult and Donation of Knowledge in the Medieval Hindu Traditions*. Studies in Manuscript Cultures 8. Berlin, Boston: De Gruyter.
De Simini, Florinda (2016), 'Śivadharma Manuscripts from Nepal and the Making of a Śaiva Corpus', In Friedrich, Michael and Cosima Schwarke (eds), *One-Volume Libraries: Composite and Multiple-Text Manuscripts*. Studies in Manuscript Cultures 9. Berlin, Boston: De Gruyter, 233–286.
Slaje, Walter (1993): *Śāradā. Deskriptiv-synchrone Schriftkunde zur Bearbeitung kaschmirischer Sanskrit-Manuskripte auf der Grundlage von Kuśalas Ghaṭakharpara-Gūḍhadīpikā*. Reinbek: Verlag für Orientalistische Fachpublikationen.
Snellgrove, D.L. (1959): *The Hevajra Tantra. A Critical Study. Part I. Introduction and Translation*; Part II. Sanskrit and Tibetan Texts. London: Oxford University Press.
Steiner, Roland (1996): 'Die Lehre der Anuṣṭubh bei den indischen Metrikern', in Hahn, M. et al. (eds): *Suhṛllekhāḥ. Festgabe für Helmut Eimer*. Bonn: Indica et Tibetica 28, 227–248.
Suvedī, Kāśīrāja Śarmā and Narendranātha Tivārī (eds) (2000): *Sauśrutanighaṇṭuḥ*. Mahendrasaṃskṛtagranthamālā 50. Dang: Mahendra Sanskrit University.
Szántó, Péter-Dániel (2017): 'A Sanskrit Fragment of Candragomin's Praṇidhāna', in *Journal of the International Association of Buddhist Studies*, 40: 225–237.
Szántó, Péter-Dániel (2012): *Selected Chapters from the Catuṣpīṭhatantra*. 2 Vols. Oxford: University of Oxford. (PhD dissertation).

Tamoṭa, Kāśīnātha (2006), *Nepālamaṇḍala*. Lilitapura: Nepālamaṇḍala Anusandhāna Guthi.
Thaker, Jayant P. (2002), *Manuscriptology and Text Criticism*. Vadodara: Oriental Institute.
Trier, Jesper (1972), *Ancient Paper of Nepal: Results of Ethno-Technological Field-work on Its Manufacture, Uses and History – With Technical Analyses of Bast, Paper and Manuscripts*. Jutland Archaeological Society Publications 10. Copenhagen: Gyldendal.
Tripāṭhī, Chandrabhāl (1975), *Catalogue of the Jaina Manuscripts at Strasbourg*. Leiden: Brill.
Tubb, Gary A. and Emery R. Boose (2007), *Scholastic Sanskrit. A Handbook for Students*. New York: American Institute of Buddhist Studies.
Tucci, Giuseppe (1932), *The Commentaries on the Prajñāpāramitās: The Abhisamayālaṅkārāloka of Haribhadra; Being a Commentary on the Abhisamayālaṅkāra of Maitreyanātha and the Aṣṭasāhasrikāprajñāpāramitā*. Gaekwad's Oriental Series: 62. Baroda: Oriental Institute.
Vaidya, Parashuram Lakshman (ed.) (1960), *Saddharmapuṇḍarīkasūtra*. Darbhanga: The Mithila Institute of Post-Graduate Studies and Research in Sanskrit Learning.
Weber, Albrecht (1891), *Die Handschriften-Verzeichnisse der Königlichen Bibliothek zu Berlin. Verzeichniss der Sanskṛit- und Prâkṛit-Handschriften*. 2. Bd. 3. Abth. Berlin: Asher.
Weissenborn, Karen (2012), *Buchkunst aus Nālandā: die Aṣṭasāhasrikā Prajñāpāramitā-Handschrift in der Royal Asiatic Society/London (Ms. Hodgson 1) und ihre Stellung in der Pāla-Buchmalerei des 11./12. Jahrhunderts*. Wiener Studien zur Tibetologie und Buddhismuskunde 77. Wien: Arbeitskreis für Tibetische und Buddhistische Studien.
Wogihara, Unrai (ed.) (1932), *Abhisamayālamkārālokā Prajñāpāramitāvyākhyā* (Commentary on Aṣṭasāhasrikā-Prajñāpāramitā) by Haribhadra. Together with the Text Commented on. Tokyo: The Toyo Bunko.
Wujastyk, Dominik (2014), 'Indian Manuscripts.' In Quenzer, Jörg B. et al. (eds), *Manuscript Cultures: Mapping the Field*. Studies in Manuscript Cultures 1. Berlin: De Gruyter, 159–182.
Yokochi, Yuko (ed.) (2013), *The Skandapurāṇa. Vol.III. Adhyāyas 34.1–61, 53–69. The Vindhyavāsinī Cycle*. Critical Edition with an Introduction & Annotated English Synopsis. Groningen: Brill & Egbert Forsten

Online and electronic sources:

Cambridge University Library (CUL):
<http://cudl.lib.cam.ac.uk/collections/sanskrit>
The Corpus of the Inscriptions of Campā:
<http://isaw.nyu.edu/publications/inscriptions/campa/inscriptions/index.html>
General Library, University of Tokyo:
<http://picservice.ioc.u-tokyo.ac.jp/03_150219~UT-library_sanskrit_ms/>
IndoSkript:
<http://userpage.fu-berlin.de/falk/>
JAINpedia:
<http://www.jainpedia.org/>
Manuscript of the Month: <http://www.manuscript-cultures.uni-hamburg.de/mom/2012_04_mom_e.html>
The Nepalese-German Manuscripts Cataloguing Project (NGMCP):
<https://www.aai.uni-hamburg.de/en/forschung/ngmcp

List of figures

Fig. 2.4.1-I: Overall layout, fols.? (NAK image 71a, 74a) © National Archives, Kathmandu
Fig. 2.4.1-II: Overall layout, fols. 34v, 51v © Cambridge University Library
Fig. 2.4.1-III: Overall layout, fols. 119v, 130v © Kaiser Library, Kathmandu
Fig. 2.4.1-IV: Overall layout, fols.? (NAK image 5a, 203a) © National Archives, Kathmandu
Fig. 2.4.1-V: Overall layout, fols. 99v, 100r © National Archives, Kathmandu
Fig. 2.4.1-VI: Overall layout, fols. 13v, 44v © National Archives, Kathmandu
Fig. 2.4.1-VII: Overall layout, fols. 41v, 42v © National Archives, Kathmandu
Fig. 2.4.1-VIII: Overall layout, fols. 46v, 48r © Bodleian Library, Oxford
Fig. 2.4.1-IX: Overall layout fols. 61rv © National Archives, Kathmandu
Fig. 2.4.1-X: Overall layout, fols. 12v, 13r © National Archives, Kathmandu
Fig. 2.4.1-XI: Overall layout, fols. 169v, 170r © National Archives, Kathmandu
Fig. 2.4.1-XII: Overall layout, fols. 6v, 7v © National Archives, Kathmandu
Fig. 2.4.1-XIII: Overall layout, fols. 36v, 37r © National Archives, Kathmandu
Fig. 2.4.1-XIV: Overall layout, fol. 10v, 11r © National Archives, Kathmandu
Fig. 2.4.1-XV: Overall layout, fols. 37v, 52v © National Archives, Kathmandu
Fig. 2.4.1-XVI: Overall layout, fols. 33v, 34r © National Archives, Kathmandu
Fig. 2.4.1-XVII: Overall layout, fol. 26rv © National Archives, Kathmandu
Fig. 2.4.1-XVIII: Overall layout, fols. 189v, 190r © National Archives, Kathmandu
Fig. 2.4.1-XIX: Overall layout, fol. 36rv © National Archives, Kathmandu
Fig. 2.4.1-XX: Overall layout, fols. 60v, 62r © National Archives, Kathmandu
Fig. 2.4.1-XXI: Overall layout, fols. 17v, 35v © Cambridge University Library
Fig. 2.4.1-XXII: Overall layout, fols. 39v, 40r © National Archives, Kathmandu
Fig. 2.4.2-I: Overall layout, fols. 26r, 67v © Cambridge University Library
Fig. 2.4.2-II: Overall layout, fols. 35v, 36r © National Archives, Kathmandu
Fig. 2.4.2-III: Overall layout, fols. 3v, 4r © Kaiser Library, Kathmandu
Fig. 2.4.2-IV: Overall layout, fols. 8v, 9r © Kaiser Library, Kathmandu
Fig. 2.4.2-V: Overall layout, fols. 20v, 21r © Kaiser Library, Kathmandu
Fig. 2.4.2-VI: Overall layout, fols. 4v, 5r © Kaiser Library, Kathmandu
Fig. 2.4.2-VII: Overall layout, fols. 2v, 3r © Kaiser Library, Kathmandu
Fig. 2.4.2-VIII: Overall layout, fols. 5v, 6r © National Archives, Kathmandu
Fig. 2.4.2-IX: Overall layout, fols. 4v, 5r © Kaiser Library, Kathmandu
Fig. 2.4.2-X: Overall layout, fols. 13v, 14r © Kaiser Library, Kathmandu
Fig. 2.4.2-XI: Overall layout, fols. 4v, 5r © Kaiser Library, Kathmandu
Fig. 2.4.2-XII: Overall layout, fols.? © General Library, University of Tokyo
Fig. 2.4.3-I: Overall layout, fols. 50v, 84v © Jinabhadrasūri Grantha Bhaṇḍāra, Jaisalmer
Fig. 2.4.3-II: Overall layout, fols. 32r, 37v © Jinabhadrasūri Grantha Bhaṇḍāra, Jaisalmer
Fig. 2.4.3-III: Overall layout, fols. 5v, 6v © Jinabhadrasūri Grantha Bhaṇḍāra, Jaisalmer
Fig. 2.4.3-IV: Overall layout, fols. 28r, 50v © National Archives, Kathmandu
Fig. 2.4.3-V: Overall layout, fols. 23r, 60v © British Library Board, London
Fig. 2.4.3-VI: Overall layout, fols. 31v, 32v © Hemacandrācārya Jaina Jñānamandira, Patan
Fig. 2.4.3-VII: Overall layout, fols. 20v, 42r © British Library Board, London
Fig. 3.2-I: An example of symbol in an earlier manuscript (reproduced by kind permission of editor from BMSC, 2002, Vol. II, Plate XIII.1, 1 A) © Jens Braarvig

https://doi.org/10.1515/9783110543087-009

Fig. 3.2-II: Symbols at the end of the text (reproduced by kind permission of editors from BMSC, 2000, Vol. I, Plate III, fol. 392r) © Jens Braarvig
Fig. 3.2-III: Symbol (reproduced by kind permission of editor from BMSC, 2000, Vol. I, Plate VIII,1, fol. 3r) © Jens Braarvig
Fig. 3.2-IV: Symbol at the end of a particular text (reproduced by kind permission of editor from BMSC, 2016, Vol. III, Plate VII, fol. 26r) © Jens Braarvig
Fig. 3.4-I: Similar symbols © Kaiser Library, Kathmandu; National Archives, Kathmandu; Bodleian Library, Oxford; General Library, University of Tokyo
Fig. 3.4-II: Similar symbols © National Archives, Kathmandu; Cambridge University Library; Kaiser Library, Kathmandu; Bodleian Library, Oxford
Fig. 3.4-III: Similar symbols © Bodleian Library, Oxford; National Archives, Kathmandu
Fig. 3.4-IV: Similar symbols © National Archives, Kathmandu; Bodleian Library, Oxford; Cambridge University Library; Jinabhadrasūri Grantha Bhaṇḍāra, Jaisalmer
Fig. 3.4-V: Similar symbols © Bodleian Library, Oxford; National Archives, Kathmandu; Kaiser Library, Kathmandu; Cambridge University Library
Fig. 3.4-VI: Similar symbols © National Archives, Kathmandu; Cambridge University Library; Kaiser Library, Kathmandu
Fig. 3.4-VII: Similar symbols © Kaiser Library, Kathmandu; National Archives, Kathmandu; Jinabhadrasūri Grantha Bhaṇḍāra, Jaisalmer
Fig. 3.4-VIII: Similar symbols © National Archives, Kathmandu; Cambridge University Library; Kaiser Library, Kathmandu; British Library Board, London; Hemacandrācārya Jaina Jñānamandira, Patan
Fig. 3.4-IX: Similar symbols © National Archives, Kathmandu
Fig. 3.4-X: Similar symbols © National Archives, Kathmandu; Jinabhadrasūri Grantha Bhaṇḍāra, Jaisalmer
Fig. 3.4-XI: Similar symbols © National Archives, Kathmandu; Bodleian Library, Oxford
Fig. 3.4-XII: Similar symbols © Kaiser Library, Kathmandu; National Archives, Kathmandu; Jinabhadrasūri Grantha Bhaṇḍāra, Jaisalmer
Fig. 3.4-XIII: Similar symbols © National Archives, Kathmandu; General Library, University of Tokyo
Fig. 3.4-XIV: Similar symbols © Kaiser Library, Kathmandu; National Archives, Kathmandu
Fig. 3.4-XV: Similar symbols © National Archives, Kathmandu; Kaiser Library, Kathmandu; General Library, University of Tokyo
Fig. 3.4-XVI: Similar symbols © Kaiser Library, Kathmandu; Cambridge University Library; National Archives, Kathmandu
Fig. 3.4-XVII: Similar symbols © Kaiser Library, Kathmandu; National Archives, Kathmandu
Fig. 3.4-XVIII: Similar symbols © National Archives, Kathmandu
Fig. 3.4-XIX: Similar symbols © National Archives, Kathmandu
Fig. 3.4-XX: Similar symbols © Cambridge University Library; National Archives, Kathmandu; Bodleian Library, Oxford
Fig. 3.4-XXI: Similar symbols © Kaiser Library, Kathmandu; Bodleian Library, Oxford
Fig. 3.4-XXII: Similar symbols © National Archives, Kathmandu
Fig. 3.4-XXIII: Similar symbols © Kaiser Library, Kathmandu; National Archives, Kathmandu
Fig. 3.4-XXIV: Similar symbols © National Archives, Kathmandu; Bodleian Library, Oxford
Fig. 3.4-XXV: Similar symbols © National Archives, Kathmandu
Fig. 3.4-XXVI: Similar symbols © National Archives, Kathmandu
Fig. 3.4-XXVII: Similar symbols © National Archives, Kathmandu; Bodleian Library, Oxford

Fig. 3.4-XXVIII: Similar symbols © National Archives, Kathmandu; Bodleian Library, Oxford
Fig. 3.4-XXIX: Similar symbols © National Archives, Kathmandu
Fig. 3.4-XXX: Similar symbols © National Archives, Kathmandu
Fig. 3.4-XXXI: Similar symbols © National Archives, Kathmandu
Fig. 3.4-XXXII: Similar symbols © Cambridge University Library; National Archives, Kathmandu
Fig. 3.4-XXXIII: Similar symbols © National Archives, Kathmandu; Bodleian Library, Oxford
Fig. 3.4-XXXIV: Similar symbols © Bodleian Library, Oxford; National Archives, Kathmandu
Fig. 3.4-XXXV: Similar symbols © National Archives, Kathmandu; Bodleian Library, Oxford
Fig. 3.4-XXXVI: Similar symbols © National Archives, Kathmandu
Fig. 3.4-XXXVII: Similar symbols © National Archives, Kathmandu; Bodleian Library, Oxford
Fig. 3.4-XXXVIII: Similar symbols © National Archives, Kathmandu; Bodleian Library, Oxford
Fig. 3.4-XXXIX: Similar symbols © National Archives, Kathmandu; Bodleian Library, Oxford
Fig. 3.4-XL: Similar symbols © National Archives, Kathmandu; Bodleian Library, Oxford
Fig. 3.4-XLI: Similar symbols © National Archives, Kathmandu; Bodleian Library, Oxford; Kaiser Library, Kathmandu
Fig. 3.4-XLII: Similar symbols © National Archives, Kathmandu
Fig. 3.4-XLIII: Similar symbols © Kaiser Library, Kathmandu; National Archives, Kathmandu
Fig. 3.4-XLIV: Similar symbols © National Archives, Kathmandu; Cambridge University Library
Fig. 3.4-XLV: Similar symbols © National Archives, Kathmandu; Kaiser Library, Kathmandu
Fig. 3.4-XLVI: Similar symbols © Cambridge University Library; National Archives, Kathmandu; Kaiser Library, Kathmandu
Fig. 3.4-XLVII: Similar symbols © Jinabhadrasūri Grantha Bhaṇḍāra, Jaisalmer; National Archives, Kathmandu; British Library Board, London; Hemacandrācārya Jaina Jñānamandira, Patan
Fig. 3.5.1-I: Realistic *puṣpikā*s after the chapter colophon and end of the last line © National Archives, Kathmandu
Fig. 3.5.1-II: Realistic *puṣpikā*s before and after the chapter colophons © Bodleian Library, Oxford
Fig. 3.5.1-III: Realistic *puṣpikā* before the chapter colophon © National Archives, Kathmandu
Fig. 3.5.1-IV: Realistic *puṣpikā*s after the chapter colophons © National Archives, Kathmandu
Fig. 3.5.1-V: Realistic *puṣpikā*s before and/or after the chapter colophons © Cambridge University Library
Fig. 3.5.1-VI: Realistic *puṣpikā* after the colophon © National Archives, Kathmandu
Fig. 3.5.1-VII: Realistic *puṣpikā*s before and after the post colophon (reproduced from Trier 1972, plate 111, n. 175a)
Fig. 3.5.1-VIII: Realistic *puṣpikā*s before and after the chapter colophon © National Archives, Kathmandu
Fig. 3.5.1-IX: Birds and realistic *puṣpikā* before and after the chapter colophon © Kaiser Library, Kathmandu
Fig. 3.5.1-X: Realistic *puṣpikā*s before the chapter colophon and after the speaker indication © National Archives, Kathmandu
Fig. 3.5.1-XI: Realistic *puṣpikā*s before and after the chapter colophons © National Archives, Kathmandu
Fig. 3.5.1-XII: Realistic *puṣpikā* before the colophon © National Archives, Kathmandu
Fig. 3.5.2-I: '*t*' similar to symbols in Fig. 3.4-XLV © National Archives, Kathmandu; Kaiser Library, Kathmandu
Fig. 3.5.2-II: Table of selected *akṣara*s, *visarga*s and *daṇḍa*s © National Archives, Kathmandu; Kaiser Library, Kathmandu
Fig. 3.5.3-I: Symbol © Jinabhadrasūri Grantha Bhaṇḍāra, Jaisalmer

Fig. 3.5.3-II: Symbol © Jinabhadrasūri Grantha Bhaṇḍāra, Jaisalmer
Fig. 3.5.3-III: Symbol © National Archives, Kathmandu
Fig. 3.6.1-I: Symbols around string-holes © Jinabhadrasūri Grantha Bhaṇḍāra, Jaisalmer
Fig. 3.6.1-II: Symbols around string-holes © Jinabhadrasūri Grantha Bhaṇḍāra, Jaisalmer
Fig. 3.6.1-III: Symbols around string-holes © Jinabhadrasūri Grantha Bhaṇḍāra, Jaisalmer
Fig. 3.6.1-IV: Symbols around string-holes © National Archives, Kathmandu
Fig. 3.6.1-V: Symbols around string-holes © British Library Board, London
Fig. 3.6.1-VI: Symbols around string-holes © Hemacandrācārya Jaina Jñānamandira, Patan
Fig. 3.6.1-VII: Symbols around string-holes © British Library Board, London
Fig. 3.6.1-VIII: Symbols around string-holes © National Archives, Kathmandu
Fig. 3.6.1-IX: Symbols around string-holes © National Archives, Kathmandu
Fig. 3.6.2.1.1-I: Symbol at the beginning of a particular section, fol. 217r © Kaiser Library, Kathmandu
Fig. 3.6.2.1.2-I: Symbols after the chapter colophon, fol. ?v © General Library, University of Tokyo
Fig. 3.6.2.1.2-II: Illustration of symbols © General Library, University of Tokyo
Fig. 3.6.2.1.3-I: Symbols before and after colophon, fol. 59r © Kaiser Library, Kathmandu
Fig. 3.6.2.1.3-II: Symbols with a particular meaning © Kaiser Library, Kathmandu
Fig. 3.6.2.1.3-III: Comparison between a florally stylised *vajra* and a modern one
Fig. 3.6.2.1.4-I: Symbols before and after the chapter colophon, fol. 160v © National Archives, Kathmandu
Fig. 3.6.2.1.5-I: Symbols at the end of the chapter, fol. 20r © National Archives, Kathmandu
Fig. 3.6.2.1.6-I: Realistic and stylised *vajra*s after the chapter colophon and colophon, fol.? © Kaiser Library, Kathmandu
Fig. 3.6.2.1.6-II: Realistic and stylised *vajra*s after the colophon and chapter colophon © Kaiser Library, Kathmandu
Fig. 3.6.2.1.6-III: Stylised *puṣpikā* and stylised *vajra* before and after chapter colophon, fol. 112r © Kaiser Library, Kathmandu
Fig. 3.6.2.1.6-IV: Stylised *puṣpikā* and florally stylised *vajra* before and after the chapter colophon © Kaiser Library, Kathmandu
Fig. 3.6.2.1.6-V: Stylised *puṣpikā* and florally stylised *vajra* before and after the chapter colophon, fol.? © National Archives, Kathmandu
Fig. 3.6.2.1.6-VI: Stylised *puṣpikā* and florally stylised *vajra* before and after the chapter colophon © National Archives, Kathmandu
Fig. 3.6.2.1.6-VII: Nearly realistic *viśvavajra* after the colophon, fol. 146v © National Archives, Kathmandu
Fig. 3.6.2.1.6-IX: Florally stylised *vajra* before the colophon, fol. 37v © Kaiser Library, Kathmandu
Fig. 3.6.2.1.6-X: Florally stylised *vajra* before the colophon © Kaiser Library, Kathmandu
Fig. 3.6.2.1.6-XI: Realistic *viśvavajra* around the string-hole, fol. 99r © National Archives, Kathmandu
Fig. 3.6.2.1.6-XII: Realistic *viśvavajra* around the string-hole © National Archives, Kathmandu
Fig. 3.6.2.1.6-XIII: Florally stylised *viśvavajra* and stylised *puṣpikā* around the string-holes, fol. 63v © Kaiser Library, Kathmandu
Fig. 3.6.2.1.6-XIV: Florally stylised *viśvavajra* and stylised *puṣpikā* around the string-holes © Kaiser Library, Kathmandu
Fig. 3.6.2.1.6-XV: Stylised *puṣpikā* and florally stylised *viśvavajra* before and after the colophon, fol. 167v © Kaiser Library, Kathmandu
Fig. 3.6.2.1.6-XVII: Various symbols © National Archives, Kathmandu

Fig. 3.6.2.1.6-XVIII: Stylised and realistic *puṣpikā*s, stylised *vajra* and realistic *viśvavajra* © National Archives, Kathmandu
Fig. 3.6.2.1.6-XX: Stylised *puṣpikā* and florally stylised *vajra*s © National Archives, Kathmandu
Fig. 3.6.2.1.6-XXI: Stylised *puṣpikā*, florally stylised *vajra*s and *viśvavajra*s © National Archives, Kathmandu
Fig. 3.6.2.1.6-XXII: Stylised *puṣpikā* and florally stylised *viśvavajra* © National Archives, Kathmandu
Fig. 3.6.2.1.6-XXIII: Stylised *puṣpikā*, florally stylised *vajra* and *viśvavajra* © National Archives, Kathmandu
Fig. 3.6.2.1.6-XXIV: Stylised *puṣpikā* and florally stylised *viśvavajra* © National Archives, Kathmandu
Fig. 3.6.2.1.6-XXV: Stylised *puṣpikā* and florally stylised *chattra*, *vajra*s and *viśvavajra* © National Archives, Kathmandu
Fig. 3.6.2.1.6-XXVI: Stylised *puṣpikā*, florally stylised *vajra*s and *viśvavajra*s © National Archives, Kathmandu
Fig. 3.6.2.1.6-XXVII: Various stylised symbols, fol. 74v © National Archives, Kathmandu
Fig. 3.6.2.1.6-XXVIII: Various florally stylised symbols © National Archives, Kathmandu
Fig. 3.6.2.1.6-XXIX: Comparison of florally stylised *vajra*s © National Archives, Kathmandu
Fig. 3.6.2.1.6-XXX: Comparison of florally stylised *viśvavajra*s © National Archives, Kathmandu
Fig. 3.6.2.1.6-XXXI: Florally stylised *vajra* (left) and *viśvavajra* (right) on the pillar of one of the *stūpa*s at Swayambhunath, Kathmandu
Fig. 3.6.2.1.6-XXXII: Extracted last three symbols from the second last row from the table of Śākya (reproduced from Śākya 1973, 85)
Fig. 3.6.2.1.6-XXXIII: Extracted symbols from the last row of Śākya's table (reproduced from Śākya 1973, 85)
Fig. 3.6.2.1.7-I: *Svastika* in a particular place, fol. 89v © National Archives, Kathmandu
Fig. 3.6.2.2-I: Puzzling symbols before and/or after the chapter colophons © National Archives, Kathmandu
Fig. 3.6.2.2-II: Puzzling symbols © Cambridge University Library
Fig. 3.6.2.2-III: Puzzling symbols before and after the chapter colophons © Kaiser Library, Kathmandu
Fig. 3.6.2.2-IV: Illustration of puzzling symbol, on fol. 81v1 © Kaiser Library, Kathmandu
Fig. 3.6.2.2-V: Puzzling symbols before and/or after chapter colophons © National Archives, Kathmandu
Fig. 3.6.2.2-VI: A puzzling symbol after the chapter colophon © Kaiser Library, Kathmandu
Fig. 3.6.2.3-I: Use and reuse of symbols © Bodleian Library, Oxford
Fig. 3.6.2.3-II: Use and reuse of symbols © Bodleian Library, Oxford
Fig. 3.6.2.3-III: Use and reuse of symbols © Bodleian Library, Oxford
Fig. 3.6.2.3-III: Use and reuse of symbols © Bodleian Library, Oxford
Fig. 3.6.2.3-IV: Use and reuse of symbols © Bodleian Library, Oxford
Fig. 3.6.2.3-V: Use and reuse of symbols © Bodleian Library, Oxford
Fig. 3.6.2.3-VI: Use and reuse of symbols © Bodleian Library, Oxford
Fig. 3.6.2.3-VII: Use and reuse of symbols © Bodleian Library, Oxford
Fig. 3.6.2.3-VII: Use and reuse of symbols © Bodleian Library, Oxford
Fig. 3.6.2.3-VIII: Use and reuse of symbols © Bodleian Library, Oxford
Fig. 3.6.2.3-IX: Use and reuse of symbols © Bodleian Library, Oxford
Fig. 3.6.2.3-IX: Use and reuse of symbols © Bodleian Library, Oxford

Fig. 3.6.2.4.1-I: Symbols at the end of the chapters © National Archives, Kathmandu
Fig. 3.6.2.4.1-II: Symbols at the end of the 64th chapter and end of the text © National Archives, Kathmandu
Fig. 3.6.2.4.1-III: Symbols at the end of the chapters © National Archives, Kathmandu
Fig. 3.6.2.4.1-IV: Symbols at the end of the text © National Archives, Kathmandu
Fig. 3.6.2.4.1-V: Symbols and blank spaces at the end of the chapter © National Archives, Kathmandu
Fig. 3.6.2.4.1-VI: Symbols at the end of the text © National Archives, Kathmandu
Fig. 3.6.2.4.1-VII: Symbols at the end of the chapter © Jinabhadrasūri Grantha Bhaṇḍāra, Jaisalmer
Fig. 3.6.2.4.1-VIII: Symbols at the end of the text © Jinabhadrasūri Grantha Bhaṇḍāra, Jaisalmer
Fig. 3.6.2.4.1-IX: Symbols at the end of chapters © National Archives, Kathmandu
Fig. 3.6.2.4.1-X: Symbols at the very end of text © National Archives, Kathmandu
Fig. 3.6.2.4.2-I: A series of three large symbols at the end of the text in the manuscript of the *Dīrghāgama*, fol. 454v (reproduced from Melzer 2014, 232, Fig. 2)
Fig. 3.6.2.4.2-II: Enlarged symbols (reproduced from Melzer 2014, 232, Fig. 2)
Fig. 3.6.2.4.2-III: A series of three large symbols at the end of the text in the manuscript of the *Vinayavastvāgama*, fol. 523r (reproduced from Melzer 2014, 233, Fig. 3)
Fig. 3.6.2.4.2-IV: Enlarged symbols (reproduced from Melzer 2014, 233, Fig. 3)
Fig. 3.6.2.4.2-V: A series of three large symbols at the end of the text of the *Aṣṭasāhasrikā Prajñāparamitā*, fol. 202r © Cambridge University Library
Fig. 3.6.2.4.2-VI: Enlarged symbols © Cambridge University Library
Fig. 3.6.2.4.2-VII: Three series of three large symbols at the end of the text in SDhPS, fols. 138v, 139rv © National Archives, Kathmandu
Fig. 3.6.2.4.2-VIII: Enlarged symbols © National Archives, Kathmandu
Fig. 3.6.2.4.2-IX: Symbols at the end of the text, fol. 132r(?) © Cambridge University Library
Fig. 3.6.2.4.2-XI: Symbols at the end of the text, fol. 186?r © National Archives, Kathmandu
Fig. 3.6.2.4.2-XII: Enlarged symbols © National Archives, Kathmandu
Fig. 3.6.2.4.2-XIII: Symbols at the end of the text, fol. 196v © Kaiser Library, Kathmandu
Fig. 3.6.2.4.2-XIV: Enlarged symbols © Kaiser Library, Kathmandu
Fig. 3.6.2.4.2-XV: Large blank spaces at the end of the text, fol. 144v © Cambridge University Library
Fig. 3.6.2.4.2-XVI: Large blank spaces at the end of the text, fol.? © Kaiser Library, Kathmandu
Fig. 3.6.2.4.2-XVII: Large blank spaces at the end of the text in the manuscript of the *Aṣṭasāhasrikā Prajñāpāramitā*, fol. 195v © National Archives, Kathmandu
Fig. 3.6.2.4.2-XVIII: Enlarged left blank space in which some part of the first line of the text is erased to keep the space free © National Archives, Kathmandu
Fig. 3.7-I: Symbols with foliation numbers © Jinabhadrasūri Grantha Bhaṇḍāra, Jaisalmer
Fig. 3.7-II: Symbol with foliation © Jinabhadrasūri Grantha Bhaṇḍāra, Jaisalmer
Fig. 3.7-III: Symbol with foliation © Jinabhadrasūri Grantha Bhaṇḍāra, Jaisalmer
Fig. 3.7-IV: Symbol with foliation © British Library Board, London
Fig. 3.8.1-I: Symbol on one of the folios in SP_1 and on one folio in A 38/5 © National Archives, Kathmandu
Fig. 3.8.1-II: Space-filler on one of the folios of SP_1 and on one folio in A 38/5 © National Archives, Kathmandu
Fig. 3.8.1-III: Overall layout, the folio which is now in the bundle of A 38/5 © National Archives, Kathmandu

Fig. 3.8.1-IV: Overall layout, one of the folios (220b/221a) of SP_1 © NAK © National Archives, Kathmandu
Fig. 3.8.2-I: Similar symbols in SP_3 and SP_4 © National Archives, Kathmandu; Bodleian Library, Oxford
Fig. 3.8.2-II: Similar symbols in SP_3 and SP_4 © National Archives, Kathmandu; Bodleian Library, Oxford
Fig. 3.8.2-III: Similar symbols in SP_3 and SP_4 © National Archives, Kathmandu; Bodleian Library, Oxford
Fig. 3.8.2-IV: Similar symbols in SP_3 and SP_4 © National Archives, Kathmandu; Bodleian Library, Oxford
Fig. 3.8.2-V: Similar symbols in SP_3 and SP_4 © National Archives, Kathmandu; Bodleian Library, Oxford
Fig. 3.8.2-VI: Similar symbols in SP_3 and SP_4 © National Archives, Kathmandu; Bodleian Library, Oxford
Fig. 3.8.2-VII: Similar symbols in SP_3 and SP_4 © National Archives, Kathmandu; Bodleian Library, Oxford
Fig. 3.8.2-VIII: Highlighted *daṇḍa*s or around the spaces of *daṇḍa*s before and after the speaker indication (Extracted part from 62r4 of SP_4) © National Archives, Kathmandu
Fig. 3.8.2-IX: Highlighted *daṇḍa*s or around the spaces of *daṇḍa*s before and after the speaker indication (Extracted part from 48r3 of SP_3) © Bodleian Library, Oxford
Fig. 3.9.1-I: Symbols by scribes A and B © National Archives, Kathmandu
Fig. 3.9.1-II: Single and double *daṇḍa*s by scribes A and B © National Archives, Kathmandu
Fig. 3.9.1-III: *Akṣara*s by scribes A and B © National Archives, Kathmandu
Fig. 3.9.1-IV: Space-fillers by scribes A and B © National Archives, Kathmandu
Fig. 3.9.1-V: Overall layout by scribe A (61ab) © National Archives, Kathmandu
Fig. 3.9.1-VI: Overall layout by scribe B (74ab) © National Archives, Kathmandu
Fig. 3.9.2-I: Symbols by scribes A and B © National Archives, Kathmandu
Fig. 3.9.2-II: Single and double *daṇḍa*s by scribe A and B © National Archives, Kathmandu
Fig. 3.9.2-III: *Akṣara*s by scribes A and B © National Archives, Kathmandu
Fig. 3.9.2-IV: Space-fillers by scribes A and B © National Archives, Kathmandu
Fig. 3.9.2-V: Overall layout by scribe A, fols.(?) (5ab) © National Archives, Kathmandu
Fig. 3.9.2-VI: Overall layout by scribe B, fols.(?) (205ab) © National Archives, Kathmandu
Fig. 3.9.3-I: Symbols by scribes A, B and C © National Archives, Kathmandu
Fig. 3.9.3-II: *Akṣara*s by scribes A, B and C © National Archives, Kathmandu
Fig. 3.9.3-III: Space-fillers by scribes A, B and C © National Archives, Kathmandu
Fig. 3.9.3-IV: Overall layout by scribe A, fol. 13v © National Archives, Kathmandu
Fig. 3.9.3-V: Overall layout by scribe B, fol. 44v © National Archives, Kathmandu
Fig. 3.9.3-VI: Overall layout by scribe C, fol. 79v © National Archives, Kathmandu
Fig. 3.9.4-I: Symbols by scribes A, B and D © Jinabhadrasūri Grantha Bhaṇḍāra, Jaisalmer
Fig. 3.9.4-II: Space-fillers by scribes A, B, C and D © Jinabhadrasūri Grantha Bhaṇḍāra, Jaisalmer
Fig. 3.9.4-III: Overall layout by scribe A, fol. 18v © Jinabhadrasūri Grantha Bhaṇḍāra, Jaisalmer
Fig. 3.9.4-IV: Overall layout by scribe B, fol. 37v © Jinabhadrasūri Grantha Bhaṇḍāra, Jaisalmer
Fig. 3.9.4-V: Overall layout by scribe C, fol. 281v?/286v? © Jinabhadrasūri Grantha Bhaṇḍāra, Jaisalmer
Fig. 3.9.4-VI: Overall layout by scribe A, fol. 311r?/315r? © Jinabhadrasūri Grantha Bhaṇḍāra, Jaisalmer
Fig. 3.9.5-I: Symbols by scribes A and B © Hemacandrācārya Jaina Jñānamandira, Patan

Fig. 3.9.5-II: Overall layout by scribe A, fols. 42v, 43v © Hemacandrācārya Jaina Jñānamandira, Patan
Fig. 3.9.5-III: Overall layout by scribe B, fols. 163v, 164v © Hemacandrācārya Jaina Jñānamandira, Patan
Fig. 4.1.1-I: Blank space before the chapter colophon and symbol after the chapter colophon, fol. 64a3 © National Archives, Kathmandu
Fig. 4.1.1-II: Blank space after the chapter colophon, fol. 164a3 © National Archives, Kathmandu
Fig. 4.1.1-III: Blank spaces before and after the chapter colophon, fol. 232v © Bodleian Library, Oxford
Fig. 4.1.1-IV: Blank space after the chapter colophon, fol. 15v © National Archives, Kathmandu
Fig. 4.1.1-V: Blank space after the chapter colophon, fol. 58v © National Archives, Kathmandu
Fig. 4.1.1-VI: Blank spaces before and after the chapter colophon, fol. 42v © National Archives, Kathmandu
Fig. 4.1.1-VII: Blank spaces before and after the chapter colophon, fol. 184r © National Archives, Kathmandu
Fig. 4.1.1-VIII: Blank spaces before and after the chapter colophon, fol. 8r1 © National Archives, Kathmandu
Fig. 4.1.1-IX: Blank spaces before and after the chapter colophon © National Archives, Kathmandu
Fig. 4.1.1-X: Blank spaces before and after the chapter colophon, fol. 145r © National Archives, Kathmandu
Fig. 3.6.2.2.3-XI: A series of three large blank spaces at the end of the text © National Archives, Kathmandu
Fig. 4.1.1-XII: Blank space at the end of a text, 13v © Cambridge University Library
Fig. 4.1.2-I: Blank spaces before and after the chapter colophon, fol. 78r © National Archives, Kathmandu
Fig. 4.1.2-II: Blank space at the end of the text, fol. 10r © Kaiser Library, Kathmandu
Fig. 4.1.2-III: Blank space after the chapter colophon, fol. 14v © Kaiser Library, Kathmandu
Fig. 4.1.2-IV: Blank space after the chapter colophon, fol. 1v © Kaiser Library, Kathmandu
Fig. 4.1.2-V: Blank space at the end of the colophon, fol. 30v © Kaiser Library, Kathmandu
Fig. 4.1.2-VI: Blank space after the chapter colophon, fol. 7v © Kaiser Library, Kathmandu
Fig. 4.1.2-VII: Blank space after the chapter colophon, fol. 2v © Kaiser Library, Kathmandu
Fig. 4.1.2-VIII: Blank spaces before and after the chapter colophon, 37r © National Archives, Kathmandu
Fig. 4.2.1.1-I: Gaps between *pāda*s on the folio, fol. 1v © National Archives, Kathmandu
Fig. 4.2.1.1-II: Extracted and enlarged part from fol. 1v © National Archives, Kathmandu
Fig. 4.2.1.2-I: Use of gaps, fol. 198r © Kaiser Library, Kathmandu
Fig. 4.2.1.2-II: Extracted and enlarged part from fol. 198r
Fig. 4.2.1.4-I: Use of gaps, fols. 22v, 23r © Cambridge University Library
Fig. 4.2.1.4-II: Extracted and enlarged part from fol. 22v © Cambridge University Library
Fig. 4.2.2.1-I: Use of gaps; fols.?, 74ab © National Archives, Kathmandu
Fig. 4.2.2.1-II: Extracted and enlarged part from fol.?, 74a © National Archives, Kathmandu
Fig. 4.2.2.2-I: Extracted part from fol. 2v © National Archives, Kathmandu
Fig. 4.2.2.2-II: Use of gaps; fol. 2v? (5a) © National Archives, Kathmandu
Fig. 4.2.2.2-III: Extracted and enlarged part from fol. 2v? (5a) © National Archives, Kathmandu
Fig. 4.2.2.3-I: Use of gaps; fols. 39v, 40r © National Archives, Kathmandu
Fig. 4.2.2.3-II: Extracted and enlarged part from fol. 39v © National Archives, Kathmandu
Fig. 5.1-I: Highlighted invocation © Kaiser Library, Kathmandu

Fig. 5.1-II: Highlighted invocation © National Archives, Kathmandu
Fig. 5.1-III: Highlighted invocation © Cambridge University Library
Fig. 5.1-IV: Highlighted *daṇḍa* and *akṣara* after and before the chapter colophons © National Archives, Kathmandu
Fig. 5.1-V: Highlighted *daṇḍa*s before and after the chapter colophon © Kaiser Library, Kathmandu
Fig. 5.1-VI: Highlighted *daṇḍa*s before and after chapter colophons © Kaiser Library, Kathmandu
Fig. 5.1-VII: Highlighted *daṇḍa* before the chapter colophons © Kaiser Library, Kathmandu
Fig. 5.1-VIII: Highlighted symbols © National Archives, Kathmandu
Fig. 5.1-IX: Highlighted symbols © National Archives, Kathmandu
Fig. 5.1-X: Highlighted symbols © Kaiser Library, Kathmandu
Fig. 5.1-XI: Highlighted symbols © National Archives, Kathmandu
Fig. 5.1-XII: Highlighted symbols © National Archives, Kathmandu
Fig. 5.1-XIII: Highlighted symbols © National Archives, Kathmandu
Fig. 5.1-XIV: Highlighted symbols © National Archives, Kathmandu
Fig. 5.1-XV: Highlighted symbol © Kaiser Library, Kathmandu
Fig. 5.1-XVI: Highlighted symbols around string-holes © Jinabhadrasūri Grantha Bhaṇḍāra, Jaisalmer
Fig. 5.1-XVII: Highlighted symbols around string-holes © Jinabhadrasūri Grantha Bhaṇḍāra, Jaisalmer
Fig. 5.1-XVIII: Highlighted symbols around string-holes © Jinabhadrasūri Grantha Bhaṇḍāra, Jaisalmer
Fig. 5.1-XIX: Highlighted symbols around string-holes © Hemacandrācārya Jaina Jñānamandira, Patan
Fig. 5.1-XX: Highlighted symbols around string-holes © British Library Board, London
Fig. 5.1-XXI: Highlighted quotation formulae, fol. 29r © National Archives, Kathmandu
Fig. 5.1-XXII: Extracted and enlarged quotation formulae from 29r © National Archives, Kathmandu
Fig. 5.1-XXIII: Extracted and enlarged part of the highlighted *mantra*s © Cambridge University Library
Fig. 5.1-XXIV: Partly and entirely highlighted chapter colophon © National Archives, Kathmandu
Fig. 5.1-XXV: Highlighted section colophon © Kaiser Library, Kathmandu
Fig. 5.1-XXVI: Highlighted chapter colophon © National Archives, Kathmandu
Fig. 5.1-XXVII: Partly highlighted chapter colophons © National Archives, Kathmandu
Fig. 5.1-XXVIII: Highlighted chapter colophon © National Archives, Kathmandu
Fig. 5.1-XXIX: Highlighted chapter colophon © Kaiser Library, Kathmandu
Fig. 5.1-XXX: Highlighted foliation © Cambridge University Library
Fig. 5.1-XXXI: Highlighted foliation © National Archives, Kathmandu
Fig. 5.1-XXXII: Highlighted foliations © Jinabhadrasūri Grantha Bhaṇḍāra, Jaisalmer
Fig. 5.1-XXXIII: Highlighted foliations © British Library Board, London
Fig. 5.1-XXXIV: Highlighted foliations © Hemacandrācārya Jaina Jñānamandira, Patan
Fig. 5.1-XXXV: Highlighted foliations © British Library Board, London
Fig. 5.1.1-I: An overall overview of various highlighted features in manuscripts © Cambridge University Library; National Archives, Kathmandu; British Library Board, London
Fig. 5.2-I: Notation used to document the experiments
Fig. 5.2-II: Colour examination on fol. 188v © Kaiser Library, Kathmandu
Fig. 5.2-III: XRF-spectra from fol. 188v

Fig. 5.2-IV: Examination on fol. 205v © Kaiser Library, Kathmandu
Fig. 5.2-V: Examination on fols. 65r, 68v © National Archives, Kathmandu
Fig. 5.2-VI: Examination on symbol on the fragment of fol. 10v © National Archives, Kathmandu
Fig. 5.2-VII: Point where the sharp part of the compass or similar item may have been placed
Fig. 5.2-VIII: Extracted and enlarged part from fol. 202r © Cambridge University Library
Fig. 5.2-IX: Extracted and enlarged part of the symbol from fol. 202r and part of the back side of the symbol from fol. 202v © Cambridge University Library
Fig. 5.2-X: Examined features on fol. 22v © National Archives, Kathmandu
Fig. 5.2-XI: XRF-spectra from fol. 22v
Fig. 5.2-XII: Examined features on fol. 44v © National Archives, Kathmandu
Fig. 5.2-XIII: XRF-spectra from foliation on fol. 44v
Fig. 5.2-XIV: Examined features on fol. 165r © National Archives, Kathmandu
Fig. 5.2-XV: Examined feature on fol. 51v © Kaiser Library, Kathmandu

Index of manuscripts[742]

Manuscript of the *Abhayapaddhati* (aka *Buddhakapālamahātantraṭīkā*) (see AP), National Archives, Kathmandu, 5/21 — 34, 63, 66–67, 83, 103–104, 118–125, 247, 289, 348

Manuscript of the *Abhisamayālaṅkārālokā* (see AAĀ), National Archives, Kathmandu, 3/738 — 31, 59, 67, 103–104, 117–125, 182, 243, 249, 273, 276, 281, 283, 288, 291–292, 298, 300, 346

Manuscript of the *Anāvilatantra* (see AT), General Library, University of Tokyo, Tokyo, MF14 63 014 — 37, 65–67, 81, 90–91, 118–125, 138–139, 350

Manuscript of the *Antarvyāptisamarthana*, National Archives, Kathmandu, 3/364 — 109, 116

Manuscript of the *Aṣṭasāhasrikā Prajñāparamitā*, Cambridge University Library, MS Add.866 — 188, 192–193, 197, 297

Manuscript of the *Aṣṭasāhasrikā Prajñāparamitā*, Kaiser Library, Kathmandu, 18, 114–115, 146, 193, 197

Manuscript of the *Aṣṭasāhasrikā Prajñāpāramitā* (see $AṣP_1$), National Archives, Kathmandu, 5/195 — 27, 54, 81, 83–84, 91, 97, 102, 108, 113, 142–144, 165–166, 239, 249, 281, 288, 336

Manuscript of the *Aṣṭasāhasrikā Prajñāpāramitā* (see $AṣP_2$), National Archives, Kathmandu, 3/359 — 28, 55, 87, 241, 249, 342

Manuscript of the *Aṣṭasāhasrikā Prajñāpāramitā*, National Archives, Kathmandu, 5/76 — 195, 197, 241

Manuscript of the *Aṣṭasāhasrikā Prajñāparamitā*, NGMPP E 2122/7 — 192–193, 197

MTM of the *Bālārkastutiṭīkā*, *Daśakrodhāgnisalokasaṅgraha*, *Pañcatathāgatastuti*, Kaiser Library, Kathmandu, 45 — 148–149, 164–165

MTM of the Bhaiṣajyagurusūtra and the Vajracchedikā Prajñāpāramitā Sūtra, Schøyen collection, MS 2385 — 79

Manuscript of the *Bodhisattvabhūmi*, Cambridge University Library, MS Add.1702 — 194, 197

MTM of the *Bodhicaryāvatāra*, *Āryavalokiteśvarastotra* etc., Kaiser Library, Kathmandu, 127 — 144–146

Manuscript of the *Bṛhaccūrṇivyākhyā* (see BCV), British Library Board, London, Or. 1386 — 40, 72–73, 88, 106, 128, 132, 134, 205–206, 276, 286–288, 356

Manuscript of the *Cāndravṛtti*, National Archives, Kathmandu, 5/729 — 99

Manuscript of the *Catuṣpīṭhanibandha* (see CPN), Kaiser Library, Kathmandu, 134 — 35, 63, 66–67, 83, 103, 118–125, 246, 249, 271, 288–289, 349

Manuscript of the *Catuṣpīṭhanibandha*, National Archives, Kathmandu, 4/20 — 105

Manuscript of the *Ḍākinīvajrapañjaraṭippaṇī* (see ḌVPṬ), Kaiser Library, Kathmandu, 230 — 34, 62, 66–67, 83, 103–104, 118–125, 348

742 N.B. this index lists only the manuscripts that appear in the 'main text' and therefore excludes the many other manuscripts and inscriptions referred to in the footnotes.

https://doi.org/10.1515/9783110543087-09

Manuscript of the *Dānadharma* (see DDh), National Archives, Kathmandu, 1/1321 —24, 52, 83, 99, 237, 249, 327
Manuscript of the *Dīrghāgama* — 186–187, 197

Manuscript of an 'early commentary', Schøyen collection, MS 2373/1 — 76

Manuscript of the *Gaṇḍavyūha*, National Archives, Kathmandu, 3/284 — 159
Manuscript of the *Gaṇḍavyūha*, National Archives, Kathmandu, 5/75 — 160
Manuscript of the *Gaṇḍavyūha*, National Archives, Kathmandu, 3/258 — 161, 165–166
Manuscript of the *Guṇavatī* (aka *Mahāmāyāṭīkā*) (see GV), Kaiser Library, Kathmandu, 226 — 31, 59, 66–67, 81, 103–104, 118–125, 243, 270, 288, 346

Manuscript of the *Haṃsayāmala* (see HY), National Archives, Kathmandu, 1/1076 —24, 51, 83, 102, 108, 110–111, 326
Manuscript of the *Haravijayamahākāvya* (see HVM), Jinabhadrasūri Grantha Bhaṇḍāra, Jaisalmer, 408 — 38, 69, 72–73, 89, 106, 126–128, 130, 134, 203, 206, 274–275, 288, 353
Manuscript of the *Harivaṃśa* (see HV_1), National Archives, Kathmandu, 1/910 — 23, 51, 57, 74, 83, 87–88, 90–91, 135, 236, 249, 255, 259, 261, 325
Manuscript of the *Harivaṃśa* (see HV_2), National Archives, Kathmandu, 1/455 — 27, 54, 83–84, 87–88, 92–93, 97, 102, 133, 240, 249, 338
Manuscript of the *Herukābhyudayapañjikā* (aka *Katipayākṣarā*) (see HAP), Kaiser Library, Kathmandu, 229 — 32, 60, 66–67, 103, 105, 118–125, 245, 347
Manuscript of the *Hevajrapañjikā* (aka *Ratnāvalī*) (see HP), Kaiser Library, Kathmandu, 231 — 35, 64, 66–67, 103, 118–125, 244, 249, 289, 349
Manuscript of the *Hevajratantraṭīkā* (aka *Ṣaṭsāhasrikā*) (see HTṬ), Kaiser Library, Kathmandu, 128 — 36, 65–67, 74, 83, 91–92, 118–125, 139, 144, 274, 288–289, 292–293, 300, 350

Manuscript of the *Jītakalpasūtra*/*Jītakalpacūrṇī* (see JKS/C), British Library Board, London, Or. 1385 — 39, 70, 72–73, 88, 106, 128, 131, 134, 275, 285, 287–288, 355

Manuscript of the *Kalyāṇakāmadhenūvivaraṇa*, National Archives, Kathmandu, 3/363 — 112
Manuscript of the *Kāraṇḍavyūha*/*Uṣṇīṣavijayadhāriṇī* (see KV/UVDh), National Archives, Kathmandu, 3/359 — 21, 49, 57, 89, 95–96, 132, 134, 249, 317
Manuscript of the *Khaṇḍakhādya*, Kaiser Library, Kathmandu, 233 — 92
Manuscript of the *Kiraṇatantra* (see KT), National Archives, Kathmandu, 5/893 — 11, 20, 48, 57, 83, 85–86, 88, 91, 94, 169–170, 179, 223, 231, 269, 272, 288, 316
Manuscript of the *Kulālikāmnāyatantra*, National Archives, Kathmandu, 5/877 — 110

Manuscript of the *Laghutantraṭīkā* (see LTṬ), Kaiser Library, Kathmandu, 225 — 32, 61, 66–67, 83, 103–105, 118–125, 245, 289, 347
Manuscript of the *Laṅkāvatāra*, National Archives, Kathmandu, 3/610 — 155
Manuscript of the *Lalitavistara*, National Archives, Kathmandu, 4/9 — 154, 165

Manuscript of the *Niśvāsatattvasaṃhitā* (see NTS), National Archives, Kathmandu, 1/277 — 19, 47, 57, 81, 83, 85, 89–91, 93, 250, 315
Manuscript of the *Nītisārapañjikā* (*Jayamaṅgalā*), Kaiser Library, Kathmandu, 77 — 115–116

Manuscript of the *Pañcarakṣā* (see PR), Cambridge University Library, MS Add.1688 — 13, 30, 58, 66–67, 73–74, 83, 85–86, 92, 98, 105, 170–171, 345
Manuscript of the *Pañcarakṣā*, Kaiser Library, Kathmandu, 108 — 150–151
Manuscript of the *Pañcarakṣā*, Kaiser Library, Kathmandu, 105 — 151–152
Manuscript of the *Pañcarakṣā*, National Archives, Kathmandu, 1/1114 — 150
Manuscript of the *Pārameśvaratantra* (aka *Pauṣkarapārameśvara*) (see PT), Cambridge University Library, Add.1049 — 17, 46, 57, 83, 86, 88, 93, 309
Manuscript of the *Pāramitāsamāsa*, National Archives, Kathmandu, 5/145 — 103–104, 118–125
Manuscript of the *Prajñāpāramitā*, National Archives, Kathmandu, 4/215 — 157, 166
Manuscript of the *Praśnavyākaraṇa* (see PV), National Archives, Kathmandu, 4/149 — 39, 70, 73, 89, 106, 127–128, 130–131, 134, 168, 354

Manuscript of the *Ratnakaraṇḍikā*, Kaiser Library, Kathmandu, 522 — 171–172

Manuscript of the *Saddharmapuṇḍarīka*, Cambridge University Library, MS Add.2197, 10, 111–113, 191, 197
Manuscript of the *Saddharmapuṇḍarīkasūtra* (see SDhPS), National Archives, Kathmandu, 3/678 — 28, 55, 58, 83–84, 97, 105, 143–144, 165, 185–186, 189–191, 197, 240, 249, 341
Manuscript of the *Saddharmapuṇḍarīkasūtra*, National Archives, Kathmandu, 4/217 — 158
Manuscript of the *Sādhanamālā*, National Archives, Kathmandu, 3/387 — 148
Manuscript of the *Sādhanasamuccaya* (see SS), Cambridge University Library, MS Add.1648 — 29, 56, 83, 103, 242, 267, 278, 282, 288, 343
Manuscript of the *Samādhirājasūtra*, National Archives, Kathmandu, 3/611 — 156, 165
Manuscript of the *Saṃpuṭatantraṭīkā* (aka *Prakaraṇārthanirṇaya*) (see STṬ), Kaiser Library, Kathmandu, 228 — 33, 61, 66–67, 83, 103, 118–125, 173, 246, 347
Manuscript of the *Sarvakulatattvasiddhividhivistaratantra*, Kaiser Library, Kathmandu, 143 — 195, 197
Manuscript of the *Sarvaprakaraṇasaṅgraha*, Kaiser Library, Kathmandu, 36 — 282
Manuscript of the *Śatasāhasrikā Prajñāpāramitā*, Royal Library, Copenhagen (Det Kongelige Bibliotek), Nepal 175A — 112–113
MTM, Schøyen collection, MS 2378 — 77
Manuscript of the *Siddhasārasaṃhitā* (see SSS), National Archives, Kathmandu, 7/4 — 26, 53, 81, 83, 91–92, 95, 101, 103, 334
Manuscript of the *Śivadharma* corpus, Cambridge University Library, MS Add.1645 —253
Manuscript of the *Śivadharma* corpus, National Archives, Kathmandu, 1/1261 — 94–96, 100, 102
MTM of the *Sugatāvadāna*, *Vasudhārādevīvratakathā*, National Archives, Kathmandu, 5/235 — 152
MTM of the *Sugatāvadānādisaṅgraha*, National Archives, Kathmandu, 4/1381 — 153, 162
Manuscript of the *Suśrutasaṃhitā/Suśrutanighaṇṭu* (see SS/N), Kaiser Library, Kathmandu, 699 — 18, 46, 57, 81, 83, 86–88, 90–92, 94, 136, 252, 266, 268, 272, 280, 288, 292, 294, 300, 310
Manuscript of the *Skandapurāṇa* (see SP_1), National Archives, Kathmandu, 2/229 — 16, 45, 57, 73, 78, 83, 86, 88, 95–96, 98–100, 207–209, 215, 218–219, 231, 234, 249, 255, 259, 261, 272, 288, 305

Manuscript of the *Skandapurāṇa* (see SP_2), National Archives, Kathmandu, 1/831 — 19, 47, 57, 73, 78, 85–91, 95, 99–102, 108–109, 219, 231, 235, 249, 255, 257, 259, 261, 272, 280, 288, 313
Manuscript of the *Skandapurāṇa* (see SP_3), Bodleian Library, Oxford, MS Sansk a. 14 (R) — 21, 49, 57, 81, 83–85, 88–89, 93–96, 98–102, 108–110, 174–179, 209–214, 235, 249, 318
Manuscript of the *Skandapurāṇa* (see SP_4), National Archives, Kathmandu, 4/2260 — 22, 50, 57, 83–85, 96, 209–214, 268, 273, 288, 292, 295–297, 300, 323
Manuscript of the *Svacchandalalitabhairavatantra*, National Archives, Kathmandu, 1/224 — 105

Manuscript of the *Tantrasadbhāva* (see TS_1), National Archives, Kathmandu, 5/445 — 25, 52, 81, 83, 103, 238, 249, 280, 288, 328
Manuscript of the *Tantrasadbhāva* (see TS_2), National Archives, Kathmandu, 1/363 — 29, 56–57, 83, 98, 267, 344
Manuscript of the *Tattvasaṃgraha* (see TSa), Jinabhadrasūri Grantha Bhaṇḍāra, Jaisalmer, 377 — 11–12, 37, 68, 72–73, 87, 90, 106, 128–129, 134, 198, 206, 274, 284, 288, 351
Manuscript of the *Tattvasaṃgrahapañjikāvṛtti* (see TSPV), Jinabhadrasūri Grantha Bhaṇḍāra, Jaisalmer, 378 — 12, 38, 69, 73, 85, 106, 126, 128–130, 134, 184, 201, 206, 226, 231, 352
Manuscript of the *Tattvopaplavasiṃha* (see TUS), Hemacandrācārya Jaina Jñānamandir, Patan, 178(2) — 40, 71–73, 88, 106, 128, 131–132, 134, 229, 231, 275, 286–288, 355

Manuscript of the *Yogasārasamuccaya*, National Archives, Kathmandu, 5/7244 — 86
Manuscript of the *Yogayājñavalkya* (see YY), National Archives, Kathmandu, 5/696 — 22–23, 50, 57, 90–91, 95, 324

Manuscript of the *Vajrāvalī*, National Archives, Kathmandu, 5/84 — 99
Manuscript of the *Vinayavastvāgama*, GBM 1050 — 187–188, 197
Manuscript of the *Viṣṇudharma* (see VDh), National Archives, Kathmandu, 5/344 — 25, 53, 58, 83, 86, 90–93, 97, 173, 181, 329
Manuscript of the *Viṣṇudharma*, National Archives, Kathmandu, 1/1002/1 — 85
Manuscript of the *Viṣṇudharma*, National Archives, Kathmandu, 4/1389 — 97
Manuscript of the *Viṣṇudharma*, National Archives, Kathmandu, 4/766 — 115
Manuscript of the *Viṣṇudharma*, Kaiser Library, Kathmandu, 2 — 86, 102, 105
Manuscript of the *Vītaśokāvadāna*, Schøyen collection, MS 2380/6 — 78